AF478908

The Outwardness of Art:
Selected Writings of Adrian Stokes

The Outwardness of Art:
Selected Writings of Adrian Stokes

Edited by Thomas Evans

Ridinghouse

Introduction to the Reading of Adrian Stokes

THOMAS EVANS

I have met more than one Adrian Stokes enthusiast who was first converted to his singular oeuvre by the section on Paul Cézanne in the 1947
book *Inside Out* – ostensibly an autobiography that regularly digresses
into clear-eyed reveries such as this:

> We picture him, then, on his way to his homeland which was his work,
> part of his work as surely as if he were a farmer. This was the way of his
> excitement. It could be called an obsession; in which case we would have
> to adapt his words about Monet and exclaim: but what an obsession…
>
> He strove to find for his canvas neither a tendency nor an echo of
> a mood, a waxing nor a waning: he strove for his senses to reveal, for
> his mind to recreate, a quintessential structure. And so he hurried away
> from all the incidental music of things. Yet Cézanne's painting cannot
> be called a conceptual art, for it is with the extreme complication of
> actual, even momentary, appearance that he philosophizes. The obser-
> vational truth of light, space, colour, tone and mass in their subtlest,
> no less than in their generalized, modes, are the sole materials of his
> structure. The otherness of the outside world is affirmed, not mitigated,
> by the intrusion of this artist's organizing mind.[1]

This marvellous passage gives the special flavour of Stokes's prose,
roaming as it does between vivid concretion and abstract flight, assidu-
ously sidestepping the rote phrase or cadence; also expressed here is
the preoccupation of his life's work, namely (as this selection aims to
show) the affirmation of 'the otherness of the outside world'; and further, it describes the aspirations of Stokes the writer as aptly as it does
those of Cézanne the painter, in that disciplined act of fantasy that

was his chief mode. Among this mixture of approaches are thrilling, energising contradictions: very much a performance for (and conscious of) the reader, Stokes's writing also offers the pleasures of a mind fruitfully in dialogue with itself; similarly, when ostensibly addressing a work of art, its sheer stylistic dazzle can seem to interpose itself between reader and artwork, yet do so inexplicably to the benefit of reader, author, artist, all – affirming, not mitigating, the otherness of the outside world by the intrusion of the organizing mind. If we turn to Stokes for conventional art-historical treatments, we may be bemused by his fantasies and gnomic aphorisms; if we come seeking conceptually watertight syntheses of aesthetic and psychoanalytic theory, we will encounter them often enough, though they may not prove the most compelling feature of his thinking; if we broach the work for its famously achieved prose style, it will not disappoint – but all of these traits are much more interestingly unified (and intensified) by Stokes's lifelong preoccupation with 'outwardness' in aesthetic objects, and consciousness's attendant experience of the 'otherness' of art. A highly heterogeneous thinker in the lineage of John Ruskin and Walter Pater, Stokes was careful to confound the expectations of genre, and one must cast those aside when reading him. This selection is devised with that principle in mind.

*

Throughout a half-century of sustained writing and thinking about art, architecture, aesthetics, psychoanalysis and ballet, and traversing milieus from Bloomsbury, the Ballets Russes and the St Ives artists to the London circle around Melanie Klein and the Imago Group, Stokes enjoyed a notably diverse and devoted readership, and despite the intermittent availability of his books posthumously, he continues to. Ernst Gombrich, Dore Ashton, David Sylvester, Richard Wollheim, Ezra Pound, the Sitwells, W. H. Auden, Elizabeth Bishop, John Ashbery, J. H. Prynne, Ben Nicholson, Henry Moore, Barnett Newman, Philip

Guston, Trevor Winkfield and Bridget Riley have numbered among
his fans, champions and interlocutors, and he has been the subject of
two biographies and several critical studies.[2] That Stokes has won such
a great diversity of devotees is due in part to the broad appeal of what
animated his writing throughout: his desire to extol and parse the
interdependence of the inner world's tensions with the 'otherness of
the outside world', and to celebrate art objects that affirm this otherness
through the aesthetic quality of 'outwardness'; whence also the title
of this book.

OUTWARDNESS AND OTHERNESS

What is meant by 'outwardness', in Stokes's conception? The earliest
inklings of the theme of outwardness are to be found in his first books,
The Thread of Ariadne (1925) and *Sunrise in the West* (1926), as the opening
essay in this collection shows. There it arises through the related term,
Hegelian in origin, of 'otherness':

> Nothing that is significant, however much its content may point to
> 'otherness', no sentiment evoked by the contemplation of matter, no
> sailor's soul that cries the bitterness and ungovernable non-humanity
> of the sea, no unconsidered outburst, no poetry can be spared by prose
> embroidering subtlety, stringing interconnection, indeed, the more
> 'otherness' and distinctness appreciated, the more indispensable
> are the meanings to prose, since that very intensity makes possible
> a correlative intensity of antithetical significance.[3]

In these highly speculative early books, this notion of otherness is
tied to the dialectical motions of consciousness: that is to say, identity
cannot come to rest within itself but is perpetually reconstituted by its
negation of another entity, which it folds into consciousness to produce
what Hegel calls a 'reflection in otherness within itself', or 'pure self-
recognition in absolute otherness'.[4] This is the meaning of the Hegelian
phrase, frequently to be encountered in Stokes's essays, of 'identity in

difference'. 'A *This* is posited', Hegel writes in *The Phenomenology of Spirit* (1807), 'but it is rather an *other* that is posited, or the This is superseded: and this *otherness*, or the setting-aside of the first, is itself *in turn set aside*, and so has returned into the first.'[5] In these formulations of subjecthood, later adapted and reprised by the British philosopher F.H.Bradley (through whom Stokes probably first encountered them) and grounding his assertion of the interdependence of opposites, Stokes found an articulation of the contradictory character of thought itself. As Hegel writes in the Preface to the *Phenomenology*, 'having its otherness within itself, and being self-moving, is just what is involved in the *simplicity* of thinking itself'.[6]

As this theme is developed, a transition ensues in Stokes's thinking from the mid-1920s to the early 1930s – that is, from *Sunrise in the West* and *The Thread of Ariadne* to *The Quattro Cento* and *Stones of Rimini* – in which a broad, ontological conception of outwardness is now linked to aesthetics, specifically to carving in sculpture. By 'carving', Stokes refers to art in which the stone is 'revealed' rather than 'forced into expression' (which is more or less what 'modelling' does, he implies). The carving mode, according to Stokes, is especially able to express the fundamental otherness of the world, its indifference to the coercions of self-consciousness: 'The essence of stone is its power to symbolise objectivity', he writes in *Stones of Rimini*. Stone can be coerced against this 'essence', of course, and *Stones of Rimini* contains Stokes's famous 'classification of Quattro Cento sculpture in terms of technique' and the specialist meaning he had given to the term 'Quattro Cento' in his preceding book *The Quattro Cento*:

> Wherever you find relief forms, be they ornament or figure, arabesque or swag, wherever you find these shapes, whatever their position, turning to show to you their maximum, like flowers that thrust and open their faces to the sun, wherever that is the salient point about them, then that sculpture is Quattro Cento as I define it.[7]

Here, then, is Stokes's aesthetic of 'outwardness': an art that is turned outward to show to you its maximum, in a recognition, a mimesis and a celebration of the obdurate otherness of the world. The analogy with the opening of flowers, incidentally, evokes Stokes's term 'stone-blossom' as a sculptural effect associated with outwardness, although outwardness itself is not made contingent upon the mimesis of nature. At this juncture in Stokes's writing, the celebratory tenor of this definition is foremost, stemming from his distinctly modernist and Nietzschean veneration of pagan vitality, of which the Tempio Malatestiano in Rimini, by his account, was the apotheosis.

With exhilarating focus, Stokes proceeds to undergird his subsequent treatments of sculpture, architecture and painting with this fixation, which also defines his praise of the 'turned out' body in ballet, where 'nothing is withdrawn, drawn inwards or hidden: everything is, artificially if you like, put outwards'. Ballet, unlike expressionistic modern dance, is 'classical', and the ideals of 'classical' art (given, as always, its particular inflection) will later be recruited for the buttressing of this aesthetic. In the aforementioned section on Cézanne from *Inside Out*, for example, Stokes writes:

> Classical art springs from a precise love and a passionate identification with what is other, insisting upon an order there, strong, enduring and final *as being an other thing*, untainted by the overt gesture, without the summary treatment, without the *arrière pensée* of 'thinking makes it so'.[8]

How, then, may the writer engage such obduracy? Walter Pater offered Stokes a precedent (while also supplying a model for Stokes's early style and his strategic confounding of genre). Pater's innovation in *The Renaissance* (1873) was his rhetorical positioning of emotional response to produce a simultaneous representation of the aesthetic object and the effect it produces. His preface to *The Renaissance* delineates the method:

> What is this song or picture, this engaging personality presented in life or in a book, to *me*? What effect does it really produce on me?

Does it give me pleasure? and if so, what sort or degree of pleasure? How is my nature modified by its presence, and under its influence? The answers to these questions are the original facts with which the aesthetic critic has to do; and, as in the study of light, of morals, of number, one must realise such primary data for one's self, or not at all.[9]

Such attention to affect, ostensibly unbounded by ethical imperatives (at least, not Christian ones), carries with it a set of implicitly endorsed aesthetic properties that permeate Pater's vocabulary ('sweet', 'peculiar', 'strange' and 'delicate', for example, are common, positively inflected epithets). Notoriously, *The Renaissance* is also notable for its concluding advocacy of the pursuit of intense ephemeral sensation snatched from the encroachments of mortality. Stokes's early work partakes liberally of the aesthete's literary performance of acute sensibility but rejects this authority implicitly ceded to death, instead occupying consciously a life-giving tension between libidinal and death instincts. Stokes was also to place Pater's language of affect in a fruitful tension with the hard-edged immanent aesthetics of the early twentieth-century arts, and perhaps where he found such aesthetics to be overly strident or macho, Pater may have supplied a handy tactic for lacing aesthetic perception with subversively ambiguous sensuality; one thinks here of how Pater himself undermined what he took to be the moral certitudes of Ruskin by such means.

Although Pater was ostensibly the Hegelian thinker, it seems to have been from Ruskin that Stokes drew one early conception of outwardness, as the art historian Richard Read has proposed – namely, the psyche's own compulsion toward stability in outward manifestation. In *Stones of Venice*, Ruskin describes a walk in St. Mark's Place in which a turbulent experience of disgust with urban claustrophobia and bustle is, as Read notes, 'externalized into orderly architecture' – an event of psychic stabilization echoed by Stokes in his autobiography *Inside Out*, where it is declared that 'the process of a man's existence is outward, giving shape, precise contour to the few things that lie deepest'.[10] The licence that Ruskin gives to acts of fantasy, with their strongly sexual tenor, may seem to us self-evidently freighted with psychoanalytic resonance, but in Ruskin those acts of fantasy are also determined by religious dichotomies, with which Stokes wholly dispensed. For Stokes comes after Freud, and performs a truly singular synthesis of Freudian 'phantasy' (defined as the mental expression of libidinal and aggressive impulses, and defence mechanisms against them) with Ruskinian 'fantasy'. In *The Quattro Cento* and *Stones of Rimini* more than any other of his books, Stokes's writerly acts of 'fantasy' are made to comprise a fabulous array of rhetorical modes – travelogue, historical analysis, ekphrasis, reverie – all of which are couched in a language at once florid and digressive, exacting without ever showboating a wearisome hyper-scrupulous 'attention to things'.

As his use of Melanie Klein's thought reached its most explicit engagement in the 1940s, art embodying outwardness began to be proposed by Stokes as symbolic of stabilized psychic conflict – as emblematic of the possibility of sanely maintaining contrary forces. ('Emblematic' is chosen advisedly here: another keyword for Stokes, it is made synonymous with stabilized outwardness from *The Quattro Cento* on, also connoting an aesthetic of life-affirming vitality.) By the time of *Greek Culture and the Ego* (1958), he could even allow that 'art presupposes visual (i.e. from a distance) apprehension of the object; yet while observing this otherness, art, I must add, strives also to bring the object nearer to us so as even to envelop us'.[11] The opposed (or at least only minimally reconciled) paradigms of Stokes's early work – carving versus modelling, the near versus the distant – are here more fully incorporated into what finally may be best characterized as a dialectical account of both aesthetic and phenomenological experience.

*

Some contemporaneous context for notions of outwardness may be drawn from Stokes's unique intersection with the intellectual shifts of the early twentieth century and the modernist pursuit of immanence over transcendence in art – the reverence for material itself expressed, for example, in the Imagism of Ezra Pound or the austere, shallow reliefs of Ben Nicholson. Additionally, and alongside the writings of Friedrich Nietzsche and Sigmund Freud – both formative for Stokes – we must take account of the British idealist philosopher F. H. Bradley, who was also to influence some of Stokes's older contemporaries, most famously T. S. Eliot, eventually to be Stokes's publisher at Faber & Faber. It is in Bradley's philosophy (and within it, Hegel's) that Stokes's preoccupation with the 'otherness of the outside world' finds its earliest conceptual scaffolding, which occurs through Bradley's reprisal of Hegel's conception of 'identity in difference' in the books *Appearance and Reality*, first published in 1893, and *The Principles of Logic*, published in 1883 and reissued in 1922 while Stokes was at Oxford, where Bradley taught (although Stokes did not study with him).

Though not crucial for the reading of Adrian Stokes, it must be noted that a point of distinction exists between Hegel's and Bradley's configurations of the identity of difference and identity: put concisely, for Hegel the contradictions of difference and identity produce dynamism, motion and flux, and a permeation of the dialectic throughout various successive stages, whereas in Bradley those contradictions effectively come to a halt in the fact of their unity, or identity. Bradley's influence on Stokes can be seen overtly in *Sunrise in the West* and *The Thread of Ariadne*, as Richard Read has also shown.[12] *Sunrise*, for example, opposes two very singular conceptions of 'prose' and 'poetry', extrapolating their individual meanings at length and eventually demonstrating their interdependence. Venturing to summarize the various inflections he gives them, one might say that 'poetry' designates a kind of imagined 'primitive' consciousness in which 'man has no sense of "otherness"',[13] while 'prose' connotes a kind of overly calculative, rationalist contemplativeness. (One feels apprehensive in attempting to summarize these terms at all, when Stokes extrapolates their meanings to such a wild degree.) These terms are resolved not by compromise but by being bound together in dynamic contention, a Bradleyan move that foreshadows Stokes's later interpretation of art's reparative effect

18

in stabilizing conflict. All the while, however, the accent is not on the virtues of interiority but rather on an affirmation of the world's otherness – or, as he was to write in his Cézanne reverie, the world 'affirmed, not mitigated, by the intrusion of [the] artist's organizing mind'.

THE TEMPIO MALATESTIANO

Among the protagonists of Stokes's early intellectual climate, Ezra Pound looms large for his kindred (if differently inflected) insistence upon an ethos of immanence, with its implicate values of 'attention to things' and 'truth to materials' as kinds of absolute values (onto which Stokes could fasten his Bradleyan/Hegelian dialectic). Stokes and Pound first met on the tennis courts of Rapallo, northern Italy, in 1926, by which time Stokes had published *The Thread of Ariadne* and *Sunrise in the West*. Pound had already erected a cult of personality around Sigismondo Malatesta (1417–1468), the Renaissance warlord whom he proposed as an exemplary leader and patron of the arts, as embodied by his temple in Rimini with its astounding reliefs by Agostino di Duccio, frescoes by Piero della Francesca and design by Leon Battista Alberti. Pound's acclamation of Sigismondo took the form of the so-called 'Malatesta Cantos' (*Cantos* VIII–XI), in which potted accounts of Sigismondo's military accomplishments and the construction of the Tempio Malatestiano are mingled with collaged excerpts from Sigismondo's correspondence.

By the early twentieth century Sigismondo's long-standing reputation as an unmitigated heretic had been transformed by the Swiss historian Jacob Burckhardt, who wrote of him, in his *The Civilization of the Renaissance in Italy* (1860): 'Unscrupulousness, impiety, military skill, and high culture have been seldom combined in one individual as in Sigismondo Malatesta.'[14] (Significantly, Nietzsche was one of the first close readers of Burckhardt's book, and Stokes's initial enchantment with Sigismondo's personality reads as strongly Nietzschean.) Sigismondo's life had been novelized by Edward Hutton in 1906, Corrado Ricci's book on the Tempio was published to acclaim in 1924, and the myth was securely in place that the building constituted a kind of defiant pagan monument to Sigismondo's lover Isotta degli Atti (a speculation that cannot be definitively proven, as Stokes recognized).

The Tempio certainly expresses a worldview, even a cosmology, that may be interpreted partly through the era's Neoplatonic strains, with its abundant elemental, astrological and classical iconography, and this worldview, with its implications of sensuous vitality and spiritual heresy, was especially congenial to Stokes and Pound, as we will see. In his study of Sigismondo, *Pagan Virtue in a Christian World* (2016), Anthony F. D'Elia also notes that 'The interior decorations of the Tempio are replete with male muscular bodies, only partially covered by clothing and displaying an aggressive male strength unparalleled in a Christian church in this period, where normally the only sculpted male nude is Christ on the cross'[15] – an iconography that might speak both to Stokes's then primarily gay sexual orientation and to Pound's pagan humanism. Stokes was to find ingenious, subtle ways of subverting – which is to say, rendering ambiguous – Pound's strongly heterosexual reading of the Tempio, all the while preserving the rhetoric of vitality associated with that reading.

Stokes had encountered the Tempio while travelling in Italy with the Sitwells in 1925. He commemorated the very day in *Stones of Rimini*: 'I have only found images and names and explanations and reasons and theories – in general, literary data – to express what on July 5th, 1925, I knew at once of the life, the landscape, the condition of which the Tempio is the emblem.' Initially, in *The Quattro Cento*, Stokes – like Pound – attributed the Tempio's qualities of outwardness to Sigismondo himself. By the time of *Stones of Rimini*, however, the Tempio's artists and architect occupied the centre of his analysis, a development that reflected the cooling of relations between Stokes and Pound. In *The Quattro Cento* he speaks in favour of 'artists inspired by a patron's personality, whence springs the art entirely emblematic, the art "twice over", miraculous to us who lack emblem'; likewise, 'All the fifteenth-century genius for emblem, for outwardness, centred in Sigismondo.'[16] Later, Pound was to declare in *Guide to Kulchur* (1938) that 'there is no other single man's effort equally registered', which seems to have been

20

a view held by some Sigismondo's in own time: he was credited by the humanist writer Roberto Valturio with devising the temple's pagan iconography 'from the hidden recesses of philosophy', for example.[17]

But if for Pound, Sigismondo exemplified a virile, individualistic model of the state leader as pagan warrior-patron, by the time Stokes wrote *Stones of Rimini* two years later, he had ceased to share Pound's appraisal of Sigismondo's character and was to distance himself from the former's concurrent embrace of fascism and antisemitism. (He was, however, prone to exhibit that casually essentialist view of racial identity typical of the period – despite or perhaps because of his own Jewishness on his mother's side.) Consequently, in *Stones of Rimini* it is the Tempio itself rather than its supposed conceiver that is the focus of his praise – in particular the astonishing reliefs by Agostino depicting astrological allegories. To these Stokes attributed exemplary outwardness, made possible in part, he argued, by their shallow relief and the frontal directionality of their composition (echoing his assertion, apropos of ballet, that 'nothing is withdrawn'). In a flagrant (but glorious, and rare) moment of ahistoricism, he even retroactively attributed an instinct for immanence to the Quattrocento *in toto*: 'Artisans, craftsmen of all kinds, were busy making triumphant objects for their free-living despot patrons – free-living because they had loved the near thing, perhaps in the first instance a stone wall.'[18]

'The near thing' is a phrase that usefully conjures some initial affiliations between Stokes and Pound, and indeed the larger gravitation toward effects of vivid manifestation so widespread among artists after the turn of the twentieth century. Clearly optical in its bias (though not always at the expense of other senses), the 'near' has the merit of possessing or permitting intensified presence, and for Stokes this effect in art has been attained through the sculptor's animation of stone *outward*. That there is liberty ('free-living') in the love of the 'near thing' may be understood as a Nietzschean ideal insofar as it affirms the pagan master's vitality against the servitude of a resentful morality attached to a Christian abnegation of the world.

What is 'near' connotes what is 'direct', or immediate and outward, in its impact upon the viewer's consciousness. Stokes speaks frequently and positively of 'direct' effect (in the Cézanne essay, for example; or, conversely, when Isadora Duncan is berated for the indirectness of her expressionism in *To-night the Ballet* of 1934), the word allying itself with Pound's 'direct treatment of the thing'[19] in his Imagist manifesto. (One could extrapolate further and connect both the 'near' and the 'direct' with the 'static' and the 'instantaneous' as espoused throughout *The Quattro Cento* and *Stones of Rimini*; here we verge upon the topic of the early twentieth-century romance, sometimes almost Orientalist in tenor, with the 'flash of meaning' embodied by the hieroglyph and the ideogram, as found in the early work of artists and writers as different as Pound, Wyndham Lewis, William Carlos Williams, Henri Gaudier-Brzeska, D. H. Kahnweiler and Juan Gris.) Ironically, the 'near' and its attendant cluster of terms can also be extrapolated toward a point of difference between the two writers: where for Stokes these possibilities of sculptural material must emerge of their own accord, Pound instead champions the application of human will to material (though later qualified by his lament in *The Cantos*, 'I cannot make it cohere'[20]). Over the course of Stokes's subsequent books, 'the near' was to recede in significance, or at least to admit tensions with effects of distance.

CARVING, MODELLING, VITALITY

As we have seen, *Stones of Rimini* and *The Quattro Cento* constitute Stokes's manifestos for carved outwardness in art; Quattro Cento art is art that possesses this quality, along with a set of associated virtues, such as 'stone-blossom', 'mass-effect' and 'the love of stone'. Here arises Stokes's famous distinction between 'carving' and 'modelling', defined thus in *Stones of Rimini*:

> the difference between carving approach and modelling approach in
> sculptural art can be illustrated as follows. Whatever its plastic value,
> a figure carved in stone is fine carving when one feels that not the figure,
> but the stone through the medium of the figure, has come to life.

Plastic conception, on the other hand, is uppermost when the material with which, or from which, a figure has been made appears no more than as so much suitable stuff for this creation.

Stokes's overlap with the modernist sensibility is typified by this concern, although his modernism was never of the militant stripe practised by, say, the Vorticists (as a contextual point of interest, however, *Sunrise in the West* and Wyndham Lewis's *Time and Western Man* of 1927 were often reviewed alongside each other), and Stokes was ultimately to ally himself with the more domesticated modernism of the St. Ives artists, with whom his theories found sympathy (Stokes's espousal of Quattrocento 'low' relief influenced Ben Nicholson's abstract reliefs, by the latter's own account).

Still, we can detect in his early writings that sometimes combative celebration of corporeal vitality to be found in Nietzsche, Pound or Lewis. 'We do not seek the refinement of distance', he opines in *Sunrise in the West*, 'We prefer the full-blooded'; in *The Quattro Cento*, Donatello receives praise for his 'singleness of energy and of movement'; and in *Stones of Rimini*, Agostino's reliefs are admired for their 'effect of vitality, of that stone-blossom we prize so high'.[21] (As an anecdotal aside, Stokes's fictionalized roles as the protagonists of novels by Edward Sackville-West (*The Ruin*, 1927) and Osbert Sitwell (*The Man Who Lost Himself*, 1929) suggest that he himself projected a compelling affect of Nietzschean supra-moral vitality, and the psychodramas that Stokes's character instigates in both novels, as a sort of predatory cat among the bloodless pigeons of the waning British aristocracy, give a vivid portrayal of the profile he cut in his youth.) Inevitably, as Stokes accommodated contrary effects in both art objects and aesthetic experience, this association of vitality with outwardness, carving and the emblematic becomes more qualified and open to dialectical tension:

Our relationships to all objects seem to me to be describable in the terms of two extreme forms, the one a very strong identification with the object, whether projective or introjective, whereby a barrier between

self and not-self is undone, the other a commerce with a self-sufficient
and independent object at arm's length. In all times except the earliest
weeks of life, both of these relationships, in vastly differing amalgams,
are in play together, as is shown not only by psycho-analysis but by
art, since the work of art is *par excellence* a self-sufficient object as well
as a configuration that we absorb or to which we lend ourselves as
manipulators.[22]

Those who have contemplated Stokes's landscape and still-life paintings might be bemused to learn that he had ever appeared to theorize
against the enveloping effect of oceanic sensation and occlusion, which
is among their foremost qualities.

PSYCHOANALYSIS AND AESTHETICS

Readers arrive at the books of Adrian Stokes by many routes: such,
happily, is the nature and diversity of his thinking and of his peculiar
locations in cultural history. Those who encounter the early work
through Stokes's literary and art-historical associations of the 1920s
and 1930s have sometimes found the supposed 'turn' toward Kleinianism unpalatable. Two rejoinders exist to this enduring myth: first, as
the later essays in this book show, Stokes was not generally a dogmatic
exponent of Klein's ideas, and as we will shortly see, his metapsychological bent often tended to put her ideas to more philosophical ends.
Second, the very idea of a 'turn' is erroneous: Stokes entered analysis
with Melanie Klein in 1929 (he was identified by Richard Read as the
subject of Klein's case history 'Mr B' in her 1932 book *The Psycho-analysis
of Children*[23]), and her ideas can already be detected in *The Quattro Cento*,
where the discussion of Donatello's putti alludes to a Kleinian conception of infant psychology: 'We in the West believe not only that the
child is father to the man, but that the child's intent play in modes hateful and loving, expresses a more real necessity than does the grown
god's esoteric power to lure and to destroy.'[24] He also asserts that 'in
the long run a more psychological approach is not at variance with a

24

more purely aesthetic approach. On the contrary, the former should be indispensable to the latter, and vice versa.'

Stokes's relationship to the psychoanalytic movement in Britain was rich and various, and is very much worthy of its own study. He first encountered Freud's writings in the 1920s through his schoolmate W. D. Robson Scott, who in 1928 translated Freud's *The Future of an Illusion* into English; and an acquaintance of his at Oxford was James Strachey, later to be editor of the standard edition of Freud's complete works. Stokes was thus well positioned to follow the development of Freud's writing as it appeared in English.

As for so many of Stokes's generation, *The Interpretation of Dreams* and *The Psychopathology of Everyday Life* (published in English in 1913 and 1914, respectively) were formative and revelatory for Stokes, and no doubt predisposed him toward fresh conceptions of fantasy. Another formative Freud text for Stokes seems to have been *The Ego and the Id* (1923), in which Freud proposes that 'the ego is first and foremost a bodily ego; it is not merely a surface entity, but is itself the projection of a surface... i.e. the ego is ultimately derived from bodily sensations'[25] – a notion taken up by Stokes in *Greek Culture and the Ego* (1958), where he connects ego integration with compositional integrity and object-otherness in art:

> The modern painter... insists on the separateness particularly of the object he himself creates, as well as on oceanic feeling; according to this theory, the otherness of the outside world can only be represented by the separateness and wholeness of the work of art. Yet it is a means also for realizing the structure, the stability, of the ego-figure in the very terms of object-otherness.[26]

Also vital for Stokes was Freud's controversial debut of the notion of the death drive in *Beyond the Pleasure Principle* (published in English in 1922), a thesis widely rejected by Freud's immediate acolytes – his biographer and chief British exponent Ernest Jones famously lamented that 'no biological observation can be found to support the idea of a death instinct'[27] – but one fundamental for Kleinian theory (and later for Jacques Lacan). By theorizing an urge on the part of the animate toward the inanimate – '*an urge inherent in organic life to restore an earlier state of things*'[28] – Freud contentiously detached his speculations from the realm of the clinic and of his case studies and dramatically expanded the metapsychological dimension of his work into what may be seen as a distinctly Heraclitean vision of *bios* pitched between opposing impulses (as in Fragment LXXIX: 'the name of the bow is life; its work is death'[29]).

Stokes is likely to have encountered Freud's death drive thesis via Klein, but it is useful to separate out the two theorists here, since by pitting Eros against Thanatos in a relation of perpetual negation, Freud proposed a psychic landscape well suited to Stokes's Hegelian/Bradleyan bent, and did so in a fashion that is perhaps less evocative in Klein's work (who, after all, could rival Freud for inspirational prose?). Stokes's allusions to the death drive focus not just on Thanatos but on its interdependence with Eros: the closing paragraph of his essay 'An Argument' (1943) is one example, the discussion of Piero in 'Art and Science' (1949) is another, and it forms the main topic of the late essay 'On Resignation' (1962), where he writes: 'If we allow to anxiety no component from the death instinct, if we do not admit a death instinct, a desire for absence and refusal, then the character of resignation, it seems to me, and the ease with which in some circumstances it may be assumed, remains an enigma.'[30]

In speaking of this influence, as with any terminology relevant to the reading of Stokes, it is essential to underscore how keenly felt this notion was for him; unconstrained by the requirements of dogma or academia, his thinking, not least when animated by the fixation with mortality, often reaches an urgency that colours the very pace of his phrasing. Conversely, of course, one frequently notices opposite qualities of leisurely contemplation; a pronounced virtue of Stokes's prose is that often its rhythms are those of a privileged amateur at liberty to temporalize differently.

*

Overt expression of the influence of Melanie Klein on Stokes – that is, his treatment with her, their friendship, her writings – emerged with the autobiographical volumes *Inside Out* and *Smooth and Rough* of 1947 and 1951 respectively. These books, along with *Art and Science* (1949), were his final books with Faber & Faber, who through the advocacy of Ezra Pound had published Stokes's ten books following *The Thread of Ariadne* and *Sunrise in the West*. In the early 1950s, Stokes greatly expanded his applications of Klein's ideas, commencing with a study of Michelangelo that proved excessively psychoanalytic in its methodology for his erstwhile publisher Geoffrey Faber and for many of his readers; it precipitated the migration of his work to the Tavistock Press, the (then) somewhat Klein-affiliated imprint that was to publish his next six volumes.

It is true that in later years Stokes's Kleinianism occasionally verged on the reductive, and *Michelangelo* (1955) is a work that seems to me constrained in this respect, as well as for the reasons that Ernst Gombrich levelled at Stokes upon reading it – essentially, that Stokes brings psychoanalytic theory to bear upon the personality of Michelangelo with a presumptuous ahistorical speculativeness. Undoubtedly the book expresses a conceptual negotiation, a bold shift in perspective that must have been difficult to deploy, and certainly it contains many passages of great perceptiveness. Nonetheless, nothing from *Michelangelo* appears in this selection (which is probably its most contentious omission), though the book is readily available elsewhere (reprinted in the 'Routledge Classics' series in 2002, for example). *Michelangelo*, however, is significant as a transitional publication in Stokes's oeuvre, and is also historically noteworthy for its discussion of Warburg school methodology in the chapter 'A Note on Iconography', where emphasis on iconographic interpretation is seen to occlude the discernment of nuanced feeling and meaning in form. (Stokes's relations with the scholars of the Warburg Institute could constitute yet another volume of its own.)

For readers of Stokes, a small set of Kleinian terms merit a brief elaboration here, as some of his later essays deploy them with little explanation. Klein's initial act of apostasy from Freudian doctrine was to posit that 'there is no instinctual urge, no anxiety situation, no mental process which does not involve objects, external or internal' (whereas Freud had theorized an initial objectless narcissism in infancy). She also argued that the 'fear of annihilation by the death instinct is... the primordial anxiety',[31] placing foundational emphasis on that aspect of Freudian theory which for the psychoanalytic orthodoxy of the 1920s and 1930s, when Klein began publishing, was still contentious and divisive.

For the reading of Stokes, the terms that directly stem from Kleinian theory include the conceptions of the 'paranoid-schizoid position', the 'depressive' position and 'reparation'. 'Position', first of all, is Klein's preferred term over 'stage': it refers to both a phase in child development and a state that may return at any later time in life. One might note parenthetically that the term's flexibility in this respect allows for recurrence, dynamism and dialectic in its provisionality, and Klein's thinking often seems strikingly Hegelian in this regard.

The 'paranoid-schizoid position', then, describes the fear of death that splits off and projects outward those objects that appear to threaten the psyche; first occurring at the earliest stage of ego development according to Klein, this position produces the splitting of both self and object into 'good' and 'bad' with minimal or no resolution. Here Klein's famous notion of the 'good' and 'bad' breast becomes relevant: as part-objects, they respectively symbolize a loving and a hateful mother that cannot (yet) be united in one figure (again, echoes of Hegel). The 'splitting' function is nonetheless deemed by Klein essential for psychic development because it is considered to permit the creation of a central core in the ego, from which to begin integration.

Conversely, the 'depressive position' describes the emergence of self-awareness regarding infant impulses: the experience (again, at any stage of life) of guilt and grief at the psyche's attacks upon external and internal objects, such as the mother. From this experience, 'reparation' – the effort to repair and/or accept the loss of one's objects – becomes possible, with guilt no longer inhibiting action but spurring it. Creativity is envisioned by Klein as an outcome of this maturation.

One account of Klein's impact on Stokes's thinking of 'outwardness' would be to say that her work allowed him to envision more clearly the artist not as a self-absorbed expressionist extrojecting undigested 'private' psychic matter, but as someone who supplies exemplary models of reconciliation with the world's otherness, models that are in fact precisely public – that is, facing outward and occupying its surfaces candidly, rather than directing those surfaces toward the author's interior.

In Stokes's writings of the 1940s on, there are also transpositions of earlier conceptual pairs into Kleinian terms: for example, carving is connected with 'whole-object' relationships, and modelling with 'part-object' relationships. An apparently pejorative connotation attaches to the latter, since in Klein's schema there is also a maturation from part-object to whole-object relations (though she was careful to allow for the coexistence, throughout life, of both relations, and even their interdependence). As mentioned earlier, Stokes increasingly acknowledged a coexistence of the carving and modelling modes, and this reconciliation is already evident in the introduction to *Michelangelo*, where he writes:

> Art, I believe, as well as love, offers us some share in the oceanic feeling. Yet, with the phantasm of homogeneity, of singleness, the lover experiences in the beloved her singularity: she is the acme of emotive otherness… this appreciation of the object's separate sufficiency united to a sense of identity with the pulse of things, prefigures, in my opinion, the sentiments that works of art in general stimulate in us.[32]

*

The years of Stokes's Tavistock books (1955–67) coincide with his discovery by a generation of younger art historians and theorists in Britain, among them David Sylvester, Andrew Forge, John Golding, Richard Wollheim and Lawrence Gowing. By this time his reputation in the US was also secured, with writers such as Meyer Schapiro and John Ashbery (who published him in the journal *Art and Literature*) and painters such as Philip Guston and Barnett Newman numbering among his dedicated readers. That Guston, who so explicitly allied himself to an architectonic tradition in painting (Piero, Cézanne, De Chirico), should be an admirer speaks particularly to Stokes's legacy.

ON THE SELECTION

The Outwardness of Art presents a substantial selection from Stokes's published writings with the general aim of highlighting him as a thinker of 'outwardness' and as a virtuoso of the essay form. Richard Wollheim edited a previous selection of Stokes's writings, which was published in 1972 (by Penguin in the UK and Harper & Row in the US). Wollheim's selection drew mostly from famous volumes such as *The Quattro Cento*, *Stones of Rimini* and *Colour and Form*. I also draw from these books, but expand on his selection with the addition of essays published posthumously, after Wollheim's selection (in the now rare 1973 volume *A Game That Must Be Lost*), as well as from Stokes's ballet writings, omitted from both Wollheim's collection and Lawrence Gowing's three-volume *Critical Writings of Adrian Stokes* (1978) despite their great popularity among Stokes admirers and their congruence with Stokes's broader conceptual concerns.

Wollheim also tends to excerpt paragraphs from essays in order to illustrate 'points': thus his selection is structured around sections titled, for example, 'Mass and Mass-Effect', 'Carving and Modelling', 'Colour as Medium', 'Art and the Body' and so on. Valuable as this book has proved for the dissemination of the work, this editorial tack is to my mind wildly ill-suited to Stokes's accomplishment: it butchers the supple muscularity of his thinking, which expresses itself exactly across essay form and not in 'points'. (If 'muscularity' evokes a swaggering tone, an observation by Walter Benjamin on Proust is pertinent: 'his sentences are the entire muscular activity of the intelligible body'.[33]) Consequently, readers will find in this volume only essays, or chapters from books, in their entirety.

Wollheim's organization of the material also obscures the abiding concern with outwardness throughout Stokes's diverse engagements. An emphasis on that concern in this selection has not, I hope, neglected the many other avenues down which Stokes's thinking travelled: after all, how to accommodate into that argument the eerie bizarreness of 'Face and Anti-Face', his great essay 'The Image in Form', the discussions of bodiliness in *Greek Culture and the Ego*, the nervous, restless meditations on spatial nuance to be found in the autobiographies? Late in life Stokes suggested once that *Sunrise in the West* already contained the one idea he ever had, by which I think he meant the theme of outwardness (he did not expand on the comment). If so, what a fantastic lifelong elaboration of one idea, and what testimony to the elasticity of Stokes's mind, which never hardened into stance or easy habit. The comment, if there is truth to it, makes his life's work somehow seem all the more an adventure.

Adrian Stokes: A Brief Chronology

1902   Adrian Durham Stokes born in Bayswater, west London, on
27 October, third son of Durham and Ethel Stokes.

1916   Attends Rugby School, where his contemporaries include Joseph
Macleod (later a poet, critic and writer on Soviet theatre) and
William Robson-Scott (later the translator of Sigmund Freud's
The Future of an Illusion), the three becoming lifelong friends.

1917   Eldest brother, Philip, killed in action on the French battlefield.

1920   Attends Magdalen College, University of Oxford, to study
history, changing to Philosophy, Politics and Economics. Reads
F.H. Bradley's *Appearance and Reality* and Freud's *The Interpretation
of Dreams* and *The Psychopathology of Everyday Life*. Befriends Robert
Byron and Edward Sackville-West.

1922   First visit to Italy.

1923   Upon graduation from Oxford, Stokes travels to India, Sri Lanka,
Burma, China and Canada, keeping a journal that will form the
basis of his first book, *The Thread of Ariadne*.

1925   Meets the Sitwell family in Rapallo, Italy (having met Osbert
Sitwell the year prior), and travels with them to Spain. *The Thread
of Ariadne* published by Kegan, Paul, Trench, Trubner & Co. Is
immersed in the work of Walter Pater and John Ruskin. On 25
July visits the Tempio Malatestiano in Rimini for the first time.

1926   Publishes his second book, *Sunrise in the West*, the cover of which
features a relief of Diana from the Tempio. Meets Ezra Pound in
Rapallo, with whom he shares an admiration of the Tempio, and
D.H. Lawrence, for whom he transports the proofs of *Lady
Chatterley's Lover* from Italy to London. In London he sees the
Ballets Russes perform for the first time.

1929   Following a long period of psychic crisis and a brief, unsuccessful psychoanalytic session with James Strachey, Stokes is introduced by the Freudian (later Freud's biographer) Ernest Jones to Melanie Klein, with whom he begins analysis on 5 December 1929, and who will become a lifelong friend and supporter. Publication of essays forming the basis of *The Quattro Cento*, through the advocacy of Pound, in T. S. Eliot's *The Criterion*.

1932   Publication of *The Quattro Cento*, his first book with Faber & Faber. It is lauded in reviews by Ezra Pound, Sacheverell Sitwell, Kenneth Clark and Robert Byron and admired by W. H. Auden. Meets Barbara Hepworth and Ben Nicholson, whose work he later champions.

1934   Publishes *Stones of Rimini*, with a cover design by Ben Nicholson. The book is negatively reviewed by Pound, precipitating the decline of their closeness. Moves to the Isokon building in Hampstead, north London, designed by Wells Coates. Publishes *To-night the Ballet*.

1935   Reviews ballet for the *Spectator*. Publishes *Russian Ballets*; becomes friends with and assists Leonid Massine on a collaboration with Ben Nicholson.

1936   Begins painting and exhibiting. Meets the artist Margaret Mellis at a Cézanne exhibition at the Jeu de Paume, Paris.

1937   Studies painting at the Euston Road School with William Coldstream. Befriends and assists Michel Fokine on the Ballets Russes production of *Le Coq d'or*. Paints at Aldous Huxley's Villa Huley in Sanary, Provence. Publishes *Colour and Form* (heavily revised in 1950), his last book for eight years.

1938   Finishes psychoanalysis with Klein. Marriage to Margaret Mellis.

1939   Anticipating the outbreak of the Second World War, Stokes and Mellis move to Little Park Owles in Carbis Bay, Cornwall, eventually sharing the house with Ben Nicholson, Barbara Hepworth and their children. Stokes and Mellis visit Alfred Wallis regularly and support him.

1940   Birth of Telfer Stokes in October.

1945 Publishes *Venice: An Aspect of Art*.

1946 Breakup of his marriage to Mellis. Returns to analysis.

1947 Divorces Margaret Mellis. Marries Ann Mellis, sister of Margaret, in Ascona, Switzerland, where they live for the next several years. Publishes *Inside Out*.

1948 Birth of Philip Stokes in February.

1949 Publishes *Art and Science: A Study of Alberti, Piero della Francesca and Giorgione*.

1950 Ann and Adrian Stokes return to the UK, living in Berkshire. Stokes meets the composer Robert Still, with whom he will later found the Imago Group.

1951 Birth of Ariadne Stokes.

1952 Publishes *Michelangelo*, his first book with Tavistock Publications.

1956 Moves to 20 Church Row in Hampstead so that Ariadne, having been diagnosed as schizophrenic, can receive psychoanalytic treatment with the Kleinian analyst Esther Bick. Starts the Imago Group with the composer Robert Still, the philosopher J.O. Wisdom and the psychoanalyst Roger Money-Kyrle. Later participants include W.R. Bion, Hanna Segal, Donald Meltzer, Marion Milner, Richard Wollheim and Stuart Hampshire.

1958 Meets the philosopher Richard Wollheim, at that time working on his study of F.H. Bradley. Publishes *Greek Culture and the Ego*.

1960 Becomes a trustee of the Tate Gallery. His writing is increasingly celebrated by a younger generation of art critics and theorists, such as Andrew Forge, John Golding, John Richardson and David Sylvester.

1961 Publishes *Three Essays on the Painting of Our Time*. Death of Klein.

1963 Publishes *Painting and the Inner World*, which includes a dialogue with Donald Meltzer.

1967 Publishes *Reflections on the Nude*.

1968 Becomes a prolific poet.

1972 Stokes is diagnosed with a brain tumour. Richard Wollheim works with Stokes on a selection of his writings, *The Image in Form*. He dies on 15 December.

Prose

From Sunrise in the West (1926)

At long last we have the afternoon to ourselves and we will surrender to
the contemplation that it induces. As the light thins, the stops of Time
pull out and set our ruminations to a complicated fugue. We hear the
motif of morning and recall that moment of emotion when we marched
with the ephors upon the sunrise. For since we have the afternoon to
ourselves we become more aware of the morning and of the night. Now
the orchestration thickens and the cymbals string with the violins.

Can we have a pinnacle without an abyss, Greek myths without
Polynesian absence of drainage? We judge the periods of history by our
office-stools, just as the dawn rises upon the afternoon.

The crusaders, it seems to us, were adventurous. But they did not
count the cost and anticipate consequences in the extreme manner that
we find habitual. Did *they* conceive of romance?

Obviously, the more contrasts the more contents. The more men
have differed and the longer that these differences have heaped themselves upon one another, the greater is the richness of existence for the
consciousness of man.

History is relative to us. Mere factual existence is meaningless without interpretation, and our manner of interpreting the course of history
is founded upon the interdependent differences of the events and upon
their divergence in spirit from that of our own time. Thus one age can
appear romantic only because another age is interpreted by contrast
as prosaic. This distinction is not absolute but one in which each term
is given meaning by the other. It may be argued that the distinction,
however relative, is permanent enough because it is not relative to *us*
inasmuch as the contrasts afforded by the differences of past eras suffice
to maintain the distinction, irrespective of the contrasted values of

our age. But we are only able to attribute an atmosphere to other times inasmuch as we see them as different from our own time and, therefore, every age, since it contrasts with our own, each and all are interpreted afresh. When we change, history changes too. There is no priority because the two are interdependent: they affect and are affected by each other equally. To judge that our view of history has altered, or that we have altered, is to make the same judgment. Then there has been a change all round. Change, therefore, is the absolute in history. But the meaning, change, is equally relative to the meaning, permanence and so on...

Our sense of relativity is compelling us to speak in terms of related meaning rather than of absolute existence. It is more fruitful. Existence itself is but a meaning and one, like all others, that cannot walk by itself for ever. We only attach significance to existence because we do likewise to non-existence, to life because we do likewise to death.

We considered the soul of primitive man to be fired with untutored poetry, but surely, it is only *we* who could so judge it as we look away from our network of steel to attribute to the savage a delightful inconsequence which would make overtures to Nature as he seeks to temper her brutalities with human treatment. A civilization emerging from savagery could not share this view of its predecessors. And what does the savage himself think of his state? Not as poetic, for he cannot conceive prose, not in terms of any of the contrasts by which we judge things, for there is not enough difference in his impressions for him to have more than a handful of distinctions. That is why we call him a savage. He is barely conscious because he is so ill aware of contrast and difference. He probably does not conceive his 'state' at all because his distinction of being and not-being is blurred.

Existence is only recognized when endowed with attributes. Strip it of these and we can no longer give a content to existence. Each age has re-endowed the stark occasions of the past with attributes, with significance, interpreting history in contrast to itself. The background of history is bound up with the foreground of our lives, the meanings of history serve as an indispensable point of relationship in a present for which every meaning is only so by right of contrast with others.

Has history any further reality than this, is it more than so much grain to form the bread of our impressions, so much food for our sensibility? We too will become history in the future, but this conviction of mortality is also a mere interdependent meaning. 'Transitoriness is the safeguard of eternity. If men and their work were not unique, irreplaceable and irretrievable, their existence would signify nothing.'[1] It is essential to a whole world of meaning that we should see ourselves as transitory. But transitoriness, again, is no absolute that can walk by itself.

Art, and our appreciation of it, is no less relative. The intimate connection between art and what is not art may be indirect, but is always vital. Except in a wet-booted life there can be no ballet.

How can there be an invariable aesthetic standard? Poor people will tend to obtain aesthetic pleasure from music that conjures up easy visions of grand attainment and splendour. Here is enjoyed the ecstatic counterpart to the gnawing greyness that consumes so many lives. Such taste is naturally deplorable to the cognoscenti who know not the Mile End Road. The sublime order and equable composition of a Bach fugue will build a beautiful tower in the mind of the fugitive from personal pettiness. But the same piece will, naturally perhaps, be but as heavily cogged wheels to the man who tends a sewing machine. If you live in the Mile End Road and always see the grey interminability of the house lines and the lines of houses, you will not delight in composition so much as scarlet, open-handed splendour, love, warmth and magnificence.

Again, the time element confuses a purely aesthetic standard.[2] It is not always possible to distinguish 'period interest' from aesthetic enjoyment, nor is it easy for a ruin to be ugly. For ruins are triumphs of impressionism, forms not definite enough to limit the imagination, but sufficiently marked in a quiet manner to induce a memorable association of ideas to which no one can take exception. The time element can create a minor work of art with even unpromising material, having the power to transmute vulgarity and to purge the whole impression of inharmonious association. What is old cannot be vulgar, and in view of this alone, any aesthetic standard which would keep art altogether pure of 'life' has to be reconsidered. It would appear that the Hebrew folklore cannot be obscene nor Propertius too exotic for the form-room.

There is little difference between a museum and a minor art collection. A common Etruscan 'utensil', dug up, becomes an *objet d'art*, and, encased in a vitrine, finds a resting place on a sideboard by the elder Chippendale. Sometime, perhaps, hundreds of years hence, the Maison Lyons will acquire aesthetic value and tourists will derive no uncertain enjoyment from the ruins of Harrods.

Gilbert in the eighties made his aesthetic cry that –

Art stopped short
At the cultured court
Of the Empress Josephine.

Forty years have elapsed since then, and the collector now extends his welcome so far as the Great Exhibition of '51. In thirty years' time, he will be engaged in the search for drawings by Du Maurier, for the bustles and bamboo tables of the eighties – if not in ten years' time, since we have now so far developed our sensitiveness to 'date' and period interest that a few already find delight, even in the unbroken Edwardian drawing-room.

Old Masters start with an enormous advantage in their appeal to taste: their manner and their matter are things digested, assimilated, uncontroversial, comforting, with the restfulness that historical perspective always affords. Modern art, on the other hand, of its nature, prejudices the Catholic temper, inasmuch as it is a mirror of our own sensibility, taken up with the same problems, the identical difficulties, the inevitable emphases from which we would be diverted in order to compose the sense of beauty. However successful a modern picture may seem, its *point d'appui* is too close to us to allow of that state of surrender in which we can best enjoy a work of art.

Nor can the phenomena of science, though the majority of them are beyond the power of our senses to perceive, destroy our balance of related meanings. Science is concerned with existence and its blameless laws. We are impressed by the millions of unsolicited agencies that order the world, the countless, exact and exacting forces that rule the universe; we are made to feel less than the atom by geologists' time and astronomers' space and less than God by the atom; we bow before the might of the storm and the mysterious growth of the orange; we admire the provident organization of Nature, inscrutable in purpose, incalculable in abundance, careful in compensation; we are nothing before the sea, before a crevice of a rock that never pauses day or night to disgorge that exact surplus of water beyond its mathematical capacity to hold, however thunderous the gale; we are helpless before the mountains, resigned before the generations, humble at the conviction of animal descent, mere specks of dust on the road of evolution, momentary images careless beneath the stars. We may express our feeling of abasement before the might of Law in likening the universe to a one-day butterfly created by God in absent-mindedness.

Owing to modern science, Nature has become many times more overwhelming to man. The imagination is let loose to roam over figures and facts which there is no gainsaying. Since we have learned to calculate with facility, we can further conceive energies, following courses incapable of error, which are beyond our power to imagine.

Yet, in spite of this development, or rather, in truth, *because* of it, we are today far less prone to interpret experience on a naturalistic basis. For, with this vast increase of scientific realization, if we were to continue to regard Nature in the manner which prevailed forty years ago, we would, by now, be unable to justify any preoccupation with ourselves. All human activities and humane interests would have appeared to be trifling, as pins in the deserts of inhuman, sub-human and super-human vastness.

With the first onrush of science as it forced a way past prejudice, natural law and matter bade fair to subsume freedom and mind under their phenomena. This crisis could only be averted by a complete break with the consciousness of the past. We have dethroned uniformity, broken the attack of natural law and leashed the causal cycle to the relative.

For these purposes we abandon the distinction between mind and matter. Mind and matter are interdependent conceptions and, therefore, of no ultimate significance. So far from the one having the power to swallow the other, so far from matter having the power to consume mind, matter is meaningless without its counterpart, its contrast. Inhuman, sub-human, super-human, all three are impossible without the human, the norm from which they diverge.

You cannot, then, embrace the human within the super-human, mind within matter, matter within mind. The saving thought of this age is that the black might of the Himalayas, the very whirlwind of virgin snow that eternally weathers the summit of Everest, are relative to any old maid's cup of tea. Such grandeur needs such pettiness.

It may be objected that *our* impression of Everest may be relative, but not so *Everest itself*. But *Everest itself* is also a significance that must take a place in the balance of meanings. Although existence is everywhere and all meanings exist, existence is but a meaning. While we contemplate on this uninterrupted afternoon, we come to regard both things and ideas, the phenomena of science in addition to the flights of the spirit, as meanings *all* of which are relative to each other.

Having stretched distinction beyond its breaking point, we are now justified in *accepting* the events of the day as part of a woven experience, daddy-longlegs embroidered with bathroom taps.

This is the attitude of modern novelists as they uncover the subtle interconnections of significance, madeira cake and guiltiness, green bottles and penguins.

Blue vision has completed its work in the prosaic, field work which can never be undone.

Great beds of primeval life, unknown monsters that haunt the ocean floor, animal, vegetable and material activities too fine or too immense, too slow or too fast for our senses to perceive, the placid secrets of desert places, the myriad stars themselves, these, though their significance resides in our regarding them as things apart, yet, if they are called upon to usurp the whole emphasis of consciousness, then must they be written off as related, bound up for their meaning with the petty, the tedious and the tiresome.

Nothing that is significant, however much its content may point to 'otherness', no sentiment evoked by the contemplation of matter, no sailor's soul that cries the bitterness and ungovernable non-humanity of the sea, no unconsidered outburst, no poetry can be spared by prose embroidering subtlety, stringing interconnection, indeed, the more 'otherness' and distinctness appreciated, the more indispensable are the meanings to prose, since that very intensity makes possible a correlative intensity of antithetical significance. Thus does prose arrogate to itself all emotion remembered in tranquillity.

It may seem that we are here heading toward some further prose-poetry confusion inasmuch as we state that sentiment is legitimate material for the relating activities of prose. But we do not refer to the moment of emotion of which prose can take no account because it is not susceptible to 'account', but to the remembrance or anticipation of the same. All experience is fair game to prose, but when we are absorbed in an end in itself, we are concerned with another sphere the intrinsic singleness of which prose cannot touch, since this other sphere does not admit of estimation until its remembrance becomes a meaning of prose. Any sentiment that is confused with reckoning, any masquerading poetry, are within the stretches of the hours, are prose, not poetry.

But the fact that the greater part of prose's reflections is upon emotion remembered in tranquillity, should warn us from committing a serious error of overemphasis while discussing the values of prose. When we recall emotion, we are impressed by its extravagance and by its unwillingness, at first sight, to be related. Now, so far in our account of prose, we have stressed the point that all meanings are relative to each other and that no absolute values are possible. We might, in fact, be said to have elaborated the absurd dictum that 'Everything is relative.' Have we not, perhaps, set up relativity as an absolute, does it not stand alone, uncontrasted, and, therefore, meaningless? We must admit the antithesis of relativity to such an extent as not to leave relativity uncontrasted, and we will find that the final wisdom of prose is knowledge of the interdependence of the two. We will admit, then, some of the absolutist implications of emotion remembered in tranquillity. In this sense, we will allow absolutist standards, but not so as to be exalted at the expense of relative standards. The absolute derives its significance in contrast to the relative. It cannot absorb the relative. Thus only are absolutes admitted by prose, enough oneness to provide the material for interdependence, enough purpose and consistent sentiment to make life varied. When formulating a judgment, it will sometimes be best to emphasize an absolute, at other times a relative, nature.

To bring this highly theoretical attitude nearer, we will consider again, in the light of these reservations, history, art and science.

We cannot adopt a purely relative attitude towards history. There is a sense in which everything is known from the beginning, a sense for which there is no need to evoke contrast to preserve meaning. In a similar mood it is relevant to declare that the deepest springs of the human soul are constant and have always been known to man, although his power to harness them has varied. Sometimes we would condone that old fancy of ancient historians, the Golden Age. For them, savagery and ignorance are overgrowths that smother the weakly truth rather than primitive stages in development for which the more true is still beyond the reach of consciousness.

The beauty of the Greeks is not touched by subsequent events. Some pauper of Canton, although he cannot appreciate the hardness of his lot if he has never experienced tenderness, nor know the wretchedness of his poverty if all others whom he meets and whose dwellings he has entered, are as poor as himself and with as meagre belongings, yet, being a man, perhaps in some troubled dream, will know that he has missed the Golden Age. Men's bodies, as well as their souls, are fundamentally the same. The Sicilian has greater joy in existence than the Eskimo. Yet each only experiences his own climate. Whether we know what it is to be ice-bound or not, we all rejoice at the yellow sun. But when the sun is white, then are we dazed, ready to confuse the giver of life with the giver of death. The Indian is morose, not only from our point of view, but also in his own estimation. We are led to consider that some *joie de vivre* lingers in his heart.

When judging a period of history, sometimes we will presuppose these absolute meanings, at other times we will be intent upon elucidating the subtleties of relative connections. We cannot press either too hard, but in our own day, the scales must be heavy on the relative side – we will see everything *in relation with* ourselves and describe ourselves *in relation with* everything – since prose-poetry has for so long weighed down the other, being aware only of absolute values. Moreover, the full realization of relativity is the chasm that divides us from the ages and the weapon with which we would destroy false issues to make possible the pure end in itself. After we have made our reservations about the relativity of art and science, we will not revert to the absolutist side of prose. The only exception we would make is in the case of art. For when modern art is virile, as is the contemporary movement, it is natural and right for the artist to stress absolute values in his aesthetic, since, deprived of the creative patina provided by the time element, his work is judged at a disadvantage in the relative aspects of beauty that we have described.

In art, then, as in history, we cannot press the relative attitude too far. Taste varies, but there are so-called works of art that can never be in good taste and masterpieces that can never be considered rubbish. A good drawing by Picasso, the mosaics in the church of Sant'Apollinare in Classe, both are dateless. However much the artist may be the interpreter, or even the creator of his age, however much his problems may vary from period to period, yet his work will only satisfy if he discovers a means to draw out something which plays amongst the visions of all artists in all ages, something which is constant in beauty, something which pleases and of which we can never tire. This something is, perhaps, best described as 'form'; it is symbolized by the favourite explicatory gestures of an artist in his attempt to describe his work, gestures that seek to express the symphonic drawing to himself of rounded, significant harmony. In connection with 'form', the epithet 'sublime' discovers its sole justification.

There are some works of art which, whatever they may lack in the interpretive and courageous spirit that would gauge all impressions, compelling the supreme artist to be the most truly honest of men, yet are so imbued with the specific essence of art, the appreciation of which is a peculiar experience (and this is a supreme experience) rather than a vision of life as a whole – that their event is immediately and lastingly satisfying. No artist could have been more certain of the success of his work than was Palladio. He took no risks with interpretation and the expression of temperament, but concentrated upon the absolute value in art. Nothing less than the pioneer waywardness of Ruskin, who subjugated his great sense of beauty *qua* beauty to serve in the harness of an inspired fanaticism, could induce a man sensitive to art to deny the loveliness of the Loggia del Capitanio which stands opposite the famous Basilika Palladiana in the piazza of Vicenza.

We must heavily qualify, then, what we said about the music of Bach in relation to the man who tends a sewing machine. There is a sense in which we can speak of beauty *qua* beauty, irrespective of date, the specific function for which the beautiful object was designed, of its relation to the condition of the spectator and to the spirit of its time. But, on the other hand, no work of art can fly *directly* in the face of these considerations without incurring judgment in terms of the same. For such an extreme at once provokes a sense of inappositeness which deflects the attention to consider relative values and, indeed, the connection between art and life as a whole. The greatest art must always be a successful balancing of the two elements, interpretation and beauty *qua* beauty, matter and form, to attain which the artist must be possessed, not only of a vivid delight in symphony, but also of a spirit which does not contrive to refuse experience, but is keen to uncover this fragile sense to the rough fires of the soul.

When we turn once more to Nature and its independent existence, we feel more humble. We have been unbalanced by consideration of the possible *scientific* end of the world, due to a collision of bodies in space, of recurring comets, spaceborn but regular, of the possibility of life upon the planet Mars or of a journey to the moon. Scientific phenomena are

46

not only meanings related in a network of meanings, but also distinct realities with the power to disorder the whole balance of significance and to challenge the course of the most deep-set instincts. We are perhaps within sight of a century when children will be born of laboratory-fertilization and when birth will not be possible in the manner which has hitherto been considered inevitable, when receiving instruments will be invented that will have the power to detect everything that we do and even what we think, when historical sound will be recovered, and a grocer's family in Washington, Oregon, will hear the din of the battle of Arbela and the trumpeting of an elephant that crashed into the heart of the jungle in BC 3 to die alone, unseen in Asia; when the sound of the undiscovered desert, the thunder of the cooling earth-crust newly parted from the sun, will have existence for the first time in the ear of some local magnate, some Jones, some Smith.

The breadth of the immutable creeps into the brain as death climbs the legs. Amid the network of tiny compensations, the studious subtleties of personal relationships, the stiff writing on the wall spreads its sudden horror, letters of forgotten wildness and derided immediacy, syllables of interminable consequence and iron-rude apportionment, words of naked command.

Man has always felt aloof and different, and, therefore, he has attributed aloofness and difference to that which is not life. Nature has always been an enemy, in whose territory man has been ordained to live, whether, in the mode of the savage, he has sought to placate the foe by overtures which would be acceptable to hinrself, or, in the manner of modern science, has attempted to harness natural forces and regulate the body to conform to his purposes. The sea captain pits Hope and her captives, hand, compass, ship, against the ocean.

Less picturesque but more incessant is the losing skirmish of the slum against the marauding sore and tireless dirt, that grim rain of blunted missiles that dulls the sensibility of all but a few fortunates and overtaxes to madness the sensibility of this remainder, unless they refuse life by refusing experience.

Many great writers have only expressed themselves successfully by undermining the directness of words in their search for subtlety of meaning, finding evil in good and good in evil, avoiding the cliché because of its vulgar associations. Yet there comes the rare but simple moment when the unpliant word is true, when the commonplace is poetic and when the cliché is a sudden courier of tremendous tidings. These moments are the most significant to us.

But this significance cannot pull the world in tow. Once more, the absolute is only possible because of the relative, and the most profound reflections of prose are the ones concerned with the adjustment of the two. Prose can never for long countenance unsupported extremes. Science must give heed to the paradox inherent in the principle of balance, which is that any one kind of meaning cannot be all-comprising seeing that its nature is what it is, only because of something different from itself. For science, mighty truths and mighty consequences *do* hang from single threads, but unless emphasis on its counterpart of the distinctly human, for half the time at least when values should be purely relative, is respected by scientists, scientific truth can command none of the significance that it claims.

Finally, prose itself, the subtle balance between the relative and the absolute, demands a counterpart to balance and calculation. It is poetry, the purity of which is made possible by this demand of pure prose for a complement.

We have at last tracked down unmitigated calculation which is the essence of prose. For although we admit the absolutist emotion remembered in tranquillity as an element of prose, yet this absolutism cannot take the highest command as it is itself conditioned by relative values. Seeing that prosaic values make for an adjustment which seeks to take all things into calculation, prose cannot emphasize except inasmuch as emphasis is a meaning in this correlative system, a reservation, put upon his creed, which could never be tolerated by a true fanatic. Prose, seen as a whole, induces an attitude of cynicism and quietism.

It is a piazza consciousness. Seated, we appraise life walking by and marvel at the art of compensating values. Without the smaller, you cannot have the greater. Who dares to uproot such and such an evil? He endangers the good. It is the houses of Ealing and Littlehampton that give wings to the Doge's palace.

We now understand how it is that Westerners, although they have always had faith in the good, yet have been incessantly baffled by paradox in their formulations. The half-realization of poetry, the impress of emotion remembered in tranquillity, the half-realization of relativity, undistinguished, unrelated and confused in one impossible hierarchy, have meant in practice the denial of two elements by the one. As the aspirations of poetry were formulated in a manner suitable to prose, they were immediately confronted by all the subtle economy of extremes characteristic of the heart of prose. It was only the very inspired and the very stupid who, in latter developments, could profess adherence to these old rallying points. The more intelligent came home from the experience of life without a conviction.

But, now, at last, no one, when the meanings of prose are appreciated, no one can trouble the world with principles and ideals in any extreme and uncompromising form, with maxims of universal application, with theories that spin the universe about their points, with undeviating prejudices and ostracisms and moral strictures – *unless* he be inspired with the ecstasy of poetry, unless there be a fire within his being, stirred to shooting flames not by carefully courted conviction reached by taking things all in all, but by some impelling, immediate vision which, in its hour, has the might to overreach the significances of prose and in which prose consciousness can recognize its counterpart. Sincerity is not enough. The calculation that one theory better fits the facts or that a collection of startling facts requires a startling theory, is not enough. Wherever there is calculation, there is prose. The carrying to the logical conclusion, the denial and discipline for the sake of an ideal, the following out of its extreme behests according to the rules of consistency, this is not enough, it is prose. Poetry is lived, not calculated. It is not difficult to distinguish pure poetry in practice.

'No truths hang by single threads' we say in the piazza on some bright afternoon when the busy clouds above spell relativity. We are thinking at the moment of spiritualism and all the outrageous conclusions that have been based on spiritualistic phenomena. We do not deny the phenomena. Far from it. Reflecting upon what else we know about life, we expect something of that sort. It is in keeping with the daily round that there should also be dark, fantastic and unearthly experiences among men. If there were no spirit that walked by night, no horrid suspense of veiled, incredible happenings, how could other things be so eminently credible, how could the bald head of the man sitting at the next table be so ridiculously prosaic, how could we remark to the company that the typical German represents the species, is the complete *Homo sapiens* because, more than other men, he lacks resemblance in appearance or gesture or habit to any animal or to anything primeval and weird – an animal simile does not occur to one as a description – and, moreover, because this particular short, fair-haired, unshaggy frowsiness is uniquely a human attribute?

The putting on of gloves demands the haunted house, the smell of cabbage the miracle of cross-correspondence and the presence of the departed.

But let us not have any impossible stress put upon the phenomena of spiritualism. We are asked to believe that there is really no such thing as death, that what is called death is just a slight change in physical condition, that we go on living even in the space and time of the world. The spiritualist seeks to prove this by producing facts, countless facts, scientific facts, spirit messages, spirit manifestations, spirit photographs. This is where we quarrel. If he had been attracted to this theory by some lyric feeling, then his facts would be more relevant to his conclusion, would bear a more absolute emphasis. At present he trifles with exist-ence. You cannot destroy death with facts. Too much depends upon death, too many other facts. Mortality is contained in the very meaning of vitality. If we do not die, we also do not live. Moreover, the advanced spiritualist and theosophist tampers with poetry, with faith and hope which he would render superfluous by the mathematical appeal of

50

scientific calculation, by diagrams of births and rebirths occurring in accordance with law, by a routine of psychical happenings that resembles a railway time-table of arrival and departure.

The questions to which the phenomena of spiritualism have given rise are typical of the prose-poetry mentality. The question 'What happens after death?' when asked in cold blood as the result of a calculation, is meaningless. In such moments, unless we regard death as death pure and simple, we strip life of its glory. It is neither just nor sensible, seeing that we have only a conception of life because we have a conception of death, to take thus created characteristics of life and attribute them to death, and to ask questions about death, questions that are taken from the analogy of life.

But there is little doubt that an inkling of poetic aspiration nourishes spiritualism. It is the old prayer for immortality. This sentiment seeks support with facts. That, in itself, is justifiable. Yet, since facts are conceived, not as the relative, interconnected entities which they seem to those who have realized the heart of prose, but as threads from which the whole weight of the universe can be suspended, an attitude, as we have seen, characteristic of prose-poetry, this aspiration, instead of enriching meaning, may lead to a general curtailment of significance. If the spiritualist is inwardly drawn to spiritualism and is only supported by the facts, we can raise no objection. But in nearly every case he is convinced by evidence, having a minute inward sympathy which is not enough permanently to lift the matter above the level of facts.

As a result of such confusion most people with theories and beliefs of this sort are not open to counter-conviction by other facts, other arguments, for the primary spark is strong enough to ward these off, though it does not possess the strength which would enrich rather than impoverish life and which would remain uninfluenced by the narrowing implications of facts as conceived by prose-poetry.

In spite of all the deadliness of modern life, its nerve-strewn, vulgar mosaic, its darting clerks and endless rolls of linoleum that primly clasp the ferro-concrete floors, yes, because of it, we are nearer today to a supreme expression than ever was Oriental sage, heroic poet, artist flushed with the dawn. The very top-heaviness of modern life demands ballast from the souls of men. We hold the inestimable advantage over the ages of having developed to the full one side of consciousness. It is the advantage of some pieces already fixed in the solution of a jig-saw puzzle. The complementary shapes are evident. Western civilization is meagre because we have lost sight of the other pieces in a special, more methodical search. We have chosen the harder way. We are justified in our present weakness.

The necessity of prose-consciousness has been explained, the development of prose has been followed. We have pursued calculation to its limit. Only calculation recognizes limit. We have now attained completed prose, fixed pieces, however unimportant, of the jigsaw puzzle. History has been the search of poetry for her medium. It is prose.

In the leaning afternoon, when Mary sat amid the household things with work upon her, when half-an-hour later a bell would toll the half-hour, as some marauding spider spoked its glistening web among the lapses of the shadows, then an angel of God transfixed Time with arrow-flight, and stars and worlds and possibilities were overborne in one annunciation.

Jesi

From *The Quattro Cento* (1932)

No sign of Frederick Hohenstaufen in the railway station at least. They say that his mother was delivered of him in the piazza San Giorgio, afterward named the piazza Federico. Jesi, today called the city of silk because there are silk factories outside the walled town, a city upon a hill with walls pushed half-way down the slope. A light after noon rain has been prepared, falls upon the road from the station. Here, then, the town above the road that fumes into hovel doors. Before the gate there is a bridge over water that rushes to turn a mill. Inside the gate climbs old Jesi. At the moment three children under the age of six descend the steep cobbles under great eaves and long, shuttered buildings. Neither rain nor sunshine disturbs a corpse. But wait a minute! A siren yelling at the silk factories rattles every rickety shutter. Ruins are kindly; they have no shutters. They whisper through baked, uncovered lips. These buildings abound with an evil life. They are not ruins. Beneath the dust on this tin plate are the arms of Savoy. Somewhere at the back of this palazzo white-gloved, dirty-necked carabinieri are crowding in a guard-room, while somewhere on the other side of the street, a hopeless nib guided by a dry-of-mouth scrapes on sheaves of papers. Every room was long ago white-washed. Nothing ghostly about such palaces and buildings. Their floors lie too long and straight and empty down the street, much of their dirt is recent, their smell is borrowed from the roadway. Even a monastery here lives from outside, never replete, without a glow. Great *cancelli* close upon empty cellars, empty, perhaps, but for a basket of hay that seems to float above the gigantic floor, loosened from an overflow of wisps upon the tiles. Yet they live, these buildings, they serve a purpose not modern nor yet an ancient purpose as does the cathedral campanile. Forbidden to grow venerable, they sleep. Not the sleep that breaks with the light. They do not sleep in the dark. Theirs is the light but well-corded slumber of the afternoon. Without recess they are living from the outside, drawing in great breaths of air specked with noise, sound of a cough muffled by a bell, of a boy's scramble shot with the hoof of a standing cart-horse out upon the cobbles of the piazza; noises that give themselves upon the few loiterers who were not seen to move up and will not be seen to move away, noises woven into a dream of basket-firm somnolence.

Better be a beggar here than a loiterer; the beggar can position himself at dawn, watch the changing light, outsit the afternoon. But in a world already made horizontal by rain, the loiterer is put under the spell of this long, shallow sleep. Less evil in the end, if more frightening, is the life of Rococo palace and church in the south which a few basket balconies, each curved rusty railing an old rip, now suggest. Nothing dreary about the murderous southern life, a different existence of which Jesi also partakes, then, by right of balcony. With beautiful lines as if traced in a spill of cream by a jocular artist, with lines that cause to mount and curve a lipper of stucco, with awry masks and prehensile balconies, loops and twirls of iron and coloured paste, the Sette Cento nobles built their palaces in the pandemonium of southern cities. In its own day, too, the eighteenth century of the small towns must have been frightening, as are the bright-coloured Sicilian sweetmeats, harder than the cohorts of the sun, and the sugar Easter-lambs, nimble as a Sicilian landscape, creation of the people's carnival, tasting of bullock's blood. Heavily disguised, Punchinello travelled far north. Portentous England was most successfully deceived. Dickensian England is related to the grinning Neapolitan slums. Hypocrisy and larded tarts, hot negus, great fires and coaches, are good disguise. But are not the courtyards of all the inns a-jingle, like the sun spangles on a southern balcony? Do not toby caps appear at upper windows and bob and mock, their bobbets then tossed between the curtains of the heavy beds, reprobate like the Rococo grotesques, old men with evil faces swollen with toothache? And what of the ferns, the cracked frames askew, the pots, those dusty aquariums and blood-red gold-fish, those thousand bird-cages, hopping canaries scattering bird-seed – how like the crowded, crazy balconies hanging with fern and damp linen, quaking with the quick, rickety children playing with flies in the flotsam spray! There is the same flitting bat-like quality about Victorian bric-a-brac and about the smirking coffin so dear to that age, the same terrible noon-day eruptive *jingle*, though one be beautiful, supremely beautiful, the other ugly, the same jingle as is to be heard in the mirror room at Bagheria. Less awful by far is the nocturnal restlessness of the ghost, a more natural noise the one that is given by the bell cap of the medieval fool. Something evil can come to birth and swarm in sunlight, garrulous sores that have power to inform the glumness and heavy comfort of the north, making even the cold sky chatter with a profusion of glass and fern, wax likeness and canary seed.

The *lazzaroni*, mouthing sly catches of the wicked macaroni song, took easy possession of these southern palaces. Perhaps these buildings are judged entirely by their new life. But probably the whiteness of the stucco was always a lazzar whiteness, the delicate lines of the stairways never averse to the slither of rats. The small churches have an even more terrible vitality. In Sicilian Ragusa, the stunted and multiple domes, red like pizza, sprouting with a green scum, elbow their way into the alleys, squat among the teeming houses, stifle the air, hasten on the charnel smoke, just as the dwarf immensities of Hindoo temples make loud and durable recesses of the bazaar. Here as in the East, the crooked street, as it approaches a religious edifice, bursts into brighter colours, becomes crowded with the pick of beggars and those diseased, leads on to a building that has relinquished its ancestry and throbs with an epochless, evil life in turn distributed to the neighbourhood. Here is a vitality that can beat the railway though the station be near. That is the attraction of the South. A volcano is always beautiful, and always fun if care be exercised. It is clever to borrow from the strength of a volcano; everything here is volcanic. The restlessness of the Rococo ornament is a hundred times augmented by the volcanic nature of the dirt that lies about and in the church. One feels the explosion, sees the explosion in the played-out washing that hangs between the houses. The lit candles in the churches are a million fuses, the wealth of rolling twisted pillars, the priceless marbles, inexhaustible loads of powder.

Yet the life of the convulsive noon-day is less harmful than depression diffused by the afternoon towns of north Italy, by the casermas of Pisa, the hotels of Vicenza, the arcades of Cesena, the perpetual road-mending of Florence and Modena. And the beauty of good Rococo is obvious. But one should pass through southern Italy quickly. Not that Rococo buildings do not wear. Why does one complain? Perhaps beauty ought to reassure. What of this Quattro Cento palace that one has come to see at Jesi? Will it wake the town, or will it capitulate to a time of the day as does Vicenza to the afternoon, Palermo to noon, Catania, Lima and Barcelona to the evening hum broad with cisterns of shadow, cities that carry their parks as caparisoned horses their plumes?

This piazza does not seem helpful. Rain falls on a fountain of imperturbable, spewing lions, like a torrent that pours off a good mackintosh, leaving the stuff wet, but no wetter than before. The fountain faces an enormous theatre. Pergolesi, as well as Frederick Hohenstaufen, was born in Jesi. What courage to build that theatre now, but even greater courage to open it and stage a soirée at Jesi! Sitting in the café del teatro – benches and wine of the country – one gets a good view of the priest's room upon the topmost floor of the opposite building. He has the keys to the library and to the gallery with the Lorenzo Lotto pictures. Should one ring the bell, certainly a woman will lean out of a high window and in answer to the question whether the priest is at home, will say, either that he sleeps, or that he is in the church, or at the café, or out eating, or that he has been dead these three months, the *poveretto*...

So this is the building one has come to see, this square brick edifice that is in bloom. For the decrepit brick has given birth to straight stone window-frames beaded as with the pips of young fruit. Wood litters the broken-down courtyard within. The stone arches are filled up. How stone hates wood, even this afflicted stone remembers that. Afflicted? No. The miracle begins to catch the heart, the miracle of Aaron's blossoming rod. That was a Quattrocento effect, just as Moses' miracle of the splashing water from the mountain side is Baroque. But Aaron's rod is the greater wonder.

And now the East and North recede. Here is the southern effect scattering time and memories. For it is immediate, without rhythm, like the open face of the rose.

I write of the South in contrast to North and East thus brought together; not the South of the eruptive noon-day which has relation to North and East, but the South in which life is outward, spread in space.

This southern stone is neither barren nor volcanic, but the repository for humanistic fantasies, particularly those symbolizing southern compulsion to throw life outward, to objectify. In the great period of the fifteenth century, Renaissance sculptors made stone to bloom.

Such effect in relation to stone, and other effects that will gradually reveal themselves, are referred to in this book by the symbol 'Quattro Cento', actually as one word the Italian chronological expression for fifteenth century. *I will not use it at all in this its proper sense.* The special content with which I am concerned, though neglected by writers on the period, permeates the spirit and the art of the fifteenth century. But I call 'Quattro Cento' only the direct and manifest expression of this content.

And I hope in the end that my use of the term will become an idea inevitably associated with the naming of those hundred years.

I write of stone. Few Northerners and few Orientals love stone: to the majority it is a symbol of barrenness. London streets would be unbearable except for movement and noise and night. Is it not horrid so much stone standing there in the two minutes' silence; and can you think of the endless pavements without the feet upon them? Yet stone inspired the development of the visual arts, that is the southern arts, so far as 'visual' refers to arts concerned with spatial, rather than with rhythmic or temporal, values. I want to show the highest effect of mass as unrelated to suggestions of rhythm or movement, as a supreme achievement, the only mirror of human aim. I exhibit stones the opposite of barren.

But I need to introduce you gradually to southern stone. The easiest images will at first be those Venice can inspire. There, even a Northerner must observe stone; for it is omnipresent. And he can bear this omnipresence because water, though silent, courses irresistibly, stemming for a time images of death that so much stone might shower on desperate lovers of green fields. Yet since the water runs slow, stone stands among it with the minimum of distraction, between water and sky. It is rare to see a stone building rise compact and white from soil: how much more solid when grown from water that bears a gondola brushing its hollowness against the lowest moulding.

South Opposed to East and North

From *The Quattro Cento* (1932)

Atkinson and Bagenal write in their book *Theory and Elements of Architecture*: 'Now in both the Egyptian and Mediterranean cases one result of the bright light and of the excellence of the climate was that men had not only leisure to contemplate… but had also forms and colours worth contemplating. Men not only conducted affairs and lived largely out of doors in a physical sense… but also thought and mused out of doors. The "artists" and "thinkers" were able to grow old in the open air. They used their eyes and thought a great deal about what they saw, and thus they came to criticize buildings, as much from the outside on account of their shape and ornament as from inside on account of their convenience. This kind of criticism from outside in a manner leisurely yet acute, and the detachment of mind that it produces, suggests the origin of what we now call "the aesthetic attitude".'[1]

And again, in northern climates,

The hearth becomes the 'focus' of the dreams which men substitute in long dark winters for direct sensuous enjoyment… Also the fire upon the hearth – the substitute for the sun in Northern winters – must be visible… But the greatest change is felt by the type of mind we call the 'artist'. He cannot so easily, in northern countries, contemplate shapes and colours in the open air, paint on walls in the sun, or refine still further the shape of a shrine. Instead, in the intervals between more urgent activities, such as fighting or hunting, he sits in the firelight and carves the handle of a hunting knife or traces an ornament on a pot. Such objects come easily to hand, and on them he can spend his fancy. Thus in hard climates art and ornament tend to be connected directly and frequently with objects of utility. The utensil or the weapon rather than the shrine becomes the characteristic refined object, and the art expended on it has a constant reference to its use or its function. The logic and skill of the maker of beautiful weapons and utensils – the skill of the smith – suggests the origin of what is now termed craftsmanship and the craftsman's attitude to art.

The southern detachment is more direct, perhaps originally more truly aesthetic,[2] even when hidden beneath a naturalistic style which it can easily govern. As for architecture, in the South the coherence of any stone wall is always worth contemplating. Here is the mass-effect that Mother Earth can never give us; while the apertures of a building are ultimate symbols for humans, being not only apertures, but 'reveals' that vivify the mass. We know that the Egyptians, and according to Penrose, the Greeks, oriented their temples so that a particular sun-ray or star should pierce the inner sanctuary as if it were a womb to be fertilized. (In the Quattro Cento the stone bears her sons.) The Egyptians personalized not only the complete building but each aperture and member. The effect they wanted of stone building was monolithic; joints were reduced to a minimum. But this was an imitation of mud construction, and one feels their use of stone was guided almost solely by its durability; they believed in 'salvation by masonry'. So they shut the dead in a stone womb with thousands of years in which to attain new birth.

The Greeks are largely explained by their marble. They understood how it stands clear, a surface, unlike wood or mud, with little absorption, a solid outwardness, then; and in this its character there lies the key to all humanism. Indeed, there exists a parallel between the Greek and Quattro Cento position.

As a rule the Greeks used plaster on their stone to obtain a smoother, more homogeneous and more reflecting surface. But the unique Pentelic marble of Athens could be made to show a surface brighter and more homogeneous than Poros or other stone treated with plaster. Thus the beauty of the Parthenon.[3] The courses are laid dry, and so finely ground are the joints that some of the stones have actually grown together.

This does not suggest a relation to Egyptian mud design in stone because the Attic builders worked pre-eminently to magnify the tones of light reflected upward.

So great is the proportion of light reflected from the ground in the South that it is not uncommon to see the shadow above and not below, a string-course. Now in the North, most of the light is shed vertically. Walls, soffits and undersides have no longer the same significance. Thus aesthetic as well as climatic necessities mean expenditure on roof. Gone is the wall-bulwark, posited and informed. Instead the roof as a spread bat, stuck in masonry and unable to fly off. Instead of apertures as distinct symbols agleam, myopic eyes and their flamboyant, minatory lenses, the dormer windows of France.

This perpetual 'looking-out' stimulates sense of guilt in the beholder. Sometimes the Gothic cathedral is a ship moored to a reedy bank. But northern Gothic is occasionally defiant of mass-effect, of all that stone means. Wherever possible a surface is pierced, originally for light. At worst the Gothic cathedral is a ship moored in dry dock. For it is only just balanced. That is the effect as well as the actuality where the weight of pinnacles alone secure the buttresses. In these cases, as in all Gothic altogether, there is bound to be an effect of sitting up and staring, a mean betwixt the desired effect of pinnacles soaring away upwards and the constructional fact that their weight in its downward thrust secures a dangerous balance. Though not disposed to advocate that a building should express the truth of its construction, I find disturbing so vertical a contrariety.

'Sitting up and staring' suggests the strange figures that recline on elbows above Etruscan tombs. For Florentine Gothic has a similar quality, whereas fifteenth-century Gothic in other parts of Italy is often the vehicle of mass-effect freed from the northern necessity to pierce and probe and fret for light. Often what I call Quattro Cento is transparently Gothic; Gothic powers in treatment of emblem lavished on the nature of the stone. A wind-swept Gothic exuberance that forges intricate the corselets of the fierce German aristocrats, that hoods simply, classically, the eagles of the Apennines in sculpture, yet revels in the pleasant

South; such Italian Gothic of the elephantine foliage and disky bosses inspired Quattro Cento carving.

As well as possible Etruscan affinities, the Florentines showed northern traits. Their masons were the best craftsmen in Italy. Except for some of their great sculptors whose masterpieces led the Quattro Cento ('great' partly because of revolt from their tradition), they were essentially craftsmen, I mean in the sense of a few pages back. They belonged to the North in so far as they were cold with their material for all their unique skill, I might say *because* of their great skill since, for the completely self-contained work of art, a major withdrawal, a slightly inhuman sternness is essential. The artificer whittling an ivory night after night before the hearth becomes a trifle abstracted. The pattern hangs in the void, isolate but for convention. A sobriety, then, borrowed from the complete objectivity of death; economy not of design nor of emotion but of emotional transparency, must be imposed, generally by means of convention.

All art must have Form, a trick of completeness. This sobriety that I mean is a further withdrawal and realizes Form narrowly. Creation is not so fresh though it be better defined. How vulgar to gild the lily when it may be frosted for the generations! Yet in some moods you feel but the narrowness of Chinese painting however varied the examples. It is an old Spanish custom, a way they have in the Highlands. Mode of contemplation is subtle, fixed. Naturally. In northern and eastern climates contemplation is less easy and more searching. The artist rescues beauty. He dilates or abstracts, for he is not incessantly stimulated, except he surrounds himself with refinement upon refinement. Yet where the light comes up from the ground the year through they needed but a grand order for their beauty.

The greatest regional distinction that can be made in art is between the naturalistic abandon toward which southern art tends to develop (not always to advantage as in the case of some Hellenistic sculpture), and the more conventionalized art proper to the North and the far-East. The abandon, rather than the naturalism, is the point; exuberance, so vastly different from luxuriance in northern and oriental art: not the

later virtuoso exuberance of the Baroque but the exuberance that
originates solely, as it were, in the stone itself because by its nature it
is the only object from which all the primary fantasies connected with
light can be made to emerge, all the fantasies, that is, underlying visual
art as a whole. For this compact and direct exuberance only found in
Quattro Cento work and in the Buddhist and early Hindoo sculpture
of India and Khmer (to arrive at the conception Quattro Cento I needed
often to visit the Amaravati sculptures on the staircase of the British
Museum), in which beauty is not rescued but discovered, taken together
with a contemporary and crowning art[4] that treats the desire to make
manifest as a desire fulfilled, I enter a special plea in this book. For
though other art may be infinitely more 'perfect', that is to say, better
defined, more 'eternal' in its values, that is to say, with a more withdrawn and therefore better selected objectivity, no other creative power
is so tense and direct; and in so far as all life is an attempt to transform
subject into object, an outwardness of a complete not a withdrawn
subject, southern art is the mirror of human aim.

A misunderstanding that I must immediately guard against when
using such phrases as 'naturalistic abandon' in contrast to 'convention',
is that I should seem to infer an absence of 'style' in the Quattro Cento.
Actually the Quattro Cento would never have occurred if the inherent
love of a grand style which underlies the Italian genius for magnitude[5]
had not been excited by Roman studies, by rediscovery of classic forms,
by reassertion of aesthetic order. This style is today still largely made up
of Roman remembrance. Every trumpet note in Italy rings out against
the embossed side of an old triumphal car not far drawn out in the
close night of Italian time.

The triumphal side of the Renaissance has been written up. But
we best catch the sense of it when reading of some festival celebration,
probably in honour of Borso d'Este, lord of Ferrara, in which over-
loaded medieval allegories are manipulated as elements of a *trionfo*,
the acclaimed entry of a man into his town. The idea of triumph is
not primarily that of success, but, following the Roman model, that
of victory over the barbarians. As the fillet about the conquering brow

chastens the forehead, cleanses, distributes the hair, and is chastened,
so man and his enemies, human and natural, after a conflict in which
he has won by noble exertion of intellect and passionate desire, uncover
in the event a wealth of sanity and emotional coherence that scatter the
delicate agonies of man distraught and incapable.

The people of Italy in the fifteenth century were fully capable. Artisans, craftsmen of all kinds, were busy making triumphant objects for
their free-living despot patrons – free-living because they had loved the
near thing, perhaps in the first instance a stone wall.

Now the Quattro Cento was dependent for so general a manifestation on northern, and no less, as we shall see, on oriental exquisite
craft, as well as on southern temperament. I have already indicated the
importance of the Gothic spirit in the Quattro Cento. The movement
is partly that of a northern people discovering the South, the light.
At any rate the aristocracy were for the most part German stock whose
fiefs had been granted by a German Holy Emperor. Gradually and increasingly old Rome and the Mediterranean had worked on German
and Lombard blood and on imported oriental art-forms.

And here an attempted analogy between this Quattro Cento position
and the Greek.[6]

It is important to remember in Homer the special sense of beautiful
and elaborate craftsmanship everywhere displayed, and the prominence of the god of the forge, Hephaestos or Vulcan, who is indeed the
husband of Aphrodite. Beautiful craftsmanship existed at all times
as a background to Greek art. Also in Homer, columns (on the exterior
of a building) are mentioned rarely as compared with 'high roofs', and
a custom that is common to the Northern and many primitive cultures
is found in Homer, namely that of covering a building with sheets of
metal (*Odyssey* VII, 37, House of Alcinous). But the Dorian Greeks are
generally believed to be a Nordic people come south; the impression
given by Homer is of a people with a new and youthful relish for light
and for brightness. The adjectives 'bright', 'shining' and 'polished' are
frequent: the sense of surface brightness is everywhere in the *Odyssey*

and *Iliad*. The impression conveyed is of a race with a strong culture of its own but sharpened to a relish of surfaces and textures by new and brilliant climatic conditions – conditions which in the course of centuries were to modify original forms. The Homeric conception of Olympus, or the dwelling place of the gods, is the conception of a people who take conscious pleasure in light. It is explicitly described in the *Odyssey* thus: 'Not by winds is it (Olympus) shaken, nor ever wet with rain nor doth the snow come nigh thereto, but most clear air is spread about it cloudless and the white light floats over it' (*Odyssey* VI. Butcher and Lang, p.93).

My ignorance precludes my attempt to labour the Indian parallel. Early Indian sculpture in which there appears intensification of every manner, every borrowing as in fifteenth-century Italy, resembles the Quattro Cento more than does Greek culture which was occupied with imposition of order. The same Greek human standard was also the objective of the Quattro Cento but not so much as a principle of order; since they could not unravel at once the medieval hotch-potch of order and theology. The immediate object of release would be anything solid and material. The stone is carved to express bond-breaking birth. This phrase suggests low relief and arabesques and other sculpture treated pictorially, which are the primary manifestations of the Quattro Cento. But that spirit was later capable of expression in severest architectural design.

However since Quattro Cento, and indeed Italian sculpture as a whole, can with few exceptions be condemned by a purist as 'pictorial' – that is to say, not essentially plastic, – I must defend the low relief.

Representational and Non-Representational Art

From *The Quattro Cento* (1932)

The Renaissance was an intensification of all known art-forms. From
the preceding pages it might appear that that material was entirely
western; which is far from being the case. And now that I have roughly
indicated the manner of Italian genius, I can proceed to suggest with
less fear of being identified with those who find the roots of the Renaissance in Byzantine or Mohammedan or even far-Eastern culture, the
diverse heritage of linear treatment that the Quattro Cento concreted
into mass-effects.

I am aware, then, that throughout the early Christian and medieval
period, Italy was inundated with successive waves of oriental forms in
art as in life from Syrian, Sassanian, Coptic, Byzantine and Islamic cultures. I am aware that near-Eastern workmen created the later Roman
art. I am aware that all European art-forms have come to the West from
the East except for what the Classical Greeks created out of their Semitic
heritage and spread into the eastern world through Hellenistic art.
Even that art, to express the authoritative psychology of Empire, be it
Sassanian or Roman (*vide* Trajan's column with its Assyrian-like bands
of commemorative procession), or to express the authority of a spiritual
idea as that of Christ ruler of the world, tended to go back on its development and reveal at the touch of contemporary Semitism, the stylization
or expression by symbol from which Hellenic naturalism had grown.
For representation must be less objective, less realistic, more patently
a symbol, to express a solely spiritual content or the forces of Nature
in general or any generalized authority. The symbol or emblem must
be formal, abstracted, lifted away from the particular and the individual, in short, an emblem less objective than in Quattro Cento art for
instance. In the case of Semitic and, indeed, of most art, creation and

re-creation of conventionalized but living symbol, *is* the creation of art. This is safe-guarded art, a safe and confined projection of symbol. Whereas for Quattro Cento art the process is reversed. The creative act itself, the turning of subject into concrete and particular and individual form, is the symbol, one that is universal and that cannot confine and direct artists except those inspired to the pitch of so universal a range, except those for whose period art itself is the living emblem.

Further from the Mediterranean where the distant can be made near and objective, beyond Semitic centres of the fertile valleys where representational art as we have it in Europe arose, the great and popular art of nomad peoples, whether Aryan, Semitic or Mongol, has flourished, the radical art of North and East, which, for purposes of antithesis, I simplified earlier on into terms of craftsmanship.

Strzygowski writes:

Non-representational[1] art is not more backward nor more primitive than representational; it is simply different. Instead of being proud of what we have done, we of the north ought rather to deplore our excessive surrender to the histrionic feeling of the south. To personify and to anthropomorphize all and everything is to attempt the opening of every door with the one master-key 'Man', and to recede far indeed from great Nature and her secrets. It is clear enough that the present generation has deliberately turned against representation... Christians were once as far removed from representation as were the Greeks originally.[2]

And again:

In my book *Altai-Iran und Völkerwanderung* I attempted to show that in the perfected style of Islam there still survives that non-representational northern and nomadic art known to us through the work of pre-historic times and that of the later Teutonic and Turkish tribes. In the period of the great migrations, both these races advanced towards the ancient forcing houses of culture, just as the Greeks, Celts, Persians, and Indians had done in pre-Christian times. Originally none of these peoples represented; they first learned this mode of artistic expression in the south. The student of art is inclined to think that the contrast between north and south may be explained by the transition to a higher stage of culture. In the south, man passed immediately from the culture of the earlier Stone Age into a social system which sought to cast a spell on the object by representation, as the primitive hunter attempted to do when he made pictures of his game. In the north, on the other hand, formative art developed out of the handicraft of the later Stone Age. It enclosed space in borders and filled it with ornament which for the most part followed from the nature of the material and the process adopted, ornament which was therefore geometrically designed for the purpose of pleasing the eye.

I do not want to twist Strzygowski's translated words. But I must remark on the phrase 'ornament which for the most part followed from the nature of the material and the process adopted'. 'Follows', not *founded in* the nature of the material. The latter will be the case only when the artist projects into the material his own vitality by means of humanistic fantasies.

It is unnecessary for me to defend southern art against Strzygowski. I prefer it for the greater objectivity he admits. I can agree about the baleful influence of southern art on northern, though I feel that but for a classical element due to the Roman church, which kept Rome alive and made renascence possible, Gothic art could not have achieved so fine a sculpture. But today the North is dumb after centuries of Roman Church and of the Renaissance. Circumstances of the machine age (which so far from being the antithesis of the handicraft ages, is their logical outcome and final triumph), though they heighten sense of design, outstrip the arts still rooted in the handicrafts from which they arose. The South takes over the machine and will make something of it, just as formerly it has taken over crafts from North and East to compose elements of a great art.

Southern art, in the course of a development, will be identified with some conception of mass. I would identify decorative art, according to

Strzygowski the original art of all Aryan peoples, with the manipulation of line. The substitution in the preceding sentence of the adjective 'decorative' for 'non-representational', is to my present purpose because I would thereby indicate as well as pattern, the flatness on which pattern is made. The third dimension in sculpture and painting must be connected with the representing of human form from which, again, is derived conception of mass; or rather, from contemplation of the warm stone into which compact humanistic fantasies are projected, there proceeds a conception of mass. Not that linear conception can be eliminated in any art. The virtue of a mass-effect is the immediacy on which I have expatiated, that absence of music, or if you prefer, of *arrière-pensée*. Such content is narrow. As symbol, manifold symbol, elastic line, spiritual line exists even amid the greatest triumphs of mass. Everything can be interpreted by linear conception save immediacy.

On the other hand, solid objects of any sort must have *some* connection with mass. You pass a building or enter it, you revolve around, while the building remains immediate. But whereas this immediacy was magnified in the South (surely the home of architecture, the abstract art nourishing all grand scale design), in the North it is slurred over: even more in the far-East where we miss a grand touch in design.

The building and the human figure are things immediate to the senses. Hence the representational art of the South in whose light building fructifies. When, as has been the case with the visual arts of most cultures, architecture is not the parent art, there results an intrusion of music. On the other hand mass, pure mass, will convey no effects, even of human form, beyond those so abstract ones of immediacy; no subtly woven fantasies, no philosophy beyond the humanistic one of space, of the worship of beauty, of the open staring face of the rose. Comparatively few motives are eligible for immediacy treatment.[3] Southern art, then, will easily become sterile, as it is less charged with diverse emotional content than the art that is essentially, though not perhaps literally, non-representational (for some naturalism from the South has percolated almost everywhere, just as decorative conception has been carried south).

Non-representational art avoids the complete articulation prized in the South, in south Europe as in India. For the feeling that inspires non-representational art is more 'profound', while the means by which it is realized are severely disciplined by some form on whose symbolic significance aesthetic significance depends. And whereas this art, with an aesthetic so guarded, so sound, less easily becomes sterile, while it also achieves a greater subtlety of subject or content, yet the symbol thus denoted is too easily stylized, conventionalized, mechanized even, and the obligation for original effort by every artist is diminished. Non-representational art subsumed under the heading, 'withdrawn art', will never sink into the vulgarity of which southern art is capable. But, equally, artists of pronounced genius are shackled. It is an art, then, tribal at root or popular, less dependent upon individual genius the cult of which, as we know from the Renaissance, is both the cause and the result of humanism.

In decorative art, landscape will be directly symbolic: at highly civilized periods it is, foremost, the expression of a mood, of a poetic idea. Poetry is near to music. Thus the pictorial art of the far-East of which Sung 'philosophical landscape' is a major but typical achievement, a cunning elaboration of the written character. Whereas Cézanne's flowers, innocent of moods or modes, do not point beyond themselves toward anything of a different sphere to which direct reference is impossible. They expose, these flowers, the ordered world of light and space and colour.

Chapter VIII

From *The Quattro Cento* (1932)

E sotto un'alta quercia, humile e stanco,
Legato stava un gentile alepardo[1]

I have referred to the subject of non-representational and Semitic art
because I want to indicate the immense education in line and in the
soundest or safest aesthetic that Italy gained from the oriental and
Gothic culture of the middle ages. I would now stress the prominence in
Italy of Semitic forms, because, apart from their importation throughout the middle ages as embodied to varying degrees in Byzantine, Persian, Syrian, Egyptian and Coptic cultures, there subsisted on Italian
soil an ancient Semitic culture which had been far less properly hellen-
ized than in Greece. For I believe the Etruscans were Semitic or Hittite
by race. Certainly one attributes to them, besides their power of modelling and antecedent to it, the particularly *graphic* mode of Semitic, but
especially Hittite, representation; also sadistic propensities in general,
brutalities of a kind that we have always associated with the East. This
vague suggestion will supply a theme when I examine Florentine art.
For the moment I wish but to suggest an oriental substratum in Italy,
which of itself explains both how easily oriental influences were taken
up and how vital could be their transmutation into humanism.

One can too easily overlook the origins of Rome. Roman art, no less
than Roman religion, in the first place is Etruscan. Roman love for the
Greek has a coherent aspect if we imagine with what darker lore and
fiercer characterization these Latins felt imbued before the shining
Greek idealism. It was an Etruscan Italy the Romans conquered bit by
bit, Etruscan but for the Greek south and the fierce Picenes of Romagna
and the races of the Veneto. These natives, be it said, had kept their

Aryan non-representational art.

A vast difference between Romans and Etruscans springs to the eye in political organization. Whereas the Roman nucleus spreads compact, spreads in empire over the Ancient World, Etruscan temper prefers the loosest of confederacies, non-colonial and based upon the brilliant unit of true (not public school) aristocracy. So Rome could conquer Etruria bit by bit. Veii need not have fallen if the twelve cities had helped. Even her nearest neighbours, Caere, Tarquinia and Vulci, remained unmoved. Historians tell the same story about Italy at the close of the fifteenth century. Not the Romans but the vulgar French, the Spaniards, the Germans and the Swiss, reimburse themselves from Italy. But before this, as well as the lust for Roman power, the cities, the twelve cities, the hundred cities at this time of renascence intensify their separate character from peak and on the plain, large in peace and in the Condottieri warfare that crowns the less intricate struggles of medieval Italy.

Of medievalism I will not attempt a detailed recipe. But in the third volume I shall show how medieval, how oriental, Italian literary pretensions during the fifteenth century still were. In spite of the humanists' and their patrons' enthusiasm for the antique and for the revival of antique studies, little really western thought appears before the neo-Aristotelian movement in Venice that inspired Giorgione at the beginning of the sixteenth century.

Popular imagination drew upon the East in the Renaissance. I take as an instance the illuminations of the Florentine fifteenth-century *Aeneid* in the Biblioteca Laurenziana.[2] In one miniature we see the Trojans in Byzantine costume shooting arrows back to back at deer. Ducks swim the foreground. Both huntsmen and hunted posture decoratively. Another miniature shows Juno dressed like the Queen of Sheba, while the mitred Jove is no western pontiff.

As I have said, the Renaissance is an intensification of all forms; not least of the oriental. Witness the fifteenth-century cassone panels. This painting was a popular art; those rich processional scenes based on the festal cavalcades with which great nobles entertained the people, are decked out not only with oriental stuffs, but with oriental types

72

from which the people created their fantasies, even those of religion. Eastern bestiaries supply many a detail and incident, symbols such as the Assyrian one of flying birds so loved of Pinturicchio[3] were used in fourteenth- and fifteenth-century painting, decoratively and with a gusto.

Manifold symbols of oriental religions find a place, particularly in the Siennese painting. This art, put in grand movement by the freedom of Giotto, sums up a whole era that has gathered colour and design from oriental textiles. Berenson remarked in 1909 that no other European school is nearer to the painting of the far-East.[4] He considers that the influence of the mystics made for this character. An art with something in common with the far-East was adapted to express spiritual content with a grace that classical precepts, though the Church clung to them for grandeur, could not emulate. At Siena one is reminded of Indo-Persian painting.

Soulier writes of the Siennese school in the early Renaissance:[5] 'Les caractères d'Extreme-Orient, qui paraissent parfois moins accusés vers la fin du 14ᵉ siècle, reprennent une insistance nouvelle jusqu'au plein milieu du 15ᵉ et au-delà: chez Giovanni di Paolo, chez Sassetta, Francesco di Giorgio, Matteo di Giovanni, Sano di Pietro, et chez Neroccio Landi qui pousse peut-être à son paroxysme le parti pris de la grâce artificielle et de la délicate afféterie... On a voulu voir chez ces peintres un mouvement d'archaïsme: en vérité, il y a recrudescence d'influences extrême-orientales, ce qui veut dire que les causes persistent et que les apports se renouvellent.'* With that I agree in general. Consider the case of Francesco di Giorgio. It bears out the formula for the Renaissance: 'intensification of all forms'. Francesco di Giorgio

---

* 'Far-Eastern subjects, which at times appear less apparent around the late fourteenth century, become pronounced again right up to the mid-fifteenth century and beyond: in the work of Giovanni di Paolo, Sassetta, Francesco di Giorgio, Matteo di Giovanni, Sano di Pietro, and also with Neroccio Landi, who perhaps takes this inclination for artificial grace and delicate affectation as far as it can go ... These painters have typically been seen to embody an archaic movement, when in fact it is a matter of an increase in Far Eastern influences, which means that their causes persist and their contributions are renewed.' – Ed.

Martini was the great Quattro Cento architect, inheritor of Luciano Laurana, the model engineer who built, or was in charge of, 136 castles for Federico di Montefeltro; Francesco whom Leonardo and Bramante summoned to their aid because they couldn't put the dome on Pavia cathedral, who wrote his treatise on architecture praising Vitruvius and the human form as the mean of proportion, who built at Cortona Madonna di Calcinajo which vies in monumental completeness with the works of Vignola and Palladio; Francesco di Giorgio of the delicate perspective drawings: yet he painted Siennese 'primitives'.

Intensification of all forms, but to the purposes of humanism. Hence the importance of the antique, the worship of the classical world which the ignorant could but deck out with oriental finery. If I have kept the balance in these notes, it is now unnecessary for me to stress the pagan intent of the Quattro Cento or the introduction of classical architectural members, or the copying of antique bronzes, or the influence of the church in the middle ages, propagating the idea of Rome. Nor do I feel it necessary to expatiate upon the 'proto-Renaissance' of Giotto and the Pisani, an example previous to the Quattro Cento of charged and simple Gothic line caught to the South where that purity excites a grandness of style still Roman. But the time is not yet for line to be concreted into mass. The distant still is distant, sacrosanct.

These influences are better known than the oriental. I need more, then, to emphasize the fact that in the fifteenth century all this orientalizing was material for the expression of humanistic exuberance; the delicate and sensitive line, for instance, of Siennese and Umbrian painting, line which is both Gothic or Giottesque, Byzantine and Persian; as well as the rich zoning of colour won from long apprenticeship with oriental textiles – these were now modes of a western, new joy. Taken up with what Monsieur Soulier might call this paroxysm, Man was referred back to the materials from which love of colour still came and by which more than by contemplation of art, it renews itself. But whereas in the glaring East these materials are preferably precious stones and plumage, in the light of Italy marbles of all kinds are loved, marble that is vast and tonal as well as brilliant; so that there arises, principally

74

in Venice, the western art of tonal painting. But first those answering blocks of colour on cassone panels and the zonal treatment of colour by Siennese painters as a whole, had helped the greatest of all painters, the Quattro Cento figure Piero della Francesca, to articulation of form by colour.

Upon education in line and in the unlimited content that line can express austerely, the humanistic impulse superseding, there follow the greatest achievements of mass-effect.

To reinforce this dictum which, in my opinion, more than any other single statement indicates the coincident circumstances necessary to produce so great an art triumph as the Renaissance, I must consider Gothic contribution to line. Gothic line is as important to the development of Renaissance sculpture as Gothic, far-Eastern and Byzantine influences are to the development of Renaissance painting. Therefore of far greater importance to the Renaissance as a whole. For the painters, if you remember, depend largely upon the sculptors and upon their love of stone.

Of Gothic art Strzygowski writes:

Northern art renounced its proper character in so far as it conceded to the human figure in architecture a place only equalled for importance in India. A distinction must, however, be made. In India the suggestion came not from the art of the immigrant peoples in the north of the country, but from that of the older population in the south, just as further west it came from Egypt to the Greek art of Southern Europe. In Northern Europe, in Gothic art, however, the essential lies not, as in India and Greece, in the human figure itself, but in the draped figure – not in the body, but in the covering given to the body by art. The figure is subordinated to form, as in East Asia; natural shapes become merely the vehicles of rhythmical line. Moreover, these Northern figures are in organic unity with the body of the structure. The consciousness that the various parts of the organism are thus naturally enlivened leads, independently of the human figure, to a luxuriant overgrowth of vegetable and animal forms unequalled in any other art, even in the South.[6]

In the North one will expect constant reminder in construction as in detail, of wood and thicket and their tall percolating light. Gothic constructional exuberance was the art-form of a religious paean which gave in the manner of hymns and psalms the allegory of natural force. Similarly the centralized but spacious plan of an early Armenian church such as the cathedral at Ani which, though a purer expression of Aryan art-form, may be said to anticipate Gothic;[7] for it expresses doctrine. In spite of the compactness, in spite of economic planning which calls to mind the civilized Romanesque of Aquitaine, a style itself derived from Armenia, I cannot discover from these sources a true mass-effect. Such building is conceived as a whole, it is true, and compared with this planning, the columnar styles of early Roman churches seem so scrappy that one regrets with Strzygowski the triumph of the long nave in Christian art at the behest of ecclesiastics. But though you hold the plan to your eye, you cannot feel space or instantaneity. Spaciousness, yes, constructional certainty, but these were induced to foster particular emotions, Christian aspects. True mass-effect is itself an expression of worship, the worship of space, of things set in space which are destroyed by any mingling with afterthought. The clustered shafts of Thalish and Ani soar, blind arcades run, they have an aim. But mass-effect pushes out time or succession in favour of a thing complete, immutable, and so, innocent of direction. Fine architectural planning, then, economic and centralized, does not necessarily mean the kind of tension I call mass.

As for the immense constructional expressiveness of Gothic, come south it stimulated, even in large part created, the humanistic fantasy to have the stone alive. And how easily the Gothic riot of figure and vegetation, upon an access of paramount love for stone itself, became stone-blossom. A thousand years of expressiveness in line sought tense fixation in mass-effect. Gothic itself, the late Burgundian Gothic of Claus Sluter and his followers, sought compression of shape, sought to concrete rich lines into mass with the finality of a fierce and dramatic naturalism, though not based, as it was soon to be in Italy, on anatomy and the antique. So Burgundian sculpture is sometimes eccentric. For the antique imposes a sanity, a clearness by light of which each excess can be successfully perpetrated. Over Donatello's most heated excesses there presides a canon which is yet in no sense a restraint.

The Avesta tells of the power 'Hvareneh' which governs birth and sprouting, which makes the waters run. Wherever Aryan decorative art penetrated through symbolic animal, symbolic landscape and vegetation, Hvareneh images were expressed, though sunk into other religions. Strzygowski gives so diverse instances as scenes from the chase constant in Persian art, the steadfast animals cut on the façade of Spoleto's cathedral, the mosaic of river landscape in the apse of Sant'Apollinare in Classe. Vine-scroll, even though mixed with acanthus by the Romans, kept an old significance. Principally from Gothic, forces of Hvareneh were collected by the Quattro Cento, and then attributed to the stone. Hence the parallel to Indian sculpture in which Iranian decoratives such as are to be found slightly modified by Indian flora on Sarnath stupa, obtain from coalition with Dravidian forms *representational* efflorescence, particularly in the Sunga sculpture at Bharhut and in the early Andhra sculpture at Sanchi.

This subject I must defer indefinitely. I believe a case could be made out to show that Quattro Cento art alone has expressed fully the symbols of the oldest Aryan cult in history, Mazdaism.

I conclude these introductory notes with a description of a Quattro Cento masterpiece, Verrocchio's *lavabo* in the small room adjoining the Old Sacristy of San Lorenzo, Florence. For thus, before embarking on the essay, I hope the better to give the meaning of stone-blossom and incrustation and emblematic tensity. Moreover I write of this *lavabo* (a basin for priests to wash their hands and vessels) at a length which would hold up the argument in the body of the essay, where it really belongs.

Verrocchio's Lavabo

From *The Quattro Cento* (1932)

Inasmuch as Verrochio and Pollaiuolo and the other great Florentines
were principally concerned with stress and strain, – with movement –
it is obvious that composition will deviate more and more from simple
correspondence; for movement must be balanced by movement corresponding *in power*; with the result that one resolute gesture may compensate a repeated directional stress. This extremely *qualitative* nature of
the objects of balance when the main purpose is of stresses and strains,
is also true, of course, of all objects of composition be they represented
as animate or inanimate, in motion or at rest; but in the case of stresses
and strains an ever increasing complication in correspondence is necessary to avoid their cancelling each other out, instead of enhancing one
another. The sum must be a synthetic movement, generally circular,
which keeps the whole process going.

Verrocchio was a great master of design. I say it contemplating the
lavabo. This greatness, in itself, does not cause the *lavabo* to be the
masterpiece of the Quattro Cento. Raphael was a great designer. His
compositions are 'dynamic'; nevertheless he owed too much to the
compass. Raphael's hardness can never be put in relation to the Quattro
Cento. Raphael sailed very close to the wind. No one else has so nearly
succeeded in reducing art to formulae. We have paid dearly for this
copy-book talent. Today we have reckoned the cost of the Superb, the
High Renaissance.

This *lavabo* is Quattro Cento because here manipulation by design
is much more directly the proof of an exuberant clarity. It glistens,
ascended from an imaginative fund whence strong roots have shot up
in unexampled profusion, necessitous thongs and twines bound for
the light from stirred under-consciousness. But, to meet the day with

78

felicitous acclamation, emergence has recognized marks, Piero de'
Medici's signet emblazoned with diamond, his falcon balanced by
spread wings as from the dawn; and to oppose all vestige of the night,
not up, but down, not out only, but overlaying from crowded heavens
shall the most distant progeny of earth and sea emerge with age-old
abandon into the new life. So the falcon is spread upon the background,
recognized mark nearest the depleted caves of under-consciousness,
now shut with marmolite with which revolves a band of oak leaves and
acorns. In front, coming clear of this wall an urn, a cup and bath, one
inside the other; these upon their slopes and incrustations receive the
large and slow rain of beasts more primitive than to act prehensile,[1]
as scales drop inch by inch, wet thorny tissues caught by the sun as iridescent mud upon the vessels grazed to warmth and wet. The hooded
beast-rain is perpendicular: any other that struck oblique would over-
balance the stoppered urn set in the precious cup standing in the bath.
Instantaneous, two enlarging drops, not to shrink in diffusion like
water, clap the urn; arrested: then slide down the neck of the urn, now
sliding soft, they slip and gradually slide longer again, till friction
gathers them on the major curve. Thereon permeation begins within
matter and life so primitive. Urn shall have living tissues so that there
can be no roll or topple when thus held inside the cup. So beneath the
lip of the cup where scorchings, water sifting and rime have long been
encrusted, as if left to golden communion with the love-chalice after
the banquet has been drained and the guests are drunk, boars' heads
drop from the cup's pierced sides. But they are not detached, they
belong to the scaly bodies and bats' wings adhesive to the urn. This
gradual falling had inevitable momentum, snouts trickling through
beneath the lip of the solid cup. But the glissade of monster-rain is
caught, and only condensation of the boars' breath will damp the bath
below where two dolphins rear up behind the fluted stem of the cup,
panting. The glissade is over, and living ropes rage about the neck of the
urn to catch the ring. They are the tails of these boars'-head dragons.
Contiguous the background, where wind revolves the heavily garlanded
marmolite free from sediment; and on the face of the bath below, a

lion's mask looks out, while at the sides are griffins with women's heads and tails that intercoil to hoist dead weight of bath, rich cup and urn. The smooth rivets of these tails show by contrast how corrugated with flapping spines are the monsters of precious dropping above them. Marine splendours have *descended* upon the urn and crested cup, scorning the bath where priests wash their hands; marble embraced to remembrance of primeval beginnings in lime dropped by countless animals. White upon white stone, these symbols, these gradual amphibian progenitors; while the delicate mouth of the urn passed over, unencumbered, comes free from the background. There, oak in a huge wreath emblazons the green and slimy disc, setting off the architecture of the laden vessels. Ribbons stream on the wind; and where above the falcon sets on the day with his armour of plumage, the wind blows him back tense.

The monster-rain (blight to all but marble), and a tensity, incrustation and stone-blossom – how come they to be grandiose, mass *in excelsis*? First of all, there is the use of coloured stone, the porphyry rch framing the whole, and the serpentine central disc; also the dark colours of the huge lip of the cup. These make the white marble luminous, and lead the eye to the shadows at the junction of surfaces, to where, for instance, the bat wings, ribbed and ending in claws like an umbrella, cling to the urn. Hence the feeling of incrustation, surface into surface, and also of growth from within (witness the oak wreath), – of stone-blossom.

The intensive movements to which I have pointed are the outcome of subtleties in the design that merit a full-length exposition. Still more so, inasmuch as this monument finds little favour with the critics. Ever since Vasari they have attributed it as the work, not of one, but of two masters, largely independent of, or at any rate successive to, one another. And yet I can think of no monument of such complication with so compelling a unity. Here are some aspects of the design in terms of stress and strain.[2]

The falcon at the top with outspread wings faces left, and his left wing he thrusts up higher than the right. This upward and leftward stress has no simple counterpart as it would have in an ordinary 'symmetrical' design. Verrocchio used this same stress to realize the downward fall of the dragons on the urn. The transition is wonderfully carried off by the spiral-patterned stopper on the urn, spiralling up from left through right to left. Beneath, on the urn's side, the right-hand dragon's wing continues the sloping line of the eagle's body, as a downward movement to the right. For this wing reaches higher up the urn than does the wing of the other dragon, and the tail of this first dragon shears off to the right at the urn's neck, so as to leave uninterrupted the line with the eagle's body, a line helped out by the spiral of the stopper. While on the subject of the dragons' wings, I would note the extreme subtlety of their inter-arrangement. I have said why the right-hand one must reach higher than the left, but inasmuch as the right one, as well as making the connection with the eagle's left-upward stress, is the means of carrying on that stress in a right-downward form, it must also reach down lower than the left-hand wing. The claws of the wings fit into each other's spaces – the bottom claw of the right-hand wing being the lowest – and when the top of this wing is reached a space has been gained, so that it is higher than the left-hand wing. How is this: is the right-hand wing larger than the left? No, but they are in different positions. The right wing is spread out to a shape suitable to carry the downward stress, while the left wing is folded and therefore shorter. These shapes have other purposes to serve beside this trick, as I shall describe. For it is the attribute of so ideal a design that every line serves to carry at least one stress and one strain with perfect harmony. The diagonal stress movement – upwards to the left, downwards to the right – is now carried round the bottom of the bath by the griffins. Were they symmetrical, these snaky bodies doubling on themselves and diminishing in tails would turn inwards or outwards both together; but the left one coils inwards, the right one outwards, and so, taken up with the knot of these tails beneath the lion's head – left goes under right – the eye seizes upon a series of coils moving round to the left griffin's head. Thus, the right diagonal stress rounds the bottom of the monument and comes through to the left. But such a rotation is not a sufficient guardian of eternal living held to the instant, not in itself the means of a perennial source of vitality expected from the greatest art. And indeed, it is at this very point, where the tails knot below the lion's mouth, that the mystery resurges, the strain in answer to the stress is here distributed to the formal circles of infinity. The right-hand griffin allowed the stress to pass along her body and be carried off to the left. But she is pulling out to the right all the same, and the part of her body that pulls against the stream is stronger, more rigid, tauter, less mobile. Another prop or break resisting the stress, is the wing of the left dragon, thin and spiky, obstinate, pointing upwards and to the right. The angle of the falcon's body, too, though making the left-upward movement of the diagonal stress, betokens a wind that blows the bird back, so that the right-upward strain of the left dragon's wing, as well as the stress, is upheld by him. All the same, the diagonal stress in its upward and to-the-left division, is still far too strong, heightened as it is because the space on the left of the falcon with his uplifted claw on the ring is more crowded than the space on the right of him. Also the knotting of the tail of the left-hand dragon about the urn is more elaborate than in the case of his fellow, and adds considerably to the weight of the left-hand side. Against this left-upward thrust both the downward-right diagonal stress and the upward-right diagonal strain, are combined. But they are not enough, not if the pre-eminent movement of the whole is to be the slow downward-right of the tight dragon's wing on the urn. To perpetuate a solution (one puts it that way) Verrocchio hit upon an invention as bold as any I know.

Without counteracting his stresses and strains, he achieves a supreme balance by (*a*) deliberately placing the centre of the cup marked by Piero's emblems to the right of the main centre which passes down the middle of the urn, and beneath the cup, down the middle of the lion's head upon the bath. The cup has been turned on its axis slightly to the right. The dragons' heads are in the conspiracy. They are equidistant from the centre of the cup, but *not* from the centre of the whole design. The left head has been brought forward, the right pushed back. Again, the left head is bulkier[3] than the right, and so makes up for the

82

space relinquished by the cup as it was turned from the background plane. These heads were the handles by which the cup was turned. We are back in the realm of masks. On a former occasion they were the heads of primeval monsters set on a serious function. Here is interplay of the formal and the dynamic.

(*b*) (The second way the right side is emphasized so as to achieve balance without confusing a pre-existent movement.) The key to this is Piero's crest with its ribbons on the cup. Again an emphasis on the emblem which has provoked all this creation, and which was shifted from the centre for the previous most spectacular feat of balance. These ribbons are agitated by a wind that blows from left to right, the same wind that blows back the falcon on top and the ribbons about his claws. The flutterings, in accordance with the left origin of the wind, are very faithfully produced. But the climax in this extraordinary feat of compensation is clockwise movement of the wreathed marmolite disc, running from the top left-hand ribbon attached to the wreath, round through the right to the bottom left-hand corner. This time, then, the wind is a rotary movement: look at the different ways the ribbons double. They are not agitated indiscriminately, but to a vital purpose.[4] But finally, this movement is equivocal, neutral; for of the clockwise motion, three-quarters of a circle are completed, and the wind drops at the bottom left-hand corner – see how the ribbon there curls back on itself. So, the rotation has supplied as well the left *down* diagonal stress which the left-hand dragon's wing now echoes. This second function of the clockwise moving wreath makes it the complement to the movement of intercoiled spinous tails where the original stress was softened and rounded.

So, what with the eagle pressing to the left and driven to the right; what with the wreath moving to the right, stopping on the left; what with the diagonal stress cut out of a circle, a circular stress and the resurgence of strains from a knotted tail; what with both dragons' wings moving up and moving down, to left and to right independent of each serving far more intricate correspondences – yet they are a pair, so are the griffins, so are the wings of the falcon, so too the independent ribbons are pairs – were ever shapes more plain yet intricate, movings so simple, inevitable, yet subtle to run on for ever, to run on without compensation: when from another angle it all is compensatory, though headed off by layer upon layer of redistribution, the sources hidden; when five or six emphases, all different, are clear and do not contradict one another when the whole is a mass, whole, shaped, striking the eye, a manifestation of completeness and of resurgence... surely it is a unit representative of all art, which, breaking from the ideal marbles, becomes circumfluent and gives back to life the spirit of life redoubled.

Should it appear that a disproportionate space has been given to this monument, I plead not only that it is a great and neglected work, but also that it is the masterpiece in sculpture of the Quattro Cento spirit. And this helps out a definition. For here and in the sculpture at Rimini one witnesses culmination in the humanizing of the elemental, one witnesses common release humanized, articulated by the voracity of emblem, of one individual's actuate *virtù*. In comparison with the *lavabo*, the Colleoni as emblem is but a memorial, the *virtù* concentrated, pointed, cut free to flaunt the campo, not a contagion in the stone seen and unseen, but a quality, a public reputation, not the almost anonymous inner and personal life transfigured in accomplishment of solidity, the marble consumed. And after Colleoni, the vital Quattro Cento spark was extinguished, and art engages to figure forth the *flow* and *rhythm* of unexcelled vitality. Thus the Baroque. In the Quattro Cento that very flow was the genius that sprung to be solidified, to be turned to instantaneousness in the strong marble core.

Man never lived so deep in other ages, so uninhibited. Externalization has been more facile or crooked, and in art the near taken to the distant, not the distant to the near. Formal living has meant not only formal art with attitudes of discreet mistiness, but also for such chinkless spreading of externalization, has meant arts which magnify the successive, which manipulate various music; arts hostile to mass, to permeation of the solid requiring the full sap. While Romantics, excusably roaring, dissipate the horizon and glean random prophecies from the clouds.

Classical and Romantic, all of it is abstraction, not infusion. Where since the Quattro Cento has the whole spirit rushed to inhabit, rather than to generalize, particularize?

And that the *lavabo* should display such liberty, such a flow of design, yet fulfil itself solely as a tense concretion, makes it the point of convergence between the grandest emotional triumph and the greatest subtlety in artistic perpetuation, coincidents that uniquely glorify the capturing alive of the life-flux by traps of tangible stone; a glory, be it said, synonymous with civilization. For what else is civilization but a converting of formless power to organized show, to outwardness? More, to toss the deep to the surface, the contriving of outwardness, is the labour of all humanity, but the joy of humanism and of art. Death is the name for complete objectivization; the subject to be converted has been eliminated. Timelessness is complete. Detached thought is near death, is death's instrument, turning life to stone. It is more profoundly evincive to turn stone to life. Primitive man and the poet are more profound than Buddha. Every subjective attitude, however naïve, is preferable to objectivization achieved by the wholesale denial of that to be objectivized. There is a revelation of life and a revelation of death. Both are needed, they imply each other. Both are needed for untrammelled living. (The Quattro Cento sometimes struck perfect balance.) Revelation of life made possible by that of death, gives us consciousness; we feel living: and revelation of death made possible by that of life leads us to conceive the world, objects, to make ourselves manifest, to objectify, to concrete the flow of living into personality so there be passions and passionate intellect to the purpose of their expression. Spirit generally suffers thin, and death in season, out of season, employs his endless suction. Life becomes too sublimate. Deep life has not come up, but escapes unfledged to hunger in the void. No concretion, but inhumanly to abstract is now the deadly showing. Whereas showing should be victory over death thus 'used' by life and thus compelled to serve life, to give eternity to content, to quality, to feeling experienced in the present. Death is the end; that finality should be won to life as self-expression. Beyond this, as that which defines life and bounds it, as that which moulds life and destroys it, as that which determines the process of satisfaction and the end or final satisfaction, death should have no other significance for man. When triumphant, death is vile. Complete objectivity is horrible when life is conquered though not drained. The purity of death is easily come by, so too is the grasp of Nirvana when life is pale, when what is to be expressed is not at all lively. Such preoccupation is childish, impudent, cheating. But further, death itself pales if not fed by any blood of life; and as there is nought but life and death, since when one is in part denied so must be the other, a brood of sunken alivers proclaiming but the lively dead as they pass through the wheels of re-incarnation – some such shallowness can prevent all values.

But whether consciousness, the gift of death to life, has any right to stand aloof from life, whether, after all, death brings to life just a little that is beyond the life-death relationship, it is not our place to wonder, not till we have surpassed the Quattro Cento in self-expression and 'used' death to the uttermost for the purposes of living.

The Quattro Cento in Florentine Art[1]

From *The Quattro Cento* (1932)

I. DONATELLO

My account of Donatello is inadequate for any but my present purpose. The attainment of Donatello is so immense, I mean the translation of that which moved him into forms of art is so personal, his inventions are so original, so purely artistic, that it gives me some cause for dismay to find that it would be quite irrelevant for me to describe his work from the angle of pure aesthetic value. But the psychological approach is not the nonsense it was some thirty years ago, since, meanwhile, criticism has dilated upon purely aesthetic value. Indeed, there is now the danger that the more literary aspects of art, the aspects in which the co-ordination of art and life are implicit, the only aspects that are fit subject for literature, will be overwhelmed by considerations of pure aesthetic. Is it not time again – for we have learned the anti-Ruskin lesson well – to re-estimate the spirit of the Renaissance, to attempt anew the co-ordination of the spirit of western man with his art; or must we refuse to the Italian subject any consideration which, at present, owing to ignorance and to our distance from African civilization we cannot bestow upon Negro sculpture?

Of course in the long run, a more psychological approach is not at variance with a more purely aesthetic approach. On the contrary, the former should be indispensable to the latter, and vice versa. I have by no means attempted their separation, since neither exists as a pure entity and since only for a partisan purpose does their division seem to exist. But I, too, redress a balance in the appreciation of Italian art. My concern with Donatello is solely in his relation to the Quattro Cento spirit. Indeed the theme of Donatello as artist, as artist in isolation, the theme of the *inventiveness* of his power to transmute the Quattro Cento stimulus into various forms of art, would be one slightly dangerous to my own. For while admitting its necessity to the Quattro Cento, I decry the Florentine power to translate emotions painstakingly into forms of art, – of which Donatello's art is the supreme outcome, – in favour of an anonymous spirit whose servants are more nearly children of their age, in favour of artists inspired by a patron's personality, whence springs the art entirely emblematic, the art 'twice over',[2] miraculous to us who lack emblem. The Florentine attitude was indispensable to the Quattro Cento, and vice versa; their relation mirrors that in art criticism between the more psychological and the more aesthetic approach; and in decrying Florence in favour of the rest of Italy, I seek to redress exactly that same balance as I do in favouring a more psychological approach. But in the case of Florence versus the rest of Italy, my partisanship is better founded. For even when an arrogant psychological approach was supreme, indeed, at all times, Florence has won every honour. This badly founded reverence for Florentine achievement is hard to uproot. For it dates back to the excellent writings of Vasari, the most successful booster in all history. How these Renaissance boosters have got away with it! Pope Pius II, the first redoubtable journalist, is another case in point. I attempt to show him up – for it is not too late, in fact the need is still urgent (see today's *Daily Mail*) – in the next volume.

In wandering back from the general to the particular it will be best to lean on this fact; in the first decades of the fifteenth century at Florence, the larger commissions of Donatello, Ghiberti and Luca della Robbia were given to them by the Signoria, the great Guilds and the Cathedral authorities. The vague personalities of public bodies must be flattered by creations that are monumental or profusely dramatic. A greater power of co-ordination will be required of the artist, and a more individual aesthetic than the one which can be so largely imposed upon him from without by the miraculous clarity in the life of a princely patron. The artist who works for impersonal societies hopes to please, not one, but several or many, minds. Esoteric or emblematic significance in his work is likely to lack the tension of projected fantasy that I seek out, unless the society is as real, or more real, than a person. And in fifteenth-century Florence, the great Guilds were breaking up, the Signoria was overshadowed by the leading families, and corporate religious fervour was not at its height.

Now Donatello's works belong largely to the Quattro Cento. He created Quattro Cento emblematic tension though he was generally engaged on the less personal contract, less personal, for instance, than the contract Matteo de' Pasti undertook for Sigismondo Malatesta at Rimini. Naturally enough, Donatello's greater effort, when successful, means a wider achievement. His emblems are more universal. So significant was the putto in his hands that, though no longer emblem, it became essential as a decorative motive to many subsequent arts.

Donatello was in revolt from the statuesque. But he could create Quattro Cento effects only with the material to hand, with the monumental and with rhythm enlarged to an exuberance. Sometimes one sees these two elements imperfectly welded. The Virgin of the Annunciation high relief in Santa Croce, is monumental, Junonian – she has even been called Baroque. Ovoids on the frieze are brutally large and plain. On the other hand the rest of the décor shows immense exuberance. In general one can associate exuberance with the relief, while the statuary which soon flourished in Florence, especially the nude statue, could serve to express a monumental plainness.

Although there was waywardness in his tormented savagery, Donatello felt the need for simplification, for a supreme, purely aesthetic *relevance* pervading every atom of humanistic ardour. The painters who followed him, especially in his love of the nude, found that a hard naturalism heightened by hard colour, could provide such a relevance, making of the aesthetic content a brio as abstract as possible, one of anatomical stress and strain. But into such aesthetic realization, and into his unequalled knowledge of the antique,[3] Donatello sent a passion which is altogether Gothic, a revolutionary passion, therefore, here in Florence. Medieval hardihood wins outburst in the sharp and peaked violence of some of his heads. The Umbrian eagle flapping coruscated wings, now no longer lone, is an image that haunts so much of Donatello's triumphant marble. Distraught is the anguish at entombments, but that pain is hammered out into rhythm. The gamin, eagle-sharp, is now no longer lone, and the protestant valour of St. George, he, forerunner of the more intense Christian public-school boy, acknowledges the slum-child shoulders of the St. John, the youthfulness, the pathetic fitness of these shoulders; and the slip of a David wears his locks long, the Greek petasos crowning the slum-child.

Donatello's supreme co-ordination of the new sensuousness was a stone-blossom; but not through the simpler fantasies of flower and foliage. He saw the passionate thronging of youthful bodies. The press upon the Pontevecchio, fire behind the eyes pulsating the blood, up out of the low quarters the quick children he imagines to stretch upon their wildest activities. The gross crowd, sole moisture of these barren streets, human luxuriance that overruns the receptive valleys, – these he disentangles for singleness of energy and of movement. The slum children cannot group about him too long. Their energy drives the air to ventilation. Every child is a newly victorious *amorino*. There is tempered steel in the strain, and no more than any Roman need Donatello be fastidious. Nakedness, however slight the form, achieves an irresistible tension, an irresistible repose, consummate in self-reliance. The fecund slime from which they grew, still clinging, is dried to brittle stone as the putti flash their limbs. Swollen with vigour they enhance rhythm beyond the powers of music. Such a stampede, a thunderous lilt, not heard, – as if the ear already deafened, the resourceful eye could store in its depth with one glance a succession of tune which will astound the ear when inaudibility lifts, which will overwhelm the shallow ear again and press down against the sides of the head – such is the rhythm of the putti as they move in their compartments on the pulpit at Prato above the long wrought bronze capital, above the monumental console, such the dance that can never run down, too strong and too subtle for the plodding ear, dance sudden and final in the corridor behind the columns of the encrusted singing gallery at Florence.

90

In the symbol of the putto, the new ambitions of the body found
a wide expression. The animal functions of infants are in themselves
symbols to adults of the most profound release. They should have been
permitted us: they are symbols of the freedom we cannot win. We relish
it that children, when unquestioning in their acts, do not shock. The
putto is a pagan emblem to those overburdened by sense of guilt, an
emblem that corresponds to so universal a desire for freedom that indecency of putti was indecency to no one. An Agostino di Duccio putto
(now hidden, it is true, by a canopy) at Rimini urinates above an altar:
even the Catholic Church, mounted as she is on sense of guilt, has
turned a blind eye.

Donatello took full advantage of this fact that blithe infants do not
shock. His putti are fierce on their pleasures, intense, even precise
enough, in their sexual romps. The stone and clay bear sons by the sculptor, not daughters. Out of the hundreds of nude forms attributed to
Donatello, two only are female, the bronze figure with cornucopia in
the Berlin Museum and the Eve at Padua. This fact is very significant.
What is true of Donatello is true of the early Renaissance as a whole. For
no other art, not even the Greek, shows so marked a preference for the
male nude, a figure far less easily composed to beauty than the female
nude. Such unique choice shows a predominance in sculptural fantasy
of a feeling for spatial values alone, of a feeling for mass, for material
as being the fruitful female block that will give birth to the most *active*
shapes full of prolific sap. From the stone comes a new, fearless energy.
And to push this fantasy further, since the architect's building is female,
set on the earth like Giorgione's woman by the running stream, the sculptor's attendant statuary are her lovers and sons rather than her daughters or a mere projection of herself. But only sculptors with a passion
for the material, stone, will keep so close to this primary fantasy that on
their low relief they create for the stone her children in the image of male
human infants. And so the marble putti who play along the marble of
Donatello's singing gallery, are the most intense manifestation of stone-
blossom: also the most humanistic. A certain humanity, as an expression
of human love for the near objective world in contrast to the distant,

yet relentless, spiritual hierarchy, is attributed to material. Once more stone is not only the medium of humanistic fantasy, but is the near object, object pure and simple, the love for which originates the anti-sense-of-guilt, the humanistic, attitude. Humanism as an intellectual movement is but a pale offshoot of such emotion.

Now Donatello's putto is certainly derived from the pagan *amorino*, and the putto's prankish turn was no doubt evolved from the slightly genre, or naturalistic, treatment, already evident at Florence in the fourteenth century, of the Virgin and Child group. Donatello's putti are nearly always winged, partly because such crinkled surfaces appealed to his love of incrustation, still more because wings enormously help suggestion of movement, of dynamic passage and of air currents made to whistle. It is as if a dust arose with the dance along the singing gallery; for the putti's wings are set off by a background of black and white mosaic flecks. The putto makes the air move. Indeed he is associated with all the elements. He bursts stone like earth, at Rimini he rides the dolphin, his tempestuous energy kindles a flame that withers tasteful ornamental foliage poor in sap, and heats the luscious growth to a vibrant, tropical bulbosity. The putto is elemental force under the symbol of the infant's animal nature. He is the emblem of Europe. For instead of the generative principle in terms of dark god and fetish or in terms of some cavernous concept of female seclusion, instead of the Indian *yaksi* beautiful though she be, or the jerky satyr who overruns the clear Greek horizon to hairy glades, we of the West have symbolized fecundity by the infant, by the play of infants in whom the primary desires that make the adult world limitless, subterranean, dark, are seen bright and immediate and in their least unsettled state. We in the West believe not only that the child is father to the man, but that the child's intent play in modes hateful and loving, expresses a more real necessity than does the grown god's esoteric power to lure and to destroy. And since the putto is unguarded, without reserve, he symbolizes as well as the necessity, the ideal of emotional externalization that I have identified with the Quattro Cento spirit. He symbolizes the process of living, that lies between Life and Death, the translation outwards of the formless flux of passions, to definite, concentrated, objective form. Adult intelligence brings the artistry to living, but only in the child can you discover the material that is worked. The Quattro Cento men uncovered that material in art, always first on the field. And now science as well insists on the sexual life of the child and learns from him. And since we know today that the child also is broken by his impotent passions, his cry and his gurgle are likely to remain for us symbols not only of Life, but also of living.

Naturally the Renaissance putto is first of all symbol of joy and freedom. Donatello swells his contours. His putto is a powerful plaything both in muscle and in sex. Donatello is safe-guarded by the 'innocence' which has been so irrationally attributed to the child. The putto is such an infant as every actual infant would like to be, and so with his games. He is a creation of Donatello's, so special, so imbued with unsuspected meaning, so emblematic of an age, that I must insist again that Rococo infants and such-like are not putti[4] at all. In fact any work in which the putto appears, is bound to be not only fifteenth century but Quattro Cento. And here I must distinguish the putto from other and contemporary infants, for instance, the della Robbia kind. As one would expect, Florentine artists were shy of Donatello's putto. Even Desiderio whose work is Quattro Cento for quite different reasons, generally changed putti into children and young boys. Rossellino and Majano followed him. They favoured especially the delicately featured young boy in bust or as guardian of a tomb. Representations of the more youthful saints, particularly the San Giovannino or young Baptist and St. Sebastian, belong to this vogue. Pollaiuolo the truculent, avoided both putto and child, both Donatello's avowal and its negation. Verrocchio returned to the putto, but not to the crowd of them. He represents them alone, a little timid, though still bulbous in form. Otherwise, it is outside Florence that Donatello's putto lives, particularly in Eastern Italy. Donatello himself worked for ten years in Padua and planted there the Quattro Cento emblems. Sculptors imitated the putti in San Antonio, but painters, principally Mantegna and, then, Giovanni Bellini, transformed them back into sweet children.

Except for his wings, one might have thought that the bronze putto in the Bargello, standing impudent on two snakes, represented the infant Hercules, so robust his shape. He wears soaken workman's trousers looped up on the hips by a huge belt, but fallen down before and behind below the parting of the legs. Other of Donatello's putti wear shirts, but when they have a hand free they often raise the shirts above their stomachs. The thin trousers of this bronze putto serve only to enfatten and to crease his legs like the slickest slime. The belt could easily cover his genitals if the useless trousers were torn away. Instead, debonair belt and fallen trousers frame them. His luminous, bloated form is made swift by tossing hair common to his kind and by wings attractive to a stinging dust. Oh the dust of the studios, the hack hack, pieces flying and stinging, and the secretious putti ruent in this hailstorm! Are they dank leather trousers, made up of an old apron? They will flap pleasantly against the softness. There is a trumpet call again in these textures, leather on vibrant flesh the most delicate, the most alert part of which scatters enclosures just as the tiny sun edges away from itself by radiance, to an enframing margin, the huge and shredded clouds.

Putti mourn on the socle of Gattamelata's statue at Padua. For the strong, plain oval socle represents a tomb. But the games of putti are wild. They make water to trumpet and bronze water-containers to gong. And not only to damps but to the processes of sea-life are they habituated. For Donatello used shell-forms and other incrustation. Witness the magnificent encrusted shell-form under the head of Giovanni Crivelli, and the twisted enframing posts of the Pecci slab in the cathedral, Siena. For Donatello's twisted posts always express a long-wound notching by millennial currents, as do the sea-tressed tendrils[5] he invented. Again, there are the pairs of dolphins holding between them thick crusty shells along the parapet of the singing gallery in San Lorenzo.

Turning to architecture, such power in rhythm, so deep a life, will, it is obvious, shake the architectural members. There will be overlapping of marble rolled back by the devices of incrustation, compression that leaves unusual shapes. Donatello came back from his second visit

to Rome thoroughly dissatisfied now with the swift regularities of
Brunelleschi. The differences of these two artists over the decoration
of the sacristy at San Lorenzo is extremely significant. Rhythm still
underlies the Florentine art, but Donatello has felt in Rome the instantaneousness of the medieval Cosmati work, has felt the precedence of
colour for rhythmic purposes over linear successions. It is now that he
works on the pulpit at Prato, now that he introduces Roman tessellation
behind the putti on the cathedral singing gallery. Draughtsmanship is
taboo. The processes of encrust require the variable colours of crystallization, and the most palpitating rhythm is that of the dizzy flecks
which invade with their swarm all the brightest objects of sunlight,
the most silent; for they are too quick, too grandiloquent for sound,
too continuous as within the beat of the pulsating heart. It was then
he designed the magnificent balustrade in the sacristy of San Lorenzo
made out of marble shells beneath the slab, and of great shoots of
marble oak issuing from their vase to the pattern of volutes. No doubt
Brunelleschi took exception to the coloured marbles and the massive
doorways.

But mass *in excelsis*, that complete appearance, arresting as the open
face of the rose, a vital steadiness, a forcible concurrence without any
throbbing, behind and beyond all rhythm, could hardly be arrived at
in Florence. Rhythm swells and breaks here, finally to settle into the
fugues of the Baroque. Donatello's second visit to Rome both made the
development inevitable, and led him meanwhile to his greater Quattro
Cento works. On this visit he carved a beautiful tabernacle now in one
of the sacristies of St. Peter's. The rebellious waves of travertine are
petrified and encrusted as if by a prolific reproductiveness of the minute
life that their seas contain.

In the Piazza Signoria, Florence, *haute* is the Renaissance. Cellini's
swaggering Perseus holds a baulked Medusa head. For already limbs
are stone, compact groups that turn their never-ending cartwheels.
Neptune winds his head toward the gleaming David. Satyrs sense their
conchs and blow brazen water at the sun. The messenger of the gods
proclaims vengeance to a swarthy god. Full-breasted daughters faint,

and ripple at the knee. Some gorgeous seam in the fullness of time fills out the anile nudity of old man Neptune, gives him a brassy strength through which the dark tremors of youth never will pass, a warrior's head set to the jaunty fabricating of an old man's gaunt peccadilli. Huge, he presides over the slippery water-sprites. High is the sun of the Renaissance, too hipped with proclamation! These bodies have a cream upon them. Every day the sun warms up tons of blood. Well-practised Perseus has an evil nakedness, though his step be firm. Andromeda's hair flies stiff as though caked with mud. Within the decade Perseus will fatten. A portly Roman, he will finger his toga on his way to the boring baths. For soon the heat of his florid nakedness will have to be stored and clothed between bouts of exhibition.

And then, beneath the enormous pile of the palazzo Vecchio, without shelter, stronger, even in the distance, than the great wall of building, a metal point of lightning amid the circumambient marbles – and you see as you draw close how precious is Donatello's *Judith*, how emblazoned her underhood and simple robe, how fierce the classical simplicity of their folds. For in this strange manner did Donatello approach the early Greeks, as did the best of the old Gothic sculptors. Embodiment of passion, strict passion, of a tension which must be new (for it cannot last), Judith has raised the sword to strike off the head of Holofernes' sleeping form. But the anger is no longer pure Semitic. Other powers have reinforced the Jews and fallen out with them. Attention wanders to the exquisitely relaxed, the soft anatomy of Holofernes over which presides this Helleno-Gothic Fury, this animus of the lean Umbrian eagle, austere and powerful, peaked. Such was the austerity which lay sometime in the souls of the Roman Fathers, now galvanized by the soft and plastic form of the slumbering pagan tyrant. But new feelings coalesce; it is a miracle, the Renaissance. Judith's scriptural fury shall animate the nude. Upon her triangular pedestal, rich and sharp pedestal, are three bronze reliefs of putti dynamic in game, winged and furious in their natural courses. Some fly to an embrace; they won't feel the bruise; some tumble about the graven basin. The feet of others trample lightly over the loud and surfeited lord of

96

fountains. One alone is chained. He calls for help, but the others are deafened. Perhaps clear sound of trumpets will organize his slovenly shape, calm his fear, and he will be free with the rest.

II. MICHELOZZO

I want to make only a curt reference to Michelozzo on two points where he touches the Quattro Cento, other than those already mentioned. Michelozzo and Donatello collaborated in several contracts. Discussion has been heated over their respective shares of the work. In view of the new light thrown on Michelozzo in connection with the Annunziata,[6] I feel that the simple, massive design of the John XXIII tomb between two antique pillars in the Baptistery, is primarily his. And just as Alberti's Roman breadth is saved for the Quattro Cento by the immediate, arresting emblems with which his collaborators emblazoned the Tempio encasement, so Michelozzo's heavy design attains a constriction, a tensity of incrustation from the hands of his collaborators, Donatello and Pagno di Lapo Portigiani, who, though avoiding here much ornament, are probably responsible for such details of the design as the shell-forms in the niches and in the semi-circle above, and for the general notched effect of the carving.

The Naples tomb on which Donatello and Michelozzo collaborated,[7] is not a Quattro Cento work, but a hybrid, a cold adjustment, though some of the sculpture is beautiful. Michelozzo worked with Donatello on the pulpit at Prato. Again, I attribute to Michelozzo the massive console, that heaviness so easily made a means of incrustation by the pictorial powers of Donatello. The lovely bases to Michelozzo's pillars of the Annunziata tabernacle show the power in his developed style to transmute the Brunelleschi line-game into a concourse. Michelozzo has gathered all the runners together and drilled them as one man.

His façade for Sant'Agostino at Montepulciano is one of the few Quattro Cento church façades. The Gothic shapes are emblematic: altogether different in feeling, then, from the 'neo-Gothic' of the Santa

Croce window. Two zones of pilasters treated in a manner that calls to mind the Quattro Cento Cancelleria palace at Rome, are separated by a zone of deep Gothic niches. In the upper zone, beneath the pediment, there is a deep *occhio* or 'eye' window. The lunette of the door surmounted by Gothic tracery, shelters a sculptured group. There is depth, and from this depth the stone blossoms into straight pilaster, so that the wall-space becomes vital as a nourishing-ground.

III. DESIDERIO DA SETTIGNANO

Donatello was the prime revolutionary. As with the painter Andrea del Castagno, a brutal animation was the humanistic counter to the cold Florentine aesthetic also in their bones. Donatello is the most profound of Quattro Cento artists. But the monumental aim, I have said, leads quickly to the Baroque where the monumental, with conventionalized complications of rhythm, aspires to approach the enfolding quality of mass, itself without connection with the monumental other than being non-monumental, non-rhythmic. But previous to formalization, while yet every detail is a treasure of dynamic sensibility, the Quattro Cento is created, how richly and with what tension some masterpieces of Desiderio da Settignano, of Antonio Pollaiuolo and of Verrocchio, further demonstrate.

First of all Desiderio. His revolutionary feat is perhaps the most subtle. It would, however, have been impossible without the example of Donatello, though he was away in Padua during the early years of Desiderio's short life. To all three, to Desiderio, Pollaiuolo and Verrocchio, Donatello gave the model for compositions in which balance radically depends on *quality* of movement or emotion, and so less (than in the case of Ghiberti's reliefs for instance) on distribution of shapes. As I have already remarked in connection with Verrocchio's *lavabo*,[8] such *dynamic* design is by no means a Baroque elaboration – though that is what is left when the vital quality diminishes – but the expression of the highest emotional tensity. This dynamic composition was Donatello's answer to the unemphasized homogeneity of Ghiberti's 'finish'. We see such composing best in bronze reliefs, those on the San Lorenzo pulpits or the series at Padua. In the relief there, for instance, representing the discovery of a miser's stone heart, a small group on the left has been entirely dissociated from the main group on the right; but owing to the dramatic or dynamic treatment of the whole, no pause, no sense of distraction ensues from this gap. A still greater design is the Deposition, in which the dead one and the sorrowing are balanced easily, though not in number, by the violent grief of a woman on the right with outstretched arms, and by two other figures. Their shapes alone, apart from the emotion they express, would not make a balance. The composition, of course, coheres in other ways as well, but the one I have isolated, though in relation to the rest, is the most important.

Now I have fully described what I consider to be the stock-in-trade of Florentine artists. So it may perhaps convey something when I assert that Ghiberti's or Luca's amalgam of coldest abstraction with the least obdurate emotionalism or 'finish', – that is to say, measure in movement attained by avoiding emphasis, by the cold working of exquisite natur-alistic representation – it is this amalgam, foreign to Donatello, with which Desiderio sought to emulate Donatello's dynamic composing, and succeeded. Desiderio was of one mind, and he was warm. He dis-sociated Luca's sweetness from his coldness. Desiderio is the only genu-ine case in sculpture of *quale visto di ogni canto*. His charm is genuine, his charming with the playfulness of children. As for workmanship, no one has ever equalled the delicacy of Desiderio's cutting. And in this connection one notices that Vasari described the ornamental friezes of the Marsuppini tomb in Santa Croce as rather dried and gauche (*spinosi*). Vasari accounts for these defects by declaring Desiderio's incomplete knowledge of the antique (in which, it is true, Desiderio shows no more than a general interest); that is, presumably, compared with the sculp-tors of Vasari's time whose lifeless 'stuck-on' mouldings do certainly reproduce the ornamentals of ancient Rome.

The delicacy of Desiderio was dynamic, his refinement fierce, so that just as Donatello revealed rhythm too profound for the ear, so Desiderio contrived a scentedness not submitted as fumes to the nose, but an ulterior fragrance seized with the eye which takes as immediate, as a revelation, what more gradually intoxicates the other senses. Sensuousness as a revelation, as an eternity of feeling, belongs only to the Quattro Cento. Energy ran loose with such concordance as to permit an appraisal; a flash of the eye, and Space captured the creatures of Time and Growth.

For once, then, for the sake of Desiderio, I concur with the myth of Florence the City of Flowers, a myth cross-grained by the cold and shapely lily, the city's emblem. But it is the smaller wild-flowers, leaves and continual fruit that garland Marsuppini's tomb. Every darkness of the cella is minimized; the sombreness of death flutters away from the winged shell placed at the base of the sarcophagus. Lightness and delicacy initiate a visible conquest over death, no less heroic than the emblazonment upon Isotta's tomb. Two children guard the sensitive foot of the urn, playing at being watchmen. No call for soldiers and funereal genii to guard the breezes of repose, no call to drag at the silky canopy when nothing is hidden, and when nothing is stark or crushed by celestial flames.

This monument has untraversable spaces between guardian children. In the zoning of it, Desiderio displayed not only measure but also great love of space in itself, he alone of Florentine sculptors. The resultant quality, enforced by the panels of coloured marble,[9] is not only one of distinctness and of roominess, but also of untraversable positions in a divine interacting; and it is significant that Desiderio's beautiful tabernacle in San Lorenzo has on its face a column-vista carved in perspective. To promote such interaction, to emphasize his spacing as quick and alive, and in view of the tepid composure of his traditions, Desiderio used methods the least sombre in the balancing of his compositions. Employing, as he does, the formulae of 'finish', Desiderio must enhance that rhythm by subtle irregularities, by far-fetched correspondence. With Desiderio a very marked degree of sophistication is attained. The composing of the children above and below the Marsuppini tomb reveals neither an instinctive nor an opportunist arrangement. The balance is too complicated. It is the same with the figures about the tabernacle – the two angels at the sides and the putti on the entablature with the infant Christ between them, balanced in benediction upon the lip of the holy chalice.

Desiderio is another revolutionary, another preparer of the Baroque. The Quattro Cento life is in him, but wedding with a Florentine bride means children of violence in the next generation. In what one suspects to be his later work, Desiderio makes particular use of ribbons and streamers for a dynamic purpose. Their correspondence is not simple; their direction must be related to the organization of the whole. The ribbons upon the frieze of the beautiful mantelpiece of *pietra morta* in the Victoria and Albert, attributed to Desiderio, illustrate this point.[10] In the Musée André, Paris, there is a Quattro Cento masterpiece, *Head of a Hero*. With extreme delicacy this strong head comes out of the marble plaque. Last to appear are crinkling ribbons attached to a fillet of bay-leaves. These ribbons spring out behind to mark the distance, one behind the other, one shorter than the other; nor yet as ornament; but they make fall and curl differently their crinkles, so as to suggest variant ambuscades of glory behind the smooth brow, behind the eager, regular features. Never was expression so ebullient while equally sensitive as in this head; recusant, Caerian, illuminated, yet toyed by tense delicacy of youthfulness.

Pointed also are the features of Desiderio's *Caesar* in the Louvre. Sensitiveness patrols Gothic eagle faces, blade-sharp now to cull the strongest flower-stem. And tendrils, bay-leaves, shall strap and scent the hair.

Later on, this pointedness was further sensitized for the drawing-room with an outcome in the Faunesque. Thus Bertoldo's beautiful statuette of Orpheus or Orion at the Bargello, the wrapt eyes far apart in the young, angled face. This Quattro Cento statuette is the loveliest I know. It is not a product of 'finish'. Critics mistakenly call it unfinished, because the viol and the bow and Orpheus' chest have not been worked up. Their crude state shows in how rough a form Bertoldo had his models cast. The grinding bow, the rough, compact viol, coin-like with rich sound, particularly the unhewn, clumsy bow, give an enormous solidity to the ecstacy and tenderness of this Orpheus, and to his slight form.

IV. POLLAIUOLO AND VERROCCHIO

With a new access of brutality, force, this time essentially forcible, was recovered. We are with Antonio Pollaiuolo, as a painter one of the principal of the Florentine 'fauves', dead set on the strains and stresses of anatomical workings at rest and in movement and in conflict. Quattro Cento exuberance in Florence now leads quickly to the *terribilità* of Michael Angelo, and to subsequent formalization in the Baroque.[11] Again the Florentine attempt at mass. It comes out of Donatello's tensity; and meanwhile Pollaiuolo belongs to the Quattro Cento. No one who has seen the bust of the brazen Condottiero in the Bargello can doubt it. The sap runs free and insolent. The restless, straining balances between the figures of Sixtus IV's monument in the museum of St. Peter's, belong still to the decades of emblazonry; so too Innocent XIII's tomb in St. Peter's. These ambitious contortions intimate a rich brutality, every nerve tremor of a once skulking soul passed into terms of vein and bounding muscle. Pollaiuolo's rebellion against the architectonic of Brunelleschi was truculent, against the limpid cella, against religion even. Those were the days when they slit your throat with a diamond, and goldsmiths belaboured the bronze with minute savagery to ends of anatomical vigour. These tombs are rich and taut as a result of this expensiveness. But Verrocchio's Colleoni,* conceived with a parallel tensity, will not be claimed for the Quattro Cento. In this work the Florentine, as did Michael Angelo later on, took the Quattro Cento exuberance altogether into his own hands. The sternness of Colleoni is too ripe for our classification, the figure too special, too conscious. He is a figure-head of the whole Renaissance as it actually occurred.

* Equestrian statue of Bartolomeo Colleoni (1480–1488), in the Campo Santi Giovanni e Paolo, Venice. – Ed.

I leave this archetype of *Forza* to the Fascists.

On the other hand, there are two early works of Verrocchio which are essentially Quattro Cento, the already described *lavabo* and the tomb of Giovanni and Piero di Cosimo de' Medici.[12] Again the cella has been abandoned, this time for a sarcophagus as precious as a casket, like St. Mark's precious as a cabinet on the table of the Piazza. Such costliness is related to the goldsmiths' art of which Quattro Cento sculpture is so often the development, surviving here to express the Quattro Cento quality of tightness, tensity, the packed dynamic. For that sense of concentration was stimulated, and perhaps indeed often originated, in the handling of jewels or antique cameos. The d'Este and the Medici were in general passionate about jewels; and Sigismondo, as we know from the inventory of his belongings and from his penury, exceeded them all in this love. Further, no religious symbols were carved on this tomb, just as the *lavabo*, though designed for the priests' ablutions, does not have one clerical reference. Pollaiuolo, too, showed distaste for Christian signs. The only other parallel is to the decorations of the Tempio.

Verrocchio's Medici tomb is a sarcophagus of porphyry with medallions of serpentine. The lid is white Carrara and porphyry. The whole is ornamented with bronze. The base is of white marble resting on four bronze tortoises. The front of the monument is in the sacristy, the back in the chapel of the Madonna, and a bronze grille of twisting cords serves as a partition. Both sarcophagus and grille, on the sacristy side, are framed by a marble band of relief forming an archway. Although the relief is crowded, and even at first sight stiff, formal, it must be resolved into a Quattro Cento expression. But the ardours of Donatello have taken a new turn. By now putti are exhausted in Florence, their revelling can break no further marbles. Driven to new courses of revolution, to new breakages of caskets that seal precious life, Verrocchio discovered a rotation of that sharp vegetable riot which Donatello passed over to goad on the urchins of his neighbourhood. Unique in their strength, spinous are the bronze acanthus leaves on the tomb, and related to the gleam of the shark's spear and tail under the scorching sun, of the dry, crinkling anatomy of the under-sea's most complicated shells. For the fertility of earth is dramatized by images of just such dryness habituated to the swirl of a redundant moisture.

Conscious, it appears, of the ocean's fruitfulness as conceived by Agostino di Duccio in his sculptures at Rimini, of Venice newly habituated to the lagoon by marbles that match the verdures of flashing fins and scales, Verrocchio confined the exuberance of acanthus blade each end, by two enormous knobbed shells of bronze replete with bronze fruit and cones. These curl below the Medici diamond.

The reliefs of the archway are made up of bunches of corn and ramage, each enclosed by the Medici diamond. Here at last in Florence – and it is this which makes it Quattro Cento – is a work inspired by the costliness of *virtù* and by the drama of significant emblem. Here, as with the *lavabo*, the Medici inspire a Quattro Cento expression, in the person of Piero de' Medici il Gottoso. The only occasion. In both these monuments the Medici diamond incites the artist to make the porphyry more precious, to make the white marble glint and plume, to souse these sharpnesses and brilliant refractions with storms of sensuous scaliness, to offer, as symbols of fertility and flower, the grandest incrustation; since the diamond can part them as through rain or yielding mould. It is highly improbable that the bronze work was gilded, inasmuch as no trace of colour can be found even in the interstices of the metal. These sombre and impressive tones were an antithesis to the bright 'innocent' colouring of the prevalent niche-sepulchral monuments. *Strength Indomitable*, that was the motto of the Medici.

With regard to Verrocchio's development of dynamic design, the subtlety in the arrangement of the bronze foliage should be remarked. This I have already enlarged on in my account of the *lavabo*.

We cannot expect another work like the *lavabo*. The rest of Verrocchio does not concern us. Some of his busts, like the terra-cotta young woman in the Foulc collection, Paris,[*] though they be beautiful, are so widely separated from Quattro Cento conception as to have a florid, an almost German, look. After Donatello, Verrocchio is the greatest of the

---

[*] Now in the Frick Collection, New York. – Ed.

Florentine revolutionaries; and it is fortunate for the Quattro Cento that at one time his art was servant to the powers of emblem. He rejected the putto for a dynamism of primitive swarming, and in contrast with Donatello he made great use of foliage, but of a new variety, spinous, prolific, over-growing, which gave the direct lie to the conventional swags and blameless nosegays of the more feeble sculptors. Otherwise, Donatello foretells Verrocchio, sometimes anticipates him. Dolphins, I have remarked, line the entablature of the singing gallery in San Lorenzo, sea-monsters writhe on the pilasters of the Miracle of the Ass relief at Padua,* and Donatello's favourite pilasters with spiral grooves, such as frame the base of the Marzocco and the Pecci slab,† were developed by Verrocchio into the spines and tendons and fins of monsters.

Now you may find these same images and an equal exuberance expressed in other periods. The point is solely the *intensity*, the *compulsion* of their showing, which keep them altogether distinct from decorated or elaborated effect, and so distinguishes them as unique. I have attempted to show how intimately connected with such compulsion was the feeling for stone. Apart from this, there were many different ways in which that same compulsion was projected in art, and all of them mean Quattro Cento work. I now suggest that Verrocchio exploited Florentine reserve itself as a tension, that the very principle of restraint was exploited as a power, a packed dynamic. Consider, for example, the famous putto with dolphin in the palazzo Vecchio courtyard. His poise is full of active inner force as yet undirected. I have said that no further work of Verrocchio can be connected with the Quattro Cento. This is because my first intention must be to distinguish clearly the Quattro Cento. But should the above sentences be understood, it will be safe to invoke affiliations.

In the unsuccessful effort to obtain trophies for the hero Leonardo, his master Verrocchio has been made to suffer. It is admitted, though,

---

* In the Basilica di Sant'Antonio, Padua.

† At the Museo Nazionale del Bargello, Florence, and Siena Cathedral, respectively.
  – Ed.

that the equivocal Mona Lisa smile belongs equally to the master.[13] But I suggest that only in the work of Verrocchio does the enigmatic find its proper context, as the foil to violence and yet as the preliminary to all action; the showing, then, of a deeper, still anonymous ferment. The correspondence of this psychological intensity still boundless, dream-like, is with the finite violence born of it. Leonardo stood outside. He would not commit himself. Quattro Cento urgency had slipped away, leaving the fascinating brood of the potentially potential. His, indeed, is the first explicit reverence for the inexhaustible fund of life. The mysterious is an abstraction. But that same boundless fund is *employed* in every work of Verrocchio. He has put Quattro Cento harness on psychological excess. You may see in his silver relief for the altar of San Giovanni, a representation of the saint's beheading.* On the right two warriors, preying, combative, beaked, a type which stimulated Leonardo to his grotesques, quarrel about the execution. Their hands are adroit talons, their perfect armour bristles beneath and above their eyes screwed to exorbitant passion. As in the neck of Colleoni, every muscle is a taut string that gets resonance from the shrinking air. Concentration of physiological force, muscular and choleric, is achieved by a goldsmith's precious, articular, care. The executioner swings his blade over the saint luxuriantly kneeling. Behind are three pages; they shrink and elongate holding one another, and slowly sway. The gesture of him on the left is extravagant. Every detail of armour is embossed. His hand waves down a beautiful salver soon to be lifted from the bottom with the torn head upon it. Meanwhile his armour eddies in a stream of life enigmatic, undirected. He is tensile, gracious, withdrawn, impartial, without apprehensiveness though murder is enacted. The past is a pool, recipient of gradual night. The future will be an awakened sun that draws to itself lone vapours. Bereft of thong and sinew, as a formlessness made ductile by surrounding exertion, did Verrocchio figure suspense. Leonardo made it isolate, mysterious. But Verrocchio loved compliance as well as power in reserve; and he mingled them.

---

* Now in the Museo dell'Opera del Duomo, Florence.– Ed.

I refer to the St. Thomas group at Or San Michele.

Verrocchio was the first *explicitly* to use Florentine reserve as a reserve of power, and the last. After him, tensity, compulsion goes. The marble is *searched* for forms, the difficulty of their showing increases, though belief in a power within the stone remains for a time. Michael Angelo's matrix from which he rarely frees his sculpture altogether, served for him in just this role of a reserve of power. He did not wish to be finally separated from the low relief, from that primitive faith in the stone's animation of which a low relief art is an expression. But actually, little reserve of power is left to the stone, little tension. The stone is spent by Michael Angelo in attaining colossal shapes, joyless, writhing supreme. Hereafter in the Baroque, there is no tensity of manifestation by stone. The Florentine reserve, exploited by Quattro Cento artists as a reserve of power in the stone, explicitly so by Verrocchio, has been broken down.

If you would measure the difference, with any Baroque monument in eye look at Verrocchio's model for the Forteguerri tomb in the Victoria and Albert. (Said to be a fake, but no matter. If it is, the faker understood his period well enough.) The design of flying angels supporting a *mandorla* with Christ reaches Baroque dimensions. One would take it for a work of the Seicento, except for the *mandorla*, and except – this is the point – for a certain tightness, a holding in reserve, so that all this extravagance of movement, seemingly uncontrollable, is controlled like that of marionettes by the fingers of their showman. This is an afterthought. But indeed, the simile is even more appropriate to the flying angels of Antonio Rossellino and Benedetto da Majano. In their cases, the string-control is apparent, and, therefore, in shameless but cold conjunction with a white, 'harmless' simplicity – disgusting. For reserve of power is not exploited dramatically, but rather as a denial of tension.

Yet, at the same time, I can now admit what I could not admit while making more subtle distinctions, namely that all fifteenth-century sculpture, particularly the Florentine, shows some tension owing to this very reserve of power. For the Quattro Cento spirit had the uniform effect on Florentine reserve, to make that spirit a reserve of power imputed to the materials the Florentine sculptors worked. Even in Ghiberti, inventor of 'finish', of fluency, one perceives a tightness of expression that is lost to the Baroque age and to subsequent ages, though Ghiberti's creations are no less fluent, and a good deal more naturalistic than those of Bernini. Is it a remnant of primitive stiffness which, though avoided in technique, and even in conception, yet remains somewhere in the whole creative process? Does the supreme charm of fifteenth-century art as a whole reside in those artists' discovery and use of 'modern' technique, 'modern' grace and perspective, to magnify the tension, the non-diffuse accumulated revelation which primitive stiffness expresses but which, in primitive art, is severely confined by that very stiffness?

I have said the Renaissance is an intensification of all forms, of all the primitive art to which it succeeds. In so broad a description I can see the art of the fifteenth century as one. I have found urgent, however, the need to distinguish where the reserve of power engendered by primitive stiffness has been denied its dramatic, revelatory effect, and where, under the title of Quattro Cento art, that tensity, fixed best in stone, has been avowed.

Stone and Water

From *Stones of Rimini* (1934)

I write of stone. I write of Italy where stone is habitual. Every Venetian generation handles the Istrian stone of which Venice is made. Venetian sculpture proceeds now, not by chisel and hammer, but under the hands, the feet, under the very breath of each inhabitant and of a few cats, dogs and vermin. See the nobs upon the ponte della Paglia, how fine their polish, how constantly renewed is their hand-finish.

Hand-finish is the most vivid testimony of sculpture. People touch things according to their shape. A single shape is made magnificent by perennial touching. For the hand explores, all unconsciously to reveal, to magnify an existent form. Perfect sculpture needs your hand to communicate some pulse and warmth, to reveal subtleties unnoticed by the eye, needs your hand to enhance them. Used, carved stone, exposed to the weather, records on its concrete shape in spatial, immediate, simultaneous form, not only the winding passages of days and nights, the opening and shutting skies of warmth and wet, but also the sensitiveness, the vitality even, that each successive touching has communicated. This is not peculiar to Venice nor to Italy. Almost everywhere man has recorded his feelings in stone. To the designed shape of some piece, almost everywhere usage has sometimes added an aesthetic meaning that corresponds to no conscious aesthetic aim. But it is in Italy and other Mediterranean countries that we take real courage from such evidence of solid or objectified feelings, quite apart from the fact that these are the countries of marble, of well-heads and fountains, of assignation or lounging beneath arcades and porticoes, of huge stone palaces and massive cornices where pigeons tramp their red feet. We are prepared to enjoy stone in the south. For, as we come to the southern light of the Mediterranean, we enter regions of coherence and of settled forms. The piecemeal of our lives now offers some mass, the many heads of discontent are less devious in their looks. When we stand in the piazzas of southern towns, it is as if a band had struck up; for when grouped at home about our native bandstand we have noticed the feeble public park to attain a certain definiteness. Similarly we are prepared in the southern light to admire the evidence of Italian living concreted and objectified in stone.

But exhilaration gained from stone is a vastly different encouragement from the one that music may afford. It is an opposite encouragement. Or rather it is something more than the bestowal of a tempo on things. For tempo, the life-process itself, attains concreteness as stone. In Venice the world is stone. There, in stone, to which each changing light is gloss, the human process shines clear and quasi-permanent. There, the lives of generations have made exteriors, acceptable between sky and water, marbles inhabited by emotion, feelings turned to marble.

Without a visit to Venice you may hardly envisage stone as so capable to hold firm the flux of feelings. Stone sculpture apart, stone is more often conceived in the north as simply rock-like. And who will love the homogeneous marble sheets in the halls of Lyons' Corner Houses? No hands will attempt to evoke from them a gradual life. For nowhere upon them is the human impress. Few hands have touched them, or an instrument held in the hand. They were sliced from their blocks by impervious machines. They have been shifted and hauled like so many girders. They are illumined in their hues beneath the light; yet they are adamant.

In writing now of Venice, I have not in mind Venetian sculpture nor marble palaces reflecting the waters between them. I refer to the less signal yet vast outlay there of the salt-white Istrian stone, every bit of it used; to bridge-banisters and fondamenta-posts made smooth and electric by swift or groping hands and by the sudden sprawls of children; to great lintels seared like eaten wood above storehouse doorways on the Giudecca; to the gleaming stanchion on the quay in front of the Salute, a stanchion whose squat cylindrical form is made all the more trenchant by the deep spiral groove carved by the repeated pull of ropes; to vaster stanchions on the Zattere, lying as long and white and muffled as polar bears... Stone enshrines all usage and all fantasies. They are given height, width, and breadth, solidity. Life in Venice is outward, enshrined in gleaming white Istrian. Each shrine is actuality beneath the exploring hand, is steadfast to the eye. Such perpetuation, such instantaneous and solid showing of a long-gathered momentum, gives the courage to create in art as in life. For living is externalization, throwing an inner ferment outward into definite act and thought. Visual art is the clearest mirror of this aim. The painter's fantasies become material, become canvas and paint. Stone the solid, yet the habitat of soft light like the glow of flesh, is the material, so I shall maintain, that inspires all the visual arts. Marble statues of the gods are the gods themselves. For they are objects as if alive which enjoy complete outwardness.

In Venice, even pain has its god-like compass. Masks of toothache, masks of suffering, snow-white, incorrigible, overhanging dark waters, these great stone heads line the base of the palazzo Pesaro on the side canal. The gondolier who enters from the Grand Canal will need to use the masks to correct his black boat. He thus polishes one or two heads, damps the swollen cheek of another, strikes a hollow roaring mouth. The cries from canal and from calli, new noises that are caught to the clammy, still livid recesses of the stone, released old and thin and ominous as echo, are as sustenance to these perennial faces...

That a stone face representing Vice or toothache should be an assistance in navigation, that misery should be exemplified as solid, attaining beauty in completeness, lends to all phenomena, even the least welcome, an almost positive zest. And see how these stones make permanent drama of the sky's shifting materials! Istrian marble blackens in the shade, is snow or salt-white where exposed to the sun. Light and shade are thus recorded, abstracted, intensified, solidified. Matter is dramatized in stone, huge stonework palaces rebutting the waters.

No: it is the sea that thus stands petrified, sharp and continuous till up near the sky. For this Istrian stone seems compact of salt's bright yet shaggy crystals. Air eats into it, the brightness remains. Amid the sea Venice is built from the essence of the sea. Over the Adriatic, mounted upon churches and palaces, a thousand statues posture, distilled agleam from the whirls and liquid tresses of the Adriatic over which they are presiding. They stand white against the sky, one with a banner, another with a broken column in her hands.

Yet this whiteness as of salt is not dazzling. On the contrary, though here the sea is petrified, it still is ruffled or is cut into successive cylinders and pillars. Istrian stone has always been hammered. It is a convention of its use which probably arose in the construction of bridges and water stairs. For this hammering, which makes the smallest surface a microcosm of the larger growths in light and shade, prevents the stone from being slippery. So, we are reminded of the substances that batten on slippery rocks and roughen them, shells with crusted grooves, or hard sponges. When such thoughts are uppermost, Istrian stone itself, Venice herself, is an incrustation.

Or again at night, Istrian is lace. The Baroque fronts are like giant fretworks that stiffen the brighter stars. Lace, in fact, has always been an industry in Venice, though more particularly at Chioggia where they have woven it large and coarse.

Again, if in fantasy the stones of Venice appear as the waves' petrification, then Venetian glass, compost of Venetian sand and water, expresses the taut curvature of the cold under-sea, the slow, oppressed yet brittle curves of dimly translucent water.

If we would understand a visual art, we ourselves must cherish some fantasy of the material that stimulated the artist, and ourselves feel some emotional reason why his imagination chose, when choice was not altogether impelled by practical, technical and social considerations, to employ one material rather than another. Poets alone are trustworthy interpreters. They alone possess the insight with which to re-create subjectively the unconscious fantasies that are general.

Agostino di Duccio's reliefs in the Tempio Malatestiano at Rimini, so far as they reflect, and even concentrate, the common Mediterranean fantasies of stone and water, for their interpretation require an account of Mediterranean geography and the dependent scope of

Mediterranean visual art seen as a whole.

An invocation of Venice has been my prologue. For the Venetian stones and waters are the Mediterranean essence: how strongly Mediterranean is this essence, you may judge from any port or harbour in the world. For, wherever it may be, the stone jetties and circumvented waters that make a port are reminders of the Mediterranean scene.

Even the port of London has its Mediterranean aspect, where at Wapping or Limehouse the stout warehouses are steeped in the river. The Genoa-like passages between them are narrow and tall: at their ends you emerge into the light and into the open, discover an array of steps, or a quay that locks the river in a seething stone or brick embrace. The stones retain an equal warmth if the sun is out, an equal radiance that contrasts with the polyp-like elongations and contractions of the water's glassiness.

The water never palls against the stone: the radiant causeway swarms. Water and builded stone vivify the one the other; they are at peace. The certainty of man-placed stones contracts the ocean's awfulness. In the port, it is as if the seas had been sifted and winnowed: upon the tall mole we can admit and gaze at their depth. Nothing is kinder to the ephemeral movements, the ephemeral reflections, refractions and shadows of water than the even-lighted masonry; no material less stalwart would provide such vivid opportunities to the water's reflective tricks.

Amid the hurly-burly of the port there exists the wideness of all space in miniature, the Mediterranean spaciousness or distinctness. In the harbour world of stone and water – this open, flat, world of different levels – there exist the broad angles which airs and winds caress, there exist the means of promenade, of conversation, of taking the evening leisurely: there are stanchions and rails and other significant shapes, stations for human attitude: there exists the scenery for gesture. Acoustic is plain in echo. Without mutual interruption, sounds glide to and fro like gulls. Bells from the towers of the upper town, or from a church reached by steps from the quay, plumb with their peals the harbour's breadth and depth.

However great its merchandise, the port is a haven, a repose, a measurer of passing things. The sun moves round, warming in turn those mammoth recording dials, the moles and quays, which the well-travelled waters lap. The scene is animated but steadfast. At night the waters are the dial. They show a shimmering rod or a hesitant patch of light. We can hardly discern the quays: we hear against them the home waters as they weigh us down carefully with the heavy finery of sleep.

What looks more apprehensive than the whiter stones before a storm, at the moment when the fall of livid ripplets against beach or mole is a distinct and almost shattering sound? This horizontal world of masonry and moving water is the ideal setting for the perpendicular rain and for the lightning. The storm passes, the dampened stones remain: even the waters are bemused and deaf to the wind. Ourselves along the wharves, perpendicular as the forest of masts upon the ships, appear intensely human: our houses stand up well above the port to which each alley leads.

Of such sort is the scenery of maritime commerce, the typical setting, we shall realize, of Mediterranean culture. For in the port we witness those elementary abstractions of visual experience which have always governed to a greater or lesser degree the Mediterranean conception of visual art. Here, in simplest form, are elements which provoke the aesthetic conception of space, here is the broad immovable masonry laid out on different levels, and betwixt these arms of stone, the moving waters. The smallest boat leaves a track on the water's face: even a thrown pebble makes enlarging circles. These liquid movements enhance a thousand-fold the solid radiance of the masonry. We come to see its stones as waywardness, as rhythm and movement, absorbed and transformed into a face of static substance; we see masonry as solid space, as an outwardness which symbolizes the sum of expression. In the clarid Mediterranean light which brings the distance near, which makes of the panorama and of all that happens there a single object, this order of stone is particularly impressive. But everywhere the light upon dressed stone shows evenly and thus recalls, when dramatized by the presence of deep yet domestic waters, the vivid outwardness of the Mediterranean scene.

This book is concerned with the imaginative meanings that we attach to stone and water in relation, so far as an emphasis put upon those meanings is essential to the interpretation of Agostino's Tempio sculpture. By virtue of this approach we discover or rediscover Mediterranean art and life, the character of limestone, the differences between carving and modelling, ancient theories of the stars. Agostino's sculpture makes cognate subjects of these.

They are never discursions. So far as this book has any aim wider than to interpret the Tempio reliefs, it is as a symptom of altered culture. Today, and not before, do we commence to emerge from the Stone Age: that is to say, for the first time on so vast a scale throughout Europe does hewn stone give place to plastic materials. An attitude to material, an attitude conceived in this book as being far more than the visual-aesthetic basis of Western civilization, can hardly survive long. The use in building of quarried stone must, we shall argue, increasingly diminish, and with it one nucleus of those dominant fantasies which have coloured the European perception of the visual world. In the work of men, manufacture, the process of fashioning or moulding, supersedes, wherever it is possible, the process of enhancing or carving material, the process that imitates those gradual natural forces that vivify and destroy Nature before our eyes. Hitherto there has always existed a ratio, full of cultural import, between carving and modelling, terms on which we thus bestow the widest application.

We emerge from the Stone Age: and perhaps the very perception of stone manifest in this book, rather than any argument adduced, proves this to be so. For what is dead or dying is more simply an object, and therefore easier to apprehend, than what is inextricably bound up with the very flow of life. Nothing in writing is easier than to raise the dead.

Carving, Modelling and Agostino

From *Stones of Rimini* (1934)

The Tempio reliefs which most concern me and which provide the majority of the illustrations [not illustr. here] are arranged as follows: lying back an inch and a half or so from a frame of moulding, they constitute, together with this frame, the surfaces on three sides of piers. These piers support arches that form the entrances to chapels. The reliefs are for the most part low, yet their forms possess many values of sculpture in the round: while the quickened mass of a human shape between wind-strewn films of drapery, the delicious torture of hair and clothing by an unseen, evocative wind upon the outer and intermediary surfaces of a relief, give to its body the effect of vitality, of that stone-blossom we prize so high. Even carved landscapes by Agostino are restless, even the countryside is drunk with this dithyrambic draught that impels to ecstatic dance as did the breezes in the sybilline cave, scattering the mad leaves of prophecy. In the relief representing the journey of San Sigismondo to the monastery of Augauno,[1] a pillar surmounted by the statue of an angel appears among the surrounding mountains like a lighthouse encompassed. Still more in the landscape representing the influxion of the moon, sea and land are mingled in supernal agitation upon which a youth rides in a boat. At the Tempio, the young Agostino evolved his style; under the influence of his patron, Sigismondo, who aroused choriambic visions, he created his master-pieces. The sea is vibrant with fish, boughs bend under the weight of birds, the active airs breed a flock of doves that descend to greet the new-born Venus from the sea to earth. The land undulates with vege-tables and animal life just as the sea with fish. But his preoccupation with sea-movement – his garments, though ostensibly disturbed by wind, cling to and disclose naked forms like seaweed waving on

116

submerged rocks, or they are like water falling clear as the bather rises to leave the pool – was undoubtedly stimulated by Venice whither he came after leaving Florence. Sigismondo made him – to his presentiment of movement added a sense of spell. A spell was upon the spirit of Agostino, the spell of Isotta[2] communicated to him by his master upon whom it first lay, a spell which when enlarged over the varying subjects of Agostino's work, brings to mind the afflicting magnetism of the moon that confounds the height with the depths, transforming landscape into the basin of a forgotten sea.

Thus, though superficially the movement expressed by these reliefs evokes a sense of air currents, yet, as we shall see later more clearly, Agostino's root preoccupation was with water forms and water movement.

But before I try to put into words the crystallization presented by this carving, of the deeper Mediterranean fantasies in connection with limestone, I mean to prospect the whole field of sculpture. Agostino achieved what he did just because he was essentially a carver of limestone, far more essentially so than were the majority of his famous contemporaries, and perhaps more so than any sculptor whose work we have. At the instance of Agostino, then, it will be possible to grasp what is the carving approach as distinguished from the modelling approach. To raise this issue is by no means to embark upon discursion. My sole aim still is to interpret the values of Agostino's sculpture. And since these are bound up largely with the imperfectly recognized virtues of carving pure and simple, so wide an issue must now be discussed for his good. Otherwise he will be appreciated and condemned in accordance with more or less irrelevant standards, that is, in accordance with considerations of plasticity or modelling by which all carving, in whatever material, is today largely judged.

The predominant virtues, then, of Agostino's sculpture demand that a basic distinction be made between what is carving conception and what is plastic or modelling conception, even though some traces of both conceptions are to be found in all sculpture whether it be carved or modelled. In view of the Germans and their horrid noun, *Plastik,* one cannot emphasize too strongly that sculptural values are not synonymous with plastic values. The values in sculpture which find but little expression in modelling are those which have been forgotten. Few people are deeply sensitive to them. Neither the German nor the Italian critics are capable of 'seeing' an Agostino relief, beyond its often indifferent modelling. This state of affairs is intensified by the currency of photographs. Photographs transmit plastic values exceedingly well, carving values hardly at all. At this point my own photographs are a hindrance. The reader who has looked at them may have wondered why I should make so prolonged a fuss about these reliefs. As plastic conceptions, the majority are by no means first-rate. Still, if the reader will follow me through this chapter, I shall offer him the true values of these reliefs in such a way that my photographs may possibly prove an advantage rather than a hindrance.[3]

So we shall now attack the vital though confused aesthetic distinction between carving and modelling. There must be a profound aesthetic distinction between them. As everyone knows, carving is a cutting away, while modelling or moulding is a building up. Agostino's virtue will shed new light upon the high imaginative constructions which common fantasy has placed around each of these antithetical processes: (imagination itself is a plastic agency, fashioning its products with fragments). Agostino's virtue will illumine afresh the field of visual art. For the distinction between carving and modelling proves to be most suggestive in relation to all visual art.

The visual arts are rooted in handicrafts. Let us keep the expression 'the Fine Arts'. For these are the useless arts, a development of handicraft that is valued, although the products possess no utilitarian function. They are the superb development of fine objects made for use. And, in turn, the handicrafts are a heightened manual skill grown from the exercise of manual labour as a whole. Every artist has more than a practical interest in labour. Just as plants, worms and insect life turn the soils and help to disintegrate the rock, just as animals crop the vegetation, so the cultivator carves the earth, hoeing and ploughing the ground, cutting the undergrowth, the trees and the planted corn. And just as the cultivator works the surfaces of the mother earth so the sculptor rubs his stone to elicit the shapes which his eye has sown in the matrix. The material, earth or stone, exists. Man makes it more significant. To wash, to polish, to sweep, are similar activities. But to weave or to make a shoe, indeed the processes of most trades, are pre-eminently manufacture, a making, a plastic activity, a moulding of things.

Plastic shape in the abstract is shape in the abstract, while carving shape, however abstract, is seen as belonging essentially to a particular substance. It is obvious that all carving is partly to be judged by its plasticity, that is to say, by the values of its forms apart from consideration of their material. But that approach alone to carving is inadequate and in some cases (Agostino's reliefs for example) is altogether beside the point. It is like judging sculpture by photographs.

Briefly, the difference between carving approach and modelling approach in sculptural art can be illustrated as follows. Whatever its plastic value, a figure carved in stone is fine carving when one feels that not the figure, but the stone through the medium of the figure, has come to life. Plastic conception, on the other hand, is uppermost when the material with which, or from which, a figure has been made appears no more than as so much suitable stuff for this creation.

In the two activities there lies a vast difference that symbolizes not only the two main aspects of labour, but even the respective roles of male and female. Man, in his male aspect, is the cultivator or carver of woman who, in her female aspect, moulds her products as does the earth. We see both the ultimate distinction and the necessary interaction between carving and moulding in their widest senses. The stone block is female, the plastic figures that emerge from it on Agostino's reliefs are her children, the proof of the carver's love for the stone. This communion with a material, this mode of eliciting the plastic shape, are the essence of carving. And the profundity of such communion, rather than of those plastic values that might be roughly realized by any material, provide the distinctive source of interest and pleasure in carved objects.

It was not inappropriate that the tool carved as an instrument for carving or to cut now a branch, now the skull of an enemy, should have had so masculine a shape. Knapped flints, rubbed obsidians and jades, are most satisfying as carving. The demands of reality and of the connections made by the fantasy are here in simple accord. One might go further. It is from such coincidence that a thus reinforced fantasy has proceeded to create visual art.

This is the point at which to emphasize the pre-eminence of stone as the material to be carved. I am not thinking of its durability, nor even of the shape it will allow. I am thinking of the equal diffusion of light that, compared to most objects, even the hardest and darkest stones possess; I am thinking of hand-polished marble's glow that can only be compared to the light on flesh-and-blood. The sculptor is led to woo the marble. Into the solidity of stone, a solidity yet capable of suffused light, the fantasies of bodily vigour, of energy in every form, can be projected, set out and made permanent. Most other statuary materials, bronze and terra-cotta, are far higher mediums of manifestly reflected lights, as if their light were not their own light. The majority of stones, on the other hand, are faintly or slightly translucent so that their light seems to be more within them. Polishing, when it is hand-polish and not a chemical polish, in nearly every case gives life and light to the stone without causing it to be so brilliant as to lose a great part of its light again in reflecting it, or to be over-confused and deadened by manifestly accepting lights reflected on to it. It is the difference between light and lights. The great virtue of stone is that unlike other hard materials it seems to have a luminous life, light or soul. Limestone in particular blends the virtues of hard and soft materials. Whatever virtues I now attribute to stone in general I have already attributed in particular to limestones and marbles.[4]

Owing to the equal suffusion of light on stone, its most gradual shapes are unavoidable, especially since they are seen in association with stone's solidity: for hardness of material gives an enormous sense of finality to shape. The obsidian that has been thinned yet rounded to a cylinder at the shaft provides one with a far greater sense of roundness than does a ball of clay. The roundness of a flint is so compact, so heavy, its roll so continuous. As for representation of the human form, it will readily be understood that in the carving of stone's hard luminous substance, it suffers all the stroking and polishing, all the definition that our hands and mouths bestow on those we love.

Polishing stone is also like slapping the new-born infant to make it breathe. For polishing gives the stone a major light and life. 'To carve' is but a complication of 'to polish', the elicitation of still larger life. Carving is a whittling away. The first instinct in relation to a carvable material is to thin it, and the first use of such material as tool or weapon required it to be sharp, to be graduated in thinness.[5] The primary (from the imaginative point of view) method of carving is to rub with an abrasive. It is possible that the forms in stone sculpture which possess pre-eminently a carving, as opposed to a plastic, significance, have nearly always been obtained by rubbing, if only in the final process. However, it is not necessary for me to enter into a discussion of technique. I think one can hold that from the deep, imaginative angle, the point, chisel, drill and claw are not so much indispensable instruments of stone sculpture as auxiliary weapons that prepare the stone for the use, however perfunctory, of abrasives. The chisel and the rest facilitate stone sculpture: and, historically speaking, it may be that these instruments were adopted from wood carving and gem carving for this purpose, rather than invented for use on sculptural stone.[6] But the only point I wish to make is that rubbing belongs integrally to the process of stone sculpture. Wood, on the other hand, is never carved by rubbing.[7] Herein lies the fundamental difference between stone and wood sculpture: for it is reflected in the shapes proper to each, whatever be the actual instruments with which they are attained. Stone demands to be thinned, that is to say, rubbed. Wood demands to be cut and even split. Wood is not only not so dense, but possesses less light seemingly its own. Typically wooden shapes are nearer to typically modelled shapes. Hence, wooden shapes need to be more emphatic. In contrast with the flattening or thinning proper to stone, more definitely circular shapes are proper to wood, conditioned as well, in the majority of cases, by the rounding tree-growth formation of its grain. But the light on stone reveals the slightest undulation of its surface; and since no stone has a general circular structure, curves depend entirely on the care with which the block has been diminished. Such forms, though they may suggest the utmost roundness, will tend in reality to be more flattened or compressed than in the case of carved wood. Indeed, as we have said, from this lack of exaggeration, from this flattening or thinning of the sphere, the slightest roundness obtains the maximum life and appeal. The light on stone is comparatively even: no shape need be stressed: where complete roundness is avoided, the more it may be suggested. So the shapes proper to stone are gradual, to which sharpness is given only by the thinned nature of the block as a whole.

Carving is an articulation of something that already exists in the block. The carved form should never, in any profound imaginative sense, be entirely freed from its matrix. In the case of reliefs, the matrix does actually remain: hence the heightened carving appeal of which this technique is capable. But the tendency to preserve some part of the matrix is evident in much figure carving, and in the case of some arts, has given rise to definite conventions: thus, the undivided knees of Egyptian granite kings and idols. My example is a literal one: for even though no part of the matrix is palpable, the conception of it may yet be imputed to some part of the form. This is the inspiration behind many of the great hard-stone Egyptian heads. In conception and execution they are pure carving; of which the proof is that nothing, no nothing, is more meaningless, more repulsive, than a plaster cast of one of these heads.

I speak of all stones as if they possessed pre-eminently the light and the texture which, in a previous chapter, I attributed to certain limestones. The majority of stones have these virtues, but to a much smaller degree. It follows that Egyptian hard stones such as granites, diorites and porphyries, are by no means the most vivid kinds of stone. They lack marble's even and palpitating light. Their extreme hardness and harsh light entail comparatively rounded shapes. Softer stones, on the other hand, tend to be diminished to greater thinness. Their curves, no less gradual, will be more capable of a varied palpitation in their defining of forms. Such definition of form by whittling and polishing marble, so that in representational art the figures themselves tend to be flattened or compressed, as if they had long been furled amid the interior layers of the stone and now were unburdened on the air, were smoothing the air, such thinness of shape appears to me to be the essential manner of much stone carving. This manner, also, preserves for us the influence of the once enclosing matrix.

Superb instances of such shape in its most direct form are provided by the little prehistoric marble figures that come from the Cyclades. Many of these figures are so thinned out that they will not stand up. The heads particularly are squashed back. Yet what roundness is suggested by the curve of the shoulders, what fullness by the slight indication of the breasts! Curiously enough, such sensitiveness to the radiance of human form and to the kindred radiance of marble, immediately proposes a Greek ancestry, although these figures antedate Achaian invasions by many hundreds of years. One will conclude, however, that this particular sensitiveness to luminous gradations of marble, Greek or not Greek, is through and through Mediterranean.

I will not stop to consider the direct evidence of such flattening in Mexican sculpture, for instance, nor attempt to elucidate it in all the major sculpture of the world. I shall not otherwise refer to the almost paper-like thinness of the earliest Chinese jades, nor explain how that though granites tend for each section to make for heavily rounded shapes, yet the colossal height of much Egyptian figure-sculpture is itself an elongation that brings them into line with pyramid and obelisk.

I pass straight on to relief. This, I contend, is a dramatized form of carving. The shape is on the surface, the matrix behind it.

It is obvious that in relief carving, especially low relief, flattened or compressed shapes can be shown to the greatest advantage; indeed, the utmost degree of compression can here serve as the direct and constant aim of the carver, an aim to which all stones inspire him. Just as an enhanced feeling of the spherical is attained in stone to the glory of stone, by elongating spheres into ovoids and into other gradually rounded shapes, so three-dimensional form may become all the more signifi-cant from being represented by the compressed shapes of low relief. Advisedly I say 'can serve' and 'may become'. For, except Agostino, no sculptor known to me has flattened into low relief almost entire figures in the round. Agostino's reliefs are the apotheosis of carving. His iso-lation, and the moderate approval that his work has won, but indicate how undeveloped, generally, is the emotion that the very idea of stone carvings would inspire; or, at any rate, how easily it gives ground to emotions aroused by considerations of plasticity.

I realize that I owe in the first place to the contemplation of Agostino's work all that I feel about stone. No other sculptor can teach so much about carving. His achievement inspires the search for its origins. As my comment, I have needed to range the Mediterranean geography and the character of limestone. For at the time of the Renaissance, above all, it was the inheritance of feeling derived from concrete objects that became intense. Agostino's qualities, of course, were in part shared by some of his contemporaries, certainly in those of their works that I have described as Quattro Cento.

A more definite search for the origin of these qualities than the one I pursue, a definite research in the technique of ancient or medieval reliefs, will explain but little. Assyrian, Mexican and Hittite low reliefs, for instance, show no large degree of flattening. Classical high relief often has the appearance of free-standing statuary that has been cut off three-quarter or half by the background plane. This matrix not only does not assist the carving value but muddles the plastic value. Classical low relief is, essentially, an engraving; in actuality, a raised surface sur-rounded sometimes by a grooved outline. This contour is clearer from the distance than a general incising of the stone would be. I rarely find a deeper inspiration behind such relief. It is intended that the figure should look as flat as possible on the raised surface. Relief is substituted for engraving merely in the interests of greater clearness. An Agostino relief is exactly opposite in conception and technique. It is intended that the figure should look as round as possible, while the lower the surfaces by which the effect is achieved, the better. So great is the three-dimensional significance of some of the Tempio reliefs, that one needs to touch their surfaces to realize fully the degree of their flatness.

In many periods of art throughout the world, low relief has too often served merely as a raised incision, a drawing or engraving in stone whose sides have been cut away to afford sharpness and definition. No wonder that our more thoughtful contemporary sculptors have no interest in relief!

I shall return to the question of relief. It is time to say something about the nature of modelling.

That with which you model in sculpture is as much a material as the stone to be carved. But plastic material has no 'rights' of its own. It is a formless mud used, very likely, to make a model for bronze or brass. Modelling is a much more 'free' activity than carving. The modelled shape is not uncovered but created. This gives rise to a freer treatment, free in the sense that it is a treatment unrestricted by so deep an imaginative communion with the significance of the material itself. The modeller *realizes* his design with clay. Unlike the carver, he does not envisage that conception as enclosed in his raw material.

If the primary carved shape is an obsidian tool or weapon, the primary moulded shape is a clay receptacle. The unglazed bowl is written with the potter's fingertips: thus he expresses the completeness of its manufacture: while enamelled pattern over glaze and slip, or on porcelain, are an elaboration of his touch, are the potter's written characters. As we shall see, the calligraphic and supremely personal element in graphic art is always to be associated with modelling conception (particularly in the case of oil painting), while painting, for instance, that essentially illuminates a certain space, the use of pigment that is more directed by some architectural conception of planes, is preferably to be classed with carving.

One can say at once of modelling forms (as opposed to carving forms) in the widest sense, that they are without restraint: I mean that they can well be the perfect *embodiment* of conception: whereas, in the process of carving, conception is all the time adjusted to the life that the sculptor feels beneath his tool. The mind that is intent on plasticity often expresses in sculpture the sense of rhythm, the mental pulse. Plastic objects, though they are objects, often betray a tempo. Carving conception, on the other hand, causes its object, the solid bit of space, to be more spatial still. Temporal significance instead of being incorporated in space is here turned into space and thus is shown in immediate form, deprived of rhythm.[8]

Modelling conception, untrammelled by the restraint that reverence for objects as solid space inspires, may run to many kinds of extreme. For instance, on the one hand there are the simple, 'pure', forms of many fine pieces of pottery, exhibiting a purity or completeness in manufacture that is foreign to the very substance of stone: on the other hand there are potential or conglomerate forms that are consciously impressed with the associative and transitional qualities of the mind's processes. The rapid content of Rodin's sculpture and, indeed, of impressionist art as a whole, serves as an example.

Characteristic of modelling is an effect of the preconceived. In any Ting ware bowl, a most complicated thoughtful conception has been realized by a simple shape; while the thrust of some all-absorbing rhythm, simple enough in its fundamental movement, has been realized in virtuoso or masterly style by Bernini, Manet and Rembrandt, in unequivocal or monumental style by Donatello and Michael Angelo. One does not encounter so prominent a masterliness, so 'wilful' a preconception in what is essentially carving. For carving entails a dependence, imaginative as well as actual, upon the material that is worked. The stone block attains vivid life under the hand that polishes. Similarly, the shape of the material on which Piero della Francesca and even Giorgione painted, was of the deepest significance to them, far more so than in the case of Rubens, for instance, or of Vermeer. These latter, in their vastly different ways, were often engaged in such potent modelling that they negatived the picture plane by their compositions, as did all the Baroque painters. Theirs was the supremely personal, the supremely 'aesthetic' touch; theirs the calligraphic omnipotence so characteristic, as well, of far-Eastern pictorial art. The Baroque calli-

126

graphy was generous, bold, adult: while the Chinese calligraphy, though far more subtle, in painting at least has always been at root an art of precocious childhood, that is to say, cunning and exquisite splodges upon a white surface.

Most developed visual art displays a calligraphic competence. Calligraphy becomes extreme only when a calligraphic draughtsmanship is that to which each of the visual arts approximates. Such was the position in Baroque times. A Baroque church, a Baroque painting, a Baroque sculpture, each of them possess the verve of experienced and rapid handwriting. All unabashed modelling conception may be put into terms of such draughtsmanship, particularly since materials are so interchangeable in modelling. All sculptural modellers should primarily be such draughtsmen. I do not mean merely that they should be able to draw, but further, that their modelling should be but a projection of this primary penmanship. The true carver's power to draw, on the other hand, is a secondary power: for it is inspired by his attitude to stone. He has sought to illuminate the stone with file or chisel: now he seeks to illuminate paper with pencil or brush, so as to articulate its evenly lighted surface. 'Illuminated manuscripts' are a just description of the painting that springs from this attitude; and to these illuminations, the painting that was inspired by the character of stone always bears some reference. There may be a strictly linear approach to contour; but in the developed pictorial art of this kind, the painter will emulate the tonal values which the actual carver reveals on the surfaces, more or less equally lit, of his block. This painter's employment of tone is distinct from all other employments of colouring: in comparison they are adventitious; whereas the former method gives rise to the painting, whether it be more linear or more 'tonal' in technique, that is most deeply founded upon tonal conception. To my mind, such is the only true painting. There are, of course, all degrees of this profundity. Thus a Piero della Francesca picture causes all nearby pictures to cease as paintings. For, in comparison, they appear to be no more than coloured designs, calligraphic brushwork, tinted drawings.

I shall not risk the further confusion of the reader at this juncture, by following up so difficult a distinction in the realm of painting. This subject, in its entirety, belongs to a subsequent volume. But, so far as it is now necessary to my interpretation of Agostino's carving, I believe it will become clearer in due course.

To turn again to sculpture proper.

I have attempted to isolate the essential carving from the essential modelling. We may now form a better idea of their interdependence. For let me admit at once that in no part of the world has there existed a sustained figure carving in which modelling did not influence, and so, extend, the carver's aim; nor have artists with the strongest plastic preconceptions disliked, for what were considered monumental works at any rate, the suggestions of carving that result from the execution of their designs in wood or stone. There is no doubt that in the majority of developed periods, sculptors have desired to combine the plasticity of poise and rhythm with those qualities of a spatial object which, it is felt, can only be translated and enhanced rather than created. Stone exhibits these qualities at their highest. And so, plastic conceptions have been realized pre-eminently in stone as well as in plastic materials; and that not only because of the greater durability of stone.

So confused a conceptual admixture, of course, is foreign to the pure plastic art of Chinese earthenware and porcelain. But in limestone Europe, the influence of stone on modelling is evident from the earliest times, particularly in the South. After the initial rapprochement, so typical of European art, the relationship is sustained with reversed roles. For the quick development of the more facile process, modelling, then constantly influences the carver. Indeed, one can make the general-ization that the greater the power of carving to absorb modelling aim, the more incessant will be the infiltration of plastic values into that carving. *Thus, the proof of the importance of stone in European art, is the preva-lence of plastic aim in European carving.* A period comes in Europe, however, when an excess of plastic aim in stone-work overpowers the nexus with carving values. As carved stone the resultant product will be empty, though it may still be lovely as modelling; since a successful plastic idea is little bound up with any one material; indeed, its entirety may be suggested by a drawing. But it is probable, since the one defines the other, that when the values proper to carving are finally lost, modelling is atrophied sooner or later. There then intervene those grotesque confusions in aesthetic values such as we attribute to the Hellenistic age and, still more, to our own immediate past. At such a time it is essential to start afresh with the primary values of carving and modelling. This is our position today.

At other times European aesthetic values are never clear. It is obvious, however, that some real nexus with stone can survive a far greater infiltration of modelling conception in Mediterranean lands whose art, I have suggested, is based directly upon the character of limestone, than in the northern countries which have emulated so rashly in this respect the Mediterranean freedom. The thousand-and-one marble figures, the Hellenistic statuary, so palpable in realistic modelling, were yet a stone display amid limestone temples, amid grove and courtyard and flowering tub, as they stained themselves with pure water above the fountain, or stood on the sky-line striking the blue with posed yet marble arm. No doubt they are almost meaningless in our northern museums: not so when they stand throughout the sun, or pale against the moon. The Hellenistic statues are poignant by the thousand, and poignant is Cassiodorus' narrative of sacked Rome, populated by 5,000 men and 100,000 ideal marble figures.

In the Renaissance, the love for stone gathered so unparalleled a force that the answering infusion of modelling values served to dramatize, in Quattro Cento sculpture at least, the values proper to stone.[9] Under the enormous stress of modelling, however, those values became more and more diffused. In any case, plastic aim was at all times the conscious aim of Renaissance artists. The Quattro Cento spirit, nucleus of the Renaissance, goes on to be little more than the fierce spur to modelling. Baroque then occupies the whole field.

The carving which appeals most to me is the fifteenth-century carving that not only withstood an enormous infiltration of plastic values, but even employed them to show the measure of its own strength, the love and understanding of stone. This is the Quattro Cento sculpture, so-called in these volumes. Quattro Cento carving is carving triumphant. Yet here again there are degrees. In love and perception of stone, Agostino outstripped all his contemporaries. To demonstrate the extent of his achievement in this respect, we shall later compare a relief by him with one by Donatello. For, compared with Agostino, Donatello himself was a modeller pure and simple.

At this point, in connection with the interdependence of modelling and carving, I perceive that some reference that bears upon the character of naturalistic art is needed. For one may imagine that, in the first place, the Hellenic modeller desired to create a naturalistic figure, not least of all because he was responsive to the flesh-like glow of the limestone rocks and buildings and statues about him, and to other humanistic influences of Mediterranean topography which, at some point, are always connected with that living yet objective condition of the stone as I too have conceived it. A plastic idea may vitalize, as well as de-vitalize, carving aim. What a stimulus it must have been to Hellenic carvers when the first naturalistic bronzes were taken from the mould! Here were the figures which the carver had vaguely attributed to his block as the fruit of his intercourse with the stone, by the modeller ripped, as it were, gleaming from a womb. In a certain imitation of the more facile process, the carver now becomes more precise in his aim, more naturalistic: the children he wants from the stone must comply more and more with his own image. His successors, however, will sooner or later dissipate the underlying style without which any form of naturalism is meaningless. But the naturalism may yet be pursued without a single real plastic or carving idea. The ideal nude ceases to have any but a pornographic interest, even perhaps for its perpetrator, whatever he may say or think – and a commercial interest, of course.

To turn once more to stone relief. Classical relief, I have said, rarely possesses superb carving value. The flattening of form, so congenial to the light and density of stone, is rarely marked. Flattening entails the use of some perspective where a scene is crowded with figures; and it was the character of classical architecture itself which ruled out any

130

such treatment.[10] A Greek temple, in particular, was so entire an expression of limestone, that a relief could add nothing structurally; while, executed in perspective, it would have disturbed the limestone geometry of the planes. It was as if architecture almost completely absorbed, and then restricted, carving aim. In some other countries, a more developed relief has still been part of the architecture without so marked a subservience. The other extreme is attained by some Indian temples in which structural conception might appear to be sacrificed to what is called ornamental carving: a misnomer; for the carving has not been conceived as distinct from the structure. It is the structure.

That will not appeal to modern taste which tends to deny, in any circumstances, a paramount sculptural value to relief. One is told that Renaissance relief is merely pictorial, merely bad painting. I trust the foregoing pages have put the boot upon the other leg; though I do not wish to suggest that a painting is inferior because it can be referred to a carving or plastic conception. If it were so, there would be no good pictures at all.

One is also told that a sculptural piece must be satisfactory from every angle; it must be entire, significant from in front, behind, on top, beneath and so on; whereas relief, of course, in worse cases than a picture, has only a front. Now the reliefs I am about to champion are to be seen from the sides as well as from the front. This has escaped everybody's notice, and it is the central point of their quality. But they have no backs. Behind them, and part of them, are slabs fitted to columns. Yet is this not to have a back? For myself, the entire piece of carving, even a primitive flint, is not the quintessential carving though it be the primary one. The carved stone that you take in your hand, that you turn over to examine every loveliness, has a created entirety which in the last resort I would rather associate with modelling. For the essence of stone is its power to symbolize objectivity. It should stand, be more or less immovable: and what better occasion for vital objectivity than when carving gives the expression to masonry itself, when relief shows the surface of the stone alive? Not often does it take this role. Quattro Cento carving, though, is of this kind, of which Agostino was the greatest master. Let me, then, if I am to convince you, define his mastery in detail, first pausing to consider the low relief that he inherited.

A few pages back I described how all the major values of stone could be glorified by the flattening and thinning of form in very low relief; how stone may thus reveal rounded forms that are yet altogether one with the matrix and with the building. Flattened shapes in relief, shapes that give *some* suggestion of the figure in the round and consequently afford *some* value to a side-view, are common enough in Byzantine, Romanesque and Gothic relief. Except, however, in some Byzantine and late Gothic pieces, the flattening is not far developed, nor could it be further developed without proper perspective. But it is a mistake to regard perspective science as something altogether unequivocal, as clearly demarcating its users from their predecessors. Wherever on flat or flattened surfaces there is a suggestion of the round, there is use of perspective of some sort. Here again is the connection between the layer-like or flattened forms natural to stone, and pictorial art in general. For the widest possible definition of a picture must be the use of flat pigment entailing some suggestion of two or more surfaces. Should pigment be used without any suggestion of a variety of surfaces, it may achieve pattern, but not painting. Painting realizes on a single plane the tones of marble surfaces. Indeed, the very same sense of round shapes that are yet flattened out, which I find proper to stone relief, is sometimes to be obtained from Byzantine pictorial art; for instance, from the compressed attitude of the mosaic sitting Virgin of Sant'Apollinare Nuovo at Ravenna. She is, in part, represented slightly sideways so that she shall the better appear to sit. As for one of the attendant Magi, his bending knees (that enable a large part of the haunch to appear), his twisting trunk, immediately put one in mind of the attitudes Agostino used in so many of the Tempio reliefs, by which he could suggest figures in the round. Again, the Byzantine terra-cotta reliefs in the Baptistery of the Orthodox* are to be connected with Agostino's works.[11]

Thus, when perspective science was discovered at the beginning of

---

* Baptistery of Neon, Ravenna.

132

the fifteenth century, it was the answer to an intensified acquaintance with stone. The Mediterranean limestone values came uppermost; and, of course, in a novel form, in a Gothic form after a thousand years or so of Christianity. But as usual the carving situation was bound up with the plastic. Given a new attention to stone that dates from the proto-Renaissance, it was not irregular that the enormous strides in technique and perspective should have been immediately contingent upon a new aim in the more facile process, modelling.

Limestone, as I have said, marble in particular, possesses a soft light. Yet it is solid and durable. Its beauty is this fusion of the virtues of hard materials and soft materials. Nay, further, the purer marble is hard and brittle, yet owing to its metamorphic, homogeneous structure, is carved by strong tools with some facility. And it is probably due also to this character of marble, that modelling, the more facile process of homogeneous soft materials, has made in Mediterranean countries an unparalleled, continuous, intrusion into the carving of stone. Some intrusion of modelling facility heightens the 'human' limestone character, as we shall see in the work of Agostino whose art reveals a combination of plastic skill with a searching respect and love for the stone.

But the majority of Florentine Renaissance sculptors had no such continuous love. Already before the 'stone rush'[12] Florentine modelling was far developed, and it was the Florentines who upon the advent of the 'stone rush' gave the new command and the new conception to the rest of Italy. In my first volume I have described this phase and its connection, so far as architecture and architectural decoration were concerned, with the dull Florentine sandstone, *pietra morta*.[13]

They loved stone little in Florence. The more typical Florentines answered to the spirit of the times, but not specifically. Their interest in carving too closely corresponded with their interest in the degree of modelling that stone could absorb. They made use of the deepened interest in stone a trifle ungenerously. Theirs was the poise, the equipoise, the cold purity of modelling conception. When I come to Florence from the Adriatic coast, I notice this at once – everywhere this poise of the bronze upon the pedestal. I have a sense of *Plastik*, I notice the prominent yet noble stomachs of the statuary, moulded, it is evident, not by eating but from outside by the sculptors. I admire the size of things, I admire greatly the poise of the open loggias and the great eaves that are like wings of wheeling aeroplanes along the streets. How they sail and wheel like the swallows who nest them! Stately, naturally stately become the figures in the narrowness below, figures once fitted in voluminous robes and locks upon high heads. As I gaze at the planes of the eaves fixed in complicated rhythm along the Via dei Bardi, high over the straight, gloomy walls, I remember Verrocchio's bronze St. Thomas with a foot balanced without the niche on Or San Michele, I feel his calm locks and pointed face and the nobleness of his cloak. The noise of the Via dei Calzaiuoli reverberating among the close grey stones, prevents this nobleness from gloominess and pride: and so it must have always been in Florence; always the plastic assurance amid turmoil.

The evidence in Florence of any essential carving is less direct.[14] It exists in the works catalogued as Quattro Cento in my first volume (the connection with fantasies of stone exuberance there described, makes them Quattro Cento), but it exists only in the large, and by no means specifically. The specific forms are the fruit of modelling, and are often enough realized in plastic materials. However, in the cutting of architectural decoration, sculptors sometimes showed less carving conception than in designs achieved with bronze or terra-cotta.

Perspective was developed by the Florentines, but was never the basis of their art. As I showed repeatedly in my first volume, the Florentine sculptors and the painters who derived from them 'used' perspective. They cared little for gradations in layers or in tone, except so far as they assisted naturalism. In carving as in modelling they realized the most realistic perspective without any intense gradation between adjacent surfaces. The foreground figures of Ghiberti's bronze reliefs are really free-standing, while the background figures are no more than outlined. Open the bronze gates or approach them from the side, and the reliefs will be meaningless, the foreground figures will be horrible and precarious bits of pointed metal. In this connection I feel in sympathy with the modern criticism of relief, especially relief on doors that presumably open and shut. But such is not the relief I hail as carving.

Since they aped in stone the extreme naturalism of Ghiberti's modelling, the Florentine cutters developed an unequalled facileness. Sometimes they anticipated the Baroque translation into stone of an extreme Baroque modelling, as when the Rossellinos hung their flying angels on the walls. These distressing figures which claim the poise of the hollow bronze although they are ostensibly marble relief, preserve their positions by being composed in reality of marble pieces that lie close on the wall surface and that are secured by a projection that passes within the wall. But there existed relief carving in Florence, exquisite relief carving, even though largely inspired by Ghiberti's plastic elegance. Desiderio could not have thus carved the swags on the Marsuppini tomb* unless he had loved the marble. Yet, if we compare him with Agostino, Desiderio is a modeller, conceives as a modeller. And the same is true of Donatello. When Desiderio or Donatello carved a Madonna and Child relief, they composed it boldly, in masses. And so, whatever the delicacy of the carving, there is little, or no, *vital* connection between one surface and the one immediately next to it. The child, although he is the front surface, will be extremely flattened, so that in composition he becomes of a mass, a plastic mass, with the mother. There are cases when a significant relation between one surface and an adjoining surface is not so much unimportant from the point of view of the general composition, as definitely undesirable. Thus the flattened top of a Virgin's head or nimbus is resolved into a rim cut away from the backround. The centrality, the emphasis upon organized mass, require the rim to be divorced from the background, so that composition be the more definite, the more precise. Such a rim, however, is contradictory when seen from the side. For, the cutting away now appears as something so blatant and emphasized as to become a main feature, a positive denial of a nexus with the background, with the matrix. In brief, there is little care of stone surfaces as valuable and related in themselves.

Lombard cutters are even more at fault. Very often the whole heads

---

* Desiderio da Settignano (c. 1428–1464), Florentine sculptor. Tomb of Carlo Marsuppini, Basilica Santa Croce, Florence.

of their crowded reliefs are cut away to an almost spear-like sharpness, apparent even from the front. It is only fair to say that of the carvers who worked principally in Florence, Desiderio is to be blamed least in this connection. He is considerably nearer to Agostino than were the Rossellinos and Majanos, or than was Donatello himself. Desiderio worked marble with a sensitiveness unrivalled in Florence. But he too seems a modeller by the side of Agostino.

Stone gradations are multiplied by an Agostino Madonna and Child relief. Graduated surfaces are the logic of its form. Each surface sponsors a fresh disclosure. What is in front (the child) is less flattened than what is behind (the Virgin). The effects of actual difference in the depth of surfaces are not diminished as by Desiderio or Donatello in favour of a plastic mass, but emphasized with perspective. Thus the forms carved on the inner layers are progressively flattened. The further into the stone the more pronounced becomes the flattening of shapes: yet the inner and background shapes suggest no less contour than the outer shapes; with the result that they are luminous even in the dimmest light, as if their contours were indeed the face of the stone-block itself. So great is the contour expressed by these gradual or flattened inter-related surfaces, that unlike the reliefs discussed above, an Agostino relief will bear examination from the side.

This is the test of relief carving. If every surface is rounded into the next so that, seen from the side, the values of forms in the round are still composed there as a face to the stone, then it is the finest relief carving. The Florentine sculptors, one and all, had little use for perspective beyond a certain point. Agostino exalted perspective, so that every gradation of the marble's slow luminous face was given life by his hands. His low relief and its background possess a vital and vibrating concomitance.

Such general statements produce small conviction. Let us compare Agostino's Virgin and Child relief in the Victoria and Albert Museum with the famous Donatello entombment that hangs on the next case, the one nearer the door. I have little doubt as to which of these two pieces the reader will prefer in photograph [not illustr.]. For the greater the modelling conception in sculpture, the less are the values lost in photograph. The photograph of the Donatello relief gives you its paint most happily. The design, the organization of masses, the elements of weight and stress and strain are clearly understood. The virtues of the Agostino relief, on the other hand, the gradual rounded cutting, the closely related equal tones and half tones, the luminosity, in part are lost. This Victoria and Albert Museum photograph is an exceptionally good one; yet the plate suffers by comparison with that of the Donatello. As for my other reproductions of Agostino's work, those plates which look the most striking are of the pieces that exhibit a more dominant plastic conception, such as the *David* and *Hercules*.

But the disparity is not merely a question of photograph. The same judgment is likely to be made in front of the reliefs themselves. For contemporary educated taste is a good deal more academic in temper than one might suppose from all the talk and would-be 'modernist' profession. Now, academic taste only feels at home with plastic conception in the widest sense. That is one of the reasons why academic sponsorship of the classic is so woeful, so doomed. Like the pseudo-modernists, academic taste can only fully recognize design alone, albeit of a different sort, but equally the plastic sort. Be it modernist or academic or whatever else, the simple, swift or 'masterly' *organization* of masses is characteristic of modelling, be it oil paint that is slickly splashed about or Le Corbusier's lightning concrete.[15] Naturally, the Florentines with their power of organization, with their complete preconception (all the values of a Florentine relief can be suggested by a sketch), are continually acclaimed unrivalled masters among the fifteenth-century sculptors. At a moderate estimate only one out of a hundred trained admirers of visual art is as sensitive to the deeper philosophies of space and tone or carving, as he is to poise and rhythm or to the plastic side of composition. The majority will fully recognize the creative verve only when it has *fashioned* something out of formlessness. They see the shape and the other attributes of a primitive flint tool, but they do not see with the same absorbed attention that it is a flint. In a word, the majority are not highly sensitive to stone. They love texture and colour of course. They know this picture has good colour and that bad colour. But there it is, just colour or colourfulness: which indeed it is when employed for plastic conception. To them the concentrated use of tone necessarily means an impressionist effect. When will they see that tone is put to more uses in a picture by Piero della Francesca than in a picture by Renoir; when will a painter come forward who is incapable of conceiving this horrible idea, colour?

I, at any rate, put in a word for carving. And, indeed, there are signs that the original carving conception is today rediscovered. Already there are painters who disdain the moulding properties of oil paint, who, so to speak, prefer to polish and scratch their canvases like the carver his stone. An attitude of such kind – rather than the often concomitant abstraction in design – is the basis of the painting we feel to be contemporary.

I do not desire to minimize the appeal of the Donatello relief, though I am not averse from anticipating its photographic advantage. Its beauty is monumental. Nothing that Agostino carved was monumental. Hence his comparative neglect by the critics. There is nothing monumental about the nature of marble. But I will not deny that the effect of the Donatello piece, in common with many other plastically conceived pieces, is enhanced by the fact that it is carved in marble. And, of course, in such carving, some of the Renaissance general love for stone obtains expression. But this relief in no way qualifies as one of Donatello's Quattro Cento works; unlike, in this respect, the reliefs on the base of the *Judith*, which, although bronze, display the tense animation and exuberance that was primarily imputed by that age to flowering stone surface. Or, if you prefer, such humanistic eruption was imputed to all materials. But I have argued sufficiently that stone has a pre-eminent objectivity for which a flowering is most desired. It is the concrete thing, the sculptor's ideal object.

Here is, then, in the Donatello relief, the modeller's organization of masses realized in marble. The Christ's body is everything. Even in photograph you can follow the modelling of his stomach which is made

138

'anatomical' in the mode that is common to Florentine sculpture of this period. On the other hand, the further wing of the foreground angel on the right is no more than sketched in. *As surfaces*, the figures traced in the background, the background heads and the nimbi, have no aesthetic relation whatsoever with the masses in front. These background shapes are relevant only to the composition as a whole, that is, as shapes; which is not enough relationship for carving conception. But apart from the background shapes, in foreground, too, there is shown small feeling for changes in surface as significant in themselves. To Donatello, changes of surface meant little more than light and shade, chiaroscuro, the instruments of plastic organization. The bottom of the angels' robes is gouged and undercut so as to provide a contrast to the open planes of Christ's nude torso. The layers of the stone are treated wholesale. Though some of the cutting is beautiful in itself, the relief betrays a wilful, preconceived, manner of approach. In brief, the composition is not so much founded upon the interrelationship of adjoining surfaces, as upon the broader principles of chiaroscuro. Stress and strain is the point: anatomy, the then unrivalled plastic subject, is the point.

There exists a tendency for composition to be thus broadly organized whenever the sculptor has made a design and delegated to assistants most, if not all, the heavy slow work of cutting the stone. Here again we see a reason, this time an unattractive one, for the interpolation in carving of plastic values. The prevalent monumental aim of European carving has, at times, entailed the gentleman sculptor of manifold commissions, who draws sometimes, and sometimes models in clay. Several recent academic sculptors are reputed not to have handled a chisel in their lives, nor any other carving instrument except at meal times. Three-feet models of war memorials – a wet day's work – have been posted to Italy to be executed there in tractable marbles by subservient masons with the mechanical aid of pointing. No wonder, then, that with few exceptions, the handful of serious sculptors who exist today concentrate upon carving and perform every stroke of their own work; no wonder they feel that they rediscover the very art of sculpture.

In the Renaissance, of course, there were hundreds of men who cut stone superbly. The most intense feeling for stone was abroad. Nevertheless, plastic conception lent itself to delegation of work, to its organization on a large scale. We see why Florentine aesthetic was so well developed, why the workshops were so big and efficient. In plastic art, at any rate, production breeds production. A plastic conception executed by able assistants does not suffer to anything like the same extent as a carving conception. The plastic conception already exists in the master's drawing. But the values of an Agostino relief, other than those of its plasticity, were achieved only in the actual carving process. Agostino's assistants in the Tempio often let him down badly; and it was inevitable that they should. One might say that the attainment of a carving conception cannot be delegated or hurried. But those peoples whose fantasies rely largely on stone, insist upon a multiplicity of statues. Thus, we realize once more that the very love for stone, for stone sculpture, entails the development of a plastic approach. For only with the aid of this approach can good sculpture become quickly extensive. And we see that when the tendency has run its course, when the original demand for stone is exhausted, a meaningless plastic sculpture, committed to academic design, remains.

We need, however, make no excuses for the cutting of this Agostino Madonna and Child low relief. It is obviously by his hand.

The most marked difference between the Agostino and the Donatello is the former's effect of steady disclosure, in direct contrast with the latter's alternating light and shade. There is always the element of disclosure in true carving. Yet, contrasted with the Donatello, Agostino's intensely low relief at first sight may seem ribbed and fretted, fussy. You miss Donatello's bold plasticity. But then you cannot realize in photograph the subtlety of surfaces that preserve the marble as wholly marble. You feel a lack of rhythm. But why always seek for rhythm in visual art, why desire that rhythm or music and other temporal abstractions be conveyed by objects; why desire from the concrete an effect of alternation, since the very process of time can be expressed, without intermittence, as the vital steadiness of a world of space, as a rhythm whose parts are laid out as something simultaneous, and which thus ceases to be rhythmical? Rhythm, surely, is not so proper to visual art as immediacy; there is, surely, a certain priority of carving over plastic conception. Plasticity or rhythm in architecture and sculpture of the South has always retained some pronounced immediacy of effect through the dramatic presentation of feeling. In the visual arts of North and East, on the other hand, rhythm too frequently impairs spatial significance: too often those arts in essence are a visual kind of music. And how few appreciators of visual art understand anything about art, except about music and literature!

Agostino's tonalities elude you. You cannot, for example, realize from the photograph the effect of the apparently straight, if ridged, surface of the Virgin's undergarment that appears beneath her left hand. Carved, not modelled, are the carefully flattened heads, slow in roundness, yet so great in roundness that they will 'read' from an angle. Should you go to the Victoria and Albert, contrast in this respect the two Florentine reliefs, one on each side of the Agostino. They are absurd when viewed from an angle, when you see them as you stand in front of the Agostino. The poignancy of his shapes is not so much in themselves, as in their relations with his other shapes. This relationship is a much tighter one than in modelling. There is a poignant beauty in the triangular shape beneath the Virgin's wrist, inside her cuff. This shape is nothing in itself: for carving conception bestows an immense content and power on what, by itself, would be the most insignificant of forms. Notice the impassable little space between the Virgin's cheek and the child's head. It has the meaning, the shapefulness, of the intervals between forms in Piero's paintings. Such irremediable position between objects, shapes that are thus so far determined by their intervals, do not lend themselves, after a certain point, to the bold organization of masses that we admire in the Donatello. And why 'bold'? Because such plastic organization runs counter to the purely spatial conception of which stone is the symbol.

Yet I will not deny that Agostino himself is an offspring of Florentine modelling as I have defined it; that unless he had learned his trade in the Florentine school,[16] he could never have developed so facile and flowering a technique, nor attained such naturalism; that some of the Florentine modelling clichés remained with him. But I have already admitted a constant interrelation between what I have called modelling and what I have called carving. I admire the infusion of such modelling into such carving so long as it enhances the layer formation of the stone. Further, I am willing to champion any marble piece, however 'modelled' its forms, where there still exists some wide reverence for stone, some evidence or remembrance of stone culture such as the Mediterranean limestone culture. I give these Florentine plastic stone statues and reliefs preference, as carving, over much northern cutting that may have a minimum of direct plastic aim but which, none the less, pulsates with rhythm. Northerners have never loved stone deep down; and no other material directs the fantasy to pure non-rhythmic space.

This conception, non-rhythmic space, is difficult to define more closely: so let me again apply its sense to one detail of the reliefs before us. Whereas in the Donatello relief the angel's face on the Christ's arm is a most definite (and plastic) transition, on the left of the Agostino relief we see one face, as it were, causing other faces. The essence of the carving, and of truly spatial, non-rhythmic approach in general, is the juxtaposition of similar tones, of related contours, of intrinsically related forms. Every part is on some equality with every other part, an organization that is foreign to the come-and-go of rhythm. Work of this intensely spatial kind recalls a panorama contemplated in an equal light by which objects of different dimensions and textures, of different beauty and of different emotional appeal, whatever their distance, are seen with more or less the same distinctness, so that one senses the uniform dominion of an uninterrupted space. The intervals between objects have assumed a markedly irreversible aspect: there it all is, so completely set out in space that one cannot entertain a single after-thought. In visual art, the idea of forms however different, as answering to some cogent, common, continuous dominion that enforces the bonds between those forms in spite of their manifold contrasts, gives rise to the distinctive non-plastic aim: and this idea was inspired, above all, by the equality of light on stone, an equality that dramatizes every tonal value. In Piero della Francesca's painting, by the religious reverence for spatial intervals, by tonal and perspective organization, all feeling, all movement, all rhythm, all plasticity itself, was translated equally into panorama terms. His pictures express the metaphysics of space or colour or tone. They are free of 'atmosphere', psychological or physical, as they are of anything emphatic.

See once more how shape causes shape in the Agostino relief. The Virgin's arm lies tight to her diaphragm. There is the impression of a surface growing inward. This helps out the slight indication of the breasts. In the Donatello, an angel's hand is put flat on the Christ's body. It directs attention to the torso: it is a *general* tactile reminder. One obtains from the Donatello none of the sense of surface making surface to flower. Agostino was the master of undulation in the stone. His stone becomes a hotbed of shape. See the angel's head at the bottom of the relief, his hand clinging to the frame as if he had emerged from the back layers and had passed through the Virgin to the front, or as if the stone were a sea in which he rocked by his hand to and from a breakwater. Also, notice the poignancy of the child's curving shoulder juxtaposed upon the face of an angel behind, from which the shoulder's roundness graduates. Face and shoulder give each other shape. This is an excellent example of Agostino's use of tone, or, perhaps in case of actual untinted carving, one should just call it surface juxtaposition.[17] At any rate, compare this surface transition with the deep shadow around the shoulder and arm of the angel on the left of the Donatello relief. There are no such gross and plastic shadows in Agostino's carving. His placing of a shoulder against a cheek behind, similar contours without a shadow between, remind one of Piero della Francesca's yet greater juxtapositions of similar tones, unaided by the actual changes of surface that facilitate this feat in carving. Piero delighted to display his extreme virtuosity in the employment of tone by using a practically identical colour for something portrayed far behind, juxtaposed to something portrayed well in the foreground. So complete his skill and so essential is it to his conception of painting, so completely is that conception realized, that with a fair amount of intelligence one might look at his *Flagellation* at Urbino* every day for a year, without noticing in the picture a very astounding instance of that feat.

This is the painting that presumes light, a more or less equal light, another word for space as a homogeneous medium, in which all things are set out. Piero could turn transition and movement into the finality of such space. Lights, on the other hand, *lighting effects*, or an emphasis upon chiaroscuro, these are to be connected with rhythm or poise, not primarily with stone. Northern European and Northern Asiatic painters have generally conceived light as the agency of atmospheric effects: when left to themselves they have been, of all pictorial artists, the least connected with stone, the furthest committed to modelling conception. Such is the case of many sculptors, too, who have avoided the introduction of specific modelling shape and idea. This avoidance has availed them little, whatever strength and superficial purity, whatever profound absence of vulgarity, their more puritan temper has evolved.

Piero's and Agostino's conception depends upon an almost hieratic use of perspective. In terms of perspective was the religion of equal light, of space, of stone, expressed in that time. Anyone may experience this finality who is familiar with the air of southern lands. It is not because of marked difference in tone or in distinctiveness that you perceive this wall to be behind this wall. The bricks of the farther house-wall are just as clear, just the same colour. Each object stands in order, reduced to a common relationship by a common medium. You are aware of space: every process seems exposed as objects, all of them all at once in their degrees. More especially, just as the sun has gone down after a hot day, things stand. A luminous whiteness, as yet untrammelled by the dizzy approach of night, is common to sea, to road, to house. Stone gleams, the dust is white: what is of dark hue is dark, what is darker is blacker without mitigation. The sun has disappeared suddenly leaving the world arranged. After the long dazzle of the day, your eyes see the world exposed by a neutral medium which is but the

---

* *Flagellation of Christ* (c. 1468–70), Galleria Nazionale delle Marche, Urbino.

144

fresh, caressing air. The evening stirs: the concrete world stands concrete. What was the passage of the sun has turned into space, and all that is left of passage are the invisible airs. Otherwise every phase, all subjective conditions, appear to have been transformed into objects arranged in neutral unbroken perspective.

It is when thus light or space imposes so uniform a dominion on objects that difference in tones seems uniquely real and poignant. There is nothing atmospheric about them. The relationship between objects becomes the essential part of their shape; and this their relationship is of tone and of perspective. Light marble pre-eminently, in most of its conditions and in most lights however dim or however violent, enjoys this tonal condition, since the equal light on stone tends but to mark its shape.

Once more I am back to the subject of Agostino. I have previously mentioned the tonal qualities of his cutting. I must now say more about his uses of perspective. Although much of Piero's finality in spatial exposition may be traced in his art, Agostino was also concerned in showing movement as a ferment on the surface of the stone. For both purposes he used exaggerated perspective: since both the tonal relationships and the ferment proper to his stone could be dramatized only by gradual curves, that is to say, by the flattened or perspective treatment of form. To describe exhaustively the method of its employment by Agostino would need a volume to itself, entailing an intensive technical study for which I am not equipped. I can but indicate a few general principles, remark a few details, a few characteristics of his carving.

In the first place, to show developed perspective in carving, it is necessary to carve relief. Having argued a connection between perspective and stone, I now bring it forward to recommend the low relief, or at any rate, Agostino's relief in which the perspective cult is celebrated. Renaissance relief perspective is based on the same conical projection as painting perspective, with the difference that painting is projection on one plane, low relief on at least two planes: thus the latter's perspective is complicated by the thickness of those planes. Also, since the joining of actual surfaces must not be obscured by the use of perspective; on the contrary, should thereby be magnified, less simplification is desirable than in the case of picture perspective. High relief does not suffer this complexity to the same degree, yet has the difficulty in crowded scenes of one figure obscuring another, especially as seen from an angle. But those sculptors who loved, rather than employed, perspective, as far as possible avoided crowd scenes of the type that can only be treated in high relief, or in some combination of high and low. Agostino's best work is of low-relief single figures which manifest clearly the flattening he employs, and its integral connection with the block.

As I have often remarked, for such degree of flattening, perspective was essential. It is almost as if his figures were conceived in the round and were then pressed into low relief, so great is the roundness that is intimated by care of stone surfaces. His perspective tricks dramatize to the full the propensities of stone: and since form in the round is there squashed out, the whole of that form is to be grasped from any angle. In sculpture, such immediacy can be attained only by relief; and I think no one except Agostino has managed it, and he by no means invariably. Not more than twenty pieces or so in the Tempio Malatestiano are first-rate, one or two reliefs by his hand at Perugia, and the Madonna and Child reliefs, the one at Florence, the other at the Victoria and Albert. We do not know how much else of the same sort has disappeared.

The ovoid is the perspective appearance of the sphere. The ovoid is the flattened sphere. Hence the ovoid, the thinned sphere, is the prevailing shape in Agostino's work. As he needs must work with ovoids, he began to visualize everything in terms of that form. Throughout his work he has given us this key. Thus, for instance, when he represented clouds, they are cut to pure ovoidal shapes. Fingers, of course, and fish were dear to him. So too, globular hair-locks and the elongated contour of breast or stomach, buttock or thigh, beneath tight strands of transparent drapery. Such transparency, again, affirmed the slight translucence of the marble. He also used drapery to enshroud the whole figure and reduce it to his dominant shape. *History* and *Rhetoric* in the Tempio are oval forms.

Agostino had various ways of enforcing perspective. Most forms in

146

his reliefs have a perspective of their own apart from their contribution to the general perspective. Occasionally this individual perspective is in opposition to the more general one, but, at the same time, the former thereby makes the latter poignant. Still, the particular, and sometimes even contradictory, perspective of details, while it yet must fit in and help to make the design, also puts emphasis upon graduation of surface and neutralizes a simple modelling assessment of general masses. This perspective treatment is not peculiar to Agostino's work. To some degree it appears in all Quattro Cento carved and modelled relief. In all representation, of course, there is the tendency to show the lower half of an object or figure as seen from above, and the higher half as seen from below. Such a mixture of perspective is common everywhere. It is the most simple means of showing more of the object or figure than would a strictly eye-level representation.

But see to what extent and to what resultant shape Agostino employed this principle. Let us turn once more to the Madonna and Child relief. The general principle obtains for the relief as a whole. At the top, the head of the Virgin is inclined slightly downward and to the left, as she looks at the child. Her face we see from below; but since she tilts her head downward we see well above her forehead, we see her hair, veil, crown and nimbus on the back of her head. (The edge of the nimbus is bevelled inwards so as to bring it forward.) We see two-thirds of her head owing to perspective flattening. We would see even more of her head if it were not turned to the side as well as inclined downward. The right side of her face is shown as far as the further edge of the eye. This right side is so flattened that in actual dimension it is only half as long as the distance from the nose to the further edge of her left eye. The ear is shown in complete profile, the angle at which an ear is most significant. It is a complicated ear, *in rapport* with the shell forms of the niche behind. The child's face is seen definitely from below, whereas the angels' heads adjoining, and those on the other side of the relief, are on eye-level. Moreover, whereas we see the child's face from below, *we see the top of his head and even parts of the back of it from above*. Otherwise, so much of the head could not be represented. This transition from one perspective to another passes muster because the head is tilted to the side and downwards, while the eyes look slightly up. Yet the perspective is even more complicated than this. Parts of the face we see on eye-level, and the ear, like the ear of the Virgin, is represented in complete profile.

At the bottom of the relief, the child's right foot, foreshortened on the outward-tilted framework, is seen entirely from above in accordance with the general perspective.[18] Yet we can see slightly underneath his left foot. Also contradicting the general perspective, though at the same time reflecting its plan on a small scale, the tilted angel's face whose chin abuts on the bottom frame is seen on eye-level, if not from below; while the top of his head, like the top of the child's head, is seen from above. The perspective of the vase on the right is also independent of the relief's general perspective. The vase's base is seen from above, its middle on eye-level, its lip from below. Such was the usual way of treating vases and candelabra in Quattro Cento arabesques.

These various perspectives cohere: in this manner several aspects of an object were represented, while individual perspective, so far as it was the microcosm of the general perspective, emphasized that general perspective, that sense of many aspects. To some degree you will find such treatment in all Quattro Cento work, whether it be stone, bronze or terra-cotta, and in all work that approximates to being Quattro Cento. And this helps out a classification of Quattro Cento sculpture in terms of technique. *Wherever you find relief forms, be they ornament or figure, arabesque or swag, wherever you find these shapes, whatever their position, turning to show to you their maximum, like flowers that thrust and open their faces to the sun, wherever that is the salient point about them, then that sculpture is Quattro Cento as I define it.* Decoration sculpted with that feeling will never look 'stuck on'. For hand in hand with vertical perspective goes horizontal perspective, the flattening which means gradual and rounded shapes that issue from the block. Of such flattening, Agostino was the supreme master.

Consider the child of the Virgin and Child piece, consider how much of his body is shown by this low relief. You say it is like painting. This, as criticism, means nothing to me. For I can here see and touch all the values I love in stone. Painting is an offshoot of such carving. The Egyptians sometimes carved the legs and head in profile, the rest of the body as frontal. Agostino's figures are a softer stone development of the Egyptian aim. A characteristic attitude, of which the child is an example, is a sideways bending of one or both knees, thus bringing in the curve of a buttock; or arm thrown across the body bringing in the shoulder and even the shoulder blade. The first attitude requires one leg in rounded profile, so that one sees almost the whole calf, while the other leg, represented frontally, is, when the cutting has been crude, so flattened as to appear without a shin bone. Furthermore, the bending knees cause the part of the legs between knees and thighs to be represented at a receding angle that is easily foreshortened; which, in turn, enhances the circular and ovular swirls, represented on eye-level, around the stomach and the hips. The trunk is often bent slightly forward over the knees, while the shoulders and head turn slightly the other way. This attitude entails a nodal vortex about the stomach and around the hips, out from which the rest of the figure undulates. Such figures appear to float rather than stand. The effect is increased by swirling hair and swirling drapery that now conceal, now disclose, limbs and breasts.

These figures appear to be embedded in some buoyant white liquid such as mercury. The soft yellowish and luminous Greek stone was cut by Agostino to show its original liquidity and condensation. The bodies of the floaters are thus enmeshed and carried, but their heads float higher and rest upon the buoyant surface. From the knees to the navel, there is a swirl, a vortex, in the typical Agostino figure. This tends to endow the males also with the female contours and the female suction. Looking at the relief of Diana and of the other planets, and particularly the one that represents the spring tides under the aegis of Diana, one feels the vast seductive influence of the moon. Not till the last words of this volume shall I have set out to my own satisfaction this lunar mythology and all that it means. I must show Isotta as the moon, and Sigismondo who built the Tempio as her counterpart. For directly, even more, indirectly, the Tempio celebrates Sigismondo Malatesta's love for Isotta.

The floating image must now give place to another. Agostino's figures inhabit every plane of the waters. If they float near the top, they also lie upon the bottom whence they seem to pierce each ripple as it passes. The Tempio is at Rimini on the Adriatic coast. Ripples come low and in quick succession upon that beach in summer. On arriving last June, I walked to the end of a small jetty. A white-enamelled iron chair stood upon the sea-bed. From the jetty I clearly saw it standing in the depth, with its round back elongated to an oval or shuddered to an ellipse. What indeed was its shape? But there it stood. I thought at once of Agostino's sculpture in the Tempio, of those flattened forms in which an influence was at work. In general it was a water influence. The reliefs were marble and dry; but they were luminous: and thereupon I felt the whole deep connection of limestone and water.

Next day in the Tempio I saw the Mediterranean countries as water and water-life congealed into stone: I saw the elements in flux and trees growing from a crested marble wave. Venus is represented as coming to land in a chariot drawn by two white swans. Around her legs and piled up behind her are the waters. The topmost wave is smooth, without a ripple. It is the shapely mountain side. On one summit there grows a myrtle tree, the aromatic evergreen shrub of limestone soil. The rose flowers in a valley of intermediate swell. The relief of the influxion of the moon shows land peaks and similar trees encompassed by the flood. The trees are tinted black in both reliefs. They are the dark evergreens of the Mediterranean light, trees that flourish from the limestone whence by temple or on promontory they show off the pure sculpture of marble. A youth rides the buoyant flood in a boat. But should Diana's mingling influence relax, his boat would be left high and dry on the back of a whale or sea-dragon. For half the seas have attained the same degree of solidity as have the mountains of liquescence. The creation of further limestone is in hand. The influence at work keeps the flood encompassing the shores to which an elephant comes in alarm.

Such pregnant waters, such trees, such pyramidal peaks beneath the ovular clouds, figure also in the relief of the Crab. Rimini, the Adriatic and the hinterland are again represented. The limestone layers are the waters. Notice the river Marecchia flowing between the hills and out into the Adriatic. It is the rainy, the torrential flow. In such waters Aquarius or Ganymede stands. They flow behind him from the ovular clouds that muffle his left arm. Clouds, like so many torpedoes, hide Mercury's knees, and upon his head is the pyramid as a pontifical mitre. From his knees to his navel and again about his head there is a vortex. It is the whirring night from which Diana emerges clean. It wraps the loins of the Twins, sucks evil Saturn, hurls up the dripping Virgin, encircles the Dance and distributes her wiry coils of hair. But the predominant vortex is about the hips. These swirling eye-level middles that disclose so many attitudes and so many surfaces, tend to put 'out of drawing' the upper part of a figure's trunk. But three lovely reliefs at Perugia show best how profound is the style based upon this mannerism. Agostino gave back to marble its primeval eddies. This vortex is sometimes recalled and set to work by the incision of a few curving lines in the background.

Where no vortex appears in the middle of a relief, the idea of it yet lingers. In the relief of the influxion of the moon, this centre, represented on a level with the eye, is the first big pyramid with the tree in front of it. Hence a further poignancy. To the pyramid, to the new limestone accruing from the waters and their life, is attributed the concentrated powers of the whirlpool whose beauty, now that it is a smooth stone, may be shown by a thin and gradual shape in complete objectivity. Here is expressed in unconscious parable the whole appeal of limestone, the whole underlying mythology of Mediterranean art.

Finally, in the matter of stone and water, I refer again to the shape of fish, to their extreme yet rounded flattening, to the predominance of the oval form. No wonder the representation of marine life has always delighted the Mediterranean limestone carvers. But it was only in Quattro Cento carving that marine decoratives, principally in the shape of dolphins, attained a paramount exuberance. There is nothing stylized and ornamental about Quattro Cento dolphins or sea-centaurs or scorpions. Yet fish are the fundamental carving shape. Fish slither and wriggle in Quattro Cento relief and arabesque. The stone is alive with them. Putti, with the marble dust in their eyes, ride the dolphins; a fluke is sometimes cut clear from the background. The block itself wells over larger deep-sea forms within. Shells encrust the architectural members. They are not stuck on: they cling; but also they flower there, bloom there: they are also stone-blossom. For the water and the water-life from which the marble was formed, in their stone shapes symbolize also the cliff, the earth, its flower and its fruit. Such shells express the first geological concretion in the history of the marble, serve to symbolize the later fruitfulness of the soil which covered it from the skies. Thus sea and land upon whose intercourse Mediterranean civilization has depended, were celebrated as one in the marble. Either as land or as sea-fruit are the shells and acorns. In the last analysis, stone-blossom and incrustation are different aspects of the same principle. Marble, then, was the prime instrument of Humanism. For such fantasies as found their home in marble, were humanistic fantasies. Therein was implicit the friendliness to man, the 'natural' unstrained exuberance which treats of elemental nature with so little anxiety in proportion to its dynamic strength. The tension is all of life: from death is borrowed but its objectivity, its unmitigated petrification.

It may seem that I use the sculpture of Agostino to further a set of ideas. I have written of particular work by him in relation to chosen photographs. Like a doctor with a nervous patient, I have avoided bringing to the reader's notice realities which might dampen his ardour. It is full time to make some reference to the actual condition of Agostino's work in the Tempio.

The Tempio was never finished, and most of what exists of the original work was done in a hurry and under difficult circumstances, as I shall relate in the next volume. Agostino was the master sculptor in the Tempio: by no means all the reliefs were the work of his own hand. We know the names of his numerous workmen, but nothing about their respective skill. Few of the reliefs have the degree of finish possessed by the Madonna and Child in the Victoria and Albert Museum; and it will be obvious that skill in actual execution is far more important to a carving design, as has been said, than to a modelling design in which, however unfinished or rough, the 'idea' may well be apparent in full force. On many reliefs in the Tempio the marks of the claw are distinguishable. In some figures, the very subtle flattening technique, as executed by assistants, has been grossly simplified. (But when one has grasped Agostino's carving 'idea', so much more difficult to understand than a modelling 'idea', one does not mind.) Perhaps the body of a figure has been flattened successfully, but the floating head, for which prominence was desired, has been treated crudely with higher, too much higher, relief.[19] Some reliefs were partly coloured and have now lost their tints, or have since been badly treated with modern colours. The first chapel to the left has been ruined by a modern attempt to restore it in fifteenth-century style. The draughtsmanship of nearly all the reliefs is, as one would expect, by no means eminent: but in many cases, too many cases, it is definitely inadequate.

Still, for those who are sensitive to stone, I do not exaggerate the Tempio's revelation. As for others, I believe that many faults they find in the internal architecture as well as in its sculpture, reflect both such people's obliviousness to carving, and their search for the modelling upon which their aesthetic values are based. Plate 17 will have many admirers.* It is lovely, but not so much as carving. It is a plastic figure. These powerful furrows possess the rapid Donatellesque organization. Gideon, on the other hand, is lovely as carving. His nakedness has a gradual yet revelatory virtue that comes of its flattening, at one with the block and with his immense shield whose edge is rounded. The conception of Hercules is midway between that of David and that of Gideon. Hercules is beautifully flattened: we can see round the calf of his further leg. But the upper part of his body is 'constructed' on the emphatic principle, so is his girdle with its deep furrows. David is the most modelled relief in the Tempio, if we except some of the very inferior infant games and shield-bearer reliefs to the second chapels on the right and left. We shall not look for Agostino's execution among any of these.

---

* The plate [not illustr.] illustrates Agostino di Duccio's relief of *David with the Head of Goliath* at the Tempio.

On the other hand, it is interesting to note that Agostino was a very fine modeller in the specific sense of the word. For instance, the coloured plaster relief by him in the Bargello at Florence is a superb piece of modelling. Here are the swift or loose organization of masses, the deep shadows.[20] He understood the large-scale treatment also, a plastic treatment that was soon to develop into the Baroque, a style still further removed from carving conception. This clay Madonna and Child relief is as purely modelled as the Victoria and Albert piece is carved.

In Quattro Cento carving, plastic aim, however strong, is yet subservient to the love of stone; an ideal situation for the cutting of medium hard stones, marbles and sandstones. In the case of hard stones, modelling skill is most likely to be altogether out of place. Their obdurate hardness has never served as so broad a repository for the elastic images of men. However, the cutting of hard stones is better appreciated in this age. The hard stones' resistance to plastic aim saves it from being entirely judged by the usual modelling standards. Sensitiveness to carving goes as far as that. But medium hard stone sculpture, when it contains an evident plastic infusion, particularly fifteenth-century marble, is less fortunate; since it is judged entirely in terms of plastic qualities which do not reflect its deeper character.

To one important aspect of Agostino's carving I have made little reference, since no photograph can illustrate it. I refer to the subtle undulation in his reliefs of their backgrounds. One may say that as a rule the block tends to be less cut away at its top and at its bottom. In many of the Tempio reliefs, as well as by heads that are in higher relief than bodies, this tendency is expanded by the bottom-most sections being of still higher relief and serving as ground for the figures. All Agostino's subtlety was used on some of these pedestals, on their shapes and curves and sections. They help to show how deep the block has been cut. Occasionally they are rounded to the sphere or ovoid so that the feet shall the better slope for us to see on top of them.[21] Sometimes the pedestal is used to represent rocks, with a few flowers incised on their barrenness whence grows an aromatic tree. Mars' scythed chariot descends a precipice. But it is in no great danger.

A hurricane blows it back, blows back his ovular shield, pins it to the block, hurls back his cloak and the tree on which his eagle has perched. Mars himself gleams; and the wolf whose hide seems mail-clad-hard, is unruffled by the wind.

Capricorn, of the full ovoid udders, reaches up a peak to nibble the mountain oak. She balances upon the naked stone. See how it is cut to fundamental stone shapes, to gradual curves and smooth ripples; not gouged, not furrowed.

Mars' chariot is seen from above, Venus' chariot from more or less the eye-level: but Diana's chariot is seen from below. Water and fishes gush out beneath it. The horses which draw the chariot, however, are represented on eye-level. Diana herself with rinded moon in her hand is represented from below.

The background is tinted dark. Owing to the mixture of perspectives, Diana is given a dazzling height above us. She is truly in the sky, above the clouds at her horses' feet. She steers above us straight out of an enormous night. At the same time, due to the flattening[22] of shape performed with the porridge-coloured Greek[23] marble, she is a luminous figure, she is the moon herself.

The Diana relief is the bottom one of the pier, the Venus the top one. *Yet Diana's chariot we see so much from below, while Venus' chariot is represented on eye-level.* This curious mingling of the heights and the depths has the magnetic quality of moonlight, moonlight of the luminous, brown shadow, moonlight which can cause even the mountains to appear like ridges in the basin of a waterless sea.

And so, under the aegis of the moon, goddess of waters and fish, goddess with the luminous marble face, I take leave of Agostino for the present.

This chapter is finished; but a postscript seems inevitable.

The fine arts are rooted in the handicrafts, the handicrafts in various manual labour whose vastly traditional character, to put it mildly, is changing. Of what kind, if any, is to be the new skill, the new handicraft? I have no intention of pursuing the subject. Instead, I call attention to one contemporary change which is simple enough, but which in itself upsets the whole balance between carving and modelling.

I have defended the low relief by pointing to its direct connection with masonry, with stone architecture. Hitherto, stone or otherwise, all developed sculpture has been founded on an association, at least, with architecture; if not specifically with buildings, then with monuments, shrines, tombs and so on. Except in the case of fetishes and other small personal objects, architecture and sculpture have in every stone-using civilization gone hand in hand: or, rather, sculpture has been dependent upon building. This connection mirrors the pre-eminence that stone has enjoyed as the desired building and carving material, has ensured the preservation of some possible carving values amid the usual growth and eventual dominance of modelling conceptions. But today stone is no longer the desirable building material. What is more, *modern building materials are essentially plastic*. These materials have little emblem of their own. With an armature of steel, Le Corbusier can make you a room of any shape you like. He can express speed with a building. Rooms will be fashioned. Their organization will be simple sheer design that has no use for trappings, least of all for sculpture.

Everywhere the slower carving processes are superseded. Manufacture, modelling, has superseded its fellow. Such, we have seen, was always the Europe trend, though it was sustained, paradoxically enough, partly as a result of the great ambitions of European peoples in carving processes.[24] Synthetic materials take the place of age-old products in which fantasy is deposited. The majority of our pavements and of our new buildings are made of synthetic stone; not merely concrete, but synthetic stone that can be fashioned to almost any effect that is desired! You need to know something about stone to distinguish it from this moulded product. Modern scientific power of synthesis fashions a fundamentally new and plastic environment.

Stone architecture is prolonged but a moment by synthetic stone. Stone architecture dies, the mother of the European visual arts for more than two thousand years. In Europe of the historical period, brick and mud and clay and wood construction never superseded stone. They had their individual life; still they were largely substitutes for stone. At any rate European men have always built with stone when they could afford it and obtain it. But today stone architecture is dying. The creations of Le Corbusier and others show that building will no longer serve as the mother art of stone, no longer as the source at which carving or spatial conception renews its strength. Architecture in that sense of the word, indeed in the most fundamental sense of the word, will cease to exist. Building becomes a plastic activity pure and simple: whereas, in the past, building with stone or its equivalents has not been (at best) a moulding of shape with stone, so much as an order imposed on blocks from which there results an exaltation of the spatial character of stone.

Mountains and pebbles still exist: but so far as stone loses its use as a constructive material, it loses also power over the imagination. Civilized man is surrounded by natural objects the intensity of whose imaginative import will continue to diminish.

What future is there for carving, or for the full spatial conception?[25] I have remarked that the strength of such modern painting as is truly contemporary is founded upon a reaction from modelling values in favour of carving values. But should the growth of plasticity, of manufacture, in labour and in art, overpower carving activities altogether, there is then no future for visual art as hitherto conceived by the European races.

The Tempio: First Visit

From *Stones of Rimini* (1934)

Rimini is not an attractive town. There are the sands and the Adriatic, flat hotels and villas stretching half a mile from the shore with hardly a stop. But these are cut off from the town by the dirty, jagged knife of the railway. You are then in a town of cobblestones, in no way picturesque; a country-town that sprawls almost in the northern manner of industrial suburbs. What abruptness abounds is harsh and without colour. The port where the river Marecchia flows into the sea beside the bathing establishments, the Roman bridge over the Marecchia, the Roman arch on the Flaminian road, these are points of interest; but as centres of departure and as points of reference in the mind, they do not 'work'. The streets, of no great length, seem endless as the Commercial Road. For whither could they lead? Not back to any great distance in the past in spite of the superb Roman bridge and the Roman arch, in spite of the Rubicon which was one of the streams just north of the Marecchia and of Rimini. The Rubicon served as boundary between Roman Italy and Cisalpine Gaul. But Rimini has lost the keen air of a frontier town, and if you were expecting some link with Julius Caesar, you will in your disillusionment find the other extreme; you will find the sprawling country-town (neither on the sea nor off it) to be made up of dull and hopeless interiors, innocent of aspidistra, but all the more *triste* for that, because bare and cold in winter; inevitably the retreats of *Risorgimento* memories and other comfortless yet Italian Victoriana. You will not, it is true, see the same old man every day, but each day different old men who exhibit a certain unnecessary presence of mind: can they not (they are thinking), should they want to, take the tram up to the beach, up to the Romagnol Lido that is hacked by the gales of winter? So the depression diffused by the more indifferent deadness of other nearby towns, Pesaro or Fano or Cesena or Forli, where the hotels are enormous provincial palaces converted into chambermaidless tombs that lie over noisy streets, is more impressive. There, the gloom of heaping roofs and bolted and unbolted wooden blinds may well shatter you.

But it would seem that the spirit of Rimini is diffused and scattered, over-harried by shunting and important trains, just because that same spirit stands isolated, though conserved, in the silent stone of one building. Noises pass away from it. And if you would liquefy the energy, all the life both of the town and of the district, all the life that here stands concentrated in stone, if you want a Gothic and even Roman Rimini, you must follow the fantasies and the noisy researches of these pages, each of them stimulated by contemplation of the one building, the Tempio Malatestiano. Perhaps my task seems an unnecessary one. Perhaps you have seen, or you will be able to see, the building for yourself. At any rate here are some photographs. And for my part, why should it be worth my while to transpose in terms of drama what is immediate and objective to the eye? At best, I shall be creating in an inferior art, inferior in objective realization, working many impressions that could be obtained in five minutes at Rimini. Certainly, though I have studied the subject on and off for six years, I have added no new intensity of feeling to my first 'ignorant' impression of the Tempio. I have only found images and names and explanations and reasons and theories – in general, literary data – to express what on July 5th, 1925, I knew at once of the life, the landscape, the condition of which the Tempio is the emblem. My excuse must be that the potential content to be gathered from looking at the Tempio will be understood by the majority of cultured people, or even noticed by them, only when some-one has done his best to transpose that same so objective content into images and ideas: and then, not into poetry pure and simple. There must be a good deal of explanation as well.

So, as heretofore, I shall take the reader step by step. Each cadence and each break will be a transposition into rhythm of what these stones mean, each fact and each idea will correspond to a carved emblem; and the literary form, with its self-conscious come-and-go, with protagonists and drama, must emulate the white certainty of Alberti's encasement.

On that first visit to Rimini I knew little of Sigismondo Malatesta who built the Tempio, beyond the name. It is easy enough for me to give you at the outset the whole of my knowledge of that time. I need but copy out a paragraph or two of Baedeker (1909) as follows:

Rimini, pleasantly situated about ½M. from the Adriatic at the mouth of the *Marecchia* and the *Ausa* (the ancient *Aprusa*), with 29,545 inhab. and extensive fisheries and silk-manufactures, is frequented by Italians and Hungarians for its sea-bathing. A fine avenue of plane trees leads from the Porta Marina (see below) to the beach. The shifting sands are apt to obstruct the harbour.

Rimini, the ancient *Ariminum*, a town of the Umbrians, became a Roman colony in 268 BC, and was the frontier fortress of Italy in the direction of Gaul, and the termination of the *Via Flaminia*. The town was extended and embellished by Julius Caesar and Augustus. During the Exarchate it was the northernmost of the 'Five Maritime Cities' (*Pentapolis Maritima*), which were ruled over by one governor. The other four were Pesaro, Fano; Senigallia, and Ancona. In 260 Ariminum became an episcopal see, and in 359 a council against Arianism was held there. The town afterwards belonged to the Longobards.

In the course of the 13th cent. the Malatesta made themselves masters of the city. In 1288 Giovanni lo Sciancato ('the lame'), surnamed also Gianciotto, put to death his wife, Francesca Polenta of Ravenna, and his brother Paolo il Bello (an event from which Dante derived the episode of 'Francesca da Rimini' in the 5th canto of the Inferno, and Leigh Hunt the materials for his 'Story of Rimini'). During the following century this family ruled the greater part of the Romagna, and also, for a time, the mark of Ancona. Under Louis the Bavarian they became viceregents of the emperor, but Cardinal Albornoz afterwards succeeded in reducing them under the power of the pope. The Malatesta family, divided into the Pesaro and the Rimini branches, distinguished themselves as condottieri, but also as patrons of learning. The most famous scion was

Sigismondo, son of Pandolfo (1417–68), who united the gifts of a great military leader with the most violent passions. He attracted painters and scholars to his court, in order to secure immortality for himself and his mistress (afterwards his wife), the clever *Isotta*. – In 1528 the people revolted against the Malatesta and placed themselves under the authority of the pope.

A broad road leads from the *Station* to the Porta Marina, within which it is called Via Umberto Primo. After 4 min. we follow the Via del Tempio dei Malatesta to the left, passing a dilapidated Renaissance palazzo.

San Francesco (*Duomo, Tempio dei Malatesta*), originally a Gothic edifice of the 13th cent., was magnificently remodelled in the Renaissance style in 1446–55[1] by Sigismondo Malatesta from designs by *Leon Battista Alberti* and under the superintendence of *Matteo de' Pasti*. The windows of the original building are retained.[2] Of the façade unfortunately the lower part only has been completed, while the dome intended by Alberti to surmount the choir is wanting. The choir itself was restored in 1709. On the plinth are the initials and arms (the elephant and rose) of Sigismondo and Isotta, who were to have been buried in the arcades on either side of the portal (see below).

The vaults of the S. side contain the sarcophagi of poets and scholars whom Sigismondo entertained at his court. In the first four are the remains of *Basinio* of Parma and *Giusto de' Conti*, the poets; *Gemistus Pletho* (died 1451),[3] a Greek philosopher whose corpse Sigismondo brought hither from his campaigns in Greece; and *Roberto Valturio*[4] (d. 1489), the learned engineer. In the others repose several physicians and a bishop of the 16th century.

INTERIOR. To the right of the entrance is the Tomb of *Sigismondo* (d. 1468). Most of the plastic ornamentation of the chapels was executed by *Agostino di Duccio* of Florence. FIRST CHAPEL on the right: above the altar, St. Sigismund of Burgundy, patron-saint of the founder; by the pillars, allegorical figures of the virtues. SECOND CHAPEL OF THE RELICS (Santuario; closed), containing a (restored) Fresco by *Piero della Francesca* (p.62; '*Petri de Burgo opus* 1451'): Sigismondo Malatesta kneeling before his patron St. Sigismund, with the castle built by him on the right. – In the

CAPELLA DI SAN MICHELE the 3rd to the right, is the *Tomb of Isotta* (d. 1470),[5] on the left, erected as early as 1450, with the motto 'tempus loquendi, tempus tacendi' at the top. The archangel on the altar by *Ciuffagni*,[6] is a portrait of Isotta. By the pillars, angelic musicians. – FOURTH CHAPEL on the right: by the pillars, the planets and other fantastic representations from a poem by Sigismondo[7] in honour of his mistress. – FOURTH CHAPEL on the left: by the pillars, allegorical figures of the sciences. – THIRD CHAPEL on the left: Children's games, probably by *Simone di Nanni Ferrucci*,[8] a pupil of Donatello. – The FIRST CHAPEL on the left is named the Cappella dell' Acqua from an ancient statue of the Madonna, represented as sending rain. On the left is a sarcophagus for the reception of the ancestors of the founder, with two reliefs, representing the House of Malatesta in the Temple of Minerva and the Triumph of Sigismondo. By the pillars, above the elephants, two portrait medallions of Sigismondo.[2]

That is what I read in the train from Ravenna. I had heard, of course, that at Rimini there were to be found a fine example of early Renaissance architecture and some sculpture of the same date. I had stayed long enough in Venice to realize that the infinite love for stone by which it had been made so variously emblematic, was especially related to the art of the early Renaissance. As yet I had no knowledge of Florence. Florence was my ultimate goal in which, as it happened, I was to be almost bitterly disappointed. But meanwhile I could see the early Renaissance in Venice and near Venice. First I stopped at Ferrara, then at Ravenna to see the Byzantine churches and the mosaics. As it happened, the visit to Ravenna from which I came direct to Rimini, was most fortunate. For thereby I was able at once to gather connections between the Byzantine achievement and the Tempio.[3]

On the way from the station at Rimini there is some fine sixteenth-century brick-work: San Girolamo. I found a custodian to open up the interior. On the ceiling of the choir there is 'St. Jerome in the Desert' by Guercino. 'Who painted it?' I asked her. She was full of assurances, though taken aback. 'Sigismondo, Sigismondo Pandolfo Malatesta'; and giving her worst idea an emphasis as is the way of some Italians, she repeated the name with impressive satisfaction. 'And Isotta made the holy water basin?' About this she could not but agree as there seemed no alternative: though the marble was hardly a courtesan's material.

Sigismondo and Isotta, I realized, were fixed ideas in people's minds; or were they just substitutes for Paolo and Francesca? But in any case my curiosity about the Tempio was increased. For it seemed unusual that stone memorials by themselves should feed popular romantic misconception: in comparison with poetry, that is; especially post-medieval building. Could it be the Tempio itself which was causing the Riminesi to evoke the names of Sigismondo and Isotta in an art encounter with foreign bathers? And I would have known – so I thought – the Sigismondo and Isotta story if it had been extensively 'written up'. What was the story, and did the stones speak? Surely there was no gesticulation, no eloquent statuary. And how did a more compact architecture suggest a story?

Here is the Tempio façade on the left. I nearly passed it by; it is so compact. Nothing draws you: it is silent, without rhythm. It is steadfast like a blind face. The fact that it is unfinished starts not one single speculation. Do you wonder what expression the blind man had when he used to see? No: his face is complete as it is. This is no shrine, no temple, but a church; Gothic San Francesco upon which Alberti has built a classical encasement. You can see the brick of the old San Francesco above where the stone encasement is unfinished. That is the only modulation.

Stone is rare in these parts. Aemilia and Romagna are poor in stone. The Istrian of which the façade is built does not weather so well as that in Venice; it does not come from the best quarries.[4] But the blocks are strong and deep. How sudden are these dense white stones in the sprawling town! The encasement is tall, steep for its length. The proportions of the four three-quarter columns and of the blind arches between them upon the high stylobate, are beautiful, strong, serene. The mouldings, delicate enough in composition, are so uncompromising in their certainty and relevance as to be ferocious – in the way that a mathematical conclusion drawn from a dense conclave of figures can be relentless yet sublime. Science and art, delicacy and strength, were never so close together as in the early Renaissance. The façade neither goes up, nor down, nor across. It stands white and strong. Nothing could be more foursquare than the box-like imposts upon the stylobate, from which the columns rise. I would prefer to have avoided this word, 'rise', because of its directional meaning; though if I were describing a Greek Temple I would use it willingly. But the Tempio façade is far too compact to afford any sense of directional emphasis. This compactness can only be gained by the ligature of arches and by avoiding at the same time their more usual effect of progression. It is true that the massive centrality of the door is emphasized: one is aware that this façade is a very careful composition: and the setting-off point of all design as we conceive it today, is some principle of centrality, its emphasis or avoidance. Yet the ratio between the shapes, between the oblong imposts, the depth of the stylobate ledge, the blankness of the blind arcades, and the triangular depth of the pediment, overcome the massive centrality in favour of a general steadfastness. Whatever their design, this is a characteristic of all Quattro Cento buildings.[5] Their architects abhorred centrality, since it entails progression from both ends of a building, as much as they abhorred a decentralized rhythm. Yet they employed arches. Their conception of composition was less plastic and infinitely more alive than ours. They obtained their effects with classical forms yet without academic manoeuvre, often without variations of any kind. And in this context, Bernini, Sir Reginald Blomfield and Le Corbusier are to be classed together in the opposite camp. A modern architect may doubt whether a building upon identical arches, with an identical arcade above, without variation, without central feature, could possibly 'come off', far less afford the highest sense of the steadfast. Let him look one day if he will, at the Procuratie Vecchie by Mauro Coducci in the Piazza at Venice. And what is true of the horizontal lay-out in Quattro Cento buildings is often true also of the vertical. The Quattro Cento architects who built with masonry were less prone than we to talk of 'good' and 'bad' design (just like that), as if all aesthetic considerations could be reduced to the simplified mechanism which an inevitable use of these adjectives suggests. They were less concerned with plastic purity. They wanted each stone to be beautiful: as far as possible they avoided the situation in which one group of stones surrenders a more positive function in order to give emphasis to another group of stones. The Quattro Cento conception of proportion was without severity and without extravagance. If you take care of the material's significance, proportion will largely take care of itself. They achieved sublime proportion with the minimum of cunning and the maximum of feeling. The rather empty Vitruvian 'rules' were a good enough conscious aesthetic; for architects inspirited them. Again, sometimes the proportions arc unsatisfactory and it does not seem to matter much.

All architecture deserving the name possesses *some* carving, as opposed to a plastic, significance of this kind. It is, at root, the character imputed to limestone itself which has immortalized the employment of classical members in architecture. Only thus, from the angle of the material's fitness and liveliness, rather than from the more conscious angle of pure design, does proportion in architecture attain sublimity. And since, tomorrow, if not today, building becomes in all respects a purely plastic art, it will less confuse the values of this art if we find another name for it, foregoing the term architecture altogether.

So much for the plan – a better word nowadays than design – of the Tempio façade. On the flanks there are deep bays, portentous as an aqueduct. The first five bays on the right side have a sarcophagus apiece. Behind are the brick walls and the Gothic windows of the interior.

As I look, the tense *cohesion* of the encasement impresses me so forcibly that already my mind has received the full stimulus that will need to find expression in such phrases as 'stone blossom' and 'incrustation', suggesting an almost *organic* connection between architectural members and between background and ornament. This quality provides the fundamental difference from nearly all other architecture, and particularly from other buildings, be they Greek, Roman, Brunellesque, High Renaissance, 'Classical', Baroque, Empire, or whatever else, that employ entirely or in part, one of the classical orders. Employment of classical pillars or pilasters nearly always means an impression of distrib-uted weight and coherence. But see how that impression is intensified on the Tempio façade into something far more dynamic, see how the pilasters are grown from the wall space, grown steadfastly like a flower, without palpitation; see how incrusted is the effect of this most classical pediment within the central arc. You can no longer distinguish archi-tectural members. The thing is organic, one, everlasting.

In Ravenna I had seen something lasting, something complete and certain. The Byzantine mosaics, and to some extent the architecture too, possess a deep religious assurance. This art celebrates the triumph of Christianity and of statecraft. Certainty is so great, content so deep, that expostulation is not only unnecessary, but impossible to its style. Yet the Byzantine achievement pales before that of the Tempio façade. For we admire here, not the certainty of the objective world gained for religious or political concepts, but objectivity itself, stones themselves, which are celebrated and dramatized as a content rather than as the means to realize or express a content.

As I stand before the Tempio, every tune falls away from my head. I encounter the stalwart face of the rose. Upon the broad stylobate there grows the Malatesta shield quartered with the monogram $. A massive wreath circles the shield, joined on either side to a tongue-like leaf of the Malatesta rose. This shield and upright rose with long and gripping leaf, alternate, except for the occasional interruption of an elephant or other emblem, in a zone of decoration along the façade and down both flanks. It is not a structural part of the design: but thus to call the shields and roses 'decoration', tends to obscure their quality, their qual-ity of growth from the stone slabs. They exhibit the stone alive: and, indeed, the forms of the roses in particular and the technique of their carving are most unusual. I did not grasp at first how very conventional-ized are their forms: the sense of exuberant naturalism they immedi-ately convey, hides at first the actual simplification of their structure. Their four petals curve uniformly inward; from the stout stalk below, the leaves branch out.

No wonder I noticed first the exuberance of this growth: there is

something almost monstrous about these turgid stalks! The Malatesta
rose is a tropical growth in miniature, an immense trunk with huge
subsidiary shoots such as would stifle a deserted town within a year.
It belongs to the foraging kind of vegetation that is almost animal.
These roses are on the stylobate at Sigismondo's behest, to provide a
forest for his heraldic elephants and to support his shields.

The stalk or trunk of the rose shoots from a massive sheath whose
fibres loop outward, and whose length curls round to be a basis for
the whole form. The sheath's end, however, curls up and divides into
flukes or scrolls.

Now this stylized fantasy of the rose affords no effect of stiffness or
of abstraction. Almost every shape is worked out to an effect of exuberant naturalism. Since the forms are not in any way copied from nature,
it is as if the sculptor had invented a naturalism of his own, as if he lived
in some world where these forms were natural. Whence springs the
elephantine impregnation that distinguishes Sigismondo's emblems?
The top and bottom of the 'I' in the $ monogram are fluked in the same
manner as the root of the rose sheath. A connection between Isotta and
the rose – that is, if 'I' stands for Isotta and 'S' for Sigismondo – suggests
itself.

The Tempio had shut that first day, so I examined the outside carefully: and when later I was clothed with the patchy night of Rimini, my
impression of the building dwindled (but with no relaxation of steadiness) to an image of one of the roses carved on the stylobate. This upstart
flower was in dynamic relation with the masonry whose mouldings it
overlapped. I was conscious in the fifteenth-century architecture and
sculpture, of a tension to reveal itself, to make manifest. The forms in
the stone put the structure at a tension similar to the most vibrant second of a singer's longest note. All is shown, put outward. I felt strongly
the compulsion to make life no less objective than the stone into which
all human passions were translated by this art.

During that night, lovely shapes grew upon the surface of my sleep
as upon the stone. So next morning when I walked into the Tempio,
I recognized the reliefs that are luminous in the dim light. I saw the tall

and tempestuous Gothic chapels on either side of the nave as a dense, highly coloured, outburst that needed, for its fixture outside, encasement by Alberti's majestic white stone. My concern on entering was not as to the design of the interior (which cannot fill anyone with particular satisfaction), but as to the force of emblematic sculpture that demanded so casket-like an encasement. The flatness of this interior Gothic, high upon the walls of which diminutive yet squat pilasters flower, heightens the luminosity of the reliefs on the chapel piers. The wall-spaces are emblazoned with Sigismondo's $ and with the rose. Elephant trunks, as plumes to a casque, break out above Isotta's tomb. $ is carved in balustrade: shield-bearers in the upper zone between the chapels and upon the entrance wall carry the mark upon their shields: everywhere the 'S' licks over and under the 'I' just as the rose-leaves embrace the shields upon the stylobate. There is elephantine foliage around the Gothic arches to the chapels: the predominant colours, blue and gold amid the stone hues, look personal and keen, interspersed in vault and spandrel above the porridge-coloured Greek marbles of the reliefs: everywhere there are coloured discs nailed to wall-fronts; centres of gravity like navels.

The first three chapels on either side are all that concern us:[6] for beyond the third chapels there is only eighteenth-century adaptation. Each pier of the chapels has three lots of three oblong reliefs. One lot is on the outside plane, another on the inside, and the remaining one between the other two below the arches. At whatever angle you stand to these piers, you will see at least one, and probably two, zones of relief; and they will be catching the light differently. On the piers of the first chapels, relief is high: on the piers of the other chapels, relief is low. The reliefs of the third chapels were those which principally concerned us in Chapter IV and will concern us again. But let us now see as well some other aspects of the Tempio, many of which are to be connected with the name of Matteo de' Pasti.

My first impression, however, was of the luminous figures on the further pier of the third chapel on the right, the reliefs of Diana, Mercury and Venus, though I had progressed but a few paces from the entrance.⁷ But, before proceeding up the church, let us look in at this first chapel on the right, the sculptures on whose piers are nearly in the round. The piers are scooped out into niches to contain these figures. At the bottom of each pier a box-like base, emblazoned with Sigismondo's emblems on its three sides (the fourth side of each pier and base joins the wall), rests square upon the nicely calculated black backs of twin basalt elephants. The weight that pours down their flanks and their close ears, causes their foreheads to be bulbous: but only their trunks that rest upon the plinth between their forelegs are notched and wrinkled to the strain.

I did not notice any bizarrerie in this architectural arrangement: for my impression was not of something exotic nor even profuse. On the contrary, reinforced no doubt by theatrical elements which might so easily have appeared Baroque and which emphatically did not, my impression was of tightness and compactness to a degree I had not known before. The stone, I felt again, shows everything upon its surface, steadfast like the open face of the rose.

Except that they denote this rare tension, the reliefs are not remarkable. Indeed, those of the prophets and sibyls on the piers of the opposite chapel are negligible.

In a sense, the design of the deeply cleft piers is 'bad' structurally; while the mingling of Gothic with classical mouldings upon the bases is clumsy and ill-adjusted. But does it matter at all, is it not part of the effect? See again the tension and steadfastness of this arrangement: see how the garlanded shield upon the square base curves like a flower to its fixity above the elephants' foreheads. The mouldings are no more monstrous than the florid Malatesta rose itself expressing a very personal myth we feel. See how tight is the fixture of the Virtues guarding their cavernous niches with which they are carved in a single piece. The *singleness* of the exuberance, the alliance of surface and depth, are the means by which the tension to make manifest appears so solid.⁸

There are two very low-relief, life-size, angels carved on each flanking wall inside the chapel. They support canopies held at their apex high up on the wall by angels of fuller relief. The low-relief figures are among the masterpieces of Agostino di Duccio. By distortion, by the use of drapery, from their attitudes, many aspects of sculpture in the round are achieved. Thus, no statue, no work cut free of a case of stone, nor even a higher relief, can emulate their quality of apparition.

The sense of fixture, obtained from the statuary on the piers and from the elephants below them, conjoined with the apparitions upon the walls, makes this first chapel an epitome of the Tempio's character.[9]

I leave for last mention the chapel's balustrade, since it summarizes all that has been said. Its qualities are of thickness, thick, replete, cornucopia, thick shields, thick round pieces, solid wheels of stone, broad and loud and smooth on their rims; and of apparition, the apparition of the peacock's spread tail, of finery notched and crusted, in fact of all associations with the shell form, loved by the Renaissance, a form here shown on its side encased by a half rim; one feels that the swags alone bumping up between the round pieces, curb and fix their propensities to roll. The stout hand-rail of the balustrade and the course below press the round pieces between them with such violence that, since their roundness is not squeezed into an ellipse, we feel the more their solid strength whose thickness we can see. No doubt this is the work of Pasti. For Agostino invented a compression of such forms that made of them ovoid elongations. As do the shields, the round shapes, heaviest of coins, possess on their faces the low sculpture of emblems. And we pass within the chapel to see their other sides, as if they were upright struck coins, so rich and so heavy that, rather than turn them, we must walk round. Here again we see carved the upstart rose, poised upon the wheel like a winged monster that hovers taut and undarkened on the face of the early sun. Here on the next coin-like shape, an ancient Malatesta emblem, the three heads.

Discs, rim within rim, characterize the jambs of the square-framed doorway next to the first chapel, and of the corresponding doorway opposite. In the moulding of the discs, in their adjustment to the rectangularity of the whole design, in the reliefs on the panels between the discs, the latter door is preferable. But it lacks the sculpture above the pediment of its fellow and also the coloured marbles[10] between the jambs and the rectangular frame: and it is the other doorway, the entrance to the Cella delle Reliquie, that is the lovelier of the two.

The modern purist may condemn this doorway for the rather clumsy admixture in its design, of square, oblongs and circles, among which the triangle of the pediment and the forms contingent on the pediment's boundaries, are uncomfortably placed. But, of course, judging from a photograph he cannot take into account the colours of the marbles or the particular *brio* of the carving which this cumbersome geometry serves to enhance.[11] Current vulgarity, current lack of emotional coordination, have driven the purist to relish above all else the indisputable shapes, the indisputable scaffolding, around which all plastic conception has been built. Nowadays, the scaffolds themselves are the only aesthetically possible new buildings: their extreme no-nonsense geometry provides some reassurance amid emotional chaos. The purist, however, ignorant of carving values, is not free of a pronounced monotony in his perceptions. Sensitive to draughtsmanship, insensitive to the liveliness of stone, he cannot perceive the emotional content of these disc-like forms with their alternating convex and concave centres, a stone-blossom and an incrustation between which the outward and inward curving shield in the pediment holds the balance: the same shield holds the balance also between the juxtaposed square and circular forms that our purist so thoroughly dislikes.

When Pasti designed the doorway under the deep influence of his patron's *virtù* and with the whole unconscious surge of humanistic aim behind his art, knowingly or unknowingly he had for his particular inspiration Sigismondo's shield with the Malatesta chequers quartered with the $. Sigismondo's valour in the field, his pride in war, the very clanking of the battlefield, shield on shield, boss against boss causing indentation, the torn canopies on the great horses' backs held by bossy buttons of gold, the approximation of real and heraldic, of naturalism and of an invented naturalism to express it – all these aims and impressions associated with the shield as an emblem and as an artistic motif are amplified and enhanced by Pasti's door. The model for such amplification was Sigismondo. Another sign of Sigismondo was the elephant;

the elephant that amplifies his neighbourhood, trumpeting up the sky, trampling the earth, banging wide through thickets that gather rank behind him upon the murmurous grass.

The pediment has many deep rifts: upon them ride Agostino's miraculous dolphins, lashing up their tails on to the backs of the broad putti astride. They glisten in white marble (the doorway itself is of the porridge-coloured Greek), kept to a triangle by the great rectangle of tooth ornamentation which expresses an enlargement[12] of the chequered armorial upon the shield. The curving, inclined elegance of this shield itself, its square and circular attributes, are enlarged by the close interplay, both tall and wide, of the squares and circles already remarked, and by their concave and convex mouldings. The mouldings that enclose the niches with their prophets are again an abstraction of the shield shape, being upright oblongs with their shorter lengths curving in and out respectively. The medallion that figures on the centre of the beam frames an elephantine *Fortezza* holding her two bits of broken column, two tusks found in the undergrowth.

Elsewhere the chequers and the rose. The trough-like mouldings around the discs with emblems on the jambs are an extension of the manner in which the $ has often been carved in the Tempio, that is, with a trough in the 'I' and similar segments in the 'S' which serpentine where the letter curves under or over its fellow. This licking 'S' has relation also to the leaves that bind the shields and other emblems on the stylobate: the flukes with which the 'I' is generally terminated top and bottom – and sometimes the 'S' as well – are related to the similar treatment of the rose's sheath and of the dolphins' tails. The steady face of the rose, in turn, has many extensions: the stout garlands around the coloured marble discs that lie between the jambs of the door and the tooth frame; the garlands about the discs in the spandrels of the façade, and many other garlands.

It is worth remarking the exact position of the discs with trough-like mouldings on the jambs of this door: the manner in which they replace the inner mouldings of the jambs and the manner in which they meet the transverse moulding (as in a latchkey); also the intervals that the disc mouldings make with the ledge over the beam. In original and spontaneous niceties such as these there resides the flower-like and steadfast effect of Quattro Cento carving.

The traveller should by now have grasped the main trends of the Tempio's imagery. And so when he moves along the right to the second chapel, the one with Isotta's tomb, he should receive the full impact from the blue and gold baldacchino and from the elephants' heads upon the casque. He should welcome the chapel's balustrade with its columns in the style of such Venetian bridges as the Ponte della Paglia. In their symmetry and lighter hue, the small, stout pillars of transient porridge-colour may suggest to him the elephant's trunk. For these columns, and those of the corresponding balustrade to the chapel on the other side, are the only free-standing columns of the Tempio, inside or out; and the shape between column and rail may easily suggest the massy convergence by which the elephant's forehead lengthens into a proboscis. Moreover the seething grey surface of the rail above, in its deliberate broadness and generous angles receiving the light, suggests some smooth brain or switchboard that directs a dynamic force.

Upon the live rail putti are rooted. In each case putto and rail are the same block. The putti are the only non-relief figures in the Tempio[13] with the exception of the enthroned San Sigismondo upon the altar of the first chapel, the archangel Michael upon the altar of the second chapel, and the shield-bearers at the base of the upper pilasters between the chapels. All these statues are only seen from the front. In fact they are far more frontal in conception than the reliefs. But the putti with their shields, at one with the rail, are designed for many angles of approach. When you pass inside the chapel you do not review a row of uniform behinds. For each putto has shot up differently from the smooth tumultuous stone; each presents his shield at a different angle. Wherever you go there will be some with their backs to you, seemingly convulsed; yet they will be turning their heads to see if you have seen, while they control or lean on their thick shields, although these are almost as big as themselves. The putti have a swollen vigour, an elephantine[14] lustiness. They are heavy, alert; they grew where their shields grew. A ribald precocity results from their oneness with the rail. They are never separated from their mother whom they ride and trample, each upon his block.

The shields have their emblems. One putto leans with all his weight on an outward tilted shield that is reversed, with the rose upon it upside down. At least one other mourns: and that should be their role. However gay in themselves, they are professional mourners. For here on the wall of the chapel depends Isotta's tomb weighted and supported by Sigismondo's elephants. Above, two trunks wave the pedestrian motto 'Tempus loquendi, tempus tacendi'. The catafalque, furrowed like a monster's hide, discloses a sarcophagus on which three times is carved the magic date 1450. Underneath the slab a yet more magic date is recorded, the year 1446 in which Sigismondo first possessed Isotta.[15] Time is jumbled about in the Tempio. Isotta's tomb was built when she was young and alive: was built in no mood of premonition, but to feign a triumph over death by lifting the sarcophagus on to the backs of sage and glorious monsters; and by delivering the funeral procession to the antics of eternal putti that stamp about their mother's body; and by fixing everywhere the steady rose. So in the reliefs upon the entrance piers, putti pack the face of the stone, handling such closely ordered instruments as harp and organ.

We have seen enough for a first visit: let us leave before the mental picture becomes blurred. That picture, though, requires for its greater precision a few touches that will convey the circumstances of Sigismondo's life. While enduring these few pages we shall lean on the brecciated rail of the balustrade to the next chapel, since we may the more easily reflect there upon Sigismondo.

On the piers of this chapel are the planet reliefs[16] to whose significance the subsequent chapter is devoted. We lean on a perforated balustrade[17] of Verona marble, a Quattro Cento masterpiece. Below us are the generous rubbed forms that the uncertain substance of this marble makes essential,[18] and to which, in any case, its glowing hues incite. The twin elephant heads serve as the epitome of that massy growth we have attributed to the Malatesta rose and other emblems. Around the trunks curls a blunt scroll with the motto 'Tempus loquendi, tempus tacendi', a time for the elephant's shrill assertion, a time for the elephant's weighted secrecy. His genius for instant revelation inspires all Sigismondo's emblems. We take his motto as our text.

Sigismondo was an aristocrat and a condottiere or soldier of fortune by profession, as had been so many previous Malatesta. A dominant aspect of his life is clearly mirrored by the disadvantage under which one so proud of his family started, and by the greed and craftiness of his original enemies. Sigismondo was illegitimate. His father, Pandolfo Malatesta, died when he was ten. The two next years Sigismondo spent at the Rimini court of his uncle, Carlo Malatesta. Both the father and the uncle were famous condottieri and men of culture. Carlo died. The Papacy was closing in on those lands that the Malatesta had held as papal vicariates for two centuries. All through the fifteenth-century the Popes were designing to recover the direct tenure of this and other fiefs in Umbria, in the Marches and in Romagna. At the beginning of the sixteenth century Cesare Borgia brought the policy to a successful conclusion, and the families of Montefeltro, Malatesta, Manfredi, Ordelaffi and Baglioni, to name but a few, were sooner or later deprived.

Without parents, with traitorous advisers, Sigismondo was fighting to hold Rimini at the age of thirteen. His brother Galeotto who ruled at Rimini on the death of their uncle was a religious maniac: so on his own initiative Sigismondo saved the capital of the Malatesta dominion already divided between several branches of the family. Galeotto died. Rimini became not only Sigismondo's city but his lair. He designed and built the first castle intended to withstand artillery; and there he made his court which, though small, was one of the most cultured in Italy. Full of pride and invention in war, he set Valturio to write his famous *De re militari*.

Sigismondo won his way, soon to be the boldest as well as the most incalculable soldier of his time. No task, no trouble, no privation was too great for him when in the mood. But his means were never equal to the scale he required. The Tempio is the solid manifestation of an intense and lifelong vaunt. He was over-sized, he was the elephant caught in the small jungles of Italian policy.

Violent his life but not extravagant. His libertinage was sometimes terrible because undisguised. He did not favour insurance policies taken out with God or man. He did not justify his actions; since he thought he could transfuse anything into his blue day. Respected in Italy for his bravery and skill in war, his noble birth and his humanism, Sigismondo championed the interests of Pope Eugenius: the Florentine state owed him everything, the Venetians employed him time and time again. But he made good enemies. Spider-men knew at once their natural foe. Alfonso, king of Naples, frustrated in his attempt, one that had had prospect of success, to conquer Italy, frustrated by the irresponsibility, as he thought, and by the military genius of Sigismondo, became vindictive. Sigismondo got him on the quick, also Pope Pius II for whom the humbling of Sigismondo became an emotional need. In these vendettas causing his downfall, Sigismondo stimulated resentments out of proportion to their apparent causes. Not his behaviour alone, but his personality, amounted to a most penetrating reproach against anyone settling into a house: and, after the peace of Lodi, all Italy was settling in. Aragon had achieved Naples; Sforza Milan; Cosimo was firm in Florence; Venice had moderated her territorial ambition; Eugenius IV and Innocent V had made Rome habitable for Popes.

Sigismondo's craftiness was too closely charged yet abrupt for his permanent success over more naïvely opportunist and, indeed, more cautious, contemporaries. Thus he desired for himself the sagacity of the elephant, choosing a large animal since he could not exercise moderation in a manner less astonishing than the one of elephants. In truth, each frustration added to his fury and to the scale of his designs. But he knew that patience and tact were virtues required for his triumph. Hence the wry and cumbersome motto 'Tempus tacendi, tempus loquendi'. At first, in the matter of Isotta, it was *tempus tacendi*, possibly because of the powerful and useful connections of his Sforza wife. A few years later it was the full *tempus loquendi*, entailing the reinvestment of the whole of San Francesco, not ostensibly or primarily, it should be said, for the sake of Isotta, but according to the twin Greek inscriptions[19] on the encasement's flanks, to celebrate his triumphs in war. This phase was closed finally by Pio's denunciation,[20] excommunication and crusade of 1461.

No amount of historical research provides us with 'the truth about Isotta', the nature of her spell over Sigismondo. We know little more than that he finally married her and that she was regent in Rimini when Venice sent him to Greece against the Turks on his last campaign; and that she was his heir. We gain no picture of Isotta from the Court eulogies: Renaissance poetry could tell nothing of the quality of Sigismondo's love. Yet we may know it even better than if we were living with both of them, since the dominant or underlying aspect of that love was projected, more or less unconsciously as I believe, in some of the Tempio masterpieces which it inspired. No direct approach elicits their full content. We shall feel the pressure of the emotion they exhibit only when we shall have found in what circumstance the fantasies of stone and water, of influence from the stars, and of the pervasive female seductiveness could be identified.

And so we now leave the Tempio: but we must gather again in front of these representations of the planets to collect an entirely different concourse of words, which, joined to those already in our possession, will form a new and final likeness of these reliefs, the most magnetic part of Agostino's work.

Barrel-Organ and Street

From *To-night the Ballet* (1934)

Ballet dancing is the only art today that is completely professional. You may have a genius for movement, but unless your frame is schooled unremittingly, it cannot be expressive in the highest sense. The other arts were once as closely professionalized. It follows – and hence a large part of its contemporary appeal – that ballet is the sole art that flourishes upon the basis of a traditional style.

Gesture and bodily movement are more subtle than language. Occasionally we see someone walking across the room 'meaningfully' just as we have read of a character in a novel. But that is probably because the person in question also has just been reading a novel.

I shall make use of diverse means to convey, not so much my impression of ballet as the necessity of ballet for me, the supreme pleasure I gain from watching it. Were it possible to describe any ballet to my satisfaction, there would be little necessity to go to it. I want but to excite the reader's interest, his propensities of appreciation, so that he may be led to learn a pleasure that he cannot obtain elsewhere.

Historically speaking, gesture is no doubt a far older means of communication than speech. The human body is more interesting than the human voice, at any rate in the theatre. You cannot make a spectacle with disembodied voices. Pantomime is the essence of the theatre, the essence of a spectacle. At the circus, animals as well perform in dumb-show. Their cries and howls and the trainer's starched words of command are but the accepted music to this pantomime. In a sense, in the theatrical sense, all plays are spectacles or pantomimes to which words are the music – that is, so far as they are plays, something played in a theatre, spectacles, so far as they are drama, and not merely the dramatized vehicle of poetry, doctrines, and anything that might be read in a book. Ballet is the only pure form of the theatre today with any popularity.

Music, we observe, or whatever corresponds to it, is essential to pantomime. Otherwise pantomime would be dumb charade. Music gives a tempo, a rhythm, that raises the dumb charade to the level of a spectacle. The music does not merely accompany the charade, but, in ballet at least, gives it a further *raison d'être*, whereas the words of a play afford the entire *raison d'être* to the gestures of the actors. Ballet is living visual music, music articulate and definite as speech. Think what a wonderful thing that is to the less cantankerous lovers of music!

We know the healing power of music, healing to ourselves, I suppose, but healing, so it appears, to things, to inanimate objects. The man who is enjoying his wireless concert sees his room, however dreary, no longer as a dead or dying mist of hard things, but as something definite if unpleasant, no longer crouching but upright, a *mise-en-scène* in which the music takes place. Think how the streets spring to life when the bolder kind of barrel-organ grinds its tune! At once the streets become a *mise-en-scène*, the movement of passers-by and of traffic becomes a ballet of a sort. So many things that lay in pieces in the mind and which were projected into the external world as piecemeal, rhythmless, living death, are gathered together, organized and drilled by the music: and so we see the street differently. We survey the intervals between pedestrians: the fact of their succession alone has taken on an almost heroic meaning. We discover the rhythm of their walk. Life again proceeds, outward as a spectacle: past and future have gathered and organized themselves in the physical movements that are the present. We see things as new, just as the external world seems to appear as if for the first time on an early spring day. Music that breaks in upon the scenes of movement gives rebirth not only of feeling but of perception.

Was not the old silent film and its accompanying music a kind of ballet? The analogy is, if anything, closer in the few modern silent films, in Flaherty's *Tabu* for instance. The Chief of all the isles has appeared over the horizon in a chartered European ship. The entire population of an island in the southern seas go out to meet him in their canoes.

They run together on to the beach as the news reaches them among the palms and the waterfalls. The music is Smetana's *Moldau*, in which the long breasting tune helps those swift native boats to navigate the gentle swell. In itself this music epitomizes the endless runnels and eddies of northern and central Europe, the pregnant irresistible flow from soft and miraculous snows that clarify themselves into the waters of spring: yet upon the screen we watch southern natives gathered from the stones and palms and tired waterfalls, crowd the seas of the echoing lagoon. The action does not interpret the music, nor the music the action. They would appear to belong to different atmospheres. Yet they cannot be held apart, since the picture they compose is unforgettable. This music that contains the force of brimming inevitable floods and the deep upheaval of the icy spring, here bestows a character of freedom and of unison upon the concourse of canoes that ride a gentle southern sea. The dark navigators are ennobled: they take on an almost Viking glamour from the heroic and pulsating starkness of unseen northern wastes to which, in turn, they give their warmth. Their smallest movements are heroic as they go full of eagerness, full of freedom, to perform their ritual. And, in this mass movement of men, illuminated for us by the clear southern day, we see the redemption of those unattended northern streams.

Such power to bestow, as it were, an apotheosis upon music by thus transposing its content or by some other means of dramatization, is most characteristic of the ballet; whereas many other forms of dancing, as we shall see, prefer to 'follow out' the music with movements almost equally continuous. Such a dancer as Isadora Duncan was really a most unconventional kind of conductor. In less inspired moments she followed the music as a bear might pursue a mouse. This 'interpretative' dancing does not make the music itself unforgettable. On the other hand, there are many who might think that they would not care to have their music transmuted by ballet. Yet everyone tends to attach associations of place and time and incident to the music he hears. The associating of ballet with music is but a superlative imprint upon it of this kind. All the same, music of the most ambitious emotional or intellectual flights is very rarely employed for ballet. Massine, however, with great boldness has devised a ballet to the music of Brahms' Fourth Symphony. In this case little transmutation is attempted nor is the music 'interpreted' in that literal yet hierarchic manner so loved of the German dancers. From the point of view of the Brahms lover, Massine's interference is unobjectionable. He has used the music better than we have used it in our own lives. In general, one can say that the treatment of music in ballet is nearly always tactful and frequently inspired.

Now the ideal spectacle, one that can be indefinitely repeated, is always self-contained but yet composed of diverse and even divergent ingredients. Within these divergences the imagination of the spectator finds perpetual scope; and it is the endless processes of the imagination of which we never tire. Thus the movement of those paddlers in the film *Tabu* are perennially stimulating. It would be otherwise, however, were there not brought together in this one episode the vast tide of the rainbow northern snows which the music expresses and the midday embarkation upon the southern sea which the music serves. This re-inforcement of an image by elements snatched from entirely different conditions, coincidents that form a definite whole, and the fact of their coincidence, stimulate the imagination enormously, provide an entire shelter for the spirit each time the experience is repeated. And, indeed, all spectacles should offer in this way something definite to the imagination with which it can play endlessly, some definite figure, some profound nucleus, a consolidation of different traits as we find them in the figures of Punch or Harlequin or in the mechanical naturalism of marionettes.

The connection between music and action, then, should be one of harmony rather than of identity. We do not ask of the barrel-organ that it should directly interpret our streets. It is the Neapolitan song or *Cavalleria rusticana* hammered out over the dim November squares that makes surrounding things so poignant at that moment, in a certain primary essence so like a ballet. This most definite consolidation of different climates provokes a *mise-en-scène* from the neighbourhood for our memories and for our movements. The most naïve kind of music

181

often serves ballet best, though, at the same time, some element of wit must be induced from this naïvety. There is, as Nietzsche said, a music in which the spirit dances as opposed to the music in which the spirit swims. The latter is the transcendental music, the former is an outward thing suitable to the streets and to the theatre. Nearly all European music, other than the intensely German, belongs to this former category in some degree. Occasionally one of the pleasures of a really good ballet is the use therein of music which one would have thought to be confined inevitably to the concert hall.

What happens when Mendelssohn's *Fingal's Cave* is used to articulate life upon the Thames estuary and the surrounding morass? In a recent film we were taken on board an old man's fishing smack in the Thames estuary. *Fingal's Cave* was the music. The old man in great clumsy boots, his coarse lunch with the dull English sky like a tent of goatskin over him and over those glum, wide waters; the giant merchant ships appearing and disappearing in the gloom; the return to Billingsgate, the sale of the old man's catch of shrimps – this was raised almost to the pitch of ballet by the music of *Fingal's Cave*. We found a rhythm, a pulse in those dull, prosaic waters; we saw the greater and statelier ships pass by as the fisherman cast his nets and squelched his boots; we saw a fresh rhythm in this slow, heavy life because by means of the music there was mingled with it, there came to exist the sensation of an inner dizzy life in those waters beneath a mist that hung over dawn or shrouded the peaceful afternoon: and ever the tide was running like a trumpet beneath the sea or like the eager rush of contrapuntal eddies.

I should like to pursue this general theme of music in relation to action so constantly experienced in modern life. I must content myself with observing that music, or, at any rate, enhanced concerted noise of every description, is today the concomitant of most people's waking hours. That is one reason why the ballet possesses a particular relevance to ourselves, the art in which sound and movement are so perfectly adjusted that their relationships provide perennial images to the mind.

Music with dance is distinguished from music with mere general action as described above, by the element of synchronization. The relation between music and movement in dancing is a heightened one. It is as if when the barrel-organ struck up in the street below, not only did the ordinary movements of the passers-by become suddenly a vivid thing, but they too being conscious of it, heightened and stressed their movements and actions into a dance, an implicit response to the beats of the music. This response is not always describable as a synchronization. Indeed, some of the loveliest moments in ballets, from the musical point of view alone, are when the dancers hold a pose. But the point I want to make now is that apart from other relations between music and movement, there is a general pleasure in their synchronization, so characteristic of the dance: and it is obvious why this pleasure should be. For synchronized movement may give an enormous power and precision to the music: it can enforce the music, enforce its sway, make it a bodily thing. We all know the impotent conductor, the bogus Isadora, the lover of jazz who cannot keep even his face still when a favourite tune is played. He is bearable, however, if we feel that he does not seek so much to interpret the music with the movements he makes in time, as to enforce it *à la Beecham*.

Any action is pointed by the synchronization of a precise sound. Just think of the noises employed at a music-hall to stress the *tours de force* of acrobats. It is as if instead of thumping the earth they struck a real musical sound by the brilliancy of their leaps: every time they hit the bell. An almost omnipotent neatness of movement is thus expressed; and since we wish that all our aims were executed with this intense organization, this slick clock-work precision, we derive pleasure from the synchronization of any noise that seems to denote the power of human movement. Also, the lighter yet quicker this synchronized movement, the more exciting it is as a rule. And we may here note in passing that outside of ballet there is no form of the dance capable of this true allegro.

No form of the dance; but what about Mickey Mouse? Apart from Uday Shankar, the Indian dancer, Mickey Mouse and *Silly Symphonies* were the only things that helped to fill the gap for the London ballet lover between the death of Diaghilev and the arrival of De Basil's Les

Ballets Russes de Monte Carlo. This sounds rather rude to those organizations in London that still provided us with ballet. But so far as their efforts were tentative and imitative, it was inevitable that they should fill us with nostalgia for the rarefied air which Diaghilev had taught us to expect. Unpretentious Mickey Mouse does not fill one with any nostalgia. But in Walt Disney's miniature theatre of grotesques we recognize an art at least related to the glories and sublimities of ballet. We recognize immediately the quality of expressive yet infinitely precise movements which make the synchronized sounds so lovable. There is a patness in everything that occurs, the vital wit that belongs to situations expressed in terms of agility or graceful movement: and closely connected is the economy of such movement as a means of expression. In *Flowers and Trees* the trees use their branches as arms just as in a ballet the dancers would use their arms as branches. There is a possible beauty in the economy of these transpositions, there is beauty and wit in the lilies that raise their tapered leaves to stifle their yawns. In the cartoon as in the ballet the same evidence of intense observation exists and the same exhaustiveness. Every possible facet of a situation is exhausted and exploited from the angle of interrelated movements. Everything is shown as a virtuoso exploit. In this way we gain a sense of completeness, as if all inner forces thus reached an outer consummation. Closely allied in the matter of movement is the element common to both of variation on a theme. The basic, but often disguised, theme in a ballet is, if not the classical technique, at any rate the ballet deportment, the ballet style. In the Mickey Mouse cartoon the variation is always of the title figure himself as in a Charlie Chaplin film. Disney generally provides something to correspond with the *corps de ballet* and an ensemble near the end, and thus the struggles of the principals are relieved by some charming co-operation or unison on the part of figures that come to aid or to accompany the hero. This development of the action is also characteristic of a ballet. Towards the end, the principal movements that have inspired a ballet are generally gathered together in a finale.

But such resemblances are more superficial. The deeper resemblance lies in the compactness of movements and of the meanings they express. This economy or compactness, this deftness or certainty, breeds style, the quality by which profundities are made effortless. So long as in the ordinary course of events Mickey Mouse is debonair, he cannot fail to express the world.

It is obvious that later on I shall have to devote a good deal of space to defining ballet and distinguishing it from other forms of the dance. For all other forms known to me fail to communicate this sense of completeness, of consummation, of all inner ferment externalized in the form of display. In the intensity of this quality my profoundest satisfaction lies, and it is the same quality that characterizes any true theatrical idea.

The process of living is the attainment of expression, the conversion of inner ferment into definite action and thought. Expression always needs a framework: otherwise it tends to evaporate. The technique and conventions of ballet dancing serve as a framework by which experience may be translated into terms of movement, into a visual kind of music. Just in what way ballet dancing is so perfect a framework is a question I shall tackle in time. Let me only say now that in this form of dancing nothing is withdrawn, drawn inwards or hidden: everything is, artificially if you like, put outwards: and, in the interests of this effect, all movement is raised on to a level of airiness, grace and ease. For, to give the greatest pleasure, the effect of turning feeling outward as movement must possess the appearance of great facility, exuberance and ease. Artificiality is never far absent from ballet nor indeed from any profound manifestation of the theatrical idea. Nothing natural or supernatural is so complete and self-contained. But does not Mickey Mouse express a good deal more with his tricks than do the protagonists of the realistic and expressionistic film, or many leading London actors who walk on to the stage and behave like themselves?

To my mind a Punch and Judy show is a far better entertainment than Noël Coward's *Cavalcade*. Mickey Mouse, like Charlie Chaplin, like the Harlequin, like the ballet dancer, like marionettes, like the pre-Wagnerian opera singers, like the Clown, is a mask, a figure, an emblem.

Nothing escapes. The propensities of such a figure have been organized on an artificial level where they may be completely known. Art needs these limitations, because feeling is better expressed in such terms. I stress and defend the artificiality of the ballet just because it is so often attacked. In reality, the modern ballet is a very wide conception giving rise to few archaic forms. Movement may be entirely 'free', with small suggestion of artificiality. Yet it remains ballet dancing just because somewhere in the background, if only in the training of the dancers, the conventional ballet technique is immanent. Where it is no longer immanent, dancing ceases to be ballet dancing. Only in this negative form can we define ballet today. But in order to gain from ballet the full pleasure, it is essential to understand the meaning of that classical technique in which both the dancers' bodies and their dispositions are continuously trained. Moreover, classical ballets are always performed among the modern ballets. The season would not be endurable without some classical ballet – I mean if one goes almost every night.

Let us return to Mickey Mouse for another analogy to ballet. The devastating fire in *Flowers and Trees* is put out by the birds. In airplane formation they fly perpendicularly up to the clouds, piercing them with their beaks. In response, in answer to this movement, the heavy rain-drops fall from the rent clouds. Again, in *Bears and Bees*, half the fun is in the dense formation of the bees as they launch their attack on the bear who has stolen their honey, and in the patterns they make throughout the pursuit. Such groupings and interarrangement of shapes, whether in the positions of a dancer's limbs or in the pictures made by the *corps de ballet*, are perhaps the most obvious feature of this entertainment. Perhaps the most obvious stimulus of a ballet is to the plastic sense. The word 'picture' with its association of the *tableau vivant* is unfortu-nate in this connection. For in a good ballet there is nothing gratuitous about the grouping: it is not a display that means little. We watch not only visual or plastic music but a visual poem. Indeed, it is preferably a poet who provides the story of a ballet. This idea is communicated to the composer of the dancing, the choreographer, and to the com-poser of the music. The other chief collaborator is the designer of the costumes and of the scenery. The painter's scope is enormous. In the days of the Diaghilev Russian ballet it used to be a special pleasure to watch in movement the 'palette', as the art critics say, of some great modern painter like Picasso or Matisse. Every moment the dancers made fresh groups, fresh pictures that revealed further the painter's thought. It is difficult to devour with the eyes a static or lifeless thing with so gross an appetite.

What a feast Diaghilev used to provide with his dancers, his painters, his poets and composers; and yet one could never have enough, so great was the glamour. We saw his older ballets at the same time, and also some classical ballet. Petipa's and Ivanov's *Swan Lake* to the music of Tchaikovsky, Benois-Stravinsky-Fokine's *Pétrouchka* and Marie Laurencin-Poulenc-Nijinska's *Les Biches* comprised the first-night programme of one season, I remember. It was a typical programme.

Think of the scope of ballet in which a poetic idea, music, painting and dancing can simultaneously reinforce one another. Diaghilev showed the modern world the fullness of this scope.

And the ballet tonight, what are Les Ballets Russes de Monte Carlo doing tonight? They are the legitimate inheritors of the old ballet and perform many of Diaghilev's ballets as well as their own creations. Massine and Woizikovsky are still there. What is your choice of images to carry away from the performance tonight? Unless you go, you cannot experience dreams in the flesh, an inner world on an illuminated stage, with an orchestra before it, an inner world externalized with all the insistence and the verve of which the outer world is capable. What is your choice of images? Perhaps it is *Jeux d'enfants* tonight. Then the stage takes a brand new stamp. It is no mere suggestion this newness, this décor by Miró. You will see emblazoned that newness of paint that children try to lick off, the whiteness and the scarlet with the curving parabola of black. But this new or toy world of debonair colour and pure diving shapes convenient to the hand that would touch them, would curb their motion – a solid wheel of scarlet, for instance, or a drum stick that will dip and rise – symbolizes an ideal adult culture. There is today bright certainty in many things. There is the produce of

Woolworth's, millions of new cheap things that are not tawdry; bright nails, bright tacks, well designed enamelled hooks, simple gleaming objects by the thousand within the reach of each stretching hand, balls of every texture, new as paint. They are not baubles or tawdry knick-knacks. Since they are serviceable the gaiety of these things lies with their simplicity and their newness.

Behold the two spirits who invoke objects beloved of the hand. The spirits are themselves closely sheathed in the abstract brightness of black and white; they are, as it were, enamelled. What precision in their movements, what precision in the controlled masculinity of Bizet's music, his *petite suite d'orchestre*.

Ballet – and later we shall see the reason – has a special predilection for toys that come to life. These new and debonair objects, then, are toys. Enter the Top, Baronova or Toumanova, both of them very young dancers of extraordinary verve. Baronova does this part best. She spins. Enter the child, Tatiana Riabouchinska. People often talk of dancers moving like deer or does. Riabouchinska really possesses this extremely youthful kind of movement. No dancer is lighter than she, few dancers can move at such an extraordinary pace. Later on, we witness the fire of Lichine and the wonderful tempo that Woizikovsky carries about with him. Look out for his slow *jetés*. In the *pas de deux* and the *pas de trois*, the rocking and the swaying of nursery love indicate the tenderness of love in general as something uniformly bright. In the *pas de trois* Bizet's music, here marked *petit mari*, *petite femme*, directly reinforces the conception of a simple and therefore sustained tenderness that nowhere falters nor shows excess.

We watch this philosophy, these images, these aspirations: we see them as graceful movement. There is nothing transcendental about ballet. The music displaces air, for it has become the dancers' bodies. The painter's imagination has bred not images, but human beings as images.

Impressions of Ballet

From To-night the Ballet (1934)

In a glitter, as if vociferous, of music, amid the very knees of a climax, the male dancer revolves with *tours en l'air*, lands after a spin ten times as tense as the stiffening of the body in fear or ecstasy, lands in a flashing arrested pose, still as a statue – our applause breaks in as the *corps de ballet* carry on – one seemingly supreme moment follows another; there is scarcely time to watch as each dancer exhausts her resources on her separate part or in unison; tour de force follows tour de force, applause breaks out in spouts; for it is the last night of a successful season. The Russian ballet leaves us and the audience is largely composed of devotees who have come time and time again. One can watch ballet night after night with increasing pleasure. The interaction of all these different arts, treasures that the dancers transmute into compact human movement, sustains delight.

Ballet has a multitude of moods and phases. But this last performance shows what is the predominant, the essential, ballet deportment. The male dancers are heroic: they carry glory, the danseuses glamour. The audience, you will find, believe in these poses and applaud them. You cannot overlook altogether the excitement of ballet if you manage to get in on a last night.

Still, it may mean no more to you than a rather glamorous spectacle or display, something of which one could easily see too much. The adagio of a classical ballet may almost have bored you. The admittedly ethereal ballerina who twists round on one toe and then extends the other leg at right angles in an arabesque, the perpetual yet silent acclaim expressed by her administering partner as he holds her up, turns her round, lets her go – these conventionalized movements and gestures that interrupt the miming of some romantic story, may seem at first to be anything but profound. You may feel that it would be a torture to see these things night after night. And, indeed, a classical ballet night after night is a strain to watch for most people unless they have first learned to love ballet in its more modern aspects. In that case the classical technique on which all ballet is based, provides an entirely different content to the imagination. We then find that one classical ballet on the usual programme of three ballets an evening, gives a heightened meaning to the other ballets and is itself heightened by them.

I shall discuss the classical ballet later in Chapter IV. But let it be understood here and now that the commonest idea of ballet dancing, of the sleek black-haired Pavlova poised with fluttering arms, a sinking, dying, swooning swan, a wraith, an ethereal Victorian apparition, is derived from an effect that seems gratuitous, devoid of any contact with reality more comprehensive than the one of the fairy story, only when one is ignorant of ballet's essence. Classical ballet is great enough to stand by itself: and the fact that today, unlike traditional forms in the other visual arts, it still has relevance, an enhanced relevance even, provides one of my main contentions. Yet I doubt whether this contemporary relevance would have been apparent, would have survived so vast an accumulation of nineteenth-century trapping, had we not been introduced to it as part of the vital Russian ballet, in company, that is, with so many ballets that are divergences from the classical technique, interpreted and even inspired by contemporary painters and musicians, though executed by classically trained dancers. In London as in Paris it was the twenty years of the Diaghilev seasons that created the vast and devoted ballet public.

How did one become a devotee, how did one grasp the point of ballet? Certainly not after one visit. No one, however experienced, can 'take in' a ballet the first time, since there is too much to take in: certainly no one, or scarcely any one, is going to realize the point of ballet as a whole from one evening's entertainment, however enjoyable.

I think one's devotion is largely founded upon accident. You go one night and it happens that the very next night you are asked to go again: and you happen to see one of the ballets repeated after only twenty-four

190

hours. It is possible that on this second occasion, while your memory of the first occasion is still fresh, some group, some progression of steps, some gesture even, will imprint itself so deeply on the mind, so gently and so comfortably encased in a musical phrase, that it will not merely haunt you like a tune pleasant or objectionable, but will seem an emblem, a talisman that you carry with you on the tops of buses or down into the tubes – in fact, a vivid insight that feeds perpetually upon a definite picture in the mind. And from this one insight, this one picture of vitality in the externalized form of stage movement by which the gigantic world is enclosed as a *mise-en-scène*, there may grow a lust for the ballet as an art revealing all forms of life under vivid and glamorous conventions.

It is something like falling in love. A picture, an essence, has become wedged in the mind and one never knew it. All devotion no doubt has a similar genesis and, obviously, I cannot at once indicate why at the present time one should be so liable to fall in love with ballet. But at least this can be said now: that fine choreography, fine ballet dancing, is strong in abstract or generalized qualities yet provides for emotions the most poignant emblems on a romantic plane. The romantic ballet *is* the classical ballet, as we shall see. This state of affairs is not without a particular relevance to ourselves since we tend to demand an increased precision even from the lyric mood.

The genesis of my own full devotion to ballet was due to a perception of this romantic-classical quality and occurred in the following way. By pure chance I happened to see the Diaghilev ballet on two successive nights and on each of these nights they did *Carnaval*. Still, I doubt whether I should have noticed what I did had I not already known the music. Again, *Carnaval* is an exceedingly good ballet and a simple one. Long may it survive! I think that perhaps of all ballets it offers the best chance to the potential devotee. Being neither a true classical ballet nor a very modern ballet, it serves as a link that strengthens Ballet. In any case, one must see really fine performances on a large stage – I was going to say, one must see the Russian ballet with the original Bakst setting. However, it will be best if I confine these remarks to my own experience.

Carnaval is a ballet in which some of the Commedia dell'Arte figures such as Harlequin, Columbine and Pantaloon pursue their amorous flights upon the stage.

Harlequin, Pierrot, how much these masks mean to us though we know nothing of their history! We watch the pierrots for hours at the seaside, hoping, hoping that they will give us the character that their costumes have suggested to the mind: occasionally they do. Pulcinella, Polichinelle, Punch – the Punch and Judy show is still to be seen in our streets and we must stop to watch although we cannot hear a word for the traffic and nothing much ever happens except Toby the dog and Punch dealing out whacks. We have bestowed such an omnipotence on these figures overwhelming or tragic in love, perennially yet romantically the same like so many dolls or fetishes for adult minds. These figures still possess the incorrigibility of their Italian temperaments. But there is never enough for them to do. Even at the old Pantomime Harlequinade, the triumphs of the lithe Harlequin are at the expense only of policemen and sausage merchants: there is little scope for Harlequin's obstreperous magic.

Carnival! Another magic word! For the sake of this word alone we will endure the seaside carnival of flowers; and so common is the nostalgia that it may happen that on those seaside occasions, sweltering or otherwise, something of the carnival spirit is captured. But on the whole we get painfully little beyond the word. We go willingly to the ball dressed and masked as Harlequins: we observe that the Venetian Carnival will never live again.

We are wrong. We can take some measure of these things in Fokine's ballet to the music of Schumann. The original Diaghilev setting was by Bakst. A period, of course, must be suggested, a date given. Harlequin, and at least one other mask in the ballet, Pantaloon, have been living for five hundred years. Since Schumann's music is itself called *Carnaval* and since the association of the Commedia dell'Arte figures with a carnival is by no means very ancient, and already denotes a romantic or nostalgic feeling for those figures, a date in the not distant past was chosen, the date of the music itself, the Viennese Biedermeier period of 1830 or so. This ballet inspired by Schumann's music is an evocation of Schumann just as *Sylphides* is an evocation of Chopin. Now Schumann's *Carnaval* was perhaps the first expression, the first formulation of that nostalgia which identifies the Commedia dell'Arte figures with the carnival. Several of the characters in the music, such as Estrella, are Schumann's invention. He invented these titles because they furthered his romantic and evocative theme. But in the ballet which itself evokes the spirit of Schumann, romantic and evocative themes that impregnate the music, though reinforced by the décor and the costumes and by the style of the dances themselves, are yet reduced to terms of the Mediterranean, to terms of classical precision and immediacy. And so this nostalgia is converted into the pleasure of an answered prayer. Harlequin, the elusive Harlequin of Schumann's imagination, is on the stage, virile and elastic, possessed of a mocking assurance, happy in his romantic silk shirt, more lithe and graceful than ever now that his rascality has been so romantically conceived. Thus the Harlequin in the ballet, the Harlequin we know and not the original Italian Arlecchino who was a servant or a thief, is, by means of that delicious expenditure of northern feeling upon the southern and catholic nature of ballet technique, restored full of honours to Brescia, his home, and to the Veneto, as well as promoted to the Venetian Carnival.

The situation is typical of ballet. For ballet technique, in the perfect outwardness of its stylized forms, is akin to the dominant Mediterranean mode of projecting emotion as we find it in Mediterranean visual art. Just as the Gothic spirit achieved a wide emblazonment under the sun of the Italian Renaissance, romantic impulses attain a concrete and definite fulfilment within the ballet framework without loss of their fluent strength.

Like the ballet technique, the Commedia dell'Arte figures, as they have come down to us, have received a predominant French stamp. Columbine and Pierrot are almost entirely French variations upon Italian themes. Still, it is Harlequin, the part created by Nijinsky, who dominates the ballet just as Arlecchino dominated the seventeenth- and eighteenth-century Commedia dell'Arte theatre.

After I had seen *Carnaval* the second time I found these masks had been restored to me. But more than this. I had grasped the point about ballet in general, the manner in which ballet orders the world of the imagination. The one impression was inseparable from the other.

The moment of revelation for me was the entrance of Harlequin and Columbine, an entrance which is, indeed, one of the greatest moments that have been contrived in dancing. The stage is empty: the music plunges into rather fierce, almost accusing respirations. Then, as a new and precise melody begins, they come moving close together, with hands joined across their bodies, Columbine with tiny steps upright on her points,[1] Harlequin slightly crouched as he makes light bounding paces drawing the knees up high, a feline canter. And thus they move as one. It is Harlequin's paces, of course, that are in time with the music. They go round in a circle before they separate. This movement occurs later in the ballet. It is the symbol of gaiety, of the sureness of their love. And if I praise ballet for the ease of its manner in the projection of every kind of emotion, at the same time I realize that it is the romantic openness with which it treats the relation between man and woman that is its mainspring from the literary point of view.

But in what way does the entry of Harlequin and Columbine epitomize the formal qualities of the classical technique, in what way do we learn from this one impression to love ballet as a whole? *Carnaval* is not strictly a classical ballet. Indeed, Fokine, Diaghilev's first choreographer, performed the greatest and the first revolution in the ballet of modern times. Fokine co-ordinated and intensified the essential, as opposed to the period, elements of ballet dancing. His was a re-creation rather than a destruction of the classical technique. In this respect, too, the greatest moment is the entry of Harlequin and Columbine. We here see the male and the female dancers performing closely together the essence of their respective ballet movements. Columbine, the ballerina, is on her points. She is an alighted insect, a butterfly with closed wings, caught within the elastic mesh of love. Those two feet that move at right angles to the floor are, as Gautier said of Sofia Fuoco's *temps de pointe,*

194

'like two steel arrows rebounding from a marble pavement'. And yet it is in this delicious mode that the woman's earthiness, her closeness to earth, is suggested, and far more succinctly suggested than by the heavy, barefoot or sandalled dancer, the expressionist dancer, who slowly enacts a kind of dream, whose movements infer that the stage is but a poor substitute for swards and woods. The ballerina, on the other hand, is an incarnation of the theatre. In accordance with the theatrical idea she externalizes the brutal world as something succinct, shows us the deepest emotions as something theatrical or outward and self-contained. And so, instead of mere earth, we become aware of the formal intensity of spatial intervals. That is her art. The same divergence exists between the effects of a good painting and of a canvas by a tortured yet arrogant amateur.

The dancer on her points, then – and it is the convention of ballet that only danseuses use points, although male dancers with their stronger feet could easily excel the women in this respect – makes us conscious of the plane of the stage on which she moves or poses. Her taut figure gives an added meaning to her ground on which she has alighted. In ballet the woman is the earth and water, the man the fire: both are etherealized. The male dancer is a firework, a figure of combustion. When Harlequin enters with Columbine it is as if his prancing steps were pistons driven up from beneath the stage which Columbine upon her points restores.

And so, from this *pas de deux* you may gather once and for all one aspect of ballet's formal profundity and of its consequent power as emblem. There are several introductions to this same theme in *Carnaval*. Of all choreography Fokine's work is the most complete. It was his aim to deliver the ballet plot from its feeble excuses for dancing, to conceive a ballet rather than the excuse for ballet dances. He succeeded. Every movement in *Carnaval* helps to construct the plot or atmosphere: there exists throughout a gradual crystallization of that atmosphere. The ballet opens with fugitive entries and exits, mere glimpses. It ends with a grand finale in which each character attains the epitome of his role. One might mention the Chiarina-Eusebius episode as an introduction to the Harlequin-Columbine theme in its formal aspects. Chiarina dallies on the points before the impulse comes to bestow the favour of the rose. Eusebius (Massine) is love-lorn, an easy prey to the archness of this virgin. Eusebius' invocations, though still graceful, are burdened with the white load of love: there is no bounce, no *ballon* in his movement: yet, once that he has caught both the roses of Chiarina, he pursues her off in a rapid goose-step: he is once again the piston, the combustive force that shoots up the stage.

Then there is the beautiful *pas de trois*. Chiarina in a mask with two companions surround and confuse the impetuous Florestan. They bundle him off. There supervenes upon the music an arch yet romantic seriousness, almost self-caressing. Something is sustained there, yet it is something, as so often in ballet, eminently volatile. For Chiarina, now wan and imperious, has drawn herself up to her full height: she beckons to her companions with long slow gestures of icy emotion. Tremulous yet imperious upon their points, each touches the white gloves of the other. They contemplate intently: slowly moving with rapid tiny steps upon the points, they share with each other the virgin's secret armoury of cruelty: they move in a suspense and then, as if drawn apart by three directions of the compass, by their far-flung destinies, still on points they leave, their right arms outstretched to one another, their gaze still fixed to the front. They disappear separately yet at the same instant, leaving the stage empty, it is true, but rich in its form as a homogeneous plane after the passage over its surface of an ever-lengthening triangle. Chiarina is the apex. Still facing the audience she passes out backwards: when she reaches the backcloth she moves to her right and disappears between overlapping curtains. The last we see of her is the outstretched arm, the white unwaving glove.

And is it nothing to perceive the equivocal female hauteur as thus complete, as thus translated into vivid and graceful yet pure geometry?

So much for *Carnaval*. Fokine is a genius, a great genius: and so was Diaghilev who brought the Russian ballet to western Europe. As I write I am thinking always of Diaghilev's ballet and of its successor, Les Ballets Russes de Monte Carlo, of which Colonel de Basil is the director and Massine the *maître de ballet* and principal dancer.

How much with one week of his ballet Diaghilev could give to our lives! On the framework of the classical ballet he emblazoned the only emblems of our time that seem no less sure, no less positive, than those we admire in the past. And if the first period of the Russian ballet, the Fokine period, was the greatest, Diaghilev contrived until the end to provide us with ballets that made us kings of our environment. Perhaps the later ballets could not have stood so well by themselves: but supported throughout the season by the older Diaghilev ballets and by one or two classical ballets, contrasted and supplemented thus, they gained as did the others a further poignancy. In the later ballets particularly, contemporary preoccupations with formal and abstract aspects of art obtained their most vivid realization. They appeared in ballet not so much as something saved from the world as the creation of a new world. I do not mean that the great Picasso, for instance, excelled himself only in his décors for ballet. I mean that only in co-operation with the old and glamorous geometry of ballet could the genius of a Picasso, of a Stravinsky, of a Satie, assume that wider air of relevance, a power to compel a whole mass, a heterogeneous audience. In terms of ballet the formal preoccupation of modern painting achieved an emblematic power that otherwise it so obviously lacks. All the decorative and absolute qualities of modern painting which each painter seeks to transcend, or rather, to which in his mind he has attached particular and interpretative contents that the public at large are slow to recognize, obtain an amplified realization when in the service of ballet. The painter's feelings about the world at large are transmitted as well by the action of the music and of the dancers. His abstractions do not lose their purity when thus exploited by the vivid scene of ballet. They merge with the geometry of the dance which has always been expressive. Ballet, in turn, is glorified by this alliance. Miró's setting for *Jeux d'enfants*, possibly the best work this painter has accomplished, is a case in point.

The modern ballet owes a very great deal to modern painters. Frequently it is the sketches of the painter which, more than anything else, decide the most general spirit of a ballet. And then, the enlargement of this spirit by the choreographer helps the painter to amplify his designs, whereas his studio conceptions are possibly too concentrated or isolated, and are fully grasped only by the most ready minds.

Bakst, though hardly a modern painter in this sense, was perhaps the chief instrument of Diaghilev's first or exotic period, the period of *Schéhérazade*. The achievement of Bakst enlarged the role that pictorial art can play in ballet. Diaghilev was not slow to act upon it.

The co-operation itself by which a ballet is produced, stimulates artists to excel themselves. Painter, composer, the originator of the story and *maître de ballet* inspire and reinforce one another, working to articulate a definite image – a rare situation in the arts today. For the modern artist, be he painter or musician, is self-conscious, isolated yet well-informed. He has no definite position in the world yet all the ages press upon him together, so large and so catholic is our knowledge. He tends to become a microcosm of Art itself, constantly working through, sometimes backwards, sometimes forwards, in a minute, economic yet generalized fashion, the larger cycles of aesthetic development. The modern artist is the guardian of the aesthetic idea which he has defined, encompassed as he is by a vulgar well-informed coterie. He is a monk largely given over to abstraction. Picasso is a monk, a bishop, a Pope.

Diaghilev was successful in dragging modern artists from their monasteries. Diaghilev, man of the world, made secular princes of these monks. But even he could not have done so without the rallying point of ballet. The ballet is the only art the traditional forms of which are in the main perfectly relevant to our own times, the only European art, then, that seems to be in full flower. We live, perhaps, in the High Renaissance of ballet. It is the only art today that can circumvent our lives. In ballet alone can we bear wholeheartedly to contemplate our European traditions. For ballet dancing is the European way of dancing. In the scheme of this technique whole eras of our civilization are embodied. In ballet alone do the eighteenth and nineteenth centuries support the twentieth. Ballet is our major reassurance, our sole grip upon continuity, the sole ancient art that lives, and more than that, lives at its height, revitalized by the modern spirit. And this we owe to Diaghilev who created the modern ballet, projected contemporary thought into terms of ballet.

He is dead: we have witnessed a period of confusion. Moreover, ballet dancing is widely attacked in the name of 'free' expressionist movement: while those who with asinine English jauntiness have initiated ballets full of Diaghilev reminiscences lifted out of their contexts, and who yet pay no direct homage to him nor even admit to remembering him, have come near to making us despair of ballet. Luckily not everyone has a small mind. The scope is there: ballet is on the rise again. We have gained full pleasure from Massine-Miró's *Jeux d'enfants* and Chabrier-Balanchine's *Cotillon*. We must cling, as yet, for our full contentment to the Russian ballet, to Massine's large ballet company.

Diaghilev could never have achieved what he did except for another factor, the Russian spirit that clung to his productions, even to the later cosmopolitan ballets as we shall see. The Russian element was his original driving force. He brought to western Europe the perfected instrument of the European dance infused with Slavonic passion. Thus, the European form of the dance externalized for us a new country, an unknown culture. The stage on which *Prince Igor* was performed, opened up for us the whole stretch of the trans-Caucasian plains and of their history. A form of music was revealed to western ears, Russian music, a westernized and recognizable embodiment of the folklore from the most elusive distances. This Russian element gave the standard of a ballet's content to Diaghilev. If he brought about the renascence of the ballet as a whole, it was because, in the first place, he used the ballet form to stabilize the Russian Renaissance. For *Renaissance* always denotes the maturity of northern emotion which seeks projection in an outward or self-contained southern form, the assured and balanced southern form. The ballet technique as we shall presently see in greater detail, is an outward medium of this kind, reducing even the more overwhelming passions to the steady light of brilliance. The Russians had long paid homage to Mediterranean civilization, particularly to Italian architecture, both infusing those forms with the native spirit and schooling the native exuberance to seek expression through those forms. Of this development, and of a later and self-consciously Russian development in opera, it was the good fortune of ballet to be the heir. And so great is the achievement in ballet from the days of Petipa and Tchaikovsky to the day of Massine or Balanchine, that it is doubtful whether the Imperial Russian and Winter Palace atmosphere can be entirely dispelled from the ballet of today. It is significant that the Bolsheviks who love the maximum confusion of art with politics, that the Bolsheviks guard the classical ballet jealously, that Stalin himself was present recently at a revival of *Casse-Noisette*, the ballet that centres around an aristocrat's ballroom and the sugar-plum fairy of rich pre-revolutionary childhoods. The Bolsheviks have attempted to free ballet from any Imperial taint. They have for the most part failed: and rather than dispense with classical ballet which is still the only possible point of departure for any innovation, they revive Tchaikovsky's *Casse-Noisette*.

The resources of ballet, then, were fully developed when ballet became the vehicle of the Russian Renaissance. Not only Nijinsky, not only Karsavina, not only these and other dancers of genius were gathered around Diaghilev, but Bakst and Benois, Stravinsky, Golovin. Their work gave the model for that concerted effort in which one man inspires another, that rush, that triumph of feeling which modern art as a whole so signally lacks.

Co-operation and the sense of production that it breeds, belong always to the theatre. Here is one source of the theatre's glamour; a glamour which today attaches to no other art. We talk of 'a show', a rather bedraggled expression but one which, none the less, implies the essence of theatrical display. For the theatre is a showing, a demonstration: that is its attraction. All works of art, we have said, are translations of inner or personal ferment into some objective form. The theatre is the literal presentation of life and movement before the lights and before the audience. The spoken drama is not 'a show' to the same extent as the music-hall, still less than the circus or the Harlequinade or the ballet. The presentation is more nearly complete, more concrete, more *theatrical* when thought is translated into movement: and it is

200

over the matter of theatrical presentation that other forms of the dance today fall so far short of ballet. Indeed, it is in the much criticized 'turning out' of the thigh, the leg and the foot and the continuous presentation of the face to the audience, that resides so much of ballet's theatrical strength. But more of this anon.

The glamour of 'a show', then, belongs to its character as life in the form of a corporeal façade. Life in terms of actual physical revelation is bound to be reassuring. Out of the dark and gloomy wings, on to the stage before the footlights, 'the show' emerges and there it is sustained. Out of the brains of many collaborators, from many sources, many homes, 'the show' is gathered each night. A multitude of different occupations concur for the nightly presentation. When the sun goes down each night the theatres show the fruit of work for our pleasure.

Ballet, I think, to a far greater extent than any other branch of the theatre, sustains this feeling of 'a show'. It is expressed in the very manner that the dancers come before us. Instead of into the pit of the circus around which the audience is arranged, the dancer must enter the long stage for the pleasure of an audience facing one way. This entry needs a higher concentration or organization of movement, a greater synthesis, as if life were to be fully expressed by two dimensions. Indeed, ballet grew from the ceremonies of royal audience, from processions, cavalcades and masques before it reached the narrow platform of the stage.

And now join the dancers in the wings. One moment they are practising pirouettes, *battements*, *fouettés*, talking, gossiping in groups. Their movements remind one of the sudden leaps, the abrupt miniature actions of animals absorbed in each other at the corner of a street: and like the dog or cat that leaves the street conclave, one of them suddenly runs off though he seemed absorbed, he runs, he dances on to the stage, see how he leaps into the glare in time with the music: he has taken the plunge without semblance of hesitation: he arrives as if he has never begun to dance because he has never stopped dancing: you witness the height of dramatic presentation, the heightening into superb movement of a mechanism, the human mechanism which, internally at least, if not externally, is never still.

Other forms of the dance are less suited to the stage: for they do not carry so high, so theatrical a glamour. In other forms of dancing the stage itself, and therefore the entry on to the stage, do not always possess so clear a significance.

Why is this so, what is the deeper root of ballet's glamour? For assuredly the brilliancy of the ballerina and of the *corps de ballet*, the feats of virtuosity, the manifold co-operation, the large company, the large orchestra, an eager audience, these are accessories, some of them – fine dancing on a large stage, for instance, an efficient orchestra – indispensable accessories to the glamour of ballet; but they do not in themselves explain that glamour.

I must turn once more to the spatial abstractions that underlie the ballet spectacle. I am thinking again of that flat space, the stage itself, the boards that are the common ground of all theatrical performance. Ballet, I maintain, is superlative stage work just because it endows the stage with more profound significance than does any other theatrical display.

There is magic, it is said, in the footlights. Yes, there is magic in the brilliancy of the stage, in that brilliantly lit rectangle on which all attention is focused. But how rarely justified is this concentration on a point, how rarely sustained except on the part of the audience with all their eyes directed. When I watch a ballet, though, I am acutely conscious that this rectangular space of the stage is assaulted from *every* side. Three arts have combined to reveal life there, three arts direct their searchlights on this space. In many forms of entertainment, dancing or singing, music and painting combine their powers: but not their full powers. Is the décor of an opera of the same importance as the décor of a ballet, and does the slow process of opera *illuminate* the floor of the stage as does the moving, ever changing ballet? And then, can other kinds of dancers assault the stage as do the cylinders of the male ballet dancer's legs as if pumping up from beneath, or the suspended oval of the ballerina's form gracing the stage in an attitude? No, certainly not. For ballet dancing is theatre dancing at its highest. The underlying principles of this technique were formulated during the course of the seventeenth century, the greatest period that the European theatre has known.

Imagine a Diaghilev ballet in progress. The stage is assaulted from every side. We, an ardent audience, are a battery from the front (and some of the strength of that battery is gauged in the intervals and renews our expectation of the next ballet). In front of us is the conductor and his orchestra making music that is directed on to the stage above them. Behind, there is the backcloth or scenery that in their turn thrust the stage forward. The major lights are at the sides: but they are nothing compared to the assaults of the dancers who issue thence, dance, go off, and very likely come on again from a different wing.[2] And if during a ballet the stage is left empty while the music continues, we feel that we gaze on the ocean bed when the battery of seas have rolled away: we notice the feather a dancer has lost or some stage property that needed to be cast down and relinquished in the heat of the action, we see these things as the derelicts that enrich the ocean bed, dead fruit of dramatic situations.

I do not deny that all stage performance and dancing of whatever kind suggest this battery of the seas upon the ocean bed. Dancing is specifically an assault upon space, an assault of love, a similar assault to that of the carver upon his stone or that of the farmer as he ploughs the earth. For the reasons we have given and for others that will appear in due course ballet is the most spectacular mode of assaulting space. We would now discover in what lies the glamour, the excitement of this act upon the stage.

First of all we must enlarge our idea of the stage. The ballet dancer possesses a marked carriage. His head, arms and torso are poised. Something is happening in the air around him as well as upon the floor. If we are sitting in the front stalls we scent and feel the air of the stage when the curtain goes up. The dancer makes of that air a thing that seems tangible to us. The stage is not a mere flat floor. It is all that lies behind the proscenium arch: it is a box open upon one side, the side to the audience, a box with small apertures on the flanks, mice-holes from which the dancers come before us. (How poignant is the entrance of the mice in *Casse-Noisette!*)

What is the deeper significance of this box? It is perhaps a house in section, like a doll's house when the façade has been taken off. We see the life that goes on inside: every detail is revealed to us. The assault upon the stage, then, that I have described, is an act of consummation, a love that elicits, extracts, the inner life. But what, in turn, is the significance of a box's or a house's rectangularity? We are familiar with the theory that classical buildings are based upon human proportions. To a less degree all square buildings, I think, exhibit a humanism of this kind, for they reflect in geometrical form the most general aspect of our awareness of our own bodies, conscious as we are of possessing a front and a back with arms and ears at the sides. And so, in a sense, the child who peers inside the doll's house and the audience who gaze at the dancers in the stage's rectangular box lying open to them, enjoy in fantasy the inner processes as tangible objects, that is to say, enjoy as tangible objects that are beautifully arranged, the ceaseless unconscious life inside the body. When, in the ballet *Les Matelots*, Sokolova of the inimitable carriage used to walk slowly on to the stage, turn her back on the audience and, with legs apart and with hands clasped behind her, stood contemplating the backcloth while the music expended itself on a cheerful, mounting phrase, we witnessed a profound symbol of doleful, sustained inner scrutiny redeemed by that element of ballet wit by which even the more obscure and tangled emotions are made compact.

In this connection we may readily understand why architectural settings have played so large a part in the European theatre. The play that took place *outside* buildings, showed openly the inside of action, in front of action's façade thus dramatized into the high externality of charged yet changeless stone. In the sixteenth-century theatre of Serlio, a background of ordinary houses was the setting for all comedies, a background of grand architecture for tragedy. The Commedia dell'Arte characters moved for centuries in front of similar scenes. The European theatre is largely a dramatization of the Italian life of the street. It is no wonder that Diaghilev went to Venice each year. Is it not a pleasure to walk through Soho on the way to the theatre of an evening, or past the outdoor furniture that litters Covent Garden?

204

And if I were allowed but one generalization with which to explain
the glamour of the theatre as a whole, I should say that it resided in this:
the projection of man's interior physical and mental life into terms of
the outside world, and particularly into terms of man's exterior, of the
appearance and the movement of his body.[3]

All art, I have said, is a projection of inner ferment into objective
form. The distinguishing character of the theatrical art and of ballet in
especial, is the drama of this presentation upon a stage, within an open
box assaulted from every side, and of its direct and literal transposition
of inner ferment into terms of action and of movement. Words and
song may be the adjuncts, but they are not the essence of the theatre.
The Elizabethan age was a great period of the theatre, not only because
many Elizabethan plays were superb poetry, but also because that
poetry was largely inspired by, and at the service of, the Italian conception of the theatre, and because in those days this true theatre was
popular. The true theatre, I have said, leaves a great deal to the imagination of the audience. Under the guise of characters in a story, the true
theatre is concerned directly with conventional figures, prototypes,
symbols, fears, aspirations which each man carries about inside him and
which he sees, on coming to the theatre, externalized and dramatized
within the open box of the stage. We know what the clown and other
masks will do, and they do it and we enjoy it. They are really mechanical
figures just like the figures young and old that we carry about inside us,
assimilations that form so large a part of our spiritual anatomy.

It pleases grown-ups no less than children to arrange the figures in
a toy theatre. We are controlling and guiding mechanical behaviour to
which, as found in ourselves, we are largely the slaves. The puppet is not
the model of a man but the model of a human mechanism in action.
The puppet-show no less than ballet displays the essence of the theatre.
From puppets, the bridge is easy to dolls and fetishes out of which the
theatre grew. A child that occupies herself with her doll is playing at the
theatre with far better sense that Mr. Maugham or Mr. Coward in their
plays, musical or otherwise. The marionette, as Gordon Craig has said,
is the human personality that never alters, but only reacts to each

situation. Dolls and toys are the same, and so are the Italian *zanni*, the masks upon which the European theatre has largely relied; so too are the ballet dancers. In the modern theatre, puppets and dancers alone possess the full force of non-utterance.

There is added piquancy in the theatre when the toys or marionettes are actually human beings, when they sing as in the *Barber of Seville* or *Don Pasquale*, when they dance or when they are speaking characters so subtle yet so inevitable as were the Harlequins or Scaramouches of the Commedia dell'Arte plays. How delicious, too, in ballet is the effect of feigned puppets coming to life! The theme of toys that come to life is a frequent one, common to *Coppélia*, to *Casse-Noisette*, to *La Boutique fantasque* and to *Jeux d'enfants*. It is also, in some sense, the subject of *Pétrouchka*, possibly the most profound of the ballets.

Pétrouchka is a ballet that compares favourably with any masterpiece of tragedy. Pétrouchka, a puppet, comes to life, though to an incomplete and mechanical life that fills him with a maddened desire for 'freedom'. This figure serves to express transcendental aspirations and what is sometimes called – but not by Russians – 'divine discontent'. There are two other puppets, the Moor and the Ballerina. The Ballerina is unexceptional as a puppet who comes to life. The Moor is animal rather than human, whereas Pétrouchka suffers an intolerable mental strain. The vivification of these puppets is controlled by an ancient oriental Charlatan who exhibits them to the crowd. Their booth has been set up in a square of St. Petersburg at a time of popular fête. 'As the magician touched the three hanging puppets', wrote Madame Nijinsky in her book about her husband, 'they came to life. Nijinsky's Pétrouchka made one convulsive movement like dead matter suddenly charged with electricity. This *pas de trois*, danced in a mad tempo, is the quintessence of choreographic technique, and, while the face of Pétrouchka is blank, his scintillating feet execute steps of incredible virtuosity.' Something transcendental is thus conveyed to us without resort to expressionism.

When the puppets run down to the front of the stage we see that Pétrouchka is performing his rigmarole distracted yet impelled. He is a maddened fool of a prisoner. In an excess of vitality with which the

Charlatan had not reckoned, he transcends his puppet state. He is romantically in love with the Ballerina, a normal animated puppet who can but fear his ungracious paroxysms, his mechanism tainted with overcharged emotions. She prefers the handsome, strong, exotic Moor, a normal barbarian who attacks and then worships the cocoanut fetish with which he plays in his cell. The Moor's reactions are limited. Unlike Pétrouchka, the figure of the intelligent human being as the neurotic, he does not fear that he is ugly or unaccountable. Pétrouchka in his cell is wedded to his suffering. He examines his grim puppet limbs, he scrambles on the walls and bangs his head upon the door jambs. It does not occur to him, nor to us, that even his fingerless hands might open the door as does the Ballerina who visits him and runs away frightened by the antics that her appearance evokes. Pétrouchka is in no condition to improve upon circumstances: this drives him to greater fury. He shakes his fist at the watching image of the Charlatan upon the wall through which he bursts, only to return and sink to the ground. Pétrouchka's fear and horror at his own crass self have been his undoing. It is the upper layer of his mind, his rudimentary sense of shame, that imprisons him. He blames the Charlatan, an obvious figure of Autocracy. But in so far as, however faintly, Pétrouchka symbolizes the white, distracted, Christian and European side of the Russian temperament that is put in opposition to the black fatalism of the Moor, the Charlatan serves also as a section of Pétrouchka's mind in so far as it is an outward and conscious omnipotent power that inhibits and tortures his passions. Pétrouchka's pathetic yet grim antics are the frenzies of introspection and cruel self-supervision. Still, our sympathies are with him rather than with the resplendent and animal Moor: Pétrouchka's conflicts seem no less real. Owing to the atavistic Russian force of the music they are endowed with an animal directness, the cruel animal pathos. One feels it takes as much to silence Pétrouchka as it took to kill Rasputin.

Stravinsky's score, a masterpiece of the first magnitude, expresses this hard-wrought Russian fibre with an intensity that even the novels of Dostoevsky can not approach. We are reminded of the direct snuffles and yells of animals. Pétrouchka is not hysterical. His paroxysms and his pathos possess the unqualified shrillness of animal sobbing. As for the Moor, he is a fierce yet panting and cistern-like mute who gobbles anything to hand. This music is no less sustained than the activity of a dog who runs and snuffles blithely, barks and runs and runs, or the vitality of a proud, stamping horse that will career until it drops. The Ballerina is the neat sugared plum with which such a horse should be fed.

This music shows us the crowd of the first and last scenes using the crude edge of the cold as a whip to their prancing spirits. They incorporate and exploit the rhythms of a jolting sledge that makes deep striped lines in snow and sludge, of the proud canter of horses untiring in that keen air, of the reins lifted from the horses' backs and dropped there to set them going faster. There exists in the music every form of respiration during the dance, the drinking in and the expenditure of that young air, rhythmic breathing that will be used in deep sleep, fierce animal pumping and the serious gaiety of mouths slightly open in pleasure. When, with faces thus set, the two blithe Ivans shoot their legs out at all angles in a cobbler's step (*Prisiadka*), we recognize the proud and masculine poise that Pétrouchka envies.

The square is still full though an evening snow has begun to fall. A scuffle starts within the booth. Out rush the three puppets. Pétrouchka's jealousy and interference in the matter of the Ballerina have infuriated the Moor. This time he is chasing Pétrouchka in earnest. He strikes him down with a sword: the people gather round amazed. A police officer goes to look for the Charlatan. The silenced crowd watches the death agony, the spasms of pain, the inarticulate last attempt to speak, to explain, to explain away. Pétrouchka dies and we hear his sombre soul jogging clear like a bear on the run. In the darkening light the Charlatan comes to reassure the crowd. 'It is only a puppet,' and he holds up a figure of sawdust, a Pétrouchka of sawdust. The people disperse joking and in the music we hear the lingering respiration of the next day that will glint in vast Russia after the passage of the oncoming night. Pétrouchka is sawdust, at rest. The Charlatan trudges off trailing the dummy. The Pétrouchka theme breaks into the music. The Charlatan

glances at the dummy he trails. At that moment the same old gesticu-
lating Pétrouchka appears on top of the booth, a ghost that frightens
the Charlatan off. Autocracy can make and destroy but it cannot eradicate. Man seemingly can make puppets of his passions, awaking them
and destroying them as he thinks fit, but when this is done with cruelty
they will rise up and shake him from his balance. As he runs away the
Charlatan's hat falls off. And now the ghost of Pétrouchka as well as
Pétrouchka himself is inanimate, gradually still, partially revenged,
utterly useless, dead.

Pétrouchka shows us a theatre within a theatre, a ballet within a
ballet, mechanical principles within puppets. It mirrors the successive
layers of the human process, layers that are not smooth but cross-cut
and widely interrelated. The façade or outward appearance is symbolized, of course, by the ever-moving vigorous crowd of the first and last
scenes. The music for this outdoor life opens with a sustained and popu-
lous shrillness that is penetrated only when the street dancer lays down
her mat before dancing to the street-organ. The façade of shrillness
then breaks, we hear underneath a street-organ tune recording the large
continuity of the people who will return finally to their houses and to
their beds, whose life, taken in the broad, is that nameless, over-ancient
epic of which all barrel-organs speak. Then, even before the street dancer has completed her performance, the eager music of the fête begins
to hustle the street tunes with a traffic of impatient sleigh bells: the
folds of the fair descend again. They are not broken until the Charlatan
with his persuasive flute emerges from the curtains of the booth which
he will presently fling aside to disclose his puppets fixed in their boxes
as if awaiting birth.

I have described this ballet at some length but I do not feel that I have
explained a hundredth part of its meaning. I could begin again and
describe it from another angle. But the more often I did so, the further
away I should be from expressing the succinct impression that the
ballet itself conveys. When the artist's emotions are sufficiently intense
for him to be working with vital symbols, many meanings no less

complicated in their inter-relationships than are his feelings, tend to converge simply in his work. In *Pétrouchka* we watch the inner life displayed succinctly for all its complication, not because such an effect was the conscious aim of its creators, but because those creators were men of genius imbued with a deep sense of the European theatre to terms of which they brought their own Russian fervour and their Russian themes. And I would emphasize in the name of *Pétrouchka* that the externalization by ballet and by the European theatre generally, of inner states, is not effected through symbols without substance or through expressionist or dream-like figures. It is something more definite than the ancient Shadow theatre which, although no less common throughout the world than the Marionette theatre, is to be principally connected with China and Japan. In the shadow theatre, figures are silhouetted on a screen. They are a shorthand of realism, a realism without substance, a dream realism. Bereft of the open box of the stage, the inner processes that are projected are not fully projected; they remain inner processes.

One might say that Lotte Reiniger's silhouette film *Prince Achmed*, released in 1926, is at the opposite extreme to Walt Disney's creations. But the cinema as a whole is in essence an expressionist or German art suitable for suggestion rather than statement, is concerned with a shorthand realism rather than with a projection that requires the full light of the stage. The growth of the cinema should help to purify our conception of the theatre. Surely the theatre can now be left to its own devices. But there is little sign that the people of the theatre would have it so at present. Meanwhile, when the ballet is not in London we go to the cinema.

The Classical Ballet

From *To-night the Ballet* (1934)

The classical technique may not provide the reader's chief interest in the modern ballet: but he will now see that the classical technique underlies, and indeed defines, dancing which is ballet dancing. And it follows that anyone who has taken sustenance from the ballet spectacle and who, by the same token, cannot stomach the German schools of the 'free' dance, will have interest and reverence at least for the classical technique. Moreover, it is probable that the frequenter of the ballet, in the process of becoming an enthusiast, will choose, rather than avoid, the nights on which *Swan Lake* or *Sylphides* or *Casse-Noisette* or *Coppélia* or *Giselle* are performed, the five classical ballets which have been constantly performed in London during the last few years.

The bearing of the classical dancer, we have said, is characterized by compactness. The thigh muscles are drawn up, the torso rests upon the legs like a bust upon its base. This bust swivels and bends but, in most adagio movements at any rate, the shoulders remain parallel to the pelvis bone. Every bend, every jump is accomplished with an effect of ease and of lightness. Perhaps nothing is more typical of the brilliancy of ballet than the manner in which the ballerina turns her head in a pirouette. Her eyes are fixed upon a point in space; as she turns, her head revolves last and comes round first with the eyes fixed on the same point. Thus by the fixed eyes that revolve in a flash back to the same position and fix the audience again, the volition as well as the actuality of speed, accuracy and brilliance is expressed.

The 'turning out' of the classical dancer's thighs, legs and feet, give the broad base-line for jumping and turning and enable a balance that could not otherwise be attained. All the five positions are 'turned out': the second and fifth positions allow the dancer to move sideways easily without turning the body. 'Turning out' is the essence of ballet and we must pause to examine its aesthetic significance. Hitherto I have attempted to argue on general grounds that ballet is the most 'externalized' form of the dance, an embodiment of the ideals of the European theatre. It will now be possible to make the conception more precise by treating it in terms of 'turning out'. For 'turning out' means that the dancer, whatever the convolutions of the dance, continually shows as much of himself as possible to the spectator. When he stands in the first position facing the front, we see his feet and his legs in profile. The ballet dancer is, as it were, extended. We realize it best in the adagio, a supreme test for the ballerina. When, facing us, she bends forward over her front leg in an arabesque, the foot of the raised rear leg is turned out and tilted upward. A downward pointing foot not only would make an ugly line but would spoil the effect of openness, of disclosure and of that suspension slightly above the ground by which objects are best defined. Again, when the free leg is extended in front and is brought round in the execution of a *grand rond de jambe* to the second position *en l'air*, leg and foot are once more turned outwards. The late Monsieur André Levinson, famous as a ballet critic, had a special affection for this position. It typified for him the openness of the dance. In all such convolutions of the adagio the ballerina is showing the many gradual planes of her body in terms of harmonious lines. While her arms and one leg are extended, her partner turns her slowly round upon the pivot of her straight point. She is shown to the world with the utmost love and grace. She will then integrate herself afresh, raise herself on the points, her arms close to her body in the fifth position *en bas*, her feet close together, the one slightly in front of the other. It is the alighting of the insect, the shutting of wings, the straightening into the perpendicular of feelers and of legs. Soon she will take flight and extend herself again. Meanwhile she shows us on the points what we have not seen in the arabesque or *développé*, two unbroken lines from toes to thighs.

Compare this sublime fulfilment, this perfect intercourse expressed in planes, with the progressive spirals of Spanish dancing that betray its oriental ancestry or with the coils of mesmeric tension which the Indian or Javanese dancer builds up and with the same form expends. The uniform outwardness of ballet avoids such alternations. If it is less intense, it is no less profound: for ballet is adjusted to the planes of the stage, composes into a precise picture, a precise sphere of feeling which the imagination grasps entire.

As a rule, the dances of other civilizations seem to us to express foremost the absorption of strength, the building up of a reserve of vitality, a kind of inner recreation. There are dances that denote the expenditure of energy: but one is still conscious that behind the movements of such dances the dancer is drawing to himself the strength of the outside world, appropriating the life of animals or of the fields, or feeding upon a cultural heritage, himself its god. Such dances symbolize an intensification of the human mystery, the wrapt human power of absorption alternating with expenditure. The more typical European forms of the dance are exactly the opposite: they show a dissolution of mystery, they express passion in terms of an uniform corporeal outwardnesss. The ballerina's body is etherealized. She seems scarcely to rest upon the ground. She is, as it were, suspended just slightly above the earth so that we may see her better. She seems cut off from the sources of her being, or rather, those dark internal sources are shown by her as something light and white, brittle as are all baubles, all playthings that we can utterly examine; yet, at the same time, so perfect is her geometry that we feel this plaything which our minds may utterly possess, to be as well the veriest essence. Her partner guides and holds her. And he – he then watches her *pas* with upraised hand, he shows her off. He has the air of perpetual triumph, and when the time comes for his own variation he bounds, leaps, bounces and rejoins the ballerina in the wings amid applause. Such is the abstract of the *pas de deux*, the crux of ballet.

In the allegro, ballet dancers move, and they move lightly and fast. Outside of ballet there is no true allegro in dancing, no fast travels that are executed with the utmost lightness and ease. All the same, a similar corporeal outwardness, we have said, is characteristic of the more typical European dances. As well as in the stately measures of palaces, ballet has its origin in dances of the people. The English country dances, dances for the village couples (whereas Morris dances, probably of oriental or Moorish ancestry, were performed by a squadron of men), some hundred years after reaching the English court, invaded the continent at the beginning of the eighteenth century. These *contredanses*, as they were called in France, have a good deal to do with the development of ballet. It is probable that they assisted the growth of allegro. Certainly, except for the minuet, and for the gavotte which was considered scandalously vivacious when first introduced, slowly trodden measures began to decline.

But apart from any historical proof, I would claim that ballet is the stylized, cultural form of the European dance (if one may entertain that conception for a moment) because ballet expresses through the agency of the human body, the very same mode of projecting feeling that characterizes all the greatest European visual art. The same fixity without distortion and without sternness, the same outwardness, is the hallmark of our art, a steady revelation that calls to mind the open face of the rose or smooth mountains in unbroken sunlight. All art is the conversion of inner states into outward objective form. But whereas the objective form is the constant in art, the degree of outwardness thereby expressed varies a good deal. It is the pleasure of many visual arts to *intimate*, by means of the objective form, an inner state: whereas, in the highest achievements of European visual art, that same inner intensity is entirely transposed into something smooth, gradual yet immediate: time and succession are converted into spatial forms, not merely symbolized by spatial forms. We like to have the mystery cleared, to see our feelings laid out as something concrete and defined. We would win for self-expression the homogeneity and the soft light of stone, stone with its gradual, even-lighted surfaces. Watching the classical ballet I am constantly reminded of Agostino di Duccio's low reliefs in the Tempio Malatestiano at Rimini, figures seemingly pressed from the round into relief, preserving many values which could be seen in a statue only if we walked round it. The values of the round are expressed frontally by these gradual surfaces. Like the limbs of the dancer, those of these

214

fifteenth-century figures are turned outwards; otherwise no synthesis could have been made of their various facets. And again, as in ballet, none of these forms are abrupt or contorted. We witness at Rimini the gradual and glowing face of the stone. In ballet the human passions are expressed by the gradual uncontorted curves and straight lines of the extended human body. There is no residuum, no veil. The human body is purged of atmosphere. All is shown. When the ballerina extends her leg in a *développé* we contemplate the essence of the European stage, a form of the theatre that is wedded to such display. This exhibition of graduated limbs is an act of virtuosity; for 'turning out' is not 'natural' but is accomplished by the dancer with an air of exuberant ease. Ballet is full of virtuoso effects. The male dancer performing *tours en l'air* is like an animated helicopter. So be it.

The character that I have called typical of European visual art and of the European theatre, is, of course, primarily a Mediterranean product which the Renaissance consolidated. For better or for worse modern Europe is the inheritor of the Italian Renaissance. We now know how greatly and how long a typical invention of that time in the visual arts like perspective, can be misused or used meaninglessly. But perspective in the first place was developed by the Renaissance artist to allow him to represent those many facets of the human form and of landscape and to order them in space. It may be objected that subsequent developments in the visual arts of Europe do not emphasize the non-contorted, if virtuoso, outwardness by which I lay so great store. Nevertheless, though it pass from one art to another, somewhere it always exists. There are many virtues in Baroque and Rococo architecture, but superficially, at any rate, these architectures do not exhibit the extreme spatiality noted above. All the same, it was from the attitude of seventeenth- and eighteenth-century deportment that the five positions of ballet dancing were taken. In Rameau's eighteenth-century handbook we may read how to make a bow and why it would be ill-bred to turn in the foot. In making his salutations the eighteenth-century gentleman gracefully showed himself, not only his front, but the sides of his legs and part of the back in the obeisance. He steps forward and he steps backwards, he shows himself in different perspectives. Such were the origins of the classical ballet as we have it today. 'When you are able to make a graceful bow,' says Rameau, 'you unconsciously acquire a taste for dancing.'

It may seem that these cultivated artificialities are not a very intense expression. That is true. Nor was there much intensity in ballet before 1780. Ballet is the last integral manifestation of the Renaissance spirit. It needed for its flowering the resurgence of northern romanticism, just as the Italian Renaissance of the fifteenth century was largely the outcome of Gothic exuberance brought to the South. Probably the earliest signs of the Romantic Movement are to be found in the famous *Lettres sur la danse et les ballets* by Jean Noverre,[1] celebrated dancer and choreographer. This book was first published in 1760.

But in reading ballet history we are aware that there is hardly a period in which some daring spirit has not visualized and even attempted to realize a wider scope. Fokine, who, more than any other of Diaghilev's instruments, created the modern ballet in which mimed action is no longer the excuse for subsequent dances but is expressed by dancing, Fokine has many predecessors, not only great reformers like Noverre and Viganò about whom we can read, but others also in earlier periods about whose work we have but the faintest indications. Noverre did for ballet what his friend Gluck did for opera. Yet over and over again, ballet tends to fall back on the safe position it can hold within opera, as a dancing spectacle thrown in between the acts. Ballet tends to stabilize and conventionalize any new ground that it has attained. Thus the romantic ballet inspired by Taglioni's dancing was soon conventionalized into the spectacle of the classical ballet as we have it today, a drama or comedy in which the action is mimed, leading up to brilliant dances of a romantic flavour.

It is perhaps dangerous to generalize on this point. Petipa, the great choreographer of the Russian Imperial theatres in the second half of the nineteenth century, varied his methods a good deal. As poetic conceptions, some of his ballets are far more intense than others. In most of them there existed the attempt to offer a new atmosphere, a new diversion. At the same time the main object was to provide satisfactory scope for the virtues of the principal dancers whose *variations* were sometimes thrust in without context. For good or for worse, the creative art of choreography has always been both inspired and limited by the aptitudes and temperaments of particular dancers. A phenomenon like Nijinsky in his own person inspired a new departure: but then there have been only one Nijinsky and two Vestris.

Music and décor were under the same servitude. But let it not be thought that I decry the classical ballets. I would give anything to see more of them. Yet I am not one of those who maintain that this, the true classical ballet, the ballet in which we see the classical *pas* performed for their own sake, innocent for the most part of any vital context, should never have been touched. Lovers of ballet will always want to see classical ballet, to see the classical *pas*, the framework of ballet, in all their purity. This will be perhaps their greatest joy. Certainly *Casse-Noisette* draws me to the theatre as insistently as do *Jeux d'enfants* or *Cotillon*, if not more insistently. But if I had not seen *Jeux d'enfants* nor *Cotillon* nor other modern ballets, I doubt whether *Casse-Noisette* would have drawn me at all. Unless I had seen how the modern ballet can create an entirely contemporary content, an art-form in which composer and painter combine with choreographer to interpret the contemporary scene or interpret other periods in the contemporary manner, if ballet had not provided my imagination with contents that I can carry on the buses and down the tubes, then I doubt somewhat whether, except for certain Italian studies, I should ever have seen the 'point' of the classical ballet. My interest might have been partially waylaid by a seeming anachronism in the treatment of the love relation, for instance. I would not have seen classical ballet as the living source of modern ballet but as a decaying art that could not be developed. The geometry of the classical ballet, the outwardness of the classical ballet and the harmonious gradualness of its forms, are an emblem of the European spirit: they will always have relevance, but it is greatly increased if other ballets are brought in closer relation with contemporary life. When we are satisfied that the dance can interpret a modern content, then we can watch with the greatest keenness the purely abstract ballet, the ballet which is, or seems at first to be, a mere excuse for the display of classical virtuosity. We soon realize, however, that these ballets too (for it is the best that have survived) provide food enough for the imagination. After witnessing the concentrated conception of a Diaghilev ballet expressed by dancing, music and décor, it is a particular pleasure to see a classical ballet in which pure dancing, the occasion for these other activities, is glorified. There exists a poignancy, too, in the very alternation of mime and dance; it is a pleasure to see dancing seize its delicate excuses, it is a pleasure to be transported into a world in which every situation attends the commentary of combined movement.

I write for my own generation, for those, like myself, whose first real introduction to ballet was through the later Diaghilev or through Massine. I did not love the classical ballet at first. But the fact that the much criticized ballets of Diaghilev's later period which some critics have stigmatized as a betrayal of the classical technique and of the ballet spirit, the fact that these later ballets, a ballet like Cocteau-Picasso-Satie's *Parade* for instance, should have in my case and in the case of others stimulated an appetite for classical ballets, is itself a sufficient answer to those critics. We would never have known how consummate was this art had not Diaghilev provided us with a feast of music, painting and wit as well as of dancing pure and simple. We would never have realized the scope of this art.

There is now in London a large and enthusiastic ballet audience. It was created by Diaghilev himself, or by the esteem which, since his death, ballet still holds. This audience would not enjoy classical ballet as they do had they not been introduced to it via the modern ballet or the prestige which Diaghilev gave it. Pavlova's company, it is true, never departed far from classical ballet. The public at large, however, went to see Pavlova, not her ballets. But whatever Diaghilev put on the stage heightened our awareness of ballet in general. First of all there was Fokine who re-created in his ballets and concentrated the classical *pas*, harnessed them to a direct expressiveness hitherto reserved for mime.

All the same, the Fokine ballets and the ballets of Diaghilev's later periods as well, were, in a sense, a diffusion of pure dancing, a diffusion that embraced the painters, particularly the great Bakst, and the composers. Both in the choreography and in these other arts the classical ballet with its abstract, self-contained dances, was harnessed to a wider expressiveness. It was in terms of this wider expressiveness that a contemporary content could be treated: and it was because of the power exhibited by this wider expressiveness that we learned to love its source, the classical ballet. Diaghilev, not Pavlova, taught us to love classical ballet, to appreciate fully Pavlova herself.

And then there was Stravinsky. *Oiseau de feu!* What can we conceive to provide a more comprehensive image of the ballet, the classical ballet! Fire and birdlike movements (the *pointe* is like the tip of a wing) are in combination an extract of the ballet soul: it was in the music, in the décor as well. Then Pétrouchka, the animated marionette, not the object of farce as in *Coppélia*, but the figure of a great and profound tragedy. The music is a masterpiece. Some critics have complained that the music overwhelms the dancing. There are ballet purists who always would have music subservient to dancing, commissioned to supply a very definite role as a mere accompaniment to the dance. These purists have much in common with Mary Wigman. There is room in ballet for every kind of relationship between music and dancing: the one kind enhances the others, just as the modern and classical ballets enhance one another. A well-devised ballet programme today gives us at least three varieties of this relationship: and that variety is part and parcel of our pleasure.

In *Schéhérazade* and *Sacre du printemps*, Diaghilev showed that symphonic music itself could be employed for ballet. There was no moonlight in the later ballets. A lyrical content was preserved with the help of the wry yet exuberant tricks of the music of Les Six. In *Les Matelots*, for instance, a ballet which has suffered so many unfortunate imitations at the hands of English choreographers, the more lyrical passages are entrusted to the wheezings of the trombone: but remember that the stage above is full of sunlight. This music and Massine's choreography provided that element of toughness, of wryness, necessary as fibre to the modern lyrical mood, a plant that extracts a soft brilliance from the glare and brass of full daylight.

In Massine's and Balanchine's ballets the classical *pas* are sometimes used, less to interpret a general idea as in Fokine's work, more to express character or situation. It is a half-ironic use of classical *pas* which yet retain the loveliness of their emblematic geometry. This characterization in really good ballets is swift and witty, profound, memorable. It is not a travesty so long as even the simplest classical *pas* are used to delineate a situation expressively. In *The Good-humoured Ladies*, one of Massine's earliest works, the ladies course round the stage with *grands jetés*, thus expressing their confusion, their sense of imbroglio. Lifar's characteristic variation in *Les Matelots* (Lifar's part was taken by Lichine in the 1933 season) was at root a classical dance. In *La Pastorale*, the tall Doubrovska as the queen of film stars used to pass her *développés* over the head of her cavalier. That was a witty and memorable movement, a disdainful adjustment of a classical *pas* to current vulgarity, a complete expression of Hollywood situations in terms of ballet. By itself such a movement might seem a travesty of ballet; but the serious beauty of dancing and of the classically trained dancers, the beauty and brilliance of the décor and much of the music, existed as well in these ballets. It was ballet, the ballet style. And then, perhaps, after the interval we were treated to *Swan Lake* or to *Sylphides*. We enjoyed each of them, *Matelots* and *Swan Lake*, to the full, and each of them partly because of the other. They were entirely different variations upon the same theme; and we realized how fruitful, how vital was that theme, the ballet style. Thus Diaghilev could employ ballet to realize the most improbable conception: there was so much glory behind him. At the same time the purists grumbled. Still, Levinson admitted that the 1925 season was saved because in the midst of these innovations Diaghilev recalled Maestro Cecchetti, most famous of teachers, put him again in charge of the troupe. The dancers performed their classical exercises each day with renewed vigour. 'Diaghilev makes pebbles with gold,' Levinson complained after watching *Les Biches* or some such ballet. And if Diaghilev did so, what a relief it was, what a proof of omnipotence, since everyone except the very best artists are always trying to make gold with pebbles. (Though to attempt to make gold with pebbles is a preferable activity in my view to the one of those London choreographers, who, mistakenly endeavouring to emulate this period of Diaghilev's ballets, imagine that they contrive art in their making of pebbles from pebbles.)

There are many fine old royalists – and I am not at all sorry that it is so – who will quarrel with me for not having dealt with the classical ballet at the beginning of this book and for not having confined myself to the classical ballet. Well, I have given my explanations. But let me now express again an unqualified love for the classical ballet. There is something hellenic about it, all the more noticeable seeing that the classical ballet is the form imposed upon a northern romanticism. This hellenism is deeply founded and therefore entirely unlike the superficial hellenism of Isadora Duncan's dancing. Ballet tends to revert to the treatment of classical subjects with which it started. The open, *physical* and graceful attitudes of the marble Greek gods in whom emotion is shown as an outward-turned body, was dramatized by the classical technique. One witnesses in ballet the release of power, not its integration, just as in the eighteenth century a man introduced himself, showed himself, by turning his feet outwards and by the wide sweep of his arm and by the slow inclination of his body. But the classical ballet as we know it today, the ballet in which the classical technique, and particularly the allegro which is so lacking in other forms of the dance was developed to its uttermost, dates from the Romantic Age.

La Sylphide, a ballet which provided Taglioni with her most famous part, was first produced in 1832. Tights had been adopted some thirty or forty years before, freeing the dancers' legs for leaps. About the same time the power to turn out the foot and the whole leg up to the thigh at an angle of ninety degrees became *de rigueur*. Before 1780 or so dancers had been content to turn out at an angle of forty-five degrees only.[2] The successes of Camargo, however, have been attributed to the fact that she was exceptionally well 'turned out' for that period. Early in the nineteenth century, dancing on points was introduced. As I have already discussed the great importance to ballet's geometry of dancing *sur les pointes*, I shall make no further comment now.

Marie Taglioni was, so to speak, the product of the same line of thought as had produced these developments, just as Liszt, the unrivalled pianist, was the product of the age which perfected the piano and produced the quintessential piano music. *La Sylphide* was both the first Romantic ballet and the first ballet in which most of the classical technique was exploited as we know it today. The romantic ballet is the classical ballet, we have said.

'Another point of interest concerning this ballet' (*La Sylphide*), writes Mr. Beaumont in his *A Short History of Ballet*, 'is that the white muslin costume designed by Eugène Lami for Mlle. Taglioni – tight-fitting bodice leaving the neck and shoulders bare, bell-shaped skirt reaching midway between the knee and the ankle, pale pink tights and satin shoes – became the accepted uniform for the dancer of the pure classical ballet.' This is the *ballet blanc* of pale tights and white ballet skirts, indicating to some people a rather faded mythology, especially if they have never seen a proper ballet but only some of the semi-ballet interludes of pantomime or of music-hall. This mythology, in classical ballet at any rate, will not seem faded to those who come to it from the modern ballet; for the latter will have taught them to appreciate the ageless and always emblematic qualities of ballet's geometry, seen at its purest when performed in the traditional costume.

Amid the glories of the Russian Imperial schools, amid the snows of the North, served by the tumultuous glint of Russian art, the classical ballet reached its height. Would that we might see the four acts of *Swan Lake* instead of the second act only![3] Petipa, a Marseillais by birth who in his early days danced in Paris with Carlotta Grisi, the original Giselle, and with Fanny Elssler, was the choreographer in chief of this great period in Russia during the last half of the nineteenth century. According to Levinson, however, it is a mistake to attribute *Swan Lake* to Petipa alone as the programmes always do, at any rate that part of the ballet which we are accustomed to see. The additional choreographer was Petipa's understudy, Ivanov, who was responsible also for *Casse-Noisette*.

I have stated that in classical ballet the music was composed to order at the precise directions of the choreographer. This is not necessarily anything against it as music. The requirements of particular dances have inspired the best composers at all periods. In the early days there were the gaillarde, pavane, volte, courante, canaries, allemande, gavotte, bourrée, passepied, rigaudon, passecaille and sarabande. Indeed, these court measures provided forms for a considerable part of seventeenth- and eighteenth-century music. Handel and Gluck wrote gavottes and sarabandes as songs in their operas. The minuet which Haydn and Mozart introduced as the third movement of a symphony, was a dance invented by Beauchamps, Louis XIV's ballet master and the original formulator of the five positions. He is believed to have evolved the minuet from a folk-dance from Poitou.

An interesting treatise might be written on the influence of European dancing upon European music. Early nineteenth-century music in particular reflects the vast influence of national and peasant dances, and it was at this time too that the waltz spread like fire. The waltz obtains an apotheosis in ballet. All these dances and the music they inspired added greatly to the variety of the ballet spectacle. For side by side with the dances evolved out of the classical exercises, the intrinsic ballet so to say, there has always existed in classical ballet many popular dances which could be added at will and which, in varying degrees, were translated into terms of the ballet technique. Popular and folk-dances, especially since the time of Taglioni, have often served as the basis of a ballet. Upon such a basis, as upon its own intrinsic movements, classical ballet builds an architectonic that closely resembles the structure of a symphony. Modern ballet is constructed in a similar way. One of the great pleasures of a good ballet is therein to witness symphonic structure as something plastic.

Some popular steps like the ancient *pas de basque* belong to the intrinsic ballet. One cannot make any absolute distinction since nearly all the movements of classical ballet may be derived from some popular or court dance, two categories which are interrelated in their turn. No definition of a living art can be absolute. The obvious adapted importation, however, is generally called a 'character' dance in classical ballet:

such, for instance, are the frequent Spanish, Hungarian, Polish and Russian dances. For these dances, though they be reduced to terms of the stage, still retain their national style. The waltz, on the other hand, which, upon its first inception from the Bavarian *ländler*, grew rapidly into a cosmopolitan dance, has become part and parcel of ballet.[4]

Even the French classical-romantic ballet, like the earlier theatre ballet and like the court ballet that preceded it, was largely composed of 'character' dances. Moresque or grotesque dances, too, have existed in ballet since the earliest days, since the seventeenth-century masques and the earlier Italian *intermedi*.

And so, when all is said and done, it is impossible to isolate the 'intrinsic classical ballet'. Yet the great style itself which orders each assimilation is immediately recognizable, and we find it just as much in those modern ballets which, from the old point of view, are composed very largely of 'character' dances. We possess a great definition of this style in the ballet music of Tchaikovsky, a definition that can never be obscured. If music owes a great deal to dancing, the ballet style itself, the style of an evanescent art, owes its one and only permanent consolidation to Tchaikovsky, composer of the scores for *Swan Lake*, *The Sleeping Princess* and *Casse-Noisette*. A Tchaikovsky ballet is ballet twice over, ballet redoubled. For this music, apart from its context, that is to say, apart from any particular dance upon which Petipa or Ivanov had decided, is always impregnated with the spirit of the classical dance in general. More than anything else it has made that conception, the classical ballet, a definite and unescapable thing.

Tchaikovsky's ballet music seems firm yet crisp. It is the opposite of music that seems moist. True, a romantic haze hovers near: but it is a haze far above that obscures nothing and in virtue of which objects gain a startling white light, dazzling contours. This music contains a white or silvery languor, a vast silvery thunder, stage thunder perhaps, though not the stage thunder of tea-trays but of the Tsar's packed sideboards of silver. *Ballon* is forever enshrined in this music, so are the ephemeral, cygnet dart-points of the *fouettés* in the *pas de quatre* of *Swan Lake*, and a host of other movements. A Tchaikovsky waltz emits that glaucous brilliance by which this dance is glorified in ballet. There is something almost terrible in the climax of such music. But watch the stage: dancers never totter: at this moment they are more superb than usual: the final note reveals an attitude, a universal precision, a closure of virtuosity that is itself an acclamation.

With what fierce springs this music unwinds itself, how superbly it dawdles and fondles the adagio of the *pas de deux*, how brisk yet tender are the variations, and overwhelming to all but the dancers are the *coda* and the *presto*! This music of the severely classical dance is itself a modern ballet: for, just as in modern ballet everyday movements are englamoured, defined by synchronization as well, so in the ballet music of Tchaikovsky the very noises of the streets, the very tooting of horns, every noise and music that stumbles, is raised to the crystal pitch of the *ballet blanc*, translucent and transparent, clear yet refractive.

The *ballet blanc* of Tchaikovsky! As I write I see the *corps de ballet* of *Casse-Noisette* in steel-blue ballet skirts amid a snow ten times more pro-fuse than the fall *Pétrouchka* can command. They are waving branched sticks with baubles at their ends. This *corps de ballet* is the snow itself which Clara must traverse with the Nut-cracker before she can gain the kingdom of the Sugar Plum Fairy. The light, silent yet careering flakes spread and mass with a continuity unusual in ballet, and therefore insistent, running to the stiff notes of wood-wind and brass: then, at the conclusion of this exhausting dance, the *corps de ballet* stand or lie piled up, waving still their white brilliant blobs as the curtain descends and rises and descends.

One has watched at twilight an almost invisible and ghostly winter's rain become illumined and compact. The rain had turned to snow. Flakes whirled and then fell slowly, for they were light.

Ballet etherealizes movement: the undulations, never tortuous, are those of snow or the swan's white neck.

The Modern Ballet and Some German Forms of the Dance

From *To-night the Ballet* (1934)

At this point, I feel, I should expatiate for a little on the use to which classical *pas* have been put in music-hall and vaudeville. I should have a word to say about the precision of well-trained chorus girls, upon their outward kicks, upon the centipede effects of their pathetic if monotonous unison. But I must hurry on before the reader loses his picture of the classical ballet, since I want to relate the classical style more closely with recent developments of ballet and with the forms of the dance today which are hostile to ballet.

The modern ballet, we have found, is to be distinguished from classical ballet primarily from the angle of expressiveness. Instead of mimed action leading up to dances, the action of a modern ballet is expressed in the dancing itself. This more homogeneous mode of expressiveness gives increased scope to the composer and to the painter. Choreographer, painter and musician are all three subservient to an image, a poetic idea: though it often happens that it is the painter or composer whose score or whose sketch provided the original image. Modern ballet employs the classical style, if not the classical technique, to realize a conception more ductile than heretofore. I need not declare again the virtues of the classical style and of the spatial abstractions implicit in the classical dance. This great heritage has been put to intensive use by those who valued it most in all its abstract purity, by great dancers like Fokine and Nijinsky, for instance. The definition of ballet does not change, the only possible practical definition, one which, of course, is by no means watertight. Still, for those who want to understand, it will be useful to say that ballet is now, as always, any form of dance spectacle in which the movement has been invented or adapted *and is executed* by acknowledged masters of the classical technique.

A dancer's body is also his mind. A great dancer trained to possess the perfect control of his body that the classical technique alone will give, cannot conceive dances that betray the ballet style, though their movements may have nothing at all to do with the five positions.[1] His dances will show neatness and finish and above all *that contained style of projecting emotion of which this neatness and finish are the product.*

Why is the link between the classical and modern ballet so all-important? First, the continuity of style and of the European theatre about which I write throughout this book is thus preserved.

The classical technique, we have said, is the European mode of the dance in rarefied form. It gives the European dancer control over every muscle of his body. It is our ABC of the dance, or rather, the five positions correspond to the musical scale, that arrangement of notes, single in themselves, on which the complexities of European music are based. We have understood that the supreme compactness which the ballet dancer alone possesses seems to have a special relevance to the ideal organization of modern life. Owing to his superb training, there is no vagueness in the movement or the postures of the ballet dancer even though he performs the loose or 'free' or heavy motions beloved of the Germans. Such movements have indeed passed into ballet and, as a rule, only those whom we feel are able to execute *pas* with virtuoso ease and lightness will convey *definite* meaning by loose or heavy movements.

But let me admit that even though ballet alone of the European arts today is able to impress us with its style, yet modern life is egregiously without style: and that, therefore, the lonely and abstracted quality of effort will tend to demand projection within the style of ballet. Indeed, the ballet style has obtained some poignancy for the grimmer aspects of the modern, and even German, soul. We have seen it in Massine's choreographic symphonies. Just as the Dorians, a northern people, descended into the sun of the Mediterranean and accepted the comprehensive steady forms of southern art, just as the Gothic spirit flowered in the Italian Renaissance, so, over and over again, northern romanticism, northern excess, has become something more concrete and more delightful, emblazoned within the style of ballet which it has thus enhanced.

To compare the German dancing company of Herr Jooss with Les Ballets Russes de Monte Carlo is like comparing a Dutch picture (and its cloying dog-like intimacy) with an Italian Renaissance picture. Jooss's dancers have not undergone the full classical training for which they are an excellent advertisement: since it is not only the choreography that lacks style, but each movement itself as executed by these dancers. Within their limits they are well trained: they have a fine precision, considerable neatness and gymnastic power: but unless that neatness, we now realize, conveys to us the sense of style as does the fishmonger's neatness in filleting a fish, it is a synchronization and little else, even though it be an expressive movement from one point of view. For, expression is nothing in itself. It must be lifted on to a ledge, a very high, a very smooth ledge. Not that Herr Jooss is not an artist. I have a great admiration for *The Green Table*. The first scene has real style, ballet style: that is to say, it is memorable, conveys a *complete* impression, provides a *definite* sphere in which the imagination of the audience can live for ever. But otherwise there is the absence of style that results from the *directness* of the symbolism, the imperfect conventionalization of expressiveness whether of face, arms or legs. As a lover of ballet I missed the blithe ballet face, the look into the distance that is practised even at the bar: I missed the head that comes round from a pirouette before the body, a mask expressive of ease, of lightness, of triumph, a convention, however, that is practical, since it saves the dancer from giddiness.

Herr Jooss's approach is too particular and too intense. The dancing of his troupe is an extremely agile romping, an extremely well conducted charade; but it is not a turning out, a display. *A Ball in Old Vienna* has a little rather facetious charm but no glamour. *Impressions of a Great City* shows even less feeling for the stage. It is cinematographic, directly impressionist, fleeting, with no more architecture than mental flow in the raw possesses.

The Green Table and Massine's *Les Présages* make a good comparison since their subject-matter is so similar. It is unlikely that many readers will have seen them both: so I will only observe that the figure of Death (Destiny in *Présages*) possesses according to Massine an antic influence

228

over the other dancers rather than a mystical, necrophilic influence. His inescapable magic, according to Massine, needs no exploitation: it is a fact which makes marionettes of us all. Massine does not describe to us the slowness of Death's hypnotism. Once again, more is left to the imagination, but our imagination has been provided with a precise figure. Dancing better expresses antics than hypnotic evolutions, at least in Europe.

The most general criticism from the ballet point of view that one will make about the Jooss dancers and those like them is in relation to their 'line'. Their limbs, and particularly their arms, lack 'line', the 'line' that is the constant pre-occupation of the ballet dancer, at any rate, in his daily classes. The gestures of miming as well are subjected by the ballet dancer to the same conception of harmony. In the modern ballet the pure lines of classical ballet are often disregarded or even reversed. Such movements are variations or departures from the pure line in which the ballet dancer is trained. However, it is not only that one knows it to be so but feels it so: for one cannot mistake the trained dancer except under such circumstances. If his line is distorted from the classical angle, we feel that it is meant to be thus: it is still 'line', for we can see that he is trained to perfect equilibrium, literally to his very finger tips. Arms, hands and fingers are studied for every movement in the classical training. This fact, coupled with the fact that the arms of Jooss's dancers are of all their anatomy the parts most open to criticism, forms a sufficient commentary upon the criticism that Jooss himself has made of classical ballet. When asked what he considered to be the principal defect of the classical technique he said, in effect, that the classical technique paid too much attention to the legs and afforded too little scope for the dancer's arms.

The reader will now perhaps understand better what brilliance a ballet training can bestow on even ordinary movements. It is not solely a question of carriage and control, it will be seen, but the far more general influence of style. Behind the successive innovations of Diaghilev there still existed the unsurpassed classical tradition and achievements of the Imperial schools. Did we not know it all the time, or, rather, feel it? It was not necessary to have the information. Every movement or pose a great dancer makes, no matter what it is, imparts something of his history as a dancer. There is a photograph of Massine standing dressed for his part in the play, *The Miracle*. Not only can one see that this is the face and the figure of a superb ballet dancer (he is standing in voluminous robes) but we feel as well that we might deduce from this one photograph, unconnected with ballet, all his principal parts as a dancer. Then again one may be sure that a dancer who every day practises the classical exercises, whose mind as well as body is imbued with this style, when he branches out and contrives a ballet with many 'free' movements, will use some of the framework as well as the technique of classical ballet. There will be a recognizable *pas de deux*, a recognizable adagio and allegro. Not always, of course, but generally.

The modern ballet in general, then, is but a wide and free exploitation of the classical technique which serves as the point of reference and sometimes as the point of departure, just as harmony and counterpoint serve modern composers. But why must I insist on this conclusion? I have given many reasons, but the chief of them, I suppose, is the attack which ballet now suffers at the hands of those who see no further necessity for dancers to be trained in the full classical technique. I have instanced Herr Jooss, I have deplored the absence of the ballet spirit, of the ballet atmosphere in his choregraphy. It would be much better if occasionally his dancers did an *entrechat* or got on to their points. So often their situation seems to suggest these movements and one feels that they avoid executing them (that is to say, *entrechats* which they could do) on principle.

We must take some account of the prestige of those dancers who are definitely hostile to ballet and who, none the less, have had a great influence on modern ballet. We must now consider some of these innovators. I do not propose to defend the ballet against them. That should be unnecessary if I have managed at all to communicate my love for ballet. What will interest us is the effect of these dancers on ballet and the extent to which we can approve of their aims.

The first and the greatest of these innovators in modern times was

Isadora Duncan. She has had no direct successor. Her achievement was entirely individual, and the same is true of all such dancers who have achieved anything. Compare this with the direct heritage of a Camargo, of a Vestris, of a Taglioni. Every great dancer enriches ballet, even dancers who are not ballet dancers.

Isadora danced barefoot and her movements were 'natural' movements. She felt that she was expressing in her person the deep tingling dance inherent in Nature. She symbolized a revolt against artificiality and virtuosity, and narrow conventions. She chose to substitute for the exhibition of the classical dance an exhibitionism. Her appeal was not of a definite imaginative content but of the widest and vaguest stimulation in the name of Life. Isadora was a remarkable personality, a phenomenon, and her aims are not without their context in our period. There was some deep truth in what she had to give. Yet a stimulation so wide and so vague has no future, no possibility of direct development except in its influence upon those who, innocent of the touch of the bogus inseparable from the claims of so universal an expressionism, supply these 'urges' with definition. It was the ballet alone that inherited the truth that Isadora contained: it was the phenomenon of Isadora that provoked Fokine to invent for ballet a wider expressiveness. Though she be endlessly imitated, her own technique or absence of technique can have no future. Her attitude to music, for instance, was in itself empty. She did not contrive from music a plastic shape. She reproduced the music, the body of the music, like a conductor. She was a dream-like, barefoot, amateur, androgynous conductor, a figure suitable, one would imagine, for television rather than for the theatre.

Isadora desired to express by her dancing the vague and universal surges that men are felt to have in common with the animal world and even with the whole of Nature. Dancing, she thought, should express Life itself, Movement itself, a conception that embraced the running of the waves and the voice of the wind. All the present-day German, Central European and American schools of the 'free' dance about which we hear so much, are obsessed, if not with the same 'philosophy' of movement, at any rate with the same degree of expressionism. And so, a certain trance-like quality characterizes the work of all these dances. Now, a mesmeric kind of movement in Oriental dancing, Indian and Javanese especially, conveys something that is most intense. These movements, often sinuous, are generally of immediate religious significance or are, at any rate, expressive of direct and definite cultural symbols. My pleasure in Uday Shankar is almost as great as my pleasure in ballet. Oriental dancing, though, cannot provide me with an equal stimulus. European 'Yoga', on the other hand, is just trance-like and expressionist (and bogus) since it is so largely the product of the vaguest of emotions, of a more or less nameless overstretching or discontent often tinged with arrogance.

The contained and definite outwardness of the true theatre and of ballet has no appeal for the German Yogis of the dance. They would but show the deeper inner ferment as the deeper inner ferment in which they have so great and so vulgar a pride. Their characteristic dances are continuous, a deep monotonous surge of mood, a come-and-go like the waves of the sea. They offer us a half-awake, half-sleeping state resulting from this crude imitation of what are thought to be the deeper layers of the mind or the dormant orientations of the body. The brilliant outwardness of European art is rejected in favour of this entirely European form of exhibitionism, in favour of the terrible and formless German 'yearning', in favour of the deeper vulgarity of the modern world. For is there anything more vulgar than a European 'Yoga' with its hasty mazy mesh of improvised gods and surges? Many performers of this kind do a great deal of dancing with their hair which they toss as a curtain in front of their eyes and then back again on top of their heads. Whatever the subject of such a dance may be, one is conscious of the emotion to possess or express emotion, an expressionism in the abstract, an unashamed exhibitionism vaunting exhibitionism.

The heads and knees in such dances go up, then the head goes down over the feet... Movements of this kind evoke the residues of experience, churning them up, the ups and the downs of the life-flow (and this is sometimes thought to be very hellenic!). It is a loose, watery, retrospective emotion. The movements express everything – and nothing.

Note the dreamy yet portentous recognition of the symbol of striving in the arm waved aloft around the head, so typical of Dalcroze conception. Contrast this movement with the ballet fourth position *en haut* in which the arms become the most graceful, the most flower-like of pennants. And again, contrast the eyes of the German dancers half-closed as in a dream, with the wide mask of the ballet face.

Talking of masks, I should be doing Mary Wigman and other famous performers of 'grotesque' *dances de concert* a grave injustice if I should seem to imply that they do not possess masks. Of course they have them, real masks (ballet dancers discarded masks in 1773), and many other accessories besides culled from the Japanese theatre, now from Javanese puppets, now from darkest Africa, etc. Such eclecticism and such accessories of style, themselves suggestive of the most rigid formalism, are paralleled by the work of many 'modern' sculptors who employ similar strictures drawn from diverse styles and often a similar uniform abstraction both to conceal and also to advance their own innate bias towards expressionism. 'Scratch a cubist and you will find a sentimentalist,' it has been said. That is not necessarily true. But what is true is that if you scratch an expressionist (a believer in the 'profound' and 'forceful' *per se*) you will find somebody who, but for arrogance, might have made a success as a bad impressionist painter.

In the foregoing paragraphs I have lumped together, unjustifiably, all the various schools of the 'free' dance. This is unfair because their aims are often most diverse. Moreover one and all, it seems, hate each other and with good reason. It is wrong to imply, for instance, that all these schools favour the soulful movements of eurhythmics. Many of them despise so-called Greek dancing as well, though not because of its heaviness but because the fashion is for darker gods and darker feelings. Exhibitionism, to be pure and frank, must necessarily possess ugliness and grossness of movement, it is found. Jerky, distorted and fat movements have come into fashion in the guise of 'grotesque' dances. The prettiness of ballet is, of course, condemned.

I am aware as I write these words that the tone I have adopted and my manner of attack resemble those of Sir Reginald Blomfield in one of his diatribes directed at modern art. Now, I do not wish to be associated with Sir Reginald Blomfield. As it happens I admire greatly those aspects of contemporary visual art which, if he knew about them, would provoke Sir Reginald Blomfield the more. Why, then, would I tend to agree with him (but I forget: he would detest many modern ballets, music, dancing, scenery, everything) if he turned his attention to dancing?

I think the explanation is as follows. While allowing to some of them an important element of discovery to which I shall refer later, I condemn the exponents of the 'free' dance in general because it is so little necessary. By that I mean that for the most part these exponents are inventing for the dance an aesthetic situation: they are copying the situation of the other visual arts, forcing it upon the dance which does not require it, or at any rate does not require it to the same degree. One will entertain, however, a certain respect for the researches of Laban. Encouraged by similar activities in the other visual arts, he has attempted to isolate the geometry of dancing (and, incidentally, he has been led to adopt or re-adopt many of the classical movements). Behind this seemingly formal and harmless research there lurks, of course, the usual gross expressionism. But that is not the point I want to make now. The point I want to make now is that owing to the fact that the dancer is, so to speak, canvas, brush, paint, subject and painter in one, the formal qualities of ballet to which I have amply referred, have at no period been overlaid. Ballet, I have attempted to explain, was the last of the great European arts to develop and the only art today in which a grand style is alive and contemporary. This is a great piece of luck for us. Owing to Diaghilev we enjoy the High Renaissance of ballet. He showed us that within the classical technique there existed a contemporary art. Many modern painters and sculptors are compelled to start at the wrong end, that is, to seek out the fundamentals of their arts or what, for the moment, they can consider to be fundamentals, before they can commence to work, instead of realizing those fundamentals in the course of more superficial studies. They may be forced to act thus (and not inspired to do so as they may think) because the fundamentals are all that remain to them in the present state of society. Yet it is possible that fundamentals in themselves provide little more sustenance than the more delightful kind of irrelevancy. Ballet is fortunate: European dancing does not need the isolation of its formal qualities. Have I not extracted some of them already from Fokine's work and from the classical ballet itself? Ballet has grown rapidly in recent years, always adding to a store. It does not need debunking.

Many exponents of the 'free' dance are content with the minimum of technique. To the majority of them the arduous ballet training appears unnecessary and 'forced'. Again, this remark sounds like an academic stricture on modern painters. 'They have no technique,' runs the complaint. 'Any child can and does make such daubs,' and by any child is meant anyone. Many modern painters have been academically trained. Modern paintings need any amount of technique sometimes in the academic sense, and where such technique is not paraded it is often the Diaghilev situation of making pebbles with gold. But that is not the point. It is impossible to define or isolate the technique of painting in general. One might well say that there are as many techniques as there are painters. But this is not equally true of dancing. In all dancing an identical instrument is employed, the human body. The diverse instruments of diverse techniques in painting is one and the same object in dancing. Leaving acrobatic and virtuoso effects in general on one side, technique in dancing is immediately defined and judged in terms of muscle control and just that. The ballet training gives the widest possible control, a vast and graduated control over every muscle.

Mary Wigman tells her pupils to dance the way they feel. No one is really in a position to teach them. I have nothing against this attitude when it is stripped of all pretension. The vast majority of even young people could not, by any stretch of the imagination, become ballet dancers. They are probably too old to begin. At the same time they may have some gift for movement. By all means encourage them to dance. Let them dance as they feel if they can do so without intending a lot of arrogant 'Yoga', and if they realize that what they desire to express by dancing is already largely defined by the severe limits of their technical power. It would be most interesting to watch within this narrow world what they did feel. They might even evolve some forms which the superior technique of ballet could exploit. I quarrel with such dancers only when they have the impertinence to think that they are the prototypes of the modern dance.

The widest accusation that one will prefer against the German fallacy is that, in the attempt to realize something 'utter' in this or that direction, they have lost sight of the stage, the scene of performance, the European theatre. They know nothing of vivacity or brilliance. There is no true allegro in any of their dances. How could there be? The dancers have not the technique. In the interests of expressing the omnipotent self they repudiate a wonderful and creative style which can be put to every other use. And we are so tired of self-expression as an end-in-itself, especially when associated with portentous and precious simplicity. Things are as they must be in those schools of the visual arts which are serious. But surely it is no particular cause for congratulation if it is true that our most acclaimed potter cannot model a pure form that is not in some sense a self-portrait. I have yet to see from Mr. Staite Murray's hands a simple pot which has not conveyed to me the feeling of a self-portrait. In more elaborate arts the element of self-portraiture is overlaid. The ballet is a spectacle in which many artists and many performers have combined their powers under the auspices of a style. Ballet needs a big stage and a big company. Wigman, on the other hand, prefers the situation of the solitary potter with a drum or two for wheel. Wigman, of course, unlike the modern potter, is an avowed expressionist. That is in her favour.

Whether we like it or not, whether we conceal it or not, expressionism is rampant today. It permeates second-rate contemporary art often under the curious aspect of debunking, abstraction and functionalism. At the same time one must recognize that, for better or for worse, an attempted pre-occupation with the deeper layers of the mind, with the inside, so to speak, of man, is characteristic of many of the more successful manifestations in contemporary art. It is this trend that, more than anything else, gives a vastly increased relevance to ballet today. Have we not seen the ballet stage as an open box in which the internal processes are externalized in a definite and immediate form? No wonder that Picasso, and even the Surréalistes, have often worked for the ballet and there attained an increased relevance for their thought. The greatest opportunity for modern art is in the theatre, that is to say, in the ballet.

Now, there is some sort of justification for expressionism in general and for the German dancers in particular, so far as expressionism is at all the crude yet impersonal symptom of cultural unrest with its concomitant strangled romanticism. But as far as dancing is concerned, this essence has been distilled by the style of ballet alone. I am thinking of Massine's *Les Présages*. Ballet today is the Picasso of the dance. That painter enforces upon northern expressionism the impersonal Mediterranean form of projection. Ballet has done the same service for the German 'free' movements.

As far back as 1913 Nijinsky's *Sacre du printemps* incorporated the contrapuntal subtleties of Dalcroze movement. One will not quarrel with Dalcroze. In fact one will recognize that he has made a contribution to the relationship of music and movement. One will not quarrel so long as his exercises are intended as education, as a training of the rhythmic sense and as a mode of physical release. Dalcroze himself has more than once declared that his dances are not meant for stage performance. But many of his followers are not so wise.

In *Présages* we see many adapted Central European movements associated chiefly with the name of Laban, and a subject which itself expresses a naked kind of striving. These are lifted, and successfully lifted, on to the glorious ledge of ballet. Wherein lies the vast difference for stage performance between the Laban movements and the Massine version of the Laban movements? I have endeavoured throughout to explain the kind of projection that ballet favours and to show why it is the proper theatrical mode. Let me sum up the difference once more with the same analogy. It is the difference between the untroubled classical art of the Mediterranean with its comprehensive mode of projecting feelings that are never consciously dissociated from the forms of art, and the 'direct' expressionist art so often characteristic of the

North when in reaction from the South, an art contorted, pettish and overdone. The ballet smooths away the excesses of this compulsive northern child so far as they are spoiling fevers. Similarly the art of Picasso is a steadying hand from the warm pressure of which all artists may take confidence.

La Boutique Fantasque

From *Russian Ballets* (1935)

Ballet in One Act.
Music by G. Rossini.
Arranged and orchestrated by Ottorino Respighi.
Choreography by Léonide Massine.
Curtain and scenery by André Derain, executed by A. Derain and
Mr. and Mme. V. Polunin.
Costumes by A. Derain, executed by Alias.
First performance on June 5th, 1919
at THE ALHAMBRA THEATRE, London

La Boutique Fantasque
Cast of first performance

The Snob	M. Stanislas Idzikovsky
The Melon Hawker	M. Kostetsky
A Cossack Chief	M. Nicolas Zverev
Five Cossacks	MM. Kostrovsky, Kegler, Okhimovsky, Ribas, Macagno
A Cossack Girl	Mme. Istomina
Dancing Poodles and	Mme. Vera Clark, M. Nicolas Kremneff
Can-can Dancers	Mme Lydia Lopokova, M. Leonide Massine
Twelve of their friends	Mmes. Klementovitch, Vera Nemtchinova, Kostrovska, Slaviska, Istomina, Wassilevska, Radina, Grantzeva, Olkhina, Petipa, Pavlovska, Mikulina
Conductor	M. Henry Defosse

The music starts on tip-toe. They are playing with plucked strings before the rise of the curtain, a good augury for ballet. Already, as we settle ourselves, we surmise the delicate tension that we shall feel when the ballerina is on her points, when she is, as it were, suspended just above the ground: taut yet aerial, she best exposes the geometry of her form.

Like the dancer's body, the overture does not convey a generalized impression only. In the repeat, the end of each phase is suffused with the plunging of kettle-drums. This delicate music is a march. We may visualize a brisk mechanism such as a fountain-jet of lithe strength that splashes resounding through floors into cellars, there to settle and thence to rise, drawn up once more through the fountain. We shall derive similar images from the ballet. At the same time this fountain effect is not in the least bit rarefied or diffuse. There is, indeed, something so robust yet graceful in the liveliness of the Rossini music that we may at once visualize the human embodiment of the fountain, the ballet dancer, particularly the Russian ballet dancer. And we may recall that *salle de la danse* at the back of the Casino (itself a *Boutique fantasque*) at Monte Carlo, where so many Russian ballets have been rehearsed, a room from which the dancers emerge on to a terrace that looks toward Italy (as does this late Rossini music) and commands a perfect view of Cap Martin lying upon the sparkling sea like a dancer's arm upon the air of the stage. The dancers have taken with them into the rehearsal room this vast sunlit theatre of natural animation: particularly, it seems, for this ballet of an animated toy-shop.

Meanwhile, now that our expectancy is at the flood, the curtain parts, revealing a drop-curtain painted by Derain. It shows a dancer holding a mask and a man with a guitar. There are curtains behind them. In the gap between the curtains there is a table with fruit on plates and a basket of flowers: behind again, a landscape in which an umbrella pine is prominent. We shall encounter this shape often enough in the ballet.

At first sight this painting suggests the inertia of things become entirely generalized. It seems to be in strange contrast with the plunging fountain of the overture. Here are the bare bones of ballet, music and dancer, before reaching the destination, a theatre. These figures are before the curtain, but there is no stage behind them. They pose near an approach to a town or (to change the metaphor as does the painting) amid the heavy odours of lodging-house equipment, mostly in costume yet partly in *déshabillé*. But the fact that this drop-curtain will rise in a moment and reveal the stage, suggests to us the swift development of theatrical time. We pass at once from what is either preparatory or completed to what is in process, from the general to the particular.

The drop-curtain has risen. It is afternoon: we are to witness a scene of commotion that will constantly remind us of waters that topple at a fountain's height. The place is a Victorian toy-shop of 1860 or so, looking out upon Nice harbour. In this ballet, as upon the drop-curtain, the Victorian *mise-en-scène* receives an airing, largely at the behest of the composer of the music, Rossini, himself a survival into Victorian times from the Rococo age.

When the curtain goes up the stage is empty for five bars of the music (though it turns out later that there are two dancers in the form of dolls at one side). In this interval we may measure the space which the dancers' movements will make significant. Apart from the setting, the stage itself has an interest for us, similar to that of a piece of sand over which the tide will play. But the assault of dancing upon the stage is an assault of love: as soon as the shopkeeper and his apprentice unlock the gate and enter the shop at the back to the strains of a clipped revolving musical-box tune, it is as if a highly efficient and fully wound mechanism, the necessary mechanism of a clock, were introduced at the back of a clock-face. Now it will go.

The shopkeeper, bending his body back and with his hands behind him, moves forward with long strides. The apprentice patters about with limp arms, cocking his shoulders. His arms are like the great flaps of a spaniel's ears, while his shoulders suggest the young forward ears of some other breed. After darting around and dusting, he comes to the centre of the stage to pick his nose. From his side there hangs a huge red handkerchief. It is the puppy's playful and breathless tongue.

While the apprentice is busy with his nose, a ragged boy slinks through the shop door intent on some small theft. He fingers the dolls on the stands.

The shopkeeper grabs the boy and with the help of the apprentice belabours him as the rhythm of the music demands. The boy breaks loose and runs for the door where, as Mr. C. W. Beaumont has put it,[1] 'He nearly collides with two old ladies about to enter the shop who, overcome with consternation, open their tiny parasols in a posture of defence.' We may here recall the umbrella pines painted upon the back-cloth, realizing that a Victorian aspect may be attributed to them. It is refreshing to find that Riviera trees as well as shiny slothful plants are in harmony with the gestures of that age.

Released from their attitude, the English old maids transmute their ruffled feelings into ice-smooth glances with the use of the lorgnette. Both the shopkeeper and his assistant are performing some literal scraping and bowing, as well they might in a ballet. Of course the ladies take advantage of their servility. They convey to the shopmen that their apologies are both useless and indispensable.

The action of the ballet so far has been at long range. But now the ladies consent to examine two dolls on revolving stands. The apprentice works the mechanism that moves their limbs. The patterns of pure mime give way to oppositions that engage the protagonists in a closer contact and which more nearly approach to dancing. The musical-box tune has returned. The workings of the *Boutique fantasque* are in full swing.

The sense of an increased plasticity is heightened by the entry of the apprentice with some miniature dolls (samples of the stock) at the end of a pole. He pokes and withdraws this bush of dolls' heads near the spinsters' faces as if they, the spinsters, were dogs begging for a bone. Both their involuntary assumption of this part and the reflexes of renewed hauteur increase their bobbing movements.

In ballet we contemplate the feelings that are expressed on the stage, intrepidly but in no wise callously. The calm and carefulness of our discernment is induced by the geometry underlying balletic articulation, a form that bestows plastic value upon movement however slight and that endows with shapeliness glances however despairing.

From this very constancy arises the constancy with which the same images can be provoked in us throughout a ballet: we may thus take our delight in imagining approximations between incidents and movements and musical phrases that are not otherwise to be connected.

These ladies, for instance, bobbing beneath the pole with its plume of dolls' heads above them, remind us of the spurting fountain that we envisaged first during the overture, and of the umbrella pines upon drop-curtain and backcloth. But again, the image may be changed at will for another of equal gaiety. For the fount of gaiety in *Boutique* is inexhaustible. A good character-ballet provides for the mind a very large field of allusiveness, although it is itself entirely definite or particularized. Never does it define except in terms of a plasticity that serves particular incident. To these slender incidents and neat movements the doors of our imagination are opened wide. The appeal of a good ballet is perennial to the imagination in the manner of the finest poems.

We may now see the old ladies differently as they bob beneath the pole of dolls; in terms of horsemen who rise and fall a short distance in the saddle, slightly wooden, it may be, in general effect, and so not altogether unsuited to this toy-shop.

This image of woodenness and the theme of mechanical responses are strengthened by the entrance of the American with his family. He is dressed in brown checks of square cut; he sucks stolidly and childishly at a corn-cob pipe. After a show of greeting between the arrivals and the spinsters and after a further inspection of the dolls, there occurs a moment of unanimous expostulation, on the part, that is, both of customers and of shopmen. The former express their appreciation, the latter warmly beat the air with ceremonious gestures. Expostulation then attains a moment of unanimous furore: the several gestures fall together to make a pattern like the fitted pieces of a jig-saw puzzle.

These rhythmic and almost mechanical gestures of politeness prepare us for the introduction on to the stage of the tarantella dolls, posed upon a trolley like huge figurines. The dolls represent Sicilian peasants: they stand square on the trolley as it is drawn to the centre of the stage. We watch a tableau of heroic peasant attitude. On the trolley is displayed that immobility of expressive gesture with which in a ballet expostulation must end.

These figures contain also a new theme. Their deportment is in contrast to that of polite society. The peasant girl is like a young bull. Something of the aura that plays around horns is seated on her red and tossed-back headdress. In a moment the dolls will leap from the trolley and dance a tarantella. Fountains of movement then play and spread larger and higher. It is a fountain worked in conjunction with a musical box.

As with all ballet dances, we sense that this tarantella has a most definite shape or span. It begins, it rages and it ceases upon the note, a well-regulated clock-work device whose propulsion seems entirely human, as indeed it is.

The dolls have ended their dance. They are put back on the trolley and wheeled off. Meanwhile the world of polite movement is revived uproariously. The two American children whirl the spinsters round in imitation of the tarantella. The children are reproved and they return to their seats and swing their legs.

The swinging of the legs to which those who take the part of child spectators in this ballet so often have recourse, contains a special interest: perhaps because of the seemingly self-generated movement of a swinging leg once it has been started, a suggestion of perpetual motion that contrasts with the timed machinery of the dolls. And then again, these swinging legs swing free, to and fro above the ground upon which the dolls exhaust their strength. Thus, by contrast, the swinging of legs from chairs heightens an impression of the stage as a space that is *consumed* by the dancers' steps: since one will conceive the effort that the dancers put forth as being no less directed than are the carver's blows upon his stone. 'Dancing is an assault on space, an assault of love, a similar assault to that of the carver upon his stone or that of the farmer as he ploughs the earth.'[2] Dancing reveals the dimensions and texture of the surface upon which it is performed. The air through which dancers move is shaped by them.

New toys are now produced, four playing cards, the Queen of Clubs, the Queen of Hearts, the King of Spades and the King of Diamonds. Before they start their mazurka they are forced by the assistant to bend or bow from the waist. When he releases his pressure they shoot back upright. One is reminded of the snapping movement with which cards are shuffled. But now that the mazurka which they dance is in full swing, one is conscious again of the plumed umbrella pines upon the backcloth, one is reminded of the wooden lilt of horsemen upon trotting steeds, of the lifting lowering head of a high fountain.

The mazurka is a dance that causes its participants to look tall whatever their size. It is the dance of the fiercest cavaliers (hence the moustaches of these kings) who, accoutred in the ballroom, envisage the tirelessness of their ancestral plains. From the long run of this dance in which occurs a rearing, entangled or syncopated motion that seems to renew impetus, we experience the sensations of the saddle on a day throughout which the horseman, tall above the circumambient plain, has ridden apt and dexterous, converting with his pliant strength each flounder into a prance, each tremor into a suave punctilious gallop.

Similarly the spurt of a fountain rides the air. It is a delight to see these court card dancers as a condensation of the liquid and ethereal. The saturated primary colours of their robes, intense blue and red and yellow, are condensations of the paler spectrum hues shown by foaming sunlit water. Such condensation is dear to the mind, a beauty become more tangible, gained for the earth's floor.

And now, heralded in the music by a slow and homely involution of the refrain with which the English ladies entered the shop, a new family of customers appear, a Russian merchant with his wife and five children. He is a huge bearded man, clothed in national costume. He has brought to the toy-shop a caravan, as it were, of progeny across those plains of eastern Europe that the mazurka has conjured up. They have come through snows to this southern climate. They are hot and extremely tired. Slowly they pace in: each time the slow tune reaches its nadir they wipe their brows.

Suddenly, in true Russian fashion, the mood of the children changes: they swarm through the shop and prance around their monolithic parents. The music iterates in more lively form the theme of buzzing curiosity already associated with the examination and comment upon the toys. The children fly hither and thither (the assistant, with his puppy-like sense of excitement, runs so violently as to disappear off the scene for a moment), but always to return to their parents.

At this point one may begin to harbour another image that is more or less constantly evoked throughout the ballet, an image of the insect swarm and of the busy excited noises from their wings. One may have remembered *Boutique* and the children's animation when, in a shop of old books, one has pulled down a volume and some insect has rocked away violently and noisily only to bump back again. In the second-hand shop or the shop of curiosities such animation belongs to death and corruption: in the *Boutique fantasque* this same animation is lifted from the shop's more wearied stock and bestowed upon children in whom it appears as a renewal of energy. The moth does not know the meaning of the book it devours: but these moth-like children are enraptured by each exhibit.

It is typical of a Diaghilev ballet that a shop of curious toys should be represented as neat, as open to the Mediterranean air, and that the intimate moth-like life, more usually associated with such a shop, should yet suggest itself; but only in terms of unequivocal delight with things that are new. Nothing dream-like or wondering, nothing German, nothing inner or internal, nothing impressionist, *nothing picturesque*. In the true theatre, inner processes, and emotions aroused by things picturesque, indeed much feeling that is vague and indefinable, will be projected as forms that are positive and particular: nor will these therefore be arid, nor consciously symbolic as a rule.

The rushings of the assistant to and fro have not been unproductive. For now there appears a most ingenious mechanical contraption, a combination toy composed of two figures which in action have different yet complementary movements. So complete is the little dance that one almost visualizes tiny and precarious rails on which a toy of such a kind would be balanced. There is a suggestion of slight top-heavy lurches common both to that tame leviathan of the streets, the tram, kept on its path by diminutive grooves of steel, and to the railed trains, propelled by clock-work, that scour the corners of the nursery at a destructive pace. This combination toy, however, is well in control and is not over-fast. In fact, one of the figures advances diagonally in a most precious fashion, while the other, a melon-seller with a hand-cart full of melons, shuffles round a half circle that meets the end of the first-mentioned figure's diagonal.

The melon-seller's shuffle and stiff sway behind his cart suggest more especially the minute, evenly spaced jerks (uphill the same as downhill) typical of cog propulsion. As for the other figure of this toy, all the unrivalled control of direction suggested by the cog seems to be implicit in his personality. He is small and he is dapper: his oblique approach should not deceive us. For he is the Snob whose aim is always compact. His stilted approach betrays no lack of confidence: in fact he is self-important, seriously so. Otherwise why should he stop to twirl in the air, why too should he twirl his moustache?

The melon-seller with the Sicilian hand-cart is his valet. The servant goes through the rigmarole of offering a melon slice, and the Snob, after one impatient refusal, treats it rapidly and passionately as a mouth-organ and hands it back. While the Snob is drawing chords from the melon slice, the solicitous butler stripes his shoes with a polishing rag and brushes down the back of his suit. Later, to the utmost consternation of them both, the Snob is run over by the hand-cart. He jumps up, twirls in the air more neatly than ever and ends the dance with the fingers of his right hand controlling his outraged moustache.

The energy with which he enforces appearances is galvanic, electric or nervous. No doubt the prototype of this comic little character is the spoilt child (riding a toy bicycle?) who is able to keep some solemn-faced adult tripping to fulfil his fancies. Indeed, his party shoes and mannikin finery suggest as much. It is the child's whim that the servant with his solemn face should trot round after him, wheeling a hand-cart of melons, no doubt a favourite fruit.

After this dance the children jump from their chairs and swarm again through the shop. Finally they discover a row of toy soldiers behind a sheet, five Cossacks with their chief. The assistant lifts each in turn and sends him bouncing sideways toward the centre of the stage. These are soft-footed toy soldiers, soft-footed in their Russian boots. Their first motions suggest that they have been rooted, but also that their roots will take new if momentary hold the instant that they are transplanted or even cast down. Each bearded soldier has a baton which he clanks on the floor during the dance that follows. These batons express the vaunt, the lordship of deadly impact that an armed man owns. Fierceness resides in the very unison of their movement. One is reminded of the warriors in the Argonaut myth who grew from sown dragons' teeth. The deep green baize of their uniforms suggests a foraging kind of vegetation, armed like the cactus painted on the backcloth.

A Cossack girl enters and is passed along to the Cossack chief at the end of the row (he is dressed in blue). She is, no doubt, what used to be called a 'garrison hack'. To my mind she is the rare, unlikely flower which is worn by some cactacious plants once in twenty years or so. Later in the ballet we shall see the Cossacks raise upon their batons a still lovelier flower.

The dance is over. The Cossacks are removed to the interior of the shop. And now the shopkeeper and his assistant are enticing toy poodles along the stage, a male and a female which, in the manner of performing animals, are upright upon their hind legs. It is not necessary to enlarge upon the pretence that they are toys since real quadrupeds in this position, displaying something that looks absurdly like a distorted human chest, always prompt one to think that they are playthings rather than animals, or else that they are semi-human. The ground is prepared, then, for dancers to take the part of performing animals, and to do so with wit.

The female runs to the middle and throws back her head and lifts a leg up backward almost to meet it. Attracted, the male dog bounds

after her. Following a moment of tense anticipation she bounds away
once more. During the amatory game the female especially shows us the
full rhythm of caprice that may be learned only from animals: neither
of them can keep sufficiently still for the other's purpose.

The wit contained in this dance is not unconnected with the fact
that it is built around the scaffolding so often used for a classical *pas de
deux*. We are reminded of the diagonal line along which the male dancer
follows the ballerina, drawn across distance by her performance of a *pas*.
Contact is renewed: then the ballerina draws apart with the same movement as before and finds another area of the stage. Thereupon diagonal
lines are balanced by circular movements effected as a rule by the ballerina with the support of her partner. (Shortly before the end of their
dance the male poodle swings his partner round.)

And now at last, posed upon the trolley, appear the *can-can* dancers.
For their advent the inquisitive music of the interludes becomes larger,
rippling, suggests a grander excitement touched slightly with commis-
eration as if for favourites, as if for nobleness. These are the thorough-
breds among dolls, these are the most waxen, the most precious, the
most fragile: and at the same time the most buoyant, like thrice-refined
essences uncorked for the occasion. Yes, the man especially would seem
to have come out of a bottle. Or else they are specimens of great beauty,
kept on a pin. See how moth-like, how wickedly genteel, is the man
with his white spats and gloves, white button hole, white face, black
hair and black velvet suit. His partner, the ballerina, is a waxen butterfly.
She and the wicked lively moth love one another. More than anything
else it is their love that gives them command of the stage. Their vigour
and their *éclat* are astonishing. At the same time they are flutterers,
dancing *at* each other like insects of the butterfly family, Lepidoptera,
in the full light of day.

As we shall see, the movements and passions of such insects provide
the image for Victorian conviviality at its height. Thus it is that the
mid-Victorian age, now so moth-eaten, is, nevertheless, restored in this
ballet to a full glamour by the stressing of features which were always
lepidopterous.

Every movement in the *can-can* is a fluttering kind: coat-tails fly, petticoats are hustled, legs titillate the air. Often enough the dancers' hands are used as fans seductive to their faces. The *can-can* is the 'naughty' Victorian dance, Parisian, strenuous, effete. In true Victorian style it is 'naughty' because it is an outrage upon 'innocence', a blasphemy against the fluttering, dear to that age, of modest souls, of maidens' hearts.

Mr. Beaumont relates that in the early productions of this ballet Massine's make-up suggested an extreme naughtiness. He used to fix on white cheeks reckless black smudges as if of hair. These must have enhanced a moth-like effect. He would belong to the species *carpophagata*, or perhaps to the *Tinea tapetzella*. Viciousness, then, no less than virtue was conceived by Victorians in the image of lepidopterous behaviour.[3]

Alas, these *can-can* dancers are dolls after all, pathetic in view of their bravado and their fame. At the conclusion of the dance they are lifted from their *écartement* for examination. The children cluster round the dolls, straighten their clothing or try their joints. Both families are interested as purchasers. The Russians buy the ballerina, the Americans the man. The lovers will be separated. It is agreed that the purchasers will return on the morrow to fetch them away. Over each *can-can* dancer is placed a cylindrical frame covered with cloth. Once more they are in the bottle, snuffed out. Their containers are then shunted to positions by the side of the door.

Meanwhile the music has changed to a tune with a quality of benediction. Far from adding point to the details of the scene, it bespeaks a generalized atmosphere connected with the putting away of the stock and the winding up of the business day and other acts similar throughout the world. The customers leave without much more ado. We are conscious of scenes behind scenes, of preparation behind daily effort: all the concentric circles of activity that result, it is hoped, in a purchase, are suggested to us by the continuous modulation of the tune. A purchase has resulted. The end of the working day is at hand.

The remaining actions of shopkeeper and apprentice will be those of habit. The apprentice pulls the flowing powder-blue curtains over the windows. He bustles about the shop conferring upon the toys that he puts away for the night the assurance of his blithe inconsequent affections. He is stirred not only by the ending of the business day but also by the very excellence of that business for the master whose interests he shares.

The master is busy with accounts. He stands at his desk. Faintly, amid the harmonious peace of evening reckoning, the music suggests to us the possibility of recrimination. The shopkeeper finds that he has not collected from the apprentice the money paid to him for one of the *can-can* dancers. The droll is called to heel, is forced, as it were, to surrender the kill he obstinately hides.

Now that the shopkeeper is at his desk, poring over a book (an account book), he seems to have the status of some traditional figure. His broad sun-hat with its blue ribbon, kept on the shelf beneath the desk, is similar to the one on the floor in the picture of St. Jerome by Catena.[4] We feel that this old man with the green eye-shade, though an ordinary shopkeeper, is familiar with the alchemy, with the effervescence, the crystallization and the fermentation that occur behind the brown doors of store-cupboards. We feel that very faintly.

Such medieval images are still common in modern life and even in the attitude of modern science. We would expect a hint of it to be derived from the ballet of a toymaker's shop. Not that there is any reason to impute to this old man a sombre lore. His shop is sunlit, airy, spacious. His hat and his green eye-shade, his white drill suit, are sensible, Mediterranean, promising ease at the café after hours.

Master and apprentice go out with their arms round each other's necks. Their mutual content and their pleasure in each other are profound.[5] Together they pull the blue curtain over the door and walk away. The hour strikes in the music. A new melody will commence. The stage is empty. Upon what have the sky-blue curtains closed?

They are the near skies of a consistent inner world. Shopkeeper and assistant have left. They are now lost to us among the cafés by the sea or at the table of their evening meal. But the spirit of harmonious working remains in the shop. We may now conceive the toys as projections, not so much of the shopkeeper's fancies, as of his disposition. Even while he sleeps his thoughts and emotions are active. The shop is within him.

But the ballet plot does not deal in dreams as such nor in other inner states. And rightly. The stage is the inner world in terms of the outer.

Two companies of toy ballet dancers now appear from the sides. For the first time the music glides, a quality enhanced by the linking of the dancers' arms over their heads, by the rapprochement and fusion of the two groups and by the red bows sewn on their white skirts. None the less, their steps and graces upon points, the first in this ballet,[6] preserve for each movement and for each dancer a separateness and a lightness: these are as a decoration and a piquancy imposed upon the tune. Such mutual contrast as well as affiliation between movement and music is similar to the relation between the colours green and red, or blue and yellow, which are opposite as well as complementary in the colour scale. We can often attribute to the music itself a motion and even a shape complementary to that of the dancers upon the stage.

When the tune is sufficiently far advanced to call attention to itself with a *fortissimo*, the Cossacks enter. Each Cossack takes two ballet dancers, one for each end of his baton. Later, there occurs a break in the melody to allow for the entrance of the Snob. He turns three somersaults over the Cossacks' batons (without his hat falling off) to a phrase of music that calls to mind in a rather forlorn key the one with which the pirouettes of his dance were synchronized. After these very different, and slightly ignominious, evolutions, he recovers his mechanized rhythm and walks slowly off, twirling his moustache.

Next, the other toys come in, each characteristically. But now that they have gone through their customary notions, there is a slight pause, a *diminuendo*. How will they proceed to their personal affairs? Doubt is set at rest by the Snob. He raises his diminutive and cuffed fist on high in protestation. He has a fierce sense of what is proper and right, particularly of what is proper. Translating his language, the melon-seller has already raised the cylindrical box that imprisons the ballerina. He guides her to the front of the stage.

She dances a little *pas seul* on points, so exquisite that she makes us feel that the floor which she prods with the straight scintillation of her points, is a stumbling, unequal thing, unworthy of the contact. And, indeed, before long she will be carried out, held aloft like a goddess on her cloud.

But now an alarm of some kind communicates itself to the dolls. Led, appropriately enough, by the poodles, they pass from side to side of the stage, listening.

All rush off: the *can-can* dancer enters bearing his partner. In our eyes too, she has earned the tenderness that is now bestowed on her. She is the representative, the fetish, the Britannia of these toys. It is as if, under the threat of separation, they have realized it for the first time. While the lovers execute a *pas de deux* the toys form a group of ascending triangular shape with the Cossack chief at the apex. One is reminded of an outdoor double staircase fronting an eighteenth-century Sicilian or Neapolitan palace. Cossacks then shuffle near in soft boots: with the ballet girls they gather round the lovers: there they enact the manipulation whereby this fetish is lifted on high. Gradually she rises, reclining above their heads upon the batons that the Cossacks hold. On the end of one baton that is held up to her she rests a hand. She rules. The cylindrical wood is an extension of her imperious finger. The ballet dancers follow the slow cortège upon their points. Their stretched arms are linked above their heads. Like a straight stalk beneath a bloom, they administer to the materialization of their common aim.

The lifted ballerina is a Tiepolo goddess reclining on a cloud: the darker blue of her bodice passes against the blue curtains of the background as against the sky.

The toys return to drollery: their rite is over. The *can-can* dancer comes in alone and strikes an attitude, a still 'shot' from his dance. Then, in imitation of his ecstatic pose, all the toys leaning back as far as they may, run through in a line. This cake-walk ends with a circle of Cossacks supporting ballet girls who kick up their legs.

And now it is day again. Shopkeeper and apprentice return to open up the shop. We have seen the clock round and beyond. The apprentice is yawning as he pulls back the curtains. But we can hear that the finale approaches: there is great moment implicit in the fugal development of the music. The final has commenced with the same entrance as the one at the beginning of the ballet. All the characterization will be resumed in an epitome.

Sure enough, the customers of yesterday troop in. They have come to carry off their purchases. But there is nothing beneath the boxes: the *can-can* dancers have disappeared. The customers vent rage on the shopmen: they beat them unmercifully and go to search elsewhere. Shopkeeper and assistant begin painfully to drag themselves to one side. While their bodies, dumb, bruised and ignominious, are thus broken the music soars into an emotional phrase,[7] providing a most poignant contrapuntal effect. This phrase is felt by us to be the utterance of those who are exceedingly misused (and do not like it), who have tried hardest to please and who have failed through no fault of their own.

Instantly there is a diversion. The Russian merchant's wife appears with the toy poodles snapping at her legs. The Snob, in high magnanimous fettle, assaults her with his kisses. All the toys return from hiding and attack the brutal customers. The children are chased and spanked. The merchant suffers the Cossacks' batons jabbed rhythmically beneath his ribs. The *can-can* dancers embrace their master and whirl him in a dance.

The customers are outside at the windows, waving their defiance and their recognition of this final alacrity in the *Boutique fantasque*. The curtain descends.

What does *Boutique* mean to us when the Russian ballet is far out of sight in the winter? Bits of the music cross the mind, melodies to which we have imputed fountain-like spurts and other motions. We may be unable to recall the dancing in any detail or even the plot. These are condensed in our minds as attributes of the music that we remember. And how blessed is this music whose mood we are able to realize in entirety, almost as if it were tangible! It contains its own form, but also the expressiveness and complementary motions of the definite scene upon the stage that we have experienced though largely forgotten. It redounds for us in poetry, far more vividly than does music once heard in personal circumstances that were particularly memorable or opposite. From such circumstances as well, all music obtains a faint balletic import: since, when heard later, it is redolent of the action that accompanied it before. But such visual associations, even when connected with the action of an opera, are nostalgic and weak as a rule. Most vividly of all things seen, movement, and especially the dance, is joined and incorporated with our appreciation of musical thought, often to the extent that the two become inseparable and complementary in our minds.

We remember the general atmosphere of *Boutique*, the smart exhibitionism of toys as an attribute of real life. The statement of function, no less concise, is our common lengthy aim. More and more we shall impute to the melodies those fountain-like spurts. For the fountain is the most lovely, the most tenuous of mechanical toys, an instrument of humanism, deft in the use of diaphanous water. Our own mechanisms of behaviour are less fluid, less beneficent.

And when we come to see *Boutique* again we shall find that those qualities that have become identified in our minds with the music, are in fact crystallized in the décor. Derain anticipated the underlying images of the ballet. Or is it he, more than any other, who created them? The still umbrella pines on drop-curtain and backcloth, with their branches supporting the compact of foliage, are like jets that restfully balance a ball at their height. We remember the tall mazurka that is to come and over which the trees will preside. Again, on the backcloth a paddle-steamer figures, first mechanism of the Industrial Age to be humanized, congenial in seascapes of a mock heroic kind. The harbour of Nice, then, and its appropriate furniture, as well as the mechanical toys, are conceived by Derain in terms of the humanistic intentions of the dance. At the sight of the cactus plants he has depicted, a growth which in this context at any rate is the outdoor undaunted Mediterranean equivalent of the aspidistra, we are ready to appreciate both the dryness of the shopkeeper's bent form (with the green curve of his eye-shade) and the batons of the green-uniformed Cossacks which they use for their drill and as supports for their partners and then, in unison, as trestles upon which the ballerina is raised to assume the attitude of a Tiepolo goddess upon a cloud, and finally to prick and prod the Russian merchant. These several functions of one instrument are typical of ballet's economy: for ballet is the art of the one unchanging instrument, the human physique. By means of the inherent geometry and gymnastic of the human form, ballet expresses all episodes with succinctness and beauty. Décor and music are the lavish concomitants, necessarily so: and the underlying economy of form sometimes obtains expression in the many uses of the same stage property, as in the instance of these batons. Not that they are, therefore, generalized objects, symbols in fact. Ballet flees all mysticism. The poetry inherent in the diverse uses of these batons is not a conscious one. Each time they are used they are the obvious means to hand.

Nor is Derain's umbrella pine a symbol of the mazurka. It has its own purpose in his composition. No, the poetry of ballet is in our own minds: it is the sum of a ballet. When the tradition and the technique of the dance and the spirit of particular invention within a company are strong, the poetry follows.

And the wit of *Boutique*?

It is supposed that the toys conceal to the utmost the fact of their mechanism. Through the pretence of naturalistic instruments of precision, there is affirmed and dramatized the balletic deportment whereby the most difficult physical feats are executed with an air of facility and of pleasure. We are not asked to consider the pains with which the dancers have achieved their control and their verve. On the contrary, we are to consider how ingenious the toil must be that could construct dolls so naturalistic as to be almost identical with dancers. In a fine character ballet the dancer lends the very facility of his art in movement to the character that he plays, whether it be the part of a toy or of an enchanted swan. This is not to the same extent the case with the spoken word of drama. The facility of the actor's voice, the beauty and brilliance of the dramatists' writing, cannot be employed so successfully as in themselves the attributes of the characters portrayed. In ballet, the dancer's virtuosity is lent to such characters, be they persons or things, as can accept it, in other words, to such persons or things as may provide a subject for ballet: the subject-matter is limited thus. Therefore, it used to be thought that only fine princes, enchanted animals, toys, dancers, nymphs, children, peasants and other *immediately* romantic figures could provide a ballet plot. Classical ballet abounds in these characters. But the work of Massine, Nijinska and Balanchine has shown us that everything, certainly everything that is vivid, may serve as the subject of a ballet.[8] The rarest inspiration, however, and a rare feeling for the romantic essence of ballet is required of the creator. We cannot expect more than one such man each decade, perhaps less. Today we are most fortunate.

Chapter Two

An augmentation upon the surface. A rose facing outward from the stem. A face, the outward part, the augmentation of all that is within the head. A true painting is of such kind: an augmentation upon the surface of wall or canvas.

Then comes the day of early spring. The air of that day is liberal, a liberality that has been veiled, obscured, overpressed and finally forgotten in the winter. We had forgotten that the skies may open: the tent of winter is asunder; the clouds sail. On this day as you approach Hyde Park the great elm trees stand up black. It is as if the sooty tunnel of winter has passed them through: they stand in the stronger light a vibrant memorial of the dim months.

Thus is time recorded by space: an augmentation upon the surface. The visual world is an accumulation of time apprehended instantaneously.

In visual art we are aware of forms as charged with a tension to be thus manifest. They are the simple showing products of complication; they are faces: they disclose, they spread: they are unfolded like the open face of the rose: a folded cycle is unfurled as a shape. Nothing else in life, it seems to me, is as final, as concrete-seeming, as this kind of manifestation conveyed by certain forms, the one miraculous sensation of fullness: and it is a source of surprise that such mode in form perception has not been isolated and enlarged upon. Its realization, however, must to some extent exist in every work of visual art.

Carving creates a face for the stone, as agriculture for the earth, as man for woman. Modelling is more purely plastic creation: it makes things, it does not disclose, as a face, the significance of what already exists. The painter of a modelling proclivity manifestly recharges a landscape with shape, with patent flourish. The painter of a carving proclivity is manifestly at pains to show that the forms there have each a face which he discloses. The first painter may very well seize upon light effects and other transitory phenomena to make a forcible pattern. He rejoices in the image of his immediate mood. There is, therefore, a greater temporal suggestion in his work, that will be absent from the work of one who rejoices in the conception of disclosure.

Where lies the perennial strength of this fantasy? It is, of course, all the figures of the inner life, of the unconscious, that are shown as a fixture, as one harmonious family, steadfast, completed as an open rose, open, revealed. The modeller on the other hand imbues spatial objects with the animus and calculation of inner life. He projects the lively feeling, though not as a disclosed state. He accumulates force and directions: he does not reveal an accumulation, an augmentation upon the surface, a mere outwardness. Stone is the symbol of the outwardness, of the hoarded store of meaning that comes to the surface. Much fierceness stands collected, just as storm-drops are calm together but undiminished in the pool. The deep life does not course in the men and women of Piero's frescoes. Their deep life stands revealed as if they were pools, millions of drops run together in a still shape.

That distinction between carving and modelling is for me one of the most fruitful in the visual arts: it applies to all of those arts. I enlarged this distinction in *Stones of Rimini*.[1] I showed that in the early Renaissance there was an architecture and sculpture that is the epitome of carving conception. Also in *The Quattro Cento*[2] I showed that there is constancy of life in early Renaissance stone ornaments, a tense communion with the plane from which they are cut. These ornaments do not give the effect of having been stuck there. On the contrary they are integral with their background plane. They appear to be more than decoration: for through them we witness powers in the wall on which they lie, just as his face shows the man.

Whatever its plastic value, a figure carved in stone is fine carving when one feels that not the figure, but the stone through the medium of the figure, has come to life. Plastic conception, on the other hand, is uppermost when the material with which, or from which, a figure has been made appears no more than as so much suitable stuff for this creation... Work of this intensely spatial (carving) kind recalls a panorama contemplated in an equal light by which objects of different dimensions and textures, of different beauty and of different emotional appeal, whatever their distance, are seen with more or less the same distinctness, so that one senses the uniform dominion of an uninterrupted space. The intervals between objects have assumed a markedly irreversible aspect: there it all is, so completely set out in space that one cannot entertain a single afterthought. In visual art, the idea of forms however different, as answering to some cogent, common, continuous dominion that enforces the bonds between those forms in spite of their manifold contrasts, gives rise to the distinctive non-plastic aim: and this idea was inspired, above all, by the equality of light on stone. In Piero della Francesca's painting, by the religious reverence for spatial intervals, by tonal and perspective organization, all feeling, all movement, all rhythm, all plasticity itself, were translated equally into panorama terms. His pictures express the metaphysics of space or colour or tone. They are free of 'atmosphere', psychological or physical, as they are of anything emphatic... Piero's and Agostino's conception depends upon an almost hieratic use of perspective. In terms of perspective was the religion of equal light, of space, of stone, expressed in that time. Anyone may experience this finality who is familiar with the air of southern lands. It is not because of marked difference in tone or in distinctiveness that you perceive this wall to be behind this wall. The bricks of the farther house-wall are just as clear. Each process seems exposed as objects, all of them all at once. More especially, just as the sun has gone down after a hot day, things stand. A luminous whiteness, as yet untrammelled by the dizzy approach of night, is common to sea, to road, to house. Stone gleams, the dust is white: what is of dark hue is dark, what is darker is blacker without mitigation. The sun has disappeared suddenly, leaving the world arranged. After the long dazzle of the day, our eyes see the world exposed by a neutral medium which is but the fresh caressing air. The evening stirs: the concrete world stands concrete. What was the passage of the sun has turned into space, and all that is left of passage are the invisible airs. Otherwise every phase, all subjective conditions, appear to have been transformed into objects arranged in neutral un-broken perspective.[3]

Of a decoration on the outside of the Tempio Malatestiano I wrote: 'The forms in the stone put the structure at a tension similar to the most vibrant instant of a singer's longest note.'

I refer to the two previous books anyone who wants to understand the full reasons why I have been led to put so general a construction on the differences between carving and modelling. I do not therefore attempt to justify it now, but I must continue to employ the distinction in reference to colour.

The colours of a picture are fine when one feels that not the colours but *each and every* form through the medium of their colours has come to an *equal* fruition. Thus is carving conception realized in painting. It will be my aim to show that colour is the ideal medium of carving concep-tion, that this wide range has the power of charged outwardness which an efflorescence upon the stone possesses; by means of colour, every form may attain equality or outwardness, each revealing the other, one showing another as its efflorescence, its child or its parent. We shall discover that in looking at a painting the eye puts one form or a col-lection of forms into another form in virtue, primarily, of chromatic relationship. The eye thus measures what has been laid out from what, what has grown from what, like a decoration from a wall. And this organic relationship as of many flowers with their foliage and with their roots, will not be confined to adjacent forms in pictorial design. Colour allows such organization to be vastly more intricate: a mutual evocation between forms must take place at all angles and at all dis-tances and in all directions throughout a picture, so that each part will seem rooted in its place and working there. (The mere balance of masses, of areas, of directions, is not in itself a statement of mutual evocation.) Thus, as well as propagating a feeling of growth between forms, as well as a feeling of material that crystallizes into a shape symbolic of its outwardness, these forms will also be equal; and many relationships will be reversible, possessing a different connotation when reversed; so that what is laid out in the whole is a sum to which each part contributes equally. Such steadiness of manifestation is lost when one form serves almost entirely as a foil to another or as a background for an emphasis. The chief potentiality of colour is then neglected, this power to subsume the diversity of hue as of plastic meaning under a more fundamental identity. The steadiness of great pictures contains diverse subject matter. It is due entirely to the painter's conception of his forms? Maybe. But it is possible that colour-sense has played a major part in his conception of form, a conception which, once held, he may also realize without the use of colour.

It will be my first aim, then, to show how one form supports the next in virtue of colour, evokes the next, vivifies it at the extreme of outwardness: to distinguish as I did in the kindred matter of reliefs, colour that seems to come out of a form, from colour that seems merely 'stuck on' or merely to tint. In a word, then, to distinguish the carving use of colour from the plastic, and to show what part colour plays in the carving conception of form in general.

In concluding these generalities, I would repeat my still wider assertion that the carving work of visual art is the concrete archetype or emblem of all artistic creation. No one can trace the manifold threads of Gaucho life upon the South American plains, the innumerable rhythms of ranch existence that are run together and augmented in its ornament, the rhythm of a tango. From these the tango grew its character. All artistic creation is like the perfect flower that shows by a certain still shape the stress and strain of roots, the gradual cycle of its nurture. Art is the face of mankind, the symbol of living, of the creating that turns emotion's multiplicity into concrete and particular and individual acts. The accumulated spirit of man would attain the immediacy of objects occupying space. In the initial attack upon colour in relation to form I shall take most of my examples from landscape rather than figure painting.

It is time to come down to detail, to examine the power of a couple of objects only in causing each other to appear thus spread.

A note on complementary colours
I must explain forthwith what is meant by complementary colours because that relationship between colours is the basis of all further relationship. 'If we look for a short time at scarlet geranium blossoms and then look steadily in another direction where there are no blossoms, we shall see spots, shaped and arranged like the scarlet flowers, but bright green in hue. After a few seconds these green spots fade and entirely disappear' (*The Enjoyment and Use of Colour* by Walter Sargent, Scribner, 1923). The vision is known as the negative after-image (hereafter called after-image) and the green is known as the complementary colour of the red we first saw, and vice versa. Thus, other things being equal, a green surface tends to redden surrounding neutral (greyed) surfaces or to cause another hue, such as orange, to move nearer to red and further from green. This is called simultaneous contrast, or, as I prefer, mutual enhancement. We shall understand later on in relation to the physiology of the eye, the reason for these phenomena. In polychromatic lights, two complementary colours together include all the chromatic rays and, therefore, fuse into a white. Complementaries afford the greatest possible contrast between two hues and yet they seem to harp on and evoke each other. Power in the working of simultaneous constrast is subject to all kinds of conditions, such as the relative areas of the two hues and, especially in the case of marked neutral or greyed areas, their relative tones (tone is the range of lightness or darkness between black and white), the presence or absence of contour lines and so on. An exposition of these matters will be found in any good modern handbook on colour. I strongly recommend the book by Mr Sargent quoted above. Scientists are now agreed that the following are the complementary relations of the six primary hues: red, sea-green: blue, yellow: orange, turquoise: violet, leaf-green. The correct list will not be found in any but the more recent books.

The blue-orange and yellow-violet errors die hard, and with some reason as far as painting is concerned, since positive enhancement, not merely the enhancement by contrast, is better constructed with these near complementaries (orange and blue is the opposition most commonly found in nature): whereas large juxtaposed areas of pure complementaries fight each other with crude weapons.

The relationship of pure hues is best conceived in the form of a circle on which each colour graduates into another on either side. Thus, starting with yellow, say, at the top and proceeding down to the right we come to orange, on to red, violet, blue, then up the other side through blue to turquoise, sea-green, and then through leaf-green back to yellow. Any diameter drawn on the circle will join two complementary colours.

The three 'dimensions' of colour are these hues together with tone and intensity. The latter is the range between the complete neutralization (greyness) and the complete saturation or intensity of a colour; whereas tone is the range between its lightest and darkest aspect. Most colour both in nature and art are to some extent neutralized (greyed) and their 'natural' tone value is either deepened or heightened. In a word, we do not often encounter pure hues.

Now, hues of equal tone and intensity do not enhance one another: they are flat, dull and stationary. Variability in all three chromatic dimensions must be employed in order to create an identity in difference, an equal insistence, an equal reciprocity between forms. The violence in opposition of complementary or near-complementary colours is alleviated sufficiently, and their activating forces thus provided with more complicated work, if one of them is neutralized to some extent (for instance, Venetian red which is roughly a neutralized vermilion is constructively active on certain shades of turquoise green), or when one colour is appreciably heightened or deepened. If we use red and blue, each at its spectrum value, they seldom look well together. But if we make the red as much lighter than middle grey as the blue is darker (coral red with dark blue), these colours will find more work to do on one another. And were it necessary to advise on the complementary relation, say, of yellow and blue, one might do worse than suggest that the lighter colour should be deepened (in tone) and the darker neutralized and heightened (in tone). Thus, deep tones of pure yellow (hard to obtain) find a great deal of scope in conjunction with a heightened blue grey (i.e. a light, neutralized blue). *This deep yellow causes the grey tone to appear more blue than it really is*. To obtain from colour the creation of colour, a *mutually* enhancing florescence, an activation that we shall soon put in relation to the one of forms, is a means of art which the carving painter never neglects. For reasons that will become apparent I shall call such colour 'organic colour'. But I would warn the reader at once from concluding that there is, or that I consider that there is, any sort of rule for the creation of such colour in a picture. The instances above are soft yet abstract, abstracted from texture, area, position and subject matter. I have for the moment divorced colour from form, but I have done so purely for the purposes of exposition in this short section. Only the total configuration is of account and that, in every case of a work of art, is made up differently.

Chapter Three

From *Colour and Form* (1937)

At Christmas time one may see in the portico of St. Martin-in-the-Fields four fir trees planted in tubs. The presence of these dark slender shapes against the whitish wall of the church is not of interest merely because of the silhouettes thus created. There is something more interesting afoot than shapes posed before a background. Indeed, I notice first of all the vivification of the church wall, bestowed by the presence of the trees. Their presence has resuscitated to a native dignity, as of fruitfulness, the Portland limestone of this portico. The very discoloration of the stone now appears fruitful because, grown from this earthiness, the trees seem to have taken their dark colour: while from the other side, owing to the presence of the green, a slight pinkish colour has warmed the stone (for, physiologically speaking, such green calls forth its complementary colour, a purplish red) as if summer warmth were stored there.

Nor is that all. The textures of masonry and tree are mutually enhancing. We have seen that it warms the stone to have her progeny there. But also the growing upward slenderness of the trees is dignified by the stone. Upon some sparse soil of limestone rock these spare forms flourish in nature. The trees have grown from the rock: deep in their black-green colour there exists the light colour of the stone.[1] *In virtue of colour relationship, then, we have seen how the dark trees have evoked a poignant darkness in the light stone, and the light stone a lightness in the dark trees.*

Thus does colour, without destroying the clear-cut, shapely, and drastic differences of tone, create for them a miraculous identity and equality, a breathing calm. Because the relationship established is one of growth and fruition attained with what at first sight might appear to be the very weapon of mere tonal altercation, we imagine the rough and living texture of the trees as some form of concentrated essence that the smoother stones have evolved. Brightness and warmth have been established in this portico, the calm radiance of classic Greece; while the December traffic perseveres in migration round Trafalgar Square.

Such mitigation in the plastic superficiality of vast tonal contrast (without sacrifice of this strength which is always necessary for the creation of pattern), provides one of the principal roles of colour in art. Great painters obtain warmth from whiteness and light from darkness, at the same time conserving tonal contrast. In so doing they offer an identity in difference, a carving steadiness. More purely plastic painters, on the other hand, use colour itself to further tonal difference. Chromatic tonal difference, of course, plays as big a part as any other factor in positive or enhancing colour relationships. But chromatic tone is employed by such painters negatively, to suggest mere black-and-white contrast with the added brightness that hue affords. Colour in their hands is primarily a more vivid form of tone, a means that enables a more drastic balance between shapes (a huge neutral area may be balanced by a segment of pure colour). Such paintings are best called tinted drawings. For the sake of the strong grasping, the perusal, the reading, the conning of a shape in relation to shapes, the umbilical cord of colour is cut: colour is used to demarcate merely, to contrast; and from such kind of organization the procedure is to composition, arrangement and balance between hostile forces, between stresses and strains, between forces that are foreign but which come together in a kind of truce because of their equal resistance to one another.

And now let me contrast the simple effect, primarily dependent upon colour, in the portico of St. Martin-in-the-Fields, with another effect equally simple in which colour plays the superficial part more usually attributed to it.

Think for a moment of an orange tree with oranges hanging like lamps between the green shiny leaves. It is a transplendent yet homely picture, not unlike that of the suffering Christmas tree hung with lights. The orange tree is flamboyant, bright – I am thinking of it in isolation and not as growing in southern countries where it often possesses great import in relation to its landscape – and that is all. For there is no (visual) poetry, no profound enhancement of the dark green leaves and the orange fruit. Those leaves, it is true, most effectively show off the pleasant spheres of the oranges that hang there, as if artificially. And it is in terms of such nursery and charming effects that many people conceive of colour. A purely external brightness.

The eye trained differently in colour (doubtless, owing to sojourn in Mediterranean lands) will always be seeing one shape as the gathering up of another. To keep to the same neighbourhood, the posts fixed in the pavement of Trafalgar Square have an interest. Their shape is not perhaps in itself remarkable – it is always comparative nonsense, though, to speak of any shape in itself and as isolated. It may be isolated in space, yet the mind will find for it relations with shapes imagined or remembered, possibly because chromatic sense cannot conceive of one colour in eternal isolation – nevertheless these posts possess a certain poignancy if one sees their shape as a gathering up, a concretion into squat vertical cylinders, of the great flat mass of the pavement's horizontal surface. This organic relationship of form exists in virtue of a similarity between the colours of the pavement and of the posts, a similarity which points to the deepening of colour in the posts. We proceed to note the intricacy of texture and of colour in these surfaces.

But suppose the posts were a staring red; it is unlikely, then, that the imaginative eye would conceive of an organic progression as existing between the horizontal and vertical planes. Seen at a little distance the red posts would jump away from a dim background of dirty pavement. Thus the most superficial plastic painters define their forms. At the other extreme there is the painter who inherits a carving tradition that has gone rotten, who merges all his forms with equal tone, a general atmosphere, a fashionable old-masterish brownness. He is wary in sensitiveness, possesses no imaginative grasp of organic colour determining form. And it is the doting nothingness of his products that provokes the cruder plastic revulsions. In all the most recent art movements of the day the carving painter and the plastic painter, both of them in revolt from some academic nothingness as the one above, ally themselves. It is a false alliance. The deeper issue in art is not understood, except by the greater artists. The work of the smaller men nearly always falls between the two stools. By that I do not wish to imply that a good picture is either of the carving or the plastic kind. On the contrary, the two elements must always co-exist to some extent. I have explained the complementary character, so to speak, of carving and modelling in *Stones of Rimini*.[2] I tried to show there that it is the very fact of the restless plastic strength characteristic of European art that has entailed at times expression of carving conception, the summit of our art.[3]

The latter always needs new material from the former, the new material that carving lays out in a manner more objective. Such was the situation in the early Renaissance owing to the dominance of the fantasy by the material, stone. But today there exists no such nexus of carving conception in everyday life. The emphasis is everywhere upon manufacture and plasticity. On the other hand, Cézanne repudiated the pure plastic aim; and so have the best of his followers. It seems useful that this position should be made clear because confusion of aim among artists is infinite. And if this conception of carving or organic colour is acceptable, I believe that the modern artist can return to a less intrusive, less spry and more generous treatment of his subject. He may well see the landscape with new eyes. Sensitiveness to the carving aspect of form will be developed only by a more imaginative attitude to colour relationships.

I have before me a picture in which is represented the deep recession of a hill. The picture plane, and in terms of the picture plane, the immediacy, the carving element (for pictures are flat surfaces and a picture must enforce two, as well as suggesting three, dimensions), is saved by three spots of colour in different parts of the picture which cause the eye to look across this plane as well as 'to look into' it. These spots vary from yellowish pink to pinkish yellow, and because of their remarkable variance in similarity as well as of their brightness, the eye immediately singles them out and sees them in relation. Such would be the case were the spots equally distinctive tones in black-and-white. But while in tone

one would immediately recognize the similarity, one would not have the call of a variation (variation not only in tone but in hue and in intensity) of yellow-pink to its fellow by which additional relations are established. In this case differences of yellow-pink remind one of the sensation of diving into a swimming bath that is colder when you strike the water's surface than in a warmer yet lighter depth that you reach after passing through an intermediate zone in which the two temperatures mingle. Though scattered through this picture, the minute areas of yellow-pink convey, even if they do not represent, the sensation of a continuous form. These colour patches by themselves could not have such effect. They are in turn determined in their mode of operation by the colours surrounding them.

The point is that this effect partially described could not be attained solely by variations of tone, chromatic or otherwise, although I am ready to admit that it belongs more nearly to a tonal effect than any I have mentioned. Colour is a glorified form of tone, but one so glorified, bringing with its two further dimensions, hue and intensity, such a host of relationships foreign to the purely linear progression of tone from lightness to darkness, that no misapprehension about the meaning of colours to the fantasy could be further from the mark than to conceive of colour as a bright yet convenient fancy-dress facilitating the perception of tonal difference. No doubt colour sense was originally evolved in the prehistoric eye to fulfil just this function. But what has been developed for practical purposes is put to different use in contemplation and in art.

Given the practical apparatus for the distinguishing of difference, the aesthetic eye seeks identity in this difference. Few phenomena in nature are more sudden, more forcible than the meeting of sea and rock. And yet if we contemplate the water seething up and over rocks, or the waves that break their backs upon cliffs, we crave that we shall find a common element in this interaction. Which is the more profound painter – the one who represents the sea's cold fury (predominantly sea-green colour) upon humpy rocks ('strong' shapes, of course, predominantly black-blue)? Like an old childless couple the sea-green and the black-blue or worse, black-brown, have nothing whatever to uphold between them. They are just 'a' and 'b' brought together in a design. A huge area of monstrously architectonic clouds will attempt, in the interests of composition, to act as mediator. It is an Academy picture, one of the less offensive, more discreet kind.

A better painter will note the intercourse between water and stone, the carving of stone by water: he will see the stone as a concretion of the liquid form. Then the rock or causeway mounts from the water as from its proper floor. Movement, restlessness, the endless to-and-fro of water lays the foundation for the statuary of substance just as does plastic exuberance for carving conception: and it is with this fantasy strongly in mind that I have written in *Stones of Rimini* of Venice, of the limestone Mediterranean countries, of their seas and of certain art-forms.

Many a good painter will probably eschew altogether a subject of sea and rocks because the imagined progression is too far-fetched for concrete realization. But he may well use his feeling for this progression or concretion in the representing of boats upon the water. Thus, the old fisherman of St. Ives, Alfred Wallis, inspirer of Christopher Wood in his last period, often paints his seas with earth colours, white and black, colours which, if gathered up, will equal in hue or in tone or by some sort of affinity, the colour of his boats. But then he has been a fisherman all his life, accustomed to conceive the sea in relation to what lies beneath it, sand or rock and the living forms of fish. For him the colour of the sea is less determined by its glassy surface that reflects the sky. The surface of his sea, seen best on grey days, is the showing also of what lies under it, and boats are further showing compact for carrying men, an elaboration of the sea-shell, a solid darkness from the depth.

Wallis in one picture has painted a red-brown boat upon a dirty white-brown sea with white icebergs at the back of the picture. The subject is a voyage to Labrador. A warm coloration is used successfully to convey the dead-cold sea of melted ice-slush. Were the hue of the sea without adjacence to the darker colour of the boat, this disintegration of ice-slush would not have been suggested. One's sense of a coloured area added up and 'going into' another, allows the impression of augmentation and of disintegration. Boat and sea are in reality bound by interaction. Without any direct suggestion of weight or movement or buoyancy, this general, as well as a particular, relationship is thus fixed. At the same time the significance of the slightest difference in colour and tone is dramatized. Great meaning of coldness belongs to the dirty white tinges in the sea, and equally to the slight reddening of the boat, haven of comparative warmth upon the waste.

Wallis' brown boat upon the slush-brown icy sea is a form of which I shall never tire because its fixture there palpitates anew and anew. Two opposite references, two worlds of feeling are merged in this earth-coloured sea to which the boat is joined, not as one form posed in relation to another, but as a form with roots in another, as it were, from which it grows and whose opposite nature it displays under the dramatic guise of rooted affinity. Within so narrow a range, the power of colour in the portrayal of difference by means of a deeper identification is used to the utmost. So often in pictures, colours do not fecundate each other but reduce each other's brightness. It must always be a characteristic of art that much should be obtained with simplified means. No colour is good colour of which this is untrue.

Painters more sophisticated than Wallis, also possessing carving vision, will accomplish identity in difference and difference in identity by more complicated adjustment. A poetic relationship between different forms, different textures and distances, may be suggested by a substitution in colour, as when Matisse takes the major blue out of his sky and puts it into the blue of curtains before a window. (I shall not attempt for the moment to discuss how this act of substitution is suggested in the picture.) A certain interchange or metamorphosis of character is effected, one aesthetically pleasing because it is a poetic restatement of that unity-cum-difference of carving conception. Both curtain and sky are enhanced in their intercourse. (But this would not be the case if from the hint of substitution our sense of the normal colour of things were outraged.)

Identity in difference is often realized by the few masters of today through a kind of addition and subtraction that the eye performs upon the colours used in the picture. I shall return again to this propensity of the eye, for it is most important to my argument. The invitation to addition and subtraction of colour – I have remarked it already in Wallis' picture and before that – is a very ancient practice in painting, but it is sometimes employed today in a manner unembarrassed by the demands of exact or even partial representation. I shall refer cursorily to a semi-representational Picasso recently exhibited at the Rosenberg galleries. The picture is called *Woman with a Mandolin.** On looking at this picture one will perceive immediately that there exists some integrating relation, more intense than the one usually described under the words 'design' or 'composition', between the figure and the chair on which she sits. This relationship depends upon a little addition sum that the eye unconsciously performs (and the eye delights in this exercise). If the area of colour of the figure's deep red dress is added to the area of pinkish colour of her flesh, the resultant colour would equal in tone the light-blue armchair on which she sits. Further, take this red and blue, their respective areas and shapes, and we shall find that the purple-brown part of her head-dress gives some sort of equivalent, both in form and in colour. Or again the black and purple-brown head-dress is a concentration or addition of the background colours that are divided into three zones. The point is not that an analysis on these lines should be literally true of the painting, but that this mode of interchange, fructification, metamorphosis, in terms of hue or tone or intensity, or by two of them, or by all three, should be suggested; not that a colour scheme should be thought out by the artist on these lines but that a conception of form, in turn based upon the family character of colour, should lead him instinctively to create a design thus integrated. In terms of two forms 'going into' a third, of one texture as the sum of another of larger area and so on, there is perhaps expressed the wished-for stabilizing, not so much of our personalities as of its qualification by those miscellaneous mixed-up archetypal figures within us, absorbed in childhood, that are by no means at peace among themselves.

---

* Stokes is alluding to the 1925 *Woman with Mandolin* now in the collection of the Norton Simon Museum in Pasadena, California. – Ed.

The colour-vision cause of this predilection for discovering two or more forms to 'go into' another is obvious if we consider after-images. 'Wherever areas of neutrals occur near areas of colour, the hue of the after-image of the colour overlays and tinges the neutral. In combinations of complementary colours the after-images are themselves complementary. Consequently, they intensify some areas and soften others' (Sargent, *op. cit.*). Thus a neutral area tends to be seen as a sum of chromatic areas which, in fact, it is. That perception is also applied to the neutralized and near-complementary hues by which opposition is reduced: the colours are more likely to figure in a carving work of art.

Let me dogmatically state that if when looking at a picture the eye is directed by the 'strong' use of tone and colour *opposition* to move continually from shape to shape, any one of these shapes, however bound together with the rest from the point of view of line and balance and mass, does not possess such spatial poignancy as when the eye rests on *any* shape in a picture and sees it as a self-sufficient shape in uncompeting relation to shapes throughout that picture. The eye construes this last apprehension in the proverbial flash of the eye and at a remarkable distance, even when the light is poor. Except in the case of huge pictures seen at close range the eye easily embraces the whole, even when it is focused on one form in that picture. Closeness of organization, therefore, by means of colour need not proceed from one form to its adjacent forms but may be effected by forms that are scattered.

Some pictures – most pictures – partly rebut this natural synthesis in the eye: one part of the picture is subsidiary to another, shows off another, by unmixed contrast rather than by a no less great difference in identity. Such forms do not grow but stand off in strong relief.

An uncompeting relationship between two shapes is one in which neither shape is subservient, in which each enhances the other to a more or less equal extent. Thus, from the angle of colour whence this conception of form is derived, although one colour 'shows off' the rest, it should itself be thereby 'shown off': between colours, activity and passivity should be equally divided; and similarly between forms. It follows that in such presentation we feel that even the mass or the form of a picture as a whole is not so much a unit standing over against us, inducing the bipolarity of tactile sensation, as a more independent self-orientated and productive mechanism equally active in all its parts, with a small wheel (one part), as it were, communicating power to a conglomeration of much larger machinery and thereby contriving for itself a place in the unity of insistence by which colour is best seen; but only because also, unlike the part of a machine, it receives power from those very brother parts to which it communicates power. A better analogy, therefore, is the one of the human body. Thus, there is a movement between colours, a simple progression in the case of adjacent hues, one more complicated in the case of an area, for instance, into which other areas 'add up' or from which they emerge possessing further relationships between themselves. But the movement has nothing except its own organic momentum, and, unlike plastic rhythm, it is not, at each change of tempo or direction, dependent as well upon a new polar relation to our own bodies.

As a rule, of course, a compromise exists between the carving and modelling mode, even in bad pictures. But frequently it is evident that a painter has done all he can with dazzling changes of tone to prevent us grasping all the forms at once. This he does in the interests of stress and strain and harsh rhythms (or even of mass) that show their strength by mounting and passing the peaks of opposition on which the eye bumps. He thinks he is interested in the purest spatial form. To my mind he is interested in form and movement that is temporal and incompletely transmuted to visual terms. But I have already admitted the value of plastic approach in the material it brings to carving approach. My bias is certainly in favour of the latter, whose products seem to me the crown of visual art. I would not deprecate the plastic approach, were the other a quarter as well understood.

I must insist, therefore, that a well-related shape as defined above, is a more definite shape. The better a picture is sustained *equally* throughout, the more significant the shape of each part of it. This is not quite the same as to assert that a picture should look the same all over, a dictum commonly accepted today. Every good modern picture has an 'all-overness'; that is to say, the rhythm as above, is carried consistently through every part: the brio of brushwork, for instance, will be transparently consistent, a sop thrown to carving values which reflects the influence of Cézanne no more than of the Impressionists. Cézanne himself admired the 'all-overness' of Impressionist pictures, but it could not content him. He started life with an almost Baroque love of a continuous, dramatic, calligraphic modelling. This remains the position of most young artists today and there they persist. Cézanne, however, almost harnessed this flourish at the behests of the equal organic radiance of the Provençal landscape. That performance was his agony. He pushed, as D. H. Lawrence has said, the apple away from him into a world more objective. His chromatic sense triumphed over his love of tonal or calligraphic exuberance. But their strength, of course, he did not forgo: it was harnessed, became sometimes the slave of gradual forms. His masterpieces possess a vociferous even tenor. By hook or by crook he got his innate, almost Greco-like, flourish into the four-squareness of space. In conjunction with extreme rotundity he insisted upon a certain flatness as of a wall carved by the air, sensitive always to the growth of the perpendicular from the horizontal.

According to Gasquet he once said: 'The whole of painting is there – to yield to the atmosphere or to resist it? To yield is to deny local colour, to resist is to give them their force and variety' as seen in an evening light. 'Titian and the Venetians worked by "localities" and that is what true colourists do.' In other words, is one to model with temporary light-effects or is one to see in local colour the breathing, living life of a form, the light as if from inside it? He also said: 'Everything we see is dispersed and disappears. Nature is always the same but nothing remains of it, nothing of what we see. Our art should give to nature the thrill of continuance with the appearance of all its changes. It should enable us to feel nature as eternal.' The accumulated material of plasticity must finally be used to realize carving conception. A line is something we reach out to, a raft for the floating spirit. But colour properly used attributes to shape an outwardness or otherness. It is a more complete, more inclusive, and indeed more courageous, sublimation.

We all arrive at this discovery towards the end of the day when in the evening the things around, at which we have glanced, finally arrest us by standing minutely described. Things now have their own light: they seem less lit from the sky. They do not stand out in a sea of shapes: all shapes stand together, separate and in communion. The character of each texture appears encouraged by the equality of revelation that an evening sky allows. The eye comprehends, does not follow. Each thing is rooted; gradation is infinite.[4]

I shall defer for a moment the equation between colour and texture. As for achromatic tone, we shall find that it differs from colour in the way that light and dark differ as concepts from warmth and coldness. The complementary principle is found in achromatic tone (i.e. in the range between black and white) although this range is hardly to be compared with the three dimensions of colour. What is not found in achromatic tone at all is the interplay between adjacents and the discovery by colours of a common factor. Thus maroon socks evoke the purple component in chocolate-brown shoes. They have this purple component in common and therefore sock seems to fit shoe with satisfaction. And, remember, a well-related shape is a more definite shape. This applies to both sock and shoe. We become aware of structure and even of movement, of one thing arising from another thing. Carving colour gives the interior life, the warmth, to composition, gives to structural conception flesh and blood as it were, a blood that passes through the joints. Colour used thus in painting is a humanistic quality attributed to the inter-working of things in space. Such colour bestows on pictorial forms however neat, though separated by tidy contour lines, the simultaneous life of the blood; to the passage of years, to the cycles of growth, to consciousness, the contiguous showing of flowers upon a windless verge.

A simple instance of such an effect is an olive tree in a typical Mediterranean landscape. In dark bark and shadeless leaves the rich colour and substance of the earth from which the tree rises has undergone a silver metamorphosis, a rarefaction: the very growth of the tree is presented to us as a thing completed or accomplished. Such effects are

not confined to neutralized colours, although the eye tires less and
derives more from them.

There is a kindred spatial poetry in a simple progression of colour
once employed at the Chinese Imperial court. The habitual robe of the
Emperor was orange embroidered with red: his attendants and the min-
isters of religion wore citron yellow. We may imagine the cluster of this
pale bright yellow deepening, weighty and glowing, in the Emperor's
robe. A more costly extraction again, potent to the point of the miraculous, from the multitude of yellow, was the thin embroidered line of
red upon the orange.

Now, I do not deny for a moment that chromatic tone plays an important part in the evocative power that may exist between two colours.
Although the effect of sock and shoe would have been minimized if the
tonal relation between the maroon and the brown were one of strong
contrast, yet, amid the complication of a picture, vast tonal differences
must be preserved and equalled out by further relationships. Even so,
there is a certain contrast between sock and shoe on which their communion depends. The shoe possesses a shiny surface in relation to the
sock, as if storing upon the surface a redundance of inner light gener-
ated from this communion.

It has been pointed out to me as a qualification of my argument that
panchromatic photographs convey most of the principal values of pictures, convey them in terms of black and white. I agree that sometimes
they do. Colour vision, being an integral part of vision, still functions
in our estimation of matters black-and-white, at any rate in the case of
a picture and especially if we have already seen it. But any photograph
would, it is obvious, appear very different to us if we were, and always
had been, *completely* colour-blind. Moreover, organic relationship will
certainly include, and perhaps be based upon, an organic progression
of chromatic tone. In black and white this progression is still available:
indeed, it is possible sometimes to gauge the greatness of a colourist by
his drawings. On the other hand, there are plastic painters using the
crudest and brightest colours who, since they obtain so little from this
strong colour, seem to me to suggest thereby achromatic tone, the

polarized range between black and white, that same range in a brighter form. I shall refer in the Appendix to the fact that many Florentine pictures are painted in this way with a great deal of care. Again, apart from a certain prettiness or glaring brightness, many effects of motley seem to me a stress upon mere achromatic tonal difference. There exists no organic relationship between such colours, and the eye jumps about relating tones that approximate.[5] The carving eye, I am convinced, always looks first amid phenomena that are diverse, for those elements which approximate. The primary power of the aesthetically trained eye is the power to synthesize.

In the act of perceiving the pattern or general organization of a picture when we first look at it, the trained eye does not tend, I am convinced, to relate the light areas with their shadows, in other words the eye does not want to take pre-eminent account of particular forms however great the emphasis given to them by the artist. On the contrary, throughout the picture the lights organize together and the darks organize together.

The lights organize together and the darks organize together. This is said from the point of view of achromatic tone. In the case of colour, the relationship is basically the same but is far more subtle, liable to every kind of paradox. The eye relates the lights together and the darks together subject to all the cross-currents of complementary colours and other factors that compensate a colour for its actual difference in tone from another colour, to an effect of greater equality between the lights and the darks, though their roles as tone is not impaired or weakened. This three-dimensional pattern element wherein similar calls to similar or near-similar throughout the mosaic of a picture, this sole emphasis upon a single unity that works, as it were, without reference to ourselves, is the first and primary quality – though misunderstood and evaded by so many artists preoccupied with the delineation of tactile form, its contrasts, its light-effects and silhouettes – that distinguishes the height of European painting from the linear or tonal progressions, conned bit by bit, of the East.[6] The all-overness of our extreme plastic exuberance already points to its final stabilization in the extreme of carving conception. The problem of our painting is, or always should be, to establish contour and pattern without sacrificing the light to the dark or the dark to the light. Hence the all-importance of colour relationship with its immense power in paradox, potent, for instance, to evoke from a dark colour not only warmth but light. In fact, in order to 'work' upon each other with *equal* power, colours more often than not require differentiation not only of intensity but also of tone.

Yet frequently in our pictures the dark patches especially have no function other than to show off the light. Now, the element of contour complicates the synthesis that the eye makes in putting the lights with the lights and the darks with the darks, complicates their relationship by the addition of roundness, distance and direction. Cézanne gave to the forms of nature an exaggerated difference between every plane, or perhaps it would be clearer to say that he multiplied those planes. At the same time in thus magnifying contour he made it more gradual, bestowed upon planes an equality among themselves by employing marked changes of hue as well as of tone. On the other hand, by his use of strong contour lines at the farthest limit of his forms he enriched his colour relationships; since a coloured shape bounded by a darker line is stronger in colour than when it is seen without a boundary. This method entailed the mass organization of equal yet unbridgeable units as in mosaic work. For contrast one might instance typical Baroque composition in which there are no units but one diagonal sweep. All the same, the lights organize well with the lights and the darks with the darks in the calligraphic Baroque mode of draughtsman-ship. Roughly speaking it was from such Baroque organization that Cézanne developed.

In the picture of bathers exhibited among the French pictures at the Burlington Galleries in the autumn of 1936, there is a good instance of the method by which Cézanne brought about an approximation between his lights and darks without sacrifice of their integrity as the means of plastic enforcement. The sky is blue in effect, the light, as it were, of the picture is blue. Yet Cézanne has used almost the same tone of blue as a shadow colour. The strong line of shadow down the spine of the foremost nude is like a flash of blue sky fastening down into the ground. Again, the strong contour lines are of the same blue. Without sacrifice of flourish a poetic approximation is created, a common entity is extracted even between sky and earth. What meaning once more for the vertical and the horizontal: how different their common entity from the superficial colour unity of those many pictures, so perfectly 'in tone' as the framers say, which look as if they were hardly there at all! The 'all-over' brownness of so much eighteenth-century painting is a feeble compromise between the Mediterranean feeling for growth or equality and the Baroque single sweep. Every kind of painting is easily degraded into compromise with its opposite.

I mention these bad pictures that are irreproachably 'in tone' and innocent of more than a touch of pure colour, lest in my insistence upon equality and close relationship I shall have given the impression that anything in the way of brightness is of necessity anathema to me. That is not the issue at all. There are Picassos in which bright reds, greens, yellows, blues and black and white show the finest kind of colour organization. I am thinking of an abstract picture exhibited at the Rosenberg Galleries and dated 1924. Each shape is subdivided in colour, and the subdivisions have their independent relations in further parts of the picture. You are conscious of all of it all at once, because if, for instance, the blue forms catch your eye, the yellow ones at the same instant engross attention; nor is your attention disappointed. I venture to say that no one else has ever brought off such perilous *tours de force* in the use of colour as I mean colour.

This evocation of form through colour and texture is but an extension of the effects I have described in terms of growth and co-operation and of the gathering up of horizontal planes into vertical shapes. In many well-coloured modern pictures the *process* of this organization as well as the organization itself is present; the material is given and also that which is, so to say, carved out of this material. In old pictures as well, sometimes the backgrounds of portraits seem to be the material upon which, we feel, the artist has worked and from which he has elicitated his foreground forms. Thus the background possesses some

significance apart from its negative role in showing up the figure.
A certain tension and equality, the tension of the spread object, obtain
throughout. We shall see this principle exploited to the full in the
pictures of Piero della Francesca. In his case we cannot speak of a background to figures: the relationship is far too positive. His background
colours and even textures are often carried into an (on the picture plane)
adjacent foreground form of an entirely different character. To give an
over-simple instance from Arezzo, the robe of a man standing in front
of a pillar carries through in its creases the fluting of that pillar. Similarly, too, in the vastly different pictures of Giorgione we have a material
worked upon; in his case, perhaps, best called a theme. In late Renoirs
we have the raw material kept raw, raw material and its elaboration
intermixed throughout. For instance, in many of his late landscapes
we are 'given' a rose-colour, a blue and a green: we find them throughout the landscape, in sky, in trees and in water, each substance thereby
qualifying the character of another in virtue of such common substance.[7]
This is where representational pictures score over abstract pictures:
a poetic relationship exists between the picture seen for its subject-
matter and when seen as an organization.

Let us now look at the matter the other way round: mutual enhancement must always be viewed from both sides. As well as a material that
is worked or carved, I see in some pictures working and developments
that in their sum give back to their material its pristine unsullied state.
A picture should be like an open concertina capable of being packed in
harmoniously. Far the most striking colour in the *Concert Champêtre* of
the Louvre is a segment of crimson hat belonging to the central seated
musician. I have always felt that the colour and form of the rest of the
picture could be folded up in that hat.

A well-coloured picture is like a spread fan, a spread peacock's tail.
To what is it that colours return, how do they lend themselves to being
packed? Lights of all hue in equal proportions make white light. Colour
is the division of white. I would define the European painter as an artist
who, as it were, carves a white canvas, divides that white (Chinese painters have never had the heart, it seems, truly to divide their white), opens

it to show the strength of colour that may evolve from it. The painter, on the analogy of the earth and its vegetation, by ploughing, as it were, a white surface, creates his own organic world, his own evening panorama. (Specularly reflected white light is at its minimum in the evening, the time at which local colour is best seen.) A division of the white flame of life in terms of graduated colour, a division so complete as to rival in completeness white, the very absence of colour: under this image I conceive the painting of Cézanne.

And I think that apart from scientific assurance on the point, we sometimes have the perception that, ideally speaking, all colours together make white. It is not, to be sure, our usual way of looking at white, even in art. But occasionally white assumes this character. I have in mind the lighthouse at Godrevy Point on the north coast of Cornwall. The lighthouse cylinder stands among a group of white-washed buildings with black barrel roofs seemingly all of one piece. These white buildings are founded in grey rock. On some days the circumventing sea has blue, yellow, green, maroon and even orange colours crested with evanescent foam as epitome. From the point in a tearing wind we look down at the island growing into firm white buildings with black roofs: the central cylinder of white outlined against the grey sky is a monument to every form and colour in sea, sky and rock.

There is a remark attributed to Titian, to the effect that the true colourist will feel the preciousness of unmixed white. Certainly few modern paintings allow one to feel it. But there are other aspects of white, as I have said. Nevertheless, the domination of white as we sometimes see it in contemporary paintings very often means little more than a refusal to give battle in the pictorial lists. The unsullied canvas is beautiful, it is vulgar to attempt to rival it except in terms of a major transformation.

From the carving point of view, paint as a substance is a meaningless plastic mud. It must therefore be divided in terms of colour, identified with the white unsullied canvas in virtue of drastic chromatic division. The use of this plastic mud in itself as providing sensations of plasticity, a role to which oil paint so easily lends itself, also has its place. Everyone learns to appreciate that: connoisseurship today in pictures is largely confined to admiring this cookery in paint, to the conning of delightful bits. The more important carving values are less widely appreciated, those matters which are more purely the concern of the eye. In my view no serious painter will ever give a thought to the lusciousness or otherwise of any particular 'passage' of a painting, in and for itself.

An Argument

(1943)

Sometimes a picture rises in the mind for no apparent reason. I may be digging and my foot may hit the spade in a certain sort of way and at the moment I have a glimpse of a road in the Pyrenees where I was walking some 25 years ago: nor has this memory been previously evoked. I suspect it is not so much something I was doing in the field that corresponded with some incident on that road, and thus evoked the memory: no, I suspect that the total configuration of image and sensation in the field, though concerned with entirely different experiences, happened to correspond in direction, feeling or pattern with a moment of my consciousness while walking that road: and this particular pattern had not come up before.

The mind, I believe, is constantly busy with the correlation of its patterns, and had I to name the content of the indubitable yeast for life which, although it varies, so seldom is altogether lost, I should say that, in terms of animal satisfaction, of accomplishment of idealism or whatever, this ever-growing store and ever-enlarging complication of patterns, were the essence. For the great part of the day of most lives – though not the night – the range is severely restricted. Those working at repetitive occupations are deeply conscious of the repetitions long after they have ceased to work. The artist, of course, and those able to study a contemplative life, are most sensitive to evocation. I know that even when I am not driven, the majority of sounds create not only images and memories but what I can only call a configuration of experience, different kinds of experience brought into one pattern, while a succession of sounds will mean a succession of configurations that together compose a far more subtle and more complicated experience. When my mind is attentive, each and every motor horn of different pitch will evoke an entirely different configuration. More matter-of-fact people, I know, under all circumstances would simply respond by thinking 'that is so-and-so's car'. Yet I believe that some sort of configuration is there, not so conscious nor perhaps so elaborate. The hoot of a train is evocative to many people. Interwoven into every mental figure of this kind is the sense of being quite simply drawn along. And yet the hoot of a train fascinates all children, even though they have never been carried in a train. The infantile satisfaction with this noise conjoined with smoke does, I believe, also underlie all the later images: and so with all configuration. It will always come back to something very simple; and here again is witness to the characteristic elaboration of the mental life wherein terms originally simple are expressed by elaborate patterns, by subtle structures of correlation and distortion. And again there is this pleasure, the pleasure of the very zest of life in the symbol, in the single experience that typifies.

A transition now to considering the nature of art as the impulse to create patterns, is easy. Indeed, there is no need to point to the analogy. Art typifies the mental flow in which much is expressed within a simple datum of the senses.

Within the terms of a particular stimulus the whole of a man's experience is expressed anew in each moment of consciousness. In the manner of a work of art, consciousness is a kind of distorted reflector of the manifold. Each aspect of the manifold has its echo in this picture within the perspective of a particular stimulus. This effectual expression of what is manifold is achieved, as in a work of art, by intensive correlation, rationalization, and indeed by distortion. Such activity is so old in us that we cannot trace without the greatest difficulty what was projected, distorted, rationalized. In this way the unconscious or semi-conscious are dragooned by consciousness. It is the fundamental activity of living, as it is an aesthetic activity. With the aid of reason man constructs infinite edifices from the ceaseless material of a few primary emotions, simple by themselves, in combination infinite of nuance. Each fresh composition uses anew the material and the memory of all previous structures.

It is strange to me that no mystique has attached itself to this process, no philosophy. For indeed, here we may perceive the matter of the basic metaphysical terms, as first of all the original terms of dualism.

Every philosophy is based upon an opposition of terms. Its aim is either to describe this interaction and find the absolute in the interaction itself or to reduce the one to terms of the other and thereby create an absolute. Language is based upon absolutes, since opposites define each other. It is worthwhile to contemplate, in a way that philosophy has not done before philosophizing, the generic pair of opposites in which our lives are cast. I am confident that here will be found all the philosophy that is needed, in fact all that is most profound. Those cursed meaningless questions, as the one about the purpose of life, will be put out of court.

The new-born baby soon becomes aware that neither his mother nor the surrounding world is an extension of himself. Henceforth, to his dying day, there remains the huge division between himself and objects, people or things. Throughout life we seek to rival the externality of things. The world of nature is not only a physical habitat and the material of science, not only the material of practical life, but the medium of every mood. Indeed without this canvas, as it were, on which to apply ourselves, by which we project, transmute and as well satisfy the simple animal needs, we cannot conceive the inner flow of the mind or the activity of the body. The body is obviously meaningless without an external world beyond it: but so too is the mind. Mental as well as physical life is a laying outward of shape within, in rivalry as it were with the laid-out instantaneous world of space. To project is to distort, etc.

That is the process, one of elaboration: whereas the fundamental spur to action, to thought, are simple and bleak, their intermingling is rich, producing an infinite range. A man is the sum of all meanings he has experienced. But it is very rare that he speaks and feels in complete equilibrium, detached from immediate circumstances, or, rather, possessing immediate circumstances as the context of equilibrium of all accumulated meanings. Nor does practical life encourage such detachment.

The most generalized apprehension we carry with us all the time is the certainty of life and of death. A parallel relationship to the interdependence of subject and object. We strive to manifest our living (subject) in rivalry with the laid-out dispositions of the outside world. In the end, we do indeed in death (object) become solely a part of the inert outside world. As well as being opposites, life and death supplement each other. It is not surprising to find that the activities of consciousness are dual and supplementary; namely the pursuit of fact necessary for practical life and for science, and the construction of fantasy, 'objective' and 'subjective' respectively in character. The fearless allocation, and thereby the further satiety of these two activities, is the proper study of mankind. (It is obvious that fantasy should have no part in science; yet it has done so in all thought anterior to science, blocked the emergence of science for thousands of years. But once the emotional expression is rationalized: that is the very breath of life... aesthetic 'truth'.) For instance, except in terms of aesthetic significance, it is meaningless, after using the idea of purpose constantly for the elucidation of fact, to harness this idea to the intimations of fantasy and ask a question an answer to which is not a craving of pure reason as is supposed but of the desire for emotional correlation of a rather vulgar kind; to ask the question, then, what is the purpose of life, or what is the purpose of death. Our images are compounded with fact, with reason, vast rationalized structures that hold in duress the fluid emotions, the grave and grand architecture of all mankind. Images encase all thought and are articulated by thought, but they are not primarily the products of thinking sense. I, even more than most men, live by fantasy. But I do not mistake it for truth.

At Venice

From *Venice* (1945)

Venice excels in blackness and whiteness; water brings commerce between them. Italians excel in the use of black and white, white stone and interior darkness. Colour comes between, comes out of them, intensely yet gradually amassed, like a gondola between water and sky.

I saw today a great grey sail patched with white, a warehouse in fact on the Giudecca it looked: it moved away to reveal such a warehouse. Commerce between mobile and static (lacking in modern streets), commerce between what thus becomes dramatically identified as well as contrasted, a deep and necessary commerce rather than an interplay, provides the clue to Venice, to Giorgione and to all the greatest art.

If we look away from the water at the white stone surrounding door and window, we seem to see all the potential whiteness in the water abrogated for the finest day, solid, geometric, still.

If we swim round a rock, we are poignantly aware of its stature. We see this hardness from below rearing out of the continuousness of water, in contrast to our slow horizontal movement on top of the water. We are on top, superficially on top of the water, but the embedded rock rises far above. It is the same relationship we have on land with a tree. The buildings of Venice appear in organic relationship with water just as trees with earth.

And it is one thing to walk past a building, another to glide past, to slip slowly in a continuous movement. The hesitancy of water reveals architectural immobility.

Those parts of any town apparent from water are deeper than the stream, still and solid. Each projection is enhanced when some of them divide the medium of water as well as that of air. The thinner air is then divided with increased clarity. And each recess obtains a static cave-like depth. From pavement to wall is a comparatively dull progression. On the water, swimming or in a small boat, we are the insects, the may-flies, buoyant. And when we disturb this translucent medium, breasting a way that has repercussion upon the shore of stone, not only immobility remarks itself but each water-level cranny is discovered. Our passage discovers the building anew. This is hardly the case with any other locomotion.

It follows that the first character of Venetian building is sheerness and height. Yet, tall brothers, Venetian palaces never lost reverence for their pollard mother, St. Mark's. The essence of Byzantine organization was in no period forgotten, but in the Gothic period and thereafter, principal windows became tall and narrow. The oblong panel, at first enclosing a pointed arch, entered an enduring relationship with the braided Byzantine curve (a relationship, however, already apparent in St. Mark's). Perhaps their original and most naked fusion is the cylindrical Gothic chimney-stacks with bell-like tops. This fusion was decocted in the Renaissance upon the partial return to Byzantine form: the relationship of oblong, cylinder and curve is the pre-eminent subject of Venetian Renaissance architecture, especially preoccupation with rectangular panel and oblong jamb to door and window or oblong face to pilaster, in association with the new emphasis upon rounded and circular shapes. The re-fusion of these elements in the form of the cylinder became the preoccupation of Venetian sculpture and, to some extent, of Venetian painting, especially when the subject was the long Venetian countenance.

Emphasis on the façade of buildings upon the rectilinear was the result of a widespread outlay of rectilinear stone in the paving and ground decoration of campi and of the piazza itself, of the steps and handrails of curved bridges. This stone flooring, and stone links above the water, bridges of a type that more or less precluded the horse, did not exist in any number before the Renaissance. Venice itself, as we think of it today, was a creation of the Renaissance. And it was at the time of the Renaissance and after, that the *liston*, the thin oblong of the most white Istrian stone, was set as an inlay everywhere, marking even the meanest apertures throughout the city.

But the first quality, as above, of Venetian building is sheerness and height. Opposing water at their bases, the palaces lean back. At water level, mouldings are so heavy and protuberant that architectural projection around the apertures aloft, appear less as projections than as incrustations at the mouths of caves raised above the sea, incrustations not only from the sea but from the moving springs within. So heavy are Venetian buildings at ground or sea level that they appear sometimes to be upside down, especially since it is rare that they are crowned with the usual projecting cornice. The untapering lightness of the higher stories, combined with the narrowness and sheerness of the whole, affords a minimum effect of weight. Weight is below: foundations are visible, all that is raised above the piles; but these projections, like the roots of trees, suggest a rising sap and strong grip captured for growth. Naturally, it is the same with buildings away from the water, and even with Venetian buildings far removed from Venice. Not even columns in Venice express the carrying of weight. Arches spring from them in a rapid curve; trabeation is not stressed. Columns project as much or more than the architraves they carry, and are not, therefore, altogether under the architraves. Ionic volutes on the capitals often appear to be without connection with the architraves. As often as not, too, and not only at the entrances of St. Mark's, twin columns upon imposts, with spaces between them, support heavy archivolts with little intervening trabeation. There is little tight linked effect of support.

Again, in humanized and ordered classical form it is the architecture of rock and cave with strong bulwark at the base, with precipice and scattered encrusted orifice. As in cliff there is no display of constructive *strength*. Each member enjoys a distinct life, each column, each capital is distinct: there is a complete equality of all the members; yet they compose together with the graciousness of all classical members: no affiliation, then, with rock-hewn temples of South America or of India where inhabited rock is indeed rock with apertures, or with strong irregular architecture in general. These palaces have that strength, but they have also the separated, civilized grace of the classical. Organization or composition though abundant and, indeed, often regular, is an organization that depends less upon opposing balances than upon a commerce, and so an identification, between disparate units. It is, therefore, an organization that approximates nearer to the one of Piero della Francesca and of other masters of equality allied to distinctness, than to the one of the draughtsman with his groups of balancing forces.

A colour, rather than a linear, organization.

Similarly, in Venice as a whole, tone so easily acquires these values ascribed to colour. Thus blackness, as well as whiteness, obtains a meaning over and above its tone value, more especially that value fundamental to profound colour relationship, identity in difference. The gondolier's seaworthy serpent, we have seen, is black between water and sky: but rather than as a silhouette whose character is to stand out, and the character of whose background is thus to be a contrasting background, the black gondola appears in organic connection with its light surroundings, an organic connection, suggestive of circulation, which belongs to colour rather than to tone. This solid blackness seems to have been extracted from the dark places of water which therefore now appear lighter. Similarly, the gondolier's rhythmic stroke sums in an orderly succession the crowded flood upon which he works.

It is rare in Venice to see bulks looming in the flood, a Turner-esque mesh ambuscading a river-mouth. What one sees nearly always rises clear from the water: the waters do not suffer it; they carve it. The concourse of waters, both in their lightness and in their darkness, are resolved as building. At the mercy of the winds, watery reflections are the impress left behind in an emptied shell. Water has no lid. An oar fathoms it, it opens just so much, closes, heals from beneath. The undulating floor of St. Mark's is water with all its colours eternally healed. Similarly the darkest windows obtain a kind of radiance from the fact of aperture above the closed waters: their darkness burns slowly and forever over the reflecting element beneath that is partly dark and partly light; just as the white stone sums and solidifies the light part. And because Istrian stone bleaches in the light, blackens in the shade, many columns and projections upon Venetian building are most dramatically, most intensely light and intensely dark. This darkness that radiates evenly has inspired as well as the characteristic chiaroscuro of Venetian painting, the extensive use of dark-coloured disks and circular holes in Venetian architecture, common in all periods.

So propitious are the black Venetian interiors as seen from outside, framed by the white or blackening stone, that however decrepit the palace above the water, something from inside, especially from the top windows, is expected to fructify. From the quatrefoils above the arches of the Doge's palace, something, we feel, comes to pass. This navel held above the pillar has a torch-like quality. Venetian Gothic, which developed circular shapes, possesses a particular still radiance in aperture. There exists in the Gothic palace windows flanked by porphyry or serpentine disks, a constant communication – and a musical one – between the inside and the outside world, as if flambeaux burnt steadily near the balconies and the palace lay open to the night music of the serenade. And how melodious this music coming from the canal which cleaves to, and carves, the palace feet and now is raised in sound to pierce the apertures above!

Circular apertures suggest a ship; and an emphasis upon aperture must be strengthened by an emphasis upon the surface in which apertures appear. Here, at any rate, we are constantly reminded of construction by the Venetian palaces. Aperture, empty space, existed first, then the skeleton, then the walls that withstand the water. In these terms, the ribs are still visible in pilaster, pillar and cornice: they are allowed to project as first defence. The wall lies behind them. And if the remaining apertures suggest caves, then the circular disks, so often in attendance upon Venetian windows, are stones that have been rolled away from these entrances. The first development from the original Byzantine architecture, was a sealing up, in the Gothic period, of the open Byzantine arcades. Byzantine secular wall-space, as we see it in the Fondaco dei Turchi, even though sheeted and embossed with emblems, does not sustain any of the above images. Where long rounded arcades are open, one above the other, there is no impression of a rock or of a cave or of a radiant darkness and lightness amassed from the reflecting water.

But Gothic builders filled up with steep walls, added ribs to the windows by dividing them with a mullion column. Nevertheless, the deep bays of St. Mark's and the precious sheeting of its walls gave the prototype, if not for these forms, then for the images employing them.

Projections from a wall, particularly in the shape of a pilaster whose thickness we can see, reinforce our sense of the wall behind them. But the greater part of a Byzantine palace wall lay too far behind deep loggias. Gothic and Renaissance builders, while at times keeping such loggias, generally contrasted them on the same plane with sealed walls, walls sealed with disks, walls whose projections suggested a further structure or framework that reinforce the walls. Conversely, when we conceive the buildings from inside rather than outside, the projections are incrustations at the apertures of caves, while the walls are the sheer rock. In short, Venetian architecture after the Byzantine period is always concerned with the wall, its thickness as a bulwark or its crystallization from the water that it rebuts. The unusual placing, at first of Gothic windows, made walls more precious, a novel way of emulating the costly or literal preciousness of the walls of St. Mark's. We are back to our original conception of the Venetian palaces, attributing to them a sheerness and height in which each orifice and carved recess has deep meaning to the mind.

We have mentioned an identity in difference as characteristic of form conceived in terms of colour: all that we have to say about Venetian architecture is relevant to the feats of Giorgione. When associated with the richness of an identity in difference, images of interchange, of transformation and of metamorphosis may serve us without a tinge of mysticism. Thus, the five blackening balustrade supports to the last window of the old prisons have white swelling breasts. They are like penguins. The black and white of sea-birds are stones in Venice. A sea-gull in Venice is of no interest. One sees it only as a finial released from a building. But the pigeons of St. Mark's are a solace to tired feet, grey softnesses above the hard and grey volcanic pavement. Feeding the pigeons is a ritual, an offering to the stones we tread.

In Venice we note particularly any transformation of material.

294

On the sides of some fondamenta, moisture causes the Istrian stone coping to mix with the brickwork below; similarly in the case of layers of stone between the brick. From mortar also, crystallizations appear on brick. Again, the copper dome of the church opposite the station has dripped greenly on the Istrian drum: the bronze statue upon the dome is similarly dyed. This building, the visitor's first sight of Venice, though unlike any other building there, in iridescent form, in a colour most unusual for Venice, symbolizes the prevailing process. This dome confounds the heights with the depths, suggesting in clear and stationary form exalted to an apex, the long tilted lift of the swell against the stone, which subsiding, reveals the greens of seaweed and of slime.

At sunset the water reflects the sky. That which the water reflected all day now it clasps and incorporates. Fusion is complete: the sky itself now rocks beneath the grandeur of yet whiter stone. This same rocking, one feels, sets the more distant churches swaying and swimming, sets their evening bells to roll. The brown prayers of the Redentore arc loosed at evening in unmoored sound: and the church slips in upon the sky-and-water, aloft the white embannered Christ upon the dome.

The richness, the salt, the hardness of the water has caked into gleaming and hammered stones, particularly on rough days when the Giudecca's sea-green canal is tipped with foam. The past in Venice seems to be the period taken for crystallization: the store of Venetian history is encased by an image of an accumulated sea-change. So deeply laid are the imaginative foundations of Venice, to such an extent has stone abrogated the meaning of soil in our minds, that decay, as we have seen, takes the form of metamorphosis, and even of renewal.

Venice is a potent symbol of the mother. As we ride the canals we move within her circulation. All we have said of Venetian architecture reflects the same symbolism. It is not surprising, therefore, to find that it worked, that is, the oligarchical Venetian government: worked with more public spirit than did any other large political organization of those centuries; and lasted longer. History gives few comparisons with the internal unity of Venice. Elsewhere political sagacity has not combated destiny with such success: no other statesmen have seen so far ahead: and by means of the supreme realism of correct prognostication, Imperial Venice perpetuated herself, artificially as it were, for some two hundred years after her needful death.

Such artificiality in astonishing unity with such realism is the measure of all Italian civilization, but more particularly in Venice where nature in exotic form conspires with good sense. Ceaselessly the waters must be carved for carrying things, ceaselessly the lagoons must be marked and dredged. The immense toil of water portage is vividly yet slowly contemplated. The ruling classes, however luxurious, could at no time isolate themselves from communal life. Their palaces could not be apart or carriages at the door. They took ship or walked with others in the midst of the sea. Here nature conspires also with beauty. Even ostentation here, even flamboyant intricate adornment are often no less effective, no less utilitarian than a racing motorcar. Thus, no other kind of craft but a gondola, and so, none less beautiful, could navigate as well the narrow canals.

When the standard of St. Mark's is ablaze on a Sunday in the piazza between two Italian flags, when one notes the crack of the six tapering pennants in the wind like the 'gives' in the body of a toy dragon – and the lion of St. Mark is most dragon-like with gold-scarlet archaic roar, with brazen wings and latin speech – when one considers that this ensign was the emblem of efficiency, foresight, strength and restraint right up to the end, it is as if some 'cunning' machine of war, some embossed and coruscated cannon spitting fire from gilt lips or carved nostril, *was* the better weapon, quicker than the machine gun, with longer range than the German colossus.

But display became more and more slow and scarlet in the a-equinous square of St. Mark's. Pedestrian pomp, secular triumph celebrated afoot with aquatic interruptions, has communicated to the deep marbles of St. Mark's an archaic, loaded dwarfishness, witness of the priest-like, ephor-like doges in solemn perambulation. Nevertheless these same doges, and very likely with the horns of satin on their heads, witnessed the sailings of the most powerful navies and richest merchant fleets in the world, bulwarks, at times the only bulwarks, of Europe against the Turk. Even in the eighteenth century the Venetian navy was still formidable. The arsenal turned out replicas of Dutch and English frigates. The massive breakwater, the Murazzi, was built from the Lido at a cost of twenty million Venetian lire from 1744 to 1751.

Let us for the moment be as if settled in Venice to live continuously through the summer, predestined long before to these waters by the dry bright winter sounds of Genoa. There is more background, the Tuscan, for our perpetuation in the sun this June, in our perpetuation among the palace shoals and the out-to-sea horizons. And here on the Giudecca where the Redentore is eager to echo other bells across the lagoon, where the long plane-less hammering of caulkers sounds all day, there are gardens towards Chioggia on the south side. Bird noises, one burst upon another, congregate, air for stones to breathe in the heat, given out in evening suspiration by long bass cries, by the sudden shattering shutting of shops; later, by the dizzy passage of guitars and of slow feet. Or else the bird cries slip across the shallows, are lost in silence before they may beat upon the reddish walls of San Lazzaro.

To such reciprocations and transformations the proud bands of Genoese winter rumour have now proceeded. At twilight the biggest ships funnel a way to the open Adriatic. They carry with them nothing of Venice: these lassitudes are not in flux. Because the stones are arranged by a thousand years of man, because the very pavements are omnipotent, rhythm remains regular, undisturbed by the less remarkable evolutions of the skies, here at their largest. Which is the released and releasing sky? There is no dust in Venice. Which indeed the clouds? All day long bright and sombre clouds carry away the storms over the undulating sea, conduct the in-bound draughts between. All movements administer to the stones.

One may know this best away from the canals, at St. Helena, at Malamocco, at the Lido, because it is surprising there. Not that these modern buildings are beautiful. Some are hideous, but most of them pleasant enough in unforced reminiscence of Venice. On the whole their contours are clean. Buildings here too are awake while the whole heaven, wind and trees are subservient. So strong the tradition of man's dominion, that it is but necessary to put up the sign 'Viale Francesco Morosini', matt black lettering on a matt white ground, in order to scatter the wilderness. Modern concrete, too, can dominate waste land, also new stones hammered throughout their surfaces as is the Venetian tradition, causing those tiny recesses which link them with the deep bays of St. Mark's. And thus, because of Venice's overwhelming impression, paradoxically the Lido, spacious and green, whose villas are like the eyes of an owl, indifferent to the day, piercing the night which they assume, may give back to one the feeling of architectural dominion if this feeling has sunk too deep amid the ancient fevers of Venice herself. The very trams that grind along the Lido are unreal, barging through the heat-haze, as sorry as cab-horses, unable to influence the habitable stucco and stone. The tram comes to rest, gives out a long somnolent sigh that mingles with the happy trees. Trees are the Venetian dogs, companions to man: forgotten their primeval savagery and forest. Natural colour is subservient, man-made colour dominant: certainty of the houses is but the servant of their tone and colour. All strength displays itself through colours and their shadows.

But we are well stocked for lassitudes in Venice, where Italy and history reach their pitch. Remembered the long salute of the Tuscan landscape this spring, the attentive, waterless, villas: the up-raised loggias of those parts, roofed like sunshades, equal to rain and to sun, open to the four winds which are withheld except to the evening nod of cypress: loggia towers like many moons risen on gradual valleys: white farm houses with big clocks, houses of noonday somnolent brightness whence the beautiful oxen disentangle the dust from the white roads. Poppies bloom amid the tides that set the cornfields and stiff bamboos in delicate motion. In the height of day the smells of flowers and animals peruse the light air, as if nocturnal. The early summer sits wide, but there is lightness in every line upon the sky.

The tall windows of Italy, steep windows of Venice! And, arrived there now, to linger through long July afternoons, to savour the counting-house gloom dim with warmed stones, though the windows are huge, of the typically Venetian charitable organization, apotheosis, as it were, of sailors' benevolent institutions everywhere, a Scuola San Marco, a Scuola San Rocco, a Scuola San Giovanni… to feel these halls now derelict of their object, still gracious, still grandiose, still superbly ship-shape, to be impelled by the frescoes of Tintoretto on wall and ceiling at San Rocco so to view them with the astonished eyes of an orphan, a beneficiary; to have the practical intention of such halls so long, so many centuries after, well in mind amid the masterpieces, is to know most poignantly that these great windows of black bottle glass give out upon the sea like portholes, is to visualize the opaque outside staircases as broad at their tops as at their bottoms, the Giant's staircase in the Ducal palace as well as the Gothic one in the courtyard in a palace at San Tomà, these and other wide stones hung between high sala and courtyard, magnifications in stone of the rope-ladders let down coiled and uncoiling in the active air above the sea. Man would seem to climb these stairs by right of pygmy-hood, just as swallows do not fail to nest in the ears of gigantic statues.

Sometime before this general magnification in stone, on another shoal of the lagoon, at Murano, sand and water began to petrify at the hands of the thrifty Venetians. Apart from glass utensils and ornaments, at Venice, probably for the first time in Europe, glass was used as window-panes. The very translucence of water was fixed to palaces affronting the sea.

Part One

From *Inside Out* (1947)

Going down the hill one morning towards Lancaster Gate, my eldest
brother remarked on an orange cloud in a dark sky: a thundercloud,
he said. And sure enough, that afternoon there was a thunderstorm.
At nearby Stanhope Gate, an old woman sold coloured balloons. It was
as if the lot had burst. I think I remember well this small event since
it symbolizes an exceptional happening. For once the glowering suspense, the feeling of things hardly redeemed, was contradicted by a
menace that came to violent fruition. The thing was done and finished
with: the storm happened and passed, and the small orange cloud had
shown it was to happen. None of the other omens I can remember was
either read or fulfilled as was this. The year would be 1908 or so, when
I was six.

I used to single out the cars in the processional traffic on the road
round the park, and count them. Their cautious, noisy explorations
without an objective, without an arrival point, a trundling round the
park, helped to create the atmosphere of grinding suspense. Meanwhile, beyond the cruel railings, the scarlet horse-buses with Tatcho
advertisements roared down Bayswater Road. The railings were cruel,
I think, because of the tramps who sat on seats outside, in waste-paper
and drowsy filth: and whatever was railed within the park, suggested
a burning-cold, a searing prohibition against those who would slink
away into the iron ivyness of copse or plantation. Other single railings
were isolated in the open parts of the park. Their usefulness would
seem to be confined to that of a threat against the couples who blunder-
ed in the dark, choosing an exposed and therefore isolated place in
which to lie. There seemed to be no love in that love-making. To the
small boy, the immersed, in-rolled couple suffered from a still greater

poverty than did the single drunks who slumbered face to the sky. The evil was poverty, not crime or drink. Poverty itself was destructive. Dirt, smell and the bleary eye, all to my mind, smart and noisome activities, were the predominant performances of poverty.

I was forbidden to sit on the seats with complicated cast-iron sides frequented by the destitute. Nevertheless, regarding these seats as forlorn homes, I was fascinated, not only by the danger imputed to them, an infection, as it were, of poverty, but by the possibility of constant acts of restitution. I would therefore implore my governess, in spite of the ban, to use these seats; and I would get behind, between the low railing at the side of the walk and the back of the seat, and imagine that I was making this last refuge, for all the bareness of board and of cold, jarring contortion of cast-iron, to 'work', whether as a ship or car or whatever purposeful vessel took my fancy.

The *underneath* of the seat, at any rate, was my discovery, this space between the seat and the low rail in front of the grass, almost roofed by the sloping of the seat's back. Those who had forbidden it, had not examined that side. Could I keep the underneath alive and thus cause the animation of the whole?

This occasional game helped me very little to endow the park and its inhabitants with health. There were vaster engines than my seat which I could not control. The machine house of the fountains, for instance, had an ominous air. A scour of mysterious steam hung over a sunken tank at the back of the engine house and was apprehended at the same time as the smell of oil and the clanking of the lethal cylinders. The cold and grinding mechanism was housed in Portland stone of a late Victorian style, both white and darkened. The fountains themselves had little grace owing to the pretentiousness of every detail of the stone lay-out. Moreover, the smell of decay was freshened by the sprayed water that dropped like pellets on the surfaces of the basins. Surplus water from the final basin poured away into the Long Water. Here was the inky-dark medium of the park suicides. My governess and I used to read outside the park police station the notices recounting, in the hope of further information which brought a reward (printed in large letters), all the crimes that had recently occurred, chiefly suicides in the Serpentine. A police description of a dead body exactly expressed my predominant impression of the park as a whole. Yet I did not altogether give up hope of infusing these remnants with life. I would return again and again to the fountains and hope against hope that the engine-house activity would spell out something good. It was indeed worse when, as so often, the fountains were not working and the water licked the lichened sides more blackly without the bombardment of pellets. To see the fountains turned on – as I often did – was a fine sight, since the spouts grew from a trickle to an inch, to a foot, to a yard, finally reaching a great height, sustained there by an eager, pumping pulse: at the summit, rainbow colours could be discerned; a thin elegant summit sometimes torn by the wind but formed again immediately. The wind might tear off the whole summit or bend the column like a tree, but the compensating power returned in the end. This entirely mechanical restitution did not please me: the power behind it was blind, exact and faithless in the sense that it did not deal in faith. Perhaps, indeed, the relentless mounting of the fountains when they were turned on, propelled by each stroke of the very extensive engine, was really most frightening to me.

The fountains played. Dirty children rushed from basin to basin: suspicious park-keepers stalked their antics, generally from afar. The keepers had boxes scattered in the park, so that their emergence could have something of the suddenness associated with the paratroop whose landing has not been observed. The keepers carried whistles. Emergence from a telephone booth is always associated by me with the fingering of something tucked away on one side of the chest, a cold, punishing little organ that it was a positive duty to handle. When a park whistle was blown near the fountains, the shrill sound seemed to travel on an eagle journey, piercing the water pellets whose clattering was considerable. In fact, you had to shout to make yourself heard near the fountains.

We called the elderly ragamuffins and tramps of the park, 'parkees'. I had wandered away from my nurse who was chatting on the walk above the fountains. Among the basins I was seized by a pack of parkees and my shouts could not be heard even a few feet away. I managed to break loose – I had the wooden handle of a push-cart with me – and regained the nurse who had noticed nothing. In spite of my remembrance, I have little doubt that no such actual thing happened. Probably the context existed; parkees spoke to me and I had been warned against such intercourse by having the fear of being kidnapped instilled in me. But a kind of feud was invented. When the nurses and their children congregated, I would glance across at the other encampment of mothers and poor children and tramp women who seemed to watch every straying movement: and perhaps, well-armed with a stick, I would run halfway in their direction, testing the evil in comparative safety.

Sometimes the positions of the opposing camps would be reversed. We would be in the fountains, and the less intent parkees (since they always inhabited these seats) would be the objects of apprehension as they sat on a stone seat with a curious round termination on the walk above, or in the high, disproportionate alcove on the hill, down from Victoria Gate.

The tall, disproportionate alcove, shallow, high and cold, with toddlers squirming on a low brown seat, was, and is today (though it be attributed to Wren), an image to me of blindness. This kind of ethical ugliness in the use of a classical form, particularly the cruel denial of shadow or depth in proportion to the height, afflicted me to such an extent that I think it has helped me in later life to find good architecture to be a particular symbol of life. Nearly all the monuments and buildings in the park, including the fountains, professed for me the same cruel discrimination.

It was little better with the forms of life abounding on the lake, or with the dogs allowed to race and bounce about for a liverish hour, or led to lamp-post or rail on a lead. Obscenely different in size, they fought each other, raced and wrestled. In conjunction with the drawing-room salutations of their owners, their curiosity about each other appeared particularly morbid. The animal world seemed a sheer importation, a waywardness controlled with distaste and severity.

It was the same with the birds, largely fed by hand. An old man would be feeding sparrows. Their hopping and twittering and mass scurries of flight seemed to express his own accumulated evasions.

There were the peacocks which could be watched between the bars of the railings at the side of the Long Water. These disconsolate birds would sometimes spread a tail. A keeper fed them and to him was attributed all the powers of their control.

Yet occasionally, at times of post-luncheon winter sunsets, there was an atmosphere of nature in the park. Smoke from bonfires and a decreasing light suggested some limit to control, and the yelling of peacocks from a nook surprisingly distant, dislodged for a time an imputed curriculum.

Nevertheless, the ducks and other water-fowl seemed no less chained than the sparrows upon the neat paths. There are two gaps by the side of the Long Water, where the railings and concealing shrubbery cease, where the path comes to the edge of the water. In these two small bays the ducks are visited and fed. Even here, there is a kind of fencing, though it is in the water. The ducks enter through gaps. The shore is edged by a sloping stone kerb. A thin line of scum, feathers, soot, twigs, laves the lower edge of the rough stones which above are whetted by the slitherings of those ducks who land to be fed. Sometimes, too, there is a collection of geese with pin-cushion foreheads, needle eyes and evident ill-temper. The easy floating of the birds on water causes the uneasy trundling and shooting necks of the birds ashore to appear painful. The swans particularly look broad and gross in this shore wrangling for crumbs. The eyes of all the birds seem to pierce their heads as the keepers' whistles pierce the fountains' spray. They have their home upon an island in the Serpentine where at night they may be self-governing, though watched, as it were, by the monotonous sentry duty of the traffic in Knightsbridge.

The swans I knew to be fierce. There were stories of a blow from a wing smashing a man's leg and of the uselessness of an opened umbrella as a guard. Sometimes they moved on the water with ruffled plumage. Once, in minatory Edwardian stateliness, a swan was seen sitting on a nest below the fountains, just to the side of the dangerous overflow from the fountains into the Long Water, a miniature eddying waterfall whose downward suction or pull was challenged, but not refuted, by the even keel of the giant bird sitting on her dry nest.

Just as in the case of the parkees, when I was older and able to row a boat I used to come as close as I dared to this waterfall-termination of the Long Water. The flow, in fact, was small. But the dangers of the park as a whole could not thus be disproved.

Where did the water go? At the other end of the lake there was a low white bridge whose several arches were perhaps not more than a foot above the level of the water. Did the water flow away here where, even a swimmer, still less a boat, could not penetrate the mystery? This white stone bridge had a certain grace: the exceedingly low arches, however, were associated in my mind with a challenge to any inquisitive and anxious head whether of water-fowl or man, who tried to share the fate, whatever it might be, of the water beyond the Serpentine.

On the further side of the white bridge there was a sharp declivity and a high though meagre waterfall. I don't think that I connected this water with a flow from the Serpentine. Later, I was to hear that most of the Serpentine water passed underground and came up in the park of Buckingham Palace. I was to be told that the Serpentine could be drained, that everything flung into it could be brought to light. All the miseries of the torn, attacked and divided mother without me and within, she who was the park and all that happened there, to be known, controlled and restored? No wonder that in many later enquiries I have sought for the clean sweep. I have had an absurd faith in the efficacy of generalization and, at times, a neurotic subservience to the behests of an apparent logic. By this would-be control I have been subservient to the same relentless animus that informed, to my mind, the face of the park.

The park, of course, was not the first desolation but it is the one I remember first, the setting down in the external world of the sum of earlier desolations. Nature, in man and beast and flower, was a thing chained and divided. It would seem that each blade of grass, smelling of London even when it grew rankest, could be examined. There were no weeds. Sheep left droppings on the grass, left them there, so it appeared, just as towards sunset some living bundle of rags would seem to be left forlorn on a green chair for the use of which a penny should have been paid.

It was not usual for us to sit on these chairs. If we did, often the ticket collector would come unseen from behind us, cutting across the grass with a town gait, with his roll of tickets and his clippers moving loosely in front of him like a sporran. This ship of the park was another examining agent.

Banked-up by gardeners, flowers were viewed through railings, a splendid array in spring near Victoria Gate, just in front of the dogs' cemetery of which you could obtain one glance from the top of a bus bound for Queen's Road. Between you and the military rows of flowers was a wide grass verge and a high railing. Nearby there was a rustic cottage. In the course of time I grew very curious concerning this and other cottages, and a well-sized house in the middle of Kensington Gardens. I had never seen anyone go in or come out, but most delicious wood smoke was often climbing from the chimneys. These cottages and their small enclosed gardens, far more than the park grass or the trees or the flowers, suggested to me the open country, unknown to me except for the landscapes I saw from the train window on the way to the seaside. Later I used to imagine myself inhabiting the house in the middle of Kensington Gardens; walking the park in the early morning, watching the dawn and later seeing the lines of trees, an unspoilt natural panorama; living in the country in the middle of London. From adolescence onwards I did what I could with my imagination to restore the park. Standing at the Round Pond, I looked across the Long Water and conjured up the vista of an eighteenth-century park, a royal park having no essential connection with the lives of children.

But it was dust-laden; every blade of grass was discerned for a metropolitan purpose. The sheep would leave wool on trees, a dubious trail in a well-known spot on all sides of which London traffic roared. In summer there was the clipping and a branding and a dip, down near the police station. The startled shorn bodies suggested a touch of extreme 'nature', a nakedness, an exhibitionism, even a sudden production of the pale body, a child's amorous game, a suicide, a thousand little boys running nude into the Serpentine on a hot summer evening, allied somehow with the world of correctitude, railings and park-keepers; with parkees and violent dirt, no less.

And so, the candles of the beautiful chestnut trees were sullied and dangerous in my eyes. Only the countless blossom of the may trees with their sweet dusty town smell, seemed poised and without potential disaster. In a polite and a young form the bloom of these trees was the microcosm of the continent of endless brick where hope lay among the clustered varied chimney pots. I remember picnics under the may trees near Victoria Gate: I remember the brown osier lunch basket with osier pin like a giant hat pin, and the contents spread on the tame grass. Two older girls with their nurses used to join our party of three brothers and a nurse. Sylvia had a reddish face and Enid was pale, with freckles, green eyes and long legs. A saga about parkees was begun at those picnics. Heat glittered beyond the tossed-up may trees in flower: between the trees traffic glinted, seen from the eye-level of the grass. This circular flow of traffic served as a kind of watchful coasting on the fringes of consciousness: at times, also, as vehicles which carried correspondence to the deeper depths of the mind, bringing thence the matter for new affinities. And yet this upward, as it were, and downward movement was expressed by a steady low-lying motion along a flat surface. There is pleasure, there is life, when movement, particularly even movement in space, when the outward world at large, takes for us the form the jaggered, shifting promontories of the mind. It is notable, however, that the first glimpse of the sea, that closer parallel to the tossing mind, has a meaning of limitless release: and words wrested from a life at sea ring true of the mind.

As I walked at the side of the traffic from the bridge over the Serpentine to Victoria Gate, the extended movement of vehicles would express for me the hostile, unforgiving expanse of the sky. To the left there was rough ground with a deep ditch, the railed boundary between the park and Kensington Gardens. The rough ground just beyond the ditch epitomized the depth of frustration and hostility. It was here, I think, after my brothers had gone to school, that I tried to make casual friends by joining to kick a football. Also, at the end of this bit of ground, by the path going down to the fountains, I had confronted a little girl with a doll-like face called Helen who was the sister of a boy at my kindergarten. I longed to get to know her. I think there were rows and fights with possible friends on this piece of ground, the scene of failures in early attempts at sociability. For me, other children, like the rest of the furniture of the park, were objects of potential danger. Any difference in upbringing and in routine indicated a lost soul: for I was wrapt by the prohibitions and rituals in which I was educated and in terms of which I still hoped to make ultimate restitution. Projected on to the face of the park and there apprehended, the struggle was ugly, torn, stern, harrowed and dirtied, redeemed slightly – and here figured a half-concealment of the most profound anxiety – by a morbid melodrama.

I was a happy boy. By that I mean that both elders and contemporaries have told me that I gave them the impression of being happy, healthy, energetic. From my parents I had love and great care. There were occasional screaming fits, I am told, when I used to shout without end, 'I want it all right'.

What did I want put right? I had best say the park, since there is very little else that I remember either of the pleasure or the pain. The park I remember well.

I shall soon try to give a picture of the other side of this predominant state but in a subsequent form. I shall show how a good mother was finally constructed, in the external world as well as in myself. Art has played an important role. This is perhaps foreshadowed by my vain scrutiny of the monuments in the park: the giant Achilles statue at Hyde Park Corner, for instance and, later, the Watts equestrian statue in the middle of the Long Walk. I had high hopes of the Watts because it was new; I remember it veiled and then unveiled. Such figures were to me stern yet impotent; figures of a father, then, who both attacked and had been attacked. These statues attempted to affront the sky yet they were recipients of fog, of bird droppings and of soot: they seemed unconnected with light. The Albert Memorial was of the category, with vain groupings and pseudo-sacred steps. Here was a great fuss about solid matter; here was a thing of arrest which, unlike the prohibiting railings, protested as well as forbade. It took many years for me to discover that art was not a kind of warning. What else was to be made of the sharp, pale, granite obelisk in the Long Walk, with the one word 'Alma', with two steps and a platform edged by a decorous iron chain?

I think it might have been different if I had been allowed to approach Kensington Palace, the sunken Dutch garden and the Orangery. The only time I saw the Orangery, at the age of eight or nine, I was much impressed. For some reason, probably a fear of infection in an enclosed space, this part of the gardens was rigorously out-of-bounds. Perhaps because of this, still more because of the deep impression of the Orangery and its mild historic associations, the extreme limits of Kensington Gardens on the west side had magic for me: so much so, that I found it difficult to decide where were the exact limits. A sense of the infinite informed this very restricted space to the east of Kensington Park Gardens. The wall was high, but gardens stretched on the further side: termination came gently. In the shadow of that mysterious wall there lay a flat green where organized games were played of a different order from the haphazard kicking of a ball in the body of the park. I thought of this piece of ground as outside the park, yet at the same time, inside it, like a historical association pursued into the present. I was later to take great comfort in history, as if the things of the park, as if all that was carried inside my mind, could be pinned down, arranged, comprehended.

Meanwhile the traffic circulated without the park and within. All existed in suspense, and in pieces, yet stuck together. My suffering was at least magnified by the Edwardian centre of Empire.

The best epitome of massive, meticulous incoherence provided by the park, was the Magazine at the end of the Serpentine Bridge. Explosive powder stood stored in this building of grey brick. A sentry always marched outside, and for all I know, does so to this day. Potential murder and death were guarded with careful pageantry. Except for the sentry's footfall there was a silence about the place, the seat of the greatest potential noise. Those stronger walls held the greater danger. I delighted in the sentry: I delighted in all soldiers. He was controlling the explosive powers within by his drilled movements.

What I remember most would seem to belong to autumn and winter. But singing of birds, in spring especially, the bursting buds on the trees, were not unnoticed: even a certain ecstasy in the air in early spring. The heart was not freed for long: the overlay of town smell and dirt, the very encouragement by the onlooker of pastoral things, denied them a reality that was supreme. Railings, decorous iron chains and park-keepers controlled such marionettes. I did not know the power of the earth. A row of hyacinths growing at Victoria Gate were 'fixed' there by the authorities like the diminutive cockade in the top-hat of the coachman-like keeper of the gate. And there was no horizon, no horizon at any time.

I associate Kensington Gardens most of all with years before I was six, Kensington Gardens rather than Hyde Park. From the time I was three until I was six, we had a very strict governess, a most patriotic Irish lady. If shoelaces came undone while out for a walk, there would be no jam for tea: if they again came undone, no cake either. This penalty fell particularly on my second elder brother to catch, for whom it was doubtless designed. I don't remember that it happened to me: nevertheless to this day I am extremely bad at improvising knots. After my brothers had gone to boarding school, Miss Drew was dismissed for maltreating me, so it is said, in the park. My mother has since told me that she had a letter from someone who witnessed the bad temper. I remember nothing about it: indeed, I remember little about Miss Drew except that she had a watch in the shape of a sword pinned to her breast, that she had moods of vivacity as well as of hot temper and that she painted pictures of battleships in moonlight.

After Miss Drew's time, the scene is more especially Hyde Park. My next caretaker was a Miss Harley, a morbidly religious middle-aged woman. Miss Drew had also been religious, a Catholic. But now I was alone, without my brothers, as if the war were already starting and the

Edwardian world were already crashing.

I had myself read in the Old Testament and had been deeply impressed by the effrontery shown by one side or the other in every issue, and by the venomous consequences. Miss Harley used to sing me hymns. She was for me the Salvation Army of morbid streets and morbid walks. Even the park sheep looked wicked and guilty, particularly the sheep, poor, smelly and sniffing. There was, I think, no talk of Christ. Perhaps it was forbidden since I was to be brought up as a simple theist at most. An essentially bachelor omnipresence, then, a bachelor blood-and-thunder, lay upon the slight hill beyond the Rotten Row, seared with paths like slow rolling tears of shame. He was a kind man – I understood that – this witness of all park love-making, sexual crimes and suicides, the magician among park-keepers as he proved himself to be in the garden of Eden or in speaking from bushes, or in hurling stone tablets out of the clouds. 'Am I my brother's keeper?' Cain had said. That was a wicked, frightened joke of Cain's.

'Time like an ever-rolling stream, bears all her sons away.' We used to sing that hymn, the thin sounds torn by the wind. I had never seen a rolling stream. I thought of it as the low thunder of the London traffic. And Time was the gloomy sky over the park, which, by turning into night, bore away the soiled fretfulness of all happenings there each day. The park monuments, then, especially the would-be works of art, possessed in my eyes an almost masochist quality in their utter poverty; impotent under the lash of Time, borne away each night to build their grimy ugliness anew each dawn. Between Marble Arch and Albion Gate there is a kind of Gothic steeple whose function is to provide several vents of drinking water. To this globuled monstrosity in particular I attributed a horrible masochism. There lingered no romance in its poverty nor in the poor frequenters; and as I was not allowed to drink such public water, I shunned it for being something blind and grey. Here stood no source, no spring... It is horrible that a flow of water, thin though the trickle, should come to represent a blindness.

But more than this. Except for that all-seeing eye, everything was blind, a skein of unseeing veins and sodden skin. Where were the eyes of those motor cars, those automobiles (under the crushed-down Renault bonnets?), those vehicles of Time itself? Vision, as well as Design, lay in the effortless sky alone.

I had the makings of a true and terrible fanatic for whom a single string of argument could trap the whole universe: I was later at one with the more inhuman speakers at Marble Arch. At another period every secret of the universe was contained for me on the walls of a big bookshop.

There were, however, rare moments when the purlieus known to me had stature. They were moments of pageantry preceded by weeks of preparation. 1910 was the year of Edward VII's funeral, 1911 of George V's coronation. I saw both processions. What stays in mind were the long thin festive poles swathed in scarlet cloth, tipped with golden spear-heads, that lined both sides of Bayswater Road. Even railings were tipped with gilt. It was not the gaudiness so much as the picking out of features, the slight rearrangement of the London forgetfulness, which gave the street a life to me. I saw, as it were, for the first time that Bayswater Road was a thoroughfare: some kind of plan appeared. But for a long time to come, apart from extreme religious fears especially for those I loved, I relied principally on the reading of history to reveal some connection in the surrounding scene.

The coronation brought soldiers to the park; thousands were encamped. A year or two before, Miss Harley had been succeeded by a Swiss, French-speaking governess, Mathilde. I think she must have been a fairly normal girl. She brought a homesick warmth. But the park held sway, and when we ate a raspberry cream-filled chocolate bar which I had been forbidden, sitting in the park on one of the forbidden seats, my pleasure was not entirely sweet. I remember particularly some bedroom slippers on which had been spilt an extremely sticky spread which I liked, called Frame food jelly. This sweetness in the wrong place was agonizing. I used to wear those slippers because the nursery stood over my parents' bedroom and my father, at that time, lay fighting for his life although his immediate death had been prophesied by doctors who were crowding the house. Later, he was to watch in a dressing-gown through racing glasses, the distant passage of the King's funeral, seen in the distance from the balcony of the house.

Both Mathilde and I worshipped the soldiers. For a time I clung to military pomp and discipline as a 'solution' of the park and its environs. In earlier years I had tried to order the universe by the arranging of lead soldiers. If one fell I was inconsolable.

And so, the face of the park came in part to be symbolized by a hybrid image of soldiers in scarlet jackets and by Marble Arch orators standing on soap-boxes. At this time, Mathilde and I sought the press of the crowd, in Rotten Row on a Sunday morning or around the band-stand of a summer evening. I have a pictorial, almost a Renoir-like, image – the only one – of those times, based, I have little doubt, on much later experiences. For it is night, a dark, still night with rain in the air. The speakers at Marble Arch are lit with their torches; the outer fringe of whispering couples are lit by the lamps. Where it is dense the crowd is dark. Hats are in silhouette, so too the railings behind the speakers. Beyond, unwhispering grass is black except where a beam of light turns an outer fringe to emerald, the tired-smelling grass that otherwise would have been long obscured.

A soldier in a red tunic detaches himself from the crowd, takes the path across the park, probably making for Knightsbridge barracks. I watch him going between the far-flung lamps, making for the centre of the park and, so it seems, for the centre of the night since the park symbolizes all. I watch him go, getting less scarlet. Steadied by the lamps, my thoughts follow him into an immense space; for he has reached the open space where the enfolding pulse of the traffic is best felt. The lights, both near and distant, stare: an iron urge is to be attrib-uted both to the soldier and to the preacher. Once and for all, I now put up the railings inside myself. I have an inspired feeling of Destiny, of Duty. I will follow out the most exacting inner imperative. With consistent dutiful fire I will equal the coldness and steadiness of the lamps: with a certain inner talisman I shall part the murmuring London sea: I shall prolong a selfless path with such resolution that the astonishing hideous pile of the Hyde Park hotel, so often figuring on the limits of vision, shall fall defeated below man's horizon...

Mathilde and I sought the crowds. Cross, genteel scents became familiar to me of a Sunday morning. The scene was shot with violent colour, of soldiers or perhaps of rhododendra. I think I attributed to these strong colours the power to strike, to hit out with the power of a dazzling wing.

We would often go to feed the ducks, either in the Long Water or in the Serpentine, taking bags of stale bread. I was aware of the possibilities of a certain ritual in the throwing of bread on the waters. The crumbs bobbed about and soaked; whereas the stale dry bread, particularly the brown, I found very appetizing. It made me hungry; I grudged the food to the ducks. However, in the feeding, the interest partly lay in trying to arrange for the ducks, or for any misguided bird on the outskirts, to have a share. Geese and baleful swans were the enemies. The ducks were defenceless and kind-hearted, unmackintoshed mothers fed on sodden crumbs. Their surrounding water looked extremely desolate. Sparrows were at our feet, gulls in the air.

There was no haze of delight in this rapacious hunger. Finally, the empty bag having been burst, the paper was put to bob on the murky water in accordance with the wind. The walk home was marked by the passage underneath the Serpentine bridge. The dirty echoing tunnel with its lingering airs was cold at all times of the year. It was as if the passage lay beneath the dark water, here at its deepest according to a notice of warning. A dog would be barking like Cerberus. In view of the thunderous echoes, additional heads would have been in keeping.

I think to this obscene hole I attributed the home of the animus that tore the body of the park to shreds; the parkee spirit that made the park poor, hungry, desolate.

Each man invents a myriad states to counter his inferno. They exist abreast of the inferno; compensations, mitigations, transferences, controls, stern deletions, reparations. And so it has been with me. I have already referred to some of the priority repairs, as it were, by which an immediate patching up was attempted. But a truly exacting person, anxious to discover a reparation of even the smallest detail, is likely to construct a state parallel to that by which inferno is summed. And indeed, it is the initial imputation, in such a strong degree, of emotional states to the external world, inferno or paradiso or both at once, which characterizes the person who will primarily be an artist, even when childhood is passed. In this, however, I do not think he is peculiar, but only extreme and exacting in the use of an omnipotence commensurate with his anxiety.

Another tunnel, a long railway tunnel, the Mont Cenis, was the approach to the counter-landscape, to the rested mother, to love and life. This tunnel was the approach; not the centre of the landscape, but a symbol of rebirth.

On the near side of the tunnel there had been the Parisian evening, a wide glow, a width beyond what I knew. Then the rush through the night, the shriek of engines, like those of peacocks, through the ancient towns of Burgundy. They banished for me the engine cries Victoria heard in Hyde Park, noises which at night had seemed deliberately to hollow an oblong trough of white upon the dark.

The Swiss mountains pointed a way in the morning. The pines too had the mountainous brow, the mountainous gesture, ranged in loftier and loftier perspective, many-armed as Siva, plated with snow.

I was prepared for Italy: I had been preparing from an early time. At the age of seven, in the years of Mathilde, I had gone to a day school. After a few terms, I started Latin grammar. I had learned from Mathilde a little French but my imagination had not been moved. I was fascinated immediately by Latin. I knew one word the first day – mensa, a table – and how to decline it. I was fascinated, deeply stirred: I can remember the scene of that first lesson, where I sat, where the desks were, where the mantelpiece was. Not that I have any gift for languages; yet I possess the image of this declension of the word 'mensa' on the first day of Latin, taught by a Miss Brown whom I liked. Of the table, for the table, by the table, each expressed by one simple word. The genitive case was the possessiveness of simple love.

It is a scrubbed, sturdy, deal kitchen table, very bright: the fact that it is solid, that it stands on the floor is beautiful. The mensa table – or rather, a nexus of such experience, since it is most unlikely to have been in isolation – was a revolution in my life, an image the 'feel' of which corresponds with an adult image of a simple table prepared for an al fresco meal, the family mid-day meal under a fig tree, with a fiasco of wine on the table, olives, a cheese and bread. With one word I possessed in embryo the Virgilian scene; a robust and gracious mother earth.

Although I continued to love Latin, and later Greek, until I came through the Mont Cenis, I did not repeat this experience so vividly.

Even as a small child I took particular note of barrel-organs, of their effect upon the neighbourhood. If their tunes were no substitute for the mensa experience yet somehow they had a connection with it; an interest, it would seem, in another Italy, in the Baroque Italy.

From what I have attributed to the traffic in Hyde Park it will be obvious that I found in sound a most effective qualification of the visual world. A street became *informed* for me by the sounds of a barrel-organ. Everything had a new angle of light upon it, a new arrangement with a centre pulsating like a heart. Thus the street was not only organized; it became an organism, it came alive. The images of dismemberment and anxious aridity that haunted me were not in this way dissipated: but an element of drama, even of 'healthy' catastrophe, was a relief. Aided by the pictures on my father's cigar boxes and on the barrel-organ and by visits to the pantomime, that distant, anglicized cousin of the Commedia dell'Arte theatre, the music in the street could provide me with a variety of scenes, populated, Baroque, catastrophic.

It is now a Neapolitan tune the Italian grinds; which says: the tall casa has painted shutters and each window a painted rococo entablature, brown upon the pink stucco of the wall. Families cluster at the rickety balconies. A man beats a carpet; the flotsam floats and swims in the sunlight towards the gay washing hanging below. Under the roof there is a broad band of fresco. (Gigantic mermaids wreck the fisher boats and tritons blow blue horns.) In a window a birdcage dangles. At first I think there is but one bird, but the hops are now frequent and I see the cage is over-populated. The tiny movements are so vivid that the great damp sheets which hang from the side of the balcony appear grey, and the bundle between the iron bars, not a little girl. You were young then too, and over the clambering terraces of houses, each with a flat square roof, you had arranged a cord that joined you to my house, a little higher up on the other side of the valley. By jerking this cord we could exchange exciting messages, words which the roar of the mills on the brook between could not silence. Inside the room is bric-a-brac, particularly ornamental feathers dusty with canary seed. The breeze softly lifts the light wooden frame of a mirror on the wall. As you jerk the cord, sirens are screaming in the harbour, tugs scurry and hoot, white figures below labour with sacks of flour while, above, smoke rises straight and blue from the black volcano.

The tune changes... Sometime the old men sat upon the mountain, each upon a stone seat. Their heads touched the blue sky. Night clattered on in valleys below and over night's invisible back a portent leaped. Another darkness, a cloud of ashes, overwhelms the feeble day. Some jump from terrace to terrace; from vineyard and from vineyard, mothers round up their children, moving like Hecubas; while below upon the lowest road the fire of the dying sun draws scarlet bands about the feet of fugitives, is now extinguished by dust, now clutches at a cart upon whose frame winnowing petals open... a cart among the rain of ashes and overtaken women bundled into fantastic attitudes: a cart, on and on, carts piled with toppling bric-a-brac crowned by sobbing children, by basket and spring that last saw the full light of day strong in the early market: on and on to the sea that rises from the bosom of a gully ahead like a gown that opens its velvet grasp and leaves the shoulders bare. Cruel, even sea, you throw no rescue ropes. Uprooted olive trees festoon the road as it rocks. Light of this last day is butchered by lava and steam: yet, every now and then, a bloody ray of seared sun-fire shoots among the fugitives.

We survivors, as we approach the gully, look back and there, sure enough, above the black of the earthquake and of the vapour, above the well-established night that glows red with illicit warmth, the old men sit agleam against a blue sky. In this cursed double night they still possess the day. Surely we wake to their tomorrow when at dawn, stiff after dead sleep upon the deck of the rescue ship, we pluck the morning air and search with sudden glance the shimmer of the cold and velvet deep...

It is noticeable that not only were these fantasies provoked by sound but contain in them the projection of a great deal of noise. Even the scenes of my early childhood sustained their life through movement, the circulation of traffic. Where there is movement there is noise, and from the noise we fashion images of movement.

In our urban life, sound qualifies *visually* scenes which otherwise are confusing and meaningless to the eye. What the eye alone might perceive is inhuman to a degree. The arts today concerned with inter-relationship of sound and movement, particularly ballet, are able to draw upon a wealth of life-giving fantasy which in one form or another is common to millions.

Thus, the barrel-organ did not restore in the fullest sense the *visual* world for me. Such was my anxiety and consequent ambition that it could be satisfied with nothing less than an instantaneous, silent mani-festation, independent of sound and of a dramatization of the passage of time: a happy coexistence, then, of things in space after the manner of mensa the table. It is possible, following an older habit, that the intrusion of sound will still provide a *point d'appui*, but it will never-theless be serving an entirely different effect.

As the train came out of the Mont Cenis tunnel, the sun shone, the sky was a deep, deep, bold blue. I had half-forgotten about my table for more than ten years. At once I saw it everywhere, on either side of the train, purple earth, terraces of vine and olive, bright rectangular houses free of atmosphere, of the passage of time, of impediment, of all the qualities which steep and massive roofs connote in the north. The hills belonged to man in this his moment. The two thousand years of Virgil-ian past that carved and habituated the hillsides, did not oppress: they were gathered in the present aspect. At the stations before Turin, the pure note of the guard's horn but sustained and reinforced the process by which time was here laid out as ever-present space.

We arrived at Turin in the late afternoon. There was a change with a wait of half an hour. On a low platform in the clean electric space – shadowless, it would seem – I stood enraptured. I watched the sky between the trains and the edge of the huge gradual curve of the station roof. The sky was now a paler blue but was still close, like the near sound of trumpets.

Day gave way to night without misgiving. Soon, in the new train, it was entirely dark. Although for the last hours of the year, the air was soft, tender, a darkness as of a perfect-fitting lid. After dinner in the restaurant car, most of the passengers had left, the table-cloths were removed. On the other side of the gangway, one table ahead, I again saw the mensa table. Not the plain deal table, it is true. But two Italians sat there with instant faces. Between them in a fiasco was the wine, and to my ears they talked like Romans. Their warm precipitation of life sustained, as it seemed to me, by the glowing reflected light of thousands of sunlit years, banished memories of Hyde Park. Instead of the Serpentine, I saw the Mediterranean, the end of my journey. In their eyes I read the pleasure of house-tops and of different levels.

We were in an electric train. While we stopped at Genoa, I could imagine a giant taut city above the Mediterranean. A young man with a red scarf escorts his sweetheart to the train. He is ugly, but he, too, holds in his eyes the pleasure of the house-tops and the different levels; of alleys between towering painted walls that float in the shade like goldfish in the sunlight.

The train began to move through Genoa. I could see through the many lighted windows of clear-shaped tenements. In every apartment, I felt, there is this happy evening return, a state of the night which is sheer acquisition; in which, like the men in the train, the inhabitants take up the night by expending the strength of a Latin day. Their talk is now the balustrades, the terraces, the balconies spread out upon the harbour, the radiant open places of the town. The ebb and flow of conversation, still more, of gesture, reconstruct the thoroughfares. As the train glided on, more and more peep shows appeared at every angle to the line. The inhabitants had no need for blinds: since no dominant misery and no surfeit of unexpressed emotion lurked inside them, there was nothing beyond the houses to be shut out.

Meanwhile in a straight passage the train was passing houses on every level to the line, now above them, now on a level with the second storey, now at the foot, now crossing a great viaduct. I had the sensation of passing through the inside as well as along the outside of the houses: never before had I been so much at home. There was every kind of light, perhaps a darkness except from the windows, perhaps a lit campo with ever-bustling happy trees tenacious of root, silent and soft, or a terraced garden with an easy iron gate and steps upon the prospect. There was a conspiracy abroad of universal triumph informing even the roads, the pavements and the harshest stucco. And when we stopped at stations beyond Genoa, at Nervi for example, and finally at Rapallo, the air held scents of flowering trees and of eucalyptus enclosing and disclosing the villas mounting on their gardens. I drove in a carriage through the town to the pension. Echoes of the horse's hooves upon the cobbles brought with them from the walls a sensation of their diurnal brightness. At the end of the ride, the horse was walking up a steep incline through the garden to the pension, a large Riviera villa set behind a balustrade. The scents intensified: there was the sound of waters falling to the sea. Church bells began, and then rang out from every side, from over-hanging levels as well as from distances; swift, hammering, light bells. It was midnight, the new year.

On waking in the morning I saw through the open French windows, over the top of a russet-red villa with green shutters, the Mediterranean, the place-name of our civilization. There was a revealing of things in the Mediterranean sunlight, beyond any previous experience; I had the new sensation that the air was touching things; that the space between things touched them, belonged in common; that space itself was utterly revealed. There was a neatness in the light. Nothing hid or was hidden. Soon, an electric train passed, gliding with ease on the hard way just below, entered a tunnel. Unlike the electric trains on London's metropolitan railway which had always been a disturbance, this train and the tunnel did not prolong themselves inside me. It seemed that for the first time things were happening entirely outside me. Existence was enlarged by the miracle of the neat defining light. Here was an open and naked world. I could not then fear for the hidden, for what might be hidden inside me and those I loved. I had, in fact, incorporated this objective-seeming world and proved myself constructed by the general refulgence. Nothing, for the time, lurked, nothing bit, nothing lurched.

As I think now of that valley at Rapallo that goes up to Mont'Allegro, as I think of the afternoon winter sunlight, I have the sensation of a sound which contains every note, prolonged, entirely sustained, as good beneath as above, a sound that provides every aural want; at the same time it is itself the epitome of complete realization. Nature spreads and mounts before me, fixed and growing, changeless in the clearness of its cycle. I have here the means of action, a demonstration, not of the purpose of life but of the power of life to be manifest; not of one thing but of the calm relationship of many things, concrete things, each bound to each by an outwardness that allows no afterthought to the spectator: an outward showing goes within him. An answering life wells to the surface, and he feels – hence the great beauty of Mediterranean landscape – that the process of a man's existence is outward, giving shape, precise contour to the few things that lie deepest; whatever the distortion they mutually endow, making the expenditure in terms of a surface we call expression, be it in action, art or thought.

The outside world, our own bodies, other people and material things point the goal of outwardness. The Mediterranean scene invokes the universal aim. In adult life, my models have been things rather than persons.

But whatever the degree, whatever the distortion, all men impute themselves to their surroundings. The broad distorted aspect of the innermost informs every particle of the huge outlying space.

Even a sense of duration or succession discovers itself occasionally as a simultaneity, as forms arranged in space. I do not think that a more direct account of my relations with people would reveal as much as this sparse account of a contemplative relation with the external world. Doubtless it is a proof of neurosis. It determines, however, without prejudice, the aesthetic aim to cause surroundings to describe matters less immediate, perhaps, but often more profound than are revealed by reminiscences; further, to illustrate (given the biological essence) that the human process is aesthetic in so far as it is outlined against the beckoning outwardness of the external world.

Of course it is basic human relationships, above all, that my two landscapes describe. Hyde Park is especially a destroyed and contaminated mother, Italy the rapid attempt to restore. In their terms, and it would seem to me in their terms alone, could I re-create succinctly the division, the incorporation of opposites.

Rapallo could not *oust* Hyde Park. After some years, however, I was to find a direction; but not at once. I had, in fact, a huge commentary with me on that first visit to Rapallo, of Kant's *Critique of Pure Reason*. I used to take it on mountain walks. For several more years I was engrossed entirely in the absolute which I had encountered compulsively first in religion and then (no less compulsively) in ethics and philosophy. After the Rapallo experience the problem had always been 'how to bring the distant things near'. This phrase recurs in many notebooks. In view of the superlative absolute, how was any preoccupation to be justified? I could not defend myself against the absence of a logical answer. Over and over again everything of value was taken away, ruthlessly, sadistically; even the Rapallo experience.

Meanwhile an interest in art, especially visual art, developed the import of a reliance. I found a period which expressed the Rapello aesthetic of life, the rush to make inside things manifest as a superlative space. When examining early Renaissance architecture and sculpture I at once recognized this passionate aim. I formed an aesthetic devolving from this art: bit by bit I was reconstructing the good mother amid continuous ruins.

Fire, slaughter, sunlight, rain: the major conflict went on; in London especially. Was there 'objective' justification for the hopelessness I felt in urban life, in suburban life, in polite or semi-polite country life; justification, I mean, warranted to every civilized person who, for one reason or another was not equipped with adequate defences? And what did the more normal man pay for his 'adequate defences'? I doubted, and I doubt, whether the material by and large of ideal inside things are to be easily found outside in terms of modern cities, or whether this outside can easily be converted to suitable inside nourishment.

However, the confrontations with which this book is *ultimately* concerned are as little as possible particular to individual conditions, even to current work or activity. Around objects as they are used or worked, or which accompany stress of any kind, a keen fantasy life is woven. This range, tinged with habit, possesses a contemplative side. But as far as the visual world at large is concerned, it is possible that after childhood most minds only rarely have the opportunities, in particular of solitude, of detachment, of suitable leisure, to step consciously on to a more intense imaginative plane. There remains, however, a low hum of insistence recorded in turns of speech, in gesture, even, and in all folklore, in all language.

I shall be attempting a generalized confrontation, however personal the reference; even, at times, an abstract setting of the mind over against the visual world.

The broad confrontation for me, particularly at Rapallo, is the piled-up darkness of the mind with the vast sunlit tangible world. To fantasy, there are as many things inside as there are outside. It is one reason, surely, why we are often appalled by the mere immensity and confusion of the outside world, by a casual or callous aspect; why we are reassured by the beauty and order of things.

A contemplative mood in some surroundings discovers an otherness that is tenuous compared to the Mediterranean. Here in Cornwall, for instance, I sometimes have the feeling that what I see out of my eyes is a projection of pictures in my head as if I were a cinema reel and the outside world a screen on which the film is projected, put in movement and enlarged.

In contemplating objects, the degree of outward orientation varies continually. I have had the sensation, very likely when travelling in Switzerland, that the railway line is piercing a man-made tunnel; while passing through a forest, that it is piercing the inner recesses of Nature whose undergrowth I can to some degree penetrate with my eyes. Not so, when travelling through a forest in England. Orientation to the landscape is different. I have not seen the track to be piercing a forest. The trees are little more than scenery to the track, backcloth to my propulsion. When walking on the track, the country is properly pre-existent. But the carriage in which I ride makes a little outside world which takes precedence in the sensation of actuality, even when I am staring out of the window. I then inhabit a substitute house and I view the country almost as something which passes this house, like a lorry seen from the dentist's waiting-room or a cloud apprehended through the window at breakfast.

Present circumstance generally forbids the wider relationship with the object. Every contemplation of the world outside must have a context, must entail a projection from inside. It still remains true that such contemplation has an increased scope so far as it is depending upon a greater apprehension of otherness; upon an *exact* concatenation in the outside world.

Sometimes of an evening in a narrow marine street a concentrated salt air blows over a wall; it is as if the very cobbles, not the waves, were hissing. These strong airs are warm, a lighted doorway is firm and open. Both air and noise blow round incessantly, are never stale. Indeed there is a calm and a freshness inter-allied, a temperance of wild air that gives some meaning to the word 'eternal'; an embrace of ferment as sleep should be.

As well as things in themselves, a wood, a house, the sea, are also symbols of physical and psychological states; fairly constant symbols; though qualified by each context, each apposition. Poets are their chief interpreters: but from some good painters, especially from the non-literary good painters, we possess also an imaginative statement of space and its objects, of the outside world *per se* as the thing that stands over against the self.

If we were to be shot or hanged within the hour, how fine and untroubled the landscape. We should feel that the ruthlessness within was already dead; or at least expiation was about to be made. And so, the exterior world would lean for us lovingly: we would feel of Nature only the wide embrace. Hitler, the slums and shipwreck would be dead in us: they would no longer qualify the landscape. How finely, how unattainably *out there* the world would look. Unattainably? We shall attain the state out there, the state of complete object, the very brother to stone, all too soon, all too completely...

In the ordinary circumstances of life it is the artist, as much as the scientist in his different way, who in this sense gives full imaginative value to the otherness of the outside world. There, as an independent and more lasting structure, as soundly related form are the basic inside figures and motive powers both physical and mental. The emphasis, I repeat, is upon the otherness of these forms and of their structure; upon their independence, at least in the greatest visual art. Even though he embraces them, the artist wills to get behind both immediate appearance and immediate fantasy or image thrust upon the appearance.

So-called ordinary people rarely contemplate in aesthetic fashion. They are unwilling sufficiently to disconnect appearance from present circumstance. It is said that the drowning man sees his life outside him as he dies. Similarly, all of us have felt that we have seen an environment 'as it really is', only when under sentence to leave it when it is no longer part of our concern, a house or a room no less than a view.

The well-known place when we are leaving it, lies close to the eye. Previously our thoughts about it have been tinged with specific matters; previously, in comparison, there was a distance between us and the thing: previously the place had appeared neither as near nor as objective. When we first arrive, still more when we leave, those are times when we 'see' the place in which we live. Waiting for conveyance to the station after ten years' stay, with nothing whatever to do except to wait, we see the room and we may feel upon us all that has happened there in terms of wainscot, wall, light and disposed furniture; we see it coolly as something independent which no longer waits upon our actions. Outside, a row of tulips is not at all a cycle of the cares of cultivation. In a manner more intense than has been possible before, we note the intervals and rhythm of their positions: we may view our life in that place in terms of their upright calm. Such contemplation is near the artist's contemplation. We see ourselves, between two cycles of action, rooted in the soil of our lives.

This wide concatenation of the outside world is more aesthetic, less passive, than those refreshing moments in which we are primarily astounded by the powerful extent of Nature; in watching a sunset, perhaps, or the fury of the sea upon rocks or the action of submerged rocks, free to the air between waves, for ever and for ever in that brief moment throwing off the maximum water before the return of the wave. Through all the sensations of vastness and of superhuman force and rhythm which such a scene gives to the senses, surely we attend a parable of inner economy, of those forces within, seemingly foreign to us. We are looking on Nature, but at the same time we look on a clearer distribution of forces within ourselves, a clearer interaction, one more Homeric, more in style and therefore more disinterested than is the case. We would that inner conflict were thus windswept, that visitation of the deeper caverns of the mind were subject to such causes as those that govern tides. And indeed they are, though it would take each of us all our years to trace such tidal movements in emotion, such governance by the few essentials. In terms of strength and space and necessity and freedom, a mental no less than a physical reminder bestows for us stark grandeur in the scene. We belong to this immense cradle of life.

In life we substitute, we repeat, we magnify, we complicate, we substitute, we repeat until the whole world is subsumed under our consciousness (childhood's world was smaller). In the course of life we embrace more and more the character of the outside world, giving ourselves to it, taking it within. At death, we and it are indistinguishable.

The more obvious process of living is a giving forth rather than a taking in. Living is ceaseless expression; ceaseless substitution, the

326

putting of one thing into many forms both of action and of thought the infinite ramification of a few themes. And so, in the more profound contemplation of our lot, we may look upon the truth within in terms of an outside ramification, the exquisite arrangement of space.

And Art? It will already be obvious that it is here regarded as the epitome of this central process.

We have our ways and means of keeping things alive: we forget nothing; and the deeper sources of our feeling are tapped by our environment, by material objects as well as by the human objects with whom we repeat original relationships. The external world is the instigator of memory: the external world reflects every facet of the past: it is the past rolled into the present. Projection, then, continuous and various projection, is the distinguishing characteristic of man. Animus (of how many kinds, infinite in gradation) impinges upon every look, every remark, every unspoken and spoken thought. Above all, as we regard what is external, ourselves speak there.

How blessed that things do not move with our thoughts. The glass on the table is still while I think, imagine, fear and love. A little contemplation of its outwardness, a little scientific or aesthetic appraisal, stabilizes the world short of the need for action or mere physical engrossment. If it were not for the still spatiality and tangibility of this glass on the table, expression would not be our lifeblood: at least, not with the colour, already apparent in the process of perception, of abstract, shiftless ideas. It is truly said that the church was founded on a rock.

Boxed up, I leave the house for the harbour. The world expands: there is a sense of freedom. Yet this larger world contains my previous thought. Anxiety, for instance, so far from being blown away on the free air, may be enlarged as it fixes on vast natural agencies. I note the rebutment of the sea by the rocks.

The evening becomes corporeal with strolling tourists. Amid a crowd's taking of leisure, contemplation of a patch of water, a breakwater, the side of a house, includes my longest questioning. They are dramatized by the strollers as by music. It is then that I drop my thought into the uninhabited water. This delving is upheld lightly amid the ease of the evening crowd. Deeper contemplation sinks out of sight yet still belongs to the scene in the way that a dog belongs, fathomless in animality, yet genial in the possession of a master strolling on the front...

Consciousness is a brisk dream of the unconscious within: the dream of utmost substitution or distortion, made vivid, made real by continuous contact with the actuality of the not-self: in this way it contrasts with the real dream state.

Yet even vast spaces are informed with our feeling, with images, maybe, of our own insides. A film of *Les Misérables* shows once more the sewers of Paris. The hero, pursued, squanders his failing strength carrying the girl, foundering in the subterranean mud and cataracts, in the slipping silky waters of dirt. Many the dangers from this tomb of suffocating, purposeful yet silent water. His head submerges. The vast under-waterway, with its occasional arches, with dim lights from above, holds firmly on the imagination, magnifies, indeed intensifies, images of the inside of the body.

There can be no agnosticism today in so far as we have ceased to formulate with any ardour those metaphysical problems to which agnosticism was applied. We do not deal in unrelated essences. Nor, at present, can any inevitable insistence be given to speculation upon the ultimate relationship of the inner and outer object. Existence, to the modern contemplator, may be observed afresh at *any* point. New peaks, new ranges, have been discovered *inside* man; new seas. The exploration only begins and will make small headway through the barbaric country of the modern world. Blind to the new vista, new religions, chiefly political, flourish on every side. It was to be expected. The unconscious is not misnamed. It cannot be enough emphasized, especially to those who have an interest in psycho-analysis.

I say this after a seven years' analysis.[1] Over and over again, something about which there did not seem to be the vestige of strong feeling, after layer upon layer of extremely cunning, masquerading resistance

328

has been undermined, showed itself to be a centre of the strongest emotion.

We are far more nearly aware of what is unconscious in the minds of other people than in our own. The unconscious is not entirely misnamed: yet this vast acrimonious territory makes itself felt at every moment: our conscious minds are vessels on the seas of our unconscious. Facets of the motivating powers are strongly reflected in the external world. Analysis reveals the unconscious without the distortions of a glass. But distortion is the very mode and matter of conscious life, the very property of mind and of all that distinguishes us from animals. In terms of projection, in terms, as it were, of the external world out there, the undimensional acuteness of original feeling is given a length, breadth and depth, taking manifold forms in all the activities of man.

There is an intense subtlety at the service of an intense crudity.

Everyone at some time or another must have been astonished in encountering a letter, say, or the result of some action that is theirs but which awakens not the slightest remembrance. As a rule there is some flicker of remembrance, but occasionally you can only accept the fact that it is your own handwriting. Generally you see that although you have forgotten about writing this letter, there is no reason why you should not have written it and forgotten about it. But occasionally, you feel that you could not have written it because it expresses some sentiment never yet entertained, a sentiment not in character.

The greater part of the situations which have determined the main channels of our love and hate and sense of guilt, are forgotten in this way, though they survive to direct our lives. For all the blaring echoes, there are many cries to which we are normally untuned. Yet so vast is emotion, we come to feel that cries from the heart rebound to us from the astronomical distances of the universe.

We are today better able to understand that much thinking, hitherto respected for a connection with the search for truth, is prompted by the desire to 'keep up morale'. This activity is not to be despised: we all must find ways of keeping up morale, but it is no longer necessary to confuse this search with the quest for truth. An essential characteristic of the future intelligent man will be his power to discover even more satisfying methods of bolstering up his morale without interfering with truth, whether it is the truth as far as it will be known concerning the external world, or himself or others, or concerning political and economic situations: not by banking on dilemmas, for instance, in science or on questions that are insoluble because they are meaningless, in general by rationalizing some wish-fulfilment as the truth; but by rationalizing some wish-fulfilment as fantasy, by imagination, by acts of love, by art.

In using the word 'morale', I mean the overlay and employment of aggressive tendencies for the hope and theory of what is constructive, in line with the love instincts: in short, a guard against destructive impulses and despair. This guard is essential: but need it deflect the grasp of reality even at the point where it might seem to be dangerous? The grim side of reality threatens *our* reality not because it is grim, but because that grimness, it is feared, might link up with, and assert, our own inner grimness. Our misfortunes remove dust from forgotten inner figures of persecution. Inner life is almost inextricably blended with external events: to reform the world seems easier than to reform oneself.

Nevertheless I think a great deal can be accomplished by honest thinking. Fantasy satisfactions will not be one whit less honourable for being called so: idealism of every kind will have a sure basis. In truth, it will be a great blow against the slavery of the mind, against stupidity.

'In its search for genuine goodness (material) and in its fear of being deceived, this age of "realism" may have overshot the mark; there is reality within us as well as without, the facts not only of our ruthlessness and greed but also of our need to love and be loving, which we suppress and do not honestly avow.' A quotation not from a religious advocate but from a book by two psychoanalysts.[2]

From the heritage of Freud we may begin to understand the long and intricate history of our love and aggression, the springs of all our lives: we can begin to understand what is most needful for our children in their initial and all-important struggles with themselves: and if, owing to no more than average capacity of love allied to a successful emotional economy, we are strong in the power of love, in the constant warmth from our inside archetypal figures who in the outside world have given love and received our love: if we are of those who are no longer so much as children that fear deep in themselves the suffocating, burning, choking omnipotence, the unrestrained power of resentment and of aggressive impulse, then today we may have the means to improve upon the perfunctory denial of primary aggression, perhaps as a form of illusion or perhaps as a sinful fault of structure, that has so imperfectly served civilization. This instinct is an inevitable component of life. We need it for self-preservation and for the element of attack consistent with any activity. If men, in the light of available knowledge and in the release of their love due, it is to be hoped, to happier upbringing in better conditions, if men allow necessity to fantasy but eschew indoctrination, admit that love's antagonist, except to the eyes, maybe, of fantasy, is no mere extraneous devil, they are likely to tear away many more injurious disguises and denials that involve also the denial of love, to harness with increasing success aggression's palpable, primal, inescapable force and thus gleefully to compel it to greatly enhanced productive uses.

We would have to recognize that many forms of aggression, envy or sour-grape denial, for instance, are modes as well of covering up fantasies of inner hate and rottenness, of reaching out for inner riches at any cost: that the lust for power has this for taproot. All evil actions own an aspect of flight from a condition which is felt to be a greater evil.

Not that a true knowledge of the depth of hate and of the mechanism of hateful thought and action as being also an attempt to preserve love, not that such knowledge can directly help the individual in avoiding these hateful mechanisms or enable him to possess satisfactory means of feeling good inside. Every spiritual economy however unsuccessful, of the sane and insane alike, is already organized to that end. But there exists small understanding of this necessity for the other person and it is very apparent what a difference in the well-being of a child a degree of such understanding on the part of the parents can make. The best hope for the future is in the happier children of more balanced parents, the only cumulative way of a vast amelioration.

Intimations from the soil and from the sky, brought along a warm wind, are also images of the within. Hitler, too, and all the crises are within us. And I see bare trees rising from a rhododendron grove like certain paramount forces from the mind. They are what is evident and of the day. They are extraordinarily clear. They are images of the mind's aspiration, of the mind, the image-fabricator.

To paint a picture is metaphorically to take things to pieces in the outside world and to put them together again; a re-enactment of an early state, since the child is bent upon just such a putting together of what in fantasy he has destroyed, bitten or torn to shreds. It is likely that this element of reparation underlies all forms of art-making as well as other kinds of 'constructive' activity. Historically speaking, the most usual manner in painting of reconstituting an object has been to create an image of the object, to re-create the object in terms of an essence rather than of a literal appearance. This is the manner of all conceptual art. A further development, in European art especially, has been to reconstitute the image more directly in terms of appearance, even of the momentary appearance due to a particular light. This is perhaps the more adult mode of organization, a greater adventure for the creative faculty in which it may well be lost; just as artistry is so often lost by children as they grow up and attempt in their drawing a greater fidelity to appearance. In the worst traditions of naturalistic painting, the image-making nexus, essential to any work of art, is entirely, or almost entirely, lost. For, such painting entertains a *preconceived image of the appearance*, involves a tricky, shoddy treatment of appearance without an image except the one which is conventional, everyday, inartistic.

Trains, shunting, trains. How the trucks knock, knob and jostle one another. I lie high up, in a hot bath: the vast window is open. I feel this experience acutely, the shunting and rearrangement of trains in the early morning, particularly while I myself am immobile, attentive: the rearrangement, re-shuffle of passenger and freight for further long striding journeys, impinges deeply on the mind. It is a residue, an echo, this shunting, in the concrete or physical form of externality down there in the cold, clear air. To me an echo, it might be taking place in the sky which is all I can see from the bath: a strange yet characteristic inversion. The echo intimates something solid, definite – I don't want to catch my fingers between the buffers – while the original is a fantasy buried deep in the mind.

We are always making up new trains within, near-unconsciously pitting different urges, different personified figures against each other with the hope that they will (with careful shuffling) draw each other along a dominant line. We are perpetually trying to manage, to harness the figures within.

It is to be wondered whether in the pre-industrial age there was a common experience from the external world that echoed the inner shunting to anything approaching the same degree of clearness: how greatly man's understanding of himself is promoted and limited by an environment merely offered to the senses or whether the invention of the steam engine, for instance, was made in man's image no less than was pre-Copernican science. How far is the external world today outside due correspondence with the inner world, and if it is, what is the cause? The spiritual import of the external world, in so far as it is qualified by the industrial revolution, still lacks interpretation. The spirit has taken kindly to the mythology allowed by railways: but otherwise, movement of the mind does not find easy direction in the world today where man has altered the appearances of Nature: at least, not as well as of old, though there are several exceptions.

Modern cities fight the mystery of the seasons and themselves receive wounds. Here in England is a nameless care in a moderate climate. Electric bulb! What an extraordinary juxtaposition! Nothing is more sudden than the switched-on light. One moment darkness, the next the radiant stare of a glass eye, brilliant, fixed, without incandescence. The dome of the bank fills with holiness at dawn. Space and measurement are diluted by oil and candle-light: in the flicker of a flame a door rears the head of portal. Night rushes on still faster as she enters the mouths and caverns that quiver on the wall. But in a cage of wire the electric bulb does not wink. At the mouth of a gusty tunnel it illuminates a white patch around which dust is blowing. The steady moon rides the night. The sore that throbs by day is soothed when pressed against the white rind of the moon; it does not bridle or pulsate. But what is this fibrous, non-pulsating electric light in the mouth of a gusty tunnel? Like a crane that cleaves the night air, we are waiting. We cannot yet humanize (such is the process of all image, of all correspondence between inner and outer) the electric light.

We begin to do so, just as with trains, with some of the older inventions, more in terms of their noise: whereas correspondence, I think, was previously obtained primarily in visual terms. Certainly, much that is specifically modern is often horrible without its noise. We are entire strangers to Oxford Street in the two minutes' silence. Plastic interplay of noise and movement gives some meaning to contemporary environment. Hence, I have suggested, the great topical content in the art of ballet.

The tons of a tram, each massive screw and indifferent bolt, the violence of unwieldy compression, this painted swan of iron and tin, feathered with screw and scraper which waddles down two frozen rivulets of steel with boulders packed between; half swan, half centipede... such images may occur when a tram is heard to pass, when the challenge is heard of this monstrous bulk to the brazen soil, as if the iron-webbed wheels had a mind to worm a way through the crust of the earth, as if the earth took up the challenge, thrust out a gritty hand, raised the taut leviathan so that he bumps and serpentines without resilience upon a palm of jagged stone traversed by veins of steel.

A perception of power comes to us very largely in terms of movement and sound. Much machinery, at rest, makes an inconsequent impression. Machines, for the most part, work or they break down. How different from the sailing ship.

But what does one expect of university towns? Only puffed clouds rolling over the scenes of former sophistry, over night alarums in crooked streets.

Along, along, along a road. May hedges still meet far ahead. Green and white the well-spread trees. We are speeding in an angled cockpit. There are slow bumps; they seem to touch, to revolve delicately the tenuous hands of the dials upon the dash-board. It is as if the passage of smooth wheels upon a smooth road in a well-sprung car was for this purpose; a transference of power, typical of machinery, ending in sensitive points as a final response: so typical that I see the car ride thus: I see thus the hedges and trees of May, the ancient house, the glowing redness of roofs; and I see Nature's machinery in man designed for the end-result of a registration of desires upon the quivering dials of consciousness.

Science, the more fructifying line of knowledge or speculation, is hard to face where it impinges upon the current beliefs of society. Obvious instances are the Copernican revolution in astronomy and Darwin's theory of Evolution. We have now reached the most difficult line or road of truth: the Freudian discoveries lead to an estimation of the nature of man which at first sight is far harder to bear. Every unconscious resistance is likely to be mobilized against it. Were this road widely used and accepted, truth thereafter would never be 'awkward': in other words, the pragmatic approach to truth would be identical with an abstract search for truth. Indeed, it is my belief that, apart from better 'living conditions', only this line of truth can increase an emotional equilibrium in men. Myth will abound no less, but let it abound as myth, as poetry, as art by which the spirit lives: in greater purity, therefore, with greater freedom than in culture hitherto. The fire of enthusiasm lies with the state that engenders it, with the aesthetic and practical uses to which it is put, not with the universality of the notions thus engendered. Fantasy has an aesthetic 'truth', defined by and defining scientific truth. This interdependent relationship will become the ultimate object of contemplation. Far, far more will be allotted to fantasy than was suspected in any previous age; in ages far less notable for science, for their grasp of reality. A paradox. Fantasy now becomes more pure as impartiality becomes more pure. Love and life cannot be ousted. They will grow yet warmer in the hearts of men when the dusty embers of universal systems based upon partialities and compulsions are raked out thoroughly.

The essence of man's cultural development has been a gradual submission to, and control of, reality, resulting in an increased substitution or a complicated deferment of emotional outlet. On the side of thought, man has rationalized neurosis and compulsiveness in terms of many speculative systems and religions; a kind of prose-poetry, detrimental to the purer prose of science which brings in its wake a purer and more voluminous poetry. If we recognize substitution as the basis of all human activity, we endow living with aesthetic values. *Art never quarrels with science.* Viewed as activities, at many points they approximate: viewed as expressions of truth, they define each other.

Part Two

From *Inside Out* (1947)

From the train one sees away in the middle distance at the top of a field in a corner, some small, rounded trees. The warmth imputed to them is fleeting, yet even so we pass out of sight rapidly. It will be cold at night in this corner of the field as well as desolate.

Clear voices of boys sound hard and deliberate against the continuous rapid language of the train. Couplings, woodwork creak: the sounds suggest a forced smile upon bloodless lips.

The rounded trees are now far behind: an agony belonged to their mute, primrose-like, immobile appeal, against the sky. The muteness is shot at by the noisy pulling back of a gritty corridor door, by a thump of steps, a great deal of peering. 'Hullo, Stokes, what kind of hols?'

The tempo quickens as the train slows down for our destination. We boys are all in black: our grins are tigerish.

Or else it is the earlier, shorter journey to a prep school. These boys are smaller, whiter, with little of the crescendo of a sprouting life. The smell of the station is profound. There is a criticism from other families in virtue of their mere existence: they are ladders to the great desolate hard self-rapture of the world beyond one's own.

Under the blare of King's Cross almost every boy is led by a parent far along the platform to be sick, sick from frightened anticipation, in front of the train that will throng him on an iron journey.

London drags out along the route; against the will it begins to thin: less and less people live here as if a curse lay on the glowering land. In the semi-country at Barnet we stamp our way over a bridge that clatters; we take brake for the school. Masters are with us, a matron awaits. There will be a fire-practice tomorrow...

To confront such deadly journeys, to serve as the Rapallo to this

Hyde Park, we shall recall Cézanne in the year 1886 or so, travelling from Paris to Aix-en-Provence (seldom to return), exchanging the swift seasons of the north for a panorama he made immovable.

First, however, it will even assist us to remember the summer wind through the plane trees of London as an invisible yet palpable wasting of time, as the hustling away of wares among which the buyer, through straining with a complete lack of indifference, could not decide. This warm wind strikes chill; the music of leaves is not heard except as an accompaniment to the ominous sound of steps upon the pavement, steps that pass, that carry with them and disperse an attempted concentration of thought. Trees of London are the harbingers of a footfall, the trees of the squares, lofty, towering, slightly swaying, the trees of the parks, the trees of the streets.

And yet, in the moment when the heart expands, rustling pavement foliage demonstrate the omnipotent powers of desire, of the compelling spirit, towering, expanding, embracing chimney-pots that have withstood so many winters. A pulsating life-blood would appear to warm the very spire of a church. Magic then belongs to movement and to repose: their division, their occasion, demonstrate the parts or attitudes of a universal breathing.

From such romantic antiphony, I, at least, pass gladly to consider the classical achievement of Cézanne, a deeply emotional, and yes, romantic, temperament. It will be found that in so doing and in reassessing shortly this painter's development, I shall have preferred my theme finally in the matter of art.

We picture him, then, on his way to his homeland which was his work, part of his work as surely as if he were a farmer. This was the way of his excitement. It could be called an obsession; in which case we would have to adapt his words about Monet and exclaim: but what an obsession. He, Cézanne – and we consider only his southern landscapes – was partner to the Provençal countryside. He sought to 'realize' his 'sensation', as he called it, in painting after nature: he sought tirelessly, starting at dawn, for the essential lie of the land. This meant in his case an enormous expenditure of a powerful inner fire, all ferocity, all love:

for these, as is the way of life, he found an object; as is the way of art, a useless object, an epitome of the life-process. He transmuted his strength, pushed it further away from himself than has any other artist, into a living-dead thing, into a Cézanne-become-a-landscape. For, remember, it was his 'sensation', no mere semblance of the countryside. He cut the cord with his fancy; the picture substituted his considerable ferocity and his remarkable love in terms of a grandiose yet razor-fine logic imputed to the outside world. His was the most direct homage ever paid to the infinite coherence of the visual world.

He strove to find for his canvas neither a tendency nor an echo of a mood, a waxing nor a waning: he strove for his senses to reveal, for his mind to re-create, a quintessential structure. And so he hurried away from all the incidental music of things. Yet Cézanne's painting cannot be called a conceptual art, for it is with the extreme complication of actual, even momentary, appearance that he philosophizes. The observational truth of light, space, colour, tone and mass in their subtlest, no less than in their generalized, modes, are the sole materials of his structure. The otherness of the outside world is affirmed, not mitigated, by the intrusion of this artist's organizing mind. His art needed a constant exercise in observation, for each new canvas a forcible detachment from the preconceived; endless thought, endless vigilance for every inch of the picture space. There was discouragement, timidity, self-distrust. But, for once, it is not agonies of mind that point the moral. Cézanne wrestled alone with the Provençal landscape, and his vision, which did harm to no one, yet sums all human activity.

And surely we may learn here of further ways to peace of mind. If when the senses are fully employed a contemplative mood supervenes, searching for interconnection, for a form, for a dominant note in this other, laid-out world beyond the body, we realize that in these terms of outside things – and we must not allow them to lean to us: they must preserve a perfect otherness – deep elements of all experience are observed and enjoyed. There is a submission to the factors of existence. Thus does a man breathe in a fresh morning. All men exercise an imaginative control, an imaginative limitation over their environment, enclosing as best they may a small world in accord with the needs of satisfying desire. But an unabashed aesthetic control (which so many thus rule out by enforcing conditional limitations) does harm to no one, depends for its sense of omnipotence upon no rationalization of prejudice, projects fantasy as fantasy, aggressive and loving, attaches a most noble imaginative logic to sensation, and, by affording so deep a sense of fitness, may allow the mind, if neurosis[1] be absent, to be free for impartial thinking at every point of reality.

May it come to that, if leisure for all will be unlimited: after an era of supreme vulgarity will have given way to a deep reliance upon more vivid uses of the mind and senses: when works of art, epitomes of all contemplation since they derive from contemplation of the face of concrete things, will be valued at a greater worth.

Cézanne withdrew from the concourse, withdrew very largely from Paris after 1886, withdrew from his friends particularly in his last twenty years. Perhaps the concourse in many more millions will come to him. He discovered a poetry that is without afterthought.

'I have nothing to hide in art',[2] writes Cézanne to Charles Camoin in 1903: and, 'What shall I wish you: good studies made after nature, that is the best thing.' Two years later to Louis Leydet: 'To succeed in formulating sufficiently the sensations we experience on contact with this beautiful nature – man, woman, still-life – and that circumstances should be favourable to you, that is what I must wish to all sympathizers of art.' Two months before he died in October 1906 Cézanne wrote in a letter to his son: 'I am sorry that I am so old in view of my colour sensations... It is unfortunate that I cannot make several specimens of my ideas and sensations; long live the Goncourts, Pissarro and all those who have the love of colour, representative of light and air.' A month later: 'Finally I must tell you that as a painter I am becoming more clear-sighted in front of nature, but that with me the realization of my sensations is always very difficult. I cannot attain the intensity that is unfolded before my senses. I have not the magnificent richness of colour that animates nature. Here on the edge of the river, the motifs are very plentiful, the same subject seen from different angles gives a subject for study of the highest interest and so varied that I think I could be occupied for months without changing my place, simply bending a little more to the right or left.' In the same month to Émile Bernard: 'I am always studying after nature and it seems to me that I am progressing slowly. I should like to have you near me for the solitude weighs rather heavily on me. But I am old and ill, and I have sworn to myself to die painting': as he did less than a month later.

In Cézanne's last letters, particularly in the letters to his son, the reader is struck by the constant juxtaposition of small requests and observations on nature or on painting. We realize that the lie of the land obsessed him, that he worked out his life there: not only in the manufacture of paintings but in front of the landscape or still-life, in his sensation before the object. But to estimate his achievement one must consider what he, for the first time in landscape or still-life painting, resisted in the object once he had settled to painting it: for instance, one must think of the low reminiscent murmur of wind among trees, along hedges; of slow thought among mounting land; of the passage of water; of soul-searching or else lyric mornings, of wrapping clouds: in effect, of the moods and evocations that we all have from nature to some degree, Cézanne by no means least. It has been said he painted portraits and landscapes as if they were still-lifes: indeed, he could resist as far as possible the seasons. Where are the voices of the fountains of Aix or the roystering yet ghostly Mistral blowing out of a blue sky; where the shuttered liquid peace of a calm Provençal afternoon? Neither in what we know of Cézanne's mature aims nor in the treatment of his subjects do we find any desire to reflect discursive messages from nature. And yet to visit Aix is at once to recall his pictures, to view them as an astonishing, faithful, mirror of that countryside, not only of the lie of the land but of the feel of the air, the character, the 'life'. It will then be no surprise to discover that Cézanne's youthful letters to Zola reveal an adolescent and a young man of extreme romantic temperament, of fervent poetry, whose roaming and bathing in his native landscape had become the centre of imaginative life. This landscape remained there, at the centre of his life. It is more true to say that his portraits and still-lifes are Provençal landscapes; while the many canvases of male bathers, particularly of the early middle period, as well as from the Louvre, from Rubens, from the Venetians, from 'Poussin after nature', derive from the passionate aquatic displays and the first freedom of the three inseparable youths, Cézanne, Zola and Baille.

Although we emphasize Cézanne's sense of structure, we must, then, also emphasize how close was his impact with nature; that at first it was a stark, even primitive, romantic onset in relation to his subjects, hinged to a Baroque complication, a Baroque posturing. His primitive simplicity, after emulating the counterpoint of Baroque design, subdued this element, especially in the early middle period, to the ends of a rectilinear grandeur that informs every inch of a painting's surface. Under the tutelage of the Old Masters whom he studied, copied and emulated all his life, particularly the Venetians, Rubens and Poussin, under the influence of Pissarro, under the influence of the deeper meaning of his native southern province, his love of Virgil and the classics, even perhaps of his own Italian ancestry, a romantic onset than which none more wild or savage or honest in primitive directness (yet from the first always subtle in counter-balance) had yet appeared in visual art, was miraculously enlarged with a majestic consensus of calm and even factual sensation; so that in spite of his life-long devotion to the art of Delacroix and of his denigration of Ingres, Cézanne's work stands to us as one of the greatest achievements of classic art; at any rate in one sense – and that perhaps the most dynamic – of the word classic. When we attempt to clarify the ultimate intention, Van Gogh, for instance, is found to stand at the opposite pole.

Classicism in the sense of a truly Mediterranean art, while keeping the broad grasp and the dignity associated with the wider use of the word, is 'close to nature', far closer than is a great deal of romantic art which treats of nature as a raw projection of emotional states, of the inside man. This classical art springs from a precise love and a passionate identification with what is other, insisting upon an order there, strong, enduring and final *as being an other thing*, untainted by the overt gesture, without the summary treatment, without the *arrière pensée* of 'thinking makes it so'.

How then did this classicist who insisted so fiercely upon the otherness of the spatial world, behave if he opened his heart when out for a walk? Gasquet's account of the lonely ageing artist whom he so passionately admired – such admiration had taken the shy and rejected Cézanne entirely by surprise – is probably a broad effect: even so, it is the text to which we feel entitled. 'He drank in the countryside with delighted eyes', wrote Gasquet; the countryside that he studied every day. 'The first pale leaves moved him deeply. Everything touched him. He would stop to look at the white road or to watch a cloud float by overhead. He picked up a handful of moist earth and squeezed it to bring it closer to him, to mix it more intimately with his own reinvigorated blood. He drank from the shallow brooks.' Earlier in this account of a walk, Gasquet wrote: 'He regretted that I was not a painter. The countryside thrilled us. He showed me, and explained to me at length, the beauty of all his conceptions of poetry and art. My enthusiasm refreshed him. All that I brought him was a breath of youth, a new faith that made him young again.'[3] It is easy to see that Cézanne was recapturing the original sense of those diurnal rushes at the landscape, with the youths Zola and Baille, which had so largely determined the channel of his life. Let the reader at once juxtapose an image of his painting where he translated this tender and ferocious pagan impetus into voluminous form. Nothing more conceptual as well as nothing less constructive seemed worthy to him.

Cézanne clung closely to nature. It is not said with the implication so familiar in art criticism today that at this one point the arch-revolutionary could not free himself, that here by a last divorce lay the best chance for his successors. It is said with the opposite implication. The validity of his abstraction, of his distortion, even, depended initially and continuously upon his emotional yet slow, painfully slow, thoughtful, consideration of mere appearance *qua* mere appearance. A sudden or conceptual management of appearances was entirely alien to him. Vollard, in describing the 115 sittings he gave Cézanne for his portrait which was left unfinished, remarks on the great proportion of the time spent by the painter in looking at the model. True, he went on with the portrait without the sitter but only, it becomes obvious, when he felt able to carry in his head a vast concatenation of appearance relationships. But not one touch would he put on except in reference to the whole, that is to say, in reference to his vision of what he wanted to subtilize as well as to abstract and emphasize in the whole. This construction, as one might call it, was a simplification of what the artist deemed to be the essential appearance, rather than an image substituted for a variety of appearances, which is the way of conceptual art. It has been possible for subsequent painters, while preserving something of Cézanne's classicism, to cut out the long agony, indeed, to impose a summary concept or image upon the object. Such achievement, though sometimes it would appear closely related to Cézanne, is in many ways at the antipodes. A super-imposed pattern of the object, though it rely upon less distortion than was employed by Cézanne in formulating his plan, may still bear no resemblance to his respectful use of an object. No artist looked harder and longer at the model. The only 'truth' he would recognize in his scheme was a concatenation of relations that corresponded with the infinite pictorial elements of an actual appearance. He was, of course, by no means a slave to the model; but that is not to say that in his search for the appearance behind the appearance he was prepared to simplify a form, unless it be to elaborate contingent forms or contingent spaces.

Conceptual art of all degrees has its great masters: but it is impossible to bring Cézanne within this fold. Indeed, he took no interest in primitive or archaic or formalized art; which is remarkable to the student who is aware that in his posing of figures, for instance, there was often an insistence upon a simple, primitive and even naïve attack which was a part of his great strength that he never forsook, a prerequisite of the subtilization and the synthesis he performed. Here, first of all, he was most original: in view of many of his successors, he would appear yet more original in not being contented with it; for, his subtilization and complication in no way mitigate or detract from this first simple onset: they indicate not a retraction but an enforcement.

344

He abominated in painting the unbroken surface whether in the earlier masters or in the paintings of Gauguin who at one time professed himself Cézanne's disciple. Cézanne would have nothing of it and Bernard says Cézanne 'spoke very harshly about Gauguin whose influence he considered disastrous'. When Bernard protested mildly that 'Gauguin admired your painting very much and imitated you a great deal', Cézanne replied furiously: 'Well, he never understood me: I have never desired and I shall never accept the absence of modelling or of gradation; it's nonsense.'[4]

If we remember Cézanne's omnipotent, almost *fauviste*, flourish in his early bohemian days,[5] if we consider what he 'worked through', it is easy to understand his revulsion from Gauguin and from the use the post-Impressionists made of his achievement, whose dismemberment he would naturally regard as disastrous. Perhaps the later letters with their emphasis upon studying after nature, reflect this same revulsion. Nevertheless, if we wish to learn more fully from Cézanne than have many of his notable successors, it may at least help us if we turn to these last letters,[6] most of them to young admirers, in which he expresses the sum of his artistic experience: and we shall find that the emphasis is in fact by no means where the Cubists chose to find it.

Thus, in May 1904, he wrote to the young painter Émile Bernard: 'I go ahead very slowly, as nature appears very complex to me and incessant effort is required. One must look at the model carefully and feel very exactly, and then express oneself with distinction and power.'

'The artist should scorn any opinion that is not based on an intelligent observation of character. He should avoid the literary spirit, which so often leads the painter astray from his real mission, the concrete study of nature – and causes him to lose himself far too long a time among intangible speculations.'

'The Louvre is a good book to consult, but it should be only as an intermediary. The true and immense study to be undertaken is the diversity of the spectacle of nature.'[7]

It was a wonderful balance Cézanne held between what he called 'intangible speculations' and the acceptance of nature as most complex, with a complexity requiring a continuous observational effort. The letter which has these phrases succeeds the famous one written to Bernard a month earlier in which he said: 'May I repeat what I told you here: treat nature by the cylinder, the sphere, the cone'; those words which, rather paradoxically, became the text of Cubism. But putting the two texts side by side we more nearly glimpse his whole achievement, especially if we add a sentence from one of the last letters to his son: 'I felt well there yesterday; I started a water-colour in the style of those I did at Fontainebleau, it seems more harmonious to me, it is all a question of getting as much affinity as possible.' Cézanne did not baulk the extreme complexity of nature, a far greater complexity than the Old Masters allowed; he learned to organize it and in so doing to 'obtain as much affinity as possible'. This last phrase elucidates the character of a modern classicism,[8] how it is possible to modulate – Cézanne's own term – in a way more contemplative than is the one of the romantic, often slap-dash, sometimes successfully slap-dash, approach, how it is possible to modulate into pictorial terms the great variety of sensation from the object.

I shall be returning to more general considerations. First, a few more passages, among many, from Cézanne's letters in which he asserts the primacy of direct study of nature. To his son he writes in September 1906: 'I am sending you a letter that I have just received from Emilio Bernardinos, one of the most distinguished of aesthetes. I am sorry not to have it in my power so as to infuse into him the idea which is so sane, so comforting and the only correct one of the development of art through contact with nature. I can scarcely read his letter, but I think he is right, though the good man simply turns his back in practice on what he expounds in his writings; his drawings are merely old-fashioned rubbish which result from his dreams of art, based not on the emotion of nature but on what he has been able to see in the museums, and more still on a philosophic mind.'

To Émile Bernard, October 1905: 'Now the idea to be insisted on is – no matter what our temperament or power in the presence of nature – to produce the image of what we see, forgetting everything that has been done before. Which, I believe, should enable the artist to express his entire personality, great or small.'9 In September 1906: 'You must forgive me for continually coming back to the same thing: but I believe in the logical development of everything we see and feel through the study of nature and turn my attention to technical questions later; for technical questions are for us only the means of making the public feel what we feel ourselves and of making ourselves understood.'

If we have this reiteration in mind we shall not misinterpret what follows in a letter to Bernard of 1904: 'Literature expresses itself by abstractions whereas painting by means of drawing and colour, gives concrete shape to sensations and perceptions. One is neither too scrupulous nor too sincere nor too submissive to nature; but one is more or less master of one's model, and above all, of the means of expression. Get to the heart of what is before you and continue to express yourself as logically as possible.' Again, the word logic. Cézanne felt strongly that he did not force the model: he enunciated its logic. The classicist object, an object, as it were, with full rights of its own, must possess an intense logic or coherence.

Finally, nine days before he died, in a letter to his son: 'The weather is stormy and changeable. My nervous system is very weak, only oil painting can keep me up. I must carry on. I simply must produce after nature; sketches, pictures, if I were to do any, would be merely constructions after nature, based on method, sensations, and developments suggested by the model, but I always say the same thing.'

Cézanne was proud to reiterate a conscientious dependence upon immediate appearance. At the same time, for each motif he would, he insisted, find the essential logic: that first and last and with every stroke between: in these terms, he knew, would pass all the 'literary' content, all the mystique, the passionate visions, the pantheistic identifications which he had felt or associated with his motifs. After all, it is only a difference of degree between this classicism and the romantic expression, a sudden sum of experience wherein there exists the very gesture to prove the fire is hot, the vision vivid.

Nevertheless, I am pretending that there is a problem, how it was that the second kind of expression should give way to the first. I want to know how it could come about that Cézanne who in his youth was the first wild man of modern art, revelling in an orgiastic omnipotence, should also have insisted with such an expense of agony upon the object as pure object, upon pushing the apple away from himself. His progress was always steady and he gave nothing up: his later expression does not reverse but includes the furious aims of the earlier.

After some attention to Corot the real influence was Courbet, the first genius of the new classicism; while the influence of Delacroix whom he loved was with him throughout his painting life. But soon the influence of Impressionism, of 'the humble and colossal Pissarro', was decisive, and in more ways than one. In the light of his contemporaneous figure compositions, it seems probable that Cézanne's conversion to Impressionism coincided with a renewed study of the Old Masters, particularly the Giorgionesque (not only on account of Manet's *Déjeuner sur l'herbe*) as well as the later Venetians. The link between the Venetian and the Impressionist styles would have been a more subtle and a more pervasive poetry.

The momentary appearance, then, the Impressionists' object, this new red-hot material for art, in Cézanne's keeping above all, came to serve a vast and timeless pictorial architecture. Not only for Cézanne but for all that group of artists, the concentration upon momentary appearance meant, as it were, surrender of all its rights to the object. A new poetry flowed freely, not to clog this objectivity but to pervade an acute exaggeration of the otherness of everyday scenes most evocative to our feeling.

But why was the former poetry not enough, even though possessing right from the start pronounced classical elements, why the drive within Cézanne's fiery, romantic disposition to refuse warmth from his pungent fires in favour of a less assertive, even if smokeless, heat? That is our pretended problem which we shall seek to solve for the sake of wider issues, though not in terms of psychology[10] but in terms of aesthetics.

We have under examination a headstrong lyrical impulse – it found no final satisfaction – which, in development, sought with ceaseless urgency a comprehensiveness, a detachment that evoked the most vital sense of the term, classical. We may compare it with an expression at the opposite extreme, a mere arrow in the air or a handful of clay appropriated and fashioned into an anthropomorphic presence. We may consider for a moment the imaginative projections of men with scant leisure, scant horizon and rough circumstances. Working as a trawler-hand, with beard and icy fingers, fumbled with heavy clothes, fish-smell, dirt and close quarters, not even the life-long artist can produce an aesthetic state without a saga. Possibly a religious, mystical or a rhythmic state that depends from some dramatic culmination. But he cannot, except flippantly, push away from him the heaving pile of struggling live fish nor gaze at it for the quality of otherness, nor thereby construct an expression to demonstrate the external world with the finality, the calm assurance of a dispensation as when on homeland, evening light removes weight from the sky, lends this weight to things.

No: such contemplation needs a caress from nature: not necessarily a softness but a coherence, a stabilization, a clarity which will provide a frame for even the harshest experience, for the peasant life, maybe, which Cézanne knew and loved. Thought has wanted the same condition for its nurture: it is no accident that the Mediterranean countries are the nurseries and the halls of factual thinking no less than of our classical art, whatever the sense of classical. When we speak of science in opposition to fantasy, we but mean impartial thinking freed of fantasy, an impartial thought which in its first days dared to find that the sun rose on a new day as a result of physical law rather than because the devout had prayed for it to reappear.[11] And so, while it is an expression of fantasy no less than romantic art, the order of classical art is less personal, an order, as it were, of fantasy facts, rejecting the wistful beauty of a fantastic and tremulous dispensation. Classical art in Europe, before it has encountered the terrible menace of polite conventions, of a mechanical pompous rule, delights to ring with pagan amplitude the contorted movements of the imagination, delights in a gusto, in a warm exuberance that pours as if from the wider apertures of the natural world. This art, then, at root, is deeply wedded to the consciousness of fact and, as we have seen, to logic, seeking to win for imaginative expression the objectivity or otherness of the factual world, to win for fantasy, for life, the exhaustive finality of death. It is the position of all art: classical art formulates the aim.

Thus our so-called problem in this case clarifies before the Mediterranean scene to which Provence belongs. With all his temperament, with all his terror of everyday problems, with all his emphatic fiery genius, Cézanne's attitude to art was catholic. Though mocked as a madman, in his thought and in his practice as an artist he exalted sanity.

He, too, experienced the openness of wine. Art for him was not a matter of intimations. What is the intimation of a blue day? There is a calm and a wide arrangement, clean spaces between things, clearness, clarity, light. We see it in England only perhaps on a still, early autumn afternoon of brilliant sunshine when the stooks and all the disposed colours stand: a biblical scene. On a blue day a song is given to the wide panorama: it is less a provoked fancy than a background or dramatization of what exists. Nevertheless, folk art everywhere is a slow extraction from the cycles of labour and country-scene, like a slow northern anger. Romantic art is fantasy speaking in terms of things: but in the south, things as themselves are captured for the mind. They have all weathers and all conditions: yet the blue day conquers.

Just as the great movement of the sea washes through our minds, so the lucidity of a still day attributes to the mind a pillared hall.

I have used the art of Cézanne to descant upon a continuous relation between emotion and the outer world. A stress on any point or points of the line of this equivalence (divided roughly, very roughly and artificially into the two zones, classical and romantic) determines both the quality of an artist's emotion and the kind of object he selects. The terms, especially outside historical Europe, have little meaning apart from a context. They are without precision and express as an antithesis what is in fact a gradual differentiation. They are, however, indispensable because by their means we can sometimes characterize broadly the artist and his object.[12] Though our concern is wider than specific art, they were introduced in order to illumine the equivalence where it is best acknowledged.

Like the difference between these two terms, so the difference between art and life is one only of degree, if living is conceived as the multiform of expression. Artistic expression or communication is self-sufficient in comparison with the interlinking activities of life, of which art is the useless epitome. We need but to refer to another truism – a work of art is a communication in terms of the data of the senses – to point to a certain rivalry here with the exposed otherness of the external world. Not only is a work of art, as a datum of a sense or senses, an object in the literal meaning, but that object expresses the universal desire to translate life into an outward attachment. The libido, according to one aspect of Freud's metapsychological thought, is primarily object-seeking.[13]

Some investigators discover in the ego a dread of being overpowered by instinctual forces per se. The ego as an organization, it is said, fears the unorganized. Thus, the ego (life itself, a physicist[14] tells us, is but intensified molecular *organization*) would seem to involve a consciousness that is more than a filter between the external and the internal. Management of instinct by the organizing ego which employs conscious thought, would seem further to involve the frequent enforcement on instinctual drives of a ramification, a projection, a substitution, culminating in culture.

Some such line of thought gives a rationale for man's ceaseless substitutive activities; interprets, for instance, the value we so often attribute to the expressing of one thing in terms of another, the value of art.

When all else of the night is black and when deep longing encounters a stretch of glimmering moonlit sea through trees, we experience in epitome the calm delirium of consciousness: as in adolescence, perhaps for the first time, not only speculative thought or abstraction but the starlit sky afford an apprehension of otherness dressed with the apparel of our passion; when the world becomes enormous and is matched by desire.

In differing degree, artists preserve the essence of this first wider rapture no less than they hold to the child's compulsion to project immediate but enclosing fantasy upon outside things.

If the two-thirds at least of the world's population which has never been properly nourished will be as well fed as the remaining third, if efficient social services and universal education are no dream, if leisure is to be almost unbounded, will art obtain the worth in a settled life that more than once it has had for an aristocracy? In the end, perhaps; and sooner if the controlling ego will be able to accept the vastly improved spiritual economy of an allocation between fact and fantasy wherein a great deal more is allowed to fantasy. But whether or not such values develop soon, it would appear that the aesthetic activity epitomizing all activity, this play which is sublime, will enrol a vast army of new addicts: they will hasten such a clear-cut division of meaning. An aesthetic appraisal of existence does not point to a huge concourse of would-be painters or musicians but to the affirmation in many more activities of aesthetic values.

We of this century have suffered a pressure from reality which finds the spirit of man unprepared: or so it seems, in spite of his creating that pressure with inventiveness. The discovery of atomic power brings to a climax our situation of imaginative unpreparedness for the environment ensuing from the Industrial Revolution. If civilization should succeed in surviving and if unbounded leisure should come suddenly, there would be a problem no less serious than those which confront us now: and we cannot guess as to the character of the equivalence which at a distant date would be contemplated most deeply between the spirit of man and the material of the outside world. (It is safer, at least once, to use this circumlocution for the arts in the future.) The crafts which have nourished them would seem to be doomed. In work the opportunities for art wane rapidly. But whether or not there would be the practice of art as now known to us, in my belief the aesthetic approach would eventually invade all rationalizations except those of science which define it.

At the moment, the heirs to a potential magnificence move among the many tortured, starved, diseased, blinded or contorted by toil. After fifty or a hundred years, after an increase of education and social services, we might have been in better condition for this overwhelming atomic gift. It is tantalizing that such immediate danger should occur at a time when painfully, slowly, through the science of psychoanalysis, a beginning is made in the understanding of the nature and economy of man's emotions and of means by which to strengthen the economy. And what if science, biochemical science, develops far-reaching power to mutate the species, while as yet the majority of scientists, like the majority of their fellow-men, need to resist the simple facts of our passions and of the infinite ramification of our substitutions? Shall the species suffer change at the hands of those who, maybe, have a strong vested interest in not experiencing what could be known about the nature of the mental life? It is the duty of every scientist, the fount of power today, to seek psychoanalytic treatment in its longest form.

Such an opinion, a demand for scientists to be yet more scientific, superb as is their tradition, will be considered ludicrous, as well as irrelevant, especially in a book that philosophizes art, by one who is not a scientist: more especially as the final words.

I can only repeat I do not think it so.

Art and Science

From *Art and Science: A Study of Alberti, Piero della Francesca and Giorgione* (1949)

There is an embodiment of fifteenth-century Italian art that is pure to the point of mystery. One of our artists is the painter sometimes accounted to be the greatest of the fifteenth century, Piero della Francesca. Two others, also supreme though their surviving works are few, Alberti and Luciano Laurana, are known to us as architects. If Alberti is first the subject, it will be with occasional reference to Piero but not because of a hard link between them.[1]

Piero and Alberti were both theorists. Vasari starts his life of Piero as of one who was a mathematician, a writer of theoretical treatises, also a painter. Piero's book on perspective, severely mathematical, does not help us to formulate his art. Most of Alberti's many writings have come down to us, including his principal aesthetic treatises. Of Laurana, the Dalmatian, we know next to nothing.

Two of our immediate heroes – Giorgione, though linked with them, must remain for a period in reserve – were of a speculative type. We may come to feel very close to Piero in his painting, though from such perfection we can infer a timeless rather than an individual aim. Many travellers have found their visits at Borgo San Sepolcro, his native place, to possess the solemnity and the intimacy of a pilgrimage, in virtue of the town and the landscape as much as of the *Resurrection*.

The case of Alberti[2] is altogether different. He was eager to give his views on every subject: and there is consistency in his teaching. We may attempt, therefore, to approach the central aesthetic of the early Renaissance through Alberti. This context has been left blank by the present writer more than once, always with the promise that it would eventually be filled. Now that the opportunity occurs, there is added the enormous stimulus of Sir Kenneth Clark's recently published essay,[3] a masterpiece of disclosure and of elucidation, presenting Alberti for the first time in the round.

We shall have little to say of Alberti's power to excel, unrivalled even at that time, of his multiform genius or physical prowess, except in so far as this power to excel was strengthened by the current faith in a reasoned perfectibility. The 'revival of learning' was partly the cause, but more the result, of a new faith in the sanity of man and of his environment.

Alberti was a wanderer, a contemplater of all Italy. As well as homelessness, he possessed deep roots in belonging to one of the great Florentine families which had been exiled. When, at the age of twenty-four or twenty-five, he was able to go to Florence for the first time, his reaction to circumstance had already caused him to express a sensitive yet robust temper in terms of a broad aristocracy of mind. He had seen a way, a hard way, for aristocratic omnipotence free of estate. Though Alberti was no more independent of favour than were the wrangling, plebeian lions of learning, yet he ordered his life, there is evidence enough to show, so that the vision of his own power and of the calm extents of his many intellectual domains reinforced a lofty aristocratic candour. And if, none the less, he was a deeply wounded man, wounded rather than embittered, to enmity and disappointment he opposed his many different talents of constructiveness and a great industry, mar-shalling them for what may be called a common-sense triumph. It was an expression, we surmise, of his tenderness, of his noble hard-won patience and of his now fanatical health. More than an aristocrat, he was a constitutional monarch of the mind, cruel and ruthless in one respect only (if we except his tirades against women), in self-discipline and in studious application to this humanist end.

In spite of persecution from some of its members of which he complains bitterly – the experience doubtless helped him to feel dissociated from any party or group – Alberti had great pride in his family's cultural achievements. Spiritual inheritor of princely men of commerce, he fostered the will to be practical and communicative in learning, as well as sound. Thus, without a trace of eccentricity he freed himself from Scholasticism. It was natural for him to write copiously on liberal lines about education or the need for prison reform or the treatment of servants, without calling in question the very structure of his society. He looked for the power of reason and good sense in all men's affairs. The term 'good sense' is joined with the word 'reason' in order to suggest the inductive originality of his mind rather than philosophical abstraction; his developed senses, particularly his acute observation allied to his learning and good memory.

So far, the subject is not dramatic; but that will come. We associate with Alberti's partisanship for the Italian language and for the new perspective art, with his roles as inventor and experimental engineer, a belief in a weight and in a gravity as belonging to his epoch, independent of an ancient dream. He was perhaps the only confident Roman of those days. The Roman heritage crowned those of Florence and the Alberti, a new empire to be exploited by the exuberance of a new candour. Applied mathematics inspired much of his view of art and through art, of all kinds of practice, allocating the novel vehement impressions from the measurable, near thing; serving as a solvent to the barriers between men and a fully independent outside world.

A few Florentine artists, chiefly Brunellesco, were the first to find in this new exactitude a sensuous inspiration. Alberti tried to build, in the *Della pittura* especially (his book on painting), the scenery for all vision. As well as discoverer he was schematist and popularizer: the condescension, the largesse of it, suited him. Accurate disposition in space, we soon realize, possessed for him a tangible, as if new-found, order as well as an extraordinary loftiness. We are reminded of the lyrical fire that could accompany careful, adult observation dismissive of magical generalities; that arose at the end of the century from the inductive Aristotelian researches of Almorò Barbaro and his followers, some of whom were to be the patrons of Giorgione.

We are approaching Alberti the new Roman yet romantic architect who was innocent of any hint of the Baroque, so electrical, so unfanciful were his sublimities; and the art at the centre of the early Renaissance which was soon overlaid. But concerning Alberti the writer on art, we must also view the dreary latter length of academic tradition still tied to

356

this same approximation between science and art long after the force of a once huge impetus was spent, judging it to be a trailing offshoot from the doctrines proposed by Alberti in his youthful treatise on painting.[4]

Let us see what they meant in the first necessitous days. It was hardly an aesthetic of naturalism. Though the lily should not be gilded and individual character affords life, yet Nature, in detail, is thorny, deficient and must be improved upon. 'Nothing in Nature is perfect,' we are told at the end of the *Della pittura*. The codification of art which always has its beginnings in Nature, is therefore made most difficult. But 'He who comes after me,' adds Alberti for his final words, 'should he exceed me in diligence and talent, will make of painting an absolute and perfect thing.'[5] This sentence does not refer to a succeeding painter but to a succeeding theorist or expounder of art. The later theorist will entirely solve the equation, as it were, in which art consists, will solve an almost mathematical problem.

Alberti's conception of perfectibility for painting does not imply advocacy of a conceptual shorthand for Nature, a simplification or generalization. It means the choice from appearances, viewed with impersonal exactitude, of those forms that express harmoniously a state of mind or exhibit harmoniously their own function: for that is beauty. Concurrently, he stresses dependence upon Nature and deprecates those who would paint 'without having an example'. The word is perhaps revealing. Nature is conceived as the wide example of order and of beauty which the artist, without distortion of any kind, must concentrate or intensify, retaining the natural balance that typifies the structure of all living things, whether it be a movement of a leg with the opposite arm, or light with dark (retaining as well an outwardness or expressiveness of pose that typifies the spirit). An applied mathematical approach – and thus did mathematics lend such power to art – brought in its train a thorough cognisance of observed relationship, of quantity and quality in terms of comparison, so that the trained eye grasped a widening order of interdependent values comprising the vast system of the outside world. The surveying of this undistorted territory, therefore, was by no means restricted to size, to perspective. Alberti's most pregnant sentences in the *Della pittura* – consider the date, 1435 – are concerned with the relativity of tonal values: and he suggests that since all visual attributes are defined only by comparison, the norm of differentiation comes from man, 'the constant measure of all things', a saying he attributes to Pythagoras: perhaps this is the correct interpretation of the saying, Alberti wonders...[6]

A measuring of phenomena served the humanism of that age to the end of supreme art, an art which therefore embraced, incorporated science. Behind Alberti's view of painting there lodged, of course, the Platonic idea of Absolute Beauty whose rules and regulations were to be appropriated. An aesthetic, drunk with outwardness, blind to any psychological consideration, which would seem, if applied to present-day circumstance, either jejune or sterile, mystic at best,[7] was the expression and the means in the early Renaissance of a sublime exuberance, of man's most comprehensive attempt to rule the universe with the least withdrawal from the world of the senses. In art it has eternity.

Alberti wrote in one of his later moral essays, the *De iciarchia*, 'Nature by herself never errs.' It would appear that when it was not a question of art the 'imperfection' of Nature lost importance. Many more cogent quotations, though not as brief, could be advanced to show how he constantly appealed to Nature for a Platonic prototype. Even in the *Della pittura* he wrote, wishing to show how ancient is the desire to paint: 'Nature also likes to paint, it seems, since we see in the fissures of marble the likenesses of Centaurs and long-haired, bearded kings.'[8] This sentence means no less than it states. The first words of the book on sculpture, the *De statua*, are as follows: 'I think the desire to represent and express the likeness of natural things has this origin. Those who will be practising the arts have chanced to see in a large tree-trunk or on the ground or in other material, an effigy of some kind which encourages them to vie with these faces wrought by Nature.'[9] And in the book on architecture, the *De re aedificatoria*, writing of fossils which he takes to be natural carvings, Alberti says: 'It is particularly remarkable that you never find on the ground one of these carved stones which is not reversed, whereby the carving is turned to the ground. It suggests that

Nature has made these things, not for men's admiration but for her own delight.'[10]

If we remember the fervent astrology and superstition of that age, we will find it remarkable that Alberti should be content with so vague and impersonal a natural agent. He refers to astrological consultations before beginning to build (for which he finds classical parallels), but offers no enthusiasm, though he would blame no one for wanting to be on the safe side: it might well be prudent. He sometimes engages upon wonder stories, especially if their poetry is judged to help as well as lighten his discourse and to illustrate his reading, but on the whole he shows a disinterest – he expresses, for instance a contempt of alchemy[11] – based less upon argument than upon a disinclination for the exotic: though he does, it is true, think there may be something in the idea for warding off lightning, by enclosing in the wall of the house a fragment of eagle or a piece of laurel or a piece of 'vecchio marino'.[12] Alberti sometimes falters when blatant superstition can be linked with a classical author or a classical myth. It would be true to say, however, that he shows no more inclination towards superstition than to the schoolmen. It would, moreover, be absurd to expect him always to be able to distinguish superstition; a cumulative work by no means finished today; perhaps no more than half finished.[13] Magic, medieval fantasies in general, are distasteful to him, being more offensive to his aesthetic appreciation of the harmonious indifference of natural forces than to his reason. We have already observed Alberti as artist, in the name of reason embracing science: now we envisage him as would-be scientist embracing art, for the sake of fantasies attached to a mathematical order. By demanding a new degree of objectivity, the simple measurements and experiments of that time wore an ennobling, a humane look.

On a larger estimate, this approximation between art and science may be found to have borne dead or constricted fruit in many seasons. But the Quattro Cento aesthetic served a tense compulsion: the objects laid out in Piero's representations and the face of Alberti's and Luciano's stone, calm, incontrovertible, yet immediate, in robust flower, pose the knotted courses of living...

The scion of a noble house who was 'cut off' because he would not go into the family business, who 'made good' in his chosen sphere, Alberti may seem to resemble the heroes of countless novels. In addition, his humourless preaching, his immense self-satisfaction and his ceaseless attempt, as Sir Kenneth Clark has pointed out, to convince his readers that virtue pays, complete an almost Victorian picture. The parallel is not without some justice; yet, though the clichés be much the same, a Victorian conception of perfectibility is as distant from the one of the Renaissance as is their art, as distant as middle-aged, post-prandial good fellowship and optimism from the ecstasy of a hard and youthful dawn. Victorian optimism, reinforced by a cast-iron belief in evolutionary progress unknown to Alberti, accompanied a now wintry academism that contrasts with his emotion and achievement though he was the ancestor. To re-establish painting after Nature on firm ground, it will first be wise to invoke against the coarse academic stupor Alberti's and Piero's passionate researches.

For the moment, however, it is necessary to come between Alberti and Piero lest we may seem to draw them specifically together in the sense of master and disciple. Though there exists at least one hypothetical instance of a reflection of Alberti's architectural form in Piero's painting, the present writer cannot find a text in the *Della pittura* for Piero's use of colour. Where Alberti treats of colour, the emphasis is almost entirely upon chromatic tone. Following on black and white, 'All colours', says Alberti, 'are means for the painter to achieve a degree of shade and a degree of light.'[14] He writes with approbation, it is true, of a certain *amicitia*, a certain amity between colours. But the phrase is employed in rounding off a passage wherein the author admires the effect of one colour against another that is far different in hue and of a contrasting tone.[15] The emphasis upon light, upon tone to which colour is subsidiary, issues from the point of view of attaining relief rather than of an even reciprocity. 'All painting is there', says Alberti in concluding the second book of the *Della pittura*, 'in outline, composition and light.'

Those passages which demand from painting nobility, *contrapposto*, compositions crowded with figures and with life, conjure up the Raphael of some seventy or more years later, as Sir Kenneth Clark points out, to a degree that is startling. Admittedly, however, the emphasis upon illumination *might* have had an influence upon Piero's system of colour or upon his master Domenico Veneziano who, with a softness, alone among his fellows attempted for itself the painting of light.[16] But is it probable that instructions meant primarily for relief would have been turned to the uses of a finer mosaic of co-ordination? Longhi's suggestion is to be preferred, of a 'Franchescan' movement between 1440 and 1460 imposed upon late Gothic painting in several parts of the Mediterranean seaboard...[17]

While we are thinking of the Raphael to come, Alberti slips in his only reference to a modern painter, Giotto, praising him without a word of qualification for the expressiveness of his poses. The praise is just; indeed, most apt, since Giotto is the father of modern painting. But a doubt rises in the mind whether Alberti, though well-placed between the two terminals, could have beheld the course between Giotto and a Raphael (whom at times he seems to envisage), a course that, though it be straight, appears vast to us, even after the telescoping performed by time. On the other hand we master easily the full implication when Alberti says that the first necessity of the painter is to know geometry or when, in his book on architecture written some fifteen years after the *Della pittura*, he speaks of the sisterhood of pillars. Neither speed nor light and shade characterize Alberti's architecture. Florentine art was no longer his focus.

There is, however, a simple explanation, apt to the text, of what Alberti visualized for painting. It has long been remarked that the Treatise is dedicated to four sculptors and to one painter only;[18] that what the sculptors had begun was as yet without wide pictorial application. Here lay Alberti's first great task to which his genius was particularly adapted. He took it upon himself to induce, as it were, the potentialities of painting from the works of sculpture around him. The clue no doubt was antique sculpture,[19] from which the image must be built up, then as now, of the Greek painting to which Alberti's classical authors referred. But the line of thought was vastly strength-ened by the contemporary sculpture, especially of Donatello who was himself swayed by antique reliefs. It is, surely, Donatello's agile and copious reliefs[20] in particular that Alberti visualized in paint, those with a strong suggestion of distance unknown to antique reliefs. Posses-sing the definite image, with his strong inclination for relevance he was quickly able to isolate the problem of the transposition, the outstand-ing question of tone (outstanding, that is, beyond perspective science). And due to this and other figments possible only in painting, the reliefs, dignified by greater space, would be set out with a subtle life as well as with stronger contrasts... It is likely that an immediate effect of the *Della pittura* was to direct the influence of Donatello on to painting.

There was no Roman school during the greater part of the fifteenth century. The first twenty years in the city were a time of ruin and bar-barity, the next twenty only a little better. Early Renaissance art, led by Brunellesco and Donatello, grew in large part amid the more ancient ruins. Yet there could be no school of Rome herself. Brunellesco first rifled the treasure house. It is not known how long he stayed: possibly his visits added up to a decade or more, possibly far less. The margin is wide, yet we do not have the sense from his buildings and from the little we are told with apparent truth, of cumulative sensibility. Instead, we feel him to have been a very active man, driven by well-defined prob-lems, the greatest of which, counterpart to his genius, was the dome for the Cathedral at Florence. Alberti also surveyed and measured the Roman remains. Unlike Brunellesco who conceivably may have spent more months in Rome, Alberti had his home there, lived there on and off for some forty years. Working in the papal administration, continu-ing to live in Rome after he had been dismissed from the service, he was the only major artist of his time who was likely to *contemplate* as well as measure the grandeur; to permit those giant ruins, arches and embossments glimpsed diurnally from the corner of the eye, to mould his mind in a sense deeper than the seeking from out the rubble a lore of engineering feats. Alberti too, we have said, went out on surveying expeditions. But the perspective of the ancient city meant a great deal more to this lonely, contemplative man. The dominant image now may not have been of the mathematic and the grandeur, of a springing and a counterpoint: the dominant image, perhaps, was in a convergence of the surveying and sight-seeing expeditions themselves, of the mass of traversed rubble, the jagged, ruined brick-work and the incorruptible face of the stone capital or carved stone aperture. Certainly in Alberti's Tempio encasement at Rimini there is a passionate stillness, a smoothness and a small carved flowering from the stone that cups and concentrates smoothness, foreign not only to Brunellesco and his school and, indeed, to Florentine art generally, but also to the posturing of painted figures advocated by the youthful Alberti of the *Della pittura*.

Added to the belief in the mathematic perfectibility of art, there was a less conscious yet unparalleled belief in the dominion of stone.[21] White stone, prime material of this Franchescan aesthetic, possesses an even, gradual radiance, revealing relations in the mode of all appearances as they stand reciprocal in an evening light. Where stone lies on brick it will have the dynamic radiance of a flower. Exuberant as is this flower of decoration from the wall, it is not to the effect of mere richness or of ornament.

Calm, steadfastness, measure, are celebrated in the chief Quattrocento buildings, affording instantaneous apprehension to the eye; exuberances of the wall whose apertures are cavernous, encrusted, whose protuberances are those of branch and flower. The more massive Antique is sometimes staid when compared with so passionate yet uncontorted a love of wall-space governed by Pythagorean-Platonic calm, amassed from dreams of self-fulfilment to rival ordered stone. The Tempio encasement transcends all other building in such respect. We may instance the unusual poignancy (since it is allied to so single or immediate an impression) of the doorway arch on the Tempio façade, a span a third greater than the flanking arches: and for the effect of stone-blossom, we may point even to the frieze of plain Roman lettering adopted by Laurana at Urbino. But in regard to decoration as in regard to the geometry, only negative precepts issue from analysis.

Although the parallel is still alive in some part of the mind, we no longer believe a work of art to be as unassuming a form as a scientific truth. Nevertheless we do well to reflect on the creative ability which could possess this belief so deeply, how that there was conjoined on occasion a perfect calm with the rediscovered world of the senses, the prolix Shakespearian world; a steady dawn with all the vigour of mid-day. We do well to know and enjoy this supreme moment of art, the model of the extent to which the soul of man can assume an outward guise.

Dr. Rudolf Wittkower, in two papers written for the *Warburg Institute Journal*,[22] has shown in the case of Alberti, and in the case of Palladio with a larger wealth of both theoretic and executed material, that we must regard references to music such as the one in the ninth book of Alberti's *De re aedificatoria* to be no generality but a precise mathematical doctrine of ratios, adopted rather than adapted from Pythagorean musical harmony. Alberti's words are: 'The numbers by means of which the agreement of sounds affects our ears with delight, are the very same which please our eyes and our minds.' In the paper referred to on Palladio, Dr. Wittkower writes: 'The splitting up of ratios for the sake of making the proportions of a room harmonically intelligible appears to us very strange. And yet, this is the way the whole Renaissance conceived of proportion. A wall is seen as a unit which contains certain harmonic potentialities. The lowest sub-units, into which the whole unit can be broken up, are the consonant intervals of the musical scale the cosmic validity of which was not doubted.'

For instance, in 1534, Titian was called in, with Serlio, to give opinion about Francesco Giorgio's memorandum on Sansovino's model for San Francesco della Vigna. This memorandum entirely identifies visual proportions with musical harmony. Titian, of course, like Giorgione, was a musician. Music ranked in the medieval *quadrivium* of the mathematical arts. The Renaissance sought to raise the visual arts within this category. 'A familiarity with musical theory', says Wittkower, 'became a *sine qua non* of artistic education.'

The Pythagorean ratios were employed primarily upon the division of a flat surface since, at the Renaissance, unlike Roman and, still more, Greek times, at the early Renaissance supremely so, *the wall was the architectural focus*, its apertures, demarcations, protrusions, which were never more fruitful to the mind. 'In the relatively short period of twenty years', concludes Wittkower, 'Alberti passed through the whole range of approaches to classical architecture which was possible in the Renaissance. He developed from an emotional to an archaeological outlook. Next he subordinated classical authority to the logic of the wall structure. And finally he repudiated archaeology and objectivity and used classical architecture as a storehouse which supplied him with the motives for a free and subjective planning of wall architecture.'[23] In accordance with his conception of the logic of the wall, Alberti, if we consider only undisputed buildings, always used pillars to support arches. Columns, rounded units which eventually he ceased to think of as being remnants of a pierced wall[24] like the arches above an aperture, provide a principle of ornament, engaged with pillars, or they may support flat entablatures like houses raised on piles. 'In practice, therefore, Alberti's conception of the column is essentially Greek, while his conception of the arch is essentially Roman – in both points he is followed by his great successors Bramante and Palladio.'[25]

We shall consider in the light of Alberti Piero della Francesca's architectural representations, though not in the sense that Piero was directly subject to Alberti's precept or example. Piero has more than once represented columned porticoes with straight entablatures. But his use of the column is determined by rectangular pictorial conception, and though we may care to look further, even to the length of considering that conception, nothing firm can be concluded on this basis alone about the relationship between the two artists. Moreover, double columns supporting arches (and little else) provide the *mise-en-scène* for the Annunciation at Perugia. These columned arches are similarly related not only to the composition of the picture but to its complicated pointed shape, that of the *cymatium* to a Gothic altar-piece, painted below on gold for the nuns of Sant'Antonio.[26] Piero's architecture is part and parcel with his non-Albertian figures and with his conception of the subject-matter, in a mode so profound as to give rise to mystic utterance. Such architecture could not have been derived by rote.[27] Except in the background of the *Madonna di Senigallia* where a doorway and window are represented which may closely reflect the work of Francesco di Giorgio, Luciano Laurana's successor at Urbino, and in the apse behind the Brera *Madonna and Saints* which (Bramante apart[28]) calls to mind[29] the Lombardi's Santa Maria dei Miracoli at Venice, soon to be begun – Piero's buildings do not reproduce an actual architecture employing the new classical members, as much as they suggest the preciousness and the smoothness of ivory conceived upon an Olympian, mathematic scale. Yet, ideal in smoothness though it be, subject to the needs not only of his design but of colour and tone (his friezes are zones of dark-coloured marble[30]), Piero's architecture translated and magnified the new concern with wall-significance, if only because of the noble affinities – indeed union – of the wall with the figures that have been projected within that orbit. His shallow mouldings and gradual curves possess a most profound intent: coffered recesses and the distinct beauty of column and demarcated pavement not only embody but most surely inspire the love of stone.

The beautiful wall, door and entablature of the Arezzo Annunciation is topped by cloud, by the figure of the Almighty and the softest blue sky. Like the rest of the building with the slow plain aperture above, like the tapering column between the Virgin and the announcing Angel, this wall, thus measured against the majesty of the holy subject, becomes the record of perfect spatial interval.

In his book on perspective Piero came near to identifying painting with this science. Except in front of his paintings it is difficult to grasp how much emotion, and in particular a sense of explicit order, how much sense of discovery could have been both stimulated and released by the employment of geometric perspective. The transcendental medieval culture was hostile to the apprehension of homogeneous space, as if the medieval Aristotelian concept of the four elements in the terrestrial zone *below* and of the divine element *above*, outmoded

366

the easy contacts of normal vision. But stress upon mathematics, both in the case of Alberti and of Piero, by itself explains nothing of their art. Similarly Platonism, neo-Platonism, was but a necessary garment, the cover of a nameless joy in things; paradoxically, since the philosophy of Plato is far from the senses, allowing no more value to the sensible world than to the individual, that other god of Renaissance man.[31] A worship of mathematics,[32] then, subject to different connections, to different unconscious tendencies, might result in an extremely conceptual, abstract or even archaic painting. As it was, renascence of the near thing, of a steady, untroubled, adult regard, the most tremendous triumph of man, provoked our science no less than our art: in the first moment of completeness, before elaboration and back-sliding, with a vast inherited iconology still undispersed, they were as one. Physical proportion took the place of medieval light from on high: verisimilitude evoked the moodless majesty of Nature.

Piero pushed this aesthetic to an extreme, he alone in painting. And whereas Alberti was able to find the Franchescan synthesis for his architecture, it may have been that from out of his more literary interest in painting, in the rhetoric of painting, he felt Piero's art to be almost a vulgarity, stilted, perhaps archaic in the application of scientific truth which he, Alberti, had first codified, treating of perspective in the *Della pittura*. There is no evidence whatsoever for this view; but in classifying Alberti with Piero, we must at the same time recognize the possibility of a situation so often met with, wherein a partner apparently takes as the one and only formula what for the other is but an initial scheme: a familiar situation that may involve acute and often bitter difference.

Piero achieved equation between true science and a majestic rapture from the earth. We sense geometry and number expressing the amplitude of love: we witness an untorn naturalism: a universal myth that is apart.

Love and the love of perspective were one, the perspective, for instance, of tilted circular shapes expressed with the slow piety of very exact drawing. Yes, piety, but more than piety, far more than the Gothic bent for the encrusted curve of a gold nimbus, inspired the corres-

pondence that is broad and temperate between his volumes. We have
from him the widest vistas and therein the equal simultaneous constancy of things; a stillness that is not archaic, a fullness without boast,
a massive self-containment in the very stream of adult life. But he delighted also to show the virtuosity, as it were, of his rooted shapes in his
fondness of temporary structures or of any such apparatus to whose
related forms he could, like the dying sun on an autumn day, unexpect-
edly attribute a durable and self-sufficient sense. Similarly his men,
even on the battlefield, in virtue of volume, of affinities between volumes and their intervals, vibrant, earthly, engrossed, possess the flux
and the chance. Piero's science serves both to distinguish exactly each
particular and to embrace it. Agitation borrows the broad arc of calm.
The geometry is at peace with a deep-rooted organic structure, product
of chromatic sense. Franchescan forms are brothers and sisters at ease
within the ancestral hall of space.

There are, then, three starting points for the critique of Piero's
painting. First, the potential coincidence of science and art in the early
Renaissance, founded on the new victories of perspective. Secondly, his
sense of colour as the basis of his sense of form. Although connections
are many between these two approaches, only the first has a literature.
To the detriment of art-criticism, form is rarely envisaged from the
end of colour. The two roads prove to be but branches of the third, the
quality of love by which Piero's bare geometry is seen by us as warm and
rich as well as noble; a nakedness of love, numbers that in bareness
may thereby be clothed with magnificence as may the study-object of
anatomist and physiologist, shared also by poets and by every human
being.

Piero's forms are familiars, we have said. No form accepts sacrifice
to the emphasis of another. Distributed by perspective they converse
through spatial simultaneity, through their affinities that search it out.
The postures of these forms acknowledge the same sublime homeliness.
Angels and princes make themselves known with the slow gestures of
a calm peasantry. Noble science gives more than the framework, gives
undying accent to the straight mysterious growing of the countryside.

368

Perspective separates, colour and form bring together in family circle the crupper on a horse and the shoulder of a hill, the fluting of columns and the hanging folds of a dress. To our eyes a slow majesty as of white oxen upon the white ribbon of a road between the terre-verte hills, belongs to the valley of the upper Tiber where Borgo San Sepolcro lies, Piero's town.

If there is an emphasis it is upon the homogeneity of space ignored by the medieval mind, an emphasis previously unknown to painting. Though a fraternal relationship between objects appeared in archaic and decorative art, the timeless unity of their space which could have permitted a wider divergence of family traits and a less summary organization, was neither comprehended nor desired. All the same, in the interests of that simultaneity, Piero, as did Cézanne whose sense of colour was equally dominant in his sense of form, preserved the two-dimensional character of the picture-space – a certain archaic flatness, then, of forms – in conjunction with a great depth and a great volume.

Piero suffered no contrast between man, his circumstance and his heavy body. The Franchescan elders are Semitic for the most part, hirsute, watchful, but it is as if their low raucous fire, subject to the architectural involucre of outwardness, cohered like a squared clod; as if the abysmal contradictions of the spirit were transmuted into the density and demarcation of a heavy turve. A transmutation, we feel (though not to the effect of those symbols that are so easily won in decorative art), a transmutation into the simultaneity of space. Space, to a less degree the perennial subject of all painting, was Piero's rigid concept: whereas conceptual art substitutes a convention for mathematical space.

When we remember his paintings we first think, perhaps, of broad calm heads, of an oaken calm, of head-dresses and blameless trees; of entablature, of foliage, linked as if by hands: of tufted ground and feet in profile on a marble floor, of open surfaces that bloom from open surfaces, spheres that respond to cylinders, fibrous hair to non-deciduous trees.

No other painter, except Giorgione and Cézanne, transposed as completely his love of life into the terms of space. Other, and usually predominant values of visual art, such as rhythm, contrast, stress, movement, arabesque, are common to all the arts however differing their sensation in each. The great poet Botticelli, for instance, to our exploring tactile sense exposes visions, sometimes restless. The transposition lacks the finality, or at any rate the immediacy, of space. Compared with Piero, Botticelli is as sea to land. One might say of all, or nearly all, the pictures in the National Gallery, compared with the Pieros they are as sea to land.

We are bound to attribute to Piero a deep contentment. The loggias and halls are not embellishments of princely life, but enlargements of an italianate street, innocent of genre. His architectural backgrounds possess great beauty; but it is less likely we shall recall Piero when looking at St. Paul's, or even San Lorenzo, than at the sight of a black-timbered farm building in the sun, a sublime demonstration of architectural meaning (since he has caused us to see it thus in element), with open doors and windows revealing a greater and more simple darkness. Outside, the sun, inside a generous darkness beyond the edges of neutral-toned apertures. The thought occurs of the square muzzle of a cow.

As well as his sheds, Piero's magnificent buildings are stalls of the greatest contentment. Their shelter is dignified, complacent, like the gesture of the Virgin in the Monterchi fresco, pointing to her pregnant stomach. There is sufficiency and amplitude both within and without the womb. Hills lie with heads, foliage with thorny hair, massive mouths on calm rounded faces. There remains always a strong ligament between light and dark, between what is spread and bark-like folds, between the rounded and the pointed. Each interval constructs an expressive pattern. In the stillness, apprehended at one glance, there is fire. The men and women of bovine lips and bovine eyes are gripped to their outward showing like trees in broad leaf. Above them stand the self-confident trees, circular, pyramidal, of thick foliage, nut, acorn, chestnut-bearing.

We may attribute a conscious application of such oaken character to the spatial settlement. Indeed, the Arezzo frescoes depict the story of the True Cross, grown from a branch of the tree of Good and Evil planted with Adam in his grave to sprout from him as did his chestnut-haired children. Further on, we observe this stubborn wood in a bridge and in a grained cross against the sky. At the last episode, the return of the cross to Jerusalem, the wood is held between two tousled trees, the link, it has been suggested, between the Old and New Testaments, between the many words that thus unstealthily would fructify.[33]

If clothes are sometimes bark, hair is breathing foliage. Man, measure of the universe, on ceremonial occasions manifests the world's geometry. Hence the towering volumes at Arezzo of the hats. But consideration of pure form, in the case of such lyrical genius as possessed both Piero and Cézanne, men of roots and strong sensuous feeling, leads to no short cut, no summary artifact. Their geometry exhibited the condensation of their far-reaching love. As is so often the case, Piero's theoretical writings mislead in the matter, for he wrote only of values responsive to rule, to scientific rule. These values, however, were in divine conjunction with his sense of the warmth between parent and offspring, between polychrome pavement and shod feet that create the spaces thereon, between grooved entablature and the creases in a band that rounds the head, between arm and peeled tree-trunk, horse and cloud, a small rich pendant and the wide spreading of lake and low hills, between a circular dark-toned hat and a porphyry disc, between hat, hand and battlement. Connection is always architectural in the sense of a division of an order: the mailed apple of a closed vizor and the rounded face of a trumpeter with his length of thin tube extending from his lips; the ring of a skull-cap and the spring of an arch; the darkness of an aperture circled with stone and the dark centres of eyes flanked with their whites; the consummation expressed in an Emperor's conical hat surrounded by heads of coiled, pleated hair against a background of arches and circular disks; the spiral grooves of ears and the straight grooves of a transparent covering that falls from the head; the winding river with light paths and white belts or curving outer hems; extended fingers and the feathered points of an heraldic eagle; the horses' hooves of opposing armies like wide-bottomed chessmen on the board; the acanthi of a Corinthian capital and the features and fingers of the Virgin, the beads and structure of her vestments; the dark head of a crossbearer against the sharp walnut-shaped centre of the grain and the ribbed clouds beyond; in a crowd, head growing from head, half a mouth against a neck or a white hem disappearing against the white of an eye; the mounting risen Christ and a dark knoll in the dawn light; the hill-protuberances beyond Battista Sforza's ivory face and the diaphanous hills beyond her husband's warted cheek... The catalogue is mechanical, since the connections are not single but profuse, ramifying in stillness. Piero's colour exploits the affinity to which we have referred in terms of shape and tone. All art exhibits connection, a bringing together. In visual art alone, and then solely in visual art deeply founded upon this colour-cum-architectural sense of form, an aesthetic communication may be explicit and immediate to the point of rebutting after-thought. It is the *réaliser* of Cézanne. Such demonstration of intellect and feeling was the crown of the Quattro Cento compulsion to make manifest. Thereafter the same chromatic sense of form to some degree persisted in post-Renaissance art refurbished, if we consider painting only, by Vermeer, for instance, by Chardin, re-enacted by Cézanne. Yet there has not been, and still there is lacking, a generalized apprehension of this side of visual art, eminent not only in painting but also in drawing, in sculpture and more particularly, in architecture whose steadfast forms and textures (not colours) have so often endowed that sensibility with archetypes.

Piero reveals the family of things. His art does not suggest a leaning from the house of the mind. He shows, on the contrary, the mind becalmed, exemplified in the guise of the separateness of ordered outer things; he shows man's life as the outward state to which all activity aspires.

The family of things. It is as if the poetry of deep affinities were identical with those objects and with their formulae; as if death's calm separation lent nobility to the pressure of each heartbeat.

There can be no art without something, however minute, of this quality; because Art, mirror of each aim, conspires to win for expression the finality of death.

No artist has been more extreme in poetic gift than Giorgione, none more sane. The rare values exclusive to painting which we have found implanted in Piero, are equally evident, though the distance is great from Piero's mathematical conception. Giorgione and Piero have in common their sanity allied to love, a supreme sense of reciprocal relation, the approach to form by way of chromatic or architectural sensibility. Piero influenced the rise of Venetian art. But turning from Piero to Giorgione, intent as we are on reviewing a similar scene, we shall have the sense of strolling, of throwing away accoutrement, of a lack of formality, where ease can never cloy since we are well aware that at any other time, under any other command, with any other antecedents, this great force, thus without uniform, without nerveless regulation, would scatter.

Of course, it is not that formal values are imperceptible in Giorgione's art. On the contrary they are very strong. Nor did he lack roots in the art of his predecessors.[34] The miracle is of bonds as naturally borne as the one of the air we all must breathe, of the freedom in subject-matter under the poetic aegis of affinities and reciprocal relations; of the just and sanguine fire in an unaccustomed mood.

Without doctrinaire emphasis, without protestation, Giorgione employed new means. To say so remarks the fusion of form and content, a fusion that Pater considered justly to be unique in figurative art, and close to music. Giorgione was the instrument of the largest revolution in the handling of paint. All the characteristic possibilities of oil painting are traceable to him; a waver, a contagion in the canvas. Prior merit may be Leonardo's in chiaroscuro invention. But Giorgione joined chiaroscuro as never again with jewel-like local colour, controlling an equal insistence throughout. From his figures and portraits we sense the movement of the blood, but otherwise there is pause. They illuminate the natural cycles; they are exemplars of life, of change, for whom sleep or the moment of pause renews in terms of unfettered afterglow the everlasting stance of objects.

At one and the same time, Giorgione brought boldness to painting and a lingering sensitiveness whose aims he completed. He demonstrated without stiffness or tension the equal insistence of things in space. Piero discovered the homogeneity of space and enlarged the science of distance. Giorgione, with Leonardo, was the first to value accurately the broad sweep of tone, to release it over draughtsmanship, attaching to this range the wider reciprocities thus engendered. His art and originality were centred in his close study of Nature, as Vasari said. The co-existence of Giorgione's observation of tonality and his poetic gifts inspired by a certain architectural and cultural ambience, is a worthy parallel, the only worthy parallel, to the co-existence in Piero's art of the new mathematic perspective and his intense love for stone as well as for man. Their chromatic approach to form was behind both appositions, entwining the terms.

Earlier painting, wrote Zanetti in 1760,[35] may have appealed to the intellect or aroused a sense of wonder, but it is not until Giorgione that paintings 'begin with sweet violence to seize on the heart'. We would not expect an appreciation of the value of a more primitive style. The interesting point is that Zanetti was writing, not of oil paintings, but of Giorgione's frescoes, some remnants of which he engraved. Although they have now entirely flaked from the walls,[36] Giorgione's frescoes, particularly those on the Fondaco dei Tedeschi, must always be regarded as central to his work. Vasari does not appear to have visited many Venetian private collections: the estimate of Giorgione as the father of the Venetian painting of his, Vasari's day, was based very largely on the frescoes and the large picture of the miracle of St. Mark at the Scuola San Marco. Indeed, were it not for the once unavoidable evidence of these frescoes to anyone proceeding along the Grand Canal, Giorgione would have become a great deal more of a myth than he is: perhaps we would have needed to invent him. The pupils and heirs who finished and repainted some of the pictures after his sudden death at the age of thirty-four, who probably carried out projects that had been merely sketched, who at first in their own separate creations sought largely to reproduce his style, Titian and Sebastiano del Piombo, were Vasari's friends, were likely to have been his principal sources for the life of Giorgione. Vasari, though to a far less extent than some writers who followed him, even closer adherents of Titian's, illustrated in his second edition the tendency to sacrifice Giorgione to Titian's fame. In regard to fame no less than to cash, Titian owned a strenuous anxiety.

'He (Giorgione)', wrote Zanetti eleven years after he had published engravings of fresco figures, 'began to lose somewhat and to soften the contours of his figures so that one is drawn within these contours. Outlines disappear in such a way that in a sense the vanishing planes suggest forms that lie beyond them.' In the same passage he speaks of Giorgione bringing painting out of its ancient timidity. The judgement may sound strange since it is more to the linear definition of a primitive treatment that we are inclined to attribute boldness. But then we have suffered much from the convenient cloak of *sfumato*. One glance at Giorgione's *Tempesta* accuses the thousands of good-taste painters and the often vain vitality in the agitated canvasses of their successors. Giorgione was bold and, from the point of view of Vasari, arbitrary. He pleased himself. (Titian raised artists' social rank by his huge prestige. It is unlikely that he took wider freedom than his much less well-known mentor.) Vasari was obviously puzzled by the 'story', the meaning, of the figures of the Fondaco frescoes. He could discover no one to tell him, he says, what they represented. It did not really trouble him, nor Zanetti, who wrote that Giorgione added to his fine grounding in art the arbitrary dictates of fantasy 'to allure and to please'. Zanetti was writing 200 years later, but this would appear to have been the judgement of contemporaries also. Many were doubtless puzzled by Giorgione's pictures and frescoes, though aware of a meaning conveyed without hindrance or protestation. There are hints that his genius overflowed into generosity and openness with others, typified by the nickname Giorgione, meaning big, and by an easy transference, big-hearted George. Such an estimate – any estimate – of his character can be impugned, of course, through the scarcity of documents or sources.

Vasari probably made his notes between thirty and forty years after Giorgione's death in 1510. He says that Giorgione was born of humble parents at Castelfranco, a little town on the mainland; that personal charm, his singing and his skill with the lute opened Venetian society to him and that he was in much demand at exalted parties; that he delighted in love; that he fell in love with a lady at a musical reception he gave in his own house; that he died of the plague, because unknown to them, his beloved had been infected.

Together with the account above of the nickname, Giorgione, these sentences exhaust the personal detail given by Vasari who was writing at greater length about the extraordinary development of his painting and of his humble and continuous application to Nature.

A host of works were attributed to him for centuries. Modern criticism has cut away, leaving at first no more than about ten extant pictures; nor are all of these from his own hand alone. The Pan-Giorgionists then resumed, this time with care and a reasonable case. Art history required a Giorgione who was not confined to the author of the *Tempesta* (which has never been seriously disputed) and a few allied works. This course is difficult. Some who admire the *Tempesta* most – the present author is among them – have had small inclination to extend the oeuvre greatly among known pictures, largely because, no doubt, the *Tempesta* is the only certain picture whose original paint is in a fair state. But consideration of the Fondaco frescoes alone causes such a position to collapse. From Zanetti's engravings we become aware of an entirely novel subtlety of posture that demands comparison wider than the one with the *Tempesta*. And so, kept in good trim by warding off the absurd attacks of the Pan-Titianists, we enter the appalling labyrinth of half-Giorgiones, fragments of originals or of copies, repaints, copies and the huge suburbs of the Giorgionesque.[37] In memory rather than before these fragments a conception emerges, compounding, perhaps, a piece of so-called self-portrait, the seated, attentive shepherd of the *Pastorale* (*Concert champêtre*) beneath the fire-light of the sun, for all the repaint the youth in the *Concert*, a figure to the left in the *Adulteress*, several portraits, a detail in the background of the *Apollo and Daphne*, the San Rocco picture, the *Venus* and the *Tempesta*, the Christ and tree of the Christ and Magdalene, St. George or St. Liberalis at Castelfranco, some of the fresco engravings, the shepherd who moves forward and the landscape in the Allendale *Presepio*, the Benson *Holy Family*, the seated, piping old man in the *Finding of Paris*…

As we return to the aspect of painting which unifies this book, Vasari (the second edition of the *Lives*) offers the ideal text. Of a figure painted by Giorgione he refers to the differing aspects that are revealed to one glance, to *una sola occhiata*. The context gives the phrase a stress. Indeed, Vasari is concerned with a property of painting which he considers to be the property of painting alone among the arts. And he refers to Giorgione in this same connection in his Preface to the whole work.

The phrase occurs in a story Vasari tells about Giorgione and some sculptors on the subject of the Colleoni statue (at the time of its unveiling?). The sculptors claimed their art to be superior because a statue could show all aspects to anyone walking round it. Giorgione replied that painting was superior in just this very respect because all the positions could be apparent in a painting for one glance, for *una sola occhiata*, instantaneously, without perambulation. And he proved it by a picture he then painted of a nude in a turning position. Clear water before the nude, polished armour to one side and on the other a mirror, reflected more aspects.

In spite of the naïve programme it could have been a beautiful picture, a kind of energetic dust-cover to a very powerful thesis. Vasari's story is probably true: for present purposes it is the perfect parable. In expressing emotion by variant shapes that insist uniformly, Piero della Francesca and Giorgione crystallized for *una sola occhiata*, in wider relation, those primarily architectural displays which had appeared on the surface of stone with such tension of outwardness.[38] Their inspired emphasis upon simultaneity entailed a lack of emphasis in any particular, but a much heightened accent upon brotherhood, upon a conception of form stemming from the ceaseless inter-communication of textures and surface colours; yet, unlike a decorative treatment, expressing deep emotional content; subsuming, also, in terms of simultaneity or immediacy, the tugging and less immediate sensations of rhythm, balance and opposition that are first objects of a tactile approach. A content of great poetry was inspired by, and inspired, this wider spatial purpose.[39]

Therefore the interpenetration in Giorgione's art of form and content arose from images, from an attitude to subject-matter which itself reflected the formal aim. This is always the case of successful art. What differs so vastly is the strength of each term and the felicity of their apposition. Stimulated by the equal showing and fraternal relationship of Quattro Cento architecture, strong without the help of hieratic formula, yet observing closely, discovering, in tune with his poetic aim, the broad sweep of tone, Giorgione sought to contain the passage of time, a man's life, in the forms of simultaneity. A literal example of Giorgionesque subject choice – an exact parallel to the naïve little story above of form – is to be found in the (to some extent) Giorgionesque painting at the Uffizi of the *Three Ages of Man*. What appears to be the same person is represented as a boy, a man and an old man: a history, as it were, made open to the glance, an attempt to translate temporal passage into simultaneous reciprocity. We recognize in Giorgionesque pastoral painting the aptness of an *old* shepherd, like the ancient who sits cross-legged, piping a continuum in the *Finding of Paris*. Examples could be multiplied. Such a very literal and rather naïve feature so common in Giorgione's lesser followers, serves to illustrate an imaginative bent whose subtleties and intensities elude any but Pater's words. It is, however, no great conceptual jump from the *Three Ages* to the *Tempesta*'s supreme poetry, or to the psychological pause which was the moment for Giorgione's portraiture, whereby features became caskets of things unsaid.

Venice inspires a sense of affinity, of equality of emphasis in the visual world, of an unchanging emblematic showing that embraces the movement of the waters. Venice, but not the population. They appear matchstick-like, out of place. Giorgione created in his frescoes by subtle

378

conceptions of posture – too sensitive, charged too accurately with feeling to be described by the term *contrapposto* with the suggestion of virtuosity – created figures that grew steadily from the wall. We may think it likely that he had painted many frescoes, at the Cà Soranzo, for example, before he painted the *Tempesta*; that then, on the same inclusive principle, he brought together a thunder-sky, a calm evening light and the perennial Venetian buildings. He had had hard experience in the accommodation of figures to his wide imaginative grasp. Now he could release the poetry which Venice inspires but which Venice thwarts in the accommodation of figures in her scenes. The *terra firma* of his childhood was different. Men 'go' with trees and brooks.

The next point can be put under the category neither of form nor of content since it concerns both equally. From Giorgione's choice of posture and, more particularly, of the complicated tilt of heads, especially in the frescoes and portraits, there results a grace or elegance often isolated in later art. But it was first a combination of aspects (for the purposes of *una sola occhiata*) which by their subtle interpenetration communicate a meaning beyond the elegant, even if the communicating voice is gracious as well as passionate. In a head tilted backward and seen from below, due to it being turned away, a view is allowed of the summit of the skull also.[40] Extreme softness and significant drawing of outline in full chiaroscuro, a range of tone that is felt continuously by the artist, not for the values of contrast but for the unanimity in difference, suggest planes beyond the contour lines that burgeon from the matrix of their background. An identity pervades the richly varied landscapes with figures whose heads of hair lie on the picture plane against foliage: a different species of foliage, different treatment of hair and a far different use of tonal range from Piero's; but the quality of the connection is the same.

The step is short to the specific terms of form. There is no more striking instance of Giorgione's form than the remarkable head of the Jew in the San Rocco picture of Christ carrying the Cross. Though the picture survives as a wreck, the shape made by this head haunts. The view is a profile, but owing to a slight tilt outward from on top, the width of the skull is seen as far as the further edge of the further eyebrow. The nostril-curve echoes the beard-curve, in to the jaw: the top of the nose is almost parallel to the contour line of the forehead: the whole nose-shape is like the front section of the skull with the beard: the ear is not dissimilar nor the shape made by the curling of the hair at the nape of the neck, nor (to instance a still smaller shape) the expressive knuckle and half-finger caught by the light. These pyramidal or pear-like or bell-like shapes – Christ's face and shoulder provide instances of the latter – are a constant unit in Giorgione's and in Giorgionesque paintings.[41] (It was soon elongated in Venetian art, as if reflected burning over the canals.) Such basic and architectural element of design in Giorgione's art was, however, indistinguishable from the needs of his imagination; so that although we are aware that his colour is unequalled, we may well remain unconscious of the formal reduplication in brotherly equal fashion, a mode, unlike a system of balance and stresses, inseparable from his use of colour; a wide contribution from significant colour to the conception of form.

The curvilinear yet pyramidal character of several Giorgione compositions has sometimes been remarked rather than the smaller and similar composite unit (it serves both form, colour and imaginative content). Though it is artificial to isolate it, an attempt must be made to find an origin in terms of form alone. Passing over Giorgione's lute, we may be reminded of the lozenge and ovoid shapes in Agostino di Duccio's reliefs at Rimini and of much other Quattro Cento stone efflorescence and incrustation differing widely from the stuck-on appearance of summary decoration. We may see in this arched shape, with its conical developments, an amalgam (suitable to the purposes of *una sola occhiata*) of the circular and rectangular, the two shapes in relation of which we are never so conscious as when we are surrounded by stone building searched by water; and we may then call to mind the extraordinary poignancy of buildings in Giorgione's landscapes, and those prime factors of classical architecture – columns upon a plinth – which are presented nude, as it were, behind the man of the *Tempesta*.[42]

The little Benson *Holy Family* has sometimes been accounted an

380

early Giorgione. It is most certainly Giorgionesque, not least because of the unstressed, bell-like, breast-like shape which brings together in love, not only the family group and the tree through the round-arch window, not only the great rock beyond; but also the rectangular brick parapet, the stones, the building and the square tower.[43] We observe how unforced, how warm, how unregimented are the affinities. A rule or regimentation is the least likely attribute of Giorgione's painting. The way was open to explore with chiaroscuro a wider world and thereby to initiate relaxed, informal yet more diverse affinities than were permissible for Piero or even for Bellini.

The jewel-like quality of Giorgione's colour is unequalled: opponents too have admitted it; and by opponents those writers are intended who were either the old Titian's friends, wishing to exalt his youth at Giorgione's expense, or who, as heirs of the Cinquecento grand manner which they took to be the summit of painting, could not allow Giorgione, since he worked on a smaller scale, to be as great. Zanetti, whom we have quoted, provides an instance of the second case. Yet he wrote: 'The strength and the relief which Giorgione knew how to give to figures did not prevent his colour, as it does in the case of other painters, from being beautiful and indeed somehow incandescent and almost aflame in his flesh tints. He managed with so much grace and "rightness" that one cannot say that he has any worthy follower at all in this respect: there has been no one to challenge his supremacy.' Only he could create between figures the telepathic contact which avoids a meeting of eyes.

It is unlikely that Giorgione was a theorist of the culture he represents, of that spirit which allowed him his divine pause by freeing him of the usual attitudes. During the fifteen years or so of his working life, Venice suffered her greatest initial reverses. Her sun began to set at the same time as her rebuilding in white stone; a pall in which she would be laid out to die, it has been said.[44] (Dissociated from impermanence, something of what is final, epitomized only by death, belongs to the spiritual outwardness of aesthetic creation.) Venice was clothing herself in white; brilliant colour was multiplying in her painting. War and disaster, as we well know, may increase the warmth of contemplation and a certain loving detachment. Giorgione worked in the most beautiful of cities. The unfurled gravity and magnificence of Venice enlarged the fever of her beauty. But Giorgione, no less than Piero, was rooted in the countryside. Vivid symbols of Venetian building lived for him in walls and farm-houses. He dispenses with the forms of crowding palaces while possessing their height in an uncrowded country air. The fever subsides: he has with him for gentle shaded slopes, for pause, for ease, for relaxation, an intercourse of square and circle, of coloured disk and shallow oblong panel wrought so plainly to the effect of equal insistence by the Venetian architect Mauro Coducci.

Instead of marbles upon the sea, instead of prismatic water and the sable interior of palace and church, instead of tidal waters, it is the earth, light on leaves, shade within the wood... As may be seen in Venetian landscape from the time of Bellini's later period, formality unbends: contours of the ground are for lying on – it is the time of *villeggiatura*, summer and autumn – for rest, for the pasturing of beasts, for the arm of night. In from the sea, aerial perspective causes hilly country to settle. More varied contour than at Venice interrupts the sky with infinite gradation, subsiding into feathery distance. Greenness is loved with an untroubled eye by one for whom marbles have been trees. But although their countryside has turned from restless tides, the great Venetian artists preserve the space of the Adriatic in the running contagion of their colour and by their mariner's sense of the richness and riotous piece of land.

The countryside was also the level tones of music. Giorgione, Sebastiano and Titian were musicians. We know that Giorgione was in great demand for his lute and for his voice.

The word 'music' today suggests an ample resonance from many sides. But the early music for voice and lute and even for the spinet, rises gently from the ground like a tenuous smoke, pervades and hangs over the scene, creating stillness by means of an accord. There is the element of a patterned dreaminess, of enchantment since music is primarily incantation. The musical equivalent nearer our own day is more defiant, more nostalgic, a cry from the heart. It is, of course, no longer by any means secular music *tout court*. But in Giorgione's time the story of Orpheus and the animals was as yet a parable of musical enchantment, of relaxation that does not scorn the tension it resolves. Giorgione's paintings seem to record the moment after the final lute note when the protagonists of his imagination were living slowly in the supervening pause (which but rarely occurs in reality between action and action or thought and thought), when all the contrapuntal tendencies that go to make the individual were fused into an unforced silence. Perhaps only a painter who was a musician could have identified his sense of pause and of silence with the simultaneity of space.

There is again the quality of Giorgione's soft contours. None of the many thousand subsequent painters who employed a similar technique has achieved as evocative an effect, evocative, that is, not only of the form the contour serves, but through form, of a pulse also, found and found again like the harmonic grip of a musical sound.

Music-playing scenes or the piping of a shepherd are common Giorgionesque subjects from which, in any case, as has so often been remarked, the spell of music is rarely absent. We sense the voice divagating upon an instrument. It is strange, therefore, that the Venetian music of Giorgione's day has not been examined in the light of his paintings, more especially since there would appear to be more than a casual connection between their spirit and a novel and contemporaneous musical vogue by which the melodious declaration of the voice was established anew. Pleasures of the ear were more valued in the Venice than in the Florence of that time: it is a difference reflected even in a variation of Neo-Platonic doctrine.[45] Thus Bembo and Betussi preferred the ear to the eye in matters of perfect spiritual beauty. Such was not the orthodox Florentine view though the Pythagorean scale was admitted to provide the canon of visual no less than of musical harmony. Music, the more abstract art, had been both exalted and inhibited by the robes of a 'science'. The fact that the less systematic (when averted from practical affairs) Venetian culture at the beginning of the sixteenth century gave ear to a warmer, more enterprising music than the Florentine, may well be a measure of greater sensuousness.

Fifteenth-century Italian music had been dominated from the North, from France and the Netherlands; but towards the end of the century a great development began of *stramvolti, sonetti, rispetti, frottole, canzonette, villanelli*, which kept a popular vein in dance rhythm.[46] Bartolommeo Tromboncino and Marchetto Cara in particular composed many *frottole* which Petrucci (1504) and later Antigo, printed. *Frottola* means fable or ballad; many *frottole* were executed in combinations of voice and instrument. The melody was given to the top voice. It cannot be doubted that this was the type of music Giorgione himself performed and for which he was in such request.

Historians of music record the rise of the *frottola* – and it was an immense vogue, dead before 1530 in company with the Giorgionesque – as an event of first importance in musical history; since *frottola* was parent to madrigal, a considerable modification in the structure of musical language. Contrasting with current polyphony, the *frottola* was an expression of fluidity and ease. 'Leurs harmonies rudimentaires', writes Prunières,[47] 'offrent le plus parfait contraste avec les entrelaces en dentelle du contrepoint franco-flamand.' Visiting foreign musicians 'se déclarèrent à écrire eux aussi des *frottole* et des *canzonetti* de diverses sortes, s'appliquant à attraper cette manière aisée, fluide et chantante des Italiens'.*

Due to the strength of Byzantine tradition, Venetians were less responsible to the pomposities of Rome. The unparticularized reference to the Antique in the form of Giorgione's *Venus* is more Hellenic[48] than Roman. Less antiquarian or expatiatory or competing, similarly without the aid of historical perspective, the culture that nurtured him perhaps enjoyed the ancient past with more affluent emotion than did the Florentine. What had been the exotic fairy-land of medieval times,

---

* 'Their rudimentary harmonies offer the perfect contrast with the lacelike interweaving of the French-Flemish counterpoint. [Visiting foreign musicians] also asserted that they could write *frottole* and *canzonetti* of various kinds, striving to imitate this easy, fluid and mellifluous style of the Italians.'

dangerous to the touch, full of dark magic, could now be better approached in the language of permeation, in the love themes of the *frottola* or *canzonetta* rising invisibly upon the air.

There must always exist a pregnant relation between a painter's understanding of music (or his lack of it) and his painting. The emphasis of this book is upon the aspect of visual art to which music offers no parallel. It cannot be proved, it can be only suggested that the distinctiveness of visual art is sometimes best isolated, best loved by those painters who, in understanding and in feeding upon, and in being satisfied by music, have less need to project rhythm, movement, contrast and other non-simultaneous sensations into their art. It could be urged, on the other hand, that just because their ears are trained and attentive, their eyes are therefore the more ready to discover or to reinforce equivalent sensations from the visual world, which they have no desire to sublimate in their painting, but which, on the contrary they prefer to accentuate at whatever the cost to the more isolated values of visual art. No rule can be suggested and it is likely that a similar connection between the two sensations often produces an opposing result. But surely Giorgione's pleasure in sound helped him to strive for the form-content perfection of music in his pictures, while eschewing many effects which are more precisely attained in music; while searching for those that are central to painting and founded upon the simultaneity of space. Giorgione's love of music enhanced the pure visual conception of his pictures. He brought to painting the remembrance, not the members, of music, the completion, the interval of silence in which, as being a mood only, he uncovered the simultaneous intervals of space. The *Concert* at the Pitti illustrates this pause.[49] In the *Pastorale*,* does the lutanist cease to play? Supported by the Brunswick self-portrait, Richter[50] has suggested that the man may be Giorgione, who sits absorbed beside the lutanist.

---

* The *Pastoral Concert* or *Fête champêtre* is now generally thought to be by Titian.

He was one of the first, if not the first, artist to paint medium-sized 'subject' canvasses, for hanging in studies and other small rooms. We can name the owners of the *Tempesta*, the *Three Philosophers*, and the *Dresden Venus* within fifteen years after Giorgione's death in the case of the last two, within twenty years in the case of the *Tempesta*. And there is some reason to suppose that these Venetian noblemen, connected by birth or by friendship, with leaders of the new culture, were not only the original owners but Giorgione's younger companions. The erratic X-ray of historical research, at no point, it is true, with certainty but with a possible inter-relationship of small facts and wider probabilities, has uncovered in fragments the ground, or, perhaps more cautiously one should say a ground, a preparation of a ground for his art.

Certainly it would be a jump to announce that the young men commissioned their pictures. It is sufficient to summon up small intellectual groups over two generations, of whom Almorò Barbaro, the great humanist, was the first teacher; some poets as well, behind whom is the figure of Pietro Bembo at Asolo. (Vasari says that Giorgione painted his portrait.) The activities of the founders of this cult were expressed very succinctly as a historical fact in a pregnant row that occurred at the University of Padua while Giorgione was a boy.[51]

The neo-Platonism of Florence did not overwhelm Venice. Barbaro translated Aristotle entire from the Greek. He cleared Pliny of six thousand corruptions. He was an exacerbated aesthete: not a philosopher but a philologist contemptuous of much of what passed for philosophy: not an arriviste nor a Papal Secretary but one of the ancestral trustees of the Venetian Republic. There was needed a hard, aristocratic distaste to counter the philosopho-magical hubbub. Among the capable Venetian families, Zeno, Foscarini, Morosini, Correr, Trevisan, Giustinian and Barbaro, beauty fostered sense.

Barbaro had no theories. He was against the would-be magic of disputes. He complained of the Germans and the Jews at Padua, chief adherents of *solvitur in ambulando*. His object was to translate accurately the entire Aristotle. Disparity with Averroist texts would be palpable.

His translation appearing in the 1480s provoked division at Padua University, the diehard stronghold of Averroism. There followed the only organized intellectual revolt of the Renaissance. The Venetian Government, with the object of attracting the *stranieri*, had forbidden Venetians the governing of the University, whereas Germans were given preferential treatment. Barbaro worked from outside. He held morning classes in a palace on the Giudecca, promising a knowledge of Aristotle in a three-year course. No mystery. The situation at Padua grew riotous; for the Averroist professors were entirely ignorant of Greek: any stripling from Barbaro's class could silence the octogenarian Vernia, most celebrated Averroist of the time. Poor Vernia had to give in, had to put aside the commentary on Aristotle which he had been preparing for thirty years. And finally, the Venetian Government, recognizing this Venetian revolution which the Germans, French and English were already taking home with them, instituted a chair of Greek.

Whether or not the *Tempesta* mirrors the Aristotelian doctrine of the four elements whereby the man would be associated with fire and air principles, the seated woman (who has just bathed[52] and is feeding the baby) with water and earth; whereby the sky and its lightning, the sunlight and the thunder-rain which will soon fall on the earth, would contain these elements naked over the township and the family; whether or not the *Three Philosophers* at Vienna are to be referred to the types of thinkers who were once engaged in the dispute at Padua – the relaxed and seated young man who seems to measure and observe *inductively* while both his middle-aged and his hoary companions suggest perambulating astrological star-gazers – whether or not any such precise references are admissible, the above, slight excursus, altogether based on Ferriguto, is most certainly not irrelevant to our subject: nor would it be, even though the particular inter-relationship of fact, interpretation and conjecture were discarded.[53] For Giorgione's art illuminates – it may be known from the constant feeling of many generations – the ideal face of our culture so often distorted since the Attic birth by Mumbo-Jumbo, beset so largely and continuously that this ideal face recedes for centuries as in a dream.

The first *Fête champêtre* is dissociated from the melancholy wilfulness which even Watteau could not escape. The ease, the *ozio*, the poetry, turned from the ocean, from the alleys and the tall Venetian light, are symbols of new being after a thousand medieval years of semi-exile. When did 'new life' assume as leniently the uncontorted mind, when was observation as lyrical yet adult? There may be a parallel in Greek, but not in Christian culture.

We will not attempt further to tie Giorgione to definite symbols as have many investigators. Yet he was the last painter whose pictures seem truly to serve as a most insistent emblem for all their freedom, for all their abandonment of hierarchic barricades. He bestowed the outdoors on the past as well as on the future. His evasion of medieval stringencies was also a last heraldic act...

Up to the period of Michael Angelo's dominant influence at any rate, the search for a conception of the outside world to mitigate the transcendental bias of the Middle Ages, is common to the Renaissance as a whole: a prerequisite, it appears, of turning to the Antique for instruction.[54] We have envisaged Alberti and Piero in realization of this theme and, with greater difficulty, Giorgione, who excels all other artists in showing man as native to the world. Like Donatello's furore, the Giorgionesque fire, whatever our mood, can never seem reprehensible. From a visionary element we may on occasion deduce northern influences which Piero – in this matter though not in others – rejected. Giorgione was not working 'from on high' to the degree of Alberti or Piero, though of course the Italianate architectonic presupposition, as well as the more particular connections that this book has sought to establish, were held in common. His earlier pictures convey the Gothic quality of emblem: a few may be parables of the thought of his time; yet we do not fear the pressure of a programme. Indeed, in this relaxed yet revolutionary art which, combining discoveries in the perception of tone, observes with such spontaneity the unhurried affectionate forms of a chromatic approach, we are confronted by a temperance of

388

Rule so hastily summoned to supplant medieval Authority; a temperance that is aflame with poetry...

Beside his dreams there lay unanxious an *inductive* spirit.

The Sense of Home

From *Smooth and Rough* (1951)

There are often two sounds on a cliff in August, the long humming of
the summer seas between the lifting of grasses by the wind. The ocean's
susurration expands fine weather. If we return in winter on a day that is
not rough, we expect to observe once more the spatial weaving of a bee,
to attend to buzzing in a sheltered patch that protrudes from the wind
like rock from swell.

Pools restore images of quiescent inner states whereby the sea,
which fills and renounces only to return, assumes the character of the
Protean mind. We infer on a cliff our separateness, recognizing tufts
visited by bees who bring the pertinacity of a closed world like figuration on a bare expanse of cloth.

If the wind rises, branches cascade, hurtle, pour. The giants of English parks, fully swaying, call with the sea's bass, detaching a surf of
leaves. A few will tap upon window-panes; theirs is the fugitive touch
of a taut dry palm succeeding the touch of finger-nail, light blows from
the external world, momentary visitations as of an overtaking passing
and receding vehicle which forces us to witness an action whose mental
counterpart is unprepared.

Slight, yet very frequent, traumatic experiences are peculiar to the
modern world.

The sheltered bay was well wooded: the trees above, below and at the
back of our house at Carbis Bay grew large for coast-land. One walked
in at the top floor of the house and could then go down to other rooms
since the garden fell away in high broad terraces. The ocean, far beneath
to the side of a lawn flanked by interlacing conifers across a sunken
lane, appeared on a level with the lower branches: between them or

aloft an expanse of ocean and air sparkled, smoked as one element in rain. On perpendicular draughts risen to great height, freshened by the trees, a hilarious shouting from bathers between the waves on the vast beach came up to us in summer.

My own room at the sea end of the house, half outside our garden boundary, looked on to the torsos or tops of many trees sapient, it appeared, in their arrest of the gardens and terraces of the gradual cliff. Beneath the nearer branches I could see across the bay to Hayle and to the sand dunes that curve round to the point of Godrevy lighthouse. The bay was often pure green; the wind would drive the surface sea-green wrinkles shorewards where they would be lost among the roots of the lower trees or be rediscovered after contact with the stabilizing temperate earth, in the topmost plumes of firs.

I had first glanced up at the house from the side-lane, below what was to be my room. I had experienced a quick hallucination – a picture without figures as I gazed at a central slatted feature roofed with copper, carrying the weather vane – a sensation of small stature and the thronging cries of children issuing like bees from this white granite hive. Later, we bought the house. My wife gave birth there to our son.

Throughout the first summer at tea-time the prospect of war opposed the green-yellow of saffron cake. During six years, except for the Home Guard, for the sale of vegetables, for market garden purchases, I rarely went outside the two and a half acres.

Visits in childhood connected me with Cornwall and with my brother who was killed in the first war. I had occasion once or twice to drive a car on the main road some ten miles behind and above the Newquay coast where we had been, above the villages whose spires were just visible in the remote sea-haze, whose names I barely remembered. It was raining on these drives from a riven mist, riven towards the sea so that I could distinguish in comparative brightness a panorama that stood for half-known feelings.

My brother, exercising a love for geology, had examined the freakish Cornish sub-soil. I was attracted later to the peninsula between the two seas, extending on the north from St. Ives to Land's End. I thought of it as the only part of Britain belonging to the geography of the Ancient World. It was certainly a fount of tin and so, perhaps, of Greek bronzes. Hills of Celtic and Stone-Age traces were once Phoenician land-marks, traversed for long after by the single file of pack-mules. On the north coast near Zennor, a wide pasture-land spreads between the surf and the hills, of Homeric scale it seems to the observer who is picking out the farm communities and noting the inhospitable sea, the isolated perpendicular stones and the network of bright walls. Warm fertile valleys that run down the other side to Mount's Bay where, they say, Phoenician tin was shipped, would accord with the sense, particularly in autumn, of ancient fire.

From the terrace of our house, at a few feet higher than the front door, parts of the roof were available to the hand. Across the bay, dunes lay open like a fan. Calm and condensation, even vastness, character-ized the lime-washed roof as Peter, companion in agriculture, and I would see it framed upon the ocean. We would be working on the land immediately above and to the side. Bending over the rows in daily discussion, we would also observe every aspect of the house. We com-manded the coast as far as Trevose Head. The lighthouse was just visible on clear days. To our right was Carn Brea with silhouetted cross on the broad summit above Redruth and Camborne.

From the main road to our entrance, this panorama topped houses and trees. If the bay were blue, I could sometimes identify it with Palermo, a well-lit, spacious depository for all tempestuous process. The mute tallness of our eucalyptus tree, with so pointed leaves, afforded pattern to the sunlight. The fir trees had lost their lower branches and had grown voluminous heads of smoky-green, a filter to the light, a brake upon darkness. The fattest birds would perch on the topmost tufts.

Every Sunday afternoon towards half past three, I would leave by the back gate, pass through the firs that sheltered our north side, to a curved sight of the ocean over the top of a small wood, a view that seemed to me Samoan. Meadow-land sloped down to the trees near the bay. I had started for the letter-box, a walk that marked division between two weeks.

But it was useless to expect immobile days of a kind in which the movement of the water at the fringe of the tide is but a spin, an iridescent skin upon the stone. The sea worked beneath stillness, less the image of spatial magnitude than of the interfused depths of the mind. The sporadic tides of war were superimposed upon ceaselessness. The sea-noise, often only a murmur, threaded those years. Sometimes we would uncover, as it were, the source, when, later on, we walked across the Lelant golf links. On a grass ridge we would come face to face with the vast transverse sand on which the sea roared. At the same instant, along the warm west currents, we became aware of soft-smelling residues of seasons other than the one of the moment. Throughout the length of vision as we paused, foam glinted in the same places. Godrevy lighthouse also, and its rock, over the rough bay, were caught by the sun.

After shopping one winter morning we walked beyond the Porthmeor beach, along the cliff and away from the sea. The road was sunk below the hedges, below the level of the wind: it led to farmhouses similarly protected by uneven ground and rocks. The swift winter sun seemed to loiter. We stayed only for a moment. What is this spread country, what are these houses, these homes?

There are two stations, St. Ives and Carbis Bay. Our house was between them, far above the branch single-track that follows, cut into the cliff, each indentation of the bay. Fields of the earliest potatoes extend below the line, run down very steeply to the sea from which they are separated by a stone hedge and a short bluff. St. Ives station is parallel to the sea across a sand beach… Once the preliminaries to a journey are settled, it is not unusual to be acutely susceptible to the place of departure. As the traveller sits on the station seat to the side of the morning London train, he will notice an emblematic intent in the movement of the waves. If it is sunny, flashes of light appear like an exordium of a dance. If the sky is sullen, then this heaving, dark, cold breast of livid tone conjoins with a deep unrest within, and perhaps brings ease, since all the vastness of sea and sky play out emotion with vicarious magnitude.

I remember sitting late in the empty St. Ives station with a friend, waiting, as we thought, for a train by which his wife might arrive from a cross-country journey. We realized later that no further train would come that night. We looked out to sea, warm and comfortable. The war was then three days old: we attempted to identify the stars, to transfer to them the fixity which had been lost to the circumstances of living. Galaxies hung over Godrevy lighthouse, something steadfast, as it were, from the sea (if only because sailors consulted them) as well as from the sky. The immense tale of light-years dwarfed the duration of the nightmare war that lay ahead. Beneath the open sky the future of our own lives moved in the darkness of the waves. But, oh yes, there were the points, the promontories of the bay: it would be as well to write a letter to so-and-so...

Carbis Bay station is high above the beach. A very steep road goes down to a gully spanned for the railway by a tall, narrow viaduct. From up this wooded gully the sea is framed by eloquent stone arches that recall classical summers of Poussin and misty-bright mornings by Claude. Fresh water descends in abundance; the sound of brook is chorded with the *basso continuo* from the beach. At a comfortable hotel nearby, towards three o'clock on a starless night, September 1940, I hammered on the door in pursuance of LDV instructions. I was carrying a message for the officer commanding the soldiers billeted there. I got no answer, I climbed through a window and shouted. I switched on a light and seeing the dinner gong I struck it loudly. The eventual silence did not relax. It was strange to assault an Edwardian somnolence to which I had always been hostile; but more especially in the month of lively danger to Britain when, at last, the pre-first-war age had assumed a golden look. I wanted to linger in the vestibule, but I realized that the soldiers must be billeted in the hotel annex on the other side of the viaduct.

Soldiers now occupied such places. They stood in the evening on the roof of a hotel in the Moorish style. As it happened, a palm tree grew from a ledge behind them. We still went down to the beach: that was what we saw when we turned for home. The perfect weather stayed.

The circumstance of the LDV corresponded with boyhood dreams. On the night we heard from a fisherman of the Dunkirk evacuation, we were keeping guard at the 'island', the promontory hill of St. Ives, using the very ancient chapel of St. Ia upon the summit. We strained our eyes into the rocks, imagining human forms. Between watches we sat in deck-chairs. Had I still been a child I would have settled the war in that one night, working upon the intricacies of the chair. This magical weapon would not have been so many years behind our gym shoes and walking sticks.

The sense of a resuscitation of an ancient ferment was rarely nourished in the Home Guard years: the Celticism of Cornwall remained torpid: the Roman camp on Tren Crom, the tors and burial grounds, had no aspect of a tryst with recent events. We looked for the enemy not to the east, nor, for the most part, from the sea, at any rate after 1940. We looked for the most part to the sky, for parachutists. In terms of cairns and ancient circles, this was a mockery of the superstition they had nurtured of stars, moon and sun. Our anxieties seemed far-fetched, delirious, rootless upon the brow of a hill. Modern ruthlessness appeared vulgar, lacking the slow ambivalence of sacrifice and carnage. If it came to an action it would not be something to which the myriad hissing and moaning of the sea at Gurnard's Head would refer. To the muttering hills with new horizons, the aeroplanes, both ours and the enemy's, were propelled, embalmed hawks.

A question of hiding! That was different; for that, the country, the lie of the land, beckoned. Stillness pervaded a period of moon during the first week or fortnight of the war. Vast, tumultuous white clouds had swept into majesty the intervening blue of the night. It was a sinister beauty because I thought that we would, that already we might, look to the sky for peril, particularly for the billowing white mushrooms of parachutists. By day, too, the sky preserved the huge stateliness of cloud in Mexican films... There followed the first air-raid warning. We went to the cellar. I came up and put my head into the radiance of a two-minute silence transposed to the summer. The sea was lulled to a caress: the sun searched a nocturnal stillness. But later, following warnings,

the sky was sometimes red at night towards Redruth and the aero-
dromes beyond: there were walloping noises as if some evil of the hills
had been traced to a certain spot. The walloping was crude, unresisted,
stopped capriciously as it had begun; a fury which in part expressed
itself by this tempo; a fury, it seemed, of impotent cruelty, impotent
in the face of the resumption of the tides and of orderly silhouette.

Invasion seemed imminent and the birth of the baby was almost
due. We planned for my wife to hide. Only a little below the house we
found a chamber cut in the rock, with a stream within it, the same
stream (said to be radioactive) that ran under the trees of the back lane.
Carbis Bay hinterland, perhaps particularly the rhododendron groves
that clothed all but the summit upon which Knill had built a sepulchre,
invited such arduous and legendary concealment.

There comes to mind, as I write, a strong impress of spatial directions. I am sitting in the deep chair of the living-room at Carbis Bay.
On my left, past the low window-sill, I see the edge and broad top of the
knee-high stout granite balustrade to the terrace; a fraction of an inch
above that, on a level with my eye-brows, the ocean's horizon. In front,
three windows face across a sunken path that I cannot see, over a grass
plot on to bushes and a granite sundial. Running away from me
(though invisible) at the sides of this narrow plot of which the right side
is considerably higher than the left, there are two paths: the lower, if
now regarded as coming towards me, leads past the terrace to the front
door; the higher is a straight drive, very broad. Both glisten with a white
surface of china clay dust. The long broad drive is the only flat 'carriage
way' in the district, except for 50 yards or so of the main road above us.
The drive continues a little beyond the house to the back entrance.
At the further end in front, some 120 yards away, there are heavy teak
gates. I hear one gate opened, then shut, and, after a pause, steps begin
to scrunch faintly on the drive. I become extremely aware of the line of
the terrace on my left beyond which I can see only the further edge of
the bay, the horizon and Carn Brea over Redruth; and of the line of the
drive in front of me along which the steps are approaching. These steps
will either continue past the house (and my right) and out of the back

gate, or else, just before the house they will take a short descending path at right angles to the drive, pass hugely by the windows in front of me and then, having turned left again across the window to that side, will end almost immediately at the front door. Does he come through the front door, the owner of the steps will have carried inside me something of the journey he has made, not merely the line of his approach, though that be predominant, but a semi-sphere as well of panorama. He contrasts with our son who first appeared in the house without coming into it as a separate being. The stranger brings another aspect, the outside-in. I have heard and felt his approach from a distance. Finally, I saw the top part of him as he passed the windows. He comes into the house and with him, as attributes, the surroundings of his passage from the gate. I have a sensation of enrichment and, possibly, of uneasiness. The house contains a new vital element.

Again I am relaxed in the low armchair. I hear the gate's soft latch some 190 yards away at the head of the drive. A pause... and the slow steps of the stranger begin. Perhaps he is turning his head, looking to his left at the garlic rows, then to the right across the lawn below him and through the trees on to the bay. He brings these things to me and, in a sense, within me. I receive their opposing textures, their detail and ensemble. The experience is more definite than one arising from lethargy as when, on the beach, we allow the sea to wash over the mind. It is as if a bird were flying to its nest or a tree were walking into the house. The less preoccupied the stranger, and the more he seems to look about him as it is interpreted by the sound of his gait, the greater the content he will bring with him. If he comes in a hurry he brings little. If he has come to visit me, the impression is cancelled, he is outside me again. Whatever the errand, whatever the directness, we will tend to be like two insects in a dance, each responding to the other's movements by a movement to the side. But those we love we harbour: we take them in with their apparel of things. My son, the inside-out, is also an outside-in: he became identified with the house. It was his trot, his oncoming or receding voice which measured its length: the few stairs renewed their steepness. He listened closely to the Cornish idiom, his father was a farmer; for me this has meant a strong tie with the Cornish soil.

On Home Guard night-watches I would leave my car, the means of agricultural transport, up a steep incline at the back of the cinema where there was a car-park used in the later years by the Americans. An adjoining engine that gave power to the cinema would be revolving with the busy, almost joyous reverberations of such apparatus at a fair. Above the hissing pumping and the throb, one heard from inside the pink, luxurious house, an immense voice, a galloping, a shriek of grinding brakes. Smell of this engine was not unpleasant and, by force of long association, seemed scented most strongly with that particular cellulose garnish upon violence that is, or used to be, inseparable from cinemas, a smell not distant from the one of the average hard-centred chocolate and of its nest of fibrous paper in the box. Here stood amid harsh accents and overstrong reverberations the house of day-dreams, offering more freedom, more light, particularly if you had come from the hills in the Land's End country, the probable venue for the Americans' recent 'exercise'. Their military expeditions and our own conduced to an image of St. Ives as a nestling outpost upon the wilds; a more ancient, more comfortable, more wooded, but equally western small town in a Western film. And, as with earth-stubbed fingers, muffled, bristling with unwieldy weapons, I dismounted from my car behind the cinema, I could have imagined myself a member, however inefficient, of the Sheriff's posse. The wildness of the coast lay in wait outside. But, since at other times I was tethered to the earth, an element of being abroad invaded the context of those evenings; out of England, beyond enclosure. A quality of agelessness invested the Cornishmen with whom I should pass the night, as if they gathered the moors within an ill-lit room. Several had served in ships and these talked of adventure in foreign parts measured against St. Ives. I began to know the map of a St. Ives day, enlarged by the presence in the Home Guard of so many bakers who used to leave us at four or five o'clock to make the bread.

In the wind and the companion cold of the harbour where we kept watch for many winter months, the parish church, the walled precincts beside the mole, looked massive, Norman; a reminder of spaciousness to the guard-room shanty and wastes of sea. Our house, invisible in the distance round two inlets, hung in the trees, miraculously of stone. I would be back soon after seven. As I dropped to sleep there, the noise of the ocean, distant from my bed, would recede further and further like a shark that has been baulked and falls astern. Yet, after these nights, coffee with milk at breakfast was a necessary clothing against an ungovernable cold, to banish the thin spray, the pieces of equipment, the heaviness and bareness of the night and the ill-ventilation. Godrevy rock with its spent lighthouse had been finally cold and lonely in the dawn, glimpsed at the end of the bay between the trees while I was walking from the gate to the house.

On harbour guard in dark nights I felt the treelessness. Fishermen would come up with torches, up steps on to the tall pier, like passengers obtaining the street from the last underground train. The earth connoted in this darkness the ingrained dirt of crack-skinned fingers or unthawed fingers picking brussel-sprouts and washing gritty leeks with January water. A night wind blew at the deserted cinema corner, making the township very small. We were joined on to the war by tales and hearsay as we searched superciliously for flashes or strange lights, staring for hours into the night face of the sea. There were only the reprehensible black-outs of some houses: no one of us in over four years discovered an object of true suspicion. We had rounds with us on watch and a bigger arsenal at home. Not a shot was fired officially except at the ranges, amid the dunes, in a landscape whose savagery it would be hard to equal. At notified intervals we were pitched against some of the elements for a short time, disciplined to see well-known roofs at unaccustomed hours of the night. To glance at them unchanged, though watched no longer, on the following day of utter fatigue, brought clearly to mind the brutal endlessness of the ways of wasting time.

In effect, we were in charge of the landscape. We sometimes used the 'lodges' of the fishermen, promoted above them as contemplators of the sea domain. Clamped for the night in the upper room of the drill-hall overlooking the narrow ancient street, I felt myself to be a more official observer of the dwindling evening life of the town than were the old women at *their* windows, who were occupying a station perhaps inherited through several hundred years. Of such kind was my astounding promotion from rootlessness in the face of an enemy threat, whereas the others had been observing for generations, at windows, on the wharves, at street corners, staring at, perhaps resenting, the stranger, imitating a defensive watch and a pricking of ears; exaggerating perils and local lore, romancing in tobacco smoke, perhaps talking too much, perhaps getting excited about nothing. Indeed, the very old, retired fishermen kept it up as we sat of an evening in their sacred 'lodges'. They were unwilling to look down on us or to resent our presence but they naturally tried to forget it. Gradually, very gradually, they would go to bed leaving the rest of the dark hours and the custody of St. Ives to us. They had rarely spoken of a time later than thirty years before. It was, of course, absurd that they should surrender *their* observation of the ocean or of the town to me, but I would look to the windows, to the black-out. Indeed, I had more duty to observe any occurrence than had the majority of respected citizens who could have been searching through the years for dereliction or oddity. The place I took, however, was more the one of an old woman at a window who had stared all her life at the house opposite: this was my choice of the privileges at hand. And so, emulating the cats in their possessive tasks, I would relish in the fading light the stone-faced dormer window opposite the drill-hall, searching each piece of flaking stone and mortar, as interweaved as the St. Ives generations.

The Sense of Loss

From *Smooth and Rough* (1951)

I cannot forgive the affliction of endless purlieus and map-less terraces, the rips in the cloud, the studs in the road, the beaten, beaten thorough-fares and the ill complacency of glazed apertures reflecting garish light but not the reverberation nor impact of the traffic. This ever-sinking ship rides no sea. Observe those flags that include the night. Talion judgment is at the heart.

This was London long before the war or wars. From an ABC restaurant in the month of Munich I used to regard a dislocated perspective of chimney pots while reflecting that it was unlikely that one of them would be extant in a year's time. London and the attaching stigma from which I could not separate myself were under threat. Hitler epitomized a greater destructiveness: over against Hitler London was, to my mind, a volatile bedraggled bird, sprawling in a snare, punch-drunk, indifferent. And now that since the war Victorian squalor and splendour are numbered, finite, I imagine that it has not only been a vast shock but also for many a psychological relief to discover dramatically that there is a decided limit to our national wealth. The sense of the awful measurelessness of London is abated, once identified with an infantile omnipotence of thinking or with some fearful animus of derogation.

For those who are under the spell of rootlessness, machines and modern cities tend to encourage an unreal view. If no interest centres in the mechanism of wealth, the machines become omnipotent, there is nothing which they cannot do, and the natural limitation to the wealth of rich people is easily forgotten: the racket of business and the black-coated life become dissociated from the mathematics which are their means. Responsibility, growth, purpose are not perceived. For this mood no one made the Underground and the Metropolitan trains. I was born among them: they were like the hills and fields of country people whose sources are shown by the seasons and the geological traces. But what wider law amasses Metropolitan ten-minute ritual of clatter, brakes, sidestepping, iron, flag and wood; what does the succession of three-minute monsters in the Tube *signify*, and the subsequent silence, knit with the noise by the line of poster smiles? We are not camping out. Streets are homes: we are compelled to think of them as expressions of average living, of our appetites, evacuations, sickness and health as well as of work and the tyranny of machines. Perhaps translation from the terms of a more modern city would be easier. In London it is as if steel were welded to miasma, to the froward Victorian age of surmise and huge disorganization. I cannot beat a meaning out of the dull yet incongruous buildings constructed by those who did not admit they were desperate or despairing; who were veiled in the fog of maniacal respectability and of the cleared throat. Monstrous expedients pervade the purlieus; gongs, bells, cracked chimes and gongs again sound at lunch time from the boarding houses of certain squares: what lacks bedizenment is frayed; but the smirk has now been lost in fog and night and in the desert of whole districts.

It used to be said that you could buy anything at certain great London stores. Why not; why not the stars? It was my presupposition that anything could be managed somehow: all was given, and if it were not, then the night indeed was black. As a child I would have needed adult intelligence to have imagined easily that London had grown and possessed a limit. Nothing in the daily surroundings spoke of an accumulated heritage, of treasure wrested from Nature, of a proud society's emblem, of constant vigilance as the price of liberty, of civilization as a patient store: whereas in the country we may always see the quick reversion to weed and jungle.

An early passion for history was an antidote to imaginative despair. But imagination, or rather the anxieties which are there propounded, cannot thus be tamed. Until latterly the paramount sense of loss was attached to London. If there is now a change, it is not because the bombs reveal finite scars in some sense limiting the size, the wealth, the poverty and, above all, the confusion, though I gratefully seize upon this imaginative inference. The degree diminishes: yet to my eyes the perennial visitors of Kensington Gardens are still the worn-out and the destitute seeking neither beauty nor space. The railings are gone, revealing no magic nakedness nor capture: the copses, once railed, secret places that hold nothing it now appears, are like whores outraged casually and still unknown.

Like monsters of a zoo, a line of lime with elm have large black trunks on the further side of Rotten Row among the trampled grass nd the low traffic roar of Bayswater Road. As a child I saw them thus, exotics captured for the town, disquieting, even indecent in their rank growth. I was fearful of their chained and smutty strength, of the squalid arbours of urban passions. Chairs were placed on the trees' further side or drawn up there by tramps and lovers. This stalwart line formed a kind of railing for licensed licence as does the public-house counter in the abstainer's eyes.

The sense of loss had to be buttoned up. I turned for reassurance very early in childhood to the clock in Star Street. It projects on an iron structure at right angles to the church spire to which it is fixed, a short squat arm thrust out not unkindly over the street. The suspension is high; the face of the clock showed, in my estimation, innocence as well as some cheerful dormant power like a row of shoes in sunlight. Earlier still I had noticed that each of two factory siren hoots, all that I heard in childhood, possessed twin notes throughout, suggesting the spaced jambs to an aperture, a finely proportioned aperture that appeared upon the surface of the surrounding turmoil. The vision faded gradually like a rainbow, to be revived by the sound of hammering from a mews or of any artifice there, or from the smell of mews hay. But in Praed Street, enfilading the queue for horse meat, wisps of straw blow, marking the intrusion of another air that cannot cleanse but dirties the more, coming doubtless from the canal that must lie to the north of the street though every approach at this point is blocked by brick and hoarding. The sudden self-exposure in these surroundings of a child decapitates the anxious chimney-pots.

There was, however, the sweet shop, the strong-lighted window glittering with mellifluous dynamite, with the exploding eroticism of the neat and sweet, sweetmeats as they were called. Several such shops served Praed Street and from those less well-to-do, the sweeter, it seemed to me, were the little tawdry eggs of sugar, and the more dynamic cocoa-nut comfits. Trays mounted to the ceiling of the window: enormous jars were taken in hand to pour an ounce. Sucking secretively at night, I reduced the blown wisps of straw to a smooth ball of stealthy ecstacy. The most poisonous colours yielded sweetness.

In those days I wore black stockings of which I was particularly ashamed. The sky absorbed the light: final things were represented by the calls of newsvendors in the dusk. What I saw outside confirmed with hideous amplification the self-distrust, the shame and the division that lay inside beneath the threshold. I had identified houses with myself or others. Some twenty-five years later I found a place to live in London where directions and influences as I formulated them, looked auspicious.

York Buildings, at the edge of the Adelphi, is a blind-alley leading to the Embankment gardens. I lived at the top of an eighteenth-century house with a small balcony under the roof, near enough to the city which held enchantment, near enough, at any rate, to some Wren churches, to St. Martin-in-the-Fields and, of course, to the Adelphi. Mild bells from nearby steeples almost dominated the uneasy age. I retreated behind the wainscot of the Strand, down a narrow passage to a more mellow time. On a day of spring the steeples rose like plants that have broken ground early, white from the winter soil. Embankment and river lay close, the whistling of tugs was heard nearby, particularly at night or in the muffled webs of a fog when their sound suggested taut ropes pulled tighter. Trams passed along the Embankment, glissading with sagacity, smoothly on a gritty surface, emitting a low hum: while, opposite the window, from the monstrous bulk, it seemed, of the Charing Cross Hotel, trains were emerging to cross the bridge, or were returning there; bringing in, taking out: while across the river in the ancient Shot Tower, presumably drops of liquid lead were falling perpendicularly to form a heap of cooling pellets at the bottom. These sounds, these movements, connecting me with the Surrey hills and beyond, gently started trains of thought. The loudest noise, more dramatic, rose occasionally from below, from the cave-like, inclined entrance of Lower Robert Street descending to the Adelphi Arches, deep beneath the house. A cart-horse and dray would be coming up over the steep cobbles of the tunnel, clouting the resonant air. I welcomed this London version of buildings upon different levels, a map which set forth levels of the mind. All such movements and directions served the immobility of Inigo Jones' York House Water Gate which endures in isolation near the end of the passage, left over after the destruction of York House and even after the river, by which the gate stood, was stowed back more than a hundred yards. A stranded mediator, a symbol of ideal access.

The bastions and stairs of old Waterloo Bridge stirred images of enduring stone in intercourse with water, however ill-starred that water with slime. So much of the visual world stands up, stretches, nearly from foundation and root, suggesting outwardness to activity. Water lies, flows, boats are recumbent, driftwood is cradled by the tide. They reflect the other half of life, the world of sleep and of the incorporated figures that we rock within us, the overlapping, the underlapping, the outside-in. It is peaceful to turn to the vast river, away from staccato outward arrangement, to eye sodden wood among ripples. The soul floats more narrowly.

Ribbon development starts very soon beyond the area of the city. Can the ornate terra-cotta porch, the unfloating terra-cotta dome in sullen light, can they fructify or flower if only once, like a cactus, in several years? I have no will now to reach through the fog to where the Marble Arch stands sham in beauty, real in expense; or down the Edgware Road, past the place where the curb is double-tiered, on to Hendon and the Welsh Harp. Yet there is an openness to be gained in the grinding air of a short journey. From the top of a bus, buying and selling at the shops appear brisk, almost to the effect of a bazaar whereby pandemonium attains an exotic tinge, whereby apertures in a wall beckon and disgorge. The cold and soot may be biting, your breath may be standing before like Vergil leading Dante, yet it is not impossible to be reminded of the outskirts of Bombay by Kilburn or by the Elephant and Castle. A sudden scent flutters on the dust... The swarming of Camden Town, of the Hampstead Road are similar, flaring in utter greyness. Such thoroughfares, when deserted, in the middle of the night, are not for contemplation or pause. They possess no line even of admonishment. It is absurd to rail against a broad warren though it be impossible to disconnect the sinister knowledge that all was made by man: to the visitor in these thoroughfares at the middle night there remains still the sense of the day-long scouring vehicles, an affliction, as it were, the root affliction of the brick and stone and glass.

How rapidly cars by day are passing St. John's Wood, quickly fading. Where the veiled sky is open there lies a spire upon it. Aspiring. The placid air holds a constant test. Dramatic sensations which we cannot avoid, appear also to be meaningless. A puff of air pushes past after each passage. Another car comes, another and another: any urgency that might be attributed to them is annulled by the opposite stream. There is silence now: a leaf falls gradually. Does the passage of cars ventilate the mind, or is there an unavoidable expectation attendant upon the approach, the overtaking; swiftly meaningless in the passing? Further thought suggests disaffection of distance, a Copernican proof that the earth is not still nor man at the centre. Our ancient towns suffer movement and noise in a mechanical form alien to the stones. But hope springs eternal as each gigantic mechanism swings by and rapidly recedes... leaving a part of us disturbed, perhaps some defence against anxiety flicked from a niche, dusted, returned. With unexpected dignity a fleck of plaster falls from a villa in St. John's Wood. Trees in the villa garden are safely rooted, attentive to the wind. Churned, hoed, snipped by each successive vehicle, *our* roots remain unknown. Yet we may feel more compact, closer knit, from this ordeal, forging along slowly, conscious of the air we must breathe. Now another car approaches, passes, recedes: human breath is caught and rejected by the mechanism.

We look to the sky, to the spire attended by trees, to the sky which the tremendous passage of a bus has failed to empurple. We turn to emptiness and perhaps to ancient grief.

The Ego-Figure

From *Greek Culture and the Ego: A Psycho-Analytic Survey of an Aspect of Greek Civilization and of Art* (1958)

I take it that sublimation, unlike substitute satisfaction, is a process through which the tie to part-objects may become an attachment to objects valued for their connectedness: it is itself a mark of some integration or wholeness in the ego. Sublimatory power implies an outcome from the depressive position whereby the realization of a whole-object loss entails the longing to repair that loss not only internally but externally in a growing appreciation of outside and independent structures. As we have seen, Melanie Klein attributes to the infant an earlier depressive anxiety in connection with the loss of part-objects, but she has been careful in so doing to emphasize that the depressive position succeeding the paranoid-schizoid phase is central and crucial for further development, i.e. for integration in the ego (Klein 1948 and 1952). Of the nature of ego-integration generally she has written:

> We may assume that when persecutory anxiety is less strong, splitting is less far-reaching and the ego is therefore able to integrate itself and to synthesize in some measure the feelings towards the object. It might well be that any such step in integration can only come about if, at that moment, love towards the object predominates over the destructive impulses (ultimately the life instinct over the death instinct). The ego's tendency to integrate itself can, therefore, I think, be considered as an expression of the life instinct.
> (Klein, 1952)

Again: 'Out of the alternating processes of disintegration and integration develops gradually a more integrated ego, with an increased capacity to deal with persecutory anxiety. The infant's relation to parts

408

of his mother's body, focusing on her breast, gradually changes into a relation to her as a person' (*ibid.*).

And again: 'I have made it clear that the processes of integration, which express themselves in the infant's synthesizing his contrasting emotions towards the mother – and consequently the bringing together of the good and bad aspects of the object – underlie depressive anxiety and the depressive position' (*ibid.*).

She had previously written:

> Returning to the course of early development, we may say that every step in emotional, intellectual, and physical growth is used by the ego as a means of overcoming the depressive position. The child's growing skills, gifts, and arts increase his belief in the psychic reality of his constructive tendencies, in his capacity to master and control his hostile impulses as well as his 'bad' internal objects. Thus anxieties from various sources are relieved, and this results in a diminution of aggression and, in turn, of his suspicions of 'bad' external and internal objects. The strengthened ego, with its greater trust in people, can then make still further steps towards unification of its imagos – external, internal, loved, and hated – and towards further mitigation of hatred by means of love, and thus to a general process of integration. (Klein, 1939 and 1948)

I cannot claim that passages such as these lend credence to the unsupported statements on which I shall soon embark. I quote them first of all because they indicate the integration I shall have constantly in mind when I use this word, as I must repeatedly, and second because they might suggest to some that in favourable circumstances the external world of things as well as people, even apart from its role as a locus for displacement, bolsters up ego-integration. Indeed, Melanie Klein herself has summarized in a footnote one of Ferenczi's (1955) *Notes and Fragments* as follows: 'Ferenczi... suggests that most likely every living organism reacts to unpleasant stimuli by fragmentation, which might be an expression of the death instinct. Possibly, complicated mechanisms (living organisms) are only kept as an entity through the impact of external conditions. When these conditions become unfavourable the organism falls to pieces' (Klein, 1946 and 1952). This is suggestive for my purpose if I am right in thinking one meaning is that physical permanence and possibly organization (projected on to the external world to be there perceived) may afford example and encouragement to the ego. No one would quarrel with that: but I must go further because I judge the evidence of all art demands it. I am going to say that an imago of ego-integration is projected and perceived as an object, i.e. this imago comes to us from the external world in the terms of a whole and independent and corporeal-seeming structure.

But before I embark on even vaguer themes, I want to mention this point: I shall be saying that works of art neither taste nor smell, an elementary fact that may have been overlooked. The discrimination, the recognition-power, of week-old infants appears to be of taste and smell in regard to part-objects. Now, there will be many reasons, other than impermanence, why taste and smell lack *direct* satisfaction in art. The one of possible interest here may lie with the aesthetic stress on whole objects, with the repudiation of those sense organs originally tied to part-object discrimination in a manner never sufficiently to be overthrown for aesthetic purposes. I think the degree of envelopment by the object in terms of taste and smell at the earliest time is relevant. I shall suggest that in art the mother must be re-created through the forms of the integrated ego-figure to which she already belongs as introjected objects. In the relationship to this aesthetic figure and similarly in the earliest signs of more mature relations to the mother, tactile and kinaesthetic perceptions are, in my opinion, uppermost. Unlike taste and smell they afford sensations which can be enjoyed through vision, at a distance, as are the so-called tactile values in a painting. My reasons for saying this are drawn entirely from the nature of the form in art as I shall present it. But I will quote from Margaret Ribble the same passage as does Melanie Klein in another context (Klein, 1952): 'Much of the quality and the cohesiveness of a child's personality depends upon an emotional attachment to the mother.

410

This attachment or, to use the psycho-analytic term, cathexis, for the mother grows gradually out of the satisfaction it derives from her. We have studied the nature of this developing attachment, which is so elusive yet so essential, in considerable detail. Three types of sensory experience, namely, tactile, kinaesthetic,[1] or the sense of bodily position, and sound, contribute primarily to its formation. The development of these sensory capacities has been mentioned by nearly all observers of infantile behaviour... but their particular importance for the personal relation between mother and child has not been emphasized' (Ribble, 1944).

I would remind you once more of the ego's hard battle to preserve integration. Here is a broad cause for identification between many persons, for their mutual respect and bond, if one supposes, as seems necessary to me, that integration is best enjoyed by perceiving it in others or in things, and that a corporeal imago of ego-integration, formalized by art and cult, is perpetually re-introjected. Such a conception provides an additional background for group loyalties wherein the ego ideal has been exchanged for the body of a leader or for other objectives held in common.

We say awareness of the self comes to us from somatic sensations; but more truly, I think, we refer here to an awareness of this or that process in this or that part of the organism whose sense of wholeness, structure, physiological and psychological, may be partly sacrificed to the over-cathexes of particular functions. In order to view ourselves not merely as continuous but as integrated we need, I submit, probably as one among several parallel ego symposia, a constant intimation of wholeness, a figure that condenses not only sensations and perceptions but principal 'good' introjections and object-relationships, a body-ego projection of its own wholeness, an awareness founded on synthesis of previous body-egos belonging to other periods of psychical growth, an empathic awareness of a corporeal figure with a generalized reference that is likely to make itself felt, according to the perceptual context, by such qualities, contributing to wholeness, as balance, rhythm, movement, texture; a figure, then, that comes best before us in the act of receiving objects, regarded as independent, which by their structure and concreteness and exact limit bring with them the sense of our composite selves. Whenever there is empathy of this kind, a version of the ego-figure – it includes the body-image – will be re-created.

It appears already how snugly the conception would apply to formal properties of works of art which they have by definition. Indeed, in view of my own prepossessions it may be thought that I am about to extend a compulsively aesthetic viewpoint. The judgment may prove justified: if so, something will possibly be revealed concerning aesthetic compulsion.

Meanwhile all will agree that cults or cultures have required the attentions of art and ritual to crystallize their entities. Where do these outer shows which, as in the individual, express cohesive being – where do they stop? It would be difficult to say: there is surely an aspect of custom, of communal obsessive acts that contributes to a shared representation of simple structure whatever the main origin of the compulsive element.

On the other hand, it cannot be thought that many cultures, when viewed from the side of ideals rather than of practical affairs, contrive specific homage for the ego's powers of integration, if we take this integration to mean a nice balance of the various parts and demands and stages of the psyche in the face of external reality. Regressive compulsions have gained outlet through other identificatory mechanisms invaluable for binding society together. Some very civilized cults foster with greater intensity more primitive identifications, an increase particularly of projective identification, a return to, the control of, the breast surrogate or even that of a pre-natal condition. We may wonder whether the need to regress is entirely the work of guilt, anxiety, and ego defence, or whether there is more direct aid – comfort, one might say – from the death instinct.

However it may be, culture, many roots of which are pre-oedipal, compounds with such 'monolithic' aims, especially by means of a religion that is 'advanced'. One cannot think that oedipal super-ego demands encompass the character of religion. The more mature vintages possess pre-oedipal bouquet. I refer especially to the ambitions, the world over, of the mystic. He sometimes eschews even a manic solution, forced back to a more primitive state both of the ego and of the super-ego, rejecting variety in object-relationship, and finally object-relationship itself, in favour of an envelopment by the Divine Ground, it is sometimes called. Mystics, in the Yoga discipline for instance, may undoubtedly achieve a stupor by which they are insensible for long periods even to their own bodies. (We should remember Freud's dictum (Freud, 1927) that the ego is primarily a body-ego.) I do not know, of course, whether such states are predominantly blissful, sublime. It is natural to suspect that on the pattern of schizophrenia, bliss will alternate, if only rarely, with appalling feelings of disintegration and persecution.

There are many less arduous mystical experiences gratifying to the senses; and they are common: indeed, any study would have difficulty in dividing those experiences from 'monolithic' moments, physiological especially and contemplative, that we all undergo.

Culture mirrors contrasting ego-states. Where one is stressed it is likely to be at some sacrifice of others, if only because of influence upon the character of the ego-ideal. But even in the instance of a palpably regressive ideal, we must suppose that the integrated ego organizes the symbols and rituals of that ideal. I shall be considering very briefly a culture that represents the other extreme in a few remarkable ways, the culture of the multiple Hellenic communities from which a possibility of science and democracy derives, as well as, for many centuries, much art. Of what I have to say a part will be common, if in a minor degree, probably to all cultures. I must remind you at once of the subjection of women in classical times, the often brutal attitude to slaves and to infants, the ruthlessness to enemies, and the almost uninterrupted state of war that issued from the economic necessities of a threadbare land over which so lucent a light shines. I must remind you also of the survival of tyrannical superstitions even in a most primitive form. On the morning of Salamis Themistocles sacrificed to Dionysus Persian youths.

Whereas most religions seek to raise or limit the barrier of death, an acceptance greater than is usual of death and decay was regarded by the classical Greeks of the Homeric or Olympian tradition to be a virtue, since it favoured godlike values of youth and activity. Guilt, depression, and paranoid anxiety belong, of course, to the picture. The gods who in Homer behave like a much interfering and incalculable and disunited upper class, must be ceaselessly propitiated or invoked with succulent sacrifice. The gods at home are the butt of Homer's humour as an aristocracy is likely to be of those who depend, even utterly, on their foibles. The gods will wrestle or plot among themselves – the world and its men are their common ground, the centre of existence – in the manner of an interplay of internal objects; but Fate, or Zeus as Fate, vastly stronger, is immovable. A Homeric deity might exceptionally be wounded. In the Fifth Book of the *Iliad*, Diomedes wounded both Aphrodite and Ares. This was not overt hubris, the great sin of pride, which comes about by believing oneself to be the god, by scorning the laws of gods and men. The universal conception, hubris, will have sprung from the wish, and then the fear, of usurping the father's place, a conflict that in the highest Hellenic culture seems to have left a horror of defences *predominantly* manic, in view both of denial and the reminder of omnipotent thinking. (I stress the word 'predominantly' because I attribute a lesser manic component to the creation of art.) The god too sheds some of his omnipotence: as well as the super-ego he may mirror the ego. Odysseus discourses wryly with Athene, one part of the self with another, or as one plotter with another (*Odyssey*, Book Thirteen). Similarly, not only in Homer but in the Athenian plays, all men, whatever the respective rank, speak to one another with an equality bred of discourse itself.

The decisive moment of the Olympian religion as presented here, occurred in the sixth century according to J.W. Mackail and Gilbert Murray (1935) when 'Homer came to Hellas', to Athens from Ionia; that is to say, the Homeric poems. They may be seen to enlarge upon an alternative to the *mana* conception of power. The *mana* of animal or god or old man is not at all the object's ego but an abstraction, a part-object. You imbibe the godly power, get the inside of the god into your inside, achieve a state of undifferentiation through a part-object, whereas a whole object, in this case the Olympian, whether or not he becomes an important part of the devotee's inner world, preserves the character of an entity in touch with a manifold world. For, there cannot be the sense of the wholeness of an object, or of its variety, without some sense of contour and limit.

A strengthening of the beneficent paternal side of the super-ego may have favoured the placid lure of whole objects. It will be appropriate further on to cite Aeschylus' *Oresteia*: in *Eumenides*, not only a primitive, tearing, maternal, pre-oedipal super-ego component is forbidden the manners of her original outlet, but both Olympians involved in the situation with the Furies, Apollo and Athene, pronounce in favour of a more balanced authority. Aeschylus' Prometheus plays – the second has been lost – were probably put on in Sicily towards the end of his life. This time the conflict grows between the ego in the person of Prometheus and a ruthless, patriarchal, and irresponsible super-ego, Zeus: the protagonists eventually compromise, to the advantage of order and justice on earth (in the psyche).

I mention so soon these small points because they indicate vividly, in the terms of the greatest art, the theme of integration for the super-ego and for the relation with the ego.

The first strength of fifth-century official religion belonged to corporate observances, to identifications with the body of the city-state, in turn identified with the very statue, the seen body of the god or goddess. There was air, measure, in the manic mechanisms employed, particularly for art: plentiful reminders of the structured ego were gained from representations of the super-ego. It seems likely that the exacting purifications required by Apollo in cases of a civil homicide, however accidental, were used partly as defences against the manic feeling of triumph. Some Hellenes cultivated distaste for strongly manic displays, or regarded them as barbarous imports. It is significant that the Greek word for madness has become our word for mania; the Greek word was also used for states of exaltation. The power to accept loss, even in the guise of jealous Nemesis, without manic denial or fatalistic identification, was part of the wider Hellenic ideal. Loss, fully admitted, stimulates reparation, resourcefulness. (Cf. the character of Homer's hero, Odysseus.) Of such kind was the very rare leaven – I claim no more – that tempered far-different and extreme attitudes. Hence Apollo's 'Nothing too much' in a land of tremendous light, and 'Know thyself'. An ability to accept loss is a first condition for some appreciation of psychical reality (Segal, 1952 and 1957). The profound need for mourning, as well as its ritual, characterizes *Iliad* and *Odyssey*. When Odysseus meets his mother in Hades – he had not known she was dead – he tries to embrace her wraith and cries: 'Mother, can you not abide the loving arms of one who yearns so sorely after you, that here, even here in Hades, we may tearfully sate ourselves with icy shuddering grief' (Lawrence, 1935).

Even so few words about Hellenic culture will suggest, I hope, a temper propitious for art. Aesthetic creativeness requires both the acceptance of loss (Segal, 1952 and 1957) leading to a reconstitution of a self-subsistent object, and some idealism or even a fusion with good objects of a kind that suggests not only a manic process (Stokes, 1956) but a partial revival of the primitive ego. I shall defer explanation of this statement. For purposes of art, the degree to which self-subsistent object-nature, innocent of transcendental overtones, can be admitted, may not always be very great (Stokes, 1955). Yet upon the pursuit, often the manifest pursuit, of part-objects and upon the oceanic states to which they lend themselves, there supervenes in art, it appears to me, an impress of equilibrium deriving from the composition of whole objects.

I now suggest a third constant process projected into the work of art, interfused with the two above, the projection of the integrated ego as a corporeal form, the main subject of this book. I think in this matter Hellenic art has been the model and indeed the despair of many civilizations.

A word on terms. I do not try, of course, to demarcate the unconscious ego from the id, nor would it be to my purpose. The ego in this book is regarded as that limb of the psyche that struggles, consciously,

416

and far more unconsciously, between the outside world, the super-ego
and instinctual urge; as the seat of defence, the source of organization
including the splitting of an object and self-splitting, the receptacle
for introjections (which have always an ego as well as super-ego aspect),
the initiator of projections, of hallucinations, and of phantasies as well
as of sublimation, reason, and reality appreciation; as the entity, in fact,
whose greater cohesiveness epitomizes the aim of psycho-analysis. It
will be thought that this should go without saying; and indeed it does.
I want to suggest how uninspiring such a description appears, contrasting with the anxious necessity likely to be felt concerning a measure
of integration; how negative in relation also with the lively demand
that aspects of the exterior world should be found to echo or, rather, to
reinforce, stability, the more appropriately so since the first function
of the ego is perception. It appears that in perception, which has been
shown by Gestalt psychology to be an act of co-ordination, we perceive
with the object a reminder of the perceiving agency, the ego; implied
in the act of perception is awareness of the perceiving agent, very likely
in regard to a past state or experience. If this be a variant of *cogito ergo
sum*, it is not intended philosophically at this late date. I affirm merely
that awareness of psychical co-ordination may be received together
with perception of objects and is known best to us in this way accompanying an image of concreteness, as part of the perception of an object;
vividly, of course, in untroubled perceptions of harmonious structures,
ideally in terms of harmonious bodies or of what may be imagined to
stand for them – that is a very wide range – since the ego is felt, at any
rate in the context of perception, to be inseparable from the body, and
is itself largely composed of introjected bodies or parts of bodies, all of
which have to be co-ordinated, if possible, as one body. I am speaking
now entirely of an integrated ego that not only sees itself (perhaps literally) in untroubled moments as stable, but sees other objects as whole
and separate. Thus, there is obviously a delight in social intercourse
additional to practical pressures or to aims more directly libidinal.
The outlets, and particularly the reassurances that are sought, will be
 of many kinds: one constant factor, I think, has reference to what might

be called a show of integration assumed to be present. I have thought of calling the species of projection I have in mind which, I submit, plays a very large role in art, the body-image; but that term has physiological associations more with the parts than with the whole. I should not quarrel with anyone who would say that the work of art reconstructs the body. On the contrary, I should agree. But I should want, as now, to comprise in that integration of the body the integration of the psyche. Also, I am not sure that the word 'image' is happy for the context. Certainly the projection is an image in the sense of a reflection; but whereas what I have in mind serves as a picture of the integrated ego, as a structural and often idealized picture, this representation is the sole means that enables the ego entity to *perceive* that integration from outside. In other words, since the ego is the organ of perception, a self-perception *in regard to structure* is best organized when it is an outer perception of the senses, possessing thus a degree of impersonality, since the reference is not primarily to the personality but to the skeleton, as it were, to a stable framework. Hence there comes about on the aesthetic side, I shall suggest, an abstracted interest in structure; hence detachment from the emotional stimulus of the artist's subject-matter, no less than deep involvement, characteristic of aesthetic contemplation and therefore of aesthetic creation.

It will now be obvious that I am not referring to what is called the personality, nor does the word 'self' assist my sense. What I have in mind starts with, and is ceaselessly supported by, kinaesthetic sensations. A sum of these sensations that serve as hidden spokesmen for the movement, the interplay, of internal objects and of other layers of the psyche, are embodied outwardly, come back synthetized, structuralized, even conventionalized, in the terms, that is, of a tactile object, furnishing us with an easily shared skeleton upon which may be moulded the individual self-esteem. I shall use for this ego-object the term 'ego-figure'. I see it as an epitome of balanced or stable corporeality, more concrete, more object-seeming than any image of what is called the personality. I hope to show that the nature of art in particular requires the hypothesis. I must stress again that this interlocking entity is always viewed

418

here as a corporeal construction whose analysis reveals somatic sensations, consorting introjects and cathected outside objects, a meaning obtained from the contemplation of others as well as of ourselves.

A need to project corporeal structures may provide, it appears to me, a further encouragement for the over-reaching mechanism of projective identification. As for art, I think I am already discussing the aesthetic means of endowing symbolic material with a potent form; and may it not be that for much rational elaboration this concrete prototype has been indispensable?

Conforming to the stability of the ego, the ego-figure offers the model for repairing and esteeming others, in terms of a body structure to be mended or treasured, in terms of a whole object that emerged originally in the wake of the depressive position when the mother could be seen restored and self-subsistent, and was thereupon introjected. Following decreased reliance upon both self- and object-splitting, integration grew in the ego, provided a basis for the projection of an ego-figure dependent, therefore, upon the framework of the introjected whole mother and, from an earlier stage, upon the introjected 'good' breast described by Melanie Klein (1956) as 'a focal point in the ego'. She writes in the same paper: 'One of the main factors underlying the need for integration is the individual's feeling that integration implies being alive, loving, and being loved by the internal and external good object; that is to say, there exists a close link between integration and object relations. Conversely, the feeling of chaos, of disintegration, of lacking emotions as the result of splitting, I take to be closely related to the fear of death.' An aesthetic object is integrated. In the light of the above quotation it is surely interesting that many aestheticians have followed Berenson in calling aesthetic formal (integrative) values, and thence the work of art, 'life-enhancing'.

There is the phrase 'respect of the person', the fruit of an attitude, often only occasional, without which culture would have been unthinkable. I suggest that projection of the ego-figure reinforces the contours of most object-relationships. 'Respect of the person' underlines libidinal value in the possession of an erotic object, and similarly heightens the import of aggression. It tends to balance disgust, reaction-formation, in regard to bodies and their products. The artist, possibly even more than the physician, needs to be a great respecter of the person in this sense, a sense that colours the admission or the defiance that is implied by a Bohemian disregard of cleanliness.

Works of art have no taste or smell; that is, their taste or smell, should they have them, are entirely excluded from the aesthetic aim and the aesthetic result. A statue soused in perfume would be aesthetically most offensive, except that our imaginative faculties would not even then treat statue and perfume together, save in regard to wetness which would be of significance as a texture. Should we conclude that some neglect of taste and smell accompanies a marked insistence on the wholeness and independence of an object?

A degree of distance helps to enforce the independence and integrity of the object. Art presupposes visual (i.e. from a distance) apprehension of the object; yet while observing this otherness, art, I must add, strives also to bring the object nearer to us so as even to envelop us, principally in terms of tactile and kinaesthetic sensations. This antinomy explains, I think, the *tour de force*, the common enough element of trickery and virtuosity; hence the virtue even of the mere fact of painting in the depicting of three-dimensional form on a two-dimensional surface. The nature of the canvas is in fact very 'other' than the represented shapes, and indeed we tend today to deprecate a paramount use of such manipulations.

Nevertheless preoccupation with envelopment and with oral need restores art, in a revised sense, within the area of taste and perhaps of smell. We speak of a taste or distaste for a phenomenon or an activity, particularly in connection with art. 'It is not to my taste', one says, meaning it may be good but it is not a form I have cultivated: it does not enfold nor do I go out to meet it.

The work of art has no taste; a satisfaction, however, provided by this thing at a distance, has often an obvious oral component; we are then both feeding from the mother and re-introjecting the image of ourselves viewed as independent structures as she is viewed. I think that particularly in the case of architecture there is a pre-eminent oral-cum-tactile appreciation: yet such a mechanism is subsidiary to enhanced recognition of another object and of ourselves. All in all, art shows us that the picture of psychical co-ordination cannot be separated from a picture of physical coherence. In concerted sound, from accompaniment, we entertain a vivid sense of co-ordination *in process*, of sounds within sounds, harmony within melody and warring voices, of bits and polarities as they become a whole that is self-sufficient. It is often much the same when we look at a view. Bits of objects controlled by projected bits of the ego, as well as internal objects, are given the air, are found reconstructed within their proper spheres throughout a panorama. What consumes, what attacks, what rejects, what envelops or is enveloped, stand together as parts of a perceptual construction, space. The reassurance, it seems to me, gained from such contemplative experience mirrors our anxiety concerning ego-integration whose importance is doubtless connected with the fear of psychosis and, maybe, of the minute splitting that Bion (1957) has described, a splitting not only of sense impressions but of thought processes. Some Greek philosophers were bold enough in intellect to attribute to common conceptions many inconsistent parts, though not rejecting them altogether as illusory; they visualized in several forms the problem of the One and the Many, a problem for which I shall give a more general interpretation. I mention it now in the context of bits, bits of objects encapsulated with bits of the projected ego, a confusion out of which ego-integration and the world of self-sufficient objects have been gradually amassed together, a process in some part to be constantly renewed and, if possible, reinforced. The work of art, often called dynamic, vital, organic, provides a figure not only of the aim but of the process.

The Luxury and Necessity of Painting

From *Three Essays on the Painting of Our Time* (1961)

Not even those who detest art will be averse to the presence of picture galleries near luxurious shops. For a moment luxury may satisfy greed and provide the riches that separate us from loneliness. We sniff a bountiful air at shop windows, contemplating possessions not yet allotted, and sometimes unenviously any magnificence, the width of a street or the span of a doorway. Entertainment seeks to bring in train such bounty, experiences that are of the nature of meals; though they but symbolize suppers, surfeit supervenes. It comes about, then, that when we are at table we may hope to incorporate far more than our food; as we watch others they appear to reabsorb what we imagine to be predominant experiences. I have had this fantasy when watching directors of galleries that exhibit paintings, at a restaurant. It seemed that theirs was very fine nourishment, with associations that differed greatly from a stuffing or emparcelling: indeed, so enduring and so various is the luxurious stain upon directors of good paintings that their actual nourishment appears to lend them the overtones of lasting reassurance that may visit others only occasionally, should the satisfaction of various appetites coalesce in the pleasure of the table.

Of course good paintings are extremely valuable, a richness that lends itself to these imaginative richnesses. The gallery director has them on his walls. He may suffer from various difficulties in connection with food; nevertheless, a modicum of the fantasy of the luxuriousness of his eating will, I am sure, occasionally at least, be his as well.

To his sanctum I attribute some Italian Baroque paintings, small, boldly painted with the raw touches that will eventually prove to have heralded the modern pictorial era. The canvasses were studies and sketches for large paintings, or for their details. In one a mushroom cloud of angels grows, as it were from the compost of an ecstatic saint who grovels upward from below: the picture vibrates with rays of a sudden flowering, but lines in one corner indicate a hard architecture, the pillars and the underside of a cornice whose grooved, stepped mass embraces the shrinking or resurgence of figures as does a basin that both holds and spills the fountain's play. The union is ennobling, an interchange or commerce we would have in ourselves between passions and the stone, since the architecture symbolizes our rational disposition unberated by death and decay, embodies a Parnassus-like bent whereby proportion and space envelop our emotions, dispersing litter on a desk and the rhythmless rush of noises from the street that link us to a chaos, otherwise inescapable, throughout the length and breadth of London ever ignoble where this painting is noble. How few are the colonnades, those tunnels with pierced sides, how small the perpetuity of silent flank and orifice, how little by which to recognize our own ideal states... As well as of the rational disposition, a good building is the monument to physique.

But it is unlikely that this director has much interest in architecture: it is not necessary today for devotees of painting: they do not acknowledge building to be the root of any grandeur and the presiding genius of graphic art. The lapse is due to failure, and to a resurgence that is taut, of architecture in our time; even more because, in view of this failure from the middle of the last century, painting, while avoiding as a rule an obvious architectural balance, has itself been inspired to fill the void, to provide the more intimate architectural pleasures, striving to envelop and to feed us without ceremony by means of clamant textures, to enwrap us with a surface, to drive us by shock into a place of safety, to declaim from a wall the need for tactile passages and transitions that were once available in lovely streets. The primacy of architecture, mother of the arts, is not first as the school of proportion and design but as the universal witness to the luxuries of art, to the aesthetic translation of mental process, as well as the scenes of living, into the terms of an absorbable substance, or of our envelopment by an object. But simultaneously there exists an emphasis upon the separateness of the artifact, upon the cake that survives our eating of it. Thus, in the name of object self-sufficiency and corporeal wholeness, art may bestow another luxury in the enshrinement of even the greatest misery, a luxury gained from the putting together of fragments of experience that have been dispersed, so that even pain coheres, owns features: a service is done thereby, a good restored. Graphic boldness and idiosyncrasy satisfy more people today than fine building surrounded by ill-advised curves and strong material and dreary roofs and the blatant, negative pretension of all urban scenes. Surely there has never before been so sterling and durable a debasement, multiplied in instances by the million, of members and materials that were once well used. It will be some time before late Victorian and Edwardian miasmas will have yielded their present air of universality.

Envelopment by building, by street, is almost unknown to Englishmen as a reassurance, but is universal in experiences of confusion or of the drugs that alleviate, such as the droplet comfort in a cottage roof, in a quaint lamp-post or a causeway too windswept for advertisements. Even so, our director has enjoyed visits to Rome; his pleasure in his Baroque paintings reminds him of cobbled roads and their smooth houses with apertures that are tall: and he has read in Wittkower of a conscious Baroque aim to envelop the spectator. 'With Caravaggio the great gesture had another distinct meaning; it was a psychological device, not unknown in the history of art, to draw the beholder into the orbit of the picture... Bernini's *St. Theresa*, shown in rapture, seems to be suspended in mid-air, and this can only appear as reality by virtue of the implied visionary state of mind of the beholder... Miracles, wondrous events, supra-natural phenomena are given an air of verisimilitude' (Wittkower, 1958). The power of this art to envelop us suggests confidence in the phantasy that an interchange infuses the complexity of relationship between substances themselves, between objects, between different arts though employed to represent a single vivid happening. Architecture, sculpture, painting merge in the representation of St. Theresa's ecstasy, just as river-god, shell, dolphin are as one with the water of the Barberini fountain.

Architecture is limited to forms without events; in many styles or periods an architectural exemplar has provided the model for translating graphic subjects into the terms of a concatenation built upon a ground bass. There are Italian masterpieces, for instance the operas of Vincenzo Bellini, whose continuous simplicity remains poignant, whose lyricism remains unmatched in a firmness far from romantic, suggesting sunlit or shaded loggias and above them, upon the wall, smooth apertures that give light, and above again the jutting features of a cornice-head.

The churches of Rome reign easily over the noisiest traffic in the world; even in this wretched sanctum in the West End of London, the Baroque paintings lend a Theatine quiet unseparated from the life of the town, as if a burst pipe that floods a building's face in patches might yet convey the image of a spring. We hang our paintings to convert not only our houses but our neighbourhoods and our neighbours.

Little understood by our director, the Baroque paintings are a sideline relegated to this narrow room. Modern paintings are his livelihood and his life. Let us go into the galleries. There he is, in the hour before the midday meal, doubtless still stimulated by pictures whose appeal fails only at the tap of another example. They titillate the appetite to absorb all things: who can say where limitation lies since these artists' aims have been to show the unknown as uniform in strong impact with the known? We have here the manner of endless bodily function as well as of hardly touched states of mind more muscular, more independent than the resonance of images in a dream yet, when viewed in terms of the intellect's categories, vague and boundless as are the spongy images of sleep so often tied to an inconsequent context, equalled occasionally by the name the modern artist puts upon his painting in the catalogue.

'I no longer invite the spectator to walk into my canvases,' writes the American Action painter Grace Hartigan (1959), 'I want a surface that resists, like a wall, not opens like a gate.' The wall, Leonardo's homogeneous wall with adventitious marks which, he said, encourage fantasy to reinforce their suggestion, has been an especial spur from the time of the Impressionists, from the time of the new negative significance of buildings in our epoch for which the picture plane, the picture surface, has become an affirmative substitute; so much is this so that much modern painting ceases to have parts or pieces, in the sense of parts that when abstracted from the whole would remain objects of beauty as of value. What price a section of an Action painting (of one section rather than another), or even of a Cubist painting or a Mondrian? The modern stress upon unity and purity, upon strict aesthetic relevance, connotes a stress upon homogeneity: in some styles the picture plane in fact resembles a blank wall to which is entrusted the coalescence of dissonances or blows directed at the spectator. Even when this is not so we are likely to discover the kindred notion of something unlimited. Unspoken experiences, bodily and mental, have always been incorporated into art through the appeal of formal relationships: but when, as now, they are offered without the accompaniment of any other symbolic content – or if there is another programme, when it is distorted or simplified even to a greater extent than in a style that has been strictly conventionalized – they readily suggest the unlimited, a concept always present to the mind in terms of a boundless, traumatic bad or a boundless, bountiful good, by which we suffer envelopment or from which we would perpetually feed.

Now, the simplest relationships, the most sporadic marks, have deep meaning: we have been shown it beyond all question. We have today an art without manners, without veneer, arresting, knock-you-down yet unbraced and unlimited, it appears, in scope: that is one reason why it must continually change so much: what is novel affords a sense of boundless possibility with which we may exchange ourselves in lieu of achievement. Modern art tends thus to be romantic, somewhat at the expense of the other fundamental draw of the work of art, as a self-sufficient entity, though this character too has been isolated and worked upon. The palpable textures of modern painting express the division and disintegration of culture as well as the ambivalent artist's restitution, often carried no further than an assembly of scaffolding. We are then left with an unceremonious image that seems to symbolize the process of art itself, of the hidden content, always immanent, whereby

426

mere space and shape touch in us sensations of pain, struggle, anxiety, or joy that we have already begun to translate into tactile and even visual sensations, since a parallel amalgam is ceaselessly registered in some part of the mind. Appreciation is a mode of recognition: we recognize but we cannot name, we cannot recall by an effort of will: the contents that reach us in the terms of aesthetic form have the 'feel' of a dream that is otherwise forgotten. This 'feel' too may be lost until it is recalled by an action in the street, by some concatenation of movement or of substances: in just this way much modern art offers us the 'feel' of our own structure, sometimes overriding the communication of particular feelings. Painting usually presents as well a specific subject-matter equivalent to the manifest content of a dream, in terms of an image of the waking world. The painter has been happiest when surrounded by an actual architecture which provided an assumption (a living style) that made it unnecessary to reconstruct *ab initio* for every work the rudiments of the body and of the psyche. Titian was adorning, not creating, the stone Venice, and Rembrandt the new Amsterdam. Architecture in the West has been the prime embodiment not only of art but of culture. There are left, of course, many beautiful places, many ordinary houses that are satisfying, particularly in the South; but it is not our ruling culture that creates them. Marinetti considered all the beauty of Italy an obstacle to his harsh idealization of the machine by which alone he felt enveloped in the unlimited way he demanded.

We will agree that the work of art is a construction. Inasmuch as man both physically and psychologically is a structure carefully amassed, a coalescence and a pattern, a balance imposed upon opposite drives, building is likely to be not only the most common but the most general symbol of our living and breathing: the house, besides, is the home and the symbol of the Mother: it is our upright bodies built cell by cell: a ledge is the foot, the knee and the brow. While we project our own being on to all things, the works of man, particularly houses or any of the shelters he inhabits, reflect ourselves more directly than will inorganic material that has not been cultivated thus. Of course buildings and the engineering involved, roads, bridges, and the rest, are so common as to be a part of a ceaseless environment. The ordered stone or brick encloses and defines: whether we will it or not, the eye explores these surfaces as if compelled to consult an oracle, the oracle of spatial relationships and of the texture that they serve. Hurt, hindered, and inspired by wall and ledge, the graphic artist has bestowed upon flat surfaces an expressiveness of space, volume, and texture equivalent to the impact, at the very least, of phantasies, events, moods. Architecture has provided the original terms of this 'language' that can rarely be put into words, though words may sometimes be found for the simple employment of the 'language' by building when taken in conjunction with the natural scene. For instance, in the fascination of gazing along a dark passage into the outside light that invades an entrance, in a subject not uncommon for seventeenth-century Dutch painters, we may become aware that we contemplate under an image of dark, calm enclosure and of seeping light, the traumatic struggles that accompany our entry and our exit, in birth and death. To look along the walls of a cave into the blinding entry would be to experience a more dramatic symbol except for the consideration that a thousand threads of conscious life bring now to the passage and to the house, to the constricted brick or stone, an appropriate association. Seeing that the projection of phantasy on to all the phenomena of Nature is ceaseless, I would not deny that the 'language' of form must have a far wider origin; but I would claim that the example of building, not least in view of a context in the natural scene, has greatly served the precision of that 'language'; nor is it irrelevant that the graphic arts have been expended in many cultures on the adornment of building; not that in pictorial art there has often figured the architectural organization. In almost all periods and styles buildings have been represented in painting: this is due not only to their commonness or to relevance for many scenes: a study of the employment of the architectural background in Renaissance art and in the theatre, shows without question that they are treated as the emblems both of ordered beauty and of a psychological tenor, in general as the presiding example of the conversion of phantasy into substance and for bestowing upon phantasy an autonomous and enduring body.

428

I shall now leave the terms of architecture and of luxury and our gallery director who loves luxury, achieves it from painting while more or less blind to building. I take leave of him because of the great distance between gallery and studio, between art as luxury and art as necessity, though the former meaning is dependent upon, and founded upon, the latter.

The calm, the architecture, the luxury of pictures, what are they to the artist? Everything, I dare to say, though the making of art is a compulsive fruit of conflict, grief, and loss, of a sadness or a lack too old and bitter, too keen though hidden, to carry for long any romantic overtone. These feelings, the spring of art whatever an artist's overt temperament may be, correspond with our own feelings of loss and confusion: none of us has escaped them; hence the reassurance and luxury, since a synthesis and restitution will have been forged in the studio.

I do not want to hint that the artist should paint with tears rolling down cheeks, misting vision, but that he projects with astuteness upon the canvas an inner need in terms of the outside objects he has chosen, so that both he and they renew life; that is, so as to figure forth a pattern wherein confusion, though it be rehearsed there, may not rule; and greed and sadistic control of the object, though they too may figure, are not unchallenged.

We have no difficulty in speaking of the painter as the artist *par excellence*, of painting as the representative of art in general. I think that this is because of the instrument, the brush, tipped with the creative material, and because the canvas is worked at arm's length, with the result that the very act of painting as well as the preoccupation with the representation of space, symbolize not only the restitutive process but a settled distance of the ego from its objects. The distance from us of our world varies continuously: the artist brings all into view, into focus, at arm's length as it were. Throughout consciousness one thing stands for another: we traffic all the time with symbols, in thought as well as in emotion; for, behind any feeling, behind the 'feel' of any argument even, there lurks another that is older and, as we proceed back, that is nearer to the source of its power over us. More than the rest of us, the artist is aware that what we see symbolizes the history as well as the aspiration of the mind: his task is to discover for them a felicitous embodiment in the outside world so that they be recognized as any object of perception is known, and better known the better the character of the object or scene represented has been seized in paint.

I am not necessarily referring to an artist's manifest aim but to the springs of his compulsion; nor do I refer in this context to anything that throws light on the immense variety of art, on the need for change. One of our most comprehensive symbolic objects – the artist is very aware of it – is the culture in which we live. In one aspect, culture and society are foods just as art itself is a food, an absorbable structure that nourishes our own. The artist absorbs his 'times', 'what is in the air'. On the other hand culture is recognized as an entity in the terms of the art it inspires; differences of culture are often measured succinctly in terms of art: and art itself, as a history of development and as a model of achievement, is another comprehensive object that the artist will tend to incorporate. Symbolic activities, art in chief, have their richest material in what is already richly and widely symbolic: the outermost ripple on the pond after the stone was cast is the one that most vividly reveals the power of the throwing and of the thing thrown. It seems that contemporary attitudes and achievements, whether or not we are sympathetic to them, provide indispensable terms for creativeness. It is well known that old works of art vary to some extent in their power of evocation, in accordance with their apparent comment upon a present cultural endeavour: and that the 'climate' of feeling is an inescapable framework for aesthetic emotion.

Our relationships to all objects seem to me to be describable in the terms of two extreme forms, the one a very strong identification with the object, whether projective or introjective, whereby a barrier between self and not-self is undone, the other a commerce with a self-sufficient and independent object at arm's length. In all times except the earliest weeks of life, both of these relationships, in vastly differing amalgams, are in play together, as is shown not only by psycho-analysis but by art, since the work of art is *par excellence* a self-sufficient object as well as a

configuration that we absorb or to which we lend ourselves as manipulators. (The first generic difference between styles lies in the varying
combinations by which these two extremes are conveyed to us.) Here is
to be observed a fundamental connection of art with the culture from
which it arises; for art helps us both to identify ourselves with some
aspect of our culture, to incorporate cultural activities or to reject them,
and at the same time to contemplate them as if they were fixed and
hardy objects. From the angle of contemplation culture *is* art – hence,
once more, the necessity of having art – since culture is most easily seen
as an object for contemplation in aesthetic terms. Moreover, a cultural
reconciliation of what is various, and even opposite, is perceived, when
reflected in art, as a symbol for the integration that we have carried out
upon contrary urges, opposite feelings, once widely separated, about
one and the same person. In painting his picture the artist performs an
act of integration upon the outside world that has reference, then, as
well as to the independence of objects, first to the re-creation and to
some resolution of his own inner processes, next in regard to the organization of the ego in a generalized sense, and finally in regard to a cultural significance. The result is an interplay between these modes of
organization to the end of making one of them more poignant since
it possesses the services of the others. Romantic art underlines an
aspect of the artist's personality, Hellenic art the generous ideal of ego-
integration, a severely conventionalized art, such as the Byzantine in
a characteristic phase, the cultural hierarchy. Throughout the history
of art, emphasis has more commonly lain here: art has been employed
to mark ritual and religion, cultural pride, social distinction and consequence. Moreover in ceramics, in all of what are called the applied
arts, only a cultural identity, by and large, is likely to survive: indeed,
the potter's compulsions, as reflected by his work, will rarely have been
apparent beyond his immediate companions, beyond the workshop:
we remain very much aware, however, that the Korean dish or Sung
bowl was an outcome not only of a tradition to which numerous artists
had contributed but of an individual who must have again, in his turn,
been subject to the aesthetic compulsion to reflect an ideal of ego

structure. The same is often true in the sphere of building. We have arrived at a further reason why the painter may represent all artists: his work usually allows us to discern other syntheses (beyond those of a style and of a culture) that underlie the practice of every kind of art. But whereas architecture does not possess the many facets of painting, it shows us the surfaces that matter most, the 'language': it surrounds us so widely that the art of painting cannot be viewed apart from architectural alternatives, volume and void, light and dark, recession and protrusion, the rough and the smooth. That is not at all to say we would have no sculpture or painting without an example of building, but only that in such case, painting and sculpture would themselves have to find a partial substitute for this absence, just as they tend to do now.

To speak of art is sometimes to estrange ourselves from the artist. He seems today often to be concerned merely with the expression of sensations, maybe sensations to touch and tear and mould material. Nevertheless, whatever he may profess, no artist, old nor modern, with the possible exception of a few child-like or naïf painters, achieved his aim without having been fired by already existing works of art, especially by the work of contemporaries. The itch to create in the aesthetic sense is perhaps a thing apart; but it follows that the artist is himself no mean connoisseur of creativeness: he understands art; he could not be much of an artist if he did not, since he is extremely sensitive to what lies together, especially to what is intentionally symbolic. There is no hard-and-fast division between the appreciator and the creator of art. Indeed, whatever his conscious interest or knowledge, I have no doubt that the artist is potentially the most highly trained appreciator, often confined in range of interest by the preoccupation of his own creative field. This is but to emphasize again in a different manner that art is a cultural activity though the fount be hidden and untutored. Were it otherwise, art would not mirror the whole man, the whole of his capacity. The fire of Van Gogh would have been of small consequence had it not consumed Vincent, the copier of drawings in the *Illustrated London News*, the admirer of Millet, and the near-contemporary of the Impressionists. Some artists today ape an effect that is untutored, but insofar as their work is notable, it will be obvious that they are, as artists, the product of modern museums. Nor do they work now in more isolation than heretofore. On the contrary, the movement, the fraternity, seems more essential: few modern paintings make their utmost point without reinforcement from others.

I sent our gallery director packing, yet he now reappears in the train of artists: we are not interested in his business acumen but in his nose. He and his smart gallery are symbols of the cultural relevance of hard agonies in the studio. Picasso is reported to have said that as a child he could draw like Raphael but that later, as an adult, it had taken him a long time to learn to draw like a child. It seems that the character of our culture has inspired an element of regression: it inspired Picasso's early appreciation of the values of negro sculpture, a very important part of his creativeness. We taste a new humility and a new arrogance, a sophistication and a barbarity in all the people and all the things surrounding us: and I do not use the word 'taste' altogether metaphorically since I would stress the oral component in our attitudes to parts of our environment: as presented by art, I have said, it does not overwhelm us since, as well as in the terms of envelopment and incorporation, we are shown an aspect of our environment and 'mental climate' by the painter as an enclosed object, at arm's length, reflecting what I have called two basic relationships to objects. They are usually experienced together; in art alone their collusion seems perfected to the extent that we appear to have the cake and to eat it without a greedy tearing, the object to incorporate and the object set out and self-contained. Surely the status of this cake is the one of the 'good' *internal* object, the 'good' breast which, as Melanie Klein (1957) has repeatedly said, formed and forms the ego's nucleus, the prototype not only for all our 'good' objects but, in the unenvious, unspoiling relationship with it, for happiness.

But it is always a prime error to search only for derivations that are positive, affirmative. I have not pointed to the fact that part of the aesthetic compulsion will have a negative basis in the component of aggression and, perhaps, of organ deficiency as well as in the threat, perhaps always present, of incipient confusion. We know of several great painters who have had ceaseless trouble with their eyes, imaginary or real. When the trouble has been imaginary we must impute to them an unconscious sense of guilt, unusually strong, in connection with the greedy, prehensile, and controlling act of vision as it has appeared to the phantasy in early years. To observe is partly to control, to be omnipotent: whereas the exercise of the cruel power continues in the making of art, it is used also to reconstruct what thereby is dismembered: in reflecting such combined yet antithetical drives, a work of art symbolizes the broader integrating processes. The aesthetic account of integration is an end-in-itself, unlike the stock syntheses that construct a character type, professional, class, or national, often valued beyond all other ego projections by unaesthetic persons. Genius displays a new mending of impulse, of feeling, with such conviction that there issues from it a novel treatment of subject-matter as of form. Cézanne applied a steel-bright knife to pattern and to distance: he introduced love and respect into an extraordinary attack upon his apples and upon the landscapes of his home. His paintings are unified by a play of glinting cuts that both bisect and glorify the contour. It is above all composers who demonstrate easily the varieties, and even the contrariety, implicit in a theme. What twists of combined feelings Mozart contrived within the clear cascade of a chamber work.

Many artists of an opposite temperament to Cézanne's will have availed themselves of his discoveries. Considered psychologically the development of art is no less complicated than the view from any other approach. But I want to stress a factor that has usually been simple, the compulsion to 'get things right' issuing in part from the fear of deformity and of aggressiveness. In the case of naturalistic painting the first test of what 'looks wrong' has been very simple. In drawing a jug how shameful it is that a side should become swollen or should be impoverished, how poignant and sacrilegious the lop-sidedness. Many present-day artists defy this fear and scan the lop-sidedness of our environment: modern art tends to conventionalize ugliness and distortion in the search for comprehensive balances: the vibrant power wanes to correct each enormity without devitalization, since art must reflect as well as affirm: idealism in art has been the face put upon some degree of truth, upon some need of balance amid discord: also the unabashed shape of the deformed jug may have this timeless quality. In the past undeformed shapes have sometimes been balanced in a picture asymmetrically: today we often see deformed shapes balanced squarely.

I have already introduced a negative approach in attributing the development of modern painting partly to the nineteenth-century vulgarization of architecture. Ugliness has strengthened not only confusion but a desire for collapse: in art we will here discern an amalgamation of negative and positive components. A collapsed room displays many more facets than a room intact: after a bombing in the last war, we were able to look at elongated, piled-up displays of what had been exterior, mingled with what had been interior, materializations of the serene Analytic Cubism that Picasso and Braque invented before the first war; and usually, as in some of these paintings, we saw the poignant key provided by some untouched, undamaged object that had miraculously escaped. The thread of life persists, in the case of early Cubist paintings a glass, a pipe, a newspaper, a guitar whose humming now spreads beyond once-sounding walls that have become clean and tactile remains. In such strange surroundings, not altogether unlike the intact yet empty buildings invented by de Chirico, the brusque accoutrements of comfort for pavement life, the one of the café, extend a great sense of calm: a simple shape and a simple need emerge from the shattering noise and changing facets of the street. Later work by Picasso is more disturbing, since he has broken off and re-combined parts of the body, often adding more than one view of these part-objects. Disruption of flesh and bone extends to the vitals, but the furor of his genius is such that the sum of misplaced sections does not suggest the parts of a machine: on the contrary, in the translated bodies, as in the rent room, of *Guernica*, there exist both horror and pathos as well as aesthetic calm: the interior of the body is not represented as a ruined closet but as part of an exterior décor. Similarly, the New York Manager of Picasso's ballet, *Parade*, wore his ribs outside his costume and outside the child's skyscraper attached to his head. In the period known as Synthetic Cubism,

Picasso and Braque had joined into whole objects upon tilted table-tops the piled-up abstract bric-à-brac accumulated in Analytic Cubism, to an enfolded effect as fresh as fruit. Strong, jagged pattern, a wrought-iron jointure, the curve of a rib blunt or acute, typify enduring characteristics in the manifold variations of Picasso's art, a giant in our times.

The distinctiveness of what we call modern art does not lie in the degree of conventionalization or of distortion or in a total neglect of appearances but in the treating by means of such methods of all experiences as if they were rudimentary; impact takes precedence of the values revealed by the last ripple on the pond. Things are already in bits and must themselves be broken up into absorbable parts. The emphasis upon strong impact is an emphasis not only upon the projection of proprioceptive or interoceptive sensations and images associated with a mere part of the body, but consequently upon the merging or incorporating function that belongs pre-eminently to our relationship with any part-object, in the first place the breast of infanthood: we cannot attribute originally to the infant an awareness of whole or separate objects either visually or imaginatively, only of highly coloured attributes or parts that in their supreme goodness or badness are assimilated with himself. In modern art, then, the wealth of adult experiences is often endowed with this primitive cast that is normally retained at such strength in adult life for some states only, such as sleep. I am here referring to a treatment in the work of art, not entirely to the effect of the work itself, which by definition brings to us also the sense of a whole and self-sufficient object. On the other hand, a unifying simplification of shape (and often a shape's mere exaggeration) to some degree figures in *all* plastic art: it facilitates the clutching impact, the easy identification, characteristic of relationship with a part-object, whereby the world is homogeneous. As well as to observe, Form induces us to partake.

We are not likely to use the word 'imaginative' in connection with modern art. This seems strange if we recall the extraordinary inventions of Picasso, for instance, syntheses of many experiences, many feelings; reflections, very often as well, of numerous cultural *nuances* past and present. Are not his phantasmagorias imaginative by definition? Yet I

436

think that even here we are loath to use the word, though we do so at once in regard to works of the early periods and to his classical reminiscences particularly in the early 1920s, to the horses and giant women by the sea and to echoes of pagan myth in representational drawings, to such a series as the one of the artist with the model. Why do we call these works imaginative whereas we make no immediate call for this word in contemplating the far greater fertility of his more recondite works? I believe the answer to be that they are more recondite in a limited sense only, since they are by no means of a hidden or etiolated manner. While it remains difficult to define the imaginative content, we are strongly aware of a constraint upon us to regard their richness as a stripping, a baring, as a defiance even of the symbolization or image-building attributed to the processes of imagination. Indeed, the word 'imaginative' is no longer in constant employment even beyond the range of professional art. Do we any more say that children are imaginative; or children's drawings? We have come to realize that *all* expressions are symbols of a further meaning. I have asked the question whether a typical child's drawing should be considered imaginative. The answer surely is No: a child's drawing finds the equivalent, without much ado, to a hidden tension in himself: hence the lesson learnt by modern art from child's art. The attempt in modern art to break down the accepted image in favour of primitive entities that it symbolizes, results in the formation of images without resonance from which we withhold the adjective 'imaginative'. In pursuing his spadework on what seems virgin ground, the artist of today sometimes manipulates appearances out of all recognition or refuses altogether to have truck with appearances other than the one of his own painting to which, as by Mondrian, the laws of the cosmos are instantly related: the world comes back with a rush in catalogue explanations, whereas what we value in Mondrian are the sensations of architecture of which we are always in need.

Though the greater part of the art of the world demonstrates varying compromises between two treatments of symbols – we can call them here the classical and modern – I do not think that the rawness of impact rescued by recent generations from primitive art and so prized in our own art today – remember, it means a raw impact of formal relationships no less than of other symbols – is likely to cease in attraction, especially since the art of the world has been assembled in photograph and in museum. But there is this point: the slower art, slower, though as strong, in formal impact, is obsessed with the variety and smooth interpenetration of things that in their sum symbolize an integration and independence of the self and of our objects, maybe at some expense of a blatant (though not an eventual) enveloping power to which I have referred. I submit, therefore, there has not been in the West an art reflective of the entire man as successful as the classical Greek and the Renaissance art at its greatest, which strove to endow symbolic objects with the full value of their own appearances.

All great art commands a strong impact, and all great art records as well the last ripple on the pond. Which aspect will be more needed in the future; will the modern concentration upon impact diminish? I have attempted to isolate the deeper necessity of these emphases: there is obviously unforgettable virtue in both.

EPILOGUE

My hope is that far from needing a more abstract treatment, what I have written above will have stimulated a modicum of consent to the following very brief summary: it embraces similar propositions I have previously put forward (1955, 1955a, 1958).

There is a sense in which we absorb the object of our attention: we speak of absorbing or imbibing knowledge while, for the moment, the rest of the world is excluded. Except for contemplative acts we do not mentally imbibe a thing as an end in itself but as part of a wider activity. Though things and their systems remain outside us, we seem to get to know them by taking them in; for the most part, however, we do not will them to flood through every atom of our being in entering the store of what we call the mind. The work of art, on the other hand,

438

though by definition a complete and enclosed system, strongly suggests to us physical and mental states of envelopment and of being enveloped. These identifications vary from strong manipulation of the object to an absorption of it and a sinking into it; I have used the word 'envelopment' as shorthand. Since art is useless, it exists solely for the contemplative act in which the senses are not the mere vehicles; the appeal is first to them. Two important results follow: as the senses are the feelers by which we apprehend the otherness of outside things, the otherness or object nature of the work of art is stressed in this act of its contemplation; yet, as I have said, the ruling attention is also engaged by the process of its absorption no less than by the more obvious projecting therein of our feelings. The great work of art is surrounded by silence. It remains palpably 'out there', yet none the less enwraps us; we do not so much absorb as become ourselves absorbed. This is the aspect of the relationship, held in common with mystical experience, that I want to stress, because the no less important and non-mystical attitude to object-otherness in aesthetic appreciation has been better admitted. Aesthetic form immediately communicates, as well as a symbolic image of an integrated ego (Stokes, 1958), the answering image of a reconstituted and independent 'good' object. This object thereupon becomes incorporated with a satisfaction that evokes in turn a more permeating ground for what is felt to be good, and so a symbol for the 'good' breast. The process entails the feeling of 'a pulse in common', of a heightened identification between the appraiser and his object: it is a process that has been accentuated in the so-called conventionalized or conceptual styles of the graphic arts; without ado they impart a generalized image imposed upon what is particular, upon what is mere appearance, transcendent equally of self and of object-nature. Evoking, through the creation of symbolic inducements, the manner of primitive attachment to a part-object (e.g. the breast), art has served ritual, religion, and every cultural aim. In this context, but more particularly outside it, that is to say, in examples which lack the focus of a narrow cultural ideal, we find an employment, as I shall show in the following two essays, for a type of experience that may be called visionary, though coupled (as assuredly it must be in the creation of art) with an insistence upon the independence of a limited, self-sufficient object.

What common analogy can we find for so strong an absorption of ourselves into other things? As a matter of fact such identification is extremely common: an element of it enters into all group attitudes, all states of contemplation and physical engrossment. The most common is surely the state of sleep wherein we discern best the 'oceanic feeling' as Freud called it, a loss of identity that he referred to the infant's satisfaction at the breast with which he is one, a part-object that does not suggest the distinctiveness from its perceiver of a whole object. (There are many methods of confusion with the object, under the stress of predominantly negative feelings, that result in serious loss of ego power. The affirmative quality of aesthetic value I have in mind is bound to be related, largely in a compensatory manner, with these mechanisms of attack and of defence.)

Dr. Lewin's so-called 'dream screen' is 'distinguished from the rest of the dream and defined as the blank background upon which the dream picture appears to be projected... It has a definite meaning in itself' and 'represents the idea of "sleep"; it is the element of the dream that betokens the fulfilment of the cardinal wish to sleep, which Freud considered responsible for all dreaming. Also, it represents the maternal breast, usually flattened out, as the infant might perceive it while falling asleep. It appears to be the equivalent or the continuation, in sleep, of the breast hallucinated in certain pre-dormescent states, occasionally observed in adults' (Lewin, 1948). Whether or not the dream screen is well authenticated, it serves to illustrate the formal value to which I would point in aesthetic experience, usually associated with a subject-matter (the dream itself). In such projections the good breast is of an illimitable character: art is here joined by religious and philosophical yearning for the absolute, so primitive and, some will think, so destructive of good sense in a pretended context of universal truth. The superb place for it is in useless art, harnessed to an equal emphasis upon object-otherness. We must realize at the same time that more generally an oral character in experience is very common; the modes of identification necessary to culture and to cultural behaviour, in part depend upon it.

Thus, in virtue of its form at least, art rehearses favourable relationships free of excessive persecution, greed, and envy. Convention, stylization, the power to generalize, are among the means of furthering the enwrapping component in aesthetic form: where one line does the job of two, in any simplification, we experience the emphasis upon singleness. But at the same time the identical formal qualities, such as pattern, that lend themselves to an envelopment theme, are the means also for creating the object-otherness, independence, and self-containment of the work of art: it 'works' on its own, 'functions' in the way of an organism: this phantasy accompanies the one of our being enveloped, but is connected with another that projects the ego in terms of an integrated figure in which opposite characteristics coalesce. The idea of beauty, I have said elsewhere (Stokes, 1958), projects the integrated ego in the terms of a corporeal figure.

I add this note in regard to Dr. Lewin's description of his dream screen as a flattened breast. One thinks at once of the flattened shapes especially of low relief in much art of the world, particularly Quattrocento low reliefs, often of the Mother and Child; and, more generally, one thinks of the picture plane in painting that is preserved at all costs by modern art: more generally still, one thinks of the little recessions, lines, and protuberances of pilasters, for instance, of the markings on frieze or cornice, by which architecture reconstitutes the body. I wrote many years ago: 'Architecture is a solid dream for those who love it. One often wakes from sleeping without any recollection of a dream but conscious of having experienced directions and alternatives and the vague character of a weighty impress in harmony with the non-figurative assertiveness of building. In architectural experience, however, changing surfaces, in-out, smooth-rough, light-dark, up-down, all manner of trustful absorption by space, are activated further than in a dream; full cognizance of space is sign enough of being wide awake. The state of sleep has thus been won for actuality.'

And so, too, I make bold to say, in art altogether.

Is-ness and Avant-garde

From *Three Essays on the Painting of Our Time* (1961)

'I habituated myself', wrote Rimbaud, 'to simple hallucination: I would see quite honestly a mosque instead of a factory... I ended by finding sacred the disorder of my intelligence' (quoted by Wilson, 1931). Any indication of the extremely good and bad in disorderly alternation, of disconnection and of compulsive equivalence, was sacred. At nineteen Rimbaud turned his back on discoveries of the deeper self through art. Not so Alfred Jarry, whose influence upon Apollinaire and Picasso was considerable as well as later upon the Surrealists. He tried to live, says Roger Shattuck, 'in foolish competition with his own work.' He 're-fused the contradictions of which he was so keenly aware and asserted the equivalence of all things'. 'The time', adds Shattuck of the 1900s, 'acknowledged the vitality of certain areas conventionally called evil and lunatic' (Shattuck, 1959). (Almost a hundred years earlier Géricault had painted the portraits of psychotics not as straight grotesques but as complicated human beings.) The element of what we now call anti-art has arisen from an exaggeration of a single aesthetic component, in the determination, as well as from the compulsion, to regress, to embrace, whatever appears more primary, to disconnect in order to bring extraneous things together so that they sprawl at all angles. These manifestations, however, stress a yearning for simultaneity, singleness, and equivalence, in due proportion proper to aesthetic experience, being an aspect of the romantic merging or identification with the object upon which the art of the last 150 years has tended to insist. Owing to this stress, the concomitant search in art for 'the inner man' has often taken a most regressive form. But the 'primitive' has then become sacred only when romantically shorn of its huge components, guilt and anxiety; in fact, there has been the attempt to deny a developed super-ego in favour

442

of a freedom that must be negatively defined. Jarry, it seems, felt himself free not to be himself, free to enjoy a deliquescence of his ego in favour of a histrionic personage whose performance was re-created each moment like a work of art.

The birth of the avant-garde was a long, prodigious labour: scores of years of research are needed for the critical reconstruction. As always, the nature of art is involved. To the indications already attempted, I add a few from preceding historical phases.

I think everyone concurs about the principal point of departure, the Romantic movement, partly prepared in the eighteenth century and before. The French Revolution was, of course, the epoch-making outer event: the stress upon 'isness' in contemporary art is still, it seems to me, a modern version of a romantic reaching for the moon. Not only did the Romantic poet vindicate 'the rights of the individual against the claims of society as a whole', but, 'with his turbid or opalescent language, his sympathies and passions which cause him to seem to merge with his surroundings, he is the prophet of a new insight into nature' (Wilson, 1931): particularly human nature in the manifold 'spiritual' relationships with objects which at the same time were seen to symbolize inner states. Thus, portrayal was known to be self-exploration in a manner more intrusive than heretofore. At the end of the nineteenth century the Symbolists were probing intimations of meaning that escaped from descriptiveness, while their opponents, the Naturalists, likewise infused the interstices of actuality with temperament. In all art of worth a new emphasis lay on the character and act of the performer behind the work, because art seemed to be creating culture rather than culture art: the individual's, the artist's achievement with himself, could appear to be more stable than society's achievement; or so the artist felt. Aesthetic qualities, formal qualities, were nearer to becoming the ego-ideal which, according to my diagnosis, they in fact should be, since they have for their subject-matter the ego's integrative processes. An isolating of the aesthetic content had begun. A subject and its treatment in our own day may be comfortably, or uncomfortably and vulgarly, opposed, whereas in the past a theme might be tragic, petty, or bestial, but its treatment, that is to say, an evident selection in the presentation of incident, had to convey a sense of fitness to which formal qualities will have lent themselves. We now often rely on formal qualities alone for the communication of calm and integration, without any of the helps of conventional appropriateness from the subject. Our artists, then, may forego the air of generality imposed upon the prosaic, or of poetry, the reference to the characteristic, needed hitherto to join with qualities more specifically formal in epitomizing, in symbolizing, the impersonal image of corporeal wholeness and psychical integration. For this reason, not only the selection of subject-matter, but subject-matter itself, has appeared to be of less importance in the making of art; whereas in the past the connection of form and subject-matter through the medium of generalization or convention has always been the very hinge that connected values purely aesthetic and the cultural values that all art serves.

Today the cultural ideal is at best the value of aesthetic process stripped of the elaboration that precise cultural ideals in the past have inspired. We represent, so far as we represent, a non-ideal conception of our surroundings or situation, confused yet forceful. A harsh and often vulgar disclaimer may intervene betwixt an anti-ideal conception and the beauty of its treatment. Beauty, of course, abject beauty, still abounds, *luxe, calme et volupté*, even in contemporary art. It is true, though, in general to say that 'uplift' or sublimity gained from art, a reconciliation with cultural endeavour, with humanitarian judgement, the titillation of the super-ego, have been transformed into ego-ideal constructions, *tout court*, into manifestations of an aesthetic process through which an individual, as has the artist, may 'find himself'; into naked models of each kind of striving encounter with our objects. We have in common a complete lack of the iconographic symbols that once enabled the arts to build symbolic structures of an evident cultural ramification. Indeed the wish to cut out all the 'nonsense', to symbolize by art 'the inner man' alone, may be said to have reinforced the ambition to possess by means of art an object rather than the symbol for it, to have stimulated, then, the constant desire for the homogeneous state I have called 'is-ness', and so, an impatience with any symbol for it and therefore, in truth, with art itself, the very means by which it may be communicated through the symbolic representation of symbolic equivalence. Hence the vulgar strain in anti-art movements.

A further paradox follows. I have mentioned that in speaking of modern art we do not call much on the word 'imagination'. Indeed, we think of visions and hallucinations as forced upon the recipient, squeezed in, as it were, between his eye-lids by an outside agency or from the depths of his mind, rather than as an active construction of the image-making faculty. This means that for what we regard to be specifically imaginative we retain the sense of a projection whose contents are better related the further they are transposed into a fictitious context, whereas to visionary experience we attribute no intellectual artifice. Baudelaire based his criticism of pictorial Realism (Courbet) a hundred years ago on a not entirely dissimilar conception of the imaginative role. Nevertheless, Baudelaire, likewise the Symbolists who were his heirs, emphasized a visionary grasp of the Real in aesthetic comprehension; a grasp that enclosed an interchange of effects between the different arts themselves. One need have no such theory in order to say, as I have said, that a unitary or visionary quality with which we may identify ourselves has entered into the creation of all art: the Old Masters' building up of monumental treatment to form a varied experience, very often causes the visionary kernel to be the more magical, an illumination for much circumstance whereby also the spectator's adult ego is notably served and flattered.

With whom shall we contrast Tintoretto? The 'Douanier Rousseau's entire career was devoted to creating the universe of a grown-up child... He incarnates his universe by painting it exhaustively and palpably close.' There is 'a single mysterious lighting from all sides, shadowless, without highlights, without any power to dissolve colour' (Shattuck, 1959). Or 'he imagines a strongly lighted distance against which he silhouettes darker forms of tree and foliage... Usually two small figures focus the eye on the foreground. This same "dream picture" haunted him from the days of *Carnival Evening* to the last jungle picture he painted' (quoted in Shattuck, 1959).

Such sentences will call to mind the visionary experiences discussed in the last essay. Picasso's banquet for Henri Rousseau in 1908 was undoubtedly a most significant occasion in the history of the avant-garde. Rousseau's pictorial dreams, elaborated in quiet suburbs during an age of some security, crystallize the contribution to avant-garde art of the naïve, the bright, and particularly of an unswerving mildness or matter-of-factness in regard to them. It could be argued that this matter-of-factness, often employed for the presentation of even imperfectly induced visions, constitutes one of the characteristics of modern art, separating it from Delacroix's vast visionary exploits, from the last great artist to be taken up with the forging of grandeur. Any masterpiece of the imagination contrasts with a truly child-like matter-of-factness.

The bridge has long been built between what is considered to be child-like and what is considered to be primitive. Champfleury, the champion of Courbet in the 1850s, is quoted by Professor Schapiro as having written: 'The idol cut in the trunk of a tree by savages, is nearer to Michelangelo's Moses than most of the statues in the annual salons', because of a vividness in common, because of 'signs of a conception' paramount in children's drawings as Rodolphe Töpffer, the Swiss educationalist, remarked in a book of 1848 (Schapiro, 1941). Some interest, then, even in the middle of the nineteenth century, some respect, had begun to be paid to the art of the child and of the savage. Professor Schapiro points out that Courbet was influenced by naïve popular prints. We can easily see that Courbet's art, so revolutionary in that he was absorbed by aesthetic contemplation of his ordinary experience at the expense of the selectiveness or appropriateness to art which was still demanded, has a mindless, visionary quality: it causes the easy justice in his perception of tone, his extraordinary naturalism, to possess an air, unique for the time, of lack of contrivance. Courbet held some devices in contempt: he was accused of being clumsy, childish, mindless, of discovering 'everything in life and nature equally interesting', to quote a criticism in 1860 of the realistic novel (Boas, 1938). A contemporary critic of his *Young Woman on the Banks of the Seine* remarked that

446

their significance was no greater than that 'of two good white cows with russet markings' (quoted in Goldman, 1959). The very accuracy in the wide sweeps of Courbet's observation, allied to a visionary mildness extended equally to all parts of a painting, seemed to make his subject-matter of neutral and even of secondary importance. His matter-of-fact attitude to the nude was felt to be particularly unfeeling. Courbet, wrote Zola, 'had the rugged desire to clasp true life in his arms, he wanted to paint in a meat and potatoes way' (quoted in Goldman, 1959). In so doing he did not envisage as a rule, though he was reviled for left-wing sympathies, a parable of peasant life or of poverty, unlike Millet whose more revolutionary social consciousness cast his art into a trad-itional symbolic mould. Few of Courbet's works 'possess any humani-tarian fervour' (Goldman, 1959). It is easy to understand that the broad back of a 'message' serves in art of however recent a date, a similar role to the conscious cultural expressions undertaken by the art of the past. That is why Pissarro considered the transcendental symbolism, re-introduced in a modern idiom by Gauguin and Bernard, to be vulgar and reactionary.

The general reflection in all art, even modern art, of culture is an entirely different case of symbolism. To us it becomes obvious, very obvious, that the Impressionists painted, symbolized by their paintings, 'the good life of the resurgent middle-class', particularly those people as they took their Sunday pleasures. Among artists at work at that time, more than others the Impressionists were the spokesmen of a positive aspect in their age, not merely of a minor spirit in that age. Yet Philippe Burty, one of the earliest admirers of Impressionist painting, justly wrote: 'Man is really an object of interest by virtue of his existence as a fact, the most interesting of all objects, perhaps, but not essentially different from trees, clothes, or the sky.' Thoré, a very perceptive critic, wrote: 'Manet's... real vice is a sort of pantheism which values a head no more than a slipper; which sometimes even grants a greater importance to a bouquet of flowers than to the face of a woman' (quoted in Sloane, 1951). The word 'pantheism' is of interest to us in view of the vision we had in the last essay of a transporting and unitary chromatic world.

As in the case of Courbet, Realism could be equated by hostile critics with indifference, indifference not only to the object represented but to an acceptable balance of contrasts. An abstractedness, away from the particular object, is not far in the future.

We are at a sufficient distance occasionally to class the great antagonists, Delacroix and Ingres, together (though Baudelaire in 1855 classed Ingres and Courbet) since each was a champion of a narrow cause that piled the fires or cooled the metal of the past. The alternatives of dying traditions were giving less and less scope to the more evident compulsive or personal approach with which they were infused by those few artists who could still successfully improve upon them with stern exaggeration. The difficulty was greatest for the ordinary 'history' painters. 'The nobility of the second Empire, like that of the first, was largely improvised' (Boas, 1938). This once dominant theme ('history' painting) had long been dethroned, at any rate in Holland. Already in the eighteenth century other qualities in art than nobility had been more esteemed (Schapiro, 1954). As well as the Dutch, supporters of Courbet might invoke Caravaggio, Velázquez, Ribera, Chardin, the Le Nain, and Goya. The ordering of the world by art, we have seen, was now to be attributed to the act of the artist independently of any nobility afforded by selectiveness in subject-matter. The Old Masters were persuasive celebrants: modern art invites the communicant, not to share an established ritual, but to contemplate a personal process. It is perhaps more companionable, no more so than the sublime work of Rembrandt who sent his inner being to inhabit the twilight of the Grand Manner. But much of our painting has at least made it clearer that the artist's work must bear witness to the immediacy of outer objects by which we live, as well as to a system of unified parts in the self. Also, we have seen, there has entered some impatience with symbolic function in favour of original, unrelated states.

These are matters that do not figure specifically in artists' manifestos. It would even be a considerable mistake to suppose that either Courbet or Manet repudiated as such the wider symbolic functions of art. Courbet called his *Burial at Ornans* 'un tableau historique' and his

L'Atelier 'Allégorie Réelle', in competition with the old symbolic style. Manet's *The Dead Christ with Angels* was exhibited in the Salon of 1864; his *Execution of the Emperor Maximilian* was exactly a 'history' painting. What he felt about the incident will have appeared cool, translated into confronting patches of light and dark material at the expense of supporting anecdotal references. The implications – they would seem entirely unwitting – of any such treatment are more clearly understood in the case of Cézanne. His boyhood friend, Zola, was Manet's most influential supporter. The doctrine of art for art's sake was given in Zola's version by his famous phrase: 'A work of art is a corner of creation seen through a temperament' (quoted in Sloane, 1951). Courbet, he felt, no less than Manet, had set down without preconception his own impressions: the artist was taking a larger hand, were he Realist or Symbolist, in deciding on the very nature of *his* world: otherwise Zola's phrase would be equally applicable to the work of Raphael. More stability or reassurance, it was beginning to be felt, could be enjoyed in contemplating the artist's personal and non-rhetorical emotion than from his protestations however imaginative. Indeed, the very process of aesthetic contriving can be in evidence, at the same time as the painting or composition that results from it: what once would have been judged sketches were now paintings. We see today that the pictorial impact of Cézanne's monumental re-creation of objects in part depends on the concomitant inner adaptation that his re-created objects stabilize. 'The qualities of the represented things,' writes Meyer Schapiro in his book about Cézanne (1952), 'simple as they appear, are effected by means which make us conscious of the artist's sensations and meditative processes of work; the well-defined, closed objects are built up by a play of open, continuous and discontinuous, touches of colour. The coming into being of these objects through Cézanne's perceptions and constructive operations is more compelling to us than their meanings or relation to our desires, and evokes in us a deeper attention to the substance of the painting.' That is to say, to speak in the jargon I have used, we are very aware in his painting of a noble ego-integrative activity both in itself and in relation to objects, a prime subject-matter as I have

449

repeatedly said, of the formal element in every art.

Professor Schapiro continues: 'The marvel of Cézanne's classicism is that he is able to make his sensing, probing, doubting, finding activity a visible part of the painting and to endow this intimate, personal aspect with the same qualities of noble order as the world he has imaged. He externalizes his sensations without strong bias or self-assertion. The sensory element is equally vivid throughout and each stroke carries something of the freshness of a new sensation of nature. The subjective in his art is therefore no isolated capricious thing, but a manifestation of the same purity as the beautiful earth, mountains, fruit, and human forms he represents.'

'If I think, everything is lost,' wrote Cézanne. 'What was lost', Lawrence Gowing commented,

was the pure character of sensation: his whole preoccupation was with perception, and not with receiving only – his attitude was far from the passivity of the pure Impressionist – but with gathering and grasping. Every touch on his canvas adds a new segment to a composite definition, uninfluenced by any that went before. The only consistency is the consistency of sensation, the kinship of one observation with another, progressively evaluated by the meditative eye. Cézanne's method, as he once said, was 'hatred of the imaginative', and we can feel that the hatred extended to all that was implied in the derived, fictitious contour of the early works. A picture now showed not only form but the history of its perception: the process of representation was made visible. Painting had in fact become the positive, appreciable action which Cézanne sought, an act of self-possession fit to measure against the world. The artist is not inferior to nature; as he said, 'He is parallel with it, unless he deliberately intervenes'. (Gowing, 1954)

The reader may find in Cézanne's quoted remarks echoes of a visionary approach as I have described it. Far more significant was the utter devotion to Form's perennial symbolic content in regard to ego-integration, the process, it seems to me, that Schapiro and Gowing so ably recount in different ways. The freeing of this content, I would suggest, is the most valuable aspect of the art of our time. I have needed to stress also, however, the concurrent enlargement of symbolic representations of symbolic equivalence or concrete thinking. In this respect there is not, of course, a straight line of development stretching from Courbet, say, to the absurdities of Dada: at every point until this last, various syntheses attempt to weld bareness, immediacy, obscurity even, with the activities of the developed ego, and vice versa. Thus Gauguin, while he re-introduced a cult of transcendental symbolism, forcing upon his subject-matter generalized meanings other than the aesthetic, employed flat areas of brilliant hue in his paintings, which suggest the non-symbolic 'is-ness' of film colour. 'Beyond the head,' wrote Van Gogh to his brother about a portrait he was painting at Arles, 'instead of painting the banal wall of the mean room, I paint infinity, I make a plain background of the richest, intensest blue that I can contrive, and by this simple combination of the bright head against the rich blue background, I get a mysterious effect, like a star in the depth of the azure sky' (quoted in Schapiro, 1951).

I think it permissible to identify in one of its aspects the 'overallness', characteristic of so much modern painting, with the visionary stamp of 'is-ness'. This character was stabilized by the immense achievement of Seurat, though he was in every way the antithesis of a mindless painter. There has never been an artist who declared more vehemently a close connection between art and science, who held with greater fervour that everything in a painting should have resulted from the artist's thoughtful participation. No less than Holbein's should Seurat's work be thought the antithesis of Action Painting. Even the smallest of his divisionist paintings are monumental, accumulated, in prolonging a scene or events in a scene. Yet, while he gives painstaking self-inclusiveness to the objects he represents, the striking immediacy of the picture plane insists upon identity of all its parts, an emphasis not so much upon unity as upon oneness.

In discussing the course of modern art it is usual to give more attention than I have done to increasing uses of abstraction. I do not believe that the isolating, which has undoubtedly occurred, of aesthetic formal values, necessarily entails even partial rejection of contingent subject-matter or of its appearances. When I read that the Cubist painter Juan Gris wrote: 'It is not picture X that manages to correspond with my subject, but subject X that manages to correspond with my picture' (quoted in Kahnweiler, 1947); I am reminded that Flaubert, sometimes hailed as the greatest exponent of Realism, could protest that art was more real to him than the events in life. No: one difficulty about subject-matter, however dim or distorted its use, lies with a disturbance that particularization of object-character may bring to bear upon the experience of 'is-ness', upon an experience as well of many things that are yet felt totally to merge into one note.

But some of our most admired younger painters today, whose pictures to the casual glance appear to be total abstractions, repudiate this impression as entirely false. Such an artist claims that he cannot work without the conviction that his painting will be the equivalent, the strongly vibrating equivalent, though in no sense the mere representation, of an outer experience. Both experiences are, as it were, equal in authenticity, the secret experience that inspires the painting and the painting intended to inspire the beholder. The painting is not the symbol of the first experience nor its record: there is no uncertainty on this point: the word used is 'correspondence': the painting corresponds with the experience. This attitude appears to be a form of compromise imposed upon a predominantly 'is-ness' aim.

Few as they are in proportion to the data to be had on every side, I have given sufficient examples, and explained enough, the symbolic projection of symbolic equivalence in modern painting, a quality that, together with the formal values entailed in reconstructing the self and the object, have been cut clear by this art which so nakedly explores 'the inner man' amid cultures that are otherwise disrupted.

I have been using the term 'form' in an unavoidably loose way, to cover the many processes by which the work of art unifies factors for the pleasure of the senses and the mind; to denote, for instance, the symbolic reconciliation of three dimensions with the two of the picture plane, or of contrasted rhythms and movements, or of shapes that are likely to achieve balance in a way that depends upon other modes of reconciliation; to denote the absorption of accents into a whole, the stimulation of bodily as well as intellectual awareness to feel this wholeness; more generally, to denote the bringing together of different kinds and different levels of significance into a cluster: a conception of wholeness underlies every effect. Throughout these essays I have attributed to the aesthetic awareness of wholeness two opposite yet combined *nuances*, the one an experience of singleness or envelopment, the other a recognition of a reconstructed and independent object. The envelopment pull in graphic art, where it notably serves the 'is-ness' asseveration, the confusing of the symbol as of subject with object, I would now designate, perhaps surprisingly, the Pygmalion theme, in honour of the most vulgar of all parables about the nature of graphic art. The life-like statue comes in fact to life; the statue is the Woman; *trompe l'oeil*, symbolic equivalence, can do no more.

On the other hand, naturalistic art, though it incorporates, as does all graphic art, the Pygmalion theme, may honour better than conceptual or iconic styles an artifact's independence and self-sufficiency, as the result of a more 'objective' mode in observing the outer world, a mode wherein a place can be found in art for recording what is incidental. We have seen that, unlike mystical experience, aesthetic experience depends upon a fair modicum of a less appropriating appreciation of the outer world, in combination with the other attitude.

Having thus treated (in the context of graphic art) of two opposing *nuances* belonging to the effect gained from art, I must briefly restore each to the other. The secret of their combination must lie with the very structure of symbol-formation. According to Freud, the primary mental processes (observable in the analysis of dreams), mechanisms such as those of condensation, projection, and displacement, create, at this primitive level, equivalences between meanings that form a cluster of significance in which no one meaning appears to have precedence of another, as does an object have precedence of its symbols for normal

453

and developed consciousness. A grouping of significance, to some extent comparable, figures in art; the very roundness of the aesthetic cluster, even the symbolic reconstruction itself of whole and self-sufficient objects, the aesthetic entity separate from its creator, contains, from the process of its manufacture, more than a trace of the primitive habit of mind, which, while providing the genetic basis of symbol-formation, can be so subject to the paranoid-schizoid stress as to inhibit a continuing development therefrom of true symbolism: in art an outcome may be a symbolic projection of symbolic equivalence or concrete thinking whose poetry becomes disproportionate to an aesthetic end.

We have seen that important aspects of the nature of graphic art, pre-eminently this one, have been abstracted a little from the past and put on view in semi-isolation by our heroes of the avant-garde.

On Resignation

(1962)

Much of what figures below assumes the general submission, published in a previous essay, concerning the death instinct as the compulsion to refuse objects, correlative with Freud's characterisation of the libido as object seeking. In arguing that the self preservative drive *vis à vis* the environment must entail a prior attitude of defence *vis-à-vis* an inner danger, I asked the question: 'If the interests of survival that the ego will serve, conflict with those of immediate satisfaction, how is the ego developed from the id, unless there be at work in the id another and negative principle that causes survival to declare itself as an immediate aim: can the instinct of self-preservation be viewed satisfactorily without a partner who typifies danger?' I said in the conclusion: 'Freud showed that the Thanatos principle as a rule operates in a close fusion with Eros: masochism was his touchstone. I have found it necessary to imagine that in all life-giving and life-preserving responses there is mingled an impulse, however faint, of refusal... The sense of loss is thereby first seen as the libidinal response to an innate refusal. I think that from the beginning the impulse of refusal is felt within other instinctual responses and tends to increase them, as might a slowly departing train the response of a man who would catch it.'

A result of anxiety is sometimes a remarkable bent for calculation. I mean by this word a reckoning concerning gain that tends to strangle spontaneity. It is very important, let us say, to be liked for the purpose of advancement: then the people with whom the suitor negotiates appear to lose in his eyes all content other than the silhouette of a dangerous counter to be coaxed, manipulated. We must all manipulate objects to some extent, but not as a rule to the length I have in mind, at the cost of stultifying any other developed attitude towards them. The well-

455

adjusted person is free to be politic without the inhuman introduction of this deadness in his feeling that arises only in some situations of extreme danger or persecution; anxiety may then produce a deadness of feeling. I choose the word 'deadness' because in avid forms of calculated behaviour I see not only the libidinal response to any threat of loss, inner or outer, at root the threat of the death instinct, but an employment also of the death instinct's spoiling or depriving character. We tend to use (and thereby drain off) some of the drive towards devaluing the object, in the very anxiety we have for its preservation. In a word, the very richness and variety of the objects about which we are anxious may tend to be reduced, even eliminated, by the anxiety itself. I suggested in the previous paper that the threat of loss, or rather of our own refusal of the object, is the first persecution. But persecution is often less painful than depression: the going back, Melanie Klein has repeatedly shown, from the depressive to the paranoid is a paramount form of defence. As we ruthlessly calculate a gain, we may be restricting in that process, by means of a numb narrowing of the objective, a possible loss. Conversely, some states of not caring, not bothering, exhibit a different exertion of the same forces. What is most threatened is, *ipso facto*, what we value most. Both in the anxiety and in the defence against it, we canalise, it seems to me, within a preservative aim, the very drive to refuse and devalue that causes the 'irrational' part of our fear. There is often a supreme acuteness in a real loss as a result of an accident that could easily have been avoided: it appears to us to be gratuitously wasteful, perverse, since we identify so avoidable a loss with the action of the perverse (as it is felt) principle in ourselves. Either we seek to reduce its threat to the good or, as by envy, the value of what is esteemed: usually both mechanisms will be employed in the compulsion to outwit the total agony of loss. The self-punishment entailed in neurotic guilt, and in its often disastrous expiation, has been similarly constructed with a refusal component wherein a devaluation of the object is re-deflected on to the self, in the interests of preserving the object.

I have had the impression that some old people's interest in the newspaper, at any rate *The Times*, is mostly confined to the Births,

456

Marriages, and Deaths announcements; in truth, I think, to the Deaths alone. It is a shock, maybe in part a pleasing shock, to see there the name of a contemporary whom one has survived, at least for a couple of days: one might, it seems, have done worse. We usually think competitiveness has been inspired by the desire to safeguard or to extend one's interests, as well as to prove potency. In the case of the contemporary's death, in the kind of instance I have in mind, there is no question whatsoever of an effect on one's interests: in no sphere has there been occasion for competition other than in this context of mere survival. Whereas it is certain that the dead person conveniently stands for a sibling or for other people with whom there has been narrow rivalry, I think, even so, that satisfaction in the misfortunes of others who are unknown to us betrays a mark of the most inclusive, the purest, rivalry, of the rivalry, that is, in ourselves between the demands of life and of death, between a desire for what becomes the gainful and a desire for absence, nothingness. Naturally, the rival claims are fused; even the urgent libidinal responses, I have suggested, to danger, such as anxiety and excessive calculation, are coloured by a refusal tinge; something of the deadness, the inhumanity, the monotony, of refusal is combined in the greedy apprehension of a gain. The power of persecutory feelings is derived from the original threat of self-destruction that could have resulted from the successful refusal of objects. In surviving a contemporary we have proved to ourselves that we have outwitted for another day or so the 'perverse' refusal of the good or of life for which we are in fear. The death component is distributed to the deceased.

I have returned to this hazardous thought, to this talk of refusal rather than of prime aggression, in an attempt to contemplate an opposite process to the one of ruthless calculation, the process of resignation, a defence that in some context or other we are likely to employ. It is not my purpose to probe every kind of surrender, such as the surrender to persecutory objects. Although other forms of surrender cannot be isolated entirely from it, the resignation to which I refer is a condition we feel to be a considerable asset, inasmuch as, so far from impoverishing, it enriches life. By no means everyone has this course open to him:

I think the very possibility would be astonishing were it not admitted that there are basic elements in common, however differently adjusted, between the resigned and the extremely calculating or grasping or envious attitudes. I have already suggested that in a hyper-calculation, deadness or obstinacy of response under the stress of anxiety combines with a strong libidinal apprehension of gain. In the state of resignation, on the other hand, a partial neglect of calculated and anxious gain may tend to free more libido for an enjoyment of the moment: in such a case there will have supervened a nearer reconciliation with one's lot, the most outstanding feature of which is undoubtedly the approach of death, and a consequent change in the matter of anxiety. If anxiety be often compounded with our refusal tendency, then it seems that a degree of resignation to loss and to failing powers would tend to sub-tract from much anxiety a part of the refusal component, now devoted to an increased acceptance of absence and death: some anxiety has been split up, defused, and the components re-allotted: the libido may then be better attuned to a proper enjoyment of the time that remains.

We shall have found that a beloved place never looked so beautiful as at the moment we had to leave it, probably for ever. The house is sold, furniture removed, luggage packed; we sit in a silent house awaiting a taxi for our own removal, a situation of no more care, involvement, responsibility. To gaze at the garden is no longer to include in the impression our concern: the moment has come when the struggling flower or weed demonstrates fully a singular peace. All perfection is close to death: there abides no further call for attack, gainfulness, and reparation: the mother is complete; we have ceased to try to restore her; instead we contemplate. It appears now that she was always whole as well as untidy and in pieces.

Thus it is that the old may rediscover the useless brilliancy of a contemplative moment and, in recognising death, lighten the anxious shadow. If we allow to anxiety no component from the death instinct, if we do not admit a death instinct, a desire for absence and refusal, then the character of resignation, it seems to me, and the ease with which in some circumstances it may be assumed, remains an enigma.

Now in psycho-analysis, death is found to be inseparable from attack, on the combined parents, for instance, or on each other's genitals, inspired by the child. We have incorporated these, and many other warring members, who heap up strife in ourselves and the mounds of decay. Must a deep recognition, then, as opposed to a denial, of our own actual, forthcoming death mean in the depths of the mind a despair of putting matters right? Does the certainty of death entail the partial recognition, at any rate, of aggressors, persecutors, victims, as ultimate and entire victors? Should we describe resignation as a grudging surrender to the persecutor? I do not expect anyone to find in this common ingredient the only interpretation. The surrender with which, in the context of resignation, I am principally concerned, seems to entail peace rather than despair, an awareness of past fructification as well as of the decay that is the outcome. There is in our dying a complication in so far as we do not believe the good to be thereby vanquished and put out: imminent decease is not always able to spell out death to the good object; like the suicide we may die in its place; we may even die in the place of others and for all. Guilt, of course, is reduced, retaliation assuaged, by the punishment of dying. Yet I do not find an argument on these lines sufficient, though sound, to explain the serene state of resignation wherein there is the capacity both to live and eventually to die in accordance with the firm prospect of which the ageing body speaks. I would again advance the hypothesis of some freeing from other emotions of the refusal component, that is to say, from persecutory fusions, though I do not suggest that the deep acceptance of death to which I refer would necessarily abrogate to a large extent any of the other negative manifestations that have accumulated throughout life, and indeed are usually intensified as the years go by; nor would I confine the power of resignation to old age.

But perhaps you would prefer that I had spoken of an original or primary and pre-persecutory masochism. It seems to me that masochism, and sadism in like case – terms that commemorate two writers associated with those genital perversions to which, in psycho-analytic usage as well, their names widely refer – it seems to me that sadism and masochism, since they have never weakened in that common and older reference, have shown themselves by no means fruitful designations of pre-genital destructiveness; they are rightfully only the analogues. Melanie Klein has demonstrated very clearly, I think, that the primary fusions with destructiveness are to be described in terms of the oral origins of greed and envy, and that envy, destruction wished on goodness as such, is the most comprehensive of the threats to what is valued, not only in the object but subsequently in the ego.[1] I shall be bringing a quality of resignation, a pre-persecutory masochistic aspect, if you like, of this fusion, into close contrast with envy, but I do not want to suggest that even the most desirable forms of resignation will have dissipated the whole strength of the primary envy: much of it remains split off from the rest of the ego in the earliest days. Nor do I for a moment suggest that the old in general are not anxious or envious: it would be absurd, if only because the aged totter over a minefield of physical perils. But I suggest that such enjoyment and happiness as may be possible stem largely from mechanisms of resignation. Any reduction in the range of anxiety, however, probably goes hand in hand with a reduction of cathexis: libido withdraws, the world narrows. The old are often persecuted by pain or disabilities that stretch to a reduced horizon. We cannot look to the senile in mind as well as body to teach us much about resignation: the macabre, ungenerous competition of the obituary column would of itself warn us from doing so.

To whom, then, shall we turn? To some old people, of course; more generally to a stable generosity of temper at any time, to those who have assuaged, rather than denied, a portion of their envy, since, as well as anxiety, envy plays a large hand in stimulating extreme calculation. Much relief flows from the ability to reject the persecution, the tiresomeness, of a ceaseless watch whereby to prove that no one has done better than oneself. The price of liberty, we have been told, is constant vigilance, a transaction of first importance, unlike this other vigilance to see that no man is more than one's equal in natural endowment. The part of envy, I would suggest, of which, under favourable conditions, particularly those of advancing age, we may more easily be free, is the part lodged in the super-ego, characterized 'by the need it provokes for punishment', since 'to persecution are added the guilt feelings that the persecutory internal objects are the result of the individual's own envious and destructive impulses which have primarily spoilt the good object'.[2] With an onset of evident decay and with death's imminence, the call for self-punishment may diminish. The prime duty of resignation, thereupon, is to furbish this exemption so that we partly cease to envy the young and thereby to torture ourselves – our envy is itself felt as a persecution – though such pleasure as we have is the same as theirs. The resigned are somewhat like artists who, in making things, had best dispense – they rarely do – with worldly calculation and enviable distinction. A fresh mind, ear, eye, are means of creativeness, of the propensity most deplored by envy. No one gambles with his life more than the artist: the work of a year may be a total failure, the work of a subsequent half-hour of greater merit. The devoted artist tries not to count the cost: his only reward without sting should be a stimulus for more work, an absorption in the life and spontaneity of the moment.

Melanie Klein has written: 'The infant's longing for an inexhaustible and ever-present breast stems by no means only from a craving for food and from libidinal desires. For the urge even in the earliest stages to get constant evidence of the mother's love is fundamentally rooted in anxiety. The struggle between life and death instincts and the ensuing threat of annihilation of the self and of the object by destructive impulses are fundamental factors in the infant's initial relation to his mother. For his desires imply that the breast, and soon the mother, should do away with these destructive impulses and the pain of persecutory anxiety.'[3] This pronouncement is fundamental in Melanie Klein's thought. She does not envisage the root of conflict as being confined to the demands of competing libidinal aims or to the demands of the libido *vis-à-vis* self-preservation: following Freud in his last system, she regards self-preservation as part of libido, as the reverse of the ever-present threat of self-destruction, a threat that qualifies every aspect of cathexis as of anxiety and accounts for such primary fusions as those of greed and envy and extreme aggression.

I have been associating with envy the deadening quality of extreme calculation and of compulsive competition. I shall now be more concerned with envy alone in its contrast and consequent tie with resignation.

I find it significant that the revulsion from the possibility of nuclear warfare is not far, far greater. The wish is likely, though unspoken, that the world may cease with our own deaths. No good, of course, could come to ourselves from that destruction of all that is good. Whereas we want good objects to survive ourselves, part of us does not want to want. The refusal component of our feeling, unable to denigrate altogether the goodness of a good object, extends the range of refusal so as to be incumbent upon everyone: let no one else, says our envious part, have what we cannot have: in this way there can come about a no-goodness and a nothingness: but if anywhere, or at any time, there is gratification, then we are missing something. I think that frustration would not necessarily arouse envy were it not that one of the reactions to frustration is the wish for the poverty or death of the object that frustrates, *not out of aggression only, but so that the refusal of it should, from this poverty, be easy*. Indeed, in the absence of gratification, the desire for some catharsis of refusal here provides, if I am right, a mainspring for the aggression. 'The object which has been devalued need not be envied any more.'[4] Paradoxical as it may seem, I have suggested that excessive calculation of gain is likewise a method of devaluation, while at the same time an anxious mode in careful preservation and in the warding off of loss. We can now clearly see that a good object conceived to be held in common, of which everyone is thought to be the potential proprietor, controverts directly the good object denigrated by envy, since envy prefers that goodness be destroyed rather than shared with another, especially with the fount of the goodness. In our happiest states, then, there is goodness for all, peace in the family. This means that the inexhaustible good breast, just because it is illimitable, can without deprivation be shared, and can, in view of sharing, be proffered, as our own beneficent bestowal, to other objects, such as siblings, whom we feel we have deprived and attacked in aggression, greed, and envy. Thus we achieve a fine defence against the pains and persecution of envy if we hold fast to this shared good breast whose beneficent power, the very object of envy, we now ourselves dispense, while still receiving as well its food not only in our own right but from the return of gifts in such a brotherhood. Surely here, more than elsewhere, exists the strength of altruism and of all good causes. In the chapter of *The Ego and the Mechanisms of Defence* entitled 'A Form of Altruism', Anna Freud brought the concept of 'altruistic surrender' into relation with envy.[5] In *Group Psychology and the Analyst of the Ego*, Freud wrote: 'What appears later on in Society in the shape of *Gemeingeist, esprit de corps*, "group spirit", etc., does not belie its derivation from what was originally envy.'[6] Subsequently, Melanie Klein has shown that envy is most painful because the good object is extremely dear to us, and it is of its very goodness that we have in the first place been envious. There will be no relief from envy, no possibility of a fruitful resignation, without a firm love towards a good object. 'Such an attitude,' she writes, 'which includes gratitude for pleasures of the past and enjoyment of what the present can give, expresses itself in serenity. In old people, it makes possible the adaptation to the knowledge that youth cannot be regained and enables them to take pleasure and interest in the lives of young people. The well-known fact that parents relive in their children and grandchildren their own lives – if this is not an expression of excessive possessiveness and deflected ambition – illustrates what I am trying to convey. Those who feel that they have had a share in the experience and pleasures of life are much more able to believe in the continuity of life. Such capacity for resignation without undue bitterness and yet keeping the power of enjoyment alive has its roots in infancy and depends on how far the baby has been able to enjoy the breast without excessively envying the mother for its possession. I suggest that the happiness experienced in infancy and the love for the good object which enriches the personality underlie the capacity for enjoyment and sublimation, and still make themselves felt in old age... All this is felt by the envious person as something he can never attain because he can never be satisfied, and therefore his envy is reinforced.'[7]

Where belief in the good object is stable, the very springs of envy may be used to enlarge anti-envious participations; moreover, in the process of resignation, I have suggested, a measure of defusion and re-allotment is evolved from the libidinal and destructive or refusing components that altogether characterise envy and make some appearance in much anxiety. A benign resignation, in which gratitude plays a part, would then be the obverse of envy and hyper-calculation, the other face of the self-same coin.

The complement of a persecuting object will often be an over-idealised object:[8] the saints stand ever on the brink of hell as of heaven. If we often observe in the looks of monks and nuns a considerable serenity, we may infer that a degree of persecution has been courted to expiate not only guilt but envy; it is preferable to be persecuted by envious feeling incorporated into the super-ego where it becomes envious of the ego's capacity for constructiveness and a many-sided happiness, rather than to be at the mercy of envy *tout court*, destructive, that is, towards the good object as such. I want to stress the very strong presence of the shared good object, over-idealised though it be, in any happy religious community; a strange companion, it seems at times, to super-ego severity. Every Catholic nun is wedded to Christ, every priest re-establishes the divine body in celebrating the Mass. The Virgin and Christ play a larger role in Catholicism today than does the patriarchal and oedipal God the Father: emissaries though they be of the Father, there is implicit in the Virgin and her Son a far softer note. Surely we cannot doubt that in the psychopathology of any religion with a universal claim, the shared, idealised breast plays as large, even a greater, part than do the oedipal parents, especially in regard to the defence against envy. Even those who attend church in order to exercise an invidious good form may be joining from moment to moment in what purports to be an anti-envy communion through the sharing of the good object.

In view of the illimitable character of the good breast, it is sometimes difficult to distinguish it from the idealised breast of a less stable origin. When based on the idealised aspect alone of the good object,

464

no resignation or serenity is firm. Melanie Klein, however, has also said that the distinction cannot be considered absolute:[9] and who can feel he has put behind him all illusions? Even posterity, perhaps posterity chiefly, is misinformed: a great part of the truth of even external events never comes out, yet many of us manage to believe that in the end justice will be done, though we reject the Last Judgement. Moreover there is no ultimate future for the illimitable good object: our descendants and mankind, with every memory and every good object, will sooner or later be wiped out. Now, idealism is designed to match an equally potent persecution; therefore it will contrive to rationalise (and perhaps even to applaud, in the manner of some Chinese Communists, so it has been said, the prospect of nuclear warfare) any disaster and destructiveness however great, whereas the owner of the unidealized good object demands a contingent goodness. Yet we must always behave as if a *raison d'être* exists, continue to scheme as if there were a final goal of the good. We elderly people will go on selling our wares, scheming for offspring, supporting a good object esteemed in common, a defence, we have seen, against envy, of more than one facet. No one claims for himself alone cliffs and sea, though they provide an experience that at the time depends upon the absence of a crowd. While it is a projection of the individual good object, our pleasure in Nature, as in art, joins us with an illimitable good object, with a fine aspect of being in general. But better than a religious devotion, love of the untouched place, of the hedgerow, of the rocks, exploits the attachment to the outside whole object as well. We gain health, refreshment, from a contemplation of natural things removed entirely from the sphere of our envy: they are, as it were, powerful people with whom we miraculously entertain a rapport that eludes jealousy, envy, and competition. Here is the mother in her own ways, sufficient for the time.

As I have said, it seems incontrovertible that the illimitable breast inspires the good cause held in common, and that altruism is a defence possessing deep roots in ground other than the stony soil of the reality principle. Moreover, the identification so necessary for making common cause has a history that dates back to the infant with the breast. But there is the phrase 'the human predicament': it has force. For me 'the human predicament' arises when a sane man with a fine trust in a good, unidealised object, is incapacitated by loss or disability or pain. I have argued that proper resignation entails an enjoyment of the moment under the roof of the good object. Obviously it applies but little in such a case, perhaps far less so than where there exists the prop of a religious resignation founded upon an idealised object that has carefully measured and matched all the conditions of persecution. If we are truly persecuted, can we be truly sane? Freud himself, not in this case his thought alone, is here a mentor and example.

I have been gradually brought back to the widest sense of the first theme in this paper; I refer to the element of acceptance of limitation at all times, acceptance of one's lot, originally an acceptance of objects, of people, as being other than oneself. We have learnt that the mother, and thereupon Nature, is subject to her own laws: the fixed aspect of outside substances has tempered to some extent the ceaseless divisions and alternations of the inner world, has qualified the shapeless ease of excessive projection and introjection. An acceptance, however partial, of the reality principle will have been prepared by the economics of emotion: in accepting, so far as we are able, hard realities, hard conditions, we may counteract some bitterness, gain a measure of reassurance from the curtailment of omnipotent powers (by the exercise of which we have assumed plentiful guilt and pain), even though we be persecuted also by hard conditions (felt to be retaliatory). Nevertheless, it seems to me that this power to accept limitation requires the hypothesis of an innate capacity for refusal, for instance in the case of the acceptance of substitutes in the place of original objects, the mechanism upon which all the richness of human development, of culture and civilisation, depends. I know that the repression of primary aims in regard to the original objects is forced on us by the anguish involved in aspects so strongly positive and negative: but how do we come partly to accept in their place, prudent though it be, diffusions and reflections while at the same time, the conservative drive, as conceived by Freud, reinforces retention and fixation? I would define acceptance as a state wherein feelings of frustration are secondary to a reassurance gained from the certainty of a degree of settled status *vis-à-vis* objects, from submitting to the painful joining of the bad with the good, a prerequisite of ego integration, yet assimilated, none the less, with trust in the beneficent breast. A measure of acceptance, as of resignation, a capacity to diminish, at least, some splitting and denial, figures largely in the psychological condition we call adult: it figures in the homage we pay to reason and reality, in the pursuit of science; it belongs to the ability to recognise the independence of the outside world, a necessity of our living but also a signpost to our death.

I am suggesting that in all the processes of integration and in a respect for reality and reason the capacity for refusal has helped to bring about a condition of acceptance of what is, even of our own eventual annihilation, the fear concerning which, as an immediate threat, underlay the primary splitting. (Defence by means of fragmentation works through an anti-linking that surely enlists the refusal drive, as did the so-called Moslems of the concentration camps, those who ceased largely to respond, even to food.) And I am suggesting that the negative force, required for these constructive roles, may to some small extent from time to time be switched from reinforcing splitting, anxiety, persecution, hate, and, above all in the matter of a fine resignation, envy. The stability of an eventual realignment will, of course, depend upon no more than a moderate congenital negative threat – otherwise splitting will have been too drastic – and upon the consequent history of ego defence that may be re-lived, and thereby revised, in the course of successful psycho-analysis.

Living in Ticino, 1947–50

(1964)

The storm had been immense along the line. I was soaked at Genoa
running thirty yards in the open to the platform for the Ventimiglia
train. When I got out at San Remo the sky had cleared, but the wind
remained in the south: the sea was pounding. I had a room high in the
hotel, with windows on two sides, at the angle of the building, I opened
all windows, let in the sea noise from just beyond the railway below.
Since the St. Ives days I had scarcely heard the sea. As if purged by its
movement, the main street – it was a very dark night – seemed still and
decorous and the young people about, calm, serene; Italians again,
outdoor figures of sky and earth. Observed in the subdued light from a
café opposite, the closed casino looked simple and uncrowded, particularly the shops built in below the upper carriage-way. I drank beer,
gazing at the retiring, discreet flashiness of this building, an impression
no doubt assisted by night. After the journey it stood for a degree of
stability and comfort: rain and movement were cleared: this steadfast
yet opulent white took possession. How different back in my room with
the pounding sea. On leaving the café I had tried to approach the sea
and I found myself in a desolate and incomplete place as if half-built,
bombed or bashed by waves. It was impossible to see the ground distinctly. I had to go back, picking very carefully the way I had come.
Up in my room above the sea again, the shutters of one window were
banging. I closed the window and then, when I got into bed, fastened
the others as the draught was too great, shutting out the sea subject to
a constant sirocco such as I had often seen and heard for days on end at
Rapallo just beyond Genoa. I had often watched from the side the exact
speed of the waves as they came into the bay. Rain would be pelting on
the ever-bright tumult of the craning tenements in Genoa itself.

As this memory faded I felt the calm of my tempestuous life to be a symbol of the mind, president to the speechless deliberations of the passions beyond the windows.

In art and architecture our eyes follow a design, an externalization of primitive force and of primitive attachment by means of a stable form. One day the artist will occupy the philosopher's throne: not the artist as we generally conceive him, no less compulsive than the mystic... One day men will learn to think of sanity as an aesthetic achievement.

We travel emotional distances, carrying the same inexhaustible luggage. As I lay on the white bed I took pleasure in a life-process that I could project into the sea and into calm buildings that range the coast lashed by rain, into the nearness of the measured, Mediterranean interval and the warmth of the inhabitants who absorb it, who appear spurred by the very extension of the external world. It is our own powers that stretch, our own experience that seems never-ending.

I was happy that reason tapers as a tower above the sea.

The rain falls, trees stand up. The sound of steady rain on leaves makes the image hold. The skies are grey, trees the greener, glistening with wet. Throughout a day of rainfall the standing up of the trees or of dripping houses, colours action and thought so that whatever is dry yet perpendicular, such as umbrellas in a stand, seems to lack benison or contact, to have become less definite or positioned, tending to float, to be emanations of a wall that is itself less ordered owing to the pre-dominance of the chords of water between sky and earth; owing to this boundless, loose-stringed harp with a complex sound of melting over-tones. Change is only of the volume of the sound... The earth receives: the giant capacity of reception mocks fires as restless.

As I walk under the arcade of Locarno's main square, I see in a clear and liquid shade a café table with a light-blue cloth that touches a stone pier. I think I would be entirely safe there: leaning against the pillar I would be able to partake utterly of every thought: I would be immobile, provided for, as in the womb yet out-of-doors: existence within and existence without would be thinly divided: in the blue tablecloth I would clutch the sky.

To explain anything we go back.

Berenson has not realized that what he calls 'lack of skill' is, in many cultural contexts, 'lack of will'. Sickert too, when he writes that Cézanne was a bungler who couldn't get the eyes in a portrait 'to go together'. He couldn't try to: he was putting *bits* together.

Particularly from art there is often gained a haunting quality as from a naked body glimpsed through trees, from an experience that at the time was noted anatomically or in terms of indecency but that proved to be a minute incident returning in a dream, in dreams, a circumstance widely evocative.

That which arrests us in a painting will not continue to do so unless it contains a structure that evokes or fits in with some aspect of what is permanent in many states of mind, in all our various relationships with objects.

When passion recedes, some are apt to turn to thoughts of dross, conceiving the dirt and filth of the physical to be the real 'reality' of the body, substituting one set of fantasies with another. Reality, like death, has no corresponding 'feel' to it: whereas the pursuit of science, the contemplation of what science reveals, has a strong emotional side, truth itself resembles numbers to which, were it possible, no association and no images are attached. In attempting to grasp what is real, we are unable altogether to disentangle emotion. This consideration must be the modern version of appearance and the *Ding-an-sich*.

An oak tree is the leg of the beloved corrugated with arteries and veins, fluted with the scaffolding of growth.

I believe we regret a loss of mass as may happen on a journey in mistaking a line of cloud for a range of mountains. I have had this acute disappointment several times, especially at sunset in India. Works of

470

art attempt to repair such a loss, the loss of the mother's body that takes over, banishes yet incorporates, a final distance.

In the imagery of music a bald head has more shape, takes longer to go over, to explore, than one of bewitching curls.

A church clock striking the hour parcels out the disordered noises of a town, submits to our reckoning the tenor of reason. The broad and easy flatness of such comprehension is like a fine wooden floor in a house set high over a town, as I had it once in Venice and again in Ascona.

The bells, in perspective of sound, proclaim the unity and calm of all visual things. Under the influence of a Sunday morning in the sun, I am reminded by the spread of the plain, by the small clusters of communities, by Locarno between lake and mountain, climbing the bright aromatic hill, by villages in Switzerland and in Italy disposed glistening upon the points above the lake, by bells near and distant, I am reminded of Athens and the early Rome, so vivid once from afar.

I was clearing up at Lower Stonehams, throwing away, making a clean sweep of more than rubbish there. I thought as I worked of the thirty years' accumulation of family emotion that I seemingly dispersed. My parents would never again come into the house: it was as if it reverted to the former owners (who had taken so much more care of it) of thirty years ago. Traces of our occupation were disappearing fast; many symbols of absence came together: the experience was painful, confused, and discoloured by a rush of time. I went finally into the garden where this mental state was shaped and limited by taking on the character of a thing. For, in the quietness of Saturday lunchtime, the gardener had left burning a steady bonfire that smouldered easily. It simplified the confused feelings I had felt in the house concerning 'the clean sweep'. But the spectacle was itself appealing because of the intense, directed and simple action it contained... Such is a work of art *vis-à-vis* emotion. I was grateful for this bonfire as if to a remaining, administering person. It performed a ritual I felt was needed: I took pleasure in the palpable image outside me of all I felt: *it*, a concrete form, was my feelings, yet calm, noble, wrapt and also more vivid than they, without the confusion or successiveness of feelings: it was new and disinterested. I had here both the essence of what I had felt and a renewal of love for an object.

The ego gains some safety through projection and then through the act of perception characterized, as we know, by orderliness or *Gestalt*. It seems that in this, the external world performs a constant role: we call it art only in those cases in which it is induced deliberately. Of course the reverse process is no less ceaseless; an aspect of the external world seen in contemplation, excites thereby associations with feelings that do not necessarily correspond with any call for action. In fact we contemplate mental states themselves only after we have endowed them with some of the definition of perceptual experience.

There is no need, therefore, to offer any special explanation for the projection of id content in art: aesthetic figuration is but a refinement of one that is far more general: nor is it remarkable that the creation of symbolism should be uppermost when questions of action in regard to the external world are in abeyance. It is more significant that symbolism permeates even the weapons for thinking, irradiates language even when language attempts most to be matter-of-fact.

Consciousness is like the unseen air surrounding us with light. Unknown to us, each sensation is qualified by every other sensation we have experienced.

We are more prone to attribute texture to a clear light than to the palpable pall of a fog.

As well as a need for some beauty, many people have a penchant for ugliness. Art is 'a criticism of life' in the sense that it is a criticism of denials; to which ugliness may be preferred, symbolized by the uncritical dog with his grown-up teeth and snarl, his unequivocal bark that is so much worse than his bite. Philistines, especially, escape: they keep to 'brass tacks' at the expense of the gold and the filth and unadorned hostility. Ugliness is, in fact, a form of culture.

Pleasure is a lighthouse flash seen across empty wastes encompassed by the sense of loss. At a death bed there is a holding of hands, the hand of any one: though we die the good object must be preserved. This concern for the object cannot be explained entirely by viewing it as a part, the good part, of ourselves. We can learn from art that there is a strong emphasis upon the status of the object as object: on the formal side it is both ourselves and not ourselves.

An area of significant space is a substitute for blind, narrow intensity.

Meals preserve a ritual, and culture an extension of the totem feast: culture is identified with the good breast and the incorproration of a self-contained mother as well as with an incorporation of what has been violently done away with: the massacre may be repeated in the appreciation: aspects of popular culture or proto-culture suggest it.

The nude is the absolute of nakedness, all too quickly attained.

The history of drugs reveals longing for the choicer monolithic states of infancy, for an undivided world that will contrast with the functioning of an analytic mind.

A gross Edwardian bowl becomes in the course of time more than an object of vulgarity: every year endows it with further independence, so that we see it more as the product of a certain kind of society than as the echo only of that society's pretension: we are then aware of a symbol's evocative power as well as of the specific content symbolized which, in turn, we begin to value.

The Invitation in Art

From *The Invitation in Art* (1966)

Since the time, nearly fifty years ago, that Marcel Duchamp sent to an exhibition in New York a porcelain urinal (described as a fountain) with the signature of the manufacturer that he, Duchamp, had attached in his own writing, we have had an excellent occasion with which to associate new reflections upon the values of art. We realize that adepts at scanning an object for the less immediate significance of its shape, a manner of looking at things that has been cultivated from looking at art, will contemplate a multitude of objects, and certainly, in an august setting, the regular curves and patterns of light on that porcelain object, with aesthetic prepossessions. With less thought for the object's function than for its patterns and shape, we project on to them a significance learned from many pictures and sculptures. But are we projecting separate experiences of art; are we not projecting an aspect of ourselves that has always been identified with them; and is not the identification an integral factor, therefore, of aesthetic experience and an aim for art? This has seemed even more likely since psycho-analysis uncovered a mechanism called projective identification by which parts of ourselves or of our inner objects may be attributed even to outside objects that, unlike artifacts, at first sight seem inappropriate for their reception. It is possibly in this manner as well that we might discover ourselves to be assimilated in an active aesthetic transformation of the urinal, an object that does not itself communicate to us with the eloquence of art. We, the spectators, do all the art-work in such a case, except for the isolating of the object by the artist for our attention.

Structure is ever a concern of art and must necessarily be seen as symbolic, symbolic of emotional patterns, of the psyche's organization with which we are totally involved. This reference of the outer to the inner has been much sharpened by psycho-analysis, which tells, for instance, of parts of the self that are with difficulty allied, that tend to be split off, and of internal figures or objects that the self has incorporated, with which it is in constant communication or forcible ex-communication. Pattern and the making of wholes are of immense psychical significance in a precise way, even apart from the drive towards repairing what we have damaged or destroyed outside ourselves.

In distinction from projections that ensue upon any perceiving, aesthetic projection, then, contains a heightened concern with structure. The contemplation of many works of art has taught us this habit. I think it is so strong only because in every instance of art we receive a persuasive invitation, of which I shall write in a moment, to participate more closely. In this situation we experience fully a correlation between the inner and the outer world which is manifestly structured (the artist insists). And so, the learned response to that invitation is the aesthetic way of looking at an object. Whereas for this context it is simpler to speak of structure, of formal relations, such a presentation is far too narrow. Communication by means of precise images obtains similarly in art a wider reference whenever the artist has created for the experience he describes an imagery to transcend it, to embrace parallel kinds of experience that can be sensed. Poetic analogy or image is apt; felicitous overtones coexist; the musical aptness of expression hazards wider conjunctions than those immediately in mind.

In visual art, too, we see without difficulty that form and representation enlarge each other's range of reference. Similarly, the same formal elements are used to construct more than one system of relationship within a painting itself, and with us who look at it. Whatever the total meaning, the perennial aspect reveals a heightened close connection between sensation significance, that is to say, impact on the perceiving instrument as it organizes the data, and more purely mental content that we then apprehend in the outside terms of sensation significance.

Referring to the character of perception, I have in mind what might be called the prejudices of vision uncovered by psychologists. I take these 'prejudices' to be an important link between the outer world and the empathic projection thereon, in ordinary and in aesthetic perception alike, of inner process. The 'forces' uncovered by the psychology of vision provide the words, the language of visual art. Whereas wide disagreement exists among psychologists as to the way that the visual world is perceived or constructed, none would deny, I believe, that the perceiver participates in what might be called the quandary of units of the visual field, which do not, or do not easily, achieve restful status. Thus, there is tension in any perceived obliquity, in any departure from an open framework: there is pull, direction, the sense of weight and movement. Even a vertical ellipse strives upward in the top half, downward in the lower. A vertical line seems to be far longer than a horizontal line of equal length; and so on. Such forces, such bents, I repeat, are the words, the language, of visual art. Not only are their implications of direction, compression, weight, pull, interference, employed by the painter to communicate the sentiment of a pictorial subject-matter, but they mirror, in their inter-working, the power that one part of the self, or one inner object, can exert over the others. Indeed, I hope it is not an outrageous conjecture concerning perception to say that stereotypes for psychical tension may be projected thereby, and that these projections in some part may have reinforced the perceptual bents to which I am referring. In any case, whether or not immured biologically in perception, internal situations remark themselves therein. We are dynamically implicated with visual stress, particularly with the enveloping use that art makes of it. When the final balancing, the whole that is made up of interacting parts, is suspended for a time by the irregularities of stresses, these same stresses appear to gain an overwhelming, blurring, and unitary action inasmuch as the parts of a composition are thereby overrun, and inasmuch as the spectator's close participation, as if with part-objects, removes distance between him and this seeming process. Much of the attraction of the sketch lies in this situation, which arises also whenever we think we find the artist at work, in his calligraphy or flourish, his gesture or touch, and, even more generally, in the accentuations of style. I have particularly in

476

mind the extreme example of Baroque paintings with a diagonal recession, invaded by a represented illumination, cast diagonally, that
cuts across figures, that binds the composition as a movement of masses,
without respect for integrity of parts of the scene, of distinct figures,
voids and substances. A principle, a process at work, seems to override
the parts. It is one aspect of the 'painterly' concept formulated by
Wölfflin, in which values of what some psychologists have called 'the
visual field' dominate certain values in 'the visual world' of ordinary,
everyday, perception. We very often associate creativeness first of all
with an ability to disregard an order elsewhere obtained, to ignore an
itch for finality in favour of a harder-won integration whose image may
still suggest an overwhelming process, no less than its integration with
other elements.

Hence the invitation in art, the invitation to identify empathetically,
a vehemence beyond an identification with realized structure, that
largely lies, we shall see more fully, in a work's suggestion of a process
in train, of transcending stress, with which we may immerse ourselves,
though it lies also in that capacious yet keen bent for aptness, for the
embracing as a singleness of more than one content, of one mode for
'reading' the elements of its construction, to which I have already referred in regard to form and image. Though they always have the strong
quality of co-ordinated objects on their own, the world's artifacts tend
to bring right up to the eyes the suggestion of procedures that reduce
the sense of their particularity and difference; even, in part, the difference between you and them, though the state with which a work is
manifestly concerned be the coming of the rains, or redemption and
damnation, or the long dominance of the dead. Most painting styles
are what we call conceptual: objects are rendered under conformity to
an idea of their genus, to hierarchic conceptions (with a comparative
neglect of individual attributes and changing appearances) favouring
the power to lure us into an easy identification with an expression of
attitude or mood. The depicting of incident thus receives a somewhat
timeless imprint, offers a relationship that at first glance saps the symbolism of an existence completely separate from ourselves. As we merge

with such an object, some of the sharpness that is present when differentiation of the inner from the outer world is more accentuated, the sharpness and multiplicity of the introjectory-projectory processes, are at first minimized. Yet I shall note, on the other hand, that under the spell of this enveloping pull, the object's otherness, and its representation of otherness, are the more poignantly grasped. But I want also to stress the opposite point by indicating in naturalistic styles, which boast far greater representation of the particular and of the incidental, that these works, if they are to be judged art, must retain, and indeed must employ more industriously, procedures to qualify the intimation of particularity, to counter the strong impression of events entirely foreign to oneself by an impression of an envelopment that embraces distinctiveness.

I now call the envelopment factor in art – this *compelling* invitation to identify – the incantatory process. I have often written of it, principally in terms of part-object relationship, particularly of the prime enveloping relationship to the breast where the work of art stands for the breast. I adopt the word 'incantatory' to suggest the empathic, identificatory, pull upon adepts, so that they are enrolled by the formal procedures, at any rate, and then absorbed to some extent into the subject-matter on show, a relationship through whose power each content in the work of art can be deeply communicated. I shall try to indicate further methods and characteristics of visual art whereby the incantatory process comes into being. I believe that much formal structure has this employment, beside entirely other employment, and that a part of the total content to be communicated is often centred upon unitary or transcending relationships, though they contrast with the work's co-ordination between its differing components, this, another content no less primary, whereby the integration of the ego's opposing facets and the restored, independent object can be symbolized. I believe that the incantatory quality results from the equation enlisted between the process of heightened perception by which the willing spectator 'reads' a work of art – often with a difficulty of which the artist makes use to rivet attention to his patterns – and inner as well as physical processes; an equation constructed or reinforced by at least an aspect of the formal treatment that encourages the sense of a process in action. There is vitality in common that suggests a unitary relationship, as if the artifact were a part-object.

I shall continue to touch on a few manifest elements in the case of naturalistic art. For it goes without saying that dance, song, rhythm, alliteration, rhyme, lend themselves to, or create, an incantatory process, a unitary involvement, an elation if you will. Thus when I wrote of this matter in 1951, I did so in terms of the manic. During the next year, 1952, there appeared in the *International Journal of Psycho-Analysis* Marion Milner's paper, renamed in the Melanie Klein Symposium of 1955, 'The Role of Illusion in Symbol Formation', where, not only in matters of art, she emphasized a state of oneness as a necessary step in the apprehension of twoness. Her key-word here is 'ecstasy' rather than 'part-object'. Her paper derived partly from ideas she had already put forward in her book *On Not Being Able to Paint* (Milner, 1950).

Of the principal aesthetic effects an incantatory element is easiest grasped. By 'grasp' I refer also to being joined, enveloped, with the aesthetic object. But whereas we easily experience the pull of pleasant, poetic, pictorial subject-matter – classical idylls, *fêtes champêtres*, and so on – there is not so much readiness to appreciate the perennial existence of a wider incantation that permeates pictorial formal language whatever the subject or type of picture. Similarly a poem, like a picture, properly appreciated, stands away from us as an object on its own, but the poetry that has gripped, the poetry of which it is composed, when read as an unfolding process, combines with corresponding processes in a reader who lends himself. Therefore my description is the incantatory process, since I feel that all art describes processes by which we find ourselves to some extent carried away, and that our identification with them will have been essential to the subsequent contemplation of the work of art as an image not only of an independent and completed object but of the ego's integration. Since, as a totality, it is an identification with the good breast, I have often submitted that the identification with processes that are thought of as in train allows a sense of nurture

to be enjoyed from works of art, even while we view them predominantly in the light of their self-sufficiency as restored, whole objects,
a value that thereby we are better prepared to absorb.

The first power that the work of art has over us, then, arises from
the successful invitation to enjoy relationship with delineated processes
that enliven our own, to enjoy subsequently as a nourishment our own
corresponding processes, chiefly, it appears to me, the relationships
between the ego and its objects, though concurrently the unitary power,
inseparable from part-object relationship, that transcends or denies
division and differences. To take the instance once more of this last
relationship from painting, Light and space-extension can be employed
to override each particularity in favour of a homogeneity with which
we ourselves are enveloped. And so, such effects in the picture – their
variety is vast – construct an enveloping *mise-en-scène* for those processes
in ourselves that are evoked by the picture's other connotations.

It is easily agreed that pictorial composition induces images of inner
process as we follow delineated rhythms, movements, directions with
their counter-directions, contrasts or affinities of shape with their
attendant voids, as well as the often precarious balancing of masses.
Predominant accents do not achieve settlement without the help of
other, and perhaps contrary, references: hence the immanent vitality,
and a variety of possible approaches in analysing a composition; hence
the ambiguity, in the sense of an oscillation of attention, that others
have noted in the interweaving of poetic images. It may be thought that
this will hardly apply to the representation of balance between static
physical forms as opposed to the representation, in which naturalistic
art excels, of movement or of stress and strain. Such immobility, however, often involves a sense of dragging weight, of the curving or swelling of a contour with which we deeply concern ourselves, since we take
enormous pleasure, where good drawing makes it profitable, in feeling
our way, in crawling, as it were, over a represented volume articulated
to this end; many modes of draughtsmanship, or of modelling, may
invite a very primitive and even blind, form of exploration. In one of
their aspects, too, relationships of colour and of texture elicit from us

the same sense of process, of development, of a form growing from another or entering and folding up into it. And, as I have said, we find ourselves traversing represented distances, perhaps enveloped by an overpowering diffusion of light. Finally architecture, possessor of many bodily references, mirrors a dynamic or evolving process as well as the fact of construction.

It is necessary to repeat that the unitary relationship between ourselves and on-going processes represented by the aesthetic object contrasts with the integration of its parts, for which we value it as a model of a whole and separate reconstituted object. In a combination that art offers, we find a record of predominant modes of relationship, to part-objects as well as to whole objects.

I want now to remark an aspect of visual art connected with what I have called the quandaries and prejudices of visual experience that provide the possibility of a stressed language. One exploitation of these quandaries lends itself to catharsis of aggression, even of a mutilating urge that, paradoxically, is sometimes more characteristic of naturalistic art than of any other. Extreme foreshortening has been described by Arnheim (1956) as 'contraction, like a charged spring'. He also speaks, not altogether without justice, of 'the rearrangement of organic parts through projective overlapping – hands sprouting from behind the head, ears attached to the chin, knees adjoining the chest. Even the most daring modern artists have rarely matched the paradoxical reshuffling of the human limbs that has been presented as an accurate imitation of nature', doing violence to simple patterns of structure, a desired norm – it is sometimes thought – for vision.

It may be useful to specify for a moment, if only with a handful of examples.

I refer very briefly to the place of the unitary breast principle in proto-Renaissance and early Renaissance naturalism. John White (1957) has described a 'growing tendency to move from the idea of things surrounded by space towards that of space enclosing and uniting things' in much art of fourteenth-century Florence and Siena. The representing of space would much later become wholly an enveloping agent, sometimes an aggressive scoop to carry us into distance, to go far beyond the canvas. But earlier, in the proto-perspective space bedecked or jewelled by Giotto, Duccio, and the Lorenzetti, there exists no such manipulation or destruction of the picture surface. Moreover, at the very same time that geometric perspective was institutionalized as a cult in the first half of the fifteenth century, there came about at the hands of those who worshipped there, particularly Piero's, a supreme use of colour, an echo between forms and intervals, whereby an equality for each shape, a lack of emphasis throughout the patterning, preserved a unified complexity of picture plane: a miraculous solution of conflicting data, perceptual and psychical, and hence of picture-making. Piero's own books reveal that he estimated perspective not at all for the new power at the artist's command of *trompe l'oeil*, but for the extension of harmony and proportion, of the laws of optics, and, indeed, of a mathematically ordained universe to be learned now fully from the image, the painting, no less than from visual experience of which it served as an image.

Thereafter, overpowering uses for perspective have sometimes been developed. Similarly, though little apparent until much later, from the time of Leonardo there has been some breaking down of the constancies that characterize the visual world, by means of the full employment of chiaroscuro, by means of insistence on a full tonal range that disregards the conventional aspect of an object usually seen to be constant whatever the illumination, just as perspective often utterly distorts, neglects, a characteristic shape of an object on which conceptual art lingers. Developing from this, we have had of late from painters the idea of a pure sensation of colour or of light. Although the psychology of ordinary vision does not support it, the abstract quality of such observation, analytic and truthful, has ennobled pictorial incident. Indeed, out of the requirement for enveloping values amid the pursuit of naturalistic detail, European artists particularly have uncovered a degree of triteness in the constancies through just observations and through the bold, embracing techniques to which they could then proceed. If what they have thus isolated in the name of naturalism has tended to disrupt both the picture plane and the enduring character of the represented objects as such, these same events have called forth unparalleled efforts for their restoration in a new, and indeed more truthful, situation of quandary, truthful especially in regard to the conflicts of the inner life. Hence the greatness, on the whole, of our art since the Renaissance, as well as the utter degradation to which it is prone.

I have been describing the suggestion of an overpowering process in the painter's deployment of perceptual truth that has been largely ignored in the exercise of practical perception. I use the word 'process' because the overpowering is felt to be going on by the spectator. I turn now to the major overall process, a reparation, in which both the good breast and the whole, independent mother must figure, a reparation dependent, it seems to me, upon initial attack. I believe that in the creation of art there exists a preliminary element of acting out of aggression, an acting out that then accompanies reparative transformation, by which inequalities, tension and distortions, for instance, are integrated, are made to 'work'. I have long held the distinction between carving and modelling to be generic in an application to all the visual arts. These two activities have many differences from the psychological angle, first, I think, in the degree and quality of the attack upon the material. Similarly, this difference of attack is relevant to the old distinction between the decorative and the fine arts where an increase of attack calls forth an increase of creativeness. But if decoration titillates, ornaments, the medium, and if larger creativeness may to some considerable extent oppose its native state, I believe that every work of art must include both activities.

A painter, then, to be so, must be capable of perpetrating defacement; though it be defacement in order to add, create, transform, restore, the attack is defacement none the less. The loading of the surface of the canvas, or the forcing upon this flat, white surface of an overpowering suggestion of perspective, depth, the third dimension, sometimes seems to be an enterprise not entirely dissimilar to a twisting of someone's arm. I am inclined to think that, more than anything else, the defacement involved of the picture plane accounts for the tardy arrival in pictorial art of an entirely coherent linear perspective. From many angles, extreme illusionism is an extreme form of art, not least in the aggressive and omnipotent attitude to the materials employed. Many – every month many more – materials are now consciously respected, set-off, in our art today; thus made purposive, their naked character bears witness to an independence of these objects. We often deprecate an entire disguise of the canvas's flatness; we advocate 'preservation of the picture plane'. But whereas the paint, for instance, stays paint in such works, a large part of the impact upon us may proceed from the fact that the canvas is so heavily loaded and scored. Always the strong impact of which defacement, I am convinced, is an attribute. It is 'seconds out of the ring' for every writer as he opposes his first unblemished sheet, innocent of his *graffiti*. It is even harder to begin to paint. With the first mark or two, the canvas has become the arena in which a retaliatory bull has not yet been weakened; no substantial assault, no victory, has begun. If a painter be so blatant, so hardy, as to fling, almost heedlessly, upon the canvas, a strong impact, he will at best create an enveloping or transcendental effect of omnipotence.

Pictures in a gallery, even the pictures in the National Gallery, make an ugly ensemble; as an ensemble the bare walls would be more pleasing. There is no doubt that the most beautiful ensembles of paintings are of those that are abstract and thinly worked, unaggressive in colour. A Ben Nicholson exhibition vivifies the walls on which it is hung. Some kinds of abstract painting, then, employ a very subtle attack. But we soon reach the strange conclusion that if attack be reduced below a certain minimum, art, creativeness, ceases; *equally, if sensibility over the fact of attack is entirely lulled, denied.* The plainer tricks of perspective drawing can be easily learned and then imposed, should the knack be greedily appropriated without a thought for the numbing distortion of the surface thus worked, and so without aesthetic sensibility. A practised artist will have become habituated, of course, to his bold marks. But he cannot be a good artist unless at one time he reckoned painfully with the conflicting emotions that underlie his transformations of material, the aggression, the power, the control, as well as the belief in his own goodness and reparative aim. The exercise of power alone never makes art: indeed it reconstructs the insensitive, the manic, and often, strangely, the academic. Art requires full-dress rehearsal of varied methods that unify conflicting trends. Such presentation causes composition, the binding of thematic material, to be widely evocative. This is more clearly shown in music than in the other arts. Musicologists tend to discover that, whereas construction is easily analysed from a variety of angles, the creative element, that distinguishes a coherent web from clever dovetailing, in general eludes analysis. Hence a vague appeal, sometimes, to 'organic unity'. I believe that it is possible to be more specific in speaking of the deep charging of these sense data with emotive significance, whereby the deployment of formal attributes becomes a vivid language, that is to say, symbols of objects, of relationships to objects and of processes enwrapping objects, inner as well as outer. The word 'symbol' here does not indicate parallel structures, but structures wherein the component parts, though possessing no correspondence with the component parts of the original objects, are interlocked and interrelated with an intensity, sharpness, regret, or other feeling-tone that belong at least to one aspect of the original object-relationships, especially to the fact of their coexistence, interpolations, and variety.

Whereas the finished work, or the work as a whole, symbolizes integration, once again while we contemplate and follow out the element of attack and its recompense, we are in touch with a process that seems to be happening on our looking, a process to which we are joined as if to an alternation of part-objects.

At the beginning of this chapter I said that naturalistic art had need, *ipso facto*, for particular exertion in initiating the incantatory process, since its apparent aim sharpens the otherness of a represented incident or scene. In conclusion, and to sum up, I think I can now better make clear, in one instance of a representational aim on which everyone is agreed, how these two objectives are combined.

Consider in painting the third dimension, the suggestion of depth. No painting of whatever kind, with any merit, is absolutely flat in effect. There will be at least a suggestion of oscillation; something tends to come forward, in a manner that intrigues the senses, in front of something else, though, in general, there be no attempt to disguise the flatness of the picture plane. The surface itself seems to have bulk. Thus, at any rate to a limited degree, illusionism, a mastery in isolating generalizations that convey it, are inseparable from painting and from the artist's sense of a creative act in his determination to discover effects for the paint that are revivifying. More clearly in naturalistic painting, the first test of its merit is the degree to which we become attached to the turn of the contours, the degree to which we are compelled to feel our way into spaces, whether populated or whether empty of shapes. This matter is at the heart of painting on a flat surface, distinguishing its appreciation from an apprehension of landscape itself which the eye constructs and contemplates without ado as a three-dimensional datum.

But there are many more ways of intriguing the spectator of a painting with space than by a pedestrian representation of depth. I have emphasized the desirability of preserving the picture plane. Yet I want now to restrict the matter to the traditional aspect, the aspect dear to art schools at any rate until very recently, the aspect of which I have been reminded by a gay bit of painting of a Mediterranean harbour that I saw in a café. One often sees such decoration, boldly painted, perhaps without much effort and even without a visit to the south. The interesting point is that the example I have in mind, and probably most examples to be found in similar places, have no aesthetic merit, far less than photographs which, for the most part, lack that element of assertive handiwork by which the artist points to his invitation. What is so wrong with the painting, what is the most obvious reason for lack of worth? Colour, design, and application of paint are not objectionable. But the aesthete would sacrifice these merits, if such they be, to the slightest poignancy in the suggestion of space. Don't misunderstand me. There is a quay, and a boat with gay sails in the water just behind it. You can't mistake the scene. The aesthete attaches not the slightest merit to that: nothing he values can be read into the scene since, for the moment, he places no value on blue waters, slim boats, and pretty sails in themselves. Before he can estimate and relate these things, he wants to be induced to feel his way over the stones of the quay, bit by bit. Again, he is not interested in the stones of the quay: he *is* interested in the breadth to the water's edge, and then in the breadth of the water between quay and boat; he wants to swim, as it were, in the empty air above them, yet again he won't mind if that which he contemplates does evocative service for, but hardly looks like, the width of a quay. There are so many ways, and always new ways, of commenting upon space, and any one of them for the moment will suffice. We want to be certain that the matter has absorbed the artist and to identify with him; we want to feel volume, density, and the air it displaces, to recognize things perhaps in the manner of the half-blind; we demand to be drawn in among these volumes, almost as if they were extensions of ourselves, and we do not tire of this process, the incantatory process at work. It is at work only because the canvas face is, in fact, flat. At the same time the restored otherness of things is asserted by these same means of true draughtsmanship, the means of all good drawings whether of things or of the figure; at the heart of aesthetic value. Surface value and depth value go hand in hand. For it is obvious that the representation of space, of depth, reflects a metaphor so unavoidable that one suspects it to be the consequence of a very old piece of concrete thinking concerning 'the layers in depth' of our mental life and individuality.

Nevertheless, incantatory rhythm and movement should be approached as well from an opposite viewpoint that reveals the vibrancy and volume of objects endowed with these qualities. The felicity of art lies in its sustaining power, in a markedly dual content, in multiple forms of expression within one boundary that harmonize. It demands usually very hard work on the part of a mentality not easily seduced and satisfied by its own products. Self-expression and art are not synonymous. Art, we have seen, is mastery within the mode of certain emphases upon reconstruction. Whatever else it makes known, art transmits an enticing eloquence in regard to the *varied* attachment to objects, and in regard to the co-ordination of the self.

Since the context has been created, I want to add a note concerning an emphasis in our surroundings. I think that normal environment has always brought home to inhabitants both the otherness of things and the sense of processes that echo or amplify inner processes as such, and even dreams as such, though these meanings may merely alternate. On the other hand, I believe that everything we feel to be out of harmony with the body's image and with the ways of natural growth or change, everything we feel today to be harshly mechanical, mirrors, in a one-sided manner, an unsettlement of the inner life. In his paper on 'The Uncanny' (1919), Freud constructed an equation between the psychologically primitive and what appears weird, outlandish, *unheimlich*, unhomely. Similarly, when contemplated as a series, the mechanical apparatus that surrounds and supports our modern living, instead of stimulating a preponderant sense of otherness in the light of an unparalleled organization of outer substances, tends rather to suggest abrupt experiences that are both stranger than this and nearer to us, though without the insinuating quality of the incantatory process in art, a setting for further content. In the environment to which I now refer, there is no provision beyond the shock of it. The beauty in our streets is mostly the one of glitter, of flashing lights; surprising, momentary signals of a confusing ramification within, yet we are arrested by a sense neither of depth nor of surface. I have spoken, in regard to art, of an enveloping effect that accompanies a represented movement. In our towns today we are largely strangers to stillness, to apparent deliberateness and silence. From the street, even buildings appear to be but boundaries or targets for the movement of traffic, whereas, in the days of the horse's clop-clop, one moved within the circulation of a whole mother who still reigned fitfully. The same harsh hallucinatory quality, from the angle of utter contemplation, that is – not everyone is prepared to contemplate it at all – inevitably characterizes much modern art of merit.

The words 'humanist' and 'humanism' are hard to define. Whatever may be meant, I am convinced that a desideratum for the humanist is an environment stimulating awareness of otherness in harmony with hopes of an integrated object, outer as well as inner. If the depressive position itself implies humanist attitudes for the adult who has embraced it well, the paranoid-schizoid position, to which the enveloping mechanisms and disconnecting noises of limitless cities pay court, certainly does not. In the old days, art was a means of organizing the incantatory element that had been felt in the length of land or in the restless sea. Today art is entirely outmoded in the choice of such phenomena by the scintillating lack of limitation of urban things in general, though it strains all the time to keep up. But, of course, in art there exist contemplative purpose, organization, a degree of wholeness. That is why art is no less a solace now, and perhaps little less an achievement, than in great ages.

On Being Taken Out of Oneself

(1966)

I discuss a possible reason why we like to be taken out of ourselves, a phrase applied to an apparent forgetfulness of the self's interests in identification with society, to the adoption of any wide cause, or even to the narrow preoccupation of routine work, indeed to any activity that seems to distract attention from the protagonists of the conflicts that we already know. 'Ourselves' of the phrase appears to be an object subjected to conscious tensions. I doubt whether we seem to forsake ourselves pre-eminently in plain object-love, in caring for our families, or in vehement preoccupation with any figure or group. These objects are closely entangled with the selves we incessantly recognise, whereas I have in mind a field of preoccupation that in contrast seems remote and free. It is this, perhaps small, element of occasional impersonality that I seek to isolate, no doubt defensive in character as are all sublimations in one aspect, and all depersonalisation. But it is not the defensive aspect with which I am concerned.

We may sometimes need new activities to replace the now more entangled activity which formerly took us out of ourselves. And so there comes about an ascending scale of greater permanence in activities that perform this service. In the case of experiences of solitude – and it is those I have in mind – many people would agree that at the top of the scale there figure, however momentarily, some contemplative states in the presence of Nature, of the sea, of trees. Though the projections involved are individual, there is common vastness in those experiences that comforts, exhilarates even. They are doubtless used at times pre-eminently as febrile manic occasions, particularly in youth. I intend to speak only of what I regard as the mature and enduring aspect. Some communion with Nature is a commonly accepted need. Witness, for example, the call for preservation of the countryside not so much in the name of agriculture as of natural scenes for themselves, empty of people. And let me remind you that the artist has often been held to possess particular interest in such communion in an even more contemplative form.

I think it would be mistaken here to read into the absorption with nature solely an image of the infant and the enveloping, nursing mother. The sea contains no plain image of nurture except the lulling slow thud of the waves or a rocking boat. On the other hand, confronted by the heaving vastness, exterior existence can recede; once more we live in the womb. There is a phrase, 'the womb of Time'. To contemplate temporal expanse is similarly calming and enwrapping. We grew unseen in the womb like the enfolded life at a tree's core. I am not content with these images alone. The infinite distances of the starlit sky from which Pascal sought refuge, take most people out of themselves similarly; thereby we self-obliterate. It could be urged that the stars are as pins of light, inextinguishable beckoning points, upon which we somewhat feed. I think that this is so. Yet we are never snugly encompassed in the coldness of unrelieved space. Obsessed with preoccupations we demand *their*, not *our* obliteration at times. But what is the great difference? We are our preoccupations, including any preoccupation with not being preoccupied. I cannot myself attribute to this last a wholly libidinal and defensive root. The night sky can momentarily reverse in us the ill proportion of affects we encounter: so may silence, all lulling, natural sound. But I believe they promise besides, thus gently, a native part of ourselves that rids us of ourselves, a part that signifies 'to disappear', though the way of it be a swallowing up by immensity or a return to the womb. The deep libidinal way of it.

On the other hand, a feeling of liberation inspired by the sight of great space does not easily suggest a desired re-entry of the womb; to those who suffer little from agoraphobia, great space usually connotes desirable freedom and independence. There is first of all freedom for the body and plentiful air. But there is also some freedom from a self that is, as it were, diluted by the immensity it can thus inhabit, doubtless a regression to a part-object relationship, in this case a form of projection that appears to be the opposite of projective identification or, rather, of most forms of projective identification, since, whereas ordinarily projective identification seeks to control the object with an active piece of the self, our aim when we fill a great space with the projection of ourselves is to find ourselves hugely diluted there. That is freedom, in the first place physical freedom: there is a tendency to run, to run wild, to attenuate our bodies to the point of exhaustion in that space. And political freedom? The doctrine of complete freedom, of Anarchy, advocates some attenuation of all ties. Liberty, in its negative aspect, expresses the desire to be free of this or that, perhaps, at root, to be free of the onus of relationships, and therefore of the self. Such depersonalisation should be examined as a mode of defence against conflict and anxiety: similarly in regard to each of the experiences to which I have referred. But on the meta-psychological level, explanations only in terms of defence would seem a shade doctrinaire or mechanical, neglectful of the quality of overdue refreshment that may belong to these experiences in the context of a busy life. Our interest here is confined, I had better say again, to a commonly valued aspect that therefore is not considered pathological.

The essence of one kind of holiday is an open vista, the sky, physical disencumberment, the freedom I have described of time stretched far. Not only that, of course, not all the time: not any of the time, it seems, as we contemplate the crowds that suffocate the beach. We soon become lonely, frightened of silence and of open things. We are not Buddhist priests renouncing a varied relationship. However, it will be apparent that I believe that part of the refreshment lies in a degree of renunciation or obliteration, not only of this or that aspect of normal mental life but, as a consequence, some reduction of the self as a complicated totality, a reduction that is fused with a part-object re-working to which we can point more easily as we fill a great space with ourselves. But if part-object working-over, momentous though it be, is not the whole crux of the matter, then there is a negative aspect also to some of the experiences that we value most highly. It could be a prime reason why we value them most highly since, in this form of attenuated projection associated nevertheless with a libidinal sorting out of the highest importance, we can project, not only without harm to ourselves or to others but for the purpose of refreshment, like sleep itself, a force in ourselves that refuses complete selfhood, possibly the force to which Freud gave the name of death instinct. And it would be a refreshment only because this reflective lack of libidinal intensity is by no means a typical state of our being; perhaps because, as well, the small degree of self-annihilation at work is borrowed from the forces that repeat the wounds of traumatic experiences, or is borrowed, and far more commonly, from the exercise of envy, of the greedy, destructive projective identification that envy stimulates. The psyche's abatement of envious feeling as the result of a momentary attenuation of libidinal aim by which resignation substitutes itself somewhat for envy, that is to say, for those unlimited envious feelings that persecute us, may provide a key to the general character of all commonly valued contemplative states. If such explanations seem far-fetched as well as unsupported, they will at least, I hope, commend the problem for psycho-analysis of common contemplative, as opposed to schizoid and manic states that confuse and overrule normal syntheses and distinctions, or prevent their growth.

I am not sure that it is not rather vulgar to imagine that the general principles or forces of our being can be the object of contemplation even through deeply sublimated forms; in view, that is, of the entire emphasis of psycho-analysis upon the buried, upon the buried and unfelt need of punishment, for instance, that is sometimes called the unconscious sense of guilt. Have we this easy access to the general nature and necessity of fusions that is altogether lacking to individual adaptations? Is not a reaching after such generality always determined, at the very least in large part, by the economics of defence? I can but repeat in answer that normal contemplative states in the presence of nature have been neglected by psycho-analysis, and that the manner of feelings there combined – not the feelings themselves in regard to objects but their wilfully withdrawn manner – may puzzle others as well as myself, insofar as we are inclined to think that this highly valued manner is not explicable in terms of defence, disavowal, or denial alone.

Another much valued experience is the contemplation of art. In view of other writing, I shall not be thought to neglect libidinal factors in saying that an attraction of art is its deadness in combination with those libidinal factors. The deadness alone, of course, is dire, especially if translated into terms of a picture's subject-matter. Kenneth Clark once told me that a woman to whom he gave a lift on the road, possessed what he triumphantly called the most primitive of all reactions to painting. Having asked about his profession, she recoiled when told that he was the Director of the National Gallery. She had been in the gallery, but never again. 'All those unmoving faces of dead people,' she added. I myself remember regarding pictures in childhood as forms of petrifaction: life, movement, gesture turned to deadness. I peered at lithographs in search of life, in search of evidence not only of the life of the painted figures but of the artist. He who looks for apples – and many people do – in the painter's representation of them, courts a desiccating experience. There is indeed a sense wherein some painters translate valued things into coloured oil. The transformation becomes life-giving when the air of unmoving finality with which art endows the objects we love, is employed to stabilise far-reaching and complex relationships. Yet it is significant that a popular conception of figurative art as macabre dies hard, an idea often transmitted by mystery films, in the visits, so common there, to antique shops or to halls furnished with portraits. Many people today prefer to hang on their walls very small landscapes that re-create the sense of freedom and of far horizon. Art is expected to bring into the home the refreshments from Nature of which I have written above, in what might be described as very small, even medicinal, doses. Such meagre works usually escape the perfection of beauty that has often been suspected of a relationship with the finality, with what might be called the 'utterness', of death.

The artist sets out for our contemplation a momentous aspect of object-relations, including an attempted re-stabilisation of the good breast that in contemplative experiences is likely to permeate other part-object relationships. This theme of re-establishment, of re-working, characterises psychical health and development, yet it is not otherwise distant from the one of fixation. As early as 1905, at the end of the first edition of *Three Essays on Sexuality*, Freud had written of a stubbornness or adhesiveness of the libido that led to fixation. This contrasts with its extreme mobility to which he often referred. In later work he sometimes adopted Jung's expression, 'psychical inertia', for this adhesiveness or stubbornness; and not only did he finally relate it to the compulsion to repeat, but in 1914, when he wrote 'From the History of an Infantile Neurosis', he used these words: 'In considering the conversion of psychical energy no less than of the physical, we must make use of the concept of an *entropy* which opposes the undoing of what has already occurred.' He spoke here also of the mental rigidity of old age. We surely see in the passage a beginning of Freud's eventual concept of the death instinct.

If, then, there is a link, metapsychologically speaking, between fixation and the dogged retention and re-working of the primary motifs that the ego has elaborated, there is no need, it might be thought, to look beyond the affirmative libidinal content in contemplative experience to the influence of Thanatos, an influence that is universal since all experiences are fusions in some degree. But contemplative states of the species I have in mind admit a portion of attenuation and depersonalisation, and even resignation, that distinguishes them from other projections whereby this vital re-affirmation is sustained.

To return to the starry night, to an empty immensity that tends to calm our so-called fevered existence. We are then liberated for once, I think, not so much *from* feelings of void and even loneliness, as *by* those feelings as well.

Nothing is humorous about the night sky, nor does humour connote attenuation of the ego: on the contrary, humour bolsters the ego up. I see, all the same, a connection with a sight of the stars in view of what Freud wrote in his brilliant paper of 1927 on 'Humour'. He attributed to the context of humour a condescending, even kindly and rescuing attitude on the part of the super-ego towards the ego: 'It means, "Look!

here is the world, which seems so dangerous! It is nothing but a game for children – just worth making a jest about!'" In this situation the super-ego acts as a parent that calms and reassures its child, the ego. Freud's instance of humour at the start of the paper is of 'a criminal who was being led out to the gallows on a Monday [and] remarked: "Well, the week's beginning nicely."'

Beneath a night sky the super-ego may comfort the ego with the thought that troubles, concerns, are about nothing in a vastness that makes all things empty, in the name of death (the seeds of which are perhaps even stronger in the super-ego than in the ego).

Now a connection between the stars and the categorical imperative (voice of the super-ego) was made by Kant in a famous remark that Freud (1933) quoted in the thirty-first of the *Introductory Lectures*. Freud wrote: 'Following a well-known pronouncement of Kant's which couples the conscience within us with the starry Heavens, a pious man might well be tempted to honour these two things as the masterpieces of creation.' And four lectures later Freud wrote:

> I may remind you of Kant's famous pronouncement in which he names, in a single breath, the starry heavens and the moral law within us. However strange this juxtaposition may sound – for what have the heavenly bodies to do with the question of whether one human creature loves another or kills him – it nevertheless touches on a great psycho-logical truth.

Thereupon, enlarging on the moral law, Freud unfortunately makes no further reference to this juxtaposition with the stars. In contrast with humour and a reassuring aspect of the super-ego, the connection between the ego's contemplation of the stars and of the stern categorical imperative seems to lie with a more austere yet manic comfort belong-ing to those renouncing situations, in which, I think, the renunciation sometimes reveals the persecution by envy. The modern cosmic scene especially counteracts all values, all good as well as bad. Nothing is worthwhile in the face of almost limitless light years and an ultimate dismemberment even of the universe. I think old envious aims as well as their renunciation are perceptible in some contemplative states.

I have suggested that it can be exhilarating for the ego, by means of contemplative experiences, somewhat to renounce itself, but not only for defensive purposes. I have suggested that throughout the psyche, including the ego, there may exist in libidinal embodiment an instinct of refusal, a desire to renounce. If there be any justice in this mode by which I have interpreted contemplative experiences in the face of Nature that are considered sublime, if there be reason for introducing to this context a mention of the dubious death instinct, then it seems that I must show that this negative force has in some sense, however generalised, a life-giving function: otherwise it could not contribute to even rare meanings essentially non-ambivalent, namely the contemplative experiences.

The task sounds perverse, especially since I do not invoke a primary masochism to explain contemplative states as I have described them, and since I have suggested that the repetition complex and the imperious persecution by envious thoughts, and by other overwhelming projective identifications, may be eased in those experiences, a sufficient explanation on these lines, it might be considered. We surely know that most mental ills and conflicts derive from divisions caused by our aggression and consequent paranoid and depressive fears. Indeed, the original persecution according to Melanie Klein is by the death instinct itself, immediately projected in the form of destructiveness. I am aware that no clinical material justifies the ascription to the death instinct as a refusing force the power to create an entirely non-ambivalent affect in fusion with libido. It must be more than enough to put the claim out of court, any confident claim. But clinical practice is not primarily concerned with the universal interpenetrations of Eros and Thanatos, with common experiences that may be beneficent, with the economic transformation, for instance, that contributes to a benign state of resignation about which I have given a paper (Stokes, 1962). Moreover this is not a confident claim, and there is a metapsychological difficulty on account of which I have attributed, in another paper (1960), a usefulness, indeed a necessity, to the libido of a death instinct. In that paper I asked:

> Can the instinct of self-preservation be viewed satisfactorily without
> a partner that typifies danger? If the interests of survival that the ego
> will serve conflict with those of immediate satisfaction, how is the ego
> developed from the id, unless there be active in the id another and
> negative principle that owing to its threat causes survival to declare
> itself as an immediate aim?

Part of the conclusion was that

> from the beginning the impulse of refusal is felt within other instinct-
> ual responses and tends to increase them, as might a slowly departing
> train the response of a man who would catch it.

That sentence contains the gist, as I had conceived it, of a positive influence upon the libido by the death instinct.

When I wrote that paper I had not realised that, of course, Freud had
foreseen the difficulty concerning self-preservation in the face of the
pleasure principle. He specifically did so in a footnote to 'Formulations
on the Two Principles of Mental Functioning' (1911), in which he said:

> It will rightly be objected that an organization which was a slave to the
> pleasure principle and neglected the reality of the external world could
> not maintain itself alive for the shortest time, so that it could not have
> come into existence at all. The employment of a fiction like this is,
> however, justified when one considers that the infant – provided one
> includes with it the care it receives from its mother – does almost realize
> a psychical system of this kind.

At the end of this footnote Freud says:

> I shall not regard it as a correction, but as an amplification of the
> schematic picture under discussion, if it is insisted that a system living

according to the pleasure principle must have devices to enable it to withdraw from the stimuli of reality. Such devices are merely the correlative of 'repression', which treats internal unpleasurable stimuli as if they were external – that is to say, pushes them into the external world.

This correlative of 'repression' is surely the beginning of another thought. It seems a far cry from 'unpleasurable stimuli' to the caution and delays imposed by the reality principle, Freud's description of which was the occasion for the note quoted above. Self-preservation requires such huge, and in many forms of life, such immediate, forestalling of satisfactions suggested by the pleasure principle. It seems that self-preservation in harness with the pleasure principle demands a built-in danger from the start, a principle of negation. There is no time to evolve the reality principle: and when in Freud's later writing, that is to say in *Beyond the Pleasure Principle* and after, ego instincts are dropped and self-preservation becomes integrated entirely with libido, the organism, whether it be a higher or lower organism under consideration, appears now to possess no more built-in variation of response as a result of conflict, since the death instinct is not considered as an active form. He had always held that in the unconscious contrary meanings lie side by side and undivorced, or rather, meanings that to consciousness appear contradictory. On the other hand, we read in Lecture 32 of the *Introductory Lectures* (1933): 'It must be confessed that we were not prepared to find that internal instinctual danger would turn out to be a determinant and preparation for an external, real, situation of danger.'

Several passages could be quoted, for instance in the paper on 'Negation', for the idea that what is bad or dangerous is immediately expelled into the external world, but the passage I have just quoted is the only one I have discovered in which Freud posits 'an internal instinctual danger' as 'a determinant and preparation for an external, real situation of danger', to repeat his words. The context is not metapsychological but oedipal. As far as I know, he did not relate this idea to the death instinct, the supreme internal threat, the supreme instinctual danger. Freud did not, in so many words, bring the onus of the death instinct to bear on the preparation of the organism against external danger. This connection, I submit, was needed for his metapsychological system, a connection that would have modified a subsequent sentence of the same lecture where Freud has written: 'It is a long step from the pleasure principle to the self-preservative instinct: the two are very far from coinciding at the start.'

This is a different view of self-preservative instinct from that of many earlier pronouncements where, as an ego instinct, he had said that at first self-preservation combines with the libido, that is to say, initially it combines with the oral drive. But if there is this gap, this absence of feeling for the adverse except in terms of unreinforced unpleasure, how does life, one will ask again, if it is not consistently protected in every conceivable way, survive? Freud himself taught those of us who accept it, about the great danger within, existing from the first moment, a danger that at once can make life doubly valuable, it seems to me, precious, threatened, to be preserved. Even so, though we allow that this danger actively threatens the human infant within, it does not help him greatly to sense external danger. Except for his cry he is utterly defenceless. Indeed, because of the strength of the death instinct, his grip on life may be tenuous, even in good circumstances. Yet this struggle, I submit, may more often strengthen striving in the sense, first of all, of acute persecution by unpleasure that puts pleasure in deeper relief. It follows that pre-natal stress also and the stress of birth cannot be regarded as general educators *by themselves* in the matter of danger, or even of persecutory anxiety.

Doubtless the infant's helplessness influenced Freud's later accounts, especially of the instinct of self-preservation. He writes in *An Outline of Psycho-Analysis*: 'The id knows no solicitude about ensuring survival.' Another sentence in this late writing runs: 'No such purpose as that of keeping itself alive or of protecting itself from dangers by means of anxiety can be attributed to the id. That is the task of the ego,' at first a feeble outgrowth only from the id. Of course there is a vast clinical background to that line of thought which seems to me to fit with Freud's conviction that the death instinct operates to say, without a precise influence upon unconscious fantasies and their derivatives, until the ego projects death instinct in the form of aggression. According to Freud in these passages, then, the id neglects both survival and death and the conflict between them, notwithstanding the fact that in the last paragraph of *The Ego and the Id* he says that 'Eros and the death instincts struggle within it' (the id). Yet it is in the *Outline* that he again formulates the dilemma inherent in conceiving that organisms are entirely subject at birth to the pleasure principle; unfettered, therefore, untutored in danger by the negative instinct that he has found necessary to posit for other contexts (but not necessary, I repeat, as a restraint upon the pleasure principle or as its booster even in regard to self-preservation, or as a condition preparatory for the recognition of external danger and so ultimately for the need of developing the reality principle). All the same he says in the passage I have in mind:

> The id obeys the inexorable pleasure principle. But not the id alone. It seems that the activity of other psychical agencies too is able only to modify the pleasure principle but not to nullify it; and it remains a question of the highest theoretical importance, and one that has not yet been answered, when and how it is ever possible for the pleasure principle to be overcome. The consideration that the pleasure principle demands a reduction, at bottom the extinction perhaps, of the tensions of instinctual needs (that is, *Nirvana*) leads to the still unassessed relations between the pleasure principle and the two primal forces, Eros and the death instinct.

As he had done before, he here visualises a link between the pleasure principle governing libido and the death instinct, an opposite interplay to the one I have suggested, since the connection he has made depends upon a common interest in the extinction of feeling. This link, it seems to me, *if it is the only one,* squares ill with the supreme antithesis of the two terms, and even with the emergence and development of life. In the slightly earlier 'Analysis Terminable and Interminable' Freud wrote: 'Only by the concurrent or mutually opposing action of the two primal instincts – Eros and the death instinct – never by the one or the other alone, can we explain the rich multiplicity of the phenomena of life.' That sentence contrasts somewhat with much I have quoted.

'Never by one or the other alone,' Freud writes. We may define life, and death too, only in each other's terms. That which conflicts may also thereby create. Without the hypothesis of a deadly negative principle that both persecutes, retards, and stimulates the strong yet complicated strands of the purposive in all our lives, how are we to account meta-psychologically for self-persecution by guilt and remorse and for their frequent promotion of striving towards reparation, integration, and truth? Two of Freud's last papers were concerned with ego defence, particularly with the defence by splitting. Klein (1957) was well attuned when advancing her conception of splitting as the first mode of defence necessitated by the warring of derivatives from the two primary principles, at a time when the ego is weakest.

What I have had in mind as the deeper content of commonly valued contemplative states in front of Nature could arise from a tentative tendency to reverse the original splitting, indeed to renounce development. Contemplation reverses action, more and more action: in the contemplative state we partly stand aside, perhaps enjoying a refusal that for once is health-giving; we do not need to split off. In the passage I have quoted, speaking of the final aim of the pleasure principle as the reduction of libidinal tension, Freud refers to the libido's 'still un-assessed' direct relation with the death instinct, in regard, that is, to some identity of their final aims. In 'The Economic Problem of Maso-chism' (1924) at any rate, Freud made it clear that he would no longer identify the pleasure principle with the Nirvana principle: the first was the modification, as yet undefined, made by libido upon the second that expressed the trend of the death instinct. One suggestion of the present paper and of my former paper claims that the death instinct could act, from the very first, also as a booster of libidinal need for which the instinct to refuse, not to partake, provides the danger. The contem-plative states of my context of course possess libidinal qualities. They can be characterized broadly as an aesthetic kind in contrast with extreme or mystical forms of contemplation that aim at nothingness. In regard to either of the alleged basic relationships between the libido and death instinct, that is to say, in regard to either the extinction or the booster theme, differing contemplative states, it seems to me, vary in emphasis. It is significant that Freud took over the descriptive term 'Nirvana' for the extinction of the tensions of instinctual needs. Nirvana is the Indian word that indicates the ultimate content of Buddhist contemplative states.

And so, if there is a sense, however metapsychological for the moment, in which Eros and Thanatos, both answerable to the Nirvana principle, work hand in glove, in which Thanatos is needed as a booster also to the opposite force, it may appear conceivable that in the vastly sublimated form of a contemplative state under a starlit sky, or in other contemplative states called supernal or sublime, an attitude of acceptance towards a very distant reflection of the creative aspect especially – but not solely – of this partnership can be symbolised. This is truly to be 'taken out of oneself', a phrase with a positive sense always, applied to a context where we might expect the dangers or persecutions associated with a principle that attenuates to be predominant, in spite of the very notable fusions with Eros that these experiences contain. Persecution may well supervene if such contemplation becomes prolonged.

There is the phrase 'the human condition'. It continues to crop up although the meaning often lapses with the utterance. Should there be such an object for contemplation, it seems that these are its occasions, the experiences to which I have adverted. And if it be admitted – a far better case, of course, would be wanted than the one I have made out – if it could be admitted that the negative principle serves a function in relation to libido, a function necessary to libidinal elaboration even while the negative principle retards and seeks to arrest, might it not be allowable that some contemplative states of short duration in which depersonalisation figures, are refreshing rather than defensive only, refreshing not only in terms of their libidinal components? Aggression, a degree of aggression, is of course necessary for survival and for development. To those who hold to the death instinct, aggression is secondary. What is true of a degree of aggression could also be true of the primary form.

Aggression, in paramount fusions with death instinct, must have outlet. We know that much of this aggression is internalised not always to the advantage either of the individual or of society. We all require to search for constructive, or at least less harmful outlets. This economic Freudian consideration applies very closely to contemplative states as I have portrayed them. And I believe that the making of art is a perfect outlet for aggression. The easiest substitute for war might be a universal making of art. You will have realised, however, that, in the liberating surrender through contemplative states to 'the human situation', I have envisaged a Thanatos hand held out to Eros as the distant object of a contemplative act. This experience, as I have presented it, not only releases from the economic viewpoint death instinct tension – I would agree that this may be the most distinctive aspect – but for once manifests a momentary lack of complication in the fusing of the two principles themselves, displays the deeds or constructive instrument, as it were, of their partnership which determines the inevitable splits and, so often, insufferable fusions, that follow fast.

I am not supposing that what I have said about contemplative states will influence anyone to view more favourably the premise of a death or refusal instinct, whereas the other thread of argument on that subject in this paper, the booster theme, is perhaps more ambitious. In ending I would recall to mind that the difficulties are not all on one side. The necessity of a radical antithesis is widely admitted: talk of the destructiveness of aggression as primary or absolute tends to transform aggression into the complete negative principle or death instinct that it was intended to replace; but this is done without qualifying the biological identification of aggression with self-preservation. Yet, if aggression be regarded as initially an aspect of self-preservation, then we ought, on the contrary, to be back with the libido and the ego instincts of Freud's first dualism and his difficulties about narcissism. And further, we should, if we are consistent, explain altogether differently such phenomena as repetition complex, the economic problem of masochism, the negative therapeutic effect or the need for illness and punishment, even the super-ego, those and other phenomena that influenced Freud to sharpen considerably the antithesis of his first dualism. But that would be, surely, to impoverish very considerably not only our meta-psychology but the common tendencies today of psycho-analytic insight.

Face and Anti-Face: A Fable

(1967)

I have a cluster of quills growing from my face. I shall write of what has happened as if commenting on the unknown.

Though they have lasted nearly ten years the shock and the strangeness persist; as I remember the pleasure of eating: what freshness had belonged to youth. Other nations continue to enjoy it. So shall we again in a few years: there seems to be a danger that this shameful experience will concern, but not more closely involve, the future.

I find little perspective in lengthy comments on the subject. With our faces set back, perspective would provide a careful analogy for its essence since what was once part of ordinary human behaviour has become, like a work of art, transposed into a concrete form. Permanent quills have usurped the place of what was once conveyed outwardly by an intermittent flicker of the eye, a glint.

After prolonged questioning the psycho-somatic correlation between the effect of the injection and the quills has been widely accepted; but not, as it were, briskly, though theorists are very few who do not regard the quills as a somatic representative of aggression and of the drive towards death, a recognition that, come what may, should radically influence speculative thought and therapeutic practice. Moreover the shameful cause of the quills, their *raison d'être*, has become a paramount component of our thoughts about their physical inconvenience.

I will refer briefly to the inconvenience of quills four inches long from the forehead and cheeks and a nest of that length from the upper lip: these also, hard and sharp at the points, stand straight out from the plane of the face. Those on the chin are unequally spaced and tilted upwards at an angle of forty-five degrees or more, so that their ends pass through the spaces between the quills growing on the upper lip.

The quills from near the lower lip reach up over the mouth behind
the tip of the nose: we twitch them continually from the nostrils. Self-
perforations are common, not only of the nose and nostrils but of the
cheeks. We suffer, we hurt ourselves and can hurt others; hence the
huge muzzles employed in the rush hour, enhancing the animal-
congregation quality of those journeys.

The advocacy, early on in fashion papers, of quill-to-quill encounter
as an elegance, pointed in fact to the electric-less acuity of the contact.
There is no sympathy in a meeting of quills. The studies sponsored
by charitable Foundations on the behaviour of porcupines have not
been useful. We eat sparely: meals take an age in spite of the dexterity
evolved with lengthy spoons and forks.

The few people who were not injected ten years ago, or since, have
not grown quills. The quills are a side-effect of the injections which
otherwise proved entirely successful. Illness, other than slight dangers
from perforation by quills, and other than terminal disease, have been
eliminated, together with many manifestations of senescence. The
wonder is that people die as regularly from natural causes as hitherto:
the average expectation of life remains steady. Nevertheless, as the
discoverers of the injection predicted, we are considerably rejuvenated
up to the last. Children have grown without ailment: most injuries do
not entail infections. There is some infant and child illness now that
injection has so largely ceased. Two years after the mass injections,
not much more than one year after the consequent growing of quills –
the first onset was comparatively slow – the enthusiasm and powerful
advocacy for the injection had vanished. And so there are many children
of eight years and less without quills: in a few years we shall have a
clear-faced youth while the rest of us will carry quills to the grave.

What I have written so far largely reflects the common moan from
which I am dissociated to the extent that I find myself attributing
immediate evil to a quill-less face. We quilled ones, at any rate the
children who have grown quills from infancy, are like animals of many
species with claws and incisor teeth, carnivorous animals who nevertheless do not, as do ordinary men, eradicate their kind; like animals

whose jaws are so hinged that they cannot chew.

It has been amply shown during the last eight or nine years that the onset of quills somewhat employs, and, may be, for those injected in infancy whose mental constellations have been weakened in their negative component by the injection, largely employs, the aggressive instinct, diverting its excesses not only from against the self but also from against others. This has been illustrated by some decrease in crime, particularly murder. It is better known by the fact, repeatedly and amazedly noted, that in the case of those who have carried violent thoughts into action, still more in the case of those who have continually used violence, the growth of quills tends to be weak: it is sometimes the case that the face has become clear. Naturally police and law-courts have taken advantage of this evidence. Many intelligent people, therefore, have become somewhat suspicious, at least, of the pristine smooth human face as we now see it in other countries. Of course foreigners laugh at our ugly spikes which we have found to shield us not only against xenophobia but against self-defeat. If no one loves an Englishman it does not mean, as once it might have done, that we are feared. On the contrary, foreigners believe our pacific intentions. They are delighted that we hurt, or at least incommode, ourselves with our emotional forest of pricks and spikes: they are delighted that we expect ourselves to assume that restraint, that limitation of destructive instinct, habitual to barbed animals: yet they know that we remain human beings who have not neglected self-preservation.

Following the growth of quills, a continuation of mass injections would have required compulsion. I fear that there is hardly any chance of it now in spite of our long campaigning. The outcome makes more sad the prevalent adulation for our smooth-faced children who are wiser than they know when they deride us as caged combatants with the foil.

I have longing no less than others for an uncluttered face. Our nights are often hideous and the frustrations of the oral bent together with self-disgust or shame are complex. Has there been less love as well as less hate? The growth of barbs is not instantaneous: it is always possible to suckle injected infants for at least six months thereafter. Finally shafts grow apace: if severed they grow again very fast, longer and even stronger. Since the innumerable attempts to eliminate them have failed, severing is practised by public performers only and by some youths who have invested manly pride in the strength of their barbs.

It has been suggested that a balance, such as existed, between love and aggression will have been upset: that the destructiveness imbibed by the infant as a result of his own projection of aggressive phantasies requires renewed projection and distribution by the male's masterful and creative, though partially aggressive, sexuality.

I do not believe that this or other mechanisms which are the fast-growing infant's implements of defence, will have been blunted by the new circumstances, although in regard to the exercise of omnipotence, secretiveness and smugness, in regard to the overtones, I think that we ourselves, and others in our eyes, may eventually appear less evil inasmuch as we are less smooth, less deceptive in demeanour. All plots were strengthened by old looks of fathomless innocence. Bearded babies, injected at birth, are more appropriately arrayed in the character of their inner world, of phantasies that build such concrete-seeming structures. If psycho-somatic illness, from which – even from this – we are now so largely free, derived from the guilty aftermath of oral aggression, from retaliation by bad objects inside, then the injection, it seems to me, has shown psychological as well as physical influence to the good. Indeed, I am inclined to reverse the usual view on the relationship between our health and the growth of spines, in saying that rather than as the side-effect or negative compensation for health, the growth is the prime cause of our health. At the least, I hold the spines to be a psychological reinforcement of the injection's physical effect.

Though every physical manifestation provides phantastic implications for the infant, in some remaining part of his mind he will not have felt the growth of spines to be 'natural', that is to say, of biological derivation: he will faintly see that his elders, his parents, are paying the same penalty for oral aggression. While this is frightening, inordinate greed loses in secrecy. I admit that the psychological effects must be most various; they must, in some cases, be deleterious. The crux is whether the growth on balance helps to distribute oral phantasies at a time when other instinctual channels are developing whereby the impact of oral disasters can be ramified. Our experience of spined infants has not been long enough for unquestionable conclusions. If, as I shall suggest, there has occurred, as a result of injection, some mitigation in later life of the worser consequences of oral drive, a valid effect upon earlier forms is reasonable expectation.

Somewhat entwined in pain we have become a sober race. It is impossible, of course, to kiss: even the bare-faced can steal a kiss only from their kind. As the source of attraction the face has ceded ground to the body, to carriage. Purged of the face, nudity has gained a more protracted status. The face, the storehouse of the stock, induced a disunited view of every other anatomical part contemplated almost solely in conjunction with the face. It was as if we once expected navels to possess a deep-set utterance.

But it is painful to vaunt our studded looks. The tossed head, the sudden eye are absent. We are hideously fanged: moreover our hair and unavoidable beards now seem another weapon, if only the gladiator's net. Performers enact in theatre, cinema and on television the old form of love-making. This has a charm which we compound with our reservations. In severing their quills those actors and actresses who are not criminals heap trouble for themselves. If the purpose is public performance, severing should be made illegal: we shall otherwise have another wave of severing on the part of the young. It is not disputed that the recent vogue was disastrous if only because the barbless interval grew less and ended, after repeated severing, in a few hours. Moreover from this practice there arose the one infection common among us, painful and dangerous. Yet those who do not tamper with their quills are immune: that has been proved beyond question.

All hope is not gone though the chance be small that an alternative government would introduce compulsory injection. One can imagine the grotesque scribbling on election posters that espoused this cause.

A better hope lies with an advance of our interests in other countries through the Fellowship of the Barbed, by means of our small colonies throughout the world. No cause has had a comparable prize, namely certain health. The price is discomfort of the face and the loss not only to the mouth but to the eyes of partiality for the luscious. (One of our posters figures Adam unable to bite the apple.) We are like clumsy pre-historic animals with boundless health and with the skills, intelligence and knowledge of other men. Though, ingrained with pain, our faces are not open to the sky nor to each other, we are less foreigners in con-fronting the countryside: we experience new friendliness with under-growth and overgrowth. I remember the traffic's roar and flicker in Park Lane at night beside the unlit park, beside this sable hinterland impenetrable to our thought as we once were, without muzzle or snout. The fecundity of creepers, trees, and all nature that displays strength, is now lodged in mind. Having sacrificed smooth brows we approach closer to furrow and hedge. Grimness antecedes our glance yet we enjoy extended brotherhood. When we encounter contradiction we find it no longer smooth. Much destructiveness or negation, I repeat, much of the power behind the blatancy of self-contradiction and denial has been converted into the psycho-somatic symptom of the quills, of their growth and continuous sharpness.

Remember the horror films and plays and the libraries of violence? They will return with smooth faces while we, the barbed, wear as a flourishing garb the area of death.

Yet we are not disgraced in making love if oral frustration, instead of increasing greed, combines with an oral quiescence. We are active, angular, light-weight: obesity is rare since we have eaten with some difficulty. It seems that it is possible, on a larger scale than before, to develop adult replacements for the full strength of the oral urge even on the part of those whose quills were grown in later life; and due to the compensatory negativism of the quills, even envy may have lost some of its pace in company with greed.

A diverting of oral urge will have influenced the hand: as with the blind our sense of touch is refined. Art has abandoned the vogue of enveloping the spectator: artists perfect masks of otherness; their works hold their distance; in this they too have quills.

The attraction of the criminal today is not his deeds but the smoothness of his face. It was thought at first that in view of the self-punishment, the expenditure of guilt-feelings, issuing from the growth of spines, crime would decrease greatly. The extraordinary aspect is surely that crime has not increased. For, not only can crime entail the catharsis of baulked greed but since many crimes tend to rid the performers of their quills and of shame, they thereby provide easier opportunities for the exercise of greed. The loss of quills, however, has not followed upon as many kinds of criminality as was once expected, a result that has taught us much about delinquency in those areas where hatred, greed and persecution are no more predominant than the desperate defences against them. The outcome, therefore, of acts of violence has not been a loss of the quills: because those acts have been subject principally to self-preservation on the part of the psychotic personality. It appears evident – and by no means in this context only – that the degree of aggression required for self-preservation remains altogether unqualified by the growth of quills, just as self-destruction is sufficient for an end in death.

Do not neglect our great discoveries, you the smooth-faced who, I fear, will have regained control, you to whom I dedicate this unequal summary. We had health, even a degree of mental health, at the cost of quills. The injection has inhibited some permutations of an instinct by stabilising many excesses – or at any rate a part of the driving force that constructs those excesses – in the form of an unrelieved, health-promising, psycho-somatic symptom, namely luxuriating quills. It is somewhat ideal.

The fact that violence has lost the attention of popular culture does not entail the absence of the criminal from its scene, the smooth-faced criminals who are in much demand as actor-lovers particularly on television. It seems to many that these beardless monsters, complexioned and smooth, alone are god-like. We are bowled over by the soft clash of their clear faces, though crimes be recorded by the smoothness of their brows and we be conscious that their health will crack. What sacrifice in their allure, what allure in the headstrong sacrifice! It is said that our quills elongate as we watch and envy. Even their fatuous speech is emollient as we dangle our attention from a weary cage of spikes, tiring of sore muzzles though the sap of health and strength is undiminished. Yet at length we may know that the hunger for smoothness is partly infantile. As I chew amid a curtain that grates and pricks and tips the bite out of every morsel, I think of my wife in whom I seem to discover roundness as her laughter. I can touch her eyes but not with my lips for fear she might be blinded. We have the power to draw blood by the slightest movement.

Every woman has had to surrender the looks of a treacherous waif, yet very little has been done to bestow on spikes a modish slant: something of their meaning has been accepted and we now see that Fashion was in part an expression of ignorance of psychic reality, and expression of boastful curiosity, of sanguine essays. In the face, eyes alone retain a glitter, without fruit-like attributes. Young people must move to show their paces, especially as the old are vigorous.

I am old. Though a propagandist I claim a predominant regard for the truth: therefore I know I will have twisted it (I wish I knew instead how much). Maybe I overestimate the positive aspects of oral deprivation as much as I minimise the new neurotic effects of this deprivation coupled with the shame and self-hatred to which the spikes may have given a handle. I must stress, however, the comfort of undecorated evidence. That is how we undoubtedly and commonly are, the spikes proclaim: and to some extent we witness the translation to which they attest in our feelings about them.

In spite of long holders, smoking has lost smoothness. But few older people are without a ball of sweet held in the mouth undisturbed, in an unshared dulcet area behind the muzzle. Our mouths are like feet enclosed in shoes. Is my thought clear, is the image vivid? The brain is smooth behind the forehead's serried points.

Is it sad that our girls lack torch-like faces? They set us alight the same, perhaps more of them than in the past. Is it sad that advertising techniques have forgone not only the face but the guiding phantasy of which the pretty girl was the object, the phantasy of both having your cake and eating it? Smiles and grins from the bill-board belong for the moment to the past: the close-up has receded into distance. The sense that used to be suggested of being pleasurably invaded by luxurious objects, every day and all day, belongs entirely to the past. The cult of Christmas has also receded together with the most tiresome, concealing, time-wasting packaging of goods. We are eager to see things plain now that we ourselves are packaged as grimly as once were wine bottles with recalcitrant caps. But if we have lost taste for the disproportionate, the need for scenes of vivid movement has grown. Games are even more popular than in the past: not many old games, of course, not those that involve entire contact which have proved as unfitting as boxing. You will have noticed for yourself that I am an elderly man whose life belongs principally to pre-injection times, whose face was already twilled with the threads of decay and death.

I have said our health is boundless. The basic conflicts are unaltered though one of their terms has been reduced in strength by means of a stable and harmless and, in view of all the factors, far less complicated exteriorisation. The infant continues to be born unfanged, defenceless, with the full wealth of aggression stored in his mind. It seems that injection may have lessened the negative component in each emotional impasse where otherwise it will have become intensified. But I find it hard to provide firm grounds for my belief that there have been considerable emotional advances in spite of the oral deprivations and as a result of the oral deprivations, not only in the case of the individual but more notably in regard to group activity and cultural achievements. I suspect that we no longer make so huge a meal of what is common in our lot, and that substitute satisfactions on the cultural level have become more subtle; and that there is a decrease in social stupefaction: we are less hungry for the group and for the leader. Some of the strength has drained, not from the proclivity to identify with others but from a uniform compulsion of so doing in group circumstances. All such activities are an extension of, a derivation from, the oral urge which has determined the original modes of relationships. And it might be thought that following the partial inhibition of direct oral satisfactions, the intricate behaviour derived from them that has existed from soon after birth would have regressively doubled rather than have become attenuated, especially since the psychic oral structure has been essential for recognition, for learning, from the earliest months of existence. It has surely become clear, however, that much of the seizing and devouring that support identificatory activities have drawn overriding compulsive power from aggression, pre-eminently when the result is confusion, confusion between self and object. These mechanisms too, and all our earliest history, remain with us; yet some negative drive has passed into the growing and into the maintenance of spines so that postures of regression lose a degree, at least, of their nimbleness. To this extent we have become new men.

Our fangs, then, should be our pride though it is hard to forgo Olympus. Music reproves uncouth masks: our state, we feel, is by no means the tip of humanity; we cannot aspire to presences portrayed by classical art. I am a grotesque whose face was poured away: but I am not persecuted to the extent of despising nobility; I do not even consider that the idealised figures of ancient art, idealised in the terms of a polished marble smoothness, serve to deny the intrinsic human character. On the contrary, I feel that those figures represent a rich variety of emotional projection. When he did not live among the many, and far more pertinent, devices of industrialised society, man himself sometimes appeared as a gleaming device. The image had become irremediably drab long before the injections, but especially so in contrast with the more recent surrounding mechanisms, particularly as we contemplated our fellows using them. We often then saw in clear outline infantile omnipotence. Moreover advertisement had brutalised the image – in this way advertisement was profound – and popular culture isolated the aggression that matched an environment that snatched away the sky. Following the injections, however, the motor car, a booster of organ potency as well as a potentially death-dealing tight little haven or home, has been far less employed as a pleasure for itself. The roads are somewhat freed and the harsh heart has deserted advertisement with the eclipse of its dim image of man. May the smooth brow be reserved for tall buildings; may we encounter Zeus anew against the sky.

Defensively brisk, smooth faces were employed to perfect deception. Those impudent dials are now rusty: they have gained the dignity of a disused alarm clock in the loss of its hands. It is good that the face is hidden, particularly the mouth, the trap; it is good to specify at that point with spikes our brutishness. Our masks are very similar except that eyes still exert predominance. But in our context eyes appear receptive, less rapacious or prehensile than of old. Perhaps vision has lost a degree of oral employment. Though none of our glances can be soft they possess an aviary eloquence within the cage. Our staid and bushy faces impose upon the smoothness of our cities a contour from the countryside, and so we no longer see the bald limpet of a face a-hover over banisters, a face from which the world of concrete appears never to recede. The strong accents of features are much reduced. Indeed the pressing together of amorous skulls always lacked the brilliance of an accommodation between knees. Most suitably, the head now looks to be a receptive brain box. We have more confidence in strangers. Supreme ambivalence and great betrayal were so often the invisible writing on brows smoother than those that now with ready bristles transcribe our temper.

There is never too much goodness for the eye: I would not say that a soft complexion was tantamount to a snare. Yet I think that we may be happier with our self-constructed blemish in an animal cast, just as we are much healthier. Hardly any adult now, cradled in beard and spike, or spike alone, resembles an overgrown baby.

I miss an accent from eye-brow or from eye-lid. All smiling heaves in shadow. But, indeed, except for the necessity of strong twitching, our faces enjoy lassitude: those muscles need no longer be prodigious. We rarely attempt to shift the weighty spines: the result would be a grimace. It is possible that the resting of the face, the partial suspension from the crowding in of faces and from being seen as a face, has contributed to large conceptions of human presence. We are the less heads and hands protruding from clothes. In fine weather we leave a shoulder bare and an arm. The area surrounding the navel has enjoyed vogue as a substitute face. (My remark about the navel was over-sanguine.) It took time, of course, to dethrone the face, to stop searching and probing the disguise, the covering, as if the face were a harem woman to be glimpsed. I have learned now to think of the voice and of the eyes as limbs.

We monsters, it appears, will soon be superseded. Our afflictions are small in comparison with the sufferings of the smooth-faced gener-tions who will succeed us. We have become a variation of man that has proved its worth, maybe an event that occurred also in the past, among hominids perhaps who had failed to shed from their skulls arboreal emblems in favour of a continuous brow. For a time at least there will be two races in England just as abroad there are colonies of the quilled among the rest.

The calm of my narrative may mislead. Over several years we have witnessed an acute struggle. Parents resist our Associations fearing for the full beauty of their children, the oldest of which are now eight plus. They have been less subject to illness than were the children in pre-injection days, in my opinion only because of a space of two years without infection, the years in which injection had been almost universal, and because all those – still the vast majority – who have been injected do not spread disease. In consequence the advocacy of quills, since it is based on the promise of health, has suffered in the appearance of urgency. Every one disputes about the price, first of all without a doubt the price of self-pricking, of facial soreness even more than of facial disfigurement. There follows the question of repast, as it is generally called, of the awkwardness, of the gradual gentle nature of the eating and drinking that has been forced on us. Naturally in popular argument these are the aspects that consume. And forms of negation, reduced in their quantity by spine-growing, tend to rally, at least in the context of these general matters, as a result of the discomfort and deprivation that it causes; also as a result of facial ugliness. But beauty, the beauty of features perfectly wedded, now attains entire coalescence with the death-wish. The untangled roots of Romanticism are brandished.

Endymion and Attis are popular names for our infants: existentialist bravado returns redoubled: the classical is becoming tantamount to the quilled. In seven or eight years when we shall have a teen-age population of the smooth-faced, a far more active hatred and aggression will be directed against advocates of injection. The practice will eventually be forbidden and hunted down. Neither the individual nor the group will have the power to preserve what they cannot hide.

Yet meanwhile, for some time, injection is available. Many enlightened parents are using it today. Can their offspring defend us against the smooth-faced?

I have tried to charge these few lines with the hesitant temper that we value of those who are spined.

The Image in Form – A Lecture

From *Reflections on the Nude* (1967)

Often in a talk[1] about art we get at least a partial division of formal attributes from representation. We say the formal relationships organize the representation, the images, on view. That's the traditional approach. On the other hand, in the theory of Significant Form, form is isolated from imagery, from the construction of likenesses in visual terms.

I am going to argue that formal relationships themselves entail a representation or imagery of their own though these likenesses are not as explicit as the images we obtain from what we call the subject matter. When later I shall refer to Cézanne's *Bathers* in the National Gallery, I shall suggest that there is far more imagery in this picture than the imagery of nudes in a landscape, a more generalized imagery, with references to all sorts of experiences, which proceeds from the formal treatment. Now I think one can say that that's obvious and indeed that it is presumed in the work of all the best writers today on current art; but it doesn't seem to have given rise to a really wide investigation of what is involved. I am going to make some suggestions about this.

The phrase 'the image in form' cropped up when I was asked to decide between two constructions at a Soto exhibition. They are made of projecting square plaques against a background of black and white lines. I said I thought one communicated a stronger image than the other. It suggested an image for an amalgam of experiences, even though that impression had not been achieved by the creation of a correspondence with recognized events as is the case where you have a subject matter. I found this abstract work to possess an image all the same, whose character would not be altogether dissimilar in the long run for those who are able to lend themselves to abstract art.

Formal arrangements can sometimes transmit a durable image.

That is not merely to say that they are expressive. There is a sense in which every object of the outside world is expressive since we tend to endow natural things, any piece of the environment, with our associations to it, thereby constructing an identity additional to the one generally recognized. At heightened moments anything can gain the aura of a personage. But in art it should not be we who do all the imaginative work in this way. The better we understand art the less of the content we impose, the more becomes communicated. In adopting an aesthetic viewpoint – this, indeed, is a necessary contribution on our part – which we have learned from studying many works of art, we discover that to a considerable extent our attention is confined to the relationship of formal attributes and of their image-creating relevance to the subject matter. The work of art should be to some extent a strait-jacket in regard to the eventual images that it is most likely to induce. Obviously any mode of feeling can be communicated by art, perhaps even by abstract art. Nevertheless the personification of that message in the terms of aesthetic form constructs a simulacrum, a presence that qualifies the image of the paramount feeling expressed. That feeling takes to itself as a crowning attribute more general images of experience. Form, then, ultimately constructs an image or figure of which, in art, the expression of particular feeling avails itself. A simple instance lies with Bonnard, with the shape of hats in his time that approximated to the shape of the head and indeed of the breast. He seems to co-ordinate experience largely through an unenvious and loving attitude to this form. He is equally interested in a concave rounded shape. Again, when we know well an artist and his work we may feel that among the characteristic forms he makes some at least are tied to an image of his own physique or of a personal aspect in his physical responses. This also would be an instance of form as an agent which, through the means of the artist's personality as an evident first step in substantiation, allows him to construct from psychical and emotional as well as physical concatenations a thing that we tend to read as we read a face. A face records more experience than its attention at the moment we look at it.

520

Perhaps all we demand of a work of art is that it should be as a face in this sense. But form in the widest sense of all, as the attempted organization that rules every experience, must obviously give rise to a strong and compelling imagery so generalized that it can hardly be absent from a consciousness in working order though ordinarily present in nothing like the aesthetic strength, since were it otherwise refreshment and encouragement that we gain from art would not be necessary. Form must possess the character of a compelling apparition, and it is easy to realize that it is the icon of co-ordination.

Integration or co-ordination of what? it will be asked. Some aspect, I have argued elsewhere, of the integration of experience, of the self, with which is bound up the integrity of other people and of other things as separate, even though the artist has identified an aspect of himself with the object, has transfixed the object with his own compulsion, though not to the extent of utterly overpowering its otherness. These perceptions of relationship that are the basis of a minimum sanity demand reinforcement. Outwardness, a physical or concrete adaptation of relationship, spells out enlargement, means certainty.

It must appear a strange suggestion that art is in any way bent upon constructing an image for sanity, however minimal, in view of the wild unbalanced strains of feeling that have so often been inseparably employed in making this image. But surely if art allows not only the extremity of expressiveness but the most conclusive mode, if it constructs of expressiveness an enduring thing, that mode must incorporate an element to transcend or ennoble a particular expressiveness of which otherwise we should soon tire. We are encouraged to experience a many-sided apprehension in art. Expressiveness – it may be infantile – becomes valuable in evolving the mature embrace by form.

In the case of abstract art we are sometimes told by the artist – and it is very understandable – that we entirely mistake his work if we insist it expresses this or that. It is itself, the artist says, it does not stand for, it does not express, anything: it is not meant to suggest associations. I think he is right in the sense he means it. He is providing us, however, in his work with an experience of spatial relationships. Now it is obvious that no experience is entirely isolated, or else it is traumatic. The experience communicated by the abstract artist, on the contrary, invites comparison with other experiences and, to some extent certainly, will point to common ground with a particular aspect of visual experience in the first place or of the relationship between experiences. Abstract art would otherwise be virtually meaningless. Hence we have here an amalgam of meaning conveyed by material that transmits an image not only optical but for the mind or memory as well; unique for the eye but generalized for the mind. Here too the form constrains us to an image, and it is not merely one of our choosing.

Aesthetic experience can be defined as the opposite, indeed often as a palliative, of traumatic experience. But I am not going to try to probe the conditions of being of which this aspect of form is the symbol. I have attempted this elsewhere, as I have said. Some of the preliminaries are straightforward – for instance, the connection with the body-image. I shall partly be confining myself to this aspect.

I have often before referred to the rough-and-smooth values in building, in architecture, that are carried over into the other visual arts and, indeed, into the textures, as we have to call them, of concerted sound. Why otherwise are we forced to speak of texture to describe appositions of instrumental sound? In truth, we cannot but speak of the surface of any work of art, and equally of shape and volume, of the articulated body, metaphors by which we assert the dynamic effect of its impression and the self-completeness. Formal values vivify such images; the inevitable metaphors derive from inevitable images that accompany our apprehension of the formal qualities. In the fifteenth-century courtyard of the palace at Urbino designed by Luciano Laurana, in my opinion one of the greatest masterpieces of architecture, we surely see the same thing, a justice and fairness in the smoothness of the pilasters on the brick wall. The strength of this wall is measured by the eloquence of its apertures and by the open arcade beneath. Each plain yet costly member of this building has the value of a limb: in the co-ordination of the contrasting materials there is equal care for each: together they make stillness that, as it were, breathes.

One must agree to a generalized and meaningful content in the relationships of the Soto construction and in the Laurana courtyard. But are they characteristic works of art, that is to say so characteristic that they can be used to illustrate a content available in all art? What of the agony, violence, irregularity, flippancy even, that appear to be inevitable in some art today, or the restlessness, the explosive disruptiveness that is also common to much of the art of the past?

I have said that the generalized content of form, an element of co-ordination as well as of allusiveness, not only does not inhibit but makes an enduring thing or body of any kind of expressiveness however extreme. When, as has been common in this country, we use the term 'expressionist' in a pejorative sense, we mean that unmistakable expressiveness figures in this or that work but is by no means richly integrated throughout the formal relationships on view, and that therefore the effect is transitory rather than enduring. It encompasses no more than one or two notes. From Picasso's *Three Dancers* at the Tate, on the contrary, we derive a shattering image that coheres. It merits a lot of study. In the Tate *Annual Report* for 1964–5 there is a remarkable analysis, I think the best account I have read of a modern painting. It shows that every piece of the canvas is emotive, contributing to the whole, and even that there are resumed two of the most expressive themes in the iconography of Christian art. I need not go into it: in fact to do so would not help my purpose at this moment, the purpose of reminding you that we are instantaneously convinced by this agitated scene, though it is disruptive and difficult to understand. But we see that every line and tone and division helps in the setting up of various relationships across and down the face of the canvas. In front of an insistently imaginative painting this tends to convince us that an emotive or poetic whole is there expressed, since the expressiveness is transmitted by a rich language of form. Were it not so it would be a bad picture. The echoes and relationships make expressiveness ring, reverberate. Poetry may be plain and simple: the reverberations, even so, are many. Similarly with the nude in visual art. Form encourages further meaning because it is itself the container of a sum of meanings;

the nude has already a variety of intense meanings, even apart from art and apart from the connection between the body and form.

In the mechanism of this reverberation prime objects, however transmuted, will figure. Parts of the body and the body itself are prime objects instituting relationships at the root of subsequent relationships of every kind. Our awareness of the violent distortions and the formal elaboration of the breast in the Picasso *Three Dancers*, leading to a round void in the middle of the dancer on the left, illustrates that the body is an object we are likely to follow keenly in transmutations imposed by the artist. I am eager to point out that an ideal Madonna by Raphael is no traitor to this wide connectiveness.

But first Cézanne and the other very great painting that we have of late welcomed to this country, *Les Baigneuses*, in the National Gallery. At first sight these figures could suggest a quorum of naked tramps camped on top of railway carriages as the landscape roars by from left to right; except, of course, that studied, monumental, they altogether refuse the character of silhouettes. They absorb, and in absorbing rule, the environment. Beyond the long seal-like woman who regards the depths of the background, the standing, studious, twin-like girls with backs to us lean across towards the trees and clouds as if to be those upright trees. All the same the stretching across the picture plane is more intense, the stretching of these governing bodies that now seem poised on the easy rack of a level moving staircase. But movement to the left is blocked by the striding figures on that side, and since movement is braked at the other end as well it is as if shunted trucks were held between two engines. The tall, contemplative figure on the further bank remembers for us the stretching movement that, in effect, has crammed the centre where the two groups of bathers meet. Rich with dynamic suggestions, the movements coalesce into a momentary composure so that even within the crowd there appears to be airiness and space. It is now that we contemplate the broad back, laid out like a map, of the sitting woman with black hair on the left. Only in art, in an image, in a concrete realization of emotional bents, such powers with their reconciliation are found perfected.

Another image comes to us in terms of the heads of hair of walnut and stained oak. It speaks to us of the strength of the trees in those women and of the tawny arena on which the bodies lie and, by contrast, it includes the circumambient blue, the knife-like blue day that these nudes have crowded to inhabit. They feed on the blue, on the distance at which the seal-woman exclaims. The close, clumsy yet heroic flesh sips the sky. These nudes are blue-consuming objects and blue is the only colour almost entirely absent from all the varieties of nourishment. The dissociation invites us to examine them more for their sculptural value, to grasp the monumentality not only of the group but of the knife-sharp, simplified faces without mouths, the alternations between astounding bulk and summary, distorted sharpness that both under-write the compositional movements and, from a faceted flatness, heighten the picture plane. The sky too is faceted, spread thick like butter.

The distorted angularity of many shoulders, the insistence upon angle and strength of line, oppose with ferocity a facile mingling of these bodies, in order to rejoin them sharply; with the result that our apprehension of the bulky, answering V shapes is a startled apprehension, as if experienced by means of the extreme flare of a forked lightning flash. Coupled with the contrasting monumentality, this sharpness persists in the impression however long we gaze. Another reconciliation is between the sheet-lightning of the enwrapping towels and the slow swathes of blue daylight that dwell on ochre-tinted flesh and ochre hair and the ochreous strand.

For me the blue embrace is the final impression, withstanding a hurricane-like flattening of the light-toned foliage and a suggestion in the shape of the right-hand bathers' group of a petal-shaped volcanic orifice erupting into a steamy cloud beyond. But the group as a whole does not appear settled or rooted to the ground. The figures almost slide on it. We sense the possibility of fresh forms burrowing up from the ground's lightness to meet the blue embrace. This sense of lightness and fruitfulness balances yet enhances both monumentality and angularity.

The left-hand group is pyramidal; incline of the tree trunks is an important element of the design, in the arrest and, on the right, in the reversal of movement. But especially in regard to so great and complex a picture I am the more unwilling to speak in the plainer functional terms of composition and design. I prefer to insist that the formal elements not only enrich but enlarge the subject matter. The fact that you do not agree with every image that I have associated with this picture does not invalidate my point. The emotive arrangements carry a number of such interpretations. Form is the container for a sum of meanings while it is from a concatenation of meanings that form is constructed, meanings that have been translated into terms of spatial significance. Without appreciation of spatial value, of empathy with bodies in space, there can be no understanding of the emotive images that form conveys. I believe that there is a nexus of meaning that we all recognize however various our explanations; it is composed from experiences otherwise divergent. The experiences will be largely individual but the power of an integrated communion between trends in concrete or corporeal terms is palpable. Let us agree that the material for creating this nexus is drawn from the artist's experiences and intentions, particularly, of course, his aims in regard to art. There are also broader limitations upon the realization of form without which we have no licence to conceive of art, matters of style, of the moment in the history of art and of the culture it mirrors, the many-sided limitations that are the concern of art history. But here, too, proper understanding depends upon an acceptance that cultural aim has been translated by all art, even sometimes without the help of iconography, into the concrete terms of the senses and within the range of our long memory for sensory experiences wherein traces of the first and primary objects are preserved. One more word about *The Bathers*. Some of the faces particularly are conceived as a series of ledges or blocks, wooden, primitive, strong. The tendency exists throughout Cézanne's development from the seventies. I believe this aspect of his work, especially in the last compositions of *Bathers*, is the first of his influences upon the evolution of Cubism. This same aspect of his influence is far more obvious upon *Les Demoiselles d'Avignon* and upon all those works that were so soon to forge the easiest of links with Negro sculpture. I cannot help speculating in the most far-fetched manner whether one day it will be possible to claim for *The Bathers* that it is among the first and perhaps the greatest works of a deeply founded cosmopolitan art which was to pre-figure the eventual evolution of a multi-racial society. That would indeed be to specify a very pregnant image implicit in form, the compulsions of which in the Industrial Age had substantiated out of the inner life a compulsion even of a history to be.

No manifestation, particularly psychological manifestation, no behaviour, no ritual, is as foreign as it was. We found a new culture from remnants that remain of our own and possibly from what we have understood of other cultures past and present. If one had to choose to say only one thing about modern art, it would have to be in relation to this, it seems to me, not as a matter of ideas, of rationalizations, but as avid necessity in regard to an externalization of the inner life, deeply qualified, as for an art activity it must be, by the social setting, by the look, by the quality of the external world on which the social setting has been projected.

The controlled tenderness of Bellini's Christian piety, as seen in *The Dead Christ Supported by Angels* (National Gallery), embraces an illumined land. That view of the body had come down to him from Attic Greece. Pentelic sanity confronts muted eloquence. The stillness of the candid dead torso dignifes life without separating it from grief. Dead, the body of Christ connects with the living who take into their minds the image of Christ as an ideal body, it is suggested here, as a chest in part, smooth, sloping, elephantine in wisdom; breathing, it seems, a warm silence. More generally we are offered images of life and death, deft angels and the mortified head of the corpse. The habit of bodies, whether sensitive or dead, is disclosed once more: we are told that in the variety of meanings to which it points a body is as expressive as a face. The partial nude always conveys the sense of disclosure: it is appropriate here to the Christian meaning. At the same time the angels perform a slow gentle wrapping of the corpse.

Many characteristics of flesh are suggested by this delineation, but only one characteristic is omni-present to which other delineations are subordinate: shape against a background.

The spaces thus contrived are roughly triangles. The angels' heads both echo and vary Christ's head, the cylinders of their arms the corpse's arms. The element of geometry or of reduplication is an armature, the aesthetic armature, to which our feelings, as if they too could be solid things, as if they could be clay, cling; that is to say our feelings of contact, our meeting with a separated object or with ourselves now encouraged to separate from the splitting of ourselves. We feel in ourselves the tautness of the angels' feathered wings, the wrinkled clinging sleeve, the arm covering in the making for the corpse below those wings. We feel in us the corpse's beautiful listless hands. Christ's right arm droops but it is half-supported by a ledge on which the fingers bend, and by the angels' enwrapping grip. That demonstration of gravity serves less the effect of momentum than of poise, so nearly compounded of compensations as to be rest.

How often is this the effect upon us of the Old Masters, particularly of paintings with nudes. In my own mind I revisit early years abroad, the sense of discovery in many galleries, the predominant effect of the pictures in relation to the discomfiture of loneliness. Art meant oasis for the body as well as for the mind but also a ritual that affirmed unalterable contact, on the whole in a fully adult sense, rescued from the excess that had obscured or depleted an embrace.

Rembrandt's *Belshazzar's Feast* in the National Gallery is far from conveying this involucre of pentelic marble; on the contrary, it shows human beings with the incorrigible character of scored, used pots. A darker conception of the body assumes a vivid clay. Hence Belshazzar's imposing pallor even though he suggests a richly feathered hen or turkey amid a treasury of filth, though the quilted magisterial stomach mounts to a plucked neck and head. Leaden with the threads of gold and silver, turban and diadem reiterate the blindness of heaped matter as does the great weighted see-saw of Belshazzar's outstretched arms. The woman recoiling on the right who spills from a cup herself suggests a rounded, stoppered vessel. The clattering gold, like all treasure, has its threat or is threatened. Amid the fur of light upon the wall incomprehensible letters speak out the traumatic counterpart sometimes associated with these bodily products.

I believe that strong feelings of such a kind, or feelings derived from them, possessed Rembrandt; they are one root of his power; and that otherwise he could not so magnificently have imposed the weighty articulation, for instance, of Belshazzar's right hand.

Many of us find Rembrandt to be the greatest of artists, I think because no artist approaches him in projecting the feel I have spoken of, the feel of presences not only substantiated from observation in the outside world but substantiated equally from the hazy presences in the mind. We are aware of a lineage for his every face far beyond the range of iconographic study. These presences are charged, weighty, condensed from the light and from the dark literally and metaphorically, with a finer drama than the apparition of writing on a wall. They are compendia, bodies that manifest the history of their growth: each speck gives power to an opaque fellow. In a very remarkable book about Soutine, just published, Andrew Forge has written of Rembrandt in similar strain. He has this sentence: 'This is his (Rembrandt's) measure, that his architecture is as ambitious as his material is earthy.'

We are sometimes shown in contemporary art heads as helmets. The projecting plane for forehead and nose folds sharply back. How beautiful the helmet-shape in Raphael's *Madonna of the Tower* (National Gallery)[2] of the shoulder's overdress, the suave shoulder bone above it, the rounded neck, the geometrical expanse of face and head turned towards us! Were the helmet-shape armour, it would not allow smoothness to the firm skin, nor stillness above the straining child. The shoulder's rotund slope is developed across the picture by the child's undeveloped, trusting arm; we give a more than usual value to the continuation since we are even ready to connect the discontinued in view of the felicity to each other of helmet-shoulder and Virgin's head, an unarmed Athene. There is added poignancy too in the more rounded head of the child pressed and tilted away by the contact with his mother's cheek, and in her hand that comes round the child's middle and in the other hand that holds his foot. The curved line of the Virgin's cheek against the darkness where the child's temple flares – there is much triangularity as well as roundness in the composition – possesses an eloquence of eyelids. The faint encircling veil that depends from the summit of the Virgin's head reinforces the group's monumentality, not least this gravity of warmth and love.

The picture's ruined state makes one wonder the more at the beauty of the whole, at the regularity of the head, at the Michelangelesque *contrapposto* of the sitting body; at the cliff-like excesses and irregular caverns of the voluminous outer garment that consorts with the smooth flat hair, with the calm landscape and the simplicity of the Virgin's face.

In considering thus the composition's sentiment we touch other states of mind as bodily things, even an account of acceptance and rejection, since visual art works pre-eminently with contrast, with relief and background, with light and dark, with emphasis and its curb, with the play of opposing surfaces and degrees of volume. The ceaseless metaphors of language are physical and physiological. We stretch them painfully in pure speculation. Art corrects abstraction. Even the good and the bad mirror their physiological derivation: what is physiologically good gives rise to what is bad when we are deprived of it or when – and that is always – it is the object of our envious selves. The language of disdain, hatred, and rejection discovers the utmost denunciation in the terms of putrefaction. We speak of the currents of our feeling as dismembered, split, or perhaps they are not crippled.

Abstractions tend to become presences in dreams. Parents from the earliest times and other people are presences within, and when the self projects part of itself it projects an object.

There are images in our lives to which we hold tenaciously; we rediscover them in their variants. These are embodied operations that allow to art a universal language.

What great demands, then, we make of the artist, and how supremely great is the great artist! This painting satisfies as a reconstruction of mother and child. The sentiment is forthright but with it the artist

530

has forged wider attachments that continue to fascinate our reflective selves. They helped the artist to typify his theme in accordance, of course, with the development and state of art at that moment, in accordance with the influence upon him from his art and from his culture, not to mention requirements of the patron. The culture served by Raphael obtained expression in his image of the subject matter that was determined also by much that he attributed to relationships in space. Or these last, it could be said, were the vehicle of a particular Christian sentiment. It makes no difference to my point which way round the matter is put. And my point is that we have not only the image of Virgin and Child presented in accordance with Italian iconography and pictorial style of the early sixteenth century but also the sixteenth-century iconography or pictorial style of relationship in man's inner world in the concrete terms of space applied to, and modified by – even inspired by – the subject of mother and child.

I can think of no other Old Master landscape painting beside Hobbema's *Brederode Castle* (National Gallery), unless it be the *Amsterdam Herring Tower*,* also by Hobbema, also in the National Gallery, and equally jewel-like in colour, that gives as strongly an impression to be discovered in most landscape, namely the impression that though one is scanning the open, the distant, at the same time one is imaginatively attending to an interior scene, an aspect of the inner life. This castle landscape, stepped from blue to red, to the dark bank, to the pink ruin and to the incontinent clouds like the disordered roof of a cave, is yet so softly and closely organized that the castle may seem to have the function of a high altar at a cathedral's end or, more simply, to suggest the centre of a cupped flower. The central mass is echoed by the forms of the bank and trees in the left foreground though they are much darker, larger, flowing or ragged. The Amsterdam townscape is somewhat similarly composed in this respect. I suggest that as well as looking on the outside world we are looking at personable figures ensconced in the mind that exert intermittent influence on the pliable forefront of our attention.

* *The Haarlem Lock, Amsterdam.*

In a changing landscape the pink buildings are these static personages, or rather the good personages who have survived every attack, whom we wish would never surrender their places; whom we want to be static even as ruins. They are shown here as receivers of the passing light and of the seasons. But there is sap in the trees, in bushes and grasses: the dark river, like the blood, like circumstance, flows in a circular channel: the river birds are community members, while the buildings are bare of all except simple structure; apertures, buttress, walls with an accretion only of fern.

Viewed as an image of mind and body the painting shows the flesh, with the forces that animate and those to which it is subject, as divided, as mingled in new combinations. Yet owing to the compelling insinuation of tone and colour a totality emerges from these divisions and admixtures, having learned from them an intimacy or warmth that now serves the central structure and its surroundings; a totality that the eye reassembles and communicates at each look.

Of such kind, I believe, is the reckoning demanded of us by the just accountancy of great paintings in regard not only to masses but to the use of paint, to tone and colour relationships, to the representation of texture, movement, light. An image of building as generic structure, rich in itself yet palpitating with the cursive endowments also of the surrounding world with which it abides in relation, has been an inherent theme of our culture and of our art since classical times, to which even this seventeenth-century northern landscape must be referred. Building has figured in nearly all our landscape painting up to the middle of the last century when architecture for the first time ceased to epitomize the co-ordination of the body and thereby the integration of the ego, of the person or the mind. Yet while the old theme was notably exploited by Corot at times, he and those who accompanied and followed him have continued to provide through the texture of their paint, or through other insistence on the picture plane, many of those surface values that an environment of architecture once had lavished.

I end on a favourite note after developing the argument with the help of a minute fragment from the variety of art. Nothing, for instance, from outside Europe. I have offered images that are, at best, sometimes appropriate to the formal elements of the pictures described – in association of course with their subject matter. Once more, as a last word, I ask you not to identify these images, these derivatives, with what I have called the 'image in form', that is, where I have spoken of it as a generalized happening implicit in all the differing manifestations a few of which I have tried to interpret. The proof of this generalized happening that seeks to dispel chaos does not rely only on such speculative, subjective assertions. Now the chaotic is at best only just behind all of us, and we discover certainty largely by a massive projection of ourselves on to the external world which we then reabsorb. This generalized happening, it seems to me, has direct bearing on the correspondence between sensuous arrangements in the outside world and the conscious – I have spoken so far only of the less conscious – images we sometimes form of our mental processes. For we find in our reflective states that simple emotions or complicated wishes both to have and not to have something, states of tension, capacities of the mind and so on, have themselves implanted as we contemplated them a residue of spatial imagery that we can watch; intersecting lines of conflict; stubborn, seemingly material, obstacles; rhyhms and intervals that correspond with the order and tempo of events, the punctuation of time; spatial images, these, of sensation and a sum of experience which, when transposed into an art activity with material, provides the means of a concrete language whose expressiveness depends upon firm links with the continuous inner images substantiating and ordering complicated experiences of the body and of the mind; but hitherto substantiating in an unfixed manner. And so we see why painting, for instance, is primarily concerned with projecting the third dimension, why we value so highly the whole range of disposition from shapes that loom to those exactly disposed, the obstinate suggestion of volume or of depth magnificently achieved in all my examples, even the Soto.[3] In any visual construction we require not only provocative nouns, so to speak, of insistent shape but equally interconnection, the action one upon another, analogous to the role of verbs upon which a statement depends. Since the glimmering nouns behind the concrete forms are strongly comprehensive yet ambiguous, the fixing verb-function of composition is likely to be many-sided. Moreover all the statements of whatever kind in a picture tend to be very closely interconnected since they are apprehended together, since their contents are simultaneously revealed. A great painter like Seurat is able to extract the utmost significance for his compositions from the slightest variation in a few dominant forms or directions.

An easy thing remains to be said; a caveat. Pictures are not problems. Nothing I have put forward, even supposing it to be correct, alters the fact that the Hobbema is a landscape painting wherein the artist communicates his pleasure, his record of a natural scene containing castle, ducks, trees, and people. This topographical value is the only value admitted by some who, for whatever reason, are entirely impervious to art. We should be in little better case than they if the considerations I have advanced, instead of supplementing or interpreting that immediate aspect of the matter, undermined it.

Psycho-Analysis and Our Culture

(1967)

The clamant reception of Lorenz's popular account of animal aggression and of Morris's *The Naked Ape* suggest considerable modification
of resistance to Darwin's book one hundred years ago. A reassurance
emerges today from our connection with the animal world. I am thinking not only of the provision in such books of an ancient lineage for the
sacredness of tribal and personal property. There is also the suggestion
that the behaviour of mammals in their communities seems in important respects milder than our own. They are delightful ancestors in view,
that is, of the concentration camps, in view of the very many pretences
and disciplines that have now slipped to reveal widely the abysses of
human nature, a shift of control in which the findings of psychoanalysis,
generally misconstrued, have undoubtedly played a part, particularly
in the matter of the outmoding of religion as well as of idealistic or
optimistic standpoints at the very time that the negativism of man has
been extensively felt as incorrigible, even without reference to psycho-
analysis. There exists in some intellectual circles today so strong a
horror of the human state that a writer, George Steiner, has urged that
alleged understanding, protestation, emotional accountancy on the
part of authors should cease in the matter of the concentration camp
horrors; that the way to measure up to enormity on this scale is silence,
drying-up, if only because words have been emasculated by the ending
they have suffered from the hypnotic techniques of advertisement and
propaganda. There is a thread of despair in many cultural expressions,
though we may be more aware of matter-of-factness or cynicism. Some
intellectuals tend to have a residual impression from concentration
camp literature and from its bearing on their own infantile intimations,
from the cases too of unpremeditated murders by adolescents in an

apparent state of sane passionless indifference, that sanity can comfortably include this indifference. Psycho-analysis does not endorse a profundity of indifference rather than of an underlying conflict. Could it be roundly conveyed that at some point or other psychopaths care, can be discovered to care, even though not for their victims, a much needed balance might ensue from this reassurance, and thereon wider understanding. This is the moment to ram home the consequences revealed by the entirely unbridled phantasmagoria of infant, child and dream. All that is most disturbing is infantile or, rather, the persistence of the infantile. Man's achievement has been his maturity, that is to say, the modifications of the infantile material. These are all acts of heroism.

It seems to me, therefore, that just as resistance to Darwin has given ground to a reassurance, however ironical – there is of course the element of making the best of the Darwinian shock – deeper knowledge of psycho-analysis, to which there has been hitherto such resistance, would further a more temperate judgement of the nature of man because, in regard to his negativism, psycho-analysis is unflinching, while on the other hand we affirm the belief – and certainly no less the child's or infant's belief – in a good object closely related to negativism or bad objects; in a good object of an everyday and physiologically-founded status that parades a homeliness far removed from the noble enthronements of the past to which it was the footstool. (Resistance, of course, necessarily remains unaltered in the psycho-analytic process. Any value there may be in what I am trying to say, depends upon some degree of validity in a distinction between the personal and the generalised resistance. Owing to the granite-strong resistances of their patients above all, as well as to the varying yet constant misunderstandings of psycho-analysis over more than fifty years, this is a distinction about which analysts themselves are likely to be sceptical.)

Apart from patients, psycho-analysis, I repeat, has some responsibility for our culture. By means of clarifications as trenchant as those of the historical and textual disciplines directly involved, it has assisted at the steady overthrow of religious revelation: it has reduced humanist rationalisations of evil, guilt and redemption, an action of particular moment inasmuch as the earlier breakdown of religion with the triumph of Rationalism in intellectual circles during the last hundred years, had cleared the way for an extraordinarily shallow grasp of the human condition, even though the Rationalist movements were fighting and conquering superstition. There is, of course, reaction today – though not towards religion against the innocent expectations of Rationalism. The advance of free thinking, the instituting of Humanist, Rationalist or Comtist chapels and their muted rites have helped to show that such abstract, impersonal yet sanguine ideas of a life-force are rather vulgar and even comic. The present cultural despair, therefore, partly arises out of the crashing of Rationalist hopes. This same Rationalist shallowness, excusable in the first flood of the early Enlightenment, is not as commonly recognised in ideas of the perfectability of man to which the only obstacle is the tyranny of economic exploitation. It was not ideas such as these that inspired the building of cathedrals or the making of any profoundly eloquent work of art. The universal religions are based on conceptions of original negativism and the hope of salvation. Stripped of strained rationalisation, their psychology is somewhat nearer to the psycho-analytic standpoint. Hence there is a duty, I feel, to defend the poetic elements in the psychology of religion; or, rather, it would be so were we unable to extract from psycho-analytic sources themselves any power that could restore to culture, and more particularly to art, a constructive sense of the *transcendental*.

This will seem a strange word to employ. Before explaining I shall repeat in a different form a part of what I have said so far.

It is very evident that a mild and sanguine view of human condition provides no inspiration to the arts. Communism promises the perfectibility of living hitherto obstructed by economic exploitation. Such a doctrine possesses the anti-aesthetic quality of all 'rational' religions. Christianity, Mohammedanism, Buddhism, on the other hand, posit what is called 'a vale of tears' springing not only from the world but from the nature of man. Though useful to tyranny and to the reduction of the masses, these beliefs and their attendant mythology and personifications have inspired the richest aesthetic material, since they are psychologically more profound. The life-force, aesthetically speaking, is null without the presence of an equally powerful negative principle that provides the scaffolding for the last-word stillness or finality of great works of art. The long echoes inside a cathedral infecting our awe there, stimulate the sense of reduplication of activity, but also of the adamantine stoniness of the stone. A pulse is unheard in this environment unless organ or choir restores activity in every vault.

Is there any future for the communal scale of such gigantic images? I think that it depends on the character of the notion of the transcendental that can be permitted to flourish.

Now in cultural contexts – and my use of the word is confined to them – 'transcendental' does not only refer to an unshared power or state beyond us but also to shared fundamental aims. We cannot experience other people's experiences but we recognise and even understand them in the terms of our own. Millions upon millions of people have existed, in the life and death of whom we have had no part: but we sense them in view of what is held in common even though as individual objects they are entirely beyond our powers. Such transcendental envisaging may lead us to contemplate in terms of a symbol the universal conditions of being and of non-being: it points to the drives or instincts. Each individual can embrace only an atom of the happenings of nature. Our imaginative conception of the rest will be homely in origin but extended in terms of analogy and contrast. Our own experience, too, far transcends what we can consciously remember or hold in mind. To comprehend feelings and phantasies widely is to be vividly sane. It is not only in analysis or after analysis that the conjunctions of passion from each stage of development are the object of much mature striving. We need the help of images that embody at one and the same time solutions both for the regard and the recoil from the body.

Religion seeks to contemplate as the transcendental or common aim a primitive object revered everywhere, perhaps wooed or placated by ritual. Religion exalts the good object into an ideal object, places it far beyond us, beyond our power to qualify or destroy it. The transcendental becomes defence and escape. For us the transcendental is that large and more varied part of ourselves with aims common to all other people. Psychologically speaking, a transcendental pre-occupation as I conceive it in non-escapist terms, expresses a projection of identity, that is to say, of that part of identity held in common which possesses for a complexity of reasons a value that we need to explore and to contemplate. It might be said to be the opposite emphasis to the one upon individual identity and therefore, in fact, upon identity. But I think that my definition is saved by the concept of maturity as the summit of identity for each of us. There could be a strengthening of individual identity by a ritual that celebrated maturity to which we would be attributing a transcendental value. I see the need for such ritual. Another contradiction has been pointed out to me here, the contradiction between maturity and ritual. Is not ritual always in some sense the celebration of a primitive object and is there not an element always of regression in the identificatory inspiration of communal fervour? But I shall continue to use the word 'ritual' even in the context of the celebration of maturity because neither the drive toward primitive identification nor the striving toward maturity will cease: and though these aims are often exclusive of one another, it is in their meeting that the height of creativity exists. I have presented the conjunction repeatedly when portraying the form in art.

I distrust religion yet I am aware of respects in which I am fortunate that there are religious people; and churches, cemeteries, processions or church bells that preside, that evoke staves for time. How rarely church bells poison the good sense of the air.

There is nothing to worship, much to accept, to contemplate in the common lot, as innocent of final purpose as a work of art. The only worthy symbols for all that is held in common, as well as for every variation of the inner life, are the projections wrought by art. But can ritual utterance be won for our common ground by means of the contemplation, a communal contemplation, of art? I don't often think so. We congregate in concert halls. I, at any rate, gain no stimulus from any audience or from the fact that others listen at the same time. One may eye one's neighbour in the concert hall primarily to judge whether he is likely to cough or to rustle chocolate papers. It is the making of some art, not the viewing, that provides a large sense of community with those present at the time: it is the players of the orchestra who are the hierophants together. And in cathedrals we may visualise past generations of the place as a white light, and present worshippers or their enactors of ritual as a subdued reflection. But is it possible for us to pool psycho-analytic insights?

I should be warned, perhaps, by the very word, the unwieldy word, 'psycho-analysis', by the emphasis upon the analytic. It is perhaps unreasonable and even heterodox to expect from this discipline an addition of even one phrase to the sum of sober poetry or ritual, to a mode of communication instant and many-sided alike, rich in tran-scendental pointers, possessing a manner of particularisation that can be widely shared. Maybe the regulative, critical or analytical role of analysis must confine absolutely: perhaps it may support the criticism of art but cannot provide specific content for its making; the analysis of living but not any attempt, however rare, at symbolic re-creation. Perhaps there should not be any communal attitude that arises from analysis towards other matters: it is no instrument here: it does not, or, rather, it should not, initiate widely contemplative states of mind whose material has been provided by analyses of states of mind.

Further, there is, of course, the difficulty of the character of psycho-analytic insights. Can they be material from which poetry is made, a future poetry? The child's and the dream's phantasmagoria, the wizards, witches, butchers and extravagant, indifferent tyrants have long made poetic appearances in the world's literature. But while psycho-analysis has established their universality, their non-fanciful actuality, their identity not only as necessitous products of the psyche but as reflectors of behaviour, such insights are compounded with others, far less downright, often of ambivalence and centred on ambi-guity: and here lies the beauty, the subtlety of psycho-analytic insight where one behaviour is the composition of two utterly conflicting trends, for instance, a symptom. Many of the applications of the word 'inhuman' commonly refer in fact to unbearable aspects of the psyche thereby projected and denied their homely nature: 'hardness of heart' makes mere deadly frost of the compulsive puritan forces that drive on with narcissistic or psychopathic fervour. Envy, meanness, cruelty obtain full description as forms of behaviour, but the human quality of the constructions that provide their continuity has, unlike the case of the good, mostly escaped comprehension even by artists, at least in regard to the positive aspect that underlies the defence mechanisms that are involved.

So can perpetual qualification become *bel canto*, the outpouring of song? Is there a song inspired by the back-handed glories of integration and maturity? Moreover, it is the prime psycho-analytic task to discover and emphasise the infantile basis of subsequent development. Could this emphasis accommodate love poetry, even supposing the status and the pretensions of adulthood had been re-defined? Nevertheless, will there not grow eventually a down-to-earth vision of living – I do not suggest that we can as yet begin to entertain it – wherein major components are no longer deeply split from one another? One would summon in its aid an image of ever-recurring patterns so evident in each analysis, in all lives. Even psycho-analytically, when seen a long way off, in perspective, after the event, they suggest the pathos and the rhyming forms of poetry. Analogies that bridge contrasting facets are telling, analogies between states as far apart otherwise as can be imagined: an analogy, perfected by a poem, between a super-ego strenuous application to correct behaviour and the cruel excesses of the psychopath, between a stern parade of bemedalled veterans and a mob of seedy teenagers sacking a sweetshop after a football match. What a cast of mind in the poet it would show. People comprehend a cast of mind, accurately embodied, though they fail to follow the insights that determine it. They can eventually accept art not only on account of the veils of symbolism but because art is felt convincingly to be a proof that a content has been truly digested as well as projected in this way. Can it be so with such analogies; will their poignancy ever be lucid and shorn of paradox; will they ever possess the aspect that is, as it were, rounded, so that it may be grasped entire by the imagination and by the artist?

Poetry enacts feeling. Some may ask: does one feel about unconscious material and if so, in what sense is it unconscious? To which one may ask in return: in finding the unconscious in analysis do we make intellectual connections only with behaviour, thereby developing the power to generalise about such connections? Certainly not. Though it may take a long time for the connections with specific unconscious material to evoke feelings widely, there are many areas in which progressing analysands have felt, have fully experienced, those connections. It is of course the core of analysis that patients should experience connections emotionally. The mere deduction is useless. As to the possibility of communication, we learn from the past that poets and artists have had the means to articulate, to hand on, the emotional impress of unconscious determinants, not in their native condition, of course, but under the veils of symbolism and sublimation. But the position of the analysed poet might seem different. Having felt the deep connections far more directly, more specifically, he might seek to express them thus directly at the cost of symbolism and therefore of communication. But I would be wrong to call him an analysed poet. He is no poet. The solution lies with the transcendental or communal aspects of the deep material whereby the poet enters the imaginative, the sympathetic, as well as the descriptive, realm. That is why I introduced earlier the concept of the transcendental, of the communal. Sympathy, empathy, imagination, are closely allied. Did we lack or play down those faculties, how would the young have even a little understanding about what it is like to be old; or how could the old perform the perhaps harder exertion of feeling what it is like to be young; possibly more difficult because the earlier state was an identity that has been obliterated by circumstance and lost, lost to the very bones?

For the moment I shall presume that one day it will be practicable to magnify, in a just and dignified manner of feeling, the elements, the transcendental elements, common to a thousand individual analyses. I envisage a congregation of analysands recalling not so much their analyses nor their analysts, as generalities of feeling they have absorbed therefrom about human relationships; set upon evoking not so much problems, defences, even objects inner and outer, as anterior drives on account of which they are constructed. Yet the drives are meaningful only in the constructions where they become personified. I imagine a perfected fable, in touch with a hundred case-histories, of the schizophrenic state. I imagine a ritual of birth and of projection and a ritual that recapitulates the growth of the psyche as far as the adult heterosexual position. The ritual might propagate ritual, a meeting-place be built for contemplation rather than for teaching. No attempt would be made to further doctrine. There would be no busts of Freud, no heroes, no history except of the psyche. Disputation would take place elsewhere. An adequate form for the fables would accommodate many glosses, would serve for a long time. This form would be compelling, if it were aesthetically satisfying, if it were beautiful. In such guise the impact of truth could be none other than an effect of its beauty. We would have created something of value in common out of what is held in common. For, except we are imbeciles, we are all potential or actual schizophrenics, paranoiacs, depressives, phobics, hysterics, and we are all potentially or actually sane. It is this chiefly about which there would have to be entire agreement to allow the contemplation in common, and in some contexts the creativeness, that I have in mind.

Who can admit to it deeply, with imagination, with feeling? Probably not all analysts, less the analysands, far less anyone else. The first impediment, of course, to psycho-analytic comprehension is anxiety. Psycho-analysis aims to reduce anxiety gradually, in phases. We want the fears of our analysands, say the analysts, neither stimulated nor assuaged by the direct influence of the environment outside analysis. The ritual activity I have forecast might prove to be at best a manic or drug-like resource, a reassurance leading to denial: at worst an instrument of anxiety.

Yet, in spite of the dangers, I do not judge it to be impossible that a ritual symbolising the psyche's evolution and disparities could be created with a character so indirect and, if you like, mythological, that the deeper content confronted those only who might demand it. The manner of art and even of religion has been such, a complex significance suited to human diversity. Some may judge that this composite element of art has today suffered fragmentation. Perhaps our sober re-working of the human spectacle alone can restore it. I myself can otherwise imagine no bond in the future of art.

That would be an immense eventual result. But the first or immediate aim of the conventicle I have in mind would be to present an average of conduct in normal circumstances. The seeming permanence of general disillusionment is the result not only of the threat from the H Bomb and from pollution but of expectation that has always been faulty. Culture, including our culture today with relaxed standards, distorts the material by employing black-and-white categories. The young especially are not conditioned to expect components that do not necessarily subtract from, though they diversify, the character of a behaviour. It should not be so surprising that each person is uneven in strength and sanity or that everyone has some persecutory reactions in the face of the ever-close proximity of aggression; or that, consequently, protection afforded by an artificial uniformity, by a code of manners, should be necessary. But though good figures need to be brought nearer to their counterparts in the presentation of maturity, I am not at all suggesting that the psycho-analytic account of average behaviour can be summarised in the bringing to light of negative components only. On the contrary, it is we who survive better than anyone else the admission of everything that occurred in concentration camps. Anxiety can take the form of psychopathic indifference: brutality may possess a component that would rid the self of what is felt to be insufferable because it is self-destructive. Remorse and forgiveness are the hard-won fruits of development. Of what account is forgiveness by a Saviour compared with the very rare non-manic forgiveness of the self by the self, a long and most arduous pursuit? It involves throughout dependence on a good, unidealised internal object whose forgiveness has already been won: it involves a powerful degree of psychical integration or maturity.

But is it possible to present the lure of such a difficult goal that belongs to life, well-being and happiness rather than to the hope of heaven: and would there be any point in outlining this aim when the realisation, we know very well, is entirely unrelated to conscious choice; in extolling as an aim in common an integrated form of identity, the key transcendental content? I feel happier on the subject of ritual fables. None the less, there would be the need to create what is called a climate of opinion, to propose standards where they are different from those that are current; to suggest the equilibrium of psycho-analytic thought. Many psycho-analytic targets might be described as 'spiritual' yet at the same time of a character that people call, or used to call, Epicurean and materialistic. The spiritual element has corporeal base. We never depart from concrete and personalised imagery. The inner life is concerned with people, parts of people and parts of the self which, whether they are introjections or more truly parts of the self, are felt to be in substantive and corporeal relation with other objects. Poets have shown that at any rate the outside world, in its very character of an actuality that intermittently we distinguish entirely, is the arena for projection and introjection. Our tenets, though, unlike the heritage of poetic imagery, would seem unsuited to romantic overtones. Yet no one sees as profoundly as the trained psycho-analytic observer how harboured as well as threatened is the life within, how stiff and blinding, for instance, the distortions may be that are the work of guilt. Living is everyone's state, the more cherished on account of inner and outer enemies if we do not throw in our lot entirely with them, those Spartan attendants, those deaths that live with us, that struggle for the mind before the body. No other doctrine, in an introverted manner, has conceived as entirely the human being to be – though he figures thus so patently in day-today judgement – a psycho-somatic entity. We alone fully realise the physiological basis of imagery: we alone know how compelling envy to be as well as love and hate, emotions to which religion also allows inevitability but not a reality that is equal, that is to say, bound up in each case with the other's power. All psycho-analytic comment on our living process can be formulated, of course, in terms of the account of sexuality, a subject about which there are likely to be few people who feel that they have heard enough. And surely one part, however small, of absorption in matters of sex is due to the awareness that what is so urgent is also in this case many-sided, redolent of the individual's history. It is first of all the physical- or concrete-seeming character of obstinate and often competing inner structures in each individual that must be emphasised. And this constructional obstinacy is not only involved of course in individual sexuality, personal relations, capacity for work. It extends to all social problems in regard to the emotions that are brought to bear: it qualifies the expression of the widest needs, of priorities, in the context of technological advance and the terrible environmental dangers involved.

Psycho-analysts have neither the time nor, it seems, the inclination to contemplate the length of their practice in regard to what might be called the pathos and sometimes the heroism of the human process as well as to the classification and explication of symptoms. Theirs is itself a heroic but unnatural vocation characterized by huge demands upon patience and the impersonal behaviour without which an analysis would collapse; by the strains particularly of the strong transference and of counter-transference. Away from the sessions, the seminars and the meetings, their requirement is for what I have heard described as 'ordinary life'. In fact, as well as family life these welcome activities may include the artistic, rather than energy devoted to appreciation and contemplation, to attitudes that are more passive. It seems a pity in this context that nearly all those who come for analysis are so markedly ill and that, in any case, prolonged resistance is universal and always wearisome; and that together with the patience and self-denial needed, in other words, due to the analyst's extremely hard and anxious work, there is much to obscure the fact that the object of his investigation, though the form is extreme, is itself a piece of 'ordinary life'. Moreover such is the position of psycho-analysis as a dubious science in our culture, and so hurtful, so dangerous, to the difficult truth the euphoria of the simplifiers and seceders, that any general contemplation may appear circumvention to a habit of mind confined in consulting room time strictly to the immediate material. It is sad that those who by their training have learned to be more receptive for hours on end than perhaps any other body of men, should be compelled outside the consulting room to modify that listening role. Thus, though they tend to revere art they are rarely disposed to undergo the labour and slowness of valid appreciation.

Now we are sometimes told that the successful waging of a psychoanalysis springs from art as well as from science. The recurrence of infantile situations is evoked by the analytic process and analytic setting. I can conceive of homage paid to this setting by means of a ritual. Would it be harmful to patients and prospective patients? Any suggestion of the artificial or of the merely theoretical is damaging to analysis. Patients are often asked not to read psycho-analytic literature. It is obvious that a conventicle and its ritual would need to be confined to old analysands.

I would say that we are hampered – there is excuse for the analysts and entire excuse for the first analysts – by the sometimes rather arrogant desire to read, to categorise, with Aeschylus, let us say, on the couch, symbols projected in the past. From a scholarly point of view this often appears to be done in entire ignorance of the context. It may become a parlour-game in the exercise of power, like Bridge, that might be informative but rarely evocative of anything that is particularly pleasant or intelligent in the player inasmuch as he works by a rule-of-thumb cleverness, in this case in an area unsuited to heavy-handedness. These enterprises, even those which have been brilliant and to some extent revealing, have done considerable harm, not unjustly, to the prestige of psycho-analysis in the intellectual world. Of course there have been thousands of psycho-analytic applications of another kind, often tenuous, half-baked, in plays and novels. They do not show prolonged reorientation and greatness of mind. I find hardly any transcendental or communal value. When such works are written by analysands, the authors, one suspects, are concerned with the presentation or sublimation of their own predominant problems which do not leave them free to experience total impingement by this new range of understanding: or else the authors do not have the time or the ambition to have the time and largeness of mind to study and contemplate at length over the years. Moreover what is most lacking in such applications is the psycho-analytic representation of health rather than of illness and excess. And whereas there has passed from psycho-analysis into culture an appreciation of the universality of ancient figures – father, mother, siblings – and the supremacy of the past which is also the supremacy of the Id, the 'threads' have few knots, no effervescence, since undertaking is lacking of the so complicated, the so many-sided, psychical structures: indeed the deeper tow imputed to life, tends to be envisaged without the fantastic rocks, without the correlations and compensations and voids in the structure of attitudes at every stage and in the interwoven stages of ego development. The ego-cum-super ego happening is not yet seen architecturally, as a township, say, as a sublimation which would provide the most satisfying environment for art, equal in aesthetic value, and a good deal more varied, than the theological systems that have inspired the past. I believe a deeper acceptance of these inner hierarchies than has been possible heretofore, alone can restore to art the exuberance of structural animation, intensified at a vital point, since outer forms will primarily reflect, not a ready-made projection, religion for instance, but the inner forms conceived to be inner that from this their nature lend themselves to revised myth. For some time the old myths have provided limited creative stimulus.

But none of us, I think, is prepared. I am aware that this paper has been, at best, of a visionary quality, especially in the matter of congregation which may be unsuitable to the magnifying of those contents that I feel must be shared if they are to exert due influence upon culture. I have mentioned contemplation of the basic drives. But, to tell the truth, I do not consider that a projection or representation of the nature of the Id for contemplative purposes, and of its curbs and developments, is feasible unless we can be more precise about Id-nature, and still more, until the negative drive, a whipper-up in some contexts of its opposite, until the death instinct, both in fusion and defusion, be entirely accepted and integrated within every aspect of psycho-analytic theory. And how can we take cognisance without the adjuncts of holiness and hocus-pocus, some sober cognisance however limited, of the

548

pre-individual, pre-object, pre-splitting fusion of drives in the Id, the basis of a communion that is even more primitive than the so-called Oceanic tie? It might be urged, on the other hand, that whereas we would have no expectation of a completed survey of the psyche, psycho-analysis is firm enough, and surely sufficiently deep, to develop in us novel attitudes, to the extent that we shall invent therefrom a non-mystical behaviour even in regard to Id representation.

For short summary I return to the uninhibited main-stream of this paper. It could well be argued that insofar as the matter of psycho-analysis is co-extensive with the details of living, the details of under-lying trends, it provides no angle for relaxed contemplative attitudes. The psycho-analytic process penetrates resistance and denial against which it is always on guard. This is a breaking-down activity that lends itself not at all to the re-enactment of cultural fables. On the other hand psycho-analytic findings are among the insights which have sapped belief in any confident wisdom about the life-process at the present time. Are we able to mitigate firmly, in a form additional to individual analysis, our culture's lack of creative communion and morale: shall we never again have works of art comparable with the cathedrals: did their creation depend upon a dogma to enforce their symbolism: is a large and overwhelming creativeness, is a communal creative activity, impos-sible without dogma, propaganda and even, at times, mass hysteria? These are among the large questions put before us. Is it the moment to re-introduce the greatest of simple statements: 'Ripeness is all'?

Men must endure
Their going hence, even as their coming hither:
Ripeness is all.

The Future and Art

(1972)

There is no art without reference to a current culture but also, I submit, there is no art without cultural attachment that rules. To take a very narrow and literal example: we know Byzantine icons and mosaics, as well as so much else, were subject to religious pattern books which determined not only the attributes but the very cast of looks appropriate for each apostle. Those precepts made the representations easy to read. But far more general than such rules and the beliefs they serve, though equally tenacious, there are usually, in my belief, composite images that often settle for striking concrete *mise-en-scènes*, sometimes architectural, that tend to symbolise, even to epitomise, a wider cultural condition: that, as well as the development of one group of artists from the preceding, as well as the amalgam with foreign styles, these unforgettable environments in a big-unit culture provide the arena for the choice of contemporary forms projected by the individual artist. Our art has no pattern books, no norms, no settled iconography whatsoever. But though he may appear to have complete liberty of conception I still believe it is impossible for the artist to formulate or to communicate in a contemporary manner entirely outside a framework of stylistic alternatives that are invented or have evolved in the shadow of just such concrete epitomes or embodiments, in our case very often concise and single, namely the urban environment and its products. For it is my belief that all modern art, every modern movement from the time of the Impressionists at least – I would like to include Courbet – will eventually be seen figured in front of this one general emotive background with which to accommodate or to supplement, on which to bring influence to bear, from which to react. This is a solid context that the diverse and contrary tendencies have in common; this is the one simple, though non-circumscribed, factor in what we call modern art. For the artist all current feeling and thinking, his own and the thinking of those who influence him, occur in the view of these concrete surroundings which are taken to impinge on the circumstances, and even to point the path, of our culture. I'm sorry to admit that if there be truth in this belief it is as much presumed as demonstrated by this lecture. I shall discuss a few aspects of modern art from this angle; and so any justification of my approach will depend on explanatory value in a very restricted field. I must add – I hope unnecessarily – that there are constant values in art irrespective of particular culture. These values, for once, have only a small part in what follows.

About the word 'future' in my title. I would find it natural if you on whom the immediate future depends, dismissed any one of my age from this theme when the considerations are aesthetic. I, too, am doubtful. But I'm certain that there is an urgent feeling we share; namely unease about, lack of belief in, the future; a very terrible ingredient in our living to which we have become accustomed. A Londoner moreover – as I said I shall be referring often to the urban scene – I have experienced throughout my life this unease, as may well have you. Although I have admired the early modern architecture especially, I have not thought it the herald of advancing civilisation. As for the Edwardian buildings in my childhood, I can truly say I experienced from them the shamelessness of pretence as if death were smug; yet in the present – any reverberation being better than none, even any pretension that has been numbered – I too cling to some of what remains. There are theorists who now consider the days of Megalopolis to be numbered. One can tolerate most things that appear finite. But meanwhile cities swell, new roads are ploughed. The future will of course be unimaginably different: that in itself causes no anxiety. By the future I mean in this talk the future for our near descendants through whom we have that degree of immortality. In old age one thinks of it more and more and more as there is less and less security that there will be a prolonged future other than for a few bereft men.

Remember the artist who at great labour and expense covered, sought to preserve one might say at first sight, or perhaps also to negate through his own omnipotent, monolithic power as in the swathing of a building's detail, a stretch of Australian coast, rocks and cliffs, with polythene. Is it, perhaps, in one part as a kind of memento of what has evoked deep response but is subject to misuse, that a handful of artists have mapped out pieces of earth themselves and called it art? Do these men, in one part, isolate a length of ground as such for aesthetic contemplation in a manner not entirely unlike Marcel Duchamp's choice of manufactured objects, his ready-mades? There has been a great broadening of the possible objects for aesthetic contemplation at the sacrifice of precise imagery, delineated symbolic content, in favour of a presentation of the pre-existent, the actual. Yet at the same time there has been a tendency to eschew many contemplative inducements in favour of a more active participation, in favour of action, change, happening, though these, like the proliferation of manufactured goods, are expected to enwrap its consumers, the artist and his spectators. I suggest that the proliferation itself of manufactured goods is epitomised by the encompassing reduplication of the ribboned urban environment where we witness the still strange intertwining as in some of our art, the intertwining of change, movement, activity with the non-resonant character of whittled objects that seem to signify only themselves, a milieu with which in a hundred contrasting ways our art has sought, must seek, to get on terms, even by dismantling what has been conceived as art for centuries in regard to the separation that used to be taken for granted of aesthetic contemplation from the state of being up-and-doing. Other artists, however, taking advantage of the reductiveness that rules our urban scene, either in terms of coloured marks or by the materials themselves as well, supply the varied textures that our streets almost wholly lack. Very satisfying, very consoling this art can be, even on the smallest scale.

Another stress, not very old, was upon the random occurrence and upon the perishable or passing, as if art were otherwise cruel to natural disorder, to the successive, to universal transience. For me this means not only the recognition of an irreversible numbness in the static aspect of our urban scene compared with which any chance concatenation is freedom, poetry, elysium, but disorder attributed to ourselves, an anarchic potentiality to which systematic sanguine thoughts from the past do not apply. Yet we know far more than has been known hitherto about the chaos, by no means romantic, by no means random though it appears random, of the psyche. Maybe happy enough, helped to confidence by much convenience and pleasure unique to modern life, we will still endure frustration, conflict, negative states: and so we would in any age; but these, I submit, are likely to find far stronger confirmation than do the positive feelings, projected on to our present urban scene. To me it appears that its indeterminacy, its non-resonance akin to destructiveness – see what fine wild use the Futurists especially made of it – can itself be interpreted as its chief echo – and art of course is the manipulation of echo – in spite of the greater variety that stems from this environment, the enlarged choice of experiences available. So an appeal to the random may attest a negative identification with our urban *mise-en-scène* created by the ordering of man. This aspect, if it is an aspect of the cultivation of the random, interests me more than the sometimes concomitant doctrine of a hidden or mystical order buried there. Though the so-called 'opting out' of the hippy may prove, in spite of schizoid connection, to have been the first sign that our species may survive the present impasse, I considered reactionary the perhaps inevitable mysticism that accompanies it. By the way, those of us who persevere in representing appearances are, by this now prosaic limitation, opters-out also of a different kind, if we work less with a false sense of a continuing past, more in reaction to a present whose actuality is estimated fully. Achievement is likely to be modest for a time, it seems to me.

Here, in the West, where we are surrounded by human triumph in means of communication, in possibilities of health and comfort, the news is always bad. I do not refer to the fact that only disaster makes perfect news at any time nor to the endemic kind of bad news, much of it arising from industrial success; unemployment, say, largely the result of what used to be called automation; not even difficulties, risks, the outcome of occasional pollution. We are more widely in the strangle-hold of a success deeply dangerous, of a failure due not only to diffi-culties easily paralleled with those of the past – there has always been depletion of soil and other resources of a particular area; there have always been painful economic shifts – but danger now from the point of view of the future of the entire human race. It is the more remarkable since in rich Western countries perennial miseries, disease, slum, shanty town, starvation, though much remain, have been reduced considerably, have waned because of science and technology as well as of political pressure. Yet dreams are abandoned that were common some decades ago. Without these hopes for the future our crippled culture is naked; and it is sad to realise that the period of fervent hope was during the last two hundred years, dating exactly from the time that industrial devel-opment begat mass misery on a larger scale in our country, began to uproot not only the traditional occupations but where people congre-gated, the face of the earth. Before long Marx's concept 'alienation' is born. Though we visualise betterment, and indeed its achievement in our time, perfect conditions, the Utopias, these are altogether out of season, as are the hopes of heaven, once the firm refuge that Utopia replaced. Even in Buddhist cosmogony, so much more pessimistic than those of the West, there is law and perpetuity of happening. In these matters most of us who are neither politicos nor mystics are disorien-tated entirely: in these matters we live neither in the past nor in the present nor in the future.

But to this state of suspension – it is my chief point – there has now accrued a limiting factor, the barrier of catastrophe that in virtue of so definite a challenge brings a feeling akin to relief. Apart from atomic warfare, the first horror to be widely recognised was the dilemma from over-population, soon joined by the pollution threat, and then we en-counter the first dilemma hugely enlarged by the threat of the immi-nent depleting of natural riches that are unlikely in most instances to be permanently replaced by substitute endeavours including, one is told by some scientists, the harnessing of atomic or the sun's energies. The species appears endangered by processes that seem nearer inevitable than the danger of atomic warfare with which we have lived for some time, the first global threat – still with us – from the side of man, a threat not only to the present but to the accumulation of the past and to the hopes of the future. I am sorry to rehearse matters equally well known or better known to yourselves. I do so because, in a rather shaky manner though it will be, I want to make some guesses at the psychological effect, and therefore about art. Moreover one needs constantly to be reminded. It is bad to entertain these problems, worse to ignore them. Now that they have been registered I think there is urgent need that they should influence, indeed determine, many attitudes over an area wider than is apparent at the moment.

Technological advance has caused these problems that in regard to their cosmic scale we feel to be unfair, a heartlessness neither willed by man nor promoted by the untouched malignity of Nature. Thus they may seem gratuitous in their emotional demand. Similarly, for the aesthetic sphere, we may well feel that the general timbre of the urban environment has not been willed; in which, from the contemplative angle, no one is truly at home. Our milieu is all by-product. At the same time, custom, legend, religion, much of what are called the cultural roots, have crumbled much of the under-pinning, in short, of any culture as that word is used by anthropologists. So, unless we have adopted a political religion, those of us in towns especially enjoy small common culture of positive effect other than as vogues expressing corporate life; that is, mostly in matters of its surface alone. Art, of course, must reflect cultural position if only because consensus is assimilated by art with integrative activities of the artist's psyche. The witness to some degree of sanity or of revolt is sought from surroundings real or imagined. The artist is the furniture removal man of great ambition, converting vague objects from the dark into chair and dresser laid on the street, insisting upon neighbourhood communion, the inner with the outer. In each sphere, however, some co-ordination must be apparent for this feat, a clue to their correspondence. In regard to the outer sphere, whether viewed in terms of urban panorama or of culture, the co-ordinating factors are not propitious.

Now, without the many, or without many of the constrictions placed upon him by his culture in the past, the artist has for a hundred years more specifically, more openly, projected his own mind and emotion in the terms of outer forms. I think we are bound to say that as one result we better understand the character of art; and of course we know far more about the psyche; but that none of this success, this knowledge, has made of living or of art a fuller achievement.

We miss, particularly from art, modes for our envelopment in wide connectiveness as well as in matters elemental. Whereas it was once the concern of artists to organise Nature for the picture of Nature, there is today the tendency to employ Nature not only for expressionism but also, as we have seen, by a degree of concrete treatment whereby to project a symbolic value. Even so, symbolic evocation of any kind seems less effective now to some who are unsure of meaning beyond the lean actuality of the object that might support it: and since a varied connectiveness involves doubts rather than assurance, many of us long to be enveloped, even brow-beaten, carried away, by a mere impression of elemental actuality; of pure or abstracted actuality.

Yet the desire to discover wide correspondence in our identifications and hence to symbolise fully, ramifies through all experience. The power to substitute, to express one thing in the terms of another as by language, the mother of art, belongs to the root of developed mental functioning. In the present context a consideration is this: whereas on the practical side man has needed to exploit Nature as best he could, from the contemplative side in all ages natural objects have been a field for his substitutions, for connectiveness through the symbolic; hence poetic power. But as well as the superhuman force as of old, all Nature now grows into a delicate object to be cherished almost with a gardener's care, though this delicacy be invisible. Shall we become proud as imaginative protectors? After all, while they flourish, even infants begin by their phantasies to shoulder some responsibility for the life-givers who tower over them. Obviously the artist will be first to envisage here fresh cultural demand, willing for Nature its own endless life, variety and strength as well as for his own, just as a child preserves his mother, reconstructs her in his mind. I see the opportunity of loving perceptual subtlety once more, and of representation by which both self and object are symbolised together.

Thinking advances connections. Art depends on contemplative attitudes to things. Watching over the external world, especially for the purposes of art, we seek reverberation, an answering response from the memory of other experiences that are connected in that context, although divergent as moods or mental states from physical forms. Thus, particularly thus, things with their relationships in space stand for figures and their relationships in the mental life. In any case every meaning has symbolic reference to previous and older meanings. Hence, from the contemplative and affirmative side, we would enlarge our home into constructions seen in space. But I suggest that we are far less at home with the urban than were our forebears, that our art often reflects distrust of its meaning and therefore of meaning. Many objects are made now by artists primarily strikingly *to be*, at the expense of much onset of connectiveness in the communication: indeed, it is sometimes defiantly asserted that these objects mean only themselves; beyond that, not only do they not represent but they must not symbolise. Though works of which this is said are not among the best of our time as a rule, they have our attention here because such bravado is the most revolutionary: it makes overt an element widely diffused; though I would agree, nevertheless, that there are growing indications of the trend that dates from Dada, as when the artist, like a séance medium invoking spirits of whatever kind, is intent on constructing a hopeful *mise-en-scène* or skeleton or atmosphere of communication, of individual expression, with the help of words themselves and/or of hypnotic visual adjuncts, rather at the expense this time of the outwardness, the self-sufficiency of objects, as if they were somewhat disembodied. This phenomenon therefore, seems to me only an oscillation from the one above.

I shall try for a moment to come closer to a conception of being at home in the world experienced by a mental picture of society as well as by art. The easy means abounded for those who have been able to contemplate a settled society, with satisfaction, and a settled cosmogony in which man has an assigned role so that custom and ritual were rich, so that his culture itself seemed an entity near to hand. Things chosen to be contemplated, part, at any rate, of the visual and aural environment, echoed, confirmed the living afoot, by means of the senses. So, for example, in the sixteenth-century theatre of Serlio, a background of ordinary houses was the setting for all comedies, a background of grand houses for tragedy. The Commedia dell'Arte characters, Harlequin, Columbine and the rest, performed for centuries in front of comparable décor. But what, ask you, is the comment of our high buildings upon the action in our streets? We have ceased to uncover in the environment a reverberation of such strength as once from church bells when they seemed to be sounding all. To what pattern are we now invited to become attuned? Contrast this absence with the extravagant achievements, the always further possibilities, of technology which are in tune with the reduplication of their products, more objects manufactured in one year, maybe, than were made in the history of man up to, say, 1900: many of them disposable but in such number as to create an extraordinary problem. (Yet in the nursery we learned that consumption regularly entails potential pollution.) So much made, so little widely emblematic.

Medical science has taught us to view the body largely as a machine, and it is easy now to imagine that the basic mechanical inventions projected physiological function. It is not as easy to understand why an approximate view of bodily function and its consequent projection appeared so late. I argued some twenty years ago that there had been in classical times, the more likely period, plenty of psychological resistance; that, unlike organic references, the mechanical analogy to the body was not, to put it mildly, inspiriting; and so it remains with machine products however beautiful they may be; emblematic of human achievement, not emblematic of human function as we would conceive it, as still it remains conceived. This is true of our urban prospect also. Somehow a disconcerting element: the machine takes over.

558

Cinematography, television, reinforced concrete, demanded new arts to employ them: artists, artisans, did not evolve those media. It follows, I think, that some young artists today try to infuse the ancient crafts of sculpture and depiction with techniques learned from sophisticated industrial practices, not for an adjunct, not only for means, but for inspiration. As throughout the modern movement, it is a courageous throw at embrace. How we long to merge into the glitter of recalcitrant materials, and how easily we are able to do so if we can find no other scene for our home. But the sensation is usually brief.

In a recent lecture, Andrew Forge referred to Constable, to his putting into landscapes his feelings about his homeland. In modern art, he said, the artist had put himself into his picture first as a result of scanning a subject to discover the more profound aspect of what he actually perceived, often at the expense of what was preconceived. Forge made the startling yet subtle point that this more abstracted concern with perception entails an expressiveness that not only antedates but pioneers the route to Expressionism and even to some forms of abstract art. Of course in the further past as well, within conventions of subject-matter and accepted style, the artist has always projected himself into his picture in the sense of predilections, in the sense of creating by means of outer forms a niche for his statue of wholeness, of reconciliation between differing trends.

But the Impressionists, Forge pointed out, were the first to demonstrate that there were often subjects for painting well beyond any range previously acceptable. Most things could make a picture: all things, one might say, would soon seem fitted for aesthetic contemplation. Hence he linked the Impressionists with a development that includes Duchamp's ready-mades; also with presentations at this moment, constructions akin to industrial products, seemingly casually arranged as works of art. I find this analysis particularly poignant in view of the lack of resonance from our streets. The great extension of subject-matter, as well as its disappearance, over the last hundred years will have been overdetermined. I would point only to the breakdown of architecture as had hitherto been achieved, and would suggest that one reason for the vast extension of subject-matter might be that the artist had felt the sense of meaningful urban surround to be at risk and that, lacking a meaningful frame, as it were, for the urban activity of the time, he searched for its reconstruction not only in the studio and the studio figure: he found it everywhere if he treated everywhere in such a way as to evoke, not architectural forms – far from it – but the contrasts and reconciliations of architectural textures. Since that time most painting has offered compensation for the loss of textures in our streets. The state of this development in the arts today shows that we must try to fan warmth from unlikely material unconfined by older patterns of response. Whenever, wherever we may, we must construct our home.

An accompaniment of these attitudes has been the regard for Nature and the materials of Nature to which Andrew Forge also referred, quoting Reynolds on the imperfection of Nature as opposed to art, the correction by art of Nature; contrasting Reynolds's view with the subsequent Romantic need – we are still in the Romantic phase though in a different manner – to sit at Nature's feet. This coincided – grimly enough – with the beginnings of the Industrial Revolution, with the unparalleled extension of the extraction of natural resources and of science. But whereas the biological aim throughout history has been the conquest, the full employment of Nature, success in recent years is such that man gobbles up the world, his own placenta as it were. I must repeat that natural riches as used at present are in danger of depletion not at all distant. Some authorities believe in the efficacy of future substitutes. I cannot argue, though it seems clear that even were the substitute endeavours that might embrace the complete victory of synthetic food and the anxious re-use of metals, were they enough to furnish a much enlarged population, these substitute endeavours could be effective only if there existed world-wide strict control of conservation, pollution, of drastic consumption cut-back, and above all of population. You may not agree. At any rate it is not disputed that ecological studies induce an awareness of the delicate balance as well as the traditional power of Nature whose interdependent processes we begin to fear will disintegrate under our touch: Nature the broadest aspect

of our home. For it is not the urban scene alone that induces some
estrangement, with no certainty anywhere of unpolluted process.
We know seas and skies are threatened, that is, our use of them is
threatened by our usages. And so, to return to art, it seems that modes
evolved in the scanning of appearances promise no future better than
their present since our faith in the essence of the things at which we
look suffers qualification. Yet there is the other thought, namely that
the natural scene, even from the practical point of view, has become,
and will increasingly become, more precious from the literal fear of
its further appropriation and poisoning by man. I can imagine panic,
stampede of panic in the face of wide disaster. I can imagine circumstances by which, for the first time, the concept, the human species, will
be an emotive term for all. It would require all, if the species at large
shall survive only through the terrible suffering of cutting back in production and consumption as well as, drastically, in the production of
offspring. It is likely that the present is the moment of greatest plenty,
confined though it is to the rich countries. Hence, to put it briefly,
respect for the unseen delicacy of an overpowering mechanism, the
world: poison, otherwise, starvation. I leave out of account the possibility of destruction and atrophy from atomic warfare.

Art tells of ourselves in terms of the external world; tells that we are
now joined to things that mean less than we would like them to do.
Each of the vastly differing aspects of the Modern Movements can be
interpreted as an attempt to get on familiar terms with these things.
Yet away from art, we contemplate them glumly. I wrote more than
twelve years ago of what I called the 'isness' of some avant-garde art.
Of course modern art is most varied and experimental: and in achievement, magnificent. But I think we are also aware of impasse in those
directions where symbolic functions of the art object are either isolated
or minimised or consciously repudiated. This last attitude itself tends
in fact to be symbolic – symbolism can never be undone – of the psyche's
negative estimations and of the projection of schizoid states. On the
other hand I regard it as a gain that, doubtless encouraged by the lack

of planned reverberation from urban environment, from haphazard technological advance, we are thoroughly learning at last the most austere lesson of Darwinian evolution. It has taken a hundred years for the complete realisation to come through that there could be no plan in such a process, no built-in design: that the emergence, as we call it, of life itself is a chance chemical concatenation of interest to ourselves. Such lack of partiality in its fullness is apt to hit the non-religious as hard as the religious, the philosopher as well as the ordinary man. We acknowledge instead the power of the drives, particularly the sexual drive. There is also the instinct of self-preservation. Survival of the species rather than of the individual, nation, race, has, or will soon, become a sublime and conscious aim that must in part reverse an aim uniform through the hundreds of thousands of years of human exist-ence, repudiating what is now suddenly an excessive control and employment of other forms of life and of geological deposits.

But moderation in the ecological interference would not apply to the probable controls, say, from genetic science over selective breeding. It is easy to see that the pushing of science forward in many directions while foregoing other immediate power that it could bring, and indeed has brought, added to the urgency of strong restraints upon produc-tion, will complicate further the problem from the psychological as well as from the economic angle. This too will have to be faced. It seems that almost impossible courses are now demanded. There is ample room for despair.

As far as we know there has not hitherto been a survival problem for mankind as a whole spread over much of the earth. When in the past an area was depleted or over-populated or had become climate-wise or predator-wise more difficult, if adaptation was impossible a move was made elsewhere. For us there will be nowhere to go. It has been put out that at the present rate of increase the world population in less than a century would be thirty billion, that is, perhaps nine times the present swollen number. No one denies the gravity. Differences of opinion are about the degree and about the immediacy, not so much in regard to population as to the aggravating factors.

What is the likely meaning for the future of art? Over and above art, we are given at least an aim, a simple aim: survival. A surge towards survival that in times of great danger, as in war, is apt to counter the surge towards death, might produce heroic affirmation of the good, of the value of life-giving processes and of brotherhood that can be summed as love. Even a little simplifying of the Western mode of life could relieve a load of vulgarity: by vulgarity I have first in mind needless, shining, obdurate wrapping, all the stimuli, particularly advertisement, of consumption as ideal. And it would signify a brake, not on invention, but on the illimitable, as it seems, manufacture of machine-made products: plastic milk bottles if there is milk, but not *endless* plastic milk bottles. I believe that beyond a certain point such man-made proliferation of dead material, unlike natural growth, is very frightening; that were it not for kindred fears, at least a few of our machines would have been developed – a prototype of the steam engine was designed and built in classical times – much earlier. We must visualise a future, then, if there is to be a rich future, cleared of the sense of limitless plastic proliferation. Materials will have better worth, better status, even the plastic milk bottle. The psychological danger from the machine has always been the degradation of object-nature. This is because our sense of the otherness, uniqueness, self-sufficiency of objects outside ourselves, the *sine qua non* of sanity, has not been of easy attainment by any of us, and is always apt to be whittled or impugned in some respect or other, particularly of course in regard to people whom we tend to enter, control or appropriate. Near the beginning of this lecture I suggested that in spite of threatened catastrophe the present challenge brings a feeling akin to relief. The limitations which will have to be recognised in the practical sphere would tend to mitigate a disproportion, viewed from the contemplative side, with which we are still by no means at home.

By a lessening – and that from necessity – of rapacious attitudes at least to substance, our affiliations could achieve fresh poetic worth, especially if men were to become better resigned to their role of human animals thoughtlessly evolved, driven on to death, sustained meanwhile by love, good feeling, by the conviction of the value belonging not only to the self but to its objects. We project on to objects inner states and we take objects into ourselves together with the projections; we introject. Inner and outer integration and stability are interdependent.

Out of the quandaries to which I have referred a new alignment on the aesthetic level could emerge. We – I speak as if we were the future – will have some thankfulness even for air, the purity of air – indeed we have it already – a pride in an unpoisonous sea though the power of the sea would still appear limitless: for a restored world, where restoration should prove still possible, the world as it would be without undue interference in the balance that has governed plant and animal life, more clearly conceived since the thought will be present that in modifying beyond a certain point we find we destroy ourselves also. This is to take Nature, rather than romantic aspects of Nature, as our familiar.

And so, whereas, if I am right, the present involvement in the creation of art objects with the haziest, or else with the most primitive and unramified, symbolic value must be linked to the hollow echo from the urban scene, with the impression of limitless non-resonance, the future visualised here as the only possible future wherein the human species will survive in a world fit for survival, could nourish an art that, by conveying a temper of restraint regarding both the material world and its organisms, might rediscover richness in variety, rather than in the brutalities of abstraction or distillation which, while themselves native to the making of art, are not of course by themselves, in isolation, necessarily the highest embodiment of completeness. But I am not denigrating forms of abstract art which I have always greatly admired, nor the varieties of Expressionism. I cannot make a comment on their probable future. I but weakly say that while it can approach an effect of cosmic contemplation, great generality, even at the same time, often expresses some affiliation with the settlement of nerveless trance. Though we lack hope and belief, we are somewhat mesmerised and stimulated by mechanical pressed-button power, a wealth, a richness. Such power may seem illimitable, able to take care of anything. Drugs, hallucination, lethargy are all the fashion as a kind of trust. The stunning impact so much sought today in art on which we rather lazily like to lean, the restriction of statement to the non-eloquence of shock, marches with the impact our urban environment best achieves as by the array, for instance, of filmy flashing lights that defies a finite space. I do not see a shock of the illimitable, of the extreme, as so strong a verve in the future should the emphasis upon the symbolic significance attached to measure, containment, limitation, interpose and thereby reinforce the variety of interacting meanings gained from different objects set together. And perhaps full-dress appearances may return in art, newly meant. But this is not at all to suggest that the milieu will cease to be powerfully technological even though the future were to belong to smaller communities than great cities: nor do I suggest that I can visualise clearly that measure in things to which I refer, in its combination with technological embrace, even in a world less at the mercy of the products of this embrace. My suggestions rely totally on the altered orientation in many spheres of which I have spoken, desperately needed in the struggle, if it is to be successful, for survival. Maybe even the journeys to the moon will prove to have fixed our feet the more firmly on this various planet.

I have long thought there might be no inevitable future for art, or, rather, for the creation of first-order masterpieces: and at the same time, in compensation as it were, that everybody becomes a bit of an artist, will attempt a mode of creativeness, an activity of aesthetic rather than utility value: sometimes as a form of therapy. But now, in view of the issues to which this talk has attempted reference, I begin to hope that the diversity in relationship between mind and external object from the angle of contemplation, this the substance of art, will again achieve comprehensive contexts if – always this 'if' – much more than a handful of men in a polluted world robbed of metal, fossil fuel, fertility, shall survive in circumstances infinitely better than those.

NOTES

Introduction
THOMAS EVANS

1 While the passage originates in *Inside Out* (London: Faber & Faber, 1947), it is more readily encountered as it was excerpted – and retitled as 'Cézanne' – by Richard Wollheim, in *The Image in Form: Selected Writings of Adrian Stokes*, Penguin Books, Harmondsworth, 1972, Harper & Row, New York, 1972, p.236.

2 The two biographies available as of this writing are Richard Read, *Art and Its Discontents: The Early Life of Adrian Stokes*, Ashgate, Aldershot, 2002, and Janet Sayers, *Art, Psychoanalysis and Adrian Stokes: A Biography*, Karnac, London, 2015. For critical studies, see Michael O'Pray, *Film, Form and Phantasy: Adrian Stokes and Film Aesthetics*, Palgrave Macmillan, Basingstoke, 2004; Stephen Bann (ed), *The Coral Mind: Adrian Stokes's Engagement with Architecture, Art History, Criticism, and Psychoanalysis*, Pennsylvania State University Press, University Park PA, 2007; and Stephen Kite, *Adrian Stokes: An Architectonic Eye*, Routledge, Abingdon, 2008.

3 Adrian Stokes, *Sunrise in the West*, Harper & Brothers, New York and London, 1927, p.94.

4 G.W.F. Hegel, *Phenomenology of Spirit*, trans. A.V. Miller, Oxford University Press, 1977, Oxford, p.10.

5 *Ibid.*, p.64.

6 *Ibid.*, p.34.

7 Adrian Stokes, *Stones of Rimini*, Faber & Faber, London, 1934, p.151.

8 Adrian Stokes, *Inside Out*, in *Critical Writings of Adrian Stokes*, vol.2, Thames & Hudson, London, 1978, p.174.

9 Walter Pater, *The Renaissance*, Oxford University Press, Oxford, 1986, p.xxix.

10 Read, *op. cit.*, pp.144–45.

11 Adrian Stokes, *Greek Culture and the Ego*, Tavistock Publications, London, 1958, pp.28–29.

12 See Read, *op. cit.*, pp.76–83.

13 Stokes, *Sunrise, op. cit.*, p.15.

14 Jacob Burckhardt, *The Civilization of the Renaissance in Italy*, Phaidon Press, London, 1951, p.21.

15 Anthony F. D'Elia, *Pagan Virtue in a Christian World: Sigismondo Malatesta and the Italian Renaissance,* Harvard University Press, Cambridge MA, 2016, p.91.

16 Adrian Stokes, *The Quattro Cento*, Faber & Faber, London, 1932, pp.128, 188.

17 Ezra Pound, *Guide to Kulchur*, New Directions, Norfolk CT, 1938, p.2; Roberto Valturio quoted in D'Elia, *op. cit.*, p.155.

18 Stokes, *The Quattro Cento, op. cit.*, pp.24–25.

19 Ezra Pound, *Pavannes and Divisions*, Knopf, New York, 1918, p.95.

20 Ezra Pound, *The Cantos*, New Directions, Norfolk CT, 1972, p.796.

21 Stokes, *The Quattro Cento, op. cit.*, p.131; Stokes, *Stones of Rimini, op. cit.*, p.105.

22 Adrian Stokes, 'The Luxury and Necessity of Painting', in *Three Essays on the Painting of Our Time*, Tavistock Publications, London, 1961, p.10.

23 Read, *op. cit.*, pp.193–214.

24 Stokes, *The Quattro Cento, op. cit.*, p.133.

25 Sigmund Freud, *The Ego and the Id*, trans. Joan Riviere, Hogarth Press, London, 1927, p.31.

26 Stokes, *Greek Culture, op. cit.*, pp.50–51.

27 For Jones's full critique of the death instinct, see Ernest Jones, *The Life and Work of Sigmund Freud*, vol.3, Basic Books, New York, 1957, pp.266–86.

28 Sigmund Freud, *Beyond the Pleasure Principle*, trans. James Strachey, Hogarth Press, London, 1955, p.36.

29 Charles H. Kahn, *The Art and Thought of Heraclitus*, Cambridge University Press, Cambridge, 1979, p.65. Kahn explains the

pun at work in a footnote here: 'Old word for "bow" (*biós*) differs from word "life" (*bios*) only by the accent, not written in Heraclitus' time.'

30 Adrian Stokes, 'On Resignation', in Eric Rhode (ed), *A Game That Must Be Lost*, Carcanet Press, Cheadle, 1973, p.71.

31 Melanie Klein, 'The Origins of Transference', in *Envy and Gratitude and Other Works, 1946–1953*, The Free Press, New York, 1975, p.53.

32 Adrian Stokes, *Michelangelo*, Routledge, London, 2002, pp.5–6.

33 Walter Benjamin, 'The Image of Proust', in *Illuminations*, trans. Harry Zohn, Schocken Books, New York, 1968, p.214.

PROSE

1 Count Keyserling's *Travel Diary of a Philosopher* (Jonathan Cape).

2 However, any lover of the beautiful who is really familiar with art, can be, and tends to be, oblivious of values created by the time element.

SOUTH OPPOSED TO EAST AND NORTH

1 Benn, 1926. In the course of the next few pages I lift several ideas from this book, to the authors of which I hereby make acknowledgment.

2 This detachment, though, since it is so facile, is very limited and has often led its devotees into most unaesthetic courses the remedy for which, as I shall show, is an introduction from North or East of a more circumscribed aesthetic.

3 Possibly, when new, the Pentelic marble was too bright and for this reason, contrary to the usual one, was toned with plaster.

4 This is a reference to such Quattro Cento artists as Luciano Laurana, Francesco Laurana, Piero della Francesca, Antonio Rizzo and Mauro Coducci.

5 As much in evidence today as ever. For instance, the new Milan railway station.

6 Atkinson and Bagenal, *op. cit.*, p.22. The same analogy could be extended to India where Aryans, still faithful to Iranian pattern, developed the representational intricacies of Buddhist and Hindoo sculpture.

REPRESENTATIONAL AND NON-REPRESENTATIONAL ART

1 This means an art that definitely avoids human representation. Animal forms are plentiful.

2 Josef Strzygowski, *Origin of Christian Church Art*, Clarendon Press, 1923.

3 That is, except when this treatment has been ordered by such great genius as inspired Piero della Francesca and Luciano Laurana.

E SOTTO UN'ALTA QUERCIA…

1 Luca Pulci, *Ciriffo Calvaneo – con la giostra del Magnifico Lorenzo dei Medici*, Giunta, Florence, 1572.

2 Reproduced and commented upon in similar fashion by Gustave Soulier, *Les Influences orientales dans la peinture toscane*, Laurens, Paris, 1923.

3 So loved too of Soulier from whom I take this point (*vide op. cit.*). He makes too much of it, while omitting to mention the oriental carpets so often reproduced in fifteenth-century pictures.

4 *A Siennese Painter of the Franciscan Legend*, Dent, London, 1909, pp.17–18.

5 *Op. cit.*, p.352.

6 *Origin of Christian Church Art*, p.97.

7 The buildings by the Armenian architect Trdat in the last quarter of the tenth century, have pointed arches as well as clustered shafts.

VEROCCHIO'S LAVABO

1 This phrase, which – I am told – is more than usually obscure, was constructed by analogy to the vulgarism, 'to act funny'.

2 Left and right in this description are from the point of view of the spectator facing the monument. As outside wings of the dragons do not appear, 'left wing' is right-hand wing of left dragon and 'right wing' is left-hand wing of right dragon. The creatures on the urn with boars' heads are dragons, while the creatures with female faces beneath the bath are griffins.

3 The right head has lost part of its snout, but the left was obviously always the bigger.

4 'It is true that the oak-leaves of the garland and the fluttering ribbons are somewhat mechanically arranged and lifeless in execution, and it is probable that these are the work of some assistant.' From Maud Crutwell's *Verrocchio*.

THE QUATTRO CENTO IN FLORENTINE ART

1 The following account of Quattro Cento activity in Florence is by no means complete. Some further reference to it will be made in the next part. I am concerned in this chapter only with the major figures.

2 See pp. 17 and 45 [NB. references here to other pages in Stokes's original books].

3 See Géza de Francovich, *Appunti su Donatello e Jacopo della Quercia. Bollettino d'arte*, 1929. The author reasserts the importance of Donatello's first visit to Rome, and with the aid of confronting photographs makes parallels between Donatello's early sculpture and antique statues, particularly in regard to realistic portraiture.

4 In future I will reserve the name 'putto' for those infants only who conform to the Donatellesque idea.

5 For instance, the ornament on the 'cheeks' of the consoles of the singing gallery in the Opera del Duomo, Florence.

6 See note 1, p.113 [NB. references here to other pages in Stokes's original books].

7 Brancacci monument in Sant'Angelo a Nilo.

8 See Part I, Section IX [NB. references here to other pages in Stokes's original books].

9 Apart from anything else, inasmuch as the coloured marble panels are not reproduced in the cast of this monument at the Victoria and Albert, its effect cannot be gauged in London.

10 See also a mantelpiece in this manner at the Museo Bardini, Florence. Verrocchio developed still further this use of ribbons.

11 Even Pollaiuolo's bronze statuettes of antique subjects such as the beautiful *Hercules* in the Pierpont Morgan collection [now in the Frick Collection, New York – Ed.], with one foot on the head of the bull precariously overlapping the pedestal, show the same tight broadness of style.

12 Also in the Old Sacristy, San Lorenzo, Florence. This sarcophagus stands on Verrocchio's slab tomb for Cosimo de' Medici.

13 Expression enigmatic also in sorrow, is common in much earlier Florentine sculpture. See the figure on the right in Desiderio's *Pietà* below the tabernacle.

CARVING, MODELLING AND AGOSTINO

1 This relief in the Castello Sforza, Milan, has been attributed to Agostino ever since Yriarte noticed it. Ricci has subsequently identified the subject and has shown that it was originally affixed beneath the throne of S. Sigismondo in

the chapel of that name in the Tempio. A cast of the relief has now been put there. The original was in the 1930 Italian Exhibition at Burlington House.

2 Sigismondo's mistress.

3 The reader, however, must bear in mind that, with the exception of the two Victoria and Albert Museum exhibits, all the carving here illustrated is architectural. The architectural arrangement of the reliefs determines the greater part of their attraction. I must apologize for my failure to obtain photographs that might show them to better advantage.

4 In Chapter II [NB. reference here to a chapter in Stokes's original book].

5 I make no reference to gems. When I speak of stone, the glass-like and fragmentary precious stones are never within my vista. Possibly to the imagination they form a subject by themselves, one for which I have little feeling.

6 See *The Technique of Early Greek Sculpture* by Stanley Casson, Clarendon Press, 1933.

7 The statement is true only in the present context, that is to say, in helping to define a trend or principle. If read literally, it is untrue. Some very hard wood forms – many instances of negro wood sculpture spring to mind – were undoubtedly attained by rubbing. But in these cases the hard wood was treated almost as stone: the basic forms are stone-like, though, to their detriment, they lack stone's even light.

8 'Objects perceived simply as related in space, encourage the ambition of every man for complete self-expression, for an existence completely externalized. Our love of space is our love of expression.' *The Quattro Cento*, vol. I, p.158.

9 Hence the popularity in the Renaissance of relief, which, we have seen (p.116, reference here to a page in Stokes's original book), may well be a dramatized form of carving.

10 See *The Quattro Cento*, p.88.

11 The probability of direct influence upon Agostino on the part of such Byzantine work at Ravenna will be discussed in the next volume.

12 One of the most obvious features of fifteenth-century Italy – and it is noted as such by contemporary travellers – was the crop of new stone buildings, and the investment of existent brick buildings with stone.

13 More usually called *pietra serena*. Cf. *The Quattro Cento*, Part II, chap. 1.

14 On the other hand, the evidence that modelling had been put on its mettle, so to speak, by the augmented appeal of stone, is direct enough. The prevalence at this time of relief modelling in clay and terra-cotta must be referred directly to the influence of stone. Also, in these moulded reliefs, as in the stone reliefs, marked flattening of form is usual, particularly of heads.

15 I am not denying the relevance today of Le Corbusier's building. I but make the point that his conceptions are purely plastic. At the end of this chapter I shall point out what difference this new (and inevitable) plasticity of building makes to the carving-modelling situation.

16 Agostino was born and trained in Florence. As a young man, accused falsely of theft, he sought his fortune on the other side of Italy. At the age of forty-five (1463), after completing his work at Perugia and at Rimini, he returned to Florence to find that the individual style that he had developed was not appreciated there. He could not attract any big commissions; though he was set to carve two colossi to be skied somewhere on the Duomo! In the end he returned to Perugia. It is a thousand pities that he, the master of low relief, was so often set to carve statues, quite apart from colossi. His later Perugian carving is for the most part lost: from the fragments it appears that in his public commissions his style

was often ruined by the needed adjustment to contemporary taste. The earlier tabernacle in the Ognissanti at Florence is a lovely work: but the necessary homage there paid (a homage that entails a modification of Agostino's style) to the reigning Rossellino type of beauty is indeed pitiable. On the other hand, the lovely Porta San Pietro at Perugia, which belongs to his last Perugian period, shows how faithful Agostino remained to the Tempio; and so do the Madonna and Child reliefs. As a rule, Agostino's statues are rather formal and exceedingly thinned, though far more frontal in conception than his best reliefs. Cf. the fragments now in the picture gallery at Perugia. One will conclude, however, that Agostino's peculiar genius for carving could have been sustained at its height only if he could have worked continually for such a man as Sigismondo. As we shall see, the very requirements of the Tempio sculpture coincided with his own bent.

17 The reader will be able to discover for himself in my photograph many other instances of such mutually enhancing juxtaposition. An obvious example is the hair of the two angels on right.

18 That is to say, the general perspective of the bottom half of a composition as represented from above, the top half from below. Cf. p.151 [NB. reference here to a page in Stokes's original book].

19 Cf. Pl. 46 [NB. reference here to a page in Stokes's original book].

20 Notice the absence of complicated perspective or of subtlety in surface juxtapositions.

21 The base of the Madonna and Child's outward-tilted framework serves a similar function, as we have seen. It is an integral part of this carving.

22 Cf. the not altogether satisfactory treatment of the horses' knees so that they won't jut out.

23 In *The Quattro Cento* I said this marble came from Verona. I am now almost certain that it is a Greek marble.

24 Cf. p.123 [NB. reference here to a page in Stokes's original book].

25 Should the reader still be puzzled by the all-important equation of 'carving values' with the 'full spatial conception', he is advised to turn back for a moment to pages 144 and 145 particularly [NB. references here to pages in Stokes's original book].

THE TEMPIO: FIRST VISIT

1 This, and the subsequent figures, refer to the note I append to Baedeker's account (endnote 2).

2 There are several minor errors in this account, and I suppose it is my duty to correct them in case an intending student should otherwise be misled. The inaccuracies are culled from the pages of Yriarte (though Baedeker has avoided many of Yriarte's errors, an astounding achievement in 1909), the Frenchman at whom the Italians have thrown too many bricks. For, though his inaccuracies, his reading of documents and his guesses, were wild, Yriarte sometimes hit the right note forcibly; as when he suggested that Agostino was chief sculptor in the Tempio (since proved by the inscription Ricci found), and when he attributed the Milan relief to Agostino. Yriarte's greatest coup was the publication of documents, relating to the Tempio, from the archives at Siena. These comprise Sigismondo's mail of December 1454 which was intercepted by the Siennese. Malatesta studies owe a great deal to Yriarte (*Un condottiere au XVe siècle*, Paris, 1882).

I merely tabulate the suggested corrections without giving my references: since a full account of them, and of their bases, would overburden what is intended merely as a precautionary note.

(1) 1447–1457 is a better date. Work also went on sporadically from 1457 till Sigismondo's ruin in 1461.

(2) This is extremely unlikely: though the matter is still disputed in certain quarters.

(3) Gemisthon Plethon died in 1450.

(4) Valturio died probably in 1475.

(5) The documents show that Isotta was living on 23rd March, 1474, and that she was dead by February 1475.

(6) It is unlikely that this is the work of Ciuffagni, nor is there anything to show that the statue is a portrait of Isotta.

(7) Alas, the poem is by someone else, nor has it any reference to the Tempio sculpture.

(8) There is nothing to support this, nor to suggest it.

3 The elucidation of this connection, and all other matters of historical analysis, are reserved for the next volume.

4 Some of the blocks were lifted from the graveyard. Tomb inscriptions can be deciphered on the façade and flanks. Sigismondo was always hard up and always on the prowl for stone. He lifted some of the port of Rimini itself. His most extensive haul probably was the Istrian stone that had been intended for a new bridge over the Metaurus at Fano.

5 But not so of Brunelleschi's unvaried arcades. See *Stones of Rimini*, p.106.

6 In the description of the Tempio quoted from Baedeker, four chapels of fifteenth-century construction are enumerated on either side. In my description, no account is taken of Baedeker's second chapels since they are not visible from the aisle, being beyond the doors that I shall presently describe.

7 The light in the Tempio is a Gothic light, that is to say, the rays come through Gothic windows behind the classical encasement. Hence one poignancy of the reappearing pagan figures that the faded barbaric light illumines.

8 Similarly, the bronze fruit upon stone panniers that form the bases to the piers in the third chapel does not strike one as an insensitive vulgar extravagance, but rather as a dubious means of tension. The bronze is like a damson mess between the planes of bread that make a sandwich, and, like the jam, the thick bronze fruit bestows a continuous authority on the planes that seemingly squash it out above and below.

9 In view of my aim to present the 'point' of the Tempio, I do not stop to remark that many of the Virtues and shield-bearers in this first chapel, and many other reliefs in the Tempio, are crudely conceived or crude and hurried in execution. Nor have I remarked that Agostino himself (it might be expected) was a mediocre and probably unwilling carver of statues. Such considerations, and an account of the Tempio's deface-ment by modern additions, can be left to others: in the case of many observers they will pretend that they see little else, although, at the same time, they will admit that there exists some general romantic charm in this interior. Thus, critics are captivated by the Tempio, though, principally in view of the unrelieved standards of plasticity by which they judge sculpture, they cannot praise it overmuch.

The thorough pedestrian critique has been performed, notably by Corrado Ricci (*Il Tempio Malatestiano*, Bestetti e Tumminelli, Milan, 1925), to whose book I am profoundly indebted. I write now – and by no means exhaustively – of those features only which inspire my theme, and which, to my mind, are all-important and neglected beauties.

10 These coloured marbles, together with those used above the main portal and as

discs on the façade, are probably some of the stones that Sigismondo stole, or bribed the monks to let him take, from the Byzantine church of Sant'Appollinare in Classe near Ravenna. In photograph the door without the dolphin reliefs looks better as design than its fellow. Moreover, the absence in the former of the mouldings on the inner side of the shields seems an improvement. But what thus appear as structural defects in the door with dolphins are actually the means of its superior colour and an integral part of its Quattro Cento steadfast effect.

11 The heavy tooth moulding of the rectangular frame loses its effect of clumsy or undue constriction when the colours and textures are seen. Then one also sees that the light but cavernous pediment has a powerful, almost Gothic, thrust that is kept steadfast and tense only by the outer moulding. The thin, reduplicated pediment lines are, as it were, the shrill cries the elephant contains.

12 An extension, in turn, of the tooth moulding, characteristic of Venetian Gothic, appears in the treatment of the manes of Diana's horses.

13 I am not, of course, taking the additions of subsequent centuries into consideration.

14 Cf. a putto on the base of the left pier in the third chapel to the left. His feet are elephant's feet.

15 It was Ricci who in 1912 found under the bronze slab with the inscription: *D. Isottae. Ariminensi. B. M. Sacrum. MCCCCL* a marble slab with the inscription: *Isote. Ariminensi. Forma. Et. Virtute. Italie. Decori. MCCCCXLVI.* Perhaps the first inscription had to be concealed as it might outrage the susceptibilities of some powerful person, probably the Pope. The 1450 inscription is repeated three times on the monument. Almost from the day of its

unveiling discussion has raged as to whether the *D* stands for *Divae* or *Dominae*, Goddess or Mistress. Such equivocation is typical of the Tempio symbols. $ may mean several things, and was probably designed to do so, partly in case one meaning had to be denied occasionally. A few more deliberate experts, notably Soranzo, hold that $ refers solely to the first two letters of Sigismondo's name. The date 1450, inscribed altogether twelve times in the Tempio, was, like 1446, a high-water mark year for Sigismondo. It was then that his position in Italy was dramatized for him in the form of the honours bestowed by Pope Innocent V at Fabriano; and it was then that the general reinvestment of San Francesco was conceived. For there is no reason to think that the adornment of the first two chapels on the right, which had been undertaken before this date, was in the first place part of any larger scheme.

16 More accurately described as reliefs of the sun, moon, five planets, twelve signs of the zodiac and an influxion caused by the moon. For brevity I shall continue to refer to them as the planet reliefs.

17 The chapel opposite with the reliefs of the Arts and Sciences has a similar balustrade.

18 See *The Quattro Cento*, pp. 73 and 74.

19 The inscriptions read as follows: Sigismondo Pandolfo Malatesta, son of Pandolfo, having survived many and vital dangers in the Italian war, bringer of victory (νίκηφόρος), for the campaigns by him concluded with courage and good fortune, to immortal God and to the City has dedicated this Temple, and in raising it has shouldered with brave heart the immense expense, leaving a noble and sacred monument.

20 It is upon the evidence of the denunciation and of the Ciceronian journalese of Pio's commentaries (thus, 'mulieres,

quorum filios e sacro fonte levavit, complures adulteriis polluit eorumque viros necavit'), in fact, upon the evidence of the purest war propaganda, that historians have acclaimed Sigismondo as a monster of crime. Yet for many years now Giovanni Soranzo has been examining these accusations and he has proved beyond doubt that the majority, at any rate, are baseless, in some cases irreconcilable with the hard facts of time and place. Since he was somewhat out of scale with his contemporaries, calumny was the usual weapon of Sigismondo's foes: but Pio's denunciation and Federico di Montefeltro's tales carried little conviction in the Italy of that time until the political motive of the Malatesta crusade was revealed, that is to say, the seizure of his lands, and until a partition of the spoils had been promised. Cf. especially among the works of Soranzo *Un'invettiva della curia romana contro Sigismondo Pandolfo Malatesta*, Imola, 1911. Also *Pio II e la politica italiana nella lotta contra i Malatesti, 1457–1463*, Drucker, Padua, 1911.

IMPRESSIONS OF BALLET

1 She is quite literally on the tips of her toes. Male dancers have been known to use points, but only as an oddity. Nijinsky used points in his *Jeux* and Dolin in *Les Fâcheux*.

2 One obtains a superb experience of this geometrical assault on space towards the end of *Cotillon*, music by Chabrier. Amid a wonderful fugue, at the moment when the last of the guests pirouettes off to the side along the middle of the stage, Baronova or Toumanova appears from the back at right angles to the departing guest and walks slowly to the centre, where she commences a series of fierce *fouettés en tournant*. All the dancers populate the stage again and move

continuously around this central figure, turning the same way as Baronova, upright now upon both points but still revolving with the impetus derived from her *fouettés*. Such is the curtain.

3 The glamour is dissipated when man's exterior has been, so to speak, denied, when each movement itself has been forced to represent or imitate an inner process. That is why German expressionist or 'free' dancing is ill-suited to the theatre.

THE CLASSICAL BALLET

1 An admirable English translation, and also of the Rameau and several other ballet classics, is available. This we owe to the enthusiasm and industry of Mr. C.V. Beaumont who publishes and sells these books and many others also that he has written on ballet, at his bookshop, 75 Charing Cross Road, WC2. The debt that ballet lovers and dancers, present and future, owe to Mr. Beaumont is very large. Possibly his most phenomenal achievement to date is his exposition of the Cecchetti method of training in classical ballet.

2 They were content also with raising their straightened legs at no more than an angle of forty-five degrees for classical *pas*. Indeed, it is doubtful whether Camargo found it necessary to wear knickers when dancing. By 1800 dancers raised their legs ninety degrees for a movement such as the *développé*. This advance is to be associated with a change of costume. As long as for their classical *pas* ballerinas were wearing voluminous eighteenth-century skirts, a greater agility was impossible. The earlier history of ballet can be most tersely written as a history of costume. It was Camargo who, in the first place, somewhat shortened the skirt and

adopted the heelless shoe.

3 This earnest wish has now been fully satisfied by the Vic-Wells production.

4 Sometimes the variations in a ballet take their names from the music alone. Thus the naming of the Valse and Mazurka in *Sylphides* refers solely to Chopin's music and not to the dances set to this music.

THE MODERN BALLET AND SOME GERMAN FORMS OF THE DANCE

1 It is as well that I say 'a *great* dancer': for there have been many classically trained dancers in recent years who have repudiated ballet. Several of the German innovators started thus. My point is that any innovation is permissible so long the classical training is vigorously kept up, and if these innovations are in some sense connected with that training, even if only in the form of contrast. But if the training itself is repudiated, then the dancing ceases to be ballet dancing: the ballet style is lost. There are also special cases in which ballet dancers are forced by their directors to forgo the fruits of their training. During the last two years a situation of this sort, it is said, has been in full swing at the Scala in Milan, one of the principal homes of ballet. It is a similar situation to those of the poor, out-of-work ballet dancers who are forced by circumstance to dance in pantomimes and 'shows' of every description. German ideas, under the title of the *Danse méditeranée*, are today predominant at the Scala. Boris Romanoff's work betrays a parallel mix-up.

LA BOUTIQUE FANTASQUE

1 Cf. his admirable description of the ballet, published by himself at 75 Charing Cross Road, *La Boutique Fantasque.*

2 *To-night the Ballet*, p.53.

3 Cf. the Victorian phrase 'to have a flutter', to bet.

4 In the National Gallery.

5 Sometimes the apprentice goes out crying as a result of his failure to keep back part of the purchase money. It is obvious that a good deal of latitude will be allowed to the interpreters of this role. Psota, the apprentice of today, is an unusually brilliant mime. While preserving the simplicity, he stresses the *gamin* side of this character.

6 That is, with the exception of the ballerina's initial steps in the *can-can.*

7 A phrase that is almost identical with the last phrase but three of the song 'If you were the only girl in the world' from *The Bing Boys Are Here.*

8 That is to say, while preserving a high standard of artistry in general conception, in choreography, décor and music. Topical ballets and *ballets d'occasion* hitherto had belonged more properly to the music hall.

CHAPTER TWO (*COLOUR AND FORM*)

1 Faber & Faber, 1934.

2 Faber & Faber, 1932.

3 *Stones of Rimini*, pp.110, 144, 145, 147.

CHAPTER THREE (*COLOUR AND FORM*)

1 I make this seemingly extravagant statement in view of the fact that green, however dark, has an associative connection with white. This is because the after-image of black is not so much white as a pale green. In other words, when the eye is dark-adapted, green or green-blue, in accordance with the Purkinje phenomenon, appear brighter, and therefore come to be associated with

the image of brightness.

2 From p.122 of *Stones of Rimini*.

3 In this connection it is remarkable that the oriental painting in coloured pattern without effects of modelling, without the delineation of shadow, should never have achieved a profound carving effect, a greatness in the use of colour.

4 The chief of several reasons for the clearness of local colour, and especially of the growth from horizontal to vertical planes in the evening light, is that since the centre of what is at any rate a diffused illumination comes from a low point in the sky, and since the eye views upstanding things from a not dissimilar angle, one is able to see more clearly all variations of vertical planes: the ground extends all the better as the architectonic base of this structure since it is now relatively far less the recipient of a direct light; whereas when the sun is higher the ground receives far the greatest share of direct light.

5 It is the same with most of the pretty Sienese primitive and mediaeval Persian paintings so often admired for their colour. In these judgements, of course, I am neglecting the psychological effect of any colour in and by itself. Such a consideration has its place in the estimation of colour by and large, but it has little immediate contact with painting. It would confuse the issue to introduce such considerations now.

6 The three dimensions of colour (hue, tone and intensity) are to be contrasted with the polarity of tone by itself. One suspects that this polarity of tone plays a part in the formation of the bipolarity of tactile sensation. In contrast, although they are not necessarily themselves directly connected, is the three-fold apparatus in the eye for the perception of hues and the three dimensions of colours thus perceived. The purely visual experience (so far as it may be isolated from its tactile component) of space as three-dimensional, would seem to link into this same nexus. And it is to be remarked that the painter who was genuinely inspired by perspective science in all its newness, Piero della Francesca (and again, only to a less degree, Bruegel), has given us the supreme realization in painting of that kind of colour, of that kind of form, that mode and quality of fantasy projection, of which I write.

7 Contrast this positive kind of 'all-overness' in which definite and contrasting factors are given and made to approximate, with the negative old-masterish veneer spoken of above.

1 Many of those who have had no occasion to look into the matter closely might be surprised, if they did, to find how sickly and often exotic a relation the current talk of psycho-analysis, particularly in many novels or in some apparently authoritative books, bears to the still little known, or rather, little understood, resistance-evoking theory and clinical practice of Freud: resistance-evoking to the ordinary psychiatrist and to the unauthorized or self-styled 'psycho-analyst' who has not had either the Freudian analysis or training, no less than to the vulgarian amateur psychologist who longs for magic and cheap Mephisto themes.

2 Cf. *Love, Hate and Reparation*, by Melanie Klein and Joan Rivière, Psycho-analytical Epitomes No. 2 (Hogarth Press, 1932). It seems to me that from such a book made up of twin lectures by two of the most authoritative analysts (based primarily on the researches of the former) and addressed to the general public with marked success, an unequalled amount of insight and wisdom may be gained

by the attentive reader. Also, there could be no less confusing mirror of the psycho-analytic approach.

PART TWO (*INSIDE OUT*)

1 Cézanne is reported by Gasquet to have said: 'L'Art console de vivre.' The practice of art is, of course, very often, perhaps always to some degree, a personal flight from life, possibly the most successful of all such flights. It is necessary for me to enlarge upon this fact which I fully recognize. But it is encumbent on me, therefore, to show that, despite this fact, the practice of art is more widely rooted in life.

2 Except where otherwise stated, the quotations from Cézanne's letters are from the translations by Margaret Kay, edited by John Rewald (*Paul Cézanne, Letters*, Bruno Cassirer, 1941).

3 Cf. *Cézanne* by Joachim Gasquet (Bernheim-Jeune, 1921). This passage is quoted by Gerstle Mack, whose translation I use, in *Paul Cézanne* (Cape, 1935). Gasquet's reconstructions of conversations with Cézanne are the source of many of the remarks attributed to him which do not come from the letters.

4 Mack, *op. cit.*, p.307.

5 At several points I find I have closely followed Roger Fry in his *Cézanne: A Study of His Development* (Hogarth Press, second edition, 1932, 54 plates). It is to be hoped this masterpiece of criticism is now in print again. It contains among other virtues an unrivalled critique of some of the paintings themselves.

6 Now available in one volume in English. Rewald, *op. cit.*

7 Mack, *op. cit.* His is the more literal and the better translation. For the text of the letters to Émile Bernard see his 'Souvenirs sur Paul Cézanne' in *Mercure de France*, September–October 1907, vol.69.

8 An infinitude of creation, particularly in the matter of the kind of form that arises from acuity of colour sense, remains to us in 'painting after nature'. Cf. *Colour and Form* (Faber & Faber, 1937).

9 Mack, *op. cit.*

10 I would bring this small detail to the notice of a future investigator. Bernard (*op. cit.*) reports Cézanne saying of his father: 'He was intelligent and good-hearted and he said of me that I was a bohemian who would die in poverty if he didn't work for me; and he made it possible for me to do nothing but paint all my life.' I believe that Louis-Auguste was, and thought himself to be, an extra-ordinary man and that on balance it was his pride to think the same of his son, once that the painting situation had been accepted. One must not forget the portraits and the youthful frescoes at the Jas de Bouffon. Even from the first there will have been some paternal pride in his painting.

This conversation, at any rate, should be put against the presentation of Louis-Auguste in many biographies, as a caricature of the mean and uncomprehending father. Cézanne's struggle with his father has naturally many aspects, not least of which is a love and an identification.

11 Such achievement of impartial thinking could have been won only after a lessening of anxiety. Thus, by an effect here attributed to the 'approachability' of the Mediterranean climate, one is reminded of a mitigation of anxiety through analysis which allows the previously neurotic psyche to entertain less rigid, because less separated and less compulsive, notions: when the good and the bad 'objects', personified within, are not kept apart with such a paramount dread; when the bad is less abysmal, can therefore be faced and thought; when,

as a consequence, the good is more genial, less fragile, and the mind is more open to the impact of 'things as they are' as well as to a belief in its own power.

On this point I quote (though not because the colour blue stood to him for goodness and security) from the conclusion to a case-history of a boy of ten who had suffered a deep depression: 'When Richard had become able during his analysis to face the psychological fact that his loved object was also his hated object and that the light blue mother, the queen with the crown, was linked in his mind with the horrid bird with the beak, he could establish his love for his mother more securely. His feelings of love had become more closely linked with his feelings of hatred, and his happy experiences with his mother were no longer kept so widely apart from his experiences of frustration. He was therefore no longer driven on the one hand to idealize the "good" mother so strongly and on the other hand to form so terrifying a picture of the "bad" mother. Whenever he could allow himself to bring the two aspects of the mother together, this implied that the bad aspect was mitigated by the good one. This more secure "good" mother could then protect him against the "monster" father. This again implied that at such times she was not felt to be so fatally injured by his oral greed and by the "bad" father, which in turn meant that both he and his father had become less dangerous. The good mother could come to life once more, and Richard's depression therefore lifted.' See 'The Oedipus Complex in the Light of Early Anxieties' by Melanie Klein, *International Journal of Psychoanalysis*, vol. XXVI.

12 I have associated our own Western conception of classicism with the grasping of the full relevance of fact. Our romanticism contains a certain revolt against fact, as well as against the artificiality of convention, in an insistence upon individual fantasy. Nevertheless, however extreme the romanticism, it cannot, in its nature as art, forego completely the formal aspects. The case of our music gives a very cogent example. The romantic movement of the nineteenth century greatly extended and enriched symphonic form. The plan, the pattern, the organization, those qualities we know of in material so much better than we know of them in the spirit, belong as well to romantic art, even if they are not enunciated with the contentment of classical art. Among the cross-currents of differing styles it sometimes happens, at any rate in Western art, that the romantic disposition *par excellence* attaches itself with the force of a discovery, with a new and vigorous love, to the capaciousness of the classical form; that is, if it be or could be made, ample. The period of the early Renaissance was of this character and the situation of Cézanne's painting was not far different. Conversely, with a similar fructifying air of triumph, a high moment of romantic conception may become for future generations the classical canon: it is the situation of classical ballet.

13 A more technical presentation oft his argument may be found in a short paper: 'Concerning Art and Metapsychology', *International Journal of Psychoanalysis*, vol. XXVI.

14 See *What is Life?* by Dr. E. Schrödinger (Cambridge University Press, 1944).

ART AND SCIENCE

1 It is likely they met often, especially at Urbino; Alberti and Piero over a long period; Laurana as well in the late 1460s.

2 Born 1404, died 1472.

3 *Leon Battista Alberti on Painting*, by Sir Kenneth Clark (British Academy,

vol. XXX. Humphrey Milford, 4*s*. 6*d*.).

4 'There is practically no part of academic teaching during the next 400 years which does not lie, compressed yet calculated, in its pages.' Clark, *op. cit.* The author opens with the remark that Alberti's treatise was the first ever to be written on painting, and concludes by showing that Leonardo, as he wrote *his* Trattato (more commonly regarded as the fount of academic shibboleths), must undoubtedly have had a copy of Alberti at his elbow.

5 II. Janitschek, *Leone Battista Alberti's kleinere kunst-theoretischen Schriften* (Vienna, 1877), p.163.

6 Janitschek, *op. cit.*, p.77.

7 At the same time we may well consider whether there is not to be found here – in the matter of identifying a measure and a divine proportion with actual sense-data – the root formula (deriving from the ideal naturalism of the Antique), not only of academism in the West, but of the prevalent architectonic patterning and the formal concepts behind the naturalism of most European pictorial art since the Renaissance: we may wonder whether there may not be found here a parent of Cézanne's or Seurat's aesthetic, for instance, and of a great deal of present-day art from the best to the worst.

Among the many reasons why the visual arts, under the aegis of architecture, were so closely interrelated before and after, but particularly during the Renaissance, foremost is the architectural impression of Antique art, offered then as now by Antique remains, particularly in Rome, a colourful version of the truth. Modern painting is, we say, pure painting. That does not conceal the fact that the leaders have sought to re-create architectonic structure without reference to other than the plainest shapes and surfaces. But can painting be

mother to the visual arts?

8 Janitschek, *op. cit.*, p.97.

9 Janitschek, *op. cit.*, p.169.

10 Bonucci, *Opere volgari di Leon Batt Alberti* (Florence, 1847), vol.4, p.309.

11 Bonucci, *op. cit.*, vol.3, p.92.

12 Bonucci, *op. cit.*, vol.4, p.362. This is the incomplete contemporary Italian text of the *De re aedificatoria*.

13 A decline in superstition should not be immediately connected with alteration in the poetic power of legend. Art drew enormous support at that time, and for centuries to come in a slowly diminishing degree, from an immense and wealthy iconography, both religious and pagan. We have only to read in Panofsky's rewarding book (*Studies in Iconology*, Erwin Panofsky, New York, Oxford Univ. Press, 1939) concerning the various, precise, alternative and even contrasting meanings of the nude in medieval iconography, to realize how wealthy were the motifs and differing stresses under the hand of the artist. If used by us today they retain no more than a tithe of their sharpness and precision. Still-life, landscape and portraiture are largely or entirely independent of iconographical meaning in the restricted sense of the term. The connection of modern art with an art serving a precise iconography, is mostly a matter of substitutes, but perhaps, none the less, all-pervasive; and it is possible that the wider vistas of modern art will best be seen from this rather demoded viewpoint.

We must also take into account the lessening after the seventeenth century of neo-Platonic magical tendencies whereby emblems, representations and harmonies could be considered as corporeal adaptations (not symbols) of supernal Ideas. This view, however vaguely held, brought fire to allegorical 'subjects'. Cf. E. H. Gombrich's very brilliant paper 'Icones Symbolicae',

Journal of the Warburg and Courtauld Institutes, vol. XI (1948).

14 Janitschek, *op. cit.*, p.131.

15 Janitschek, *op. cit.*, p.139.

16 Clark, *op. cit.*

17 *Piero della Francesca*: Roberto Longhi. English translation by Leonard Penlock (Frederick Warne, 1930), enlarged Italian edition (Milan, 1947). An aspect of the same trend is strongly reflected by some fifteenth-century sculptors of whom Francesco Laurana was chief. It is notable that he, too, may have often met both Alberti and Piero at Urbino. Cf. *The Quattro Cento* (Faber & Faber, 1932).

18 The Maso of the dedication is generally taken to be the painter Masaccio, though he had been dead some seven years. On the other hand the little known sculptor Maso di Bartolomeo whom Janitschek suggests, an associate of Luca della Robbia (another dedicatee) and of Michelozzo, was working in the Tempio Malatestiano in 1452 (two years after Alberti had made his plan). In the same year he designed the beautiful doorway to San Domenico, the first piece of Renaissance architecture in Urbino. It is by no means impossible that Alberti recommended him.

This reference to the unequalled Masaccio – if such it be – is most painfully inadequate. Or, is one to think that he was the unspoken inspiration of Alberti's treatise, especially since he was at first almost the only painter to be deeply influenced by Brunellesco's architecture and sculpture? Masaccio attained a more flowing naturalism (in the Brancacci chapel) and a greater relief, a greater realization of mass, than did the Florentine school which eventually proceeded from him as well as from contemporaneous sculpture. And this he accomplished with the simplest means and without denying the rootedness and steadfastness that issue from the

chromatic approach to form. As well as for the chief of the Florentines, Masaccio is a source for Piero. There is a certain (sometimes allied) rootedness or, at any rate, slowness, in a more primitive style to which, as well as to the newly rediscovered aims of classical architecture, both Masaccio and Piero were heirs. It is true also of Alberti as artist, of course, little less than, say, of Donatello.

19 Clark, *op. cit.*

20 For instance, the *Dance of Salome* [*Feast of Herod* – Ed.] at Lille, usually dated about 1433.

21 The contemporary scientific theory retailed by Alberti (he reserves judgement) as to the origin of stone, a gradual growing from soil and water in the earth, like a seed that is planted, is of interest from the point of view of fructification fantasies connected with stone. Bonucci, *op. cit.*, vol.4, pp.290 and 342. In his accounts of building stones, Alberti speaks of them as almost living materials. In Book 8, chap. 5 of the *De re aedificatoria*, he exclaims on the extraordinary outburst of stone building throughout Italy, how that the drab cities known to his childhood now shine in marble. For him, as for Piero, and as later for the Lombardi and Mauro Coducci in Venice, the use of slabs of precious coloured marble deriving from the Byzantine or the Romanesque, enhanced white stone.

22 Wittkower, 'Alberti's Approach to Antiquity in Architecture', *Journal of the Warburg and Courtauld Institutes*, vol.IV (1940); 'Principles of Palladio's Architecture: II', *Journal of the Warburg and Courtauld Institutes*, vol.VIII (1945).

23 Prof. Wittkower's succinct conclusion to a most brilliant and unique analysis from the technical side is perhaps a little enclosing from the side of a deliberate aesthetic choice in control of all the trends that go to make it. For the present author, at any rate, it is not the façades

at Mantua of Sant'Andrea and of San Sebastiano (second scheme) but the Tempio façade, symbolic encasement to a Gothic church, the first fresh essay, unfinished, altered in plan by constructional difficulties, that transcends all other walls in emotional power, unless it be Luciano's courtyard. Moreover it would be misleading to isolate Roman architecture from an emphasis upon the wall. An intense wall consciousness is indisputably demonstrated as well as a love of stone. For instance, the giant travertine attic storey to the Colosseum is a robust yet precious wall, rich medium of aperture, in just the fifteenth-century sense. It was inevitable, for empirical reasons alone, that this aspect of Roman architecture should have influenced the early Renaissance artists and their successors so profoundly. Even today, after the Roman and Trajan fora have been excavated, when throughout ancient Rome hundreds of pillars have been raised that were invisible in the fifteenth century, the dominant impression is still of close brick-work in vast masonry between the heavy, pregnant apertures; of the baths, of Maxentius' basilica, of the cupola and awe-inspiring walls of the Pantheon.

24 Though he did write of columns as being imaginatively such remnants of the wall. The arch-supporting column may well be thought to represent the wall's three dimensions; cf. most notably, Luciano Laurana's courtyard at Urbino.

25 Wittkower, 'Principles of Palladio's Architecture: II', *op. cit.*

26 Longhi, *op. cit.*

27 Nor can the single-storied church with its three equal vertical divisions, represented at the back of the Proving of the True Cross at Arezzo, be related even indirectly with any plan Alberti might have sketched when engaged on the reconstruction of Santa Maria Novella's

façade. Though a few features approximate, every element of the Santa Maria Novella problem and of its solution are absent. A more Albertian reminiscence in the Arezzo frescoes would seem to be the centring of the beautiful column at the Annunciation. Alberti, it will be remembered, pronounced columns to be the most sublime of ornaments.

28 In 1549 (*Ricordi overo ammaestramenti*, Fra Sabba da Castiglione) Bramante was described as 'a great perspective genius and the intimate disciple of Piero del Borgo' (Piero della Francesca), cf. Longhi, *op. cit.*

29 As do the balconies behind the Poldi-Pezzoli *St. Thomas Aquinas* and the National Gallery *St. Michael* (also late works).

30 Though doubtless Tuscan Romanesque or Proto-Renaissance façades in dark and white marble influenced Piero's architectural smoothness, yet his representation of precious stones, even in strips, and more particularly his favourite self-communing yet concerted architectural members, are more suggestive of Venice and of the Byzantine than of the striped Tuscan. And it may well be that Piero, no less than Alberti, influenced, or at least gave courage to the early Renaissance Venetian architects; just as earlier he had considerably influenced the rise of Venetian painting (for this last point cf. Longhi, *L'arte*, 1913).

As for Alberti in this connection of coloured marble, it is true enough that the tabernacle of San Pancrazio recalls Tuscan marble inlay, but the inlay of porphyry and serpentine over the door of the Tempio, and the disks, look more to the Adriatic. Alberti did not grow up 'surrounded by such monuments as San Miniato in Florence' (Wittkower, *op. cit.*); in fact he could not have seen them before he was twenty-five. He was brought up in Venice, or the neighbourhood.

Dadoes to the columns on the

Tempio façade are very like those to the columns in Sant'Apollinare in Classe. The sarcophagi beneath the arches of the flank are of a Byzantine type. Cf. the sarcophagi placed in medieval times in the exterior arcade of Theodoric's tomb, Corrado Ricci, *Tempio Malatestiano* (Bestetti e Tumminelli, Milan, 1925).

31 It is not surprising that the philosophies of the humanists abound in contradictions. The position for which the majority of them strove is clear, namely, the justification of an harmonious external world ruled by law, immanent in every detail, and an emphasis upon the individual in an universal scheme. But the feeling of certainty, even for many humanists themselves, was expressed better by art than by thought. Painting was called an art rather than science because, to give one reason, it is a *fare*, a doing. It therefore conveyed more certainty than many of those sciences. Mathematics and painting founded on the new geometric perspective, had in common a power of exposition, a demonstrability in advance of philosophical treatment. Here, in painting, was best seen the reconciliation of the individual with the type or mean, of particular nature with the ideal. Because, like a science, art makes known the state of Nature, enormous and varied knowledge was expected of the artist. Cf. *Piero della Francesca. De prospectiva pingendi*, edited and introduced by G. N. Fasola (Sansoni, Florence, 1942).

32 It is notable that in the other surviving treatise that may in part be attributed to Piero's authorship, the *De divina proportione*, he is concerned with the geometrical shapes 'behind' all visual phenomena. These shapes are the cube, pyramid, octahedron, dodecahedron and icosahedron. Cf. Fasola, *op. cit.*

33 *P. della Francesca. Gli affreschi di San Francesco in Arezzo*, Mario Salmi (Bergamo).

34 More particularly Mantegna (subsuming Donatello) and Antonello da Messina, who were vital influences upon Giovanni Bellini, Giorgione's master according to Vasari. There is also the Piero thread as in the case of Cossa and Ercole Roberti of Ferrara (where Piero had painted frescoes), a town that Giorgione may have visited. Cf. G. M. Richter in work cited below.

35 Passages quoted or referred to from Zanetti and from Vasari may be found in the documents section of G. M. Richter's monumental *Giorgio da Castelfranco*. All the known sources and documents relating to Giorgione are printed here in full (University of Chicago Press, 1937).

36 All except a shattered fragment of a figure that has now been removed from the Fondaco's wall to the Accademia. In this connection it is not necessary to take account of alleged juvenilia, a fresco frieze in the Casa Pellizzari, Castelfranco. Cf. Richter, *op. cit.*

37 Richter, *op. cit.*, prints a very extensive bibliography, up to 1936, and a chart of attributions.

38 Cf. *The Quattro Cento* (Faber & Faber, 1932) and *Stones of Rimini* (Faber & Faber, 1934).

39 Whenever, subsequent to Giorgione, this purpose has considerably weakened, while no new strength has been claimed from a different approach to painting, literary fallacies have not only held, but rioted, upon the stage.

40 The choice of such posture, the demands of or interest in *una sola occhiata*, lead inevitably to a consideration of Giorgione's preferred shapes and to the amalgam of form they express. See below.

41 There seems no reason for inferring (as does G. Fiocco, *Giorgione*, Bergamo, 1941) that Michiel's near-contemporary reference to the Christ of this picture is itself a statement to the effect that only the figure of Christ is by Giorgione's hand.

42 It has already been suggested (*Venice: An Aspect of Art*, Faber & Faber, 1945) that the Venetian early Renaissance architecture, particularly Coducci's, contained a similar chromatic approach to form, and that this architecture deeply influenced Giorgione.

43 Rock and tower are sometimes judged to be by another hand.

44 *Giovanni Bellini*, Philip Hendy (Phaidon Press, 1947).

45 Panofsky, *op. cit.* He contrasts Ficino's metaphysical presentation of neo-Platonic doctrine with Bembo's aesthetic approach, typically Venetian, in the delightful *Gli Asolani* (1505).

46 *Les Débuts de la musique à Venise*, Charles Van den Borren (Brussels, 1914); *Nouvelle Histoire de la musique*, vol.1, Henri Prunières (Paris, 1934).

47 *Ibid.*

48 The Venetians, of course, had access to the Greek islands. Their principal contribution to antique studies was from the side of the Greek language. Aldo Manuzio, who owed a great deal to the help and encouragement of Bembo particularly, produced his first book in 1494. The Aldine Press soon won fame, especially for the collation and first printing of Greek texts. The Aldine Aristotle, in five volumes, appeared in 1495–8. (*Aldo Manuzio*, Mario Ferrigni, Milan, 1925), cf. also references below to Almorò Barbaro, who belonged to the previous generation.

49 According to Schubring (cf. Richter, *op. cit.*, p.420) the spinet of this picture is the earliest known example and the player possibly Joh. Spinetus. The subject is the victory of the spinet over the old-fashioned lute.

50 *Ibid.*

51 *Almorò Barbaro*, Arnaldo Ferriguto (R. Deputazione Veneta di Storia Patria, Venice, 1922). Also Ferriguto's *I committenti di Giorgione* (Atti Reale Istituto Veneto, 1925–6) and *Attraverso i misteri di Giorgione* (Castelfranco, 1933).

52 X-ray has recently shown that underneath the man's figure there exists, incompletely sketched, a woman's figure resembling closely the one we have, though larger, with her legs in the stream. A seated figure spread thus in the foreground was not harmonious even with the rectilinear relationships of the background. She was moved (before the baby had been sketched in) higher up and to the other side. The woman, therefore, the more complicated pictorial conception, was attempted before the man, as one might expect. Some commentators, however, suppose from the X-ray evidence that an earlier conception of the picture (which Giorgione scrapped) may have been of two women, two sisters, twins. In favour of such an hypothesis it has been urged that the sketched woman and the existing woman are on the same level of paint, i.e. that the existing woman was not painted over a sketched man in harmony with what happened on the other side of the picture. The X-ray photographs do suggest, however, that the picture is well-named and that tempest, background and buildings were elaborated first as part of a landscape with figures who were to be the creatures (if also the lords) of the landscape. Cf. an article by Ferriguto in *Misura, rivista internazionale*, November 1946.

53 Though it might depend upon what were to be put in its place. Nevertheless even though Giorgione were coopted a member of a secret sodality, interested in occult 'science' (cf. *Giorgiones Geheimnis*, G. F. Hartlaub, Munich, 1925), it would be impossible to disregard the wider cultural tendencies of which he could have acted as transmitter even through so involved a mesh. Such contradiction and, indeed, the aesthetic percipience which

may be an outcome, are unlikely to be beyond any reader's experience.

54 'The Architecture of Brunelleschi and the Origins of Perspective Theory in the 15th Century', G.A.Argan, *Journal of the Warburg and Courtauld Institutes*, vol.IX (1946).

THE EGO-FIGURE

1 J.O.Wisdom has attributed awareness of the body-ego primarily to tactile and kinaesthetic sensations (Wisdom, 1953).

Bibliographic References:
Bion, W.R. (1957), 'Differentiation of the Psychotic from the Non-Psychotic Personalities', *International Journal of Psychoanalysis*, vol.XXXVIII, parts 3 & 4.
Ferenczi, Sándor (1955), *Final Contributions to the Problem and Methods of Psychoanalysis*, ed. M. Balint (London, Hogarth Press).
Freud, Sigmund (1927), *The Ego and the Id*, trans. Joan Riviere (London, Hogarth Press).
Klein, Melanie (1939), 'Mourning: Its Relation to Manic-Depressive States', *International Journal of Psychoanalysis*, vol.XX, parts 3 & 4.
Klein, Melanie (1946), 'Notes on Some Schizoid Mechanisms', *International Journal of Psychoanalysis*, vol.XXVII, parts 3 & 4.
Klein, Melanie (1948), 'A Contribution to the Theory of Anxiety and Guilt', *International Journal of Psychoanalysis*, vol.XXIX, part 2.
Klein, Melanie (1952), 'Some Theoretical Conclusions Regarding the Emotional Life of the Infant', in *Developments in Psychoanalysis* (London, Hogarth Press).
Klein, Melanie (1956), 'On Identification', in *New Directions in Psychoanalysis* (London, Tavistock Publications).
Lawrence, T.E. (1935), translator, *The Odyssey* (London, Oxford University Press).
Murray, Gilbert (1935), *Five Stages of Greek Religion* (London, Watts Press).
Ribble, Margaret A. (1944), 'Infantile Experience in Relation to Personality Development', in *Personality and the Behavior Disorders*, vol.2 (New York, Ronald Press).
Segal, Hanna (1952), 'A Psychoanalytic Approach to Aesthetics', *International Journal of Psychoanalysis*, vol.XXIII, part 2.
Segal, Hanna (1957), 'Notes on Symbol Formation', *International Journal of Psychoanalysis*, vol.XXXVIII, part 4.
Stokes, Adrian (1955), *Michelangelo: A Study in the Nature of Art* (London, Tavistock Publications).
Stokes, Adrian (1956), 'Form in Art', in *New Directions in Psychoanalysis*, ed. Melanie Klein, Paula Heimann, Roger Money-Kyrle (London, Tavistock Publications).

THE LUXURY AND NECESSITY OF PAINTING

Bibliographic References:
Hartigan, Grace, from the catalogue of *The New American Painting*, an Arts Council exhibition at the Tate Gallery (1959).
Klein, Melanie, *Envy and Gratitude* (London, 1957).
Lewin, B.D., 'Inferences from the Dream Screen', *International Journal of Psycho-analysis*, 1948.
Stokes, A., *Michelangelo: A Study in the Nature of Art* (London, 1955).
Stokes, A., 'Form in Art', from *New Directions in Psycho-Analysis*, edited by M. Klein, P. Heimann, and R.E. Money-Kyrle (London, 1955a). Reprinted in *Journal of Aesthetics*, vol.XVIII, no.2.
Stokes, A., *Greek Culture and the Ego: A Psycho-Analytic Survey of an Aspect of

Greek Civilization and of Art (London, 1958).

Wittkower, R., *Art and Architecture in Italy, 1600–1750* (Harmondsworth, 1958).

IS-NESS AND AVANT GARDE

Bibliographic References:
Boas, G. (ed), *Courbet and the Naturalist Movement* (Baltimore, 1938).
Goldman, B., 'Realist Iconography: Intent and Criticism', *Journal of Aesthetics*, vol. XVIII (Baltimore, 1959).
Gowing, L., Catalogue to Arts Council Cézanne Exhibition (London, 1954).
Kahnweiler, D. H., *Juan Gris, His Life and Work*, trans. D. Cooper (New York, 1947)
Schapiro, M., Review of Sloane (1951) in *Art Bulletin*, June 1954.
Schapiro, M., 'Courbet and Popular Imagery', *Journal of the Warburg and Courtauld Institutes*, vol. 4 (London, 1941).
Schapiro, M., *Vincent van Gogh* (London, 1951).
Schapiro, M., *Paul Cézanne* (New York, 1952).
Shattuck, R., *The Banquet Years* (London, 1959).
Sloane, J., *French Painting between the Past and Present: Artists, Critics, and Traditions, 1848–70* (Princeton, 1951).
Wilson, E., *Axel's Castle* (New York, 1931).

ON RESIGNATION

1 Klein, Melanie, *Envy and Gratitude* (London, Tavistock, 1957).
2 *Ibid.*
3 *Ibid.*
4 *Ibid.*
5 Freud, Anna, *The Ego and the Mechanisms of Defence* (London, Hogarth, 1937).
6 Freud, S., *Group Psychology and the Analysis of the Ego*, *S.E.*, vol. 18.
7 Klein, *Envy and Gratitude, op. cit.*

8 *Ibid.*
9 *Ibid.*

THE INVITATION IN ART

Bibliographic References:
Arnheim, R., *Art and Visual Perception* (London, 1956).
Freud, S., 'The Uncanny', 1919 (London, Standard Edition, vol. 17).
Milner, M. (*sub. nom.* Joanna Field), *On Not Being Able to Paint* (London, 1950 and 1957).
Milner, M., 'The Role of Illusion in Symbol Formation', in *New Directions in Psychoanalysis*, edited by M. Klein, P. Heimann and R. Money-Kyrle (London, 1955). First published under the title 'Aspects of Symbolism in Comprehension of the Not-Self', *International Journal of Psychoanalysis*, 1952.
White, J., *The Birth and Rebirth of Pictorial Space* (London, 1957).

ON BEING TAKEN OUT OF ONESELF

Bibliographic References:
Freud, Sigmund (1905), *Three Essays on the Theory of Sexuality*, *S.E.*, vol. 7.
— (1911), 'Formulations on the Two Principles of Mental Functioning', *S.E.*, vol. 12.
— (1918), 'From the History of an Infantile Neurosis', *S.E.*, vol. 18.
— (1925), 'Negation', *S.E.*, vol. 19.
— (1927), 'Humour', *S.E.*, vol. 21.
— (1933), *New Introductory Lectures on Psycho-Analysis*, *S.E.*, vol. 22.
— (1940), *An Outline of Psycho-Analysis*, *S.E.*, vol. 23.
Klein, Melanie (1957), *Envy and Gratitude* (London, Tavistock).
Stokes, Adrian (1960), 'A Game that Must Be Lost'.
— (1962), 'On Resignation'.

THE IMAGE IN FORM – A LECTURE

1 Adapted from a lecture given with slides.
2 Ascribed to Raphael. One can say with certainty that the major design is his.
3 Cf. Professor Wollheim's inaugural lecture of 1964, where he argued that a mark made on paper causes not only configuration but representation in nearly all cases. *On Drawing an Object*, Richard Wollheim (London, H. K. Lewis, 1965).

BIBLIOGRAPHY

COLLECTIONS

The Image in Form: Selected Writings of Adrian Stokes, ed. Richard Wollheim (Harmondsworth: Penguin, 1972; New York: Harper & Row, 1972)

A Game that Must Be Lost: Collected Papers by Adrian Stokes, ed. Eric Rhode (Cheadle Hulme: Carcanet, 1973)

The Critical Writings of Adrian Stokes, 3 vols., ed. Lawrence Gowing (London: Thames & Hudson, 1978)

With All the Views: The Collected Poems of Adrian Stokes, ed. Peter Robinson (Manchester: Carcanet New Press, 1981; Redding Ridge, CT: Black Swan Books, 1981)

Adrian Stokes, 1902–72: A Retrospective, exh. cat., Serpentine Gallery, London (London: Arts Council of Great Britain, 1982)

Art and Analysis: An Adrian Stokes Reader, ed. Meg Harris Williams (London: Karnac, 2014)

INDIVIDUAL BOOKS

The Thread of Ariadne (London: Kegan Paul, Trench, Trubner & Co., 1925)

Sunrise in the West: A Modern Interpretation of Past and Present (London: Kegan Paul, Trench, Trubner & Co. [1926])

The Quattro Cento: A Different Conception of the Italian Renaissance (London: Faber & Faber, 1932; New York: Schocken Books, 1968)

Stones of Rimini (London: Faber & Faber, 1934; New York: Schocken Books, 1969)

Tonight the Ballet (London: Faber & Faber, 1934; New York: Dutton, 1935; revd edn London: Faber & Faber, 1935)

Russian Ballets (London: Faber & Faber, 1935; New York: Dutton, 1936; 2nd (corrected) edn London: Faber & Faber, 1935)

Colour and Form (London: Faber & Faber, 1937; revd edn, 1950)

Venice: An Aspect of Art (London: Faber & Faber, 1945)

Inside Out: An Essay in the Psychology and Aesthetic Appeal of Space (London: Faber & Faber, 1947)

Art and Science: A Study of Alberti, Piero della Francesca and Giorgione (London: Faber & Faber, 1949)

Smooth and Rough (London, Faber & Faber, 1951)

Michelangelo: A Study in the Nature of Art (London: Tavistock Publications 1955; New York: Philosophical Library, 1956; London: Routledge)

Greek Culture and the Ego: A Psycho-analytic Survey of an Aspect of Greek Civilisation and of Art (London: Tavistock Publications, 1958)

Three Essays on the Painting of Our Time (London: Tavistock Publications, 1961)

Painting and the Inner World (London: Tavistock Publications, 1963)

The Invitation in Art, preface by Richard Wollheim (London: Tavistock Publications, 1965; New York: Chilmark Press, 1966)

Venice, with illustrations by John Piper (London: Lion and Unicorn Press, 1965; London: Gerald Duckworth, 1965)

Reflections on the Nude (London: Tavistock Publications, 1967; New York: Barnes & Noble, 1967)

BIOGRAPHIES AND CRITICAL WORKS

Bann, Stephen, ed, *The Coral Mind: Adrian Stokes's Engagement with Art History, Criticism, Architecture, and Psychoanalysis* (University Park PA: Penn State University Press, 2007)

Kite, Stephen, *Adrian Stokes: An Architectonic Eye* (London: Routledge, 2008)

O'Pray, Michael, *Film, Form and Phantasy: Adrian Stokes and Film Aesthetics* (London: Palgrave Macmillan, 2004)

Read, Richard, *Art and Its Discontents: The Early Life of Adrian Stokes* (Aldershot: Ashgate, 2002)

Sayers, Janet, *Art, Psychoanalysis, and Adrian Stokes: A Biography* (London: Karnac Books, 2015)

ACKNOWLEDGEMENTS

Many thanks to the Estate of Adrian Stokes (Telfer Stokes and Philip Stokes) for their permission to publish this volume, and their help and conversations throughout. Special thanks to Telfer Stokes for his years of assiduous encouragement of the project (and the various iterations of it), and for first introducing me to the work of Adrian Stokes. Thanks also to Ian Angus and Ann Stokes (in memoriam) for their support.

My thanks to the late Karsten Schubert and Doro Globus, former Ridinghouse Publisher, for agreeing to publish this volume. For their work on production thanks to Kitta Roos, the book designer Mark Thomson, the indexer Nic Nicholas, and to Sophie Kullmann, Ridinghouse Publisher, whose labour on the entire book has been truly above and beyond, and to whom I am immensely indebted. Thanks to type designer Peter Matthias Noordzij of TEFF, who worked closely with Bram de Does on the original design of the Lexicon type in which this book is set, for the matching $ monogram in *The Tempio: First Visit*. My especial thanks to Richard Read, who gave so freely and generously of his thoughts and time, and who undertook several readings of my introduction (any errors in which remain my own), as well as his take on the selection itself. My Stokes chronology draws on his, which can be found at www.adrianstokes.com. Note that the essay 'An Argument' was first transcribed and edited by Richard Read, and published with an introduction in *PN Review* 15, vol.7, no.1 (1980), pp.41–2.

For additional assistance and comments, my thanks to Helen Douglas, Ekaterina Guseva, Rob Holloway, Marc Lowenthal, Janet Sayers, and Trevor Winkfield.

Published in 2020 by Ridinghouse
46 Lexington Street
London W1F 0LP
United Kingdom
ridinghouse.co.uk

Distributed in the UK and Europe by
Cornerhouse Publications
c/o Home
2 Tony Wilson Place
Manchester M15 4FN
United Kingdom
cornerhousepublications.org

Distributed in rest of world by
ARTBOOK | D.A.P.
75 Broad Street, Suite 630
New York, New York 10004
artbook.com

British Library Cataloguing-in-
    Publication Data
A full catalogue record of this book is
    available from the British Library.

ISBN 978 1 909932 48 7

Ridinghouse Publisher: Sophie Kullmann

Designed by Mark Thomson
Set in Lexicon (Bram de Does)

Printed in Estonia by Tallinna
    Raamatutrükikoja OÜ

Ridinghouse